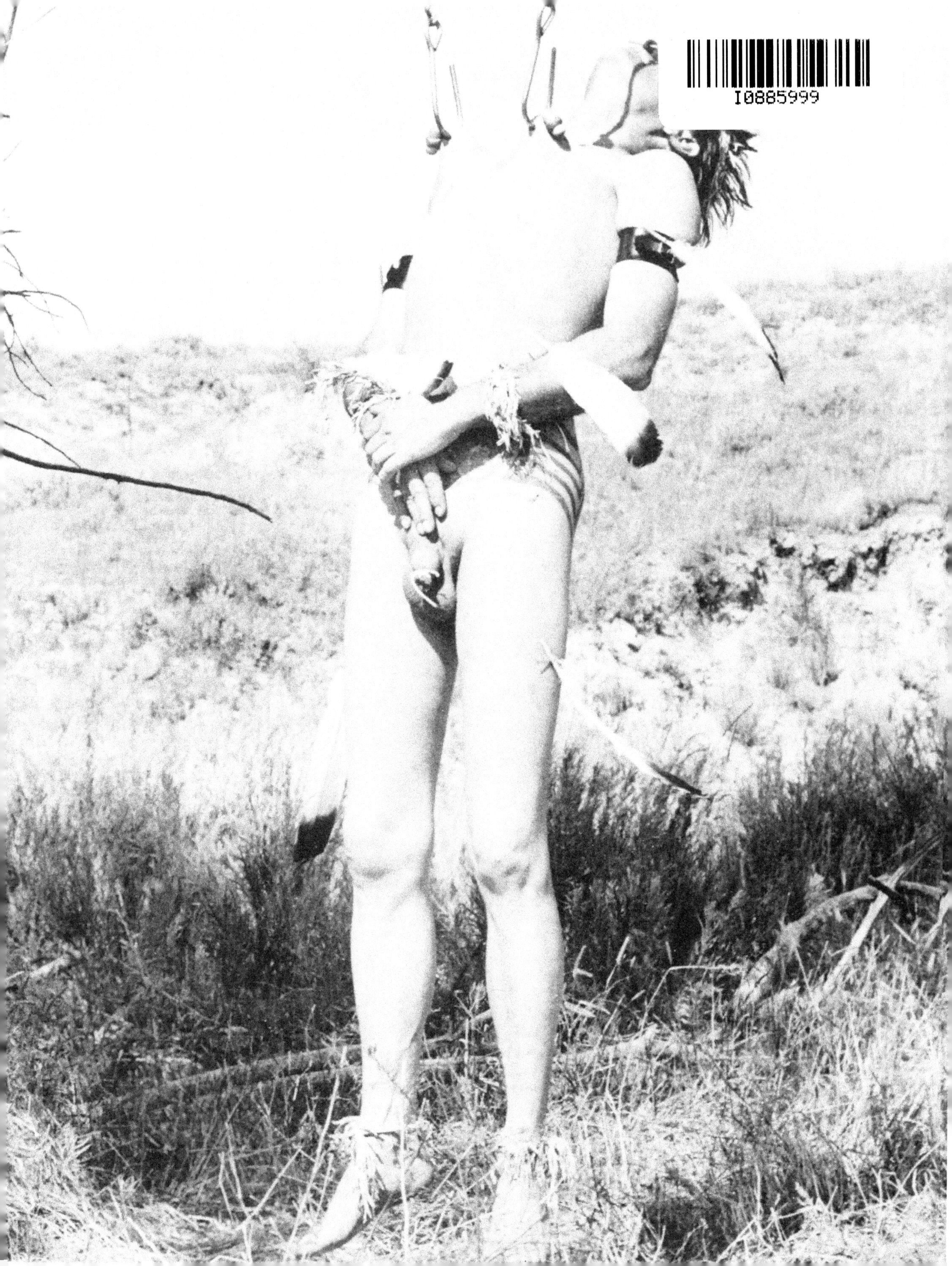

Modern Primitives Foreword

Predicting the future has never been easy, or more people would be doing just that. Two hundred years ago, Hegel offered a simple directive: the future can be defined by "more freedom and more consciousness for more people." Yet the most casual examination of history within the past hundred years reveals the truth of the aphorism: "One step forward, two steps back." Despite millions of hours of study by scholars who have investigated Capitalism, Marxism, Trotskyism, Anarchism, Situationism, Surrealism and other social/economic theories purporting to show us humanity's future — judge by results: how "freer" are more people today all over planet Earth? We're in the age of the new feudalism.

Sadly, much of the earth's populace seem enslaved by interior / mental "chains" as much as physical circumstance. "Kill the inner policeman inside yourself!" said a Situationist graffiti written in Paris walls *circa* May 1968. The Surrealists militated against religion and monotheism, yet statistically, today more people than ever seem to be succumbing to the three "religions of the book": Judaism, Islam and Christianity. The King James Bible says, "Thou shalt make no marks upon the flesh," presumably referring to tattooing and scarification, and these three religions all seem to *control the body* — especially its capacity for pleasure and adornment. Yet, the body (and the contents of the brain) is the only true "possession" any of us own — police can take away everything else and put people into a concentration camp, but humans will still retain their bodies.

It seems obvious that the full potential of the body for pleasure and beautification ought to be the birthright of every human. Why do so few people explore and "maximize" this potential?

The IDEA behind the *Modern Primitives* book was bigger than the book itself: to chart out and present all the ways that humans have historically modified and decorated their bodies D-I-Y (Do-It-Yourself; without surgery / hospitalization, and the attendant authoritarian hegemony and intrusion), and present this information unjudgmentally . . . WITHOUT MORALISTIC COMMENTARY. (No religious guilt!)

Also, *Modern Primitives* presented this data in exceptionally clear language and illustrations, from a variety of viewpoints. This was "amateur" anthropology / philosophy / aesthetics / history at its most accessible — without academic pretentiousness. Result: the floodgates were opened! For "Body Piercing," Yellow Pages telephone directory listings went from zero to dozens in cities all over the world. For "Tattoo," listings increased from single to double digits.

As with any artistic medium, body artists / practitioners aimed at taking the Art of Body Modification further. Implants represent a radical renaissance in themselves. More full-body tattoos which include facial, neck and hand tattooing have been innovated (e.g., "the Leopard Man"), along with literally dozens of piercings all over the body canvas. We interviewed one man in Germany with nearly a hundred facial piercings (he works at home as a computer software engineer). How many body piercings is it possible to have?

Our book, *Modern Primitives*, also aimed at restoring ritual, and staged suspensions (ritual hanging from hooks) signpost possibly the biggest growth territory for future artistic expansion. Dozens of iconoclasts all over the world have formed suspension groups which celebrate the phenomenon of "possession" and the attainment of the trance state, beyond endurance tests and other explorations of the shadowy area between pain and pleasure. Singing opera arias while suspended from hooks is just one of probably many more future *Modern Primitive* cross-pollinations between the arts. Meanwhile, the "Side Show" tradition is yet being preserved by groups unafraid to introduce humor and entertainment into formerly "sacred" social ceremonies.

The full scope of body modification and extreme endurance rituals appears here to stay. The personal has become social; the conceptual has become experiential; the regional has become global; the historical has become futuristic. It remains to be seen how the development of new technologies will further extend and enhance the body augmentations of the coming centuries. Meanwhile, we can travel the world to find the latest "cutting edge" conceptual / physiological breakthroughs unveiled in privately-organized piercing conferences and other social gatherings. But as William S. Burroughs once ironically observed, "It is necessary to travel. It is not necessary to live."

All physically-felt body modifications are a form of time travel linking us with both the past and the future, as we reaffirm our relationship with the only "spaceship" we may ever intimately know: the human body. The body provides the portal facilitating our deepest explorations of both Outer and Inner Space — and this is an investigation which never ends. Beyond the horizon there will always be more to discover, more to stimulate our imaginations, and more epiphanies to light up our world view. The quest continues . . .

— *V. Vale*

WARNING: Do not attempt any of the body modifications or practices described herein. If you insist on doing any, go to a professional. Neither the contributors nor the publishers will assume responsibility for the misuse of any information contained in this book.

RE/Search Publications 20 Romolo #B San Francisco, CA 94133 (415) 362-1465 info@researchpubs.com
ISBN paperback 978-889307-26-8 (contact us for 20th Anniversary Deluxe Hardback edition)
Front Cover Photo: Bobby Neel Adams, Hilary Cross tattoo by Greg Kulz; Back Cover Photo: Ken Werner
1st page: Fakir Musafar Photo by Charles Gatewood; Last page: Fakir Musafar Photo by Bobby Neel Adams
RE/Search staff & consultants: V. Vale, Marian Wallace, Robert Collison, Seth Robson, Skyler Lusteg, Andrew Bishop

TABLE OF CONTENTS

INTRODUCTION

MODERN: 1. Being at this time; now existing. 2. Of or pertaining to the present and recent times, as distinguished from the remote past; pertaining to or originating in the current age or period. 3. Characteristic of the present and recent times; *new*-fashioned; not antiquated or obsolete. 4. Everyday, ordinary, commonplace.

PRIMITIVE: 1. Of or belonging to the first age, period, or stage: pertaining to early times; earliest, original, ancient. At the beginning; anciently; originally in time, at first. 2. With the purity, simplicity, or rudeness of early times. 3. Original, as opposed to derivative; primary, as opposed to secondary; radical. 4. *Math.*, etc. Applied to a line or figure from which some construction or reckoning begins; or to a curve, surface, magnitude, equation, operation, etc., from which another is in some way derived. 6. Of colors: Primary. 7. Anything from which something else is derived.

PRIMITIVIST: A primitivist is a person who prefers a way of life which, when judged by one or more of the standards prevailing in his own society, would be considered less "advanced" or less "civilized." The primitivist finds the model for his preferred way of life in a culture that existed or is reputed to have existed at some time in the past; in the culture of the less sophisticated classes within his society, or of primitive peoples that exist elsewhere in the world; in the experiences of his childhood or youth; in a psychologically elemental (sub-rational or even subconscious) level of existence; or in some combination of these. Primitivistic themes appear in almost all literatures: they are found in classical and medieval literature; in the last Renaissance. Montaigne, in his essay *Des Cannibales*, praises the happy and virtuous life of savages living close to nature; Pope envies the untutored Indian; 18th century interest in p. receives its fullest expression in Rousseau's pietistic doctrine of the children of nature; Wordsworth attributes superior wisdom to sheep-herders and children; Thoreau tells us that "we do not ride on the railroad: it rides upon us"; the poetry of Rimbaud is a record of defiance of Europe and dogmatic Christianity in favor of an Oriental "fatherland"... D.H. Lawrence makes a similar condemnation of Western civilization and advocates a return to an older mode of living based on a recognition of man's "blood nature." Primitivists have differed widely on the nature of the evils and weaknesses of civilized life, the causes of these evils, the positive values of the primitive life, and the degree to which a regression to the primitive is possible. — *Princeton Encyclopedia of Poetry and Poetics*

MODERN PRIMITIVES examines a vivid contemporary *enigma*: the growing revival of highly visual (and sometimes shocking) "primitive" body modification practices—tattooing, multiple piercing, and scarification. Perhaps Nietzsche has an explanation: "One of the things that may drive thinkers to despair is the recognition of the fact that the *illogical* is necessary for man and that out of the illogical comes much that is good. It is so firmly rooted in the passions, in language, in art, in religion and generally in everything that gives value to life, that it cannot be withdrawn without thereby injuring all these beautiful things. It is only the all-too-naive person who can believe that the nature of man can be changed into a purely logical one."

Civilization, with its emphasis on logic, may be stifling and life-thwarting, yet a cliche-ridden illusion as to what is "primitive"provides no solution to the *problem*: how do we achieve an integration of the poetic and scientific imagination in our lives? There are pitfalls on both sides, and what is absolutely not intended is any romanticization of "nature" or "primitive society." After all, advances in science and technology have eliminated much mind-numbing, repetitive labor, and inventions such as the inexpensive microcomputer have opened up unprecedented possibilities for individual creative expression.

Obviously, it is impossible to return to an authentic "primitive" society. Those such as the Tasaday in the Philippines and the Dayaks in Borneo are irrevocably contaminated. Besides having been dubiously idealized and only partially understood in the first place, under scrutiny many "primitive" societies reveal forms of repression and coercion (such as the Yanoamo, who ritually bash each other's heads in, and African groups who practice clitoridectomy—removal of the clitoris) which would be unbearable to emancipated individuals of today. What is implied by the revival of "modern primitive" activities is the desire for, and the dream of, *a more ideal society.*

Amidst an almost universal feeling of powerlessness to "change the world," individuals arc changing what they *do* have power over: *their own bodies.* That shadowy zone between the physical and the psychic is being probed for whatever insight and freedoms may be reclaimed. By giving visible bodily expression to unknown desires and latent obsessions welling up from within, individuals can provoke change—however inexplicable—in the external world of the social, besides freeing up a creative part of themselves; some part of their essence. (However, generalized proselytization has no place here—some people should definitely *not* get tattoos. Having a piercing is no infallible indication of advanced consciousness; as Anton LaVey remarked, "I've known plenty of people who have had tattooing and all kinds of modifications to their bodies—who are really screwed up!")

Art has always mirrored the zeitgeist of the time. In this Postmodern epoch in which all the art of the past has been assimilated, consumerized, advertised and replicated, the last artistic territory resisting co-optation and commodification by Museum and Gallery remains the Human Body. For a tattoo is more than a painting on skin; its meaning and reverberations cannot be comprehended without a knowledge of the history and mythology of its bearer. Thus it is a true poetic creation, and is always more than meets the eye. As a tattoo is grounded on living skin, so its essence emotes a poignancy unique to the mortal human condition. Likewise, no two piercings can be identical, because no two faces, bodies or genitalia are alike.

These body modifications perform a vital function identical with art: they "genuinely stimulate passion and spring directly from the original sources of emotion, and are not something tapped from the cultural reservoir." (Roger Cardinal) Here that neglected function of art: *to stimulate the mind*, is unmistakably *alive.* And all of these modifications bear witness to personal pain endured which cannot be *simulated.* Although... society's machinery of co-optation gets faster and faster: a recent issue of *New York Woman* reported the marketing of *non-piercing* nipple rings ranging from $26.50 to $10,000! No doubt further attempts at commercialization lie just around the corner...

This book presents a wide range of rationales, ranging from the functional ("The *ampallang* makes sex *much* better!") to the extravagantly poetic and metaphysical. The archetypes have been investigated; nevertheless, numerous practitioners are absent—it was simply not possible to interview everyone of relevance. Many of the subjects started their experiments as children: before he was 12, Ed Hardy had begun coloring "tattoos" on his peers; Fakir Musafar was enacting various primitive rituals borrowed from *National Geographic* by the age of 14. All share in common a *creative imperative* to which they have yielded in a kind of ultimate commitment: they have granted their *own bodies* as the artistic medium of expression.

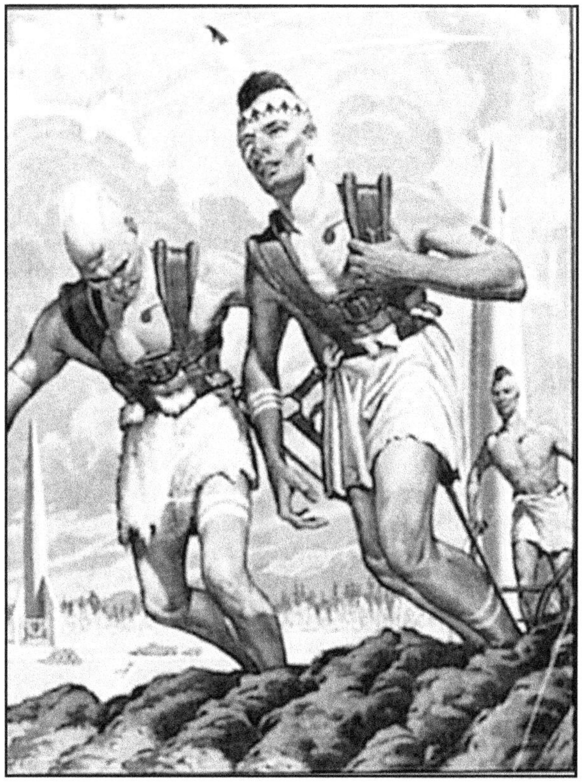

Cover painting from *Astounding Science Fiction*, June 1952.

Increasingly, the necessity to prove to the self the authenticity of unique, thoroughly private sensation becomes a threshold more difficult to surmount. Today, something as basic as sex itself is inextricably intertwined with a flood of alien images and cues implanted from media programming and advertising. But one thing remains fairly certain: *pain* is a uniquely personal experience; it remains loaded with tangible shock value. The most extreme practitioners of SM probe the psychic territory of pain in search of an "ultimate," mystical proof that in their relationship (between the "S" and the "M"), the meaning of "trust" has been explored to its final limits, stopping just short of the infliction/experiencing of death itself.

The central, pivotal change in the world of the twentieth century—the wholesale de-individualization of man and society—has been accomplished by an inundation of mass-produced images which, acting on humans, bypass any "logical" barriers of resistance, colonizing the memory cells of any receptive viewer within range. Almost unnoticed, first-hand "experience" and un-self-conscious creative activities (hobbies such as whittling or quilt-making) have been shunted aside in favor of a passive intake of images which the brain finds "pleasurable" and "relaxing": watching TV. The result: people all over the world share a common image bank of spurious memories and experiences, gestures, role models—even nuances of various linguistic styles, ranging from that of Peewee Herman to JFK to the latest commercial.

Our minds are colonized by images. Images are a virus. How does a virus work? "Viruses are not cells; they are made up merely of *genetic material*—DNA or RNA. But once inside a host cell, the virus insinuates itself into the cell's replicative processes by attaching to its DNA or RNA, and tricks the cell into producing more viruses through the same mechanisms the cell uses to copy its own genes. Thus sabotaged, the cell not only fails to perform its intended function, but also is forced to help the enemy multiply." (Robin M. Henig, *Vogue*, March, 1988) In the absence of truly unique, first-person experience in one's own RNA-coded memory cells, how can one feel confident about one's basic "identity"? And by extension, how can one, lacking unique experiences, create something truly eccentric? Virtually every experience possible in the world today: from touring Disneyland to trucking on photo safaris in Africa—has already been registered in the brain through images from a movie or TV *program*—an apt word indeed. (We are programmed, but for what? Where does the image end and reality begin?) It is cynically appropriate that the word *faux* (a pop correlative of the academic signifier, "simulation") has comfortably settled into the working vocabulary of the '80s.

All the "modem primitive" practices being revived—so called "permanent" tattooing, piercing, and scarification—underscore the realization that death itself, the Grim Reaper, must be stared straight in the face, unflinchingly, as part of the continuing struggle to free ourselves from our complexes, to get to know our hidden instincts, to work out unaccountable aggressions and satisfy devious urges. Death remains the standard whereby the authenticity and depth of all activities may be judged. And [complex] eroticism has always been the one implacable enemy of death. It is necessary to uncover the mass of repressed desires lying within the unconscious so that a *New Eroticism* embracing the common identity of pain and pleasure, delirium and reason, and founded on a *full knowledge* of evil and perversion, may arise to inspire radically improved social relations.

All sensual experience functions to free us from "normal" social restraints, to awaken our deadened bodies to life. All such activity points toward a goal: the creation of the "complete" or "integrated" man and woman, and in this we are yet prisoners digging an imaginary tunnel to freedom. Our most inestimable resource, the unfettered imagination, continues to be grounded in the only truly precious possession we can ever have and know, and which is ours to do with what we will: *the human body.*

—V. Vale

FAKIR MUSAFAR

Photographer Charles Gatewood first introduced RE/Search to Fakir Musafar in January, 1982 at a Chinese restaurant. Dressed in an expensive business suit and tie, Fakir looked the part of a 52-year-old Silicon Valley advertising executive. But during the course of dinner he proceeded to remove his tie, insert a large bone through his nose, and work two 3/8" steel circlets into each earlobe, remarking, "There—I feel *much* more comfortable." Then he unbuttoned his white broadcloth shirt and inserted twin pearl-handled daggers into two holes in his chest, forming an open "V" pattern.

Nobody else in the restaurant seemed to have noticed the transition from modern executive to modern primitive. The startling yet smoothly achieved transformation was accompanied by a brief autobiographical account citing an early influence by *National Geographic* and *Compton's Picture Encyclopedia*. Fakir saw the "primitives" depicted in their photographs not as objects of derision but as role models signifying a forgotten direction for future development and evolution. By the time he was twelve, Fakir had begun a systematic, personal exploration of virtually every body modification and ritual practice known to man—all done clandestinely until the '80s.

Since the release of the 1985 film *Dances Sacred and Profane* (in which he did the primitive rituals of a Sun Dance and a Kavandi Bearing), Fakir has given numerous lectures accompanied by slide shows, "live" demonstrations of rituals and practices, and showings of *Dances Sacred and Profane* for which he is the booking agent. He has published a series of publications titled *Body Play*, and has been featured in several videos by Charles Gatewood and others. Fakir is now world-renowned for his workshops, performances and publishing. What follows is a condensation of conversations conducted 1982 to 1986, and is representative of his philosophy and thought to that date.

■ *ANDREA JUNO: Let's start from the beginning.*

■ FAKIR: I was born August 10, 1930, at Aberdeen, in the Northeastern corner of South Dakota. At a very early age I was aware I was an alien; I didn't belong where I was. Whatever was natural, rational and sensible to me was unnatural and repulsive to other people. From the very beginning I just didn't seem to fit.

Until I reached puberty I had some strange powers, like kinaesthetic ability—sometimes I could make small objects on the table, like playing cards, jump. I went into trance states a lot, and saw faces melt and change—especially when adults were talking and I couldn't go out and play. At a very early age I had a great desire to feel strong sensations in my body.

■ *VALE: And when did these feelings begin?*

■ F: One summer when I was only six or seven, my dad took me to some dusty carnival. We saw a man in a diving suit descend into a tank of water and something like lightning hit me. Then we went to the ten-in-one show. There a man was being tattooed. Instantly I knew what was going on. Right then I had an incurable

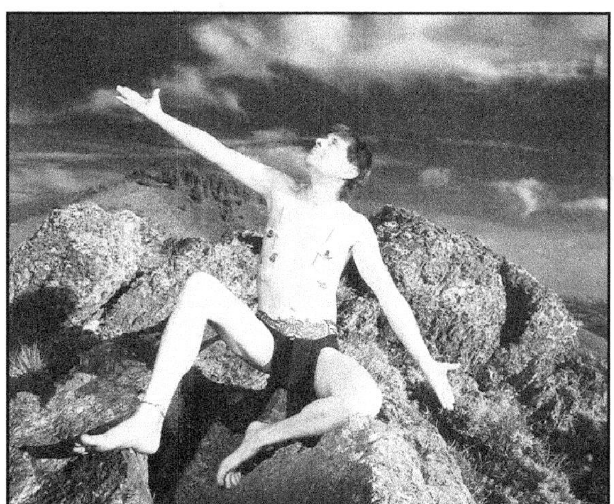

Photo by Bobby Neel Adamas.

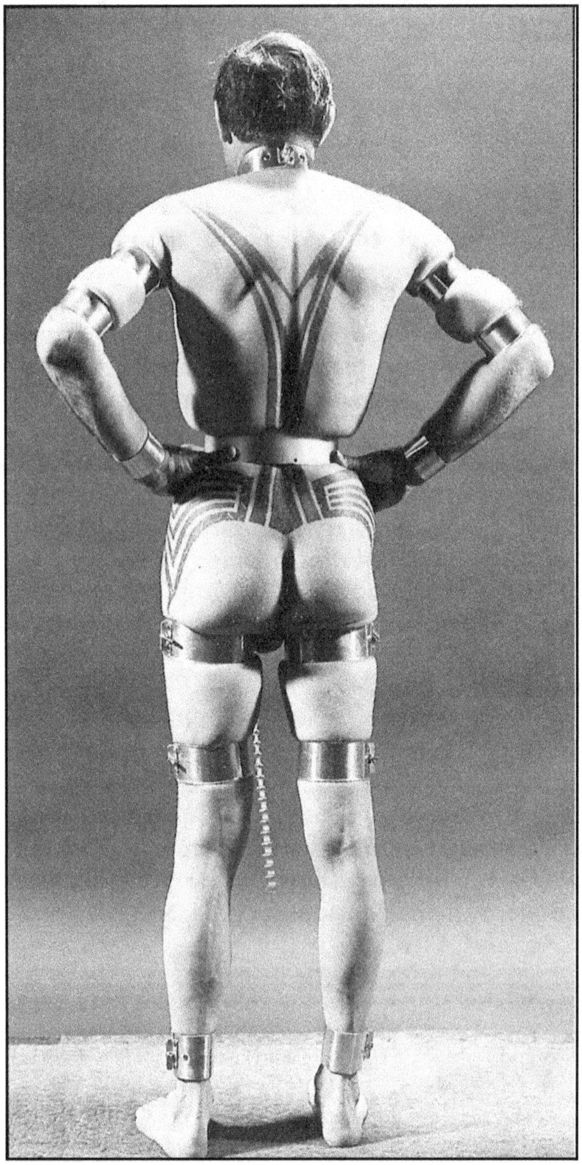

Fakir reshapes his limbs with tight metal bands.

desire to make marks on and put holes in my body, to feel these odd sensations and do things with my body.

When I was going to school, there was an immense cultural conceit about people from other lands: "Oh, isn't this quaint? Those crazy cannibals!" And the (pre-1940s) encyclopedias showed *everything*: naked natives were like butterflies and toads. People in our culture didn't quite consider them human beings. I lived through a period during which all the encyclopedias were rewritten and expurgated. After WWII, photos like these were deleted, along with the explanation of those practices. They were not considered fit for growing children—too bizarre.

And of course, like a lot of people, I grew up tempting my primitive lust by reading good old *National Geographic*. It awakened a lot of people's consciousness. Taken as a whole, the old *National Geographics* constitute quite a compendium and survey of primitive practices. Since World War II they've adopted a new "humanitarian" policy; since they finally got around to considering these natives as human beings, they can't show them naked anymore!

Theaters used to regularly show travelogue movies. One that influenced me a lot was called *Dangerous Journey*. I've had people in New York, Hollywood, and the Smithsonian Institute hunting archives and vaults for a print of that movie. But I think they've all been destroyed!

The act of doing this slow piercing and surrendering to the experience is a transcendent spiritual event. But people in this culture have few precedents for such an exercise in self-transformation.

■ *V: What was it about?*

■ F: The daughter of Theodore Roosevelt and a man named Armand Denis went on "The Denis/Roosevelt Expedition" just prior to WWII. They photographed the most most bizarre body practices in the world and put them all together in one movie. It was released in 1946. It was a shocker, believe me! It contained some of the best footage of African women getting scarification; women getting giraffe-necks (who start at the age of 6 or 7); kavandi-bearing in India—it's a fantastic film.

So as a youth I was an avid reader, and starting with "A," I read through the entire set of *Compton's Picture Encyclopedias.* These were pre-WWII, and showed a lot of primitive people, like a boy from Burma with interesting designs tattooed on his thighs—the first Iban tattoos I saw.

Below another photo of a young man from New Guinea was the caption, "He must be the talk of his village, for above all things his people admire small waists and well-spiked noses." Here the custom was for young men to be constricted in tight belts. A father would take his son to

Ibitoe from New Guinea wears the Itiburi waist belt.

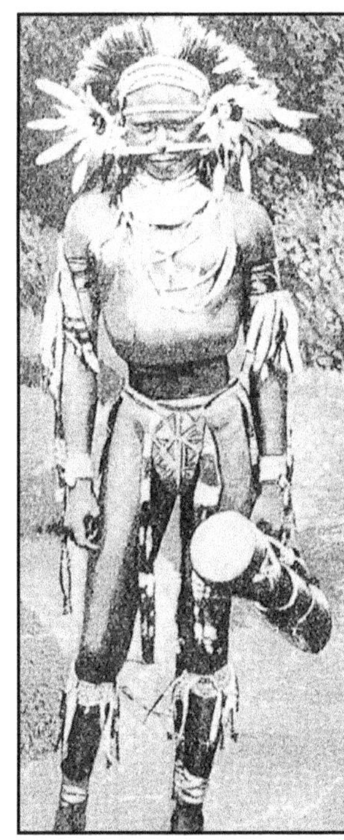

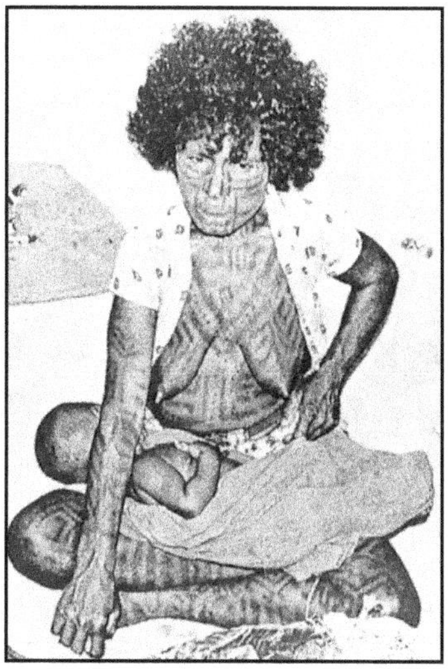

Papua New Guinea woman with tattoos.

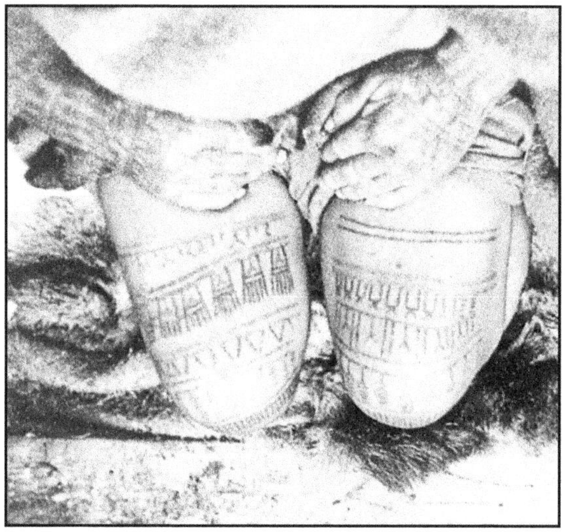

Eskimo Indian with tattoos made by pulling sooty thread through skin.

a maternal uncle and say, "Suffer my son to bear the Itiburi" (Itiburi is the tight band around the waist). The maternal uncle would say, "Yes, I accept your son. Will the son accept the Itiburi?" And the son almost always says "Yes," because it's shameful if he doesn't.

They wrap a very tight band around the boy's waist, and he has to wear it day and night, regardless of whether he can sleep and eat or not. And finally he gets used to it. Later, he does have the same choice in the matter; he can say, "I'd like my Itiburi replaced," which means they put one on that's stiffer, wider and tighter. Usually the progression is from a tight cloth to a bark belt. The result of this initiation constriction make the youth incredibly small in the middle—wasp-like.

Then the young men become dandies and sit around and put feathers in their hair and decorate their bodies all day. In a sense they become kind of effeminate in their society, while the women assume the power and provider role. (This was a matriarchal society where women select men for mates. A male with a small waist was prized because he couldn't eat too much and be a burden on the woman provider.) I was fascinated, so I became an Ibitoe to see what it was like, and fell in love with the practice. I have an early photo of myself emulating Ibitoe garb, with a very tight waistband. I wore that frequently for more than thirty years and it had quite an effect on me. My torso became totally re-proportioned: chest expanded like a pouter pigeon, waist permanently fixed at a small diameter (24" to 28"). Not too many people can claim approximately the same size waist from age 18 to 55!

A lot of photos I took back then are examples of early self-photography; some were taken with a little folding camera. I'd tie a string to the shutter button, line up the lens, move back and pull the string and take the picture.

■ *V: You've hidden these activities from your family and society most of your life?*

■ F: Yes. I started doing them in secret, generally in the basement of our house. At age 13, for example, I made my first piercing in the foreskin of my penis. I think modern primitives are *born*, not made. Early childhood experiences only open the door to what's already inside. If you had very strong inclinations in a previous lifetime, and did certain practices like change the body to a different shape, color, form and size, then when you're born again, no matter what culture you're born into, you're going to want to do what you did before. At least that's my explanation for myself.

So my first piercing wasn't quick. It was done with a clamp with a sharp point that presses little by little. It takes many hours—in this case about a day—before the little stud came popping through the other side. The act of doing this slow piercing and surrendering to the experience is a transcendent spiritual event. But people in this culture have few precedents for such an exercise in self-transformation.

I also had the desire to mark my body, so by the time I reached high school I had already made little hand needles and tattooed some designs on my chest. The first one I did turned out to be a holy symbol of North Africa, a protective "bug" of the Bedouins.

Original Fakir Musafar from Persia, circa 1800.

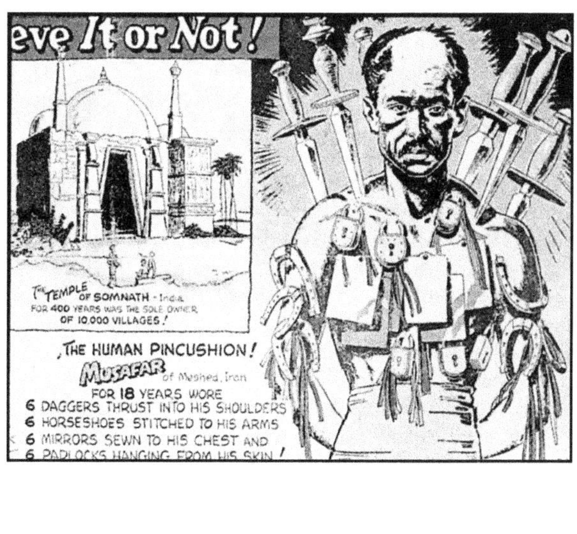

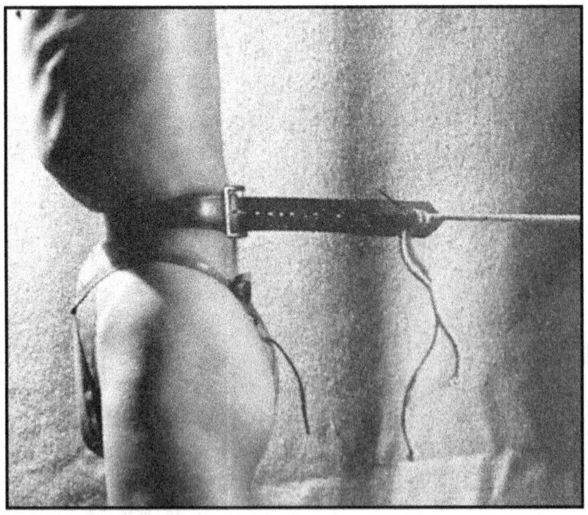

Fakir at age 19 using belt to constrict his waist to 14".

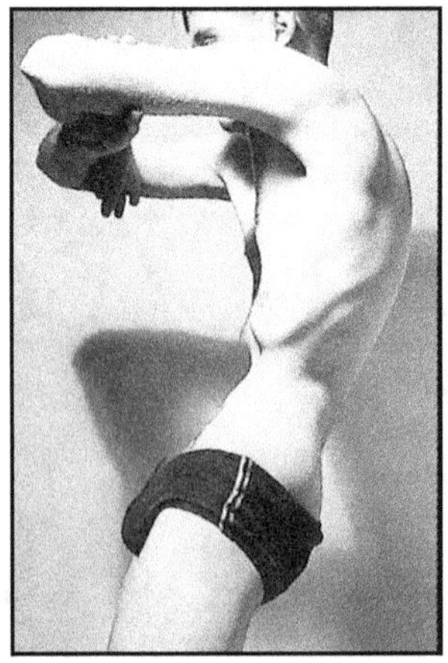

Fakir at age 19.

I did several more. At this point I had not researched how to tattoo, or the history of design, or anything—I just *knew*. I took some of my mother's sewing needles, tied them tightly together, dipped them in some india ink and pushed them into my skin. The ink ran down the needles, entered the pricked skin and lo and behold, when you wiped the ink away, there was a mark that didn't go away!

■ *V: What did you base your tattoo designs on?*

■ F: Inner visions. Similar, I suppose, to Balinese textile patterns that came from altered states and trips to another world. Same for the one on my back. Any tattoo that didn't come from inside you is not for you. Sometime the tattoo artists in primitive cultures were shamans. They envisioned the marks, tattooed them on the body, and then the person who got the tattoo was whole, complete. It was their pattern, their mark, and without that mark they were incomplete. That's part of the magic of the tattoo…

■ *V: How about your American Indian connection? How did that happen?*

■ F: Well, I grew up surrounded by Indian culture in South Dakota—strong echoes of the past. About two-thirds of the state of South Dakota in the 1930s was Indian reservations. It was the one last dead hopeless place where the White Man brought in Indians from as far away as Florida. So there were Indians of all cultures and tribal backgrounds mixed together on South Dakota reservations.

At an early age I suffered the same recurring nightmare once or twice a week. I walked down a dusty street, with incredibly long black cast-iron sewer pipes stacked up against a great yellow brick building. It was high noon, and I was all alone. I *had* to get from *here* to *there* by passing these pipes. I knew it was risky, but I started walking down this street looking at these menacing pipes. And every time I had this dream, by the time I reached the middle there would be a huge rumbling sound like an earthquake, and all the pipes would come crashing down and crush me. I went through this again and again through my childhood.

Later on in life I found out what it meant. The dream was symbolic of a real experience I had in an Indian body. At the time the Indians were being wiped out, in this previous life, I had been an Indian lad and at about age 22 was involved in an intertribal war.

■ *V: What happened, specifically?*

■ F: This event occurred along the South Dakota/Minnesota border. I'm supposed to warn our tribe of an ambush. I'm riding a pony along the banks of the Yellow Bank river where opposition Indians had made a trap of logs and debris piled very high, with some way of cutting it loose and I was crushed. I didn't know I was dead, and I tried to engage in combat. But I only had my spirit body and couldn't fight. I wandered around for about 90 years near this spot until I reincarnated in this body.

My mother came from a Minnesota German family with ten children. She had been a maverick—the first female to defy the Prussian iron-fisted rule of her father. She broke away to Aberdeen Business College and met a charming young aviator—a barn-storming young pilot who had just started a small airline company. They met at a Halloween party. I grew up in the back-cockpit of a bi-plane.

■ *V: Where did you get the name Fakir Musafar?*

■ F: From a very early *Ripley's Believe It or Not* feature, which I cut out of the paper and saved. I still have it. The original Fakir Musafar was an 19th century Sufi who wandered around for eighteen years with daggers and other things stuck in his body. He was trying to educate people in the mysteries he had discovered, but they didn't understand him or pay much attention to him. Finally he died of a broken heart.

At age 13, for example, I made my first piercing in the foreskin of my penis. I think modern primitives are born, not made. Early childhood experiences only open the door to what's already inside.

■ *V: You've got very early photos of yourself practicing your rituals. How did that come about?*

■ F: When I was doing my early experiments, I was into anything to do with fire, light, or electricity. I learned how to make gunpowder, fireworks, batteries, and also do photography.

■ *V: What were you learning by doing your "body play" experiments?*

■ F: I soon learned the value of constrictions or encumberments. Anything that's fixed on the body for

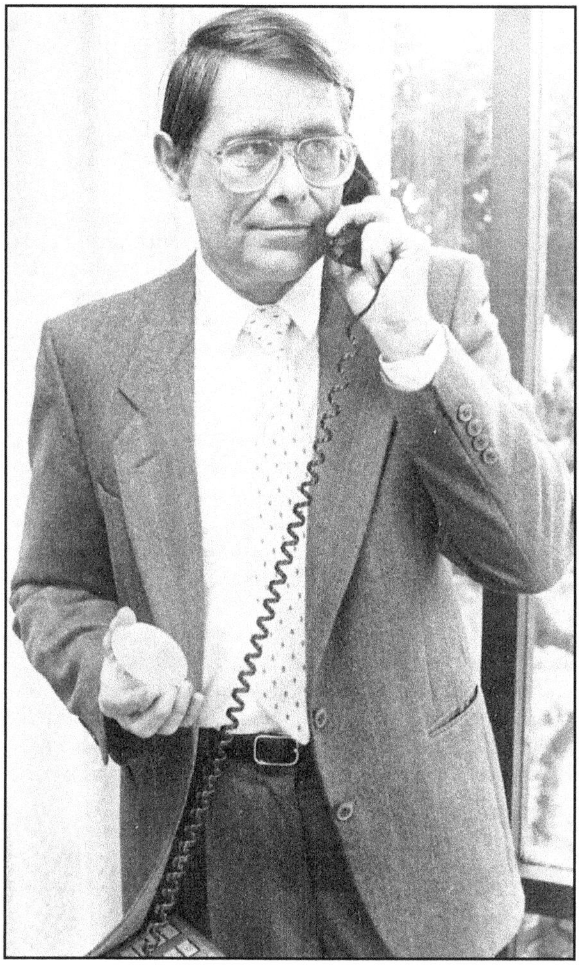

Photo by Charles Gatewood.

a long period of time changes your outlook on life. It changes your relationship to life and the body you're living in. If you put on a tight belt and wear it for 20 hours, strange things start to happen to you. Not just physically, but to your consciousness psychically and spiritually! In the basement I found some old chains and wrapped about 100 pounds of them around me and clanked around in them for half a day when my parents were gone. I shot a photograph of myself with a crude remote-control string set-up.

I also found it easy to push needles through my body; I just did this without any encouragement; nobody knew. I clipped on clothespins in fans on my body; I temporarily pierced my ears and nose. And I made photos of all these experiments. Of course you didn't run down and get these developed at the photo shop.

My uncle had loaned me a little camera he had gotten in World War I. He'd been a "Johnny Doughboy" and had kept in his pocket a 1915 vest-pocket folding Kodak camera. When I started shooting my photos WWII was going on, and film was hard to find—it was rationed. But every now and then some would arrive, and I'd rush down and wait in line and get a roll of 127 Verichrome film. I taught myself developing by reading a book, and that's where these pictures came from. These are actual prints I made [photos show progression of teenage Ibitoe waist training, piercing, etc].

■ *V: What did you learn about pain?*

■ F: One of the first altered states you can learn is to separate your consciousness from your body. You don't walk away from your body, you don't separate from your body, but the part of you that feels and thinks can separate from the feelings in the body itself. So that makes it possible for you to push a needle through. *You* don't feel the pain; the *body* feels the pain, and you observe the body recording or feeling sensation. Then it's not pain. If you can learn to separate your consciousness and your attention from your body, you can do almost anything to it and you don't feel pain! If all your attention is locked in your body, and not focused outside the body or on a specific body point, you'll feel pain. That's one of the first lessons I learned. That's an altered state. And there are hundreds of different kinds of altered states.

In a way it's a denigration, a cultural conceit, to label someone who does these activities as a "primitive." There are different societies and cultures on earth, and they've all developed different ways. Either they externalize, or they internalize. If they externalize, they develop tools which become technology or organized, rational science. That's what the Western culture is. Or, they can internalize and develop the other way, whereby they can do all kinds of physical things with magic. At this point in history, both approaches are starting to merge.

■ *AJ: You're a successful advertising executive, right?*

■ F: I suppose so; last year we grossed almost five million dollars. Although to me, that isn't really success. If I could move buildings with magic—*that's* successful!

■ *AJ: But there's something great about being able to exist in both worlds fluidly.*

■ F: Of course. And I appreciate both approaches. But I'm not saying it's easy to be a magic person in a technical culture. In college I took physics, chemistry, and became a ham radio operator and built transmitters out of scrap. They worked really well, but most of the time I did these science things by *instinct.*

Actually, science *is* magic. Take a key: most people don't really know how it works, but they trust it—to them it's really magic. They get into this iron pony with no fire in its belly, and if they go through a little ritual with this key, putting it in the right place and turning it the right way, something will happen. Magic works the same way—all of a sudden something will come to life—the car will become alive and move and take you where you want to go. People don't really know *how* it works or why, but they trust it and it works—at least most of the time

The movie *Little Big Man* showed what magic culture is about, and what a kid went through growing up in two cultures—I could identify with Dustin Hoffman. The old grandpa goes up on the hill to die, and everything's very serious. It starts to rain in his face, nothing happens, and he says, "Well, you know how it is with magic—sometimes it work and sometimes it doesn't! Ha ha ha!"

■ *AJ: That irreverence is vital. My favorite scene in* Dances Sacred and Profane *is when you arrive at this sacred spot where you're going to do this very serious ritual. Suddenly you're playing golf—*

■ F: Yes, knocking golf balls across the sacred ground! People in this country take themselves far too seriously. Magic tends to be more play.

Back to the biography: when I was 17 I had been doing these practices for awhile, and I had explored altered states. At the same time I was puttering in the basement making explosives and batteries as well as developing and processing film so I could record my body play. So on evenings, weekends, or holidays when my parents went out somewhere, I always would try to stay at home so I'd have an opportunity to do these things alone. I had to be very secretive; I couldn't let my parents know about *anything* I was doing. They would never understand. It was out of their range of experience in this embodiment or any other.

My parents had sent me to Lutheran Catechism School where I assumed the attitude of non-resistance: no matter how silly it might seem, I did anything they told me to do just to stay out of trouble. I was desperately afraid of looking like a kook; I knew I couldn't continue on doing what I thought was right if I looked like a kook; they would come down on me. So I was well-behaved. If the pastor wanted an explanation of transubstantiation, I would give it eloquently! I thought it was a crock of shit, of course. And "He died for your sins"—I never could understand that one! I didn't feel like a "sinner." Besides, only *I* can die for me; no one else can. I knew that instinctively, and nothing was going to change that.

Another thing that always bothered me was: they forced you to eat exactly on time, three times a day. I couldn't understand this; I wanted the human right not to eat, but they wouldn't allow that. There were many other things that were offensive to me: I had to cut my hair, and I didn't want to cut my hair. I was forced to live a very regulated, limited life, and my only relief was when I had a holiday or week when they went away and I could do something zany.

For example, when I was 17, I had fasted, I had not slept for 24 hours, and I put staples in a wall to pull ropes through in the outline of my body. (My book *Body Play* documents some of this.) After I had been dancing for hours with this logging chain around my body, I was getting into a numb, weary, robotic altered state—hyper-alert, however, despite lack of sleep. At 3 AM I started lashing myself to the wall, legs and torso tight. The only catch was, I wasn't sure if I could get loose, especially since my arms went numb—and it *was* possible that I could suffocate.

Actually, I wanted an experience that was right on the edge of death. Finally I got my body totally lashed to the wall, my arms in hooks, my head in a restraint, and I had a conscious out-of-the-body experience—and there's nothing else quite like that. You have a body, but it's fluid; you can walk through the walls, earth, iron... you can stay in the present, or walk forward or backward in time, just like walking into another room. You can walk into your future or go back a thousand years and see what's going on; there are no limits.

However, this out-of-body experience can be terrifying in that you have to literally go through all the symptoms of real death. And you feel them acutely. Numbness works its way up your legs; your arms go numb; finally it goes up your torso and hits your chest; you go through all the sensations of drowning or suffocating, yet you're not dead. You wonder, "Why am I not dead?" then there's a buzzing and a little light and you know your eyes work and you're still seeing things with physical sight.

At this point I just become a head—all my consciousness, all my attention located in the very center of my head. I'm still conscious of my heart beating, but it feels like I've been hung by an incredibly long rope and swung between two stone walls. My body goes *smash! smash! smash!* from one wall to the other, but it's actually my heartbeat—I'm feeling the power that makes my body go. Then at a crucial moment when this sensation is incredibly strong, there's a *snap!* like something breaks, and I hear a high-pitched sound like bells ringing.

By now I was floating, with no sensation of body or weight or anything—just warmth and comfort. Then finally, dimly, I became aware I could see, and I didn't know if I were dead or not. It was a helluva experiment for seventeen!

I realized I wasn't dead—if I were dead, I couldn't be thinking and be aware of anything, could I? I looked and saw the body pinned against the coalbin wall and thought, "I can't be looking at myself." In this state I had no fear, and it was a joyous experience. I really had a sense of knowing who I was—I was not a body, just a blob of consciousness that was really very free, and there was no time.

One of the first altered states you can learn is to separate your consciousness from your body. That makes it possible for you to push a needle through. You don't feel the pain; the body feels the pain.

I discovered that the only time you're aware of time, is when you're in a body! Because time belongs to nature; it's a part of trees getting green, having leaves, and leaves falling off. And your body belongs to nature—we don't own it, it isn't us, we just use it; it's like a house we live in. You live in a house but the house isn't you, it's your house, and you do with it as you please—if you want it pink, you paint it pink!

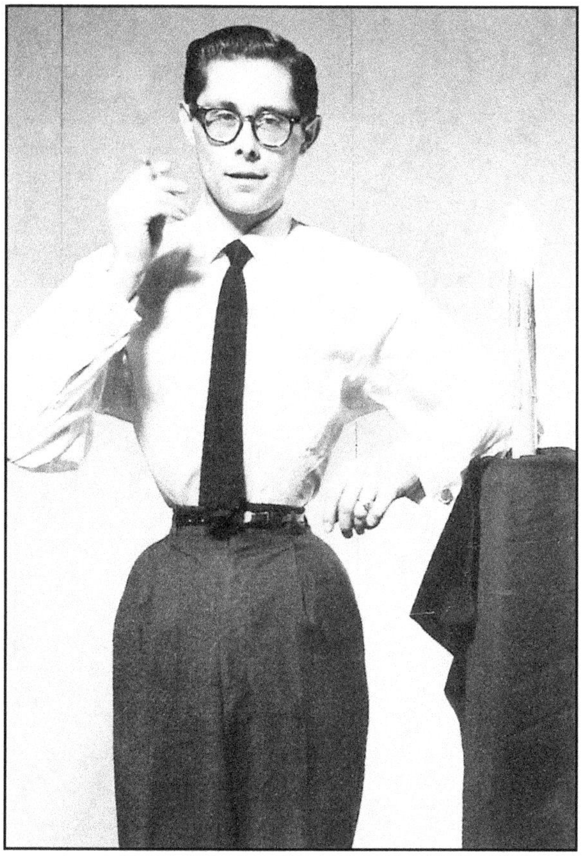

Fakir as the "Perfect Gentleman", 1959.

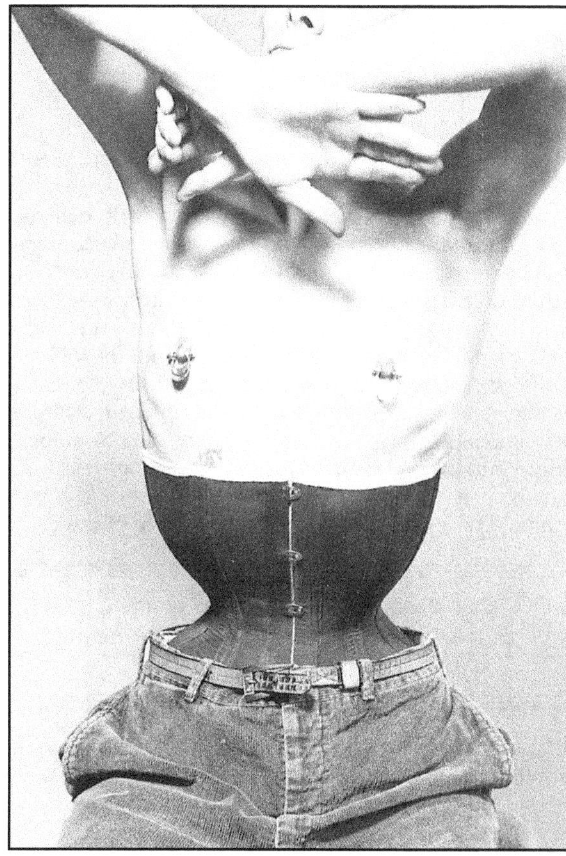

Fakir's hand-made corset with 19" waist.

Back to body play and modern primitives—they all seem to have this understanding that you live in this body but you're not your body. Although they may appear to be backward, people like Australian aborigines *know* something that people here don't know. And that's the reason they can poke holes in the body, they can tattoo it, they can decorate it—it's all just a joyous loving expression of decorating your house—an expression of the life force that lives in the house. To not do these things is *not to live*—it's to deny the purpose of why we're here. So, that's what I discovered (or re-discovered) at seventeen.

After this experience, my recurring nightmares disappeared—a lot of things changed for me. I felt more comfortable in this strange society and I went on to college to become an electrical engineer. I did just fine for two years until I hit higher mathematics where I got totally lost.

Then I became an English major. I could write sonnet after Shakespearian sonnet effortlessly—something that's very difficult for some people. But poetry is akin to magic—I was back on home turf.

■ *AJ: Wait a minute—how did you get down from the coalbin wall?*

■ F: I suspect my higher being guided me back and made the robot body automatically act, because my arms were totally dead, my legs were dead, and some parts of my body didn't come to life for hours! After I got released from the wall I collapsed and was there on the floor for some time. The whole experience lasted about five hours, and I was out of body for most of that. But once you have that experience you want it again—it's so beautiful!

So my whole life has been a constant exploration, experimentation and searching. And again it comes down to body play—the body is a crucial element. It's very hard to make music or play Tibetan bowls or work magic spells without a body—you can't *do* anything in the physical world without a body.

As time has gone by a magic power has accumulated. I use it in business; I don't make business decisions in a rational, logical way. And I've run into a lot of other business people—very successful, multi-millionaire, corporate people who, when push comes to shove, finally admit that they make their most important decisions on a magical basis. Because if they had to use rational means, they'd have no luck. But on the other hand, you must also have skills, intellect, rationality, discipline, and high standards to function effectively.

I think it's impossible for human beings to progress unless there are certain magical events that occur periodically. Whether they're done expertly by knowledgeable people or blunderingly, they still seem to work in the end. Those events are called rites of passage—initiation. They should occur a little before, during or after puberty, or you'll never ever become a really mature person. So, we have a world full of people with middle-aged bodies and child-like interiors—people who've never had a rite of passage, an initiation. Some people instinctively know this, and if society won't give them a rite of passage, they'll invent one! Teenagers will walk on the ledge of a building, scratch their initials in their arm with a safety pin, or something—run off and get a tattoo. It must be physical, it must be painful, it must be bloody, and it should leave a mark. Those are characteristics of a rite of passage.

It's a denigration, a cultural conceit, to label someone who does these kinds of activities a "primitive."

I think it would be more humane if we had wise people who were trained in magical arts to actually conduct young people through rites of passage, because they might make more advancement. If you were an Indian lad who had just reached puberty and whether you liked it or not had to undergo a Sun Dance ceremony—had your chest pierced and had to rip free over many hours—you invariably would be thrown into an altered state or two. And experiencing these altered states is what matures people—intellectually, emotionally or spiritually.

■ *AJ: I've heard people report a change in their lives after a tattoo.*

■ F: A lot of people have said that. The purpose of the tattoo is to *do* something for the person, to help realize the *individual* magic latent within them. It seems the purpose of the modern world is to wipe out *difference.* The genotypes of plants, birds, and animals originally generated more difference, more variety. Now we've got this great oppressive force that's trying to homogenize and make everything the same! And that we must resist and fight, because that's anti-life! Evil is "live" spelled backwards. Whatever would tend to crush the individual expression of life in people—that is evil.

After that experience at age seventeen, I did more serious experiments like: kavandi-bearing, where I went out of my body and floated above it. Encumberments: I put these on and wore them for weeks sometimes, and that's a helluva experience that I recommend to anybody. Constrictions: tight bands and belts all over. Penetration, bed of nails, hook-hanging by flesh hooks. Tattooing, Yoga, Contortion, Piercing.

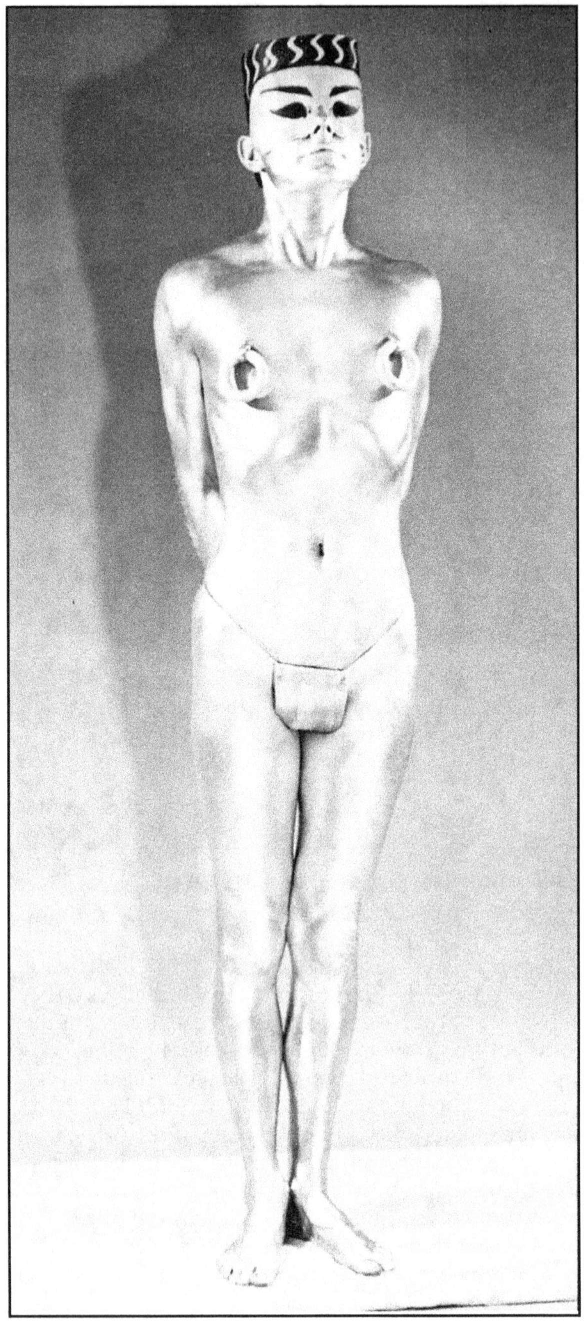

F: I do an ordeal by sealing up: all body openings are sealed up for several hours. Also I gild myself.
AJ: I thought if you totally gilded yourself, you would die after a few hours.
F: That's a myth from the movie *Goldfinger.* It's reasonably safe, although some gilt is toxic. I've been very careful to find a gilt and a way of doing this that isn't toxic; a way of applying it and getting it off. But you will run into problems and develop tremendous skin rashes, etc. if you don't get it off soon enough.
V: I thought that if you had a tiny untouched area at the base of the spine, you'd live.
F: No, that's a nice myth but it's not true. You do need to breathe through your nose and your mouth—if you stop that, you're in trouble!

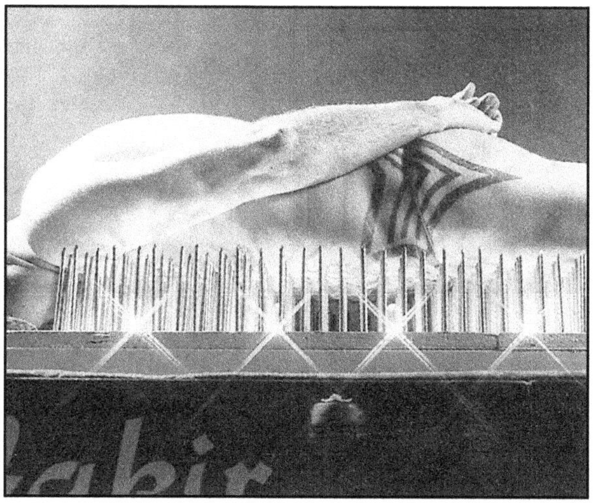

Fakir on his bed of nails.

Suspension by hooks; they do this in Ceylon for 4 or 5 hours. Enlarging my nipples. More Ibitoe experiments. And this was all secret and private.

There was more: isolation—in the mask. Gilding—you can do that for 3 or 4 hours. Corseting—the "Perfect Gentleman" [see photo] was another classic experiment for the Fakir.

■ *V: When did you start appearing publicly... showing others your secret activities?*

■ F: In 1970 I got very friendly with the *Ripley's Believe It Or Not* Wax Museum franchise owners in San Francisco, and appeared on a Bed of Swords. We had mobs you wouldn't believe. I was out in the street with chains on drumming up a crowd, then I ran back into the museum. I had a platform right at the exit and was lying on a bed of swords, and as people left they thought it was another wax dummy. One lady came over and poked me and shrieked, "Ohmigod, that's a *real person*!"

I appeared in the Renaissance Faire when it originally opened in Los Angeles. I drove down in my Mercedes every weekend for a month and appeared as the Fakir. In 1975 I appeared briefly at the Bondage, Fetish and Leather Ball in Los Angeles and disappeared when all the flash cameras started—it was fun.

Then in 1978 I totally came "out of the closet" as "Fakir Musafar" at the Tattoo Convention in Reno. I hooked daggers in my chest and whirled around in chains, chopped cabbages, and did yoga positions. Then I laid on a rack of machetes, and a belly dancer stood on me and did a little dance. Sailor Sid broke bricks across my back while I lay on the Bed of Nails. Then I found a hotel cart that valets use, hooked it up to the holes in my chest, and pulled the belly dancer on the cart across the ballroom floor for a finale.

■ *AJ: How do you view pain during your rituals and ceremonies?*

■ F: For me there is no real pain, only one thing—*sensation*. It's nice to have sensation through a body, because then you know you're alive. If you stub your toe against the bed you can feel pain because it's *unexpected*. But you can be trained in karate to knock your toes against a brick until it doesn't bother you. You have a sensation but it's not unexpected, so that sensation gets *modified*.

The negativity of pain (strong, unexpected sensation) only exists for people who are relatively undeveloped. If you have enough training, instruction and practice, you can transcend, transmute or change a sensation to anything you wish. The more you focus your attention on the pain and shift it, the less it'll bother you. The body feels the sensation, but you can learn to quickly separate your consciousness from sensation and then it isn't pain anymore.

That's what I do when I hang by fleshhooks. People say, "That's incredibly painful!" I say, "No, it's

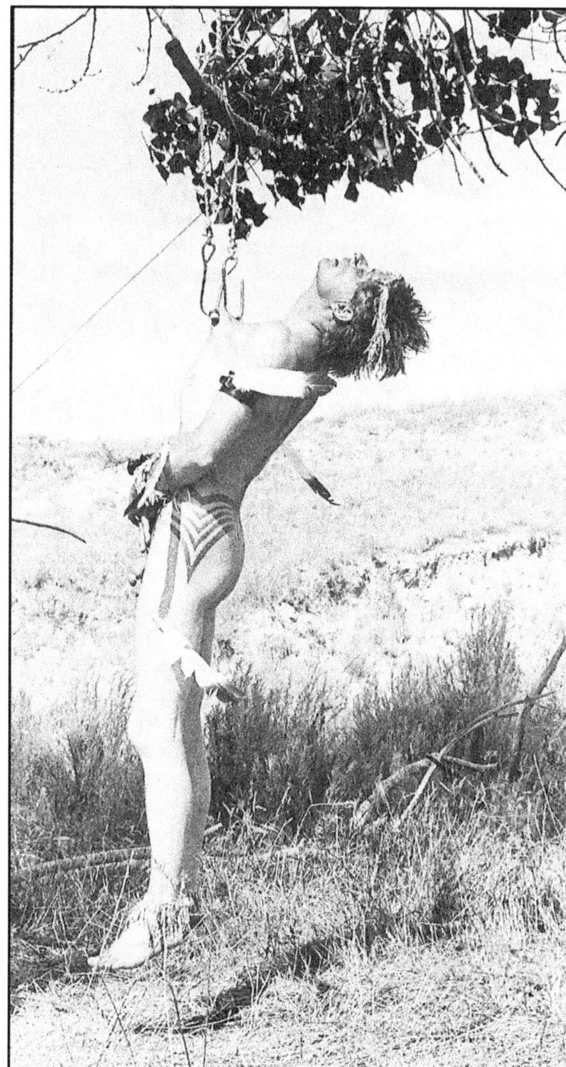

Fakir hanging by fleshhooks performing an Indian O-Kee-Pa ceremony. Photo by Charles Gatewood.

ecstatic, it's beautiful!" They say, "You're crazy—how can that be?" I say, "It depends on your training, how you've conditioned yourself and what state you go into." If, at a certain point, I don't make a transition when I'm about to go up on fleshhooks, I can't do it. I say, "No—can't do it today."

Oddly enough, the more intense pain (sensation) is, the less localized it becomes. Like lying on a bed of nails—the first ten minutes you're conscious of maybe 10 of the 40 points you're on. After awhile they all tend to merge into one another, and after more time you don't feel like you're lying on nails at all. You'd be surprised how expensive a bed of nails is these days! They shouldn't vary more than 1/8", otherwise you'll dip and one or two will poke you real hard, and that'll distract you. It's best to lay on your tummy, mainly because there's more padding on the front of your body. In the back you hit the bones of your spine.

People should all try the bed of nails—it doesn't cause any permanent damage, so why not—you might learn something! People are often surprised—it just isn't what they thought it would be. You can disconnect your consciousness on the bed of nails; it's unpleasant only until your perception shifts. You can feel this happening stage-by-stage.

■ *V: I have doubts that even your kind of training can transcend an experience like being under the electric prod and wires of an Argentine torturer.*

■ F: You're probably right. That's non-consenting brutality—something else. I doubt if many people being tortured in the Inquisition *enjoyed* it. A lot of torture was intended to be fatal. Crucifixion was intended to be fatal—Jesus did a neat yoga trick when he survived the cross. That particular crucifixion has been warped and distorted into a big cult—the biggest cult I know!

■ *V: It's funny how such a basic goal of life—to raise consciousness—is so universally perverted.*

■ F: It took a long time and a lot of "experiments" before I saw the White Light and finally met my Maker face-to-face. It was out in my garage during a hanging ceremony. And I dumped my "made identity" (ego) and went through all these steps: I was not afraid to be nude in front of people, I was not afraid feel strong sensation; I was not afraid to get sexually aroused and go beyond it; I was not afraid to go further yet and drift up into nirvana. Finally, I could leave that state and awaken to realize there was a calm, surging White Light just above me, and it said, "Hello! I'm you!" And you can't *imagine* the love I felt. I've talked to a few people who've had the clinical death experience and what many of them felt was exactly the same!

■ F: I do an ordeal by sealing up: all body openings are sealed up for several hours. Also I gild myself.

■ *AJ: I thought if you totally gilded yourself, you would die after a few hours.*

■ F: That's a myth from the movie *Goldfinger*. It's reasonably safe, although some gilt is toxic. I've been very careful to find a gilt and a way of doing this that isn't toxic; a way of applying it and getting it off. but you will run into problems and develop tremendous skin rashes, etc., if you don't get it off soon enough.

■ *V: I thought that if you had any untouched area at the base of the spine, you'd live.*

■ F: No, that's a nice myth but it's not true. You do need to breathe through your nose and your mouth.—if you stop that, you're in trouble!

MODERN PRIMITIVES

■ *V: Can you talk about the idea of "modern primitives"?*

■ F: The whole purpose of "modern primitive" practices is to get more and more spontaneous in the expression of *pleasure with insight.* Too much structuring somehow destroys any possibility of an ecstatic breakthrough in life experiences.

"Modern Primitive" is a term I thought *I* had coined in 1967 when I met Bud "Viking" Navarro and Zapata in Los Angeles. We used the term to describe a non-tribal person who responds to primal urges and does something with the body. There is an increasing trend among certain young people now to get pierced and tattooed. Some do it as a "real" response to primal urges and some do it for "kicks"—they aren't serious and don't know what they're doing. People are getting piercings in places where no one should get them! One girl got a piercing like a beauty mark above her lip, but anything she wore would get caught in her teeth! She had to give it up.

I had a problem with one young man who wanted red rubber balls sewn on him. I knew where they should be placed, but he kept saying, "No, I want them here and here"—he had made up his mind to put them in places where you can't sew them on; where they don't bounce and feel good. So he put one on his sternum and then realized it wouldn't work. Sometimes people get the "primitive" spirit but then go off on their own flights of fancy, totally ignoring something that took thousands of years of trial and error by people who did

Modern Primitive Zapata.

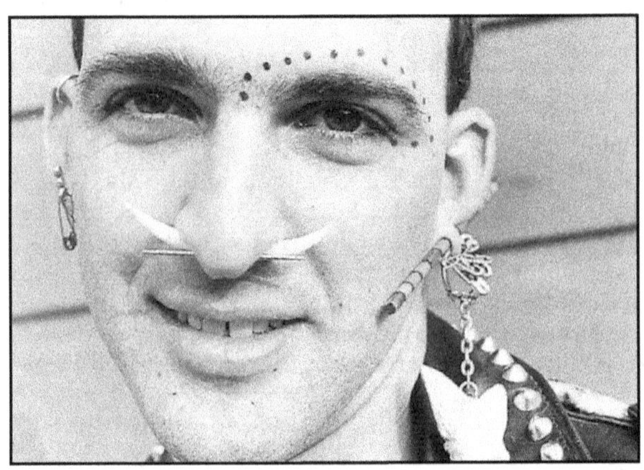

this full-time trying to find out what it's all about, for the best effects.

Bodybuilders are a modern-day *accepted* manifestation of body modification. How do they do what they do? By a semi-mutilatory process: ripping muscles that have to regrow, and when they regrow they get grosser, denser. They literally rip the muscles apart—that's what they're doing when they lift weights in a bodybuilding course. Then they have to eat tons of protein so the building process is fast.

Most other cultures revere androgynous characters and people who are different—fools, midgets, nuts—as "god-like." In this culture these people could only find a place in a carnival.

Physical difference frightens people in our culture more than anything else. You can be as aberrant as hell mentally, politically, socially, but do one little thing physical—put a bone in your nose—and boy, you're in trouble! They'll let you do almost anything as long as it isn't physical.

Most other cultures revere androgynous characters and people who are different—fools, midgets, nuts—as "god-like." In this culture these people could only find a place in a carnival, but then that faded out of vogue. Now you can't have a ten-in-one show anymore because all the freaks are in institutions or they've been patched up with plastic surgery or something—made more normal. Since 1945 it's been impossible to have a freak show—I know some people who tried to find enough freaks to have one, and they couldn't find any! It's a helluva world: you can't even find freaks anymore! Everyone "has" to look the same!

There are other cultures that are very tolerant of physical differences, but very intolerant of social or political differences—most tribal cultures are that way. They feel very threatened, and don't like people to come up with strange philosophies. They don't mind if you have bones in your nose or wherever you want to put 'em—that doesn't frighten them at all.

■ *V: What are the ways you can modify the body?*

■ F: There are basically seven different ways you can modify or work on the body; seven categories of body play:

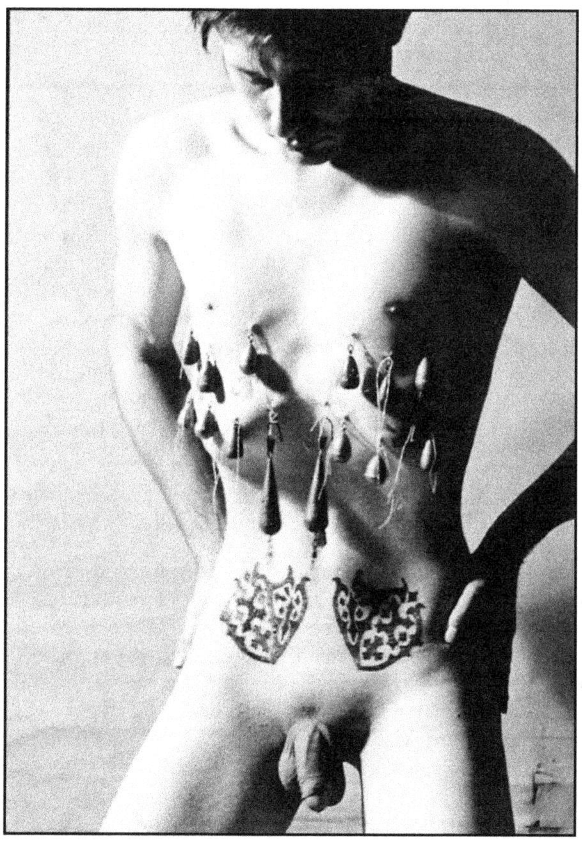

Fakir, in 1954, with two 8 oz. weights and twelve 4 oz. lead weights sewn on.

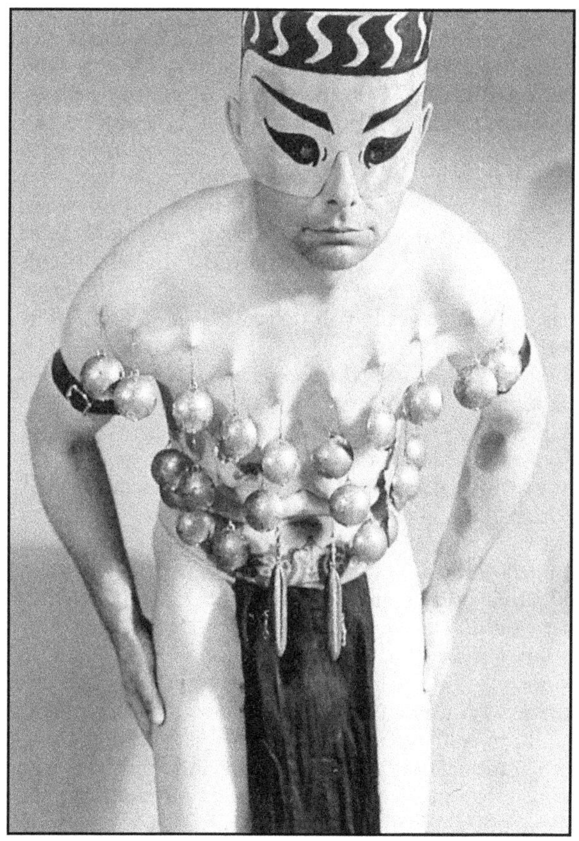

Fakir, in 1965, shown bearing 24 one-pound weights attached with fishhooks.

1) contortion
2) constriction
3) deprivation
4) encumberments
5) fire
6) penetration
7) suspension.

I recently saw a photo of a young girl in England who had started putting thin metal bracelets in her ear piercings. She started with 2, and now has about 20, which really stretch out the earlobe. And she has no connection with any cult or group; she just works with her folks in a hotel. She started doing this on her own, spontaneously. She just wanted big earholes and a lot of earrings—that's the way the primitive urge works.

■ *V: People are always asking: why should you do things like get pierced or get tattooed? You gave us three reasons: 1), religious/spiritual benefits, 2) social status or for adornment; and 3) sexual pleasure.*

■ F: Well, we're all suffering from a lot of repressive conditioning which you can't undo in just a *mental* way. Most of it has to do with sexuality and sexual energy. If you get into any practices of other cultures you're bound to be involved with a lot of sexuality in other states and guises that aren't even acknowledged as being in *existence* in this culture. And a good shamanistic answer to *Why do these things?* is *BECAUSE IT'S FUN!* It's more fun than getting on a bus and going to work in the morning. It's more fun than getting on a bus and going to college or getting a Ph.D. It's more fun for you, and it can sometimes be a lot of fun for people around you. I mean: what's wrong with that? *Is there a law against having fun?*

Experiencing ecstatic states: why would one want to experience an ecstatic state? Well, you might *learn* something out of it. You might be able to help others. You might see other worlds. There may be all *kinds* of reasons, but basically you do it because it's fun! Why not?

■ *V: There's another angle—these activities hardly cost anything!*

■ F: Yes, you don't have to have a million dollars for a polo pony. *Everybody has their own body,* and if they only realized it, they're free to do with it what they will. I often think about this when I walk down the street and see someone who has an ideal body for certain kinds of things: "If they only knew what they could do with that body that would be sensational!" But they just wouldn't understand if you tried to tell 'em.

In a more female-oriented culture like in India (as opposed to ours, which is very aggressive and male-oriented, with a great deal of suppression of the female nature in *both* males and females), it is considered perfectly rational to do things like alter and "mutilate" the body—that's part of their tradition. Their attitude is, "Why not?" Whereas we say, "This is crazy—why do *that?* Especially if it hurts!"

I know the idea is odious and alien to our culture that one would *deliberately* impose restrictions on movement and freedom of the body, but mankind throughout history has always done this. The lessons that can be learned and the life that can be led by doing this far transcend what can be learned by being *comfortable.* Being comfortable isn't necessarily living a "good" life—that's the myth, but it's not true. Living an uncomfortable life is sometimes far more satisfactory than a placid, bovine existence.

To *not* have encumberments, to *not* have holes in your body, to *not* have tattoos may be debilitating—this is something people have to consider. They may not be getting the most out of life because they *don't* do these things—that's the point. People may be missing beautiful, rich experiences because of *cultural bias and conceit.*

Twenty to thirty years ago I lived in libraries trying to find some answers to my questions. I read a lot of anthropological studies to find out everything I could about other people who lived and acted differently. I tried to get the *real stuff*—sort out the bias from the bullshit; decipher the actual reportage of what was really going on with these peoples.

■ *V: Why do you shave your body? Is there a reason?*

■ F: Well, if you try to put clothespins on your legs and they have hair on them, the pins won't stay on—they'll slip off because the hairs are slippery. Actually, a lot of primitive body activities can't be done with hair—they're just physically impossible. And something as

BODY PLAY

1. **Body Play by Contortion: "Bending Bones," "Distortion":** Gymnastics, contortionism, Yoga exercises and Hindu practices of Sadhus, the "Scavenger's Daughter," enlargement of piercings, cupping, high-heel shoes, foot-binding, stretching part of the body, etc.
2. **Body Play by Constriction: "Compression":** Bondage, tight ligatures and belts, corsets, tight clothing (like rubber or denim), cords, body presses, etc.
3. **Body Play by Deprivation: "Shut-Off,"** "Frozen": Fasting, sleep deprivation, fatigue, restriction of movement, sense isolation in boxes, cages, helmets, body suits, bags, etc.
4. **Body Play by Encumberment: "Wearing Iron":** Heavy bracelets, anklets, neck ornamentation, footwear, manacles, encasements, chains, etc.
5. **Body Play by Fire: "Burn-Out":** Sun tanning, electricity (constant and shock), steam/heat baths and boxes, the "pack," branding and burning, as in the Japanese "okyu" treatment, etc.
6. **Body Play by Penetration: "Invasion":** Flagellation, being pierced, punctured, spikes or skewered, tattooing, bed of nails, bed of swords, irritants like hair, cloth or chemical agents, etc.
7. **Body Play by Suspension: "Hung-Up":** Hung on a cross, the "witches' cradle," suspended by wrists, thighs, waist, ankles or flesh hooks, suspended by constrictions or multiple piercings, etc.

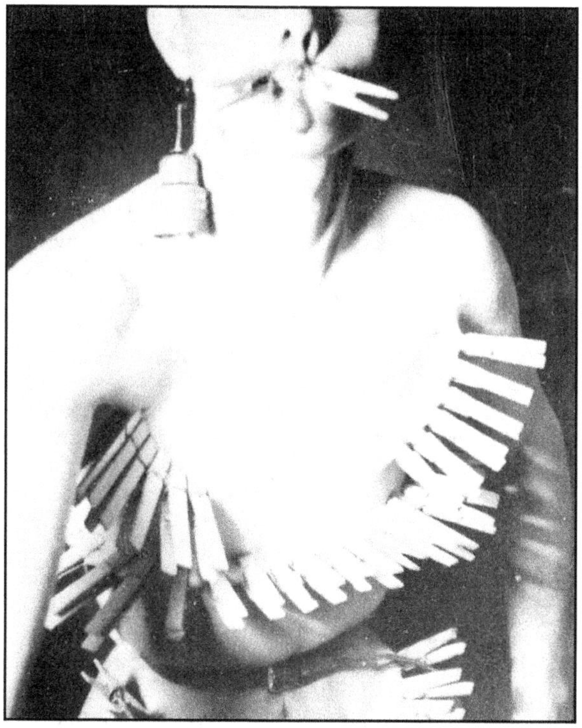

Pinching ordeal: clothespins put on body for several hours. Photo taken in 1948.

simple as putting clothespins on your body—it's actually hard to find somebody who can do this properly.

When I submit to something like getting clothespins put on me, this is not submitting to another being's will. In order for me to submit to another person's will, that person has to be spiritually much larger than I am. Whereas in a lot of SM activities, the ones submitting are submitting to people inferior to them spiritually. And that doesn't make sense. Then again, if you're really spiritually "large," you don't want anybody to submit to you as a human being. You'd rather have them submit to an *experience,* while you're just a party to it.

SADHUS & THE PENIS

■ *V: Have you ever heard of an explorer named Leonard Clark?*

■ F: I read his book, *The Rivers Ran East* describing how he escaped death many times exploring the Amazon in the early '40s. He returned to America with about fifty herbs including a birth control herb—I wonder what happened to that? The Indians probably discovered it through trial and error—who knows? Look at the example of curare—after being discovered, now it's a mainstay in modern hospital operating rooms as a key ingredient in deep anesthesia. Modern civilization could benefit from so much that primitive people know, yet because of cultural arrogance, they miss it. Clark brought back a quinine-like herb and other curatives.

I read about another explorer who claimed he found, in the Orinoco area, a tribe who had some evil-smelling fluid. They'd take people with crooked bones (like a crooked leg) and soak them in these troughs for weeks, then take 'em and straighten the bone out, like that!

But what most interested me in Leonard Clark's book was: he discovered this strange Indian tribe who believed that the male penis was where God was located. So they worshipped the penis. Selected very young males had progressively heavier weights hung on their cocks until they became stretched out incredibly long. When they reached adulthood they carried it coiled up in a little basket, and if they removed the basket it would hang down beneath their knees. But they couldn't do this to too many males, because after

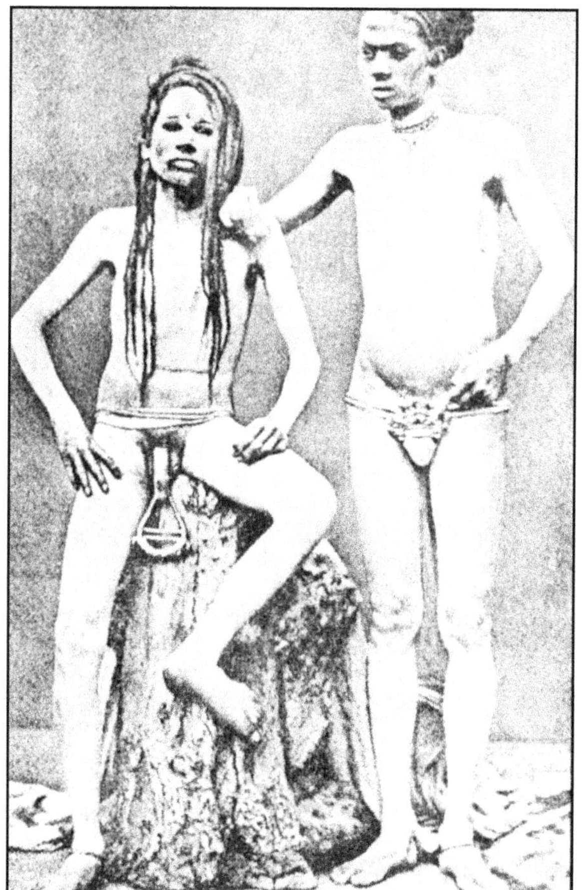

Sexual negation of Sadhu boys in India: One is stretching his penis gradually with increasing weights. It will end up 12" to 18" long by adulthood. The other has pressed his penis inside his body and the scrotum has been rolled around a rod. In time, his penis will not come out of his body.

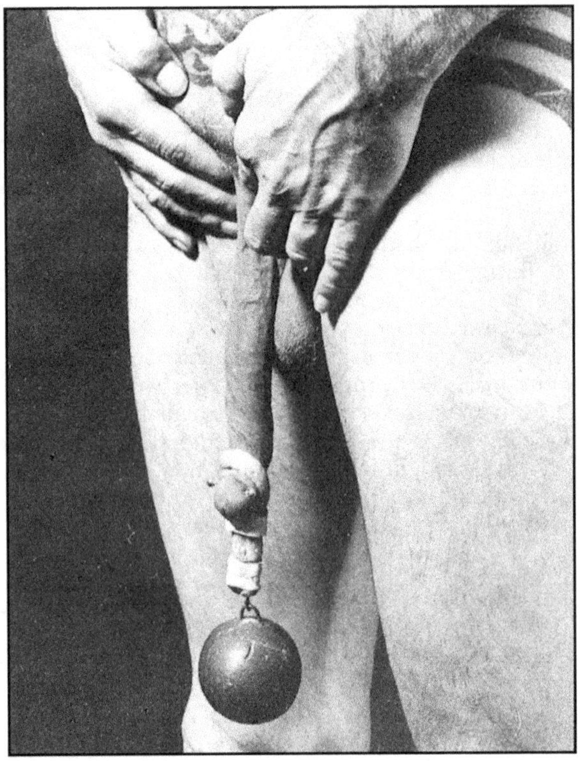

Fakir uses penis weights for temporary negation.

the "treatment" they couldn't impregnate, and then of course the race would die out.

■ *AJ: But what was the significance of stretching it out?*

■ F: Then God would have more *lebensraum*—I don't know! They would tie knots in them, too.

There are very few places in the world where that's practiced. In our film, *Dances Sacred and Profane,* we show some Indian Sadhus who have practiced the same penis weight training: they hang a little weight on there when they're pre-pubescent and leave it on all the time. As the formative ligament (which restricts the length of the penis) hasn't hardened, this stretches it. This practice has to be begun early in life or it won't work. After they get it to eight or ten inches then they can *really* get on with it and stretch it out to incredible lengths.

The mature Sadhus' penises are tied in knots, but usually there's a cloth wrapped around it. That was considered proper etiquette—they didn't let it hang out there naked. I've seen photos of Sadhus with elongated cocks but most people thought they were part of their loincloth or something; they didn't know what they were looking at.

Sadhu activity in general is underdocumented and unexplored. Why the Sadhus do what they do, and what they get out of it, is even more misunderstood. In India they are the mavericks and offshoots and cast-offs, although India has been very tolerant. But India would just as soon forget about Sadhus and shove 'em off into the corner; they don't want you to look at them.

I met an Indian filmmaker at Stanford University who was showing a documentary he'd made about India. The film took you up and down the Ganges, and in every little village and clearing there were Sadhus laying on beds of thorns, hanging upside down by their legs all day, or sitting by a pot of smoking cowshit piercing holes in the body.

I talked to him afterward and said, "I know that many of the Sadhus dishabilitate the sexual apparatus. They stretch their cock till it hangs down and is unfunctional." He smiled and said, "Yes, I have much footage of that, but I can't show it. People would never understand." *National Geographic* has avoided showing that for years. They've shown all kinds of practices, but they won't publish *that*—it would be *too much* to show Sadhus stretching and changing their sexual apparatus.

The Sadhus do a variety of other activities, like kavandi bearing, beating themselves with a ball of spikes, or sticking the body full of needles. Some of them lose their more "sacred" purposes and get carried away and get foolish and lost in what they're doing, and it becomes a profane dance. There are a lot of Sadhus that are dancing a profane dance all this while.

■ *V: Fakir, when I was in Spain I went to a club called the Casbah in Barcelona, just down from the Hotel Gaudi. There were only about twelve people in the audience, including four women. I saw a great show, all choreographed like MTV, where everyone acted out little scenarios and mouthed their lines (which the audience seemed to find very funny) but the voices were actually from a pre-recorded tape played over a big speaker system.*

The show had the usual acts, like a black man with a white woman, a woman on a cart with five different dildoes, and a dwarf who had sex with a small blonde dressed like a little girl... but the grand finale was when a man came out dressed in black. He passed out to the audience two thin, elegant black-and-gold-handled Spanish daggers. I felt one and other people felt them and they were really sharp. Then he got up, put his leg on a stool, held out his arm (it was quivering, vibrating), and with great effort, worked the dagger into his forearm and out the other side. Then he did this to the other arm. Then he pulled out his lip and did it to each cheek.

He came up to me and I had to pull out one of the daggers—it was difficult; it was really stuck. Since I did this myself, I know it was really in there. During this act several other people pulled out daggers as well. The wounds didn't bleed, but you could see a little indentation here and there. I tried to pull out my dagger as carefully as possible so it wouldn't bleed, but a little lymph trickled out.

■ F: Well there are two possibilities. This is the old human pincushion act that was around carnivals for years. However, this goes further with the thin little daggers, and I'd say it's a helluva lot better. There are

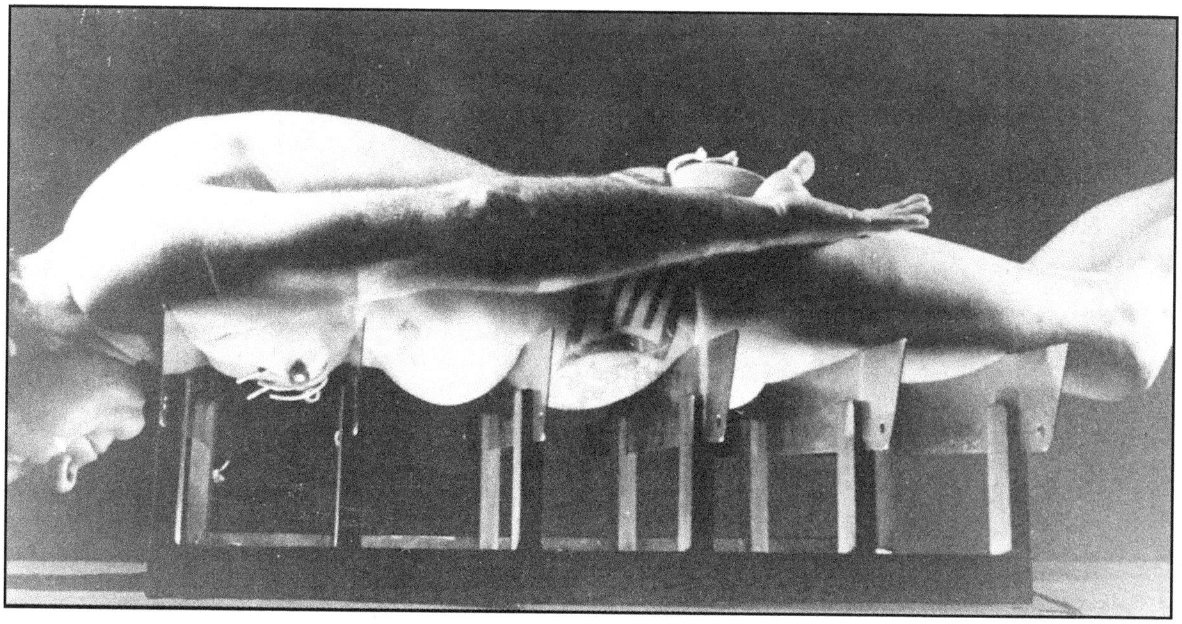

Fakir on a bed of blades.

If you're seeking an altered state, the last thing in the world you want is to have it turn into sex-especially a sexual release. If you do, then it blows it and the energy's gone. That's why these young Sadhus go to quite some lengths (literally) to permanently alter themselves.

some guys who just take needles, and they kinda get drunk on hooch all the time—this is a carnival thing—and they usually use the bicep or another part of the arm and do act after act after act. They really do literally put the needle through.

Now, I have a film that's rather interesting, taken in Spain, featuring some wandering, Middle-Eastern "fakirs." These aren't *real* fakirs, but they use that term for people who do those kind of things. One of them was taking a huge dagger—it was thick—and piercing it through the tongue. Actually, what these people do is make permanent piercings.

Now this guy, I suspect, may have had permanent piercings wherever he pierced, and he used that little indentation—that's the entrance for that piercing. Most of the time he keeps nothing in there. If you take the studs out of the piercings, after awhile they shrink 'way down, and all you can see is a little indentation which most people don't notice.

You can put piercings in the cheek; one of the more popular ones is the tongue. These Middle-Eastern fakirs performing in Spain—some of them laid on swords and on daggers and other things and that's for real. You just lay on them; as long as you don't screw around you don't get cut. I have a bed of blades I lay on; it's made up of razor-sharp machetes. I stand on them, walk on them, lay on them—stuff like that. That's part of my act. I have another one where I have a wire loop—a very sharp thin wire. You have a head of cabbage weighted with a block of wood; you push down on the wood and it slices the cabbage right in half. Then I take the wire and put it around my waist and hook it up above me and then bend forward and let my body weight go down on it and hang suspended by that wire. It sinks in and looks like it's cutting right through—it looks awful. It is not easy to do. I do about a dozen things like that.

■ *V: Anyway, for the finale, he took his penis out and he put the dagger right through it, behind the head.*

■ F: Right behind the head?

■ *V: It looked like behind the head.*

■ F: Well, he's got a hole in there. He has an apadavra, a little piercing, in there.

■ *V: Then he wrapped a rope around it—*

■ F: —and tied it to a wagon and pulled it?

■ *V: Yes! He selected a 250-pound man from the audience, sat him in a wagon and pulled him around in circles on the little stage.*

■ F: All right, *sure*. I do that too! Except I've got a cart with lights on each end and a rack on the top. I had to specifically reinforce my cart; I could haul four people easily, but after six or seven (a thousand to fifteen hundred pounds) the damn tires would go flat. So I drilled the holes in them and filled them with cement. *Now* they don't go flat!

In my act I used 7 or 8 people; each one would step on a scale and I'd ask, "How much do you

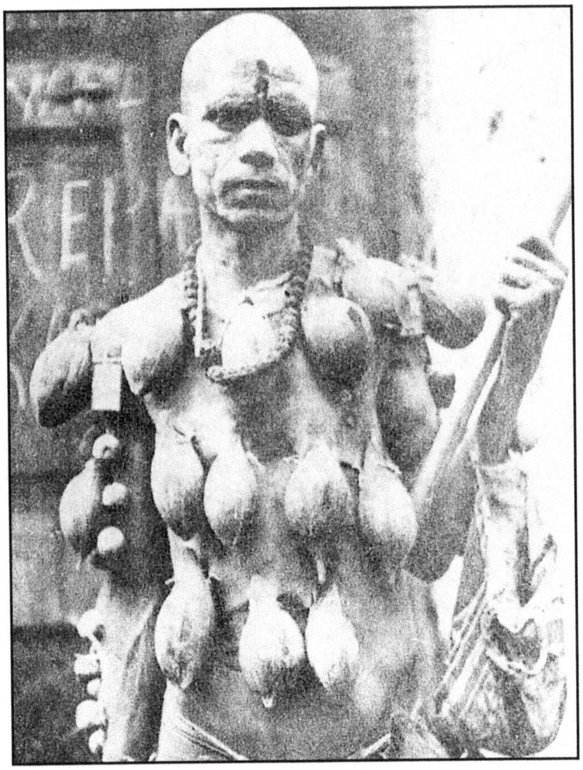

Indian Sadhu wears coconuts sewn on his body.

weigh?" They'd get on board until I had over a thousand pounds on this cart, then I'd pull it with ropes attached to my chest hooks. That was quite impressive.

■ *V: How do those Sadhus in India get to the point where they can haul a heavy cart with a rope tied to their penis?*

■ F: When you get into an altered state of consciousness, physical "miracles" can happen. There are guys in India who weigh 90 pounds and go over to a concrete block with a handle on it weighing 400 pounds—and this is physically impossible, you cannot do this medically and mechanically—and they take the handle, and get glassy-eyed and breathe strangely, and pick it up. Now you can't *do* that! It's impossible—the thing is heavier than they are by 3 or 4 times, yet they still do it.

These mysteries confound the medical people and they confound the physicists. Either the ratio of weights was altered at the time, like: the stone really weighed 300 pounds, but for an instant through the altered state of consciousness in a human being, it was like it weighed nothing at all. A common example is: a car gets into an accident and traps a little kid, and a little old lady who's 65-years-old lifts the car up. How did she do that? Well, she was in an altered state… although people here are not willing to explore that, even though people like John Lilly have tried (*Eye of the Cyclone*) without going far enough to get results. In general people in academia are afraid to go far enough to get results, so they don't get any!

■ *V: Is there much information on penis weight training?*

■ F: There's damn little anywhere; very seldom has it been mentioned in print that this was ever done *anywhere*. Only a few people have run into this in different parts of the world. However, I long since abandoned that because it would ruin my sex life with my current lover. I would not attempt to go any further with this; I almost went too far as it was!

■ *V: What do you mean? In 1985 you had your suspensory ligament cut and were starting Sadhu penis weight training. At that time you were saying "The fakir does not have sex."*

■ F: Now the fakir has found sex is a wonderful thing and is another way of expression and *enlightenment!*

■ *V: Have you turned your back on the notion of going beyond orgasm?*

■ F: No; there was a dimension that needed filling out after all the other work had been done. We're now in the postscript, and where do we go from here? Cutting the ligament and stretching the penis has [laughs uproariously] come in handy. It has made for some problems, but it has made for some interesting possibilities. I don't pop right up and stand up anymore,

Sadhu of India stitches small fruits to his back and chest every day and wears them until they dry up to pea-size. Then they are cut off and strung on long chains that are hung on freshly sewn fruits. The length of the chain shows how long and how many times he has endured this.

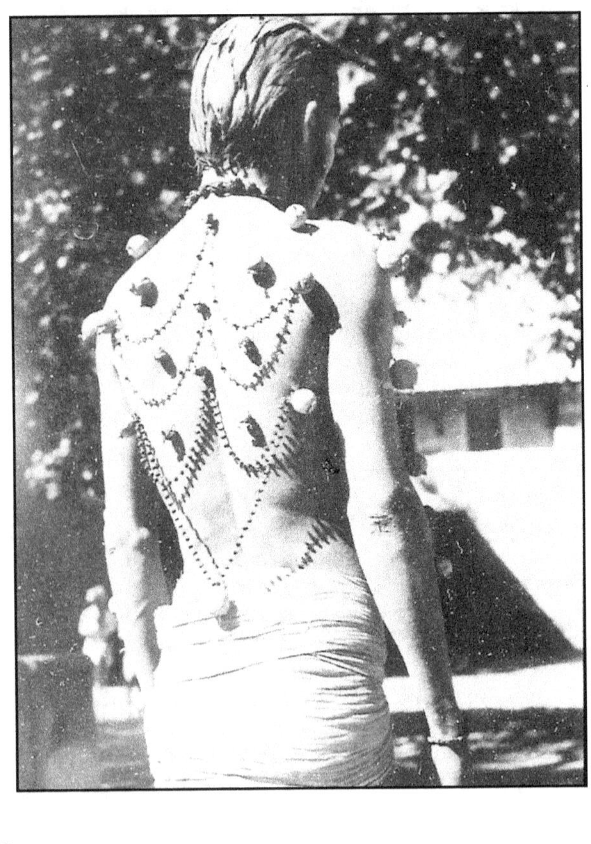

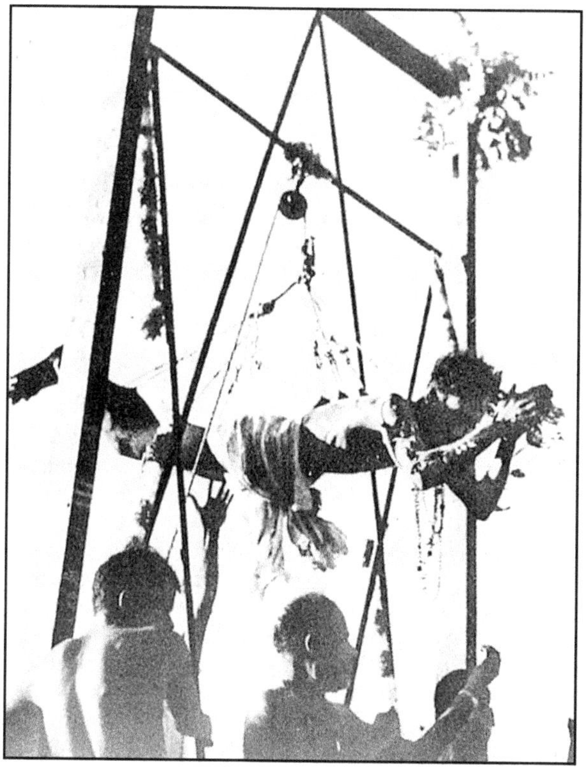

Indian Sadhus hangs from fleshhooks attached to his back.

but now I can have intercourse in ways that I could never ever have before—interesting new ways that are not possible without this. You can come at things from different directions! Let's put it this way: you can have a hard-on in *any* direction—which is really novel! And it takes a rather broad-minded and experienced woman to get used to this and take advantage of it!

■ *V: Do you regret the operation?*

■ *F: I* don't. Sometimes my girlfriend says it was a foolish thing to do, but only because in certain situations it's frustrating. And of course she has no experience before with me, so there's no way to compare with one person.

The operation made my penis about an inch and a half longer, in both the normal and erect state. If I hang this 3-lb weight on my cock for a couple of hours, my cock stretches out like rubber. Afterwards it will shrink back again. There is a limit as to how far you can stretch the blood vessels. And if you do this long enough, eventually it won't shrink back and then you're in real trouble!

■ *V: For it to not shrink back, you have to start before puberty?*

■ F: What limits your length is your ligament: a little muscle on the top of your cock that hooks up to your pubic bone. This ligament develops until about puberty. When you get erect, the cavernosa in the penis will engorge with blood up to the limit established by the ligament. But if your ligament is cut, your penis will go down as well as up; it'll be stiff in *any* direction.

There's also a Tantric technique used in India called suka training (suka means swelling). This is a way of getting a hard-on that won't come down—you can keep it for hours, days, weeks, months! However, if you have an erection for too long, it becomes very hard to get it down, and it's also *very* painful.

Through suka training men have made incredibly big cocks in India; they're manufactured—they're made. The people there have developed very interesting ways to modify the body that are very practical and that work. Like I said, our film, *Dances Sacred and Profane* had footage of Sadhus whose penises are wrapped up, but obviously they're about eighteen inches long.

■ *V: The Sadhus never have sexual intercourse?*

■ F: Not when it's that long! They also have the suka treatment which gives length and thickness (they combine both the suka and the stretching).

■ *V: Give us a more detailed description of the stretching process.*

■ F: First of all, they start early. A young man may start out with a triangular-shaped block of wood with a small hole, which he puts around his penis. He hangs little weights on it, adding just a few grams additionally every day, and wears it all day, every day. They let that

Fakir hangs from fleshhooks.

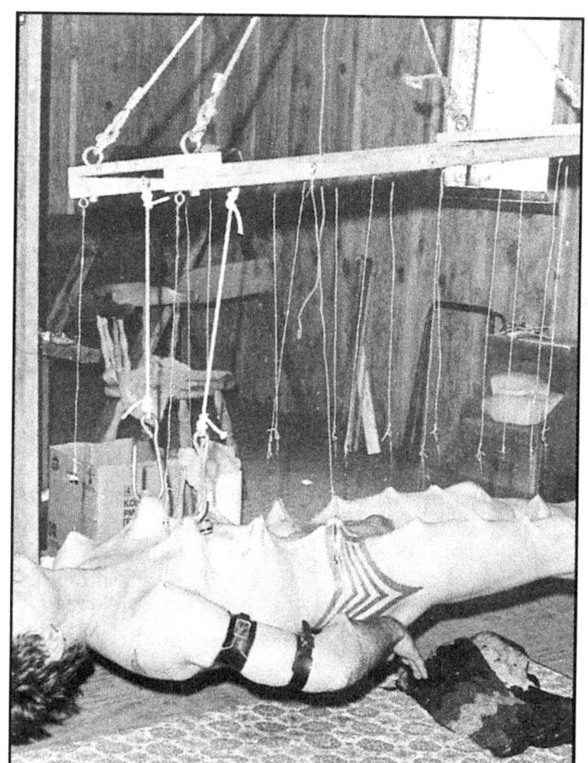

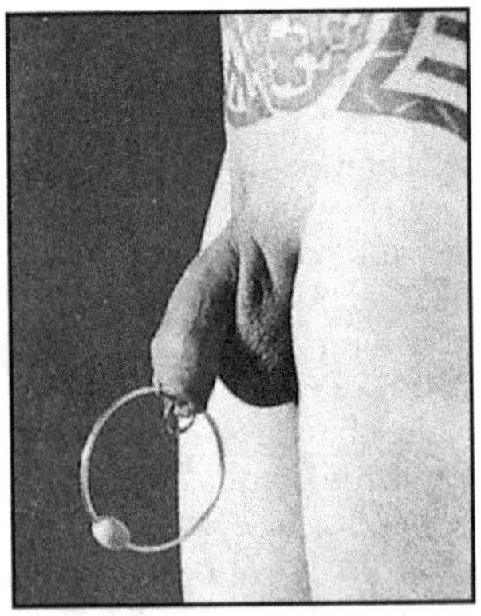

Fakir with "Oetang" ring through foreskin piercing.

hang on there continuously day and night for a long period of time—usually they dig a hole in the ground and sit there and it hangs down. Or, they may hang a loop of rope over the head of the organ and hang weights on that.

I made a special chair, like a potty chair, so you can sit down and let your cock hang down through the opening in the seat. You can also swing a lighter weight like a great pendulum back and forth—that's called the *lingam pendulum.* For this you use a padded cock ring which is fastened in the back, with a light weight (about a pound) attached to a loop on the back, and swing the organ round and round, and back and forth. The purpose of the lingam pendulum is to maintain a healthy, active organ and to make it larger. If one were to do this several hours every day, one eventually might get an improved model.

■ *V: How does cock training relate to a goal beyond sex?*

■ F: Cock lengthening falls into the category of the primitive urge for altered states. I have a photo of a young fellow who's just taken vows that he's going to stretch his cock until it hangs down to here [gestures to knee]. Then it won't be functional for normal sexual activity, but he will be aroused and on the verge of orgasm all day, every day. And in that state, he is able to go beyond...go into altered states. That's why these Sadhus do this; they deliberately choose this as a way of life. Although they may have other symbols too, such as an anklet welded on, the long braided hair, the cords around the waist.

■ *AJ: Fair, how heavy is your penis weight?*

■ F: Three pounds.

■ *V: Only 3 pounds? It feels heavier than that!*

■ F: Well it's lead so it's very compact and dense. If you put that on, the weight can ultimately hit the floor because this is a long loop and I stretch down to about that long [gestures again]. This is something I do prior to doing an altered state ceremony. After you've stretched yourself for a matter of hours, you can't get excited. But this isn't permanent, which is an advantage because some of the things tend to go into masochism...or get erotic and arousing. And if you're seeking an altered state, the last thing in the world you want is to have it turn into sex—especially a sexual release. If you do, then it blows it and the energy's gone and you can't go forward; you have to stop and do it another time. That's why these young Sadhus go to quite some lengths (literally) to permanently alter themselves.

Ultimately, when you're finally in one of these states you can fling yourself down on a bed of thorns and roll around on them and not feel pain.

■ *V: The thorns don't cause any infections or inflame the skin?*

■ F: No. In fact in some of these primitive rites, the participants actually go out of their way to dip the tip of the sword in cow dung to make it as dirty as possible, just to prove that in this state you cannot get an infection. I've done this myself: deliberately tried to give myself an infection while in an altered state, and I've never gotten one! In fact, during the the course of one ceremony I sustained some large wounds, yet within two hours all evidence had vanished—it had instantly healed over!

You see, in an altered state, your whole physical being is plastic and alterable. I've seen people change to a different sex, a different race, a different size, a totally different configuration. This was brought out in the movie, *Altered States,* and I think it can happen.

Another thing of bearing of weights is done by the Sadhus, who stitch small fruits the size of a plum on their back and chest until they dry up and shrink to the size of a hard little pea. Then they sew on another bunch on, and another. The previous little dried-up ones are cut off and strung into chains, and the number and length of chains show how long the person has endured this.

Now, since I don't have time to wait for the fruits to dry, I hang lead weights on myself. I have a 1954 photo of myself bearing 12 4-ounce lead weights and 2 8-oz weights, and another showing me bearing 22 4-ounce weights. The reason I didn't have all 8-oz ones was: that was all I had. I have a later photo showing me bearing 32 8-ounce (half-pound) weights. Still later I can sustain 24 one-pound weights on fishhooks in my body!

Believe me, this is a beautiful experience! That's why the Sadhu in India goes around every day and every night bearing milk-filled coconuts pierced into

Sexual negation by encasement. Scrotum and penis are sealed in plaster for many days.

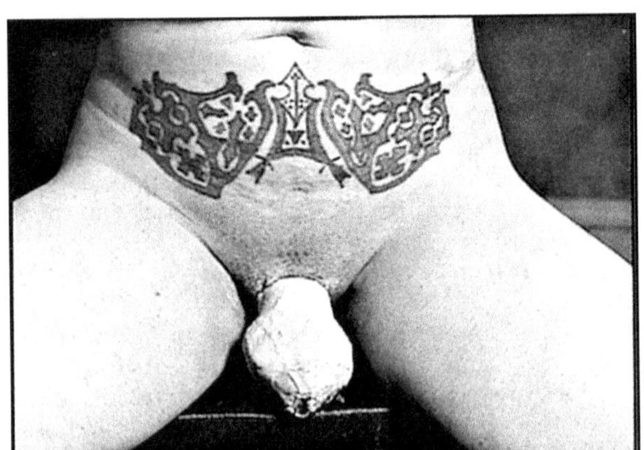

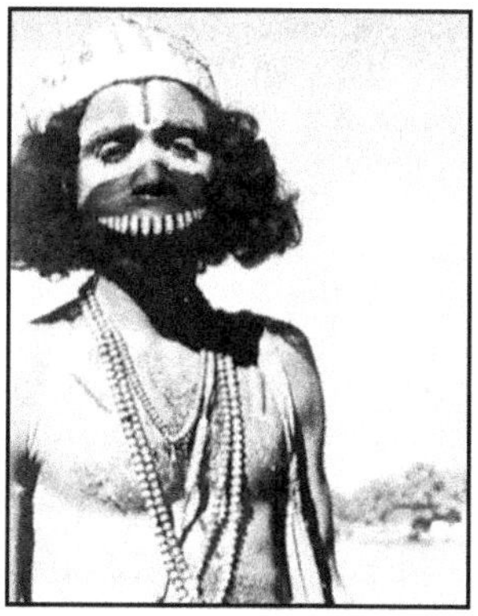

This Sadhu has his mouth sewn shut for several days to several weeks. He has a wooden plug inside his mouth and sips water through a small straw.

his body. He sleeps that way and does everything with these on, and he also wears little fruits. I have a beautiful photo of a young Sadhu girl in India who has them sewed to her cheeks and elsewhere.

There are Sadhus who experience other vows, such as never to sit or lie down again. They sleep on this sling, but never actually sit or lie down, 24 hours a day—that's their vow! Another may sit in contortions all day, and people throw down coins to support him (he may be a fakester one). I have a photo of one Sadhu wandering around with his mouth sewn shut for days or even weeks; he survives by sipping water or fluids through a little hole between his lips. Again, that's deprivation or restriction. Another Sadhu may live in a cave so small he can barely squeeze through. These Sadhus go to great lengths—why would anyone do that? [mockingly] That's pretty damn alien!

■ *V: What is your critique of SM?*

■ F: SM, in this culture, is one of the few places people can get started on the road back to their god. In this culture there are very few opportunities for this.

■ *AJ: But don't most SM people just get stuck?*

■ F: Most of them do. SM is a means of sexual fulfillment that's not just intercourse. Although—many people get worked up with the SM, and then they fuck, and *that's it.* End of subject, end of experience, end of consciousness-raising. But some people start that way and feel unfulfilled, and by accident they'll go a step beyond—their partner will take a step beyond that point, and they'll discover a strange new world just this side of orgasm that beats orgasm all to hell. The feeling you have in orgasm is weak compared to what I'm talking about—these feelings are *way* beyond—*big!*

Orgasm builds, it gets delicious, you get anesthetized, people can claw and scratch you and you don't feel any pain—*boom,* the great moment comes—*Uhhh!* and then it's all over. But this gets back to why you hang a rock on a cock: you can get to that point and keep right on climbing: 5,000 feet, 10,000 feet, 20,000 feet—*up up up!*

■ *V: Does that prevent orgasm?*

■ F: You bet it does. And eventually if you stretch the cock long enough, you get to the point where you can't have a physical orgasm at all. And that's ultra-sexual life. That's what the Sadhus do: they lead an ultra-sexual life, going around in a perpetual orgastic state.

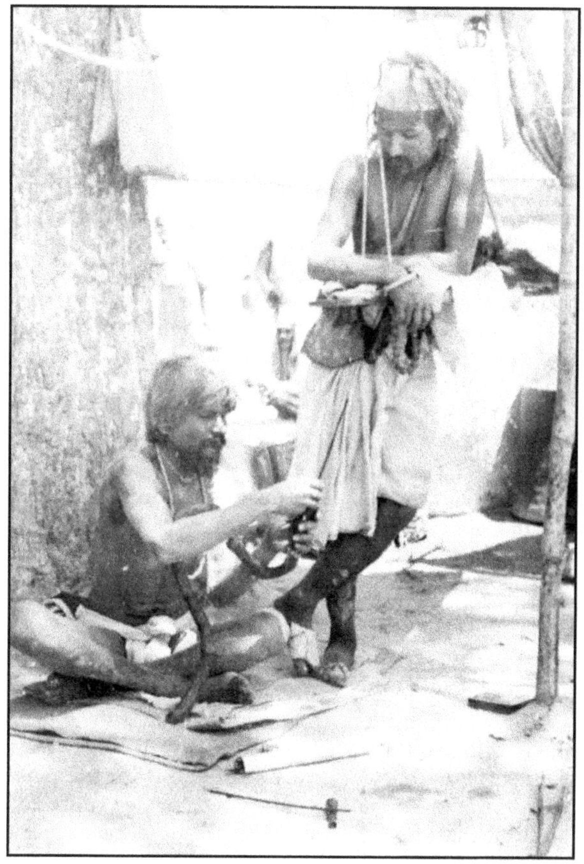

One Sadhu has vowed to never sit or lie down again. He eats and sleeps on the sling 24 hours a day. The sitting Sadhu has lengthened his penis to about 18". It's wrapped in cloth and tied in a knot.

■ *V: That sounds a little like sexual negation.*

■ F: Another kind of alteration is *containment,* in which a Sadhu pushes his penis back into his body, rolling the scrotum up in such a way that the penis ends up inside his abdomen; it's difficult for his penis to come out of the body. This is sexual negation for super-sexual, altered states of consciousness. They've been doing this for thousands of years and very few people in this culture know anything about it.

Another example of sexual negation is found in Borneo, where men may have piercings in their foreskin. If they go on a trip, their wives may insist they put a big ring called the *oetang* through the piercings and weld it closed. When they return, the ring is removed. Because when the ring is on, you can't have intercourse—you can't enter or penetrate anybody.

■ *AJ: Like a male chastity belt!*

■ F: Yes. Yet another form of sexual negation that's found in India is the *encasement.* A man may seal up his penis and balls in a brass ball and rivet everything shut (but with a little pee opening).

■ *V: Doesn't that hurt the skin at all? There's no ventilation there.*

■ F: No, you could leave it that on for months *if* you do it right. I once did an encasement with plaster and left it on for two days. I'd sealed it up with white glue, and the glue got hard as a rock—I didn't know if I could get it off! [laughs]

Encasement has to do with the flow of P.E. or primal energy. The only time most civilized men and women experience a flow of primal energy, P.E., is during sex, but P.E. is not sex, only a temporary condition that *may* occur during sex. At the moment of orgasm, that great feeling you have is primal energy but the flow of P.E. then stops. If one wants to prolong the flow of P.E. using sexual means, then you have to delay or inhibit orgasm altogether, and this is the way you do it. It's a mechanical way.

■ *V: If you do an encasement, you can't get an erection, then?*

■ F: No. In fact, what's odd is: after you're encased like that for several hours, you don't feel like there's anything inside that ball. It just hangs there, that plaster or whatever it is, and you lose all sensation that you've anything in there. It's like you've been castrated. It's a weird feeling, and you cannot get an orgasm. If you had it on for a month, then you couldn't get an orgasm for that whole month.

However, this negation is temporary. When you take it off, you'll recover, by and by. And when you take it off you'll be very, very sensitive. It's a tremendous sensation because you've been sealed up and had no feeling for that long. The slightest touch feels incredible. Curious side effect.

Now *sexual enhancement* is the other side of the coin. Women in Borneo, in certain tribes, at least, will not have sex with a man unless he has an ampallang piercing, because she doesn't feel enough sensation. The head of a penis is spongy, not very hard, and when it gets down to the end of the vagina, nothing much happens—there's no *wham* at the end of the stroke. But if you put in an ampallang, it goes down vibrating and wobbling and when you get to the end, it hits hard. The women I've tried this on have reported a tremendous kick out of it—they think it's great. That's sexual enhancement—again, an expression of the primitive urge.

Another example of sexual enhancement is ball-stretching. You can lengthen the scrotum; in one photo I have fourteen rings on. For Jim Ward this is a major expression of primal energy; his balls, without a stretcher, hang about 7 inches low. If he puts a stretcher on, that pulls them out another couple of inches.

■ *V: What does that do?*

■ F: It enhances. It's exciting, it's stimulating—try it! I haven't carried this to extremes like he has. But there are some guys who want to have balls that hang down to their knees. All this may sound crazy unless you see it in a context of expressing primal energy, the primal urge, without inhibition. Why shouldn't you try anything you want to? You're not going to be struck down by a bolt of lightning!

■ *V: What about sexual enhancement or negation for women?*

■ F: Sexual negation for women is a tough problem, partly because it's already widely practiced—mostly involuntarily. Although, in some places the women *want it*; they look forward to the day they will be occluded.

■ *V: What's that?*

■ F: The United Nations is trying to stop this practice, but in North Africa it continues to this day. Occlusion is a kind of sealing up. They take a girl when she's about 8 or 9 years old and in most cases do a clitoridectomy first (cut off the clitoris) and then abrade the edges of the outer labia, pull them together and either clamp them or stitch them together until the crotch heals up and there's nothing but a little teeny hole to piss through. And that's the negation. The woman has no stimulation there at all and cannot be penetrated until she's cut open.

■ *AJ: Is she cut open later?*

■ F: Yes. When she's married, then she's cut open. She has intercourse for for three or four days and then they sew her back up again. If she has to have a baby, they have to cut her open again.

Something similar used to be done in Australia to the men. At initiation the penis would be ripped open from the head down the urethra all the way to the balls with a sharp-edged stone or a flint. This was part of a puberty rite.

■ *V: Sounds like a drastic form of birth control.*

■ *AJ: Back to that earlier topic: a clitoridectomy and occlusion negates a woman's sexuality. Something like elongating a child's head or Ibitoe waist training may be thought of as beautifying, and the aesthetic effect doesn't seem to have negative functional consequences. But to take out a clitoris is functionally going to change that woman, totally, and that falls into the category of sexual domination and slavery that one can't condone.*

■ F: The only time we run into a possession of human beings by other human beings is in societies which have begun to accept Western "civilized" ideas and which get a cash economy. This happened to the Kalahari bushmen in Africa. You can read a whole history of how these people who are very pure get encroached upon by Westerners. They never had any possessions; no property rights—everybody shared everything until they came into contact with civilized man. Then they start discovering they've got to have money, and money buys things, and sooner or later someone says, "I own you." The idea of possession, the idea of slavery, the idea of using in bondage one person by another is strictly a civilized idea. It does not exist in the primitive world. I've researched this deeply.

Cultures such as the Arabs are not primitive and they're not civilized, so they fall into the worst crack of all. *A little bit of civilization is a terrible thing.* Like in Micronesia—Dan can tell you about that. Out there, it's gotten to the point where the young men don't even know how to row a boat anymore—if the outboard motor runs out of gas, they're in trouble. In one generation they've forgotten all the sailing and navigational knowledge that's been handed down for centuries. They're now almost a people without a past, who just want ghetto blasters and TVs.

I defy you to find one case where the people have been relatively pure, where there is any of this cruelty and ugliness we find in civilized society. It does not exist until "civilization" encroaches on them. Then, all of a sudden, there are *property rights:* "I own you," "I have five wives," etc. This happened in Africa, the most desecrated continent in the world. Every culture there that got touched by Western society became extremely cruel and possessive, and all of this shit came out. The worst aspects of Western society become assimilated.

PENIS ELONGATION

■ *V: Tell us about the doctor who did your penis-enlarging operation.*

■ F: My operation was done in Tijuana, by Dr Ronald Brown, who has a rather seedy reputation. He's done about five or six hundred sex change operations. He doesn't ask too many questions and he does it for a pretty cut rate. He's very hard to communicate with because he moves around a lot—you send him mail and it comes back.

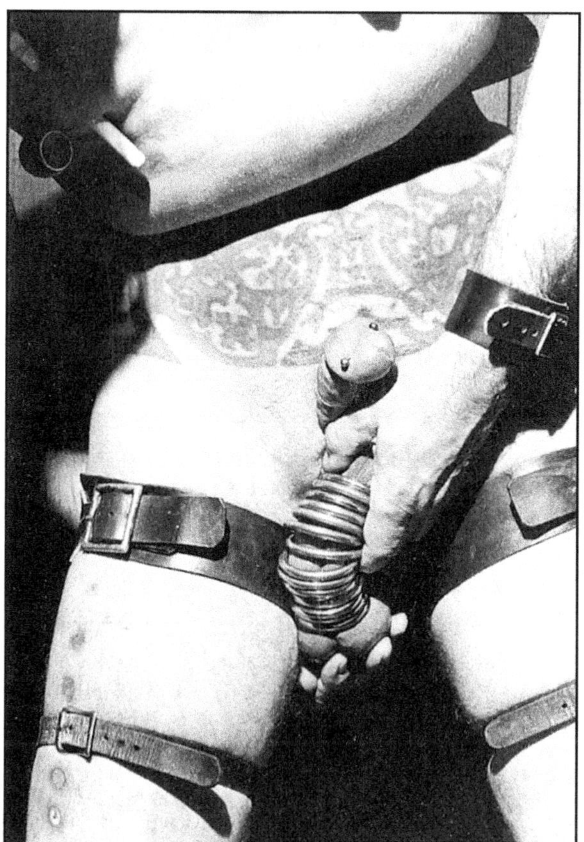

Sexual enhancement: elongating the scrotum by slowly adding a series of metal rings. Fakir is wearing 14.

I have a 2-hour video interview with him that Annie Sprinkle did down in Rosarita, walking by the beach and sitting on the coast of Baja Norte. Dr Brown is an interesting figure with an interesting life; he's probably a very good plastic surgeon. He also is a klutz—the kind of guy who gets up to go to the door and trips! He's done some interesting surgery, some of which came out quite well, and some of which, according to legend, was a horror story.

■ *V: It's hard to sue in Tijuana.*

■ F: He had his license revoked there. The last time he came up here I was post-op on my ligament, and he gave a little talk on male sexual enhancement. He sent out some notices, and it was at a motel on Van Ness Avenue, and quite a few people turned out including 2 guys whom we kinda thought were a little fishy.

I left early; he had invited us to have supper with him in the restaurant downstairs, and damned if these 2 guys didn't pinch him! (They *were* undercover agents.) He called himself Dr Brown, and since he was revoked as a doctor he could not legally say he was a doctor in California. Theoretically, a doctor that comes out here to give a talk from John Hopkins University or some other famous place in another state cannot say he's a doctor. That's the law they used against him. They put him in jail and—it was pretty embarrassing. That was his last trip to San Francisco.

I heard some terribly bad things about him from transsexual circles. He did a lot of sex changes as well as penis enhancement operations. But he also did facelifts, tummy tucks, nose jobs—he was really a plastic surgeon who graduated with honors from Columbia University Medical School. He also was a Mormon from Utah. He really is a first-rate plastic surgeon—although anyone can make a mistake!

The operation I had was a ligament-cutting operation. It costs a minimum of $2500 because it's just not that simple. It's known as the *Bihari* because a doctor named Bihari in Cairo is the only other man who did this operation *successfully*—reportedly on John Holmes. Now some people don't need this; they may suffer from immature development and mainly require testosterone treatment. Females who want to be males can receive testosterone treatment and develop quite long clitorises.

Anyway, I started to read up on this and realized it was not the simplest operation in the world, because major blood-supplying veins, arteries and nerves are literally glued on to both sides of the ligament. Therefore this operation requires a very delicate, microsurgical skill such as a good plastic surgeon possesses, who's used to peeling back one layer of skin, then another, then moving a muscle around, without damaging nerves or the blood supply. Totally different approach from a general surgeon, who basically just makes a hole, goes in and works, and then sews the hole back up. And the anesthetic required is an epidural spinal, because a true spinal is dangerous, and a general is very tricky. So Dr Brown had a surgical nurse present, his son who took photographs, and another doctor who was learning the procedure. He works in a hospital.

Not too many people get just the Bihari. Some people also get an operation which implants a pair of rods the full length of the expanded corpus cavernosum, so the penis is always erect—even when it's not erect it *looks* erect (which can sometimes be embarrassing).

■ *V: What about implanting little pearls or plastic spherules under the skin?*

■ F: They do that in India; it's a relatively simple procedure. There's space between skin layers, like in a cat. If you're careful you can cut a little incision, pull the skin layers apart, and tuck in a sterile ball (surgical steel or non-reactive plastic) inside and sew it back up again.

■ *V: How did Dr Brown learn his craft?*

■ F: He made deals with homosexuals, saying, "I won't charge you anything if you let me conduct a couple of surgery experiments *before* I finally remove your penis." It took practice learning how to cut the ligament, and you can't do it on a cadaver because everything there changes shape at death. That's why the anatomy books are wrong, because the drawings are all based on cadavers—nobody dared work on a live one! So...if you have any fantasies you want fulfilled, go visit Dr Brown!

JOHN WILLIE COUTTS

■ *V: How did you find out that other people shared your interests?*

■ F: The first clue came when I chanced across this little magazine called *Bizarre* published by John Willie Coutts. Later I contributed to it. Only 5000 copies were printed.

■ *V: How did you find the Bizarres?*

■ F: Fate! I bought them when they originally came out. John Willie Coutts was an advertising man and an illustrator In New York, and this was his hobby. His whole story is extremely interesting. He was born in Singapore on December 9, 1902, educated in England, and then worked for British Intelligence before WWII in Australia. Subsequently he lived most of his life between Canada and the U.S., but in 1957 moved to California. In 1958 one of his favorite models, 19 year-old Judy Dull, was killed by Harvey Glatman, the "Bondage Murderer." Perhaps the shock prompted him to leave; he died August 6, 1962 at age 60 in Catel, Guernsey, near France.

■ *V: When did he start publishing?*

■ F: In Montreal he began publishing in the mid-thirties but didn't hit his stride until 1946 when he started *Bizarre*, which featured his pioneering S&M/bondage photos and drawings. He invented classic personas such as Sweet Gwendoline, Secret Agent U-69, the evil Contessa "M" and her cohort "Sir Dystic d'Arcy."

I was fortunate enough to meet Coutts once (in Minneapolis at the Flame Lounge), because I kept contributing to the magazine and he could sense I was an interesting person. We talked about ultra-high heels and agreed that, in themselves, they possessed no unique charm. However, what *was* exciting was the thought that someone had to endure hours of painful training to learn how to wear them. He described the "look" of a woman who learns to master ultra-high heels as "cultivated helplessness...mobile immobility...a delicate balance always on the edge of collapse."

He traveled around a lot sponging off people. They would write fan letters, he would get their addresses and show up in Dubuque, Iowa, saying, "Hi, I'm John Willie Coutts!" and stay for a week while they wined and dined him—he loved to drink good brandy; he was an alcoholic. He photographed Bettie Page before anyone knew she existed.

■ *V: Before Irving Klaw?*

■ F: Yes, his work predates Irving Klaw by several years. Klaw reprinted his work but censored some of the Gwendoline drawings by having clothing drawn over exposed breasts and buttocks. Willie's drawings are idealized portrayals of how people should look—not only women but men. He went through the whole, the entirety, of culture and rearranged everything. He had this absolute passion for the modification of the body, tied in with bondage: all the various forms of bondage and light SM activities.

His legend and myth will persist; individuals all over the world—Spain, Germany, France, Japan—have bootlegged old issues of *Bizarre* or photos from them. Willie published one or two issues a year, although he stopped from 1947-'51 for lack of money. Then he resumed and in 1956 sold the magazine to a friend of his who published 6 more issues from '56-'59. Most people today do not understand that all this stuff started with *Bizarre* magazine. The early ones are the best; they're all drawings and art in two or three colors—beautiful.

There are all these fetishy people who really don't know what the hell they're doing. They aren't dealing with primal energies, they aren't dealing with altered states—which is what John Willie dealt with.

Today, *Bizarre* has been plagiarized beyond comprehension. And everything's a copy of a copy of a copy, and somewhere the deeper spirit's got lost. There are all these fetishy people and their hangers-on who really don't know what the hell they're doing. They aren't dealing with primal energies, they aren't dealing with altered states—which is what John Willie dealt with. He really was pioneering a kind of modern primitive activity in the sense that he was trying to reach *other levels* in his exploration of erotic sex.

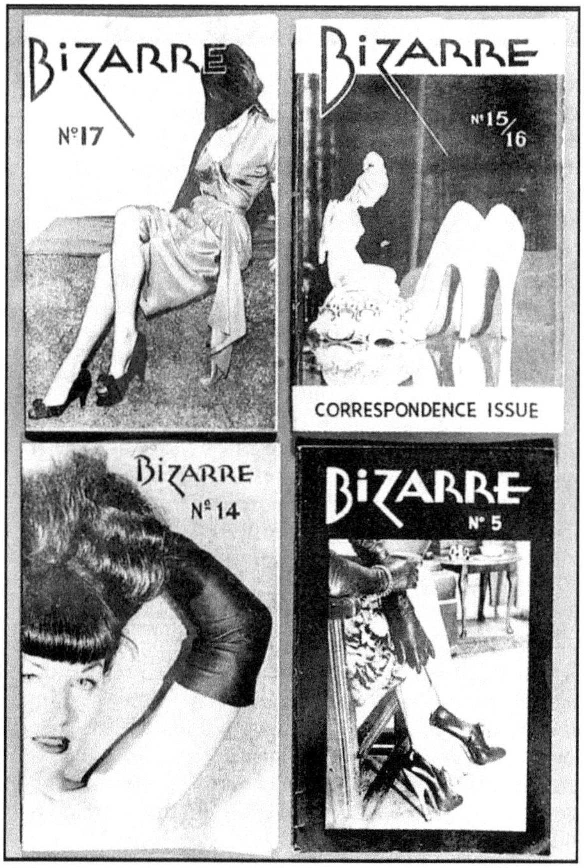

***Bizarre* magazine by John Willie Coutts.**

■ *AJ: So you think he was aware of these levels?*

■ F: Definitely! As a young person I wrote letters to him. I think he had several lovers: ladies that lived in New York who would answer the letters for him (or perhaps he himself was replying under pseudonyms; who knows). I had a long correspondence with one lady who was frequently written up with pictures and drawings of her. I still have these letters from John Willie and *Bizarre* magazine, written to me in the early '50s. And like I said, he was the first; there was never anything like this published before. Of course, he was busted a thousand times.

■ AJ: For what?

■ F: *Pornography!* This was pornography—you couldn't sell this in public, distribute it or send it through the mail or you'd be thrown in the slammer for life. In the 1940's and '50s this was pornography.

The first person who really exploited any of this was Irving Klaw. And he had such a small idea of how to do it. He would generate a series of glossy picture sets and thought that if over a five-year period he sold 500 sets, that was big business. I, in turn, had gone to Japan where I gave a lot of Irving Klaw material to a friend who placed the photos in Japanese magazines—there would be 85,000 copies the next week! [laughs] The Japanese would consume it at that rate, but here—*never!* You cannot make money in this culture catering to the tastes of people who might like that; it just does not work, it's not allowed. There are middlemen; there are gangsters here who control it all.

■ *V: What do you know about Irving Klaw?*

■ F: I corresponded with him; I have his original first catalog. He sold surplus pin-up photos from Hollywood studios—pin-up photos of Betty Grable—things like that.

■ *V: When was this?*

■ F: The '50s; the end of John Willie and the beginning of Irving Klaw butt up right against each other. The first person to photograph Bettie Page was John Willie, and she very quickly became one of Irving Klaw's hottest subjects. He'd pay maybe 25 dollars to shoot all afternoon and make a set of photos.

He managed to collect a lot of subjects, particularly women, who were willing to do *anything.* They were masochists; very heavy-duty masochists. Now that's a much maligned and misunderstood term, yet there's a component of that in everybody, and it doesn't always go where society has cast it—more often than not it goes somewhere different and takes different expressions.

■ *V: What do you mean?*

■ F: Like innocuous body play...like the old guy running in the marathon race—those are expressions of masochism. Which in many cases is one with finding your primal self.

■ *V: Socially acceptable masochism.*

■ F: What *isn't* socially acceptable? Most of it. The very notion that one would enjoy being hurt or enjoy "pain" (which is really not a valid word to use in this context) was until recently considered "sick." [laughs] Yet it isn't; it may be "normal" and "healthy"—a certain amount of it, in the right way. And *not* to express that may be unhealthy.

I think that's probably *the* premise of Modern Primitivism in general: there's a primal creative urge in all of us that's always there, and it's got to find expression *somehow*—yet our society gives us no way to express this part of us that's *very* deep and *very* strong. And some of the socially acceptable ways are kind of silly, like bodybuilding, which to most people looks ridiculous, yet it's a socially acceptable way of expressing this urge or primitive need. Having multiple-pierced ears is now pretty acceptable, whereas you'd really be a freak if you had those 10 or 15 years ago—people would have looked at you *really weird.*

■ *V: What other imitations did Bizarre spawn?*

■ F: *Bizarre* was an underground publication that was printed and distributed clandestinely; there never was more than 5000 copies printed. There were many shoddy imitations that appeared after John Willie's death, such as *Exotique* by Bermel which came out around 1957. But none of the imitators ever grasped the reality behind John Willie's publishing, which was so clearly the expression of the primal urge. They

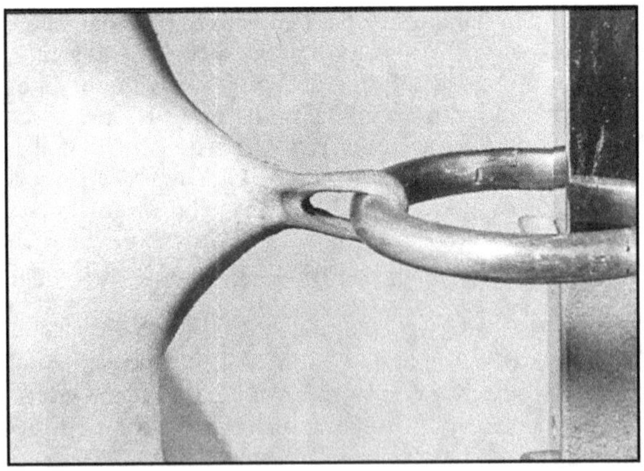

Fakir's nipple loops.

became copycats of John Willie and copycats of each other, with no depth. They're superficial and out of that developed more superficiality and fake fetishism—it's *called* fetishism but it isn't really; it's a tired copycat of the original.

In *Bizarre* physical restrictions and disabilities were idealized by John Willie and and the readers of *Bizarre* who put the ideas into practice. They photographed almost every possible variant of restriction: arms, legs, torso, head, neck, vocal cords. "If your wife is a problem at home, put her in bondage for the day!"

Did you ever hear of the Seabrook experiment? William Seabrook was a very popular writer who in 1940 wrote a book, *Witchcraft: Its Power in the World Today.* In a chapter entitled "Justine In the Mask" he describes a famous experiment he did with sensory deprivation: "It is common knowledge that when certain of the five normal senses are dulled or blanked out, whether temporarily or permanently, other senses in the normal group may tend to become highly sensitive." Seabrook took a young girl, Justine, and conducted a series of "experiments" in which first one sense, then another, would be restricted, and observed the results. After an extended period of being blindfolded, Justine could correctly identify people passing by at a distance, whether it was one man or two, or a man and a woman, or a big dog or a little dog. Finally he had made a beautiful kid leather mask which completely covered her head, and had her wear it all day with her hands tied or chained well away from her head. Eventually she ended up liking the mask, and began having moments of actual illumination, trance states, in which she traveled backward and forward in time, with occasional pre-cognitive visions. She got deeper into the primal urge and did dervishdangling, hanging half-suspended by straps all night, and traveled into deep space/time having fantastic adventures which she would relate.

PIERCING

■ *V: How did the modern resurgence of piercing originate?*

■ F: The father of the modern rebirth of piercing was Doug Malloy, an eccentric millionaire. In the early seventies he brought a lot of us together, and encouraged us. Originally there were about seven people in the U.S. who had piercings. Some lived in L.A., there was myself and one other in Northern California; another in Florida, one in New York—we were spread all over the country. Doug (not his real name) lived in a very exclusive neighborhood in Hollywood and was very prominent in the scene there. But he had another side which was very partial to piercing and other kinds of erotica of that nature. He retired early; he'd made his first million when he was something like 24, so he had plenty of time and horsepower to put into finding and putting people like us together.

All seven of us had piercings we'd made ourselves. We all thought nobody else in the world had these, until we met the others who all had felt the same way! So whenever possible, Doug would host these *T&P* (Tattooing and Piercing) parties which were like dinners in the back of restaurants in L.A. Whenever anybody was in town, everybody would get together and spend an evening swapping stories, etc.

After research and letter-writing and phone calls, we all discovered we had odd things in our piercings—old rusty safety pins, ladies' earrings, S-hooks—anything we could find; but there was nothing available that was really suitable for the kinds of piercings we had—foreskin piercings, etc. So one of the first goals we set as a group was to pool our ideas and determine the kinds of jewelry we thought would be appropriate, as well as research what historically had been used in these kinds of piercings in other cultures. That's what we did.

Jim Ward had training in jewelry-making, but at the time he was making picture frames—a very unhappy occupation. Doug backed him—bought tools, gold, any materials he needed, and Jim started a little shop in a back room of his house in L.A. Basically that's how the whole jewelry business got started—about five years before *PFIQ.* So it all started with the sharing of experiences, the T&P parties, Doug Malloy encouraging us all to get more piercings, and Jim Ward appointed the person to craft the jewelry ideas we all jointly came up with.

Jim originally opened the shop, Gauntlet, before we started the magazine *PFIQ.* I didn't think much of *PFIQ* #1, but by #2 I was in it [Jim Ward interview] and enthusiastic, and became a part of this enterprise and have been ever since.

■ *V: Tell us more about Doug Malloy's background.*

■ F: He came from a shanty in Seattle, Washington, and went to school to become an audio engineer. By the time he was 23 he was fabulously wealthy. Now he's dead so we can say his real name: Richard Symington.

He lived down in Tolucca Lake behind the Hollywood Bowl. He had a church organ in the living room, 2 other organs in the house, ten bedrooms, 2 Rolls-Royces, a 200-seat movie theater in the basement where he could show *2001* wide-screen. On Monday nights he would show movies to a lot of Hollywood celebrities.

In his studio he had a five-rank manual Wurlitzer that came out of the 20th-Century Fox Studios. It had been used to play music for Valentino and people like this in the silent movie days. When you went to his movie screenings you always heard an organ concert.

We all discovered we had odd things in our piercings—old rusty safety pins, ladies' earrings, S-hooks. There was nothing available. So one of the first goals we set as a group was to pool our ideas and determine the kinds of jewelry we thought would be appropriate.

Doug Malloy was one of the founders and inventors of muzak. Also, in 1949 he got one of the very first Ampex tape recorders on a lease, went to Europe and recorded orchestras and conductors that were vanishing. The first LPs of classical music were mostly recorded by him. As late as 1978 he was still getting royalties from those tapes. Everything he did turned to magic. When I met him, I realized he was a shaman.

■ *V: How did you meet him?*

■ F: Somehow he found out about me and called and said, "I would like to meet you." We had a nice chat for a couple of hours—didn't go too deep. But I led him into what I had been doing for 20 or 30 years. About a week later, he phoned me up and said, "That was good, but now I'd *really* like to meet you. Could I fly up and see you?"

I met him at the airport in my beat-up Volkswagen and brought him to my house where I had nothing but an old cot; I was very poor then. Before we even introduced ourselves he told me who he was, where he came from—his whole life story.

He said that ever since he was 14 years old, this little Egyptian man had been appearing to him, looking as real as anybody sitting across from you, advising him and consulting him and telling him how to run his life. Every time he followed the man's advice he made another million dollars or two!

Long ago apparently Doug had been an Egyptian, and a man had sealed him and his whole family into an airtight tomb. This man was stuck in this mode until he had redeemed himself by helping Doug; thus he'd pay back his karmic debt.

The Egyptian taught him about music and sounds, and what sounds really were. He would take Doug out and sit him down on an asteroid for long periods of time, and talk about vibrations. Now Doug had been a poverty-stricken down-and-out bum's kid in Seattle, yet by listening to this guide tell him on a certain day to do this, and then go and do that, he had made over a million dollars by the age of 24. But he didn't keep Doug from all the hazards in life; Doug kept getting into accidents—he had false hips, incredible medical problems. He always thought he was going to live to the year 2000, and he didn't—unexpectedly he fell over dead from a heart attack in someone's apartment across from the UCLA Medical Center, and he had never had any symptoms of heart disease. Surprised everybody, including himself!

He did publish a small booklet, *The Art of Pierced Penises,* which wasn't totally factual—there was quite a bit of fantasy mixed into the "history" and "practices" described. But his major contribution was getting us all together, and backing Gauntlet and thus *PFIQ.*

■ *V: Can you tell us the state-of-the-art techniques and follow-up hygiene for piercing? I saw one photo in PFIQ showing a C-clamp being used.*

■ F: [laughs] That wasn't for piercing, that was for body play. The clamps and hemostats we use for permanent piercings are surgical, from a medical supply house. But everything you need is available from *Gauntlet* [see address elsewhere]; after extensive experimentation they have selected all the supplies best suited for piercing: the needles (which are often a problem; they have to be specially made), etc. One Stop Shopping for piercing! The techniques written up in *PFIQ* for different types of piercing are based on a joint pool of knowledge which all comes together in each article as to how to best do a Prince Albert, etc.

■ *V: Saline solution?*

■ F: That's not too good for cleaning; it doesn't kill bacteria very effectively. The most neutral agent we've found is Hibiclens surgical scrub. The scrubs that surgeons use for surgery is what we prep with and clean with later on; Hibiclens is the best we've found. We still use Betadine topical as an antiseptic—that's one of the most potent there is. But for cleaning and preparations and general care after the fact, we use Hibiclens—it's more neutral and doesn't dry the skin out; it doesn't cause skin damage or bother people with allergies as easily.

Usually we swab with Hibiclens diluted with water, scrub our hands, then we use gloves (and clean the gloves, too) before we approach a body. As an added precaution, after we've cleaned the area with surgical scrub, we add a Betadine topical solution to the area we're going to pierce—the same brown iodine solution used before an OR (operating room) surgical incision is made.

If someone has a minor infection in the piercing afterwards, it's best to wash and clean all the crusty matter off the jewelry—

■ *V: You mean, slip it off and clean it?*

■ F: No—you *don't* want to move the jewelry—it'll move all by itself. The danger in this is: when you're healing, lymph and other types of matter will come out of the piercing and collect on the jewelry and turn hard. This matter is gooey before it tends to turn hard; it collects bacteria. Now if you try to run the jewelry through, and any of that matter is

BODY PIERCINGS

BY DOUG MALLOY

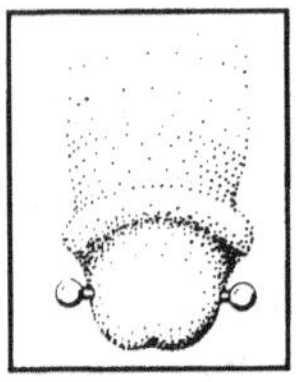

AMPALLANG

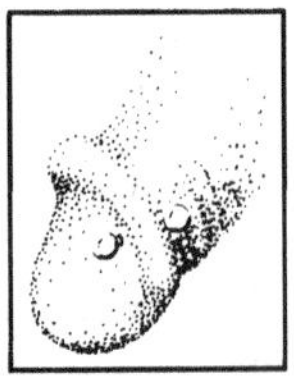

DYDOE

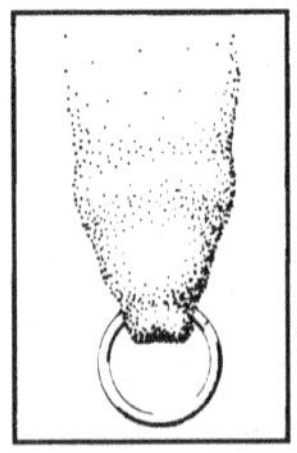

FORESKIN

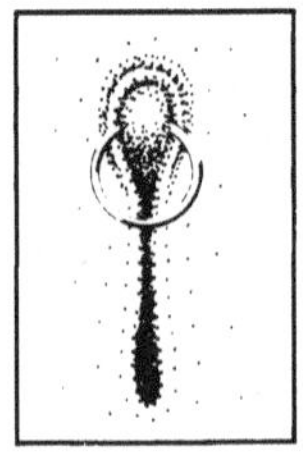

CLITORIS

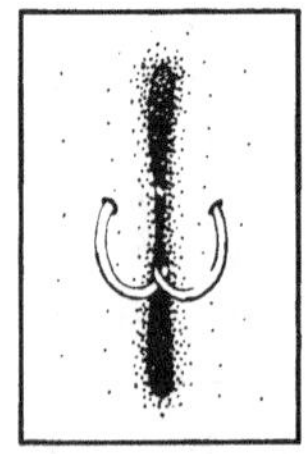

LABIA

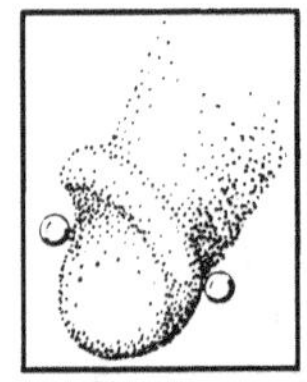

APADAVYA

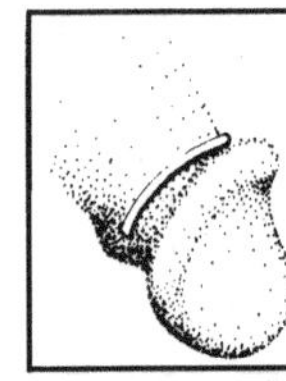

FRENUM

Piercing of the body, for a variety of reasons, is an ancient, if not always wearable, art. For many years an underground phenomenon, it is at least emerging into the light.

Piercing of the nipples is not really new. The proud Roman centurions, Caesar's bodyguard, wore nipple rings as a sign of their virility and courage, and as a dress accessory for holding their short capes. The practice was also quite common among society girls of the Victorian era to enhance the size and shape of the nipples. Today the lure of piercing is primarily a sexual one. It provides a mechanical "tit"-illation achieved by no other means. For many, especially the men and women into the bondage and discipline and S&M scenes, there is a tremendous psychological turn-on. Where possible, piercing should be professionally done as placement determines the nipple's development, shape and aesthetic effect. While difficult to obtain unless one knows a sympathetic doctor, anesthetics are available for the faint-of-heart. Healing normally takes 6 to 8 weeks and is quickest where a retainer with straight post is used.

The proud Roman centurions, Caesar's bodyguards, wore nipple rings as a sign of their virility and courage, and as a dress accessory for holding their short capes.

***Naval* piercing, a sign of royalty to the ancient Egyptians, was something denied commoners. Hence, a deep navel was highly prized. But times change. Today this piercing is becoming increasingly popular especially with young swingers of the "In" set, male and female. Possible only to those with a well-shaped navel, the piercing usually is done through the little flap of skin above the opening and retained with a ring during healing, usually 4 to 6 weeks. Later the ring may be replaced by a decorative stud or bangle selected to suit the wearer's fancy. While not a sexually functional piercing, the visual effect is sensual and directs the viewer's attention to the pelvic area.**

The Prince Albert, called a "dressing ring" by Victorian haberdashers, was originally used to firmly secure the male genitals in either the left or right pant leg during that era's craze for extremely tight, crotch-binding trousers, thus minimizing a man's natural endowment. Legend has it that Prince Albert wore such a ring to retract his foreskin and thus keep his member sweet-smelling so as not to offend the Queen. Today its function is strictly erotic, providing the ultimate in sexual pleasure to men of both persuasions. Piercing is through the urethra at the base of the penis head. The procedure is quick; the pain, minimal; the healing, rapid; and the pleasure, lifelong.

The use of *dydoes* seems to be of fairly recent origin. As they return much of the sensation lost with the foreskin, their emergence corresponds with the widespread practice of circumcision. Nor does the man alone benefit. During intercourse his dydoes provide delightful vaginal stimulation for his consort. The flagging sexual interest in many relationships has been revived with the use of these devices. Piercing is done through both sides of the upper edge of the glans. As proper placement is imperative, piercing should be done professionally.

Small barbell studs, rings, "D" rings, or clamps may be inserted according to the wearer's preference. While healing usually takes 4 to 6 weeks, continence during this period is not necessary.

The *ampallang*, relatively unknown to the Western World, but gaining foothold, is indigenous to the areas surrounding the Indian Ocean. Though sometimes done in childhood, the piercing is usually done as part of a puberty rite, the service being performed by an old woman who places the ampallang horizontally through the center of the head of the penis above the

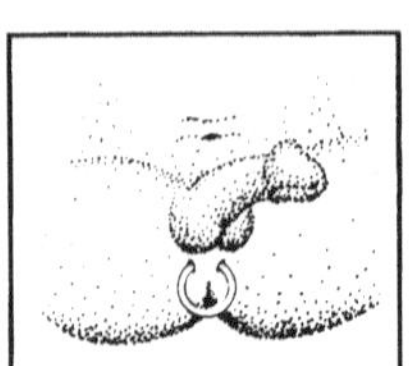

GUICHE

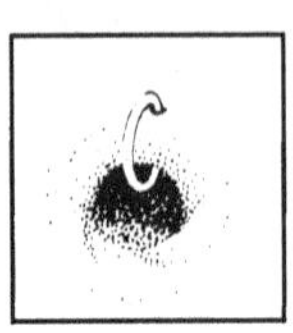

NAVEL

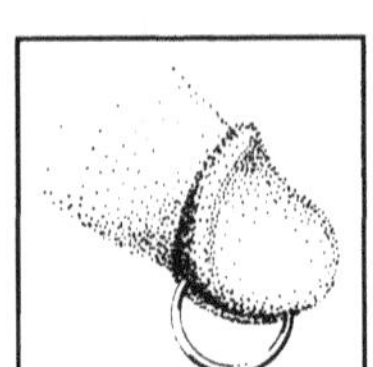

PRINCE ALBERT

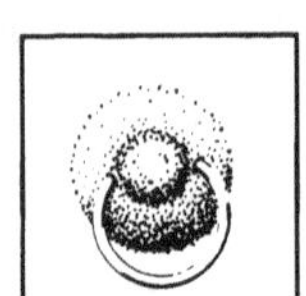

NIPPLE

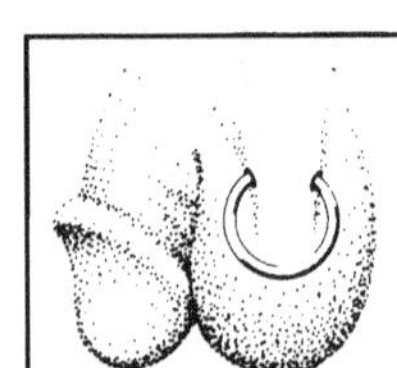

HAFADA

urethra. A metal bar retained with metal discs may be used or studs of bone, ivory, or even gold, if the man is well-to-do. As this sexual device greatly enhances the sensual pleasure of both partners, many women may deny intercourse to a man not so pierced, or specify the size ampallang he should wear if he is.

As described in the *Kama Sutra,* the ancient classic Hindu treatise on love and social conduct, the *apadravya* [apadavra, *var.*] is any one of a number of devices (antique "French ticklers" and/ or dildoes, if you will) used during intercourse to excite the woman. Among the Dravidian people of southern India, the word also refers to the device worn through the pierced male member. The piercing is generally vertical through the penis shaft behind the head, but sometimes in the head itself. It should be noted that this piercing is neither common nor widespread.

Piercing of the *frenum*, the loose piece of flesh beneath the penis head, is of European origin, having served, strange to say, the extremes of both chastity and sexual stimulation. A padlock through the frenum will prevent copulation. A special chastity device called a *Franey Cage*, secured at one end through the frenum and at the other through a second piercing at the base of the penis, prevents even masturbation. By contrast, a ring which passes through the piercing and encircles the head, fitting snugly but comfortably in the groove around the glans when the penis is flaccid, can be extremely erotic, acting to increase erection, much like a cock ring. Many men sleep with the ring flipped down over the middle finger. Ring size is important, measurement being readily obtained using a draftsman's circle template. Piercing is quick and simple, and healing rapid.

It is a proud day in the life of an Arab youth when he achieves manhood. A stag party "rite of passage" is arranged by his male relatives and friends, and one of his gifts will be a silver stud or perhaps a ring or clasp. At a ceremonial piercing this will be inserted through the left side of the scrotum between the testicle and the base of the penis. Believed to prevent the testes from ever returning to the groin from whence they descended in childhood, the *hafada,* as it is called, gives visual evidence that the youth is now and forever a man. Wealthy Arabs eventually install hafadas set with precious stones, the most highly prized (at least in the Persian Gulf area) being the Kuwait pearl. French Foreign Legionnaires have returned from North Africa wearing this genital adornment, usually only on the left side, but occasionally on both. Piercing is quick and not particularly painful, although the healing period is somewhat prolonged. While not the most erotic of piercings, it does provide some stimulation when stroked.

Even today the *guiche* (pronounced "geesh") is very common among the male natives of the South Pacific. The piercing is done, usually at puberty, through the *raphe perinei,* the ridge of skin between the scrotum and the anus, at what would be the inseam. A knife point is used to make the hole, more accurately a tiny slit, and a rawhide thong is placed in it. Less primitive individuals who have adopted this highly sensual device use more conventional piercing tools with ring or stud retainers. Either way, when healing is complete (usually 6 to 8 weeks), a bangle is attached which enhances sensation and provides a convenient grip. The guiche is one of the more erotic piercings and Westerners can benefit from its adoption. Light pressure applied to the piercing greatly increases arousal and gentle tugging on the bangle at climax prolongs and intensifies orgasm. Anyone desiring this piercing is advised to consult an experienced piercer as placement is of great importance.

The Prince Albert was originally used to firmly secure the male genitalia in either the left or right pant leg during the Victorian era's craze for extremely tight, crotch-binding trousers.

While piercing is primarily done for erotic reasons, it has often been used to prevent sexual indulgence—though to those of the bondage and discipline persuasion, even such restraint is doubtless erotic. When used for purposes of chastity it is commonly called infibulation, and both men and women have been its victims. Ancient Roman male slaves were often subjected to the practice, some form of device being locked through the perforated foreskin. With women the device was inserted through the labia. Though both piercings are not uncommon today, they less often imply chastity. In Europe the genital ring is vying with the finger ring as the symbol of betrothal. The man has his fiancee's labia pierced and ringed; and she, his frenum, usually at the same appointment. Through their mutual pain a mere intense commitment has been made. It should be mentioned in passing that piercing of the clitoris, while rarely seen, is also being done by some women who are very much into the scene. Though not particularly functional in a sexual sense, it is an eye-catching place to display ornaments. As with most piercings, those considering any such "needlework" are advised to consult an experienced piercer.

stuck on the jewelry, it'll be pulled into the piercing, you'll scratch the inside that's already healed up, and you will infect it from the bacteria that's in the dried matter. So I recommend cleaning the jewelry at least twice a day with Hibiclens and a little Q-tip, and always keep it clean. Never try to remove the ring! The only time you ought to move it is after you've cleaned it thoroughly and applied a little antibacterial lubricant, like Neosporin (some people are allergic to it), Bacitracin, Matricin—there are all kinds of brands.

■ *V: A lot of readers of PFIQ do the piercings themselves—what do you think about that?*

■ F: They have to realize that these are permanent piercings that one intends to heal and carry for the rest of your life, like a tattoo. There's always the chance that if you're inexperienced and do it yourself, it will not be properly placed. If a person goes to an experienced piercer, obviously they're going to be better off. In Los Angeles, there's Jim Ward [now in San Francisco—see his article; also Raelyn Gallina, this issue]; in the Bay Area, the Fakir; and in London, Mr Sebastian...There

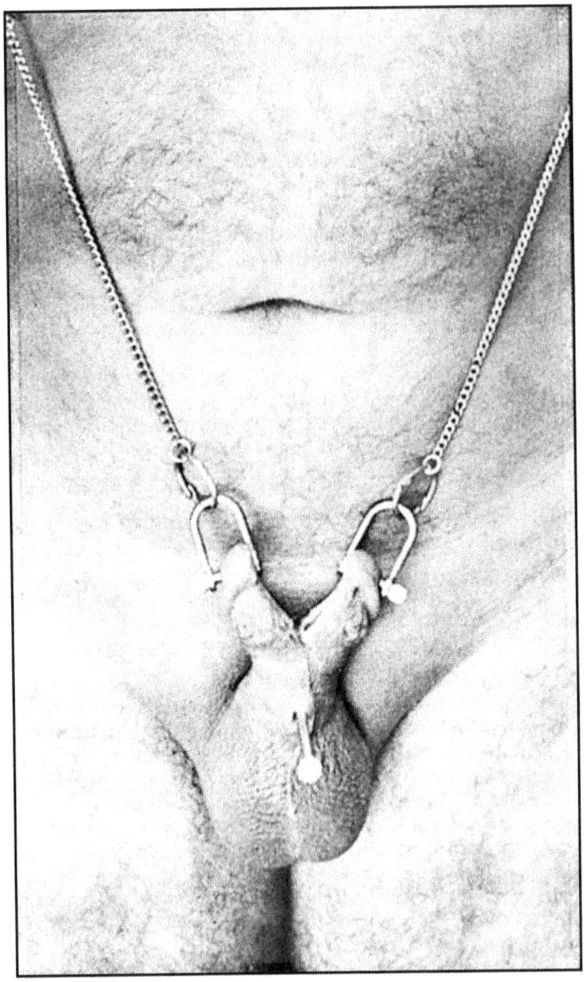

"My decision to surgically remodel my genitals was deliberate, of deep satisfaction to me, highly exciting, sexually adventurous, and erotically exhilarating... Full erections are still maintained as previously, but now in two complete, separate halves. The erotic zones of my penis are still the same, with orgasms and ejaculations functioning perfectly. Entry into the vagina requires a little extra effort for insertion, but once my penis is inside, its opened effect on the vagina's inner lining is more pronounced, giving better, female orgasmic feelings."—Carl Carroll, quoted in *PFIQ #15*. Reportedly, certain Australian aborigines perform a similar modification in homage to a totem lizard with a split penis.

aren't too many who are competent—we've heard of people who've even worked in storefronts who did not do them well—the piercings didn't last long. After a while word got around, and...

■ *V: What's the most dangerous piercing to do, that you don't recommend people do themselves?*

■ F: The ampallang would rate very high. There are times when even people who do a lot of piercings would refuse to do one on certain people, if they're built a certain way. The ampallang has to be pierced through the spongeosum covering on the head of the penis, and it has to be deep enough to heal up—it's very difficult to heal anything in that type of tissue in the first place. And it bleeds a lot, even without getting into any major *anything*, because it's loaded with blood—it's very sensitive and nerve-rich.

You have to pierce it in that spongeosum as far as possible and still not hit the cavernosum—the cavities that hold the blood during an erection. So it's a very touchy operation to hit just the right spot—very difficult piercing to make and get it just right. The danger is: if you go too deep, or in the wrong spot, you pierce the cavernosum, and that may never heal up—blood would squirt out all over forever; it could be very dangerous.

The ampallang would rate very high in danger. The danger is: if you go too deep, or in the wrong spot, you pierce the cavernosum, and that may never heal up—blood would squirt out all over forever; it could be very dangerous.

■ *V: Have you ever heard of that happening to anyone?*

■ F: Yes, I have! And they were lucky—they got the needle back up and the wound somehow managed to seal itself off. But it could have been very dangerous.

■ *V: How about the piercing in the back of the testicle sack?*

■ F: The guiche? Relatively no danger—very simple. That's just superficial—through the skin. You cannot pierce deep into the scrotum—that's very dangerous. Whoever does that has to know anatomy pretty well—you can only pierce the sac. The guiche is in a little piece of skin *behind* the testicles—there's no risk there. It's very similar to the belly button piercing. Since it's in a relatively flat skin area, these have a high rate of not healing properly, or growing out. Both tend to grow out. Whatever you put in there will gradually, little by little, migrate to the surface and grow out.

■ *V: Is that true of cheek piercing?*

■ F: Again, that's a surface-to-surface piercing. Our general policy is this: if it protrudes, pierce it. If it doesn't, don't. Anything that does not protrude from the body is subject to not healing. You can't just run a needle through the surface of your arm or hand—chances are 9 out of 10 that it'll grow out, that it'll never heal.

■ *V: What is the most common piercing?*

■ F: The nipple. Actually, earlobes are probably the safest for an amateur to pierce. We did run a survey, and of all the different types of piercings among the readers of *PFIQ* the most popular piercing, the one liked by most, was the earlobe which we're all familiar with.

■ *V: By the way, what does the dydoe do?*

■ F: The dydoes rub the sensitive area of the corona of the penis, stimulating the wearer. The ampallang,

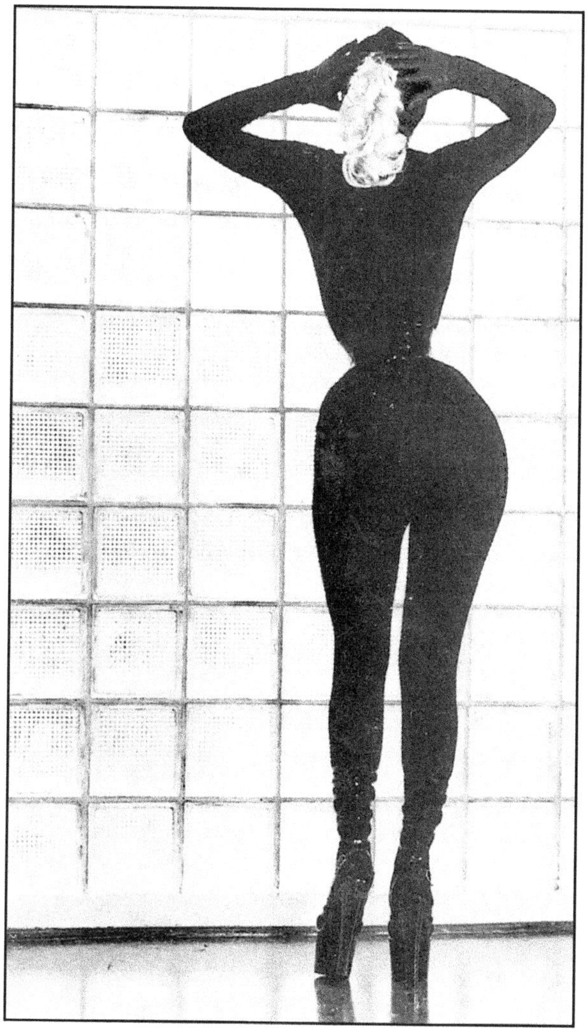

Famous German corseted woman with 17" waist.

I've heard, makes a significant difference to your partner, whether male or female, and the Prince Albert is basically for the wearer; it doesn't seem to create much sensation for the other person.

■ *V: How about the tragus [the front lobe of the ear]? Why aren't there more piercings there?*

■ F: That's very difficult to pierce; very few people know how to do it and get it to stay. After experimenting on about five people Jim Ward worked out a procedure. That has to go through a pretty chunky piece of cartilage. From trial and error on our own bodies we learned a lot about what to do when piercing through or near cartilage.

Sometimes the upper ear can be just as much of a problem; the rim is also semi-cartilage. Those are very difficult to heal. In general, when there's cartilage involved, you have to make the hole a great deal larger than what you put in it—punch out a big chunk of cartilage, then put a small object in and have the skin grow inside and around the little piece of cartilage, unlike a fleshy piercing like the earlobe—there's no cartilage there.

■ *V: What's the best metal to use, that the least number of people would have an adverse reaction to?*

■ F: We don't know. We've had people who've had troubles with stainless steel—there's nickel in any kind of stainless, and they sometimes have allergies to that or some other trace minerals that might be in stainless. On the other hand, we've had a number of people very allergic to the alloys you have to put in gold, because you can't use pure gold—that's just like butter—it's too soft.

We found out that for practical purposes 24-carat gold is too soft, so the jewelry that Gauntlet sells is 14-carat with a fair amount of alloy in it, and that sometimes bothers people. Silver is out of the question—very, very bad for body piercings. Usually ear wires are stainless or gold-plated, and very cheap earrings may be gold-plated brass, and the gold plating wears off very quickly leaving just brass which is very, very bad. Most people react very badly to brass. And there are other metals which work—I've had very good luck with aluminum in my body; it's very neutral for me. But some people have trouble with it.

Fakir emulates Ibitoe waist training, 1956.

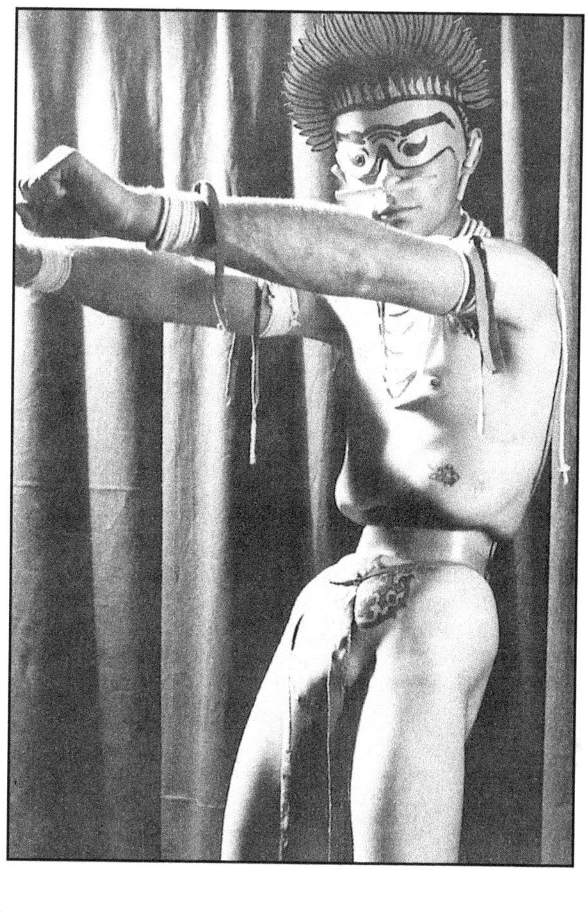

We've had *very* good luck with high-quality surgical stainless. There are some people making rings (you can't tell, because you can't run a lab-analysis on what they sell) who are not using a real good or even a surgical-grade stainless; they're using an industrial grade or something. And there have been problems, in that if you actually take their ring and put it in salt water it'll get rusty. That is not good! Good surgical stainless (which surgical instruments are made of, hip pins or implants in the body) is the only material which is really safe. And that's what Gauntlet sells.

■ *V: Doesn't Sailor Sid have fifty or so genital piercings?*

■ F: Well, he has a *lot*, although in *PFIQ* we featured a guy named Indie who actually had more. However, I'm of the opinion that quantity doesn't count as much as quality. To me, one large earhole is worth far more than 20 dinky piercings—it's a more major body modification. So the numbers are really not that important. But *where, how deep* and *how big* the hole is—that's different! That starts to assume some meaning and significance.

■ *V: And are piercings at all dangerous to the skin?*

■ F: People don't realize how strong living skin is. Just put a tiny little wire into a tiny little piercing, and then try breaking that skin—it's damn near impossible, even with hundreds of pounds pressure! Living skin is extremely strong (although dead skin is very weak). There have been tales of Indian Sun Dancers who have jerked against the cords for 24 or 48 hours trying to break it. In fact, next time I do the Sun Dance I think I'll use a triangular, serrated needle so it'll break easier!

■ *V: Do you have any comment on the person in* PFIQ *who split his penis in half?*

■ F: Again, that's an eccentric piece of self-surgery. Somehow the guy was able to figure it out and pull it off. Even for a plastic surgeon, this might be considered damn near impossible, because he was slicing something that's paper-thin. Somehow he did it, and it worked. He sent us some photos, we printed them, and that's all we know. Another thing—this person lives in Australia, and Australia and New Zealand banned *PFIQ*—they started to put surveillance on people who received the magazine, and many of the subscribers wrote us: "Please, for God's sake, we don't want to get into any more trouble with the authorities—don't send anything to us!" So our lines of communication were closed down with a lot of people because of suppressive governments.

■ *V: I noticed the latest issue of* PFIQ *contained a subscription form with a very detailed disclaimer to sign if I wanted to renew. Has* PFIQ *had any legal problems?*

■ F: No, this is just on the advice of an attorney who's pretty competent in these matters. Right now we're in an increasingly repressive period.

■ *V: Yes, not only have various satirical radio shows been banned, but Allen Ginsberg's* Howl *couldn't even be read on public radio recently.*

■ F: At one time Jim Ward and I both took *PFIQ* into the adult book market, and the gangster types you have to deal with (that you can never make a deal with, anyway), rejected them in horror. Even if a billion copies were sold, they wouldn't handle it! They could comprehend plain old hardcore sex—fucking and sucking—but putting a needle through a nose?!

CORSETS

■ *V: Tell us about your involvement with small waists.*

■ F: As I said, the *Comptons Picture Encyclopedia* gave me the yen to be the *Ibitoe*; it showed a picture of a young boy with a tightly cinched waist. So I tried it.

■ *AJ: What does cinching the waist do?*

■ F: Corseting can either be temporary, or can permanently re-shape the torso. If taken to extremes it becomes masochism—*corset masochism.* Corsets in general, when one adjusts to them properly, become very erotic. They've been used since time immemorial, back in pre-history, to cause the sensation of erotic arousal, particularly in women. Having sex with a corset on is quite an experience!

There are a number of ways you can express life through the body or use the body as a vehicle to learn something about life itself. Most primitive people know this. Among the New Guinea people, only the males decorate themselves with face paint and plumage, whereas the women seldom decorate. Same with the Nubans in Africa—the men do most of the preening, body decorations and make-up art; it's the male prerogative. This was quite a surprise: to find out there were other cultures where things were totally reversed.

Corseting goes back to ancient times and is cross-cultural. It has to do with rearranging the body, making it more attractive. In Africa the Dinka people wear corsets.

■ *V: Historically, who were the first to use corsets?*

■ F: According to Western history, the Minoans, on the island of Crete near Greece, wore belts similar to the Ibitoe; they didn't wear corsets as such. The young men and women between the ages of 15 and 25 would try to see how small they could compress their waist. We don't really know why. But they left behind a lot of detailed drawings and brass and bronze figurines that depicted these body modifications.

■ *V: Do you know any written documentation of the Ibitoe?*

■ F: It was an initiation rite that also had religious overtones. When a young man was at the proper age his father would take him to his maternal uncle and—I quote John Foster Fraser in *Quaint Subjects of the King:*

"When a Papuan boy gets to the age at which an English boy begins to think about taking to stand-up collars, instead of encasing his neck in a rampart of stiff linen, he crushes his waist into a wooden belt so tight that his ribs protrude over it like the chest of a pouter pigeon. The belt terminates at the back in a kind of tail that trails upon the ground. The more wasp-like his waist, the more airs the boy gives himself. When he

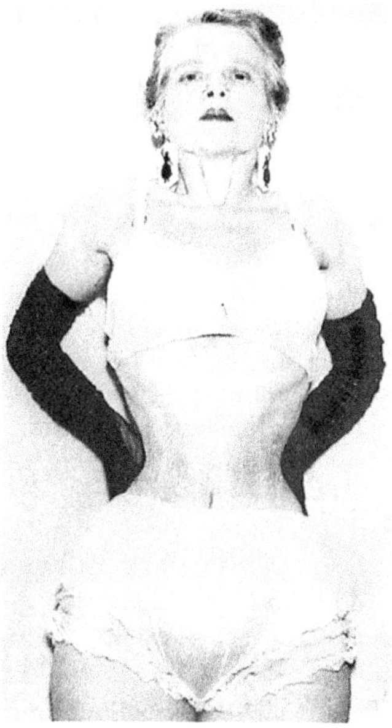

Ethel Grainger at age 50 with corset removed.

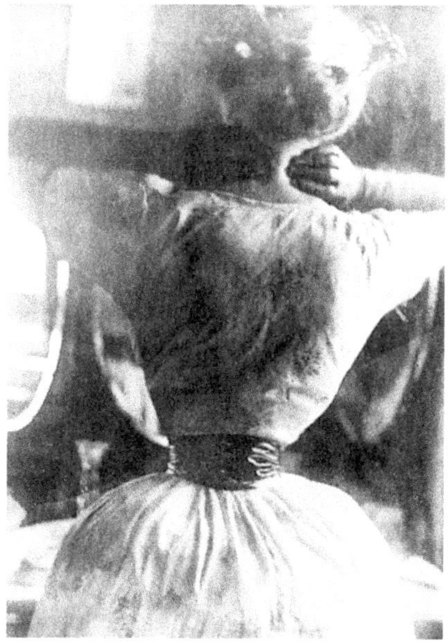

Ethel in her 40's showing her 13" waist.

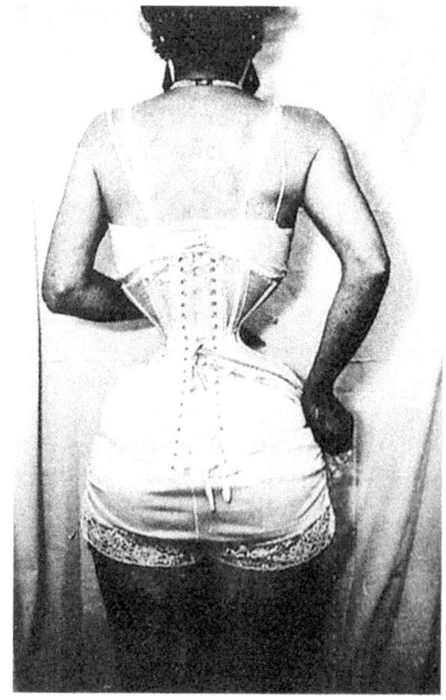

Ethel with corset.

has assumed this wooden belt he is called Ibitoe and becomes entitled to all privileges of a full-grown man including being chosen by a woman."

Another book additionally described that when a boy entered manhood, his nose and ears were pierced, and his father would ask his maternal uncle, "Suffer now that my son assume the Ituburi." The uncle would place the Ituburi on the boy. Basically, they would wind the waist very tightly with beaten soft fiber made out of bark, to compress the waist. On top of this they would put a wooden band. As part of the initiation (and this was not totally voluntary) once he had this on he was not allowed to take it off day or night, no matter how much he suffered! He had to leave it on until he adjusted to it.

■ *AJ: What does this accomplish?*

■ F: It teaches them that *they are not their bodies.* If you can remove your attention from the pressure and discomfort of the belt, then you get to a stage where it actually becomes pleasant, and it becomes *unpleasant* to take it off. The same thing goes for wearing any kind of encumberment. There is an adaptation that goes on, but the most important thing you learn is that you are not your body, you just *live* in it. People in this culture practically never have that experience.

Today there are still other cultures in which men wear corsets. Tight beaded corsets are everyday wear for the Dinka men. Color indicates age: red and black are worn by 15-25 year-olds; pink and purple by the 25-30 set, and yellow by those over 30. Now these are encumberments, restrictions, but supposedly through experiencing these people learn something, so they know something that other people don't know.

A similar lesson can come from pushing the body to its limit. Marathon runners experience this; they can get really hooked on "hitting the wall." They go so long, and finally run out of energy and their body tells them, "Quit!" but they keep going *anyway.* Then they reach a point where all of a sudden the pain sort of vanishes in a fog and they aren't really aware of the body or their legs going or their heart pounding. This is *removing* the consciousness from the body...yet another way to learn you are *not* your body. You live in it, you operate it, and if you love it and cooperate with it, it will love and cooperate with you. But it will go *way* beyond what you think you can do with it.

■ *AJ: Tell us more about the history of corsetry?*

■ F: About 500 A.D. people in European cultures wound stiff bands around their bodices. In the 1700s-1800s there were officers of Napoleon and the British Army that would waist-train with special corsets just for them. They would cut military uniforms particularly to fit these attenuated bodies. This was of course a fashion—a style, although in many cases people got hooked on it and discovered the same thing that the Ibitoe were to learn involuntarily.

■ *AJ: You mean: that they could transcend their body? What about women who wore corsets? Did all those corseted women transcend?*

■ F: In the 1880s-90s, it was extremely fashionable to have an attenuated middle. So a lot of women suffered to have this waist, just to be *au courant.* Some, however, went into it for the purposes of fashion, and came out of it totally addicted to tight lacing. Women, particularly, discovered that this practice (if done properly) can be very exotic and sexual. It put them in a state of permanent sexual arousal.

Again, corsetry was a very initiatory practice. There are a lot of stories about young girls, who were often rebellious, being forced to wear tight corsets, and how they suffered and cried and didn't sleep for 3 days—similar to what the New Guinea boys were subjected to. And if you fight body modification it can be horrible and a very negative experience.

However, it's better if the culture offers rewards, like: "It is a great honor to do this; it is making you into a man." Then you're more apt to have a good attitude. So when the little girl has the collar around her neck, she may ask, "Make it a little taller, please." Or if the young girl is being corseted in the 1880s, she says, "Could you pull it a little tighter; I wish to be smaller." Such a person would be more likely to discover something out of this.

■ *AJ: But what happens to the internal organs?*

■ F: They move to a different place—they get rearranged. In the 1800s there was a big cultural rivalry between the Germans and the French. The French were leaders when it came to really tiny waists, although Scotland also excelled, and so did Austria. There were women with waists *that* big around [forms circle with hands almost touching]. That took one hell of a lot of dedication; your whole life would revolve around this—nothing else.

The negative corset propaganda was instituted by the Germans. They wanted to denigrate the French so they got on an anti-corset campaign and came out with all kinds of phony-baloney medical evidence. It was all fake; there was no medical documentation to support these claims as to the ill effects of tight lacing. It has all been refuted; in fact, it is almost impossible to injure a human being by doing this properly. Corsetry is a very slow process and the body resists it—it's just naturally hard to *overdo* it.

■ *V: What about pregnancy? I thought that was the main objection to it.*

■ F: There were some problems there. Some women wanted to keep their tiny waists; they didn't want to get pregnant, so the corset provided an excuse. Many times this would fend off sex they didn't want. So corsets were used in this period of history as a form of liberation for females. Although, it also made them very helpless—when you're corseted this small you get very fragile, and many women overplayed that helpless aspect. That's how customs like opening doors developed, because women were physically incapacitated to a great degree.

So these "primitive" constrictions do tend to restrict what you can do in physical life. You can't run a marathon with an Itiburi on; however, I see no reason why you can't operate a computer with your neck in a brass coil!

Those Germans said that a woman's liver would burst if they laced into tight corsets, but of course that's totally untrue. They even invented little gauges to slip down inside the corset to measure the amount of pressure. By the way, this compression principle can be carried out on other parts of the body: arms, legs, virtually anywhere.

■ *AJ: How did you get into the corseting business?*

■ F: I had a grandmother who had a very small waist. All the women in her family had small waists; there were framed photographs everywhere. But the best picture was of my grandmother in her wedding dress. It was taken about 1896 when she was 18: a wee Scottish lass with frizzy hair and a tiny, belted 18" waist. Incidentally, corseting is best explored when one is very young; it gets harder and harder as you get older.

In the forties, I read a lot of corset lore in *Bizarre* magazine—that was the only source in the world of information about corset training. Of course, magazines of the late 1800s or around 1900 like *Englishwoman's Domestic* had a pretty fetish-y concept going. A little later there was *London Life;* if you ever saw a copy of that, you'd be amazed—it's another clandestine underground magazine. It was printed and circulated in very limited quantities for people who were totally on the outside of society. Because at this time you could be thrown into prison for practicing any of this.

I did a little magazine called *Fancy* that printed some of this kind of material, and I did a little corset newsletter too, back when I had the corset business. I covered body urges and body play possibilities.

The tight waist training of the Ibitoe teaches them that they are not their bodies. You are not your body, you just live in it.

■ *AJ: What's the sexual angle in all this?*

■ F: Helpless women with small waists is a sexual turn-on for men. It's also a sexual turn-on for women, if they adjust and take to this body-training. By the early twentieth century only actresses and burlesque-type people went for waist training, like Anna Hill, Flo Ziegfeld's wife—she had a 16-inch waist.

■ *AJ: So only people on the fringe of society would do this: actresses and creative people, in a sense.*

■ F: It only lived on in those few special people. Judge Roy Bean, the "Hanging Judge," fell in love with Lily Langtree who was famous the world over for one thing—mainly her hourglass figure with its 18" small waist.

■ *V: Who was the most famous?*

■ F: The most famous corseted lady of all time was Ethel Granger, who had a 13-inch waist—barely enough room for her spinal column. But she was in great health until she died at about the age of 83. Her husband died years before; he didn't wear a corset. She worked at a corset shop in London and lived in the suburbs; she used to ride a little motorbike every day about 15 miles to this corset shop where she assisted people.

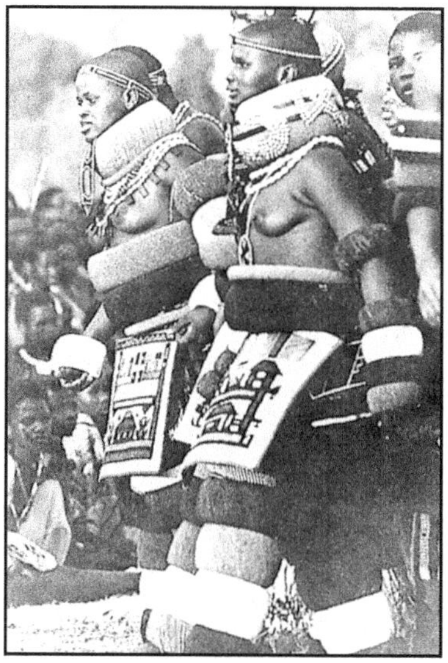

Ndebeli women of South Africa wear collars for life. The other encumberments they wear for long ceremonies.

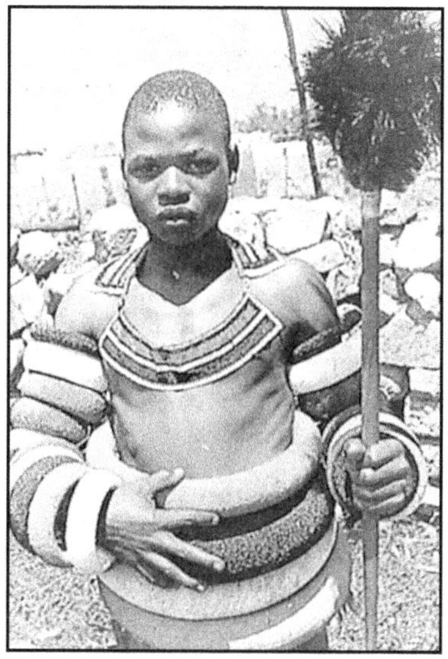

This Ndebeli boy must wear his beaded weights for a 30-day initiation.

■ *V: How did she get into corsetry?*

■ F: Her husband Will was a male who loved the domination he could exert, and she went along with it very willingly. By the mid-30s her 26" waist had been reduced to 16" and her ears had been pierced many times. By WWII her waist was down to 13" and her nose and nipples had also been pierced. Will and Ethel were really two of the most outrageous Modern Primitives in this century—pioneers! She's been in the *Guinness Book of World Records* for a long time.

She lived a healthy, full life. Her husband Will was a college professor and he didn't make much money, so they lived in relative poverty all their life in Peterborough, England. Even though she was the world's smallest-waisted woman, this wasn't worth a penny. Nobody was interested in the world's smallest-waisted woman.

Will died in 1967, and Ethel lived until 1974 when she died of natural causes, and her corset was removed. Of course her body had been modified; even without a corset she measured about 16-17 inches around the waist. She also had huge holes in her ears and nose and all over her body. I published a little booklet containing the first half of her biography, which Will wrote.

■ *V: Who else had exceptionally small waists?*

■ F: Mademoiselle Polaire, who was a show biz lady, had a 14-inch waist. As late as 1917 people were still doing this. There was a catch to things then: women in the past would slowly train themselves down to a smaller size, getting used to these corsets. Then they would have these elegant, costly gowns made to fit, and they were stuck—they couldn't take it off if they wanted to wear these gowns—this was the thing to keep them going!

Elizabeth Taylor was corseted in a number of early movies, like *Raintree County* and *Cat on a Hot Tin Roof*. I have some movies in which Diana Dors is outrageous. And in the '50s there were some contests and Mitzi Gaynor was corseted down to about 15 inches.

■ *AJ: Do you think corseting is a drugless high if you get into it long enough?*

■ F: Oh, yes, definitely.

■ *AJ: Is it like hyperventilating?*

■ F: Not really. Also, it enhances sexual experiences. There's nothing like being extremely tight-laced yourself as a male and making love to a woman who's extremely tight-laced. This is something you cannot experience any other way—all your internal organs and your sexual components are in different positions, with different tensions and so on—there's a mechanical basis for this. It's very ecstatic.

■ *V: But how did you get into making corsets?*

■ F: After I left the service, I wanted to be a lighting designer, scene designer, or technical director of a theater. So I came to S.F. State and became totally immersed in theater—basically tech-theater. This was the time of the beatnik days, with guys sitting around and playing flutes and reading poetry.

I had been in a couple of musicals and worked with people who did costuming. The vaguest thing to me was costuming—I knew a little or nothing about it, but I knew it was an essential part of theater. So I took every costuming class they had.

In the costume class I learned how to make original patterns for any body, of any style, of any period. I could start out with a watercolor sketch, then go to a live person who is going to be the character, and then make a pattern for their body, tailoring the sketch which was evolved through research.

For one of my projects I selected an 1880s ball gown, because it was the most complicated, elegant thing I could find. In the process I discovered that bodies weren't shaped the same in the 1880s; woman wore corsets that made them incredibly differently-proportioned. I was making a gown for a girl in my class who was the subject, and it didn't fit anybody because nobody was shaped right! I found out that a corset was required, and that there were no corsets available. I asked, "Why not? What *is* a corset and how is it made?" So I started researching corsets, the underpinnings of those elegant gowns.

After I left school I discovered through trial and error that the original corset patterns in books didn't work, because 'way back then women were all shorter, their trunks were shorter—all the proportions were different. The upper chest was much smaller than it is now; women's chests have expanded and become bigger.

I learned how the original corsetiers worked, and how to sculpt wire-mesh mannequins, pulling the wire into the right shapes. When you finally get the right shape, you can cut a thing to fit over it, and you've got a costume to fit somebody. The original corsetiers had made woven wicker (like that used for a chair) to these corseted shapes. They had a great knowledge of anatomy and physiology; they had to know the aesthetics and practical mechanics of the material they were working with—the whole thing.

Jim Ward and I both took PFIQ into the adult book market, and the gangster types you have to deal with rejected them in horror. They could comprehend plain old hardcore sex—fucking and sucking—but putting a needle through a nose?!

So I re-made corset mannequins for modern women. I had a book with figure dimensions for some 200 women that had been in musical shows, from all ages—5 to 50 years old. I found out they fell into about 5 basic groups, so I made a mannequin for each one of those 5 basic figure shapes of modern women's bodies. Then I altered the mannequins, allowing for the amount of expansion that would occur in the upper chest when you've constricted the waist. There's also a little expansion on the bottom—the hips tend to go out a little bit more, and in the corset era that was desirable—they liked to start with somebody who was rather chunky and train them into corsets, because you had to have some material to *shape*. If they were too skinny and slender it was difficult, because they may start out with a really small waist, but then there wasn't much to push around—the object of the corset is to push you around into a different place, and then you end up with a totally different figure.

So, I got my mannequins done, covered them with papier-mache many times, and drew my patterns directly on the dried paper. Then I took the paper, cut it off, moistened it and laid it flat, and I had corset patterns! I had the pieces; I had to study the way it was constructed, the way the bias of the cloth ran, where all the gores were—all this kind of stuff. I ended up making corsets and from the very first one on they were a success. I had made the first new patterns for modern bodies in 75 years, and they worked!

■ *V: Tell us about some current-day corset wearers.*

■ F: One of my first corset customers was a lady who was the wife of a microbiologist. They were loners and strange and withdrawn and lived in a little house with gas lights, decorated like it was the turn of the century. In the evenings they read poetry to each other, and so on. And she dressed in corsets and gowns and of course her figure looked perfectly 19th century. They had a nice fantasy going, and who's to say the quality of their life wasn't preferable to a more "modern" existence? Especially since they combined some of the best aspects of past and present.

People don't realize how strong living skin is. There have been tales of Indian Sun Dancers who have jerked against the cords for 24 or 48 hours trying to break it.

All the couples I know involving a woman with a small waist are extremely secretive. They don't want anybody to know anything about this.

■ *V: What happened to your corset business?*

■ F: After several years of effort, I found I couldn't make a living from corsets—there wasn't enough interest back then. I couldn't get enough orders to make ends meet. I loved it, though. Then I met Ruth and Lou (BR Creations); they took it over and now have a thriving business going, so maybe I was just a couple decades ahead of my time! They started putting ads in *Harper's Bazaar* and have been doing well for the last four years. I appreciate the fact that I get a 10 percent royalty. I spent a year training her how to make them and I gave her my original patterns, which took several years to refine.

Padung girls who are only 9 or 10 already have 6" to 8" coiled collars.

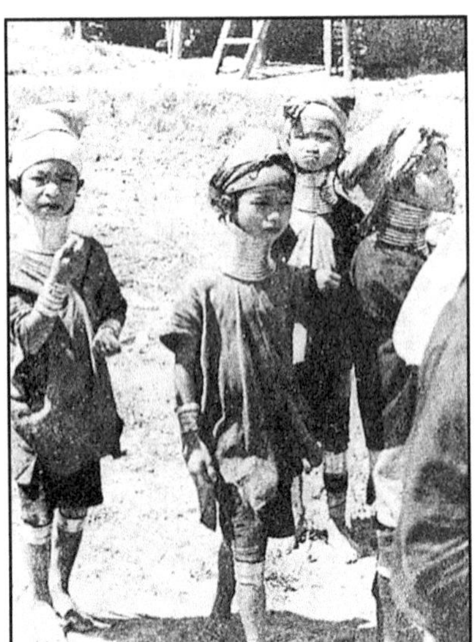

Fakir stretches his neck with metal collar.

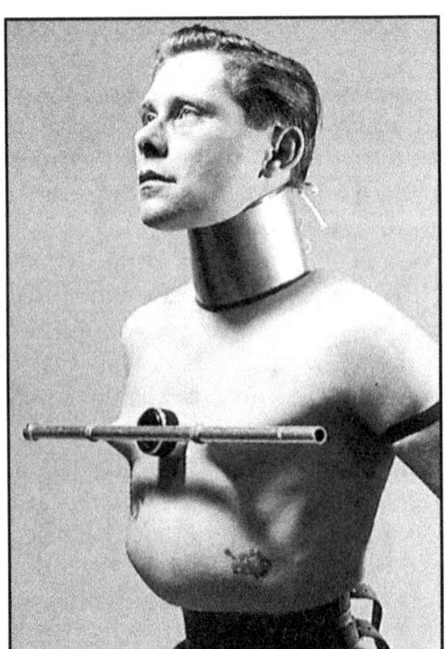

When Ruth first started, we thought if she made 3 corsets a month that would be big time. Now she's got 3 ladies working for her full-time, and she can't keep up with the demand. The business is growing and they're selling to straight people now, not just the kinky circuit. Like bridal salons—it's amazing where they're selling these things. They ran an ad in the *New York Times* and got a ton of orders from it...

ENCUMBERMENTS

■ F: The area of encumberments is very widespread. Primitive people, by and large, do not wear much clothing, and they tend to put a lot of heavy stuff on the body. Why? [laughs] What's the purpose in this? It's a restriction; it's going to limit physical movement—especially when some bracelets weigh 15 pounds apiece!

One idea favored by early anthropologists was: these were very macho societies and they wanted to keep women helpless, under control. However, it turned out that many of the societies where the women have the encumberments are matriarchal. The women of the Cuno Indians in San Blas, Mexico wear tight armbands and legbands and a big ring in the nose, yet they run the culture and tell the men what to do.

As far as the few remaining tribes throughout the world who wear encumberments go, the prevailing idea is: none of them can be brought into the 20th century looking like that. "No, we can't have this in the world; we must abolish it, and if these people won't stop this silliness, kill them!" Genocide—that's the attitude of the South Africans and a lot of people in Brazil. Their attitudes are a hundred years behind the times, but they've got the guns! And some of these practices will only survive on film, if that.

■ *V: Are there examples of encumberment in Western Society?*

■ F: Back in the days of Marie-Antoinette's court, there was an encumberment by clothing. Ladies that weighed 98 pounds wore dresses that weighed 75 pounds with hoops and a lot of other frippery. Although this form of encumberment wasn't exactly *intimate.* And also it mostly hid the body. To hide the body is counter-primitive—*important point!* And to express the primitive urge is to show the body; whatever you put *highlights* the body; emphasizes the body. There's a big difference there.

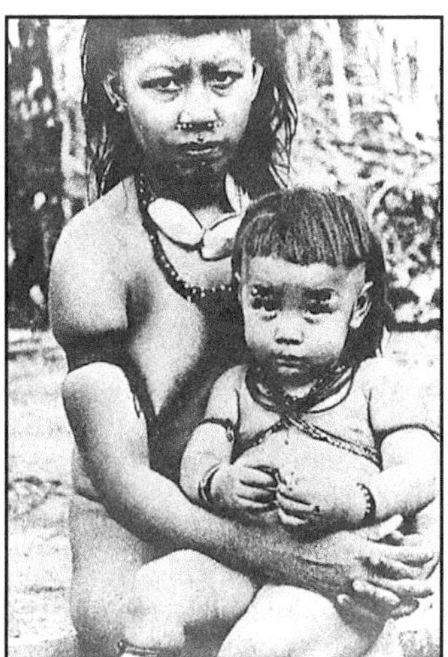

South American Indians reshape limbs with tight arm and leg bands.

■ *V: How did those Burmese women with the neck coils function?*

■ F: Well, they go around and saw wood and pound millet and do the normal chores. They're quite functional...with certain restrictions. You can't look down, you have to bend from the waist to do that. But they're regarded as beautiful and special and treated with great care.

■ A little girl will start out with rings about 3-1/2" long. Usually a ring measures about 7/16". So you can count the coils and approximate the height of the rings. I have a photo of one woman whose neck is almost 12 inches long—that's about the longest one I ever found. It's fairly common for a girl to have about 19 primary coils (times 7/16", so her neck is 8-3/8" long). There was a legend that if the women got unruly, they'd just put a rope through the coils and hang them up in the house. That turned out to be untrue; in fact the society is matriarchal and women tend to run things.

■ *V: What are the rings made of?*

■ F: Usually a very soft brass that can be bent very easily, with not a lot of copper in it—maybe a lot of tin and zinc, because they don't seem to corrode; they seem to stay pretty shiny.

■ *AJ: What happens to the skin underneath?*

■ F: It probably peels and corrodes and god knows what happens to it under there. It's probably hard to wash, especially since they wear the rings all their life.

There's a picture of an x-ray of a Padung woman's neck from *National Geographic* which clearly shows how the neck was stretched. They also printed another photo of a woman who had her coil removed, and you can see little striations where the coil had been around her neck.

■ *V: We've been seeing more people with constricting metal circlets around their arms.*

■ F: This is all a resurrection, a resurgence, a Renaissance of primitivism. It may be a bit superficial, the reasons may not be there, the experiences may not be complete, the commitment may not be very deep, the depth of what they're doing may not be very much, but nevertheless it still is a resurrection and a renaissance of the primitive urge that's been with us since the beginning of man.

Back in the days of Marie Antoinette's court, there was encumberment by clothing. Ladies that weighed 98 pounds wore dresses that weighed 75 pounds with hoops and a lot of other frippery.

■ *V: Do you know if the women with neck coils ever dance?*

■ F: Well, there are photos of ladies carrying babies on their back. I've tried putting as many encumberments as I can stand on my arms, legs, body and so on. It's quite an experience to have all that on and go out and dance vigorously for a couple of hours. You finally lose all sensation of weight and you feel very light—it's really a strange feeling. I know, because I've tried it. There's a lesson to be learned here.

Nuban girls wear armbands with a purpose of making arm grooves. The groove is permanent if you get it deep enough and do it long enough.

■ *AJ: When do you get to the point of fearing gangrene?*

■ F: Well, if you go about any of these things slowly, there's no gangrene. There *are* tales of males who went for tighter and tighter armbands until their arms hung useless and couldn't be used. But I think they're folklore. It's amazing how you can constrict the arms and limbs and not do any damage. Just like Mrs Granger, who lived a perfectly healthy life with every organ in a totally different place than it was when she started. You can get acclimated or adjusted to all of these restrictions, to the point where it's more normal to be with it than without. And function quite well. It's probably impossible for most people to damage themselves; the pain would force them to quit long before they could do any permanent damage.

Besides, one of the things you learn from wearing encumberments is a certain kind of patience and cooperation with nature; think of the time cycles of the sun, the moon, and the earth. People who try to stretch a piercing out learn they might have to work for the next five years to get a good result! People get excited when they hear about Sadhus in India stretching the penis and I say, "Sure, but you have to do it day and night for a year or two—nothing but that! And during that time you don't work for a living." Well, that's body modification!

Take Mrs Granger with her 13" waist; she had to corset-train for maybe 7 or 8 years. Look where it got her, however! But it takes damn long. It takes a patience that people today have no concept of. If you're an African woman with 15-pound brass anklets and you have to travel to another village—no big deal, you get up and clank along those 10-20 miles. No big deal—you get used to it. So it's not a short 50-yard dash; this is like running the marathon every day all day long for years! To get the primal urge out to those degrees requires very heavy commitment...

THE VENTRILOQUIST

■ *AJ: There's the showman part of you and then there's the "real" truth-seeker; how do you balance the two out?*

■ F: I started out as an amateur magician and became an expert showman. I've always been fascinated by magic; when I was in junior high school I started doing magic shows. First I tried ventriloquism. My grandmother gave me a little dummy and I learned how to talk with my mouth closed: "Hey, how are you there? Ha-ha-ha-ha!" I went up in front of a large group of people and participated in a talent show, in back of footlights, and I got the creepiest feeling I've ever had up to that time. There was something very sick about this. Since then my path has constantly been crossing with ventriloquists, until I finally met the apex of ventriloquists.

■ *V: How did that happen?*

■ F: My brother told me, "You've got to meet this guy Bob. He's been in show business and he's a ventriloquist." Since I used to do ventriloquism, too, and I had done stage magic, we met and became fast friends right away.

Bob soon met a lady who was friends with people like Art Linkletter. She decided she wanted to become a TV producer, and persuaded Papa Langendorf (of the bread company) to sponsor "The Happy Holsum Show." Bob knew I had training in writing, theater, and radio production, so they hired me to design a set and come up with a daily, scripted show with a running plot.

I was living down on the peninsula, so I quit my job and moved to San Francisco and started living in a couple of rooms on the third floor of the Dorchester hotel where they used to film *Streets of San Francisco.* We built a little studio in the basement of the Broadmoor hotel across the street, where Bob had a little apartment. Our little children's TV show went on for about 8 months on a local station.

I produced, directed and wrote the show, and he acted in it; he was the star. He was very good technically...but he was the sickest man I have ever met. He used to take rats and nail them to a board and slowly cut them apart. And he hated his dummy—they always get jealous of their dummy! I was the one who had to repair it, because he'd poke its eye out in hatred; then we'd have to do a show the next day and there was no way to quickly get a dummy repaired in San Francisco (get its eye back in and moving) so *I'd* have to do it. And there was evil connected with it—*absolute evil!*

Ventriloquism is dealing with magic, but in a very strange way. And most people who dabble in ventriloquism don't really understand what they're doing. When you get good at it, you're actually at a point of being able to conjure up things, or draw spirit energies, and what's really happening when that dummy acts alive is probably a little bit of *real life* acting in the dummy—it's not just "talking with your mouth closed." It's a spooky kind of magic; *Dead of Night* had an excellent sequence on this theme of the love-hate relationship with the dummy. And you may not be dealing with all the purest kinds of forces—you might draw some real malignant energies like Bob did—he drew hate, he drew the most malignant forces. I could see him back in time being the head of Buchenwald—this guy was really evil.

I remember one time I confronted him after I'd found the remains of rats he had sliced apart, and he just said, "So what? So what if I torture rats?" The

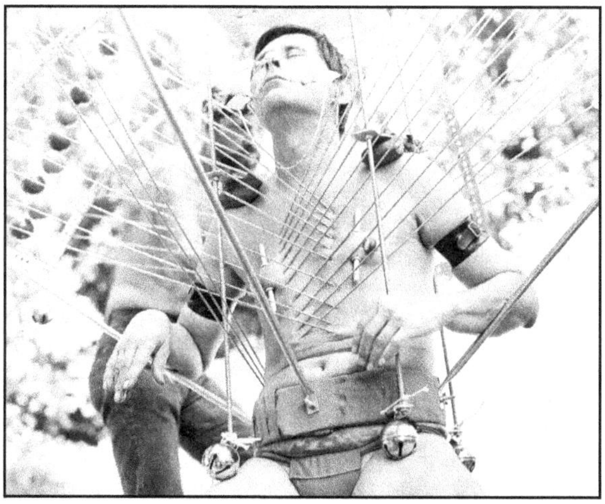

Fakir bears the "Spears of Siva" in a Kavandi-bearing ceremony. Photo by Mark Chester.

room felt like he had conjured up malignant, terribly malevolent spirits; there was the iciest feeling, the coldest draft in there that made you absolutely shrivel up like a pea. That was the most horrible thing I have ever felt in my life.

The last six weeks of the show were hell; we had to take Bob to a psychiatrist just to keep the show going. The main dummy, "Happy Holsum," kept turning into a mean, nasty sadistic character on camera, and we had to do take after re-take. When the show ended, Bob went to Australia, then back to Texas (his home state) and finally ended up in the Texas State Penitentiary for molesting young girls. I don't know what finally happened to him.

KAVANDI

■ F: Another penetration ritual is *kavandi-bearing* which is not done by sadhu professional holy men—ordinary people in India do this, usually in February during a festival—trial by the spears of Siva. A similar ritual is done in Africa. This actually is an interesting way to get into an altered state—most of these people get very glassy-eyed and ecstatic doing this.

Kavandi-bearing in India.

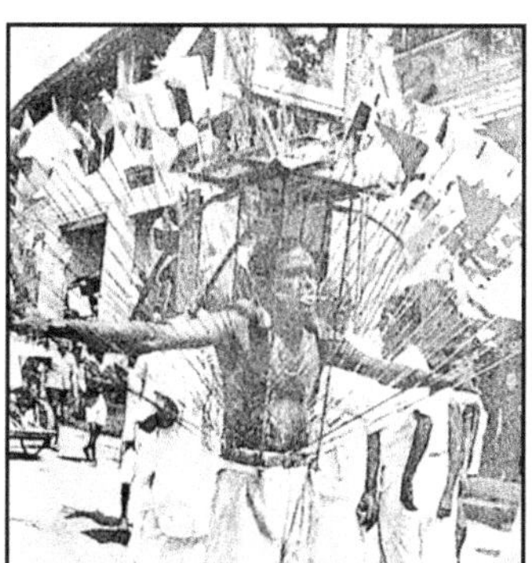

A framework is placed around your body and locked on; sharp rods with points are stuck into your skin, then you rise and dance and walk and move. The more you move, with the rattling and vibrating of the spears, the deeper they go into our skin, and the longer you do it, the deeper they go into your skin. So, you don't feel pain as you once knew it—you can get into a great state of ecstasy and you can flip off, which I've done a couple of times, into a totally altered state—in two cases I had a real out-of-body experience. I just totally left my body, lifted out of it, floated up above and watched this body like a robot running around, going crazy, with these spears jangling and clanging in the framework. But the people with me got nervous because I kept running around smashing into the door, and they were afraid I'd run out into the street, which probably would have scared anybody who happened to be walking by outside...

Kavandi-bearing in India is done for several reasons: "I had a good year, and everything is great! I'm going to do the kavandi to celebrate this and express my joy!" Another reason may be for intervention: "My wife is sick and she can't bear children. I'll do this hoping to contact powers and ask them to please help me in this situation." There are many reasons for doing this, but people seem to think this connects them with life energy and forces greater than them.

SUN DANCE

■ *V: Tell us about the Sun Dance.*

■ F: Jim Ward and I were both fascinated by the American Indian Sun Dance. I had a little background; I had talked to old men who had done it or had seen it, because I grew up in South Dakota on an Indian reservation. But I never *saw* a Sun Dance; they didn't do this—it was against the law. The legend and what was supposed to happen was wonderful, but we knew that we were not Indians and we could never have access to doing this as an Indian. So we decided, being non-blooded Indians, and not knowing all that much about the myth and heritage behind it, that we would go out into the wild, into Wyoming, and do a Native American Sun Dance as best we could, our way. That was captured on film for *Dances Sacred and Profane.*

It starts out with Jim Ward and I at Devil's Tower some days prior to the actual Sun Dance. We went there primarily because I'd been there before; it's a great energy generator. It gets you prepared, and powers and energizes you so you have the strength to do something like the Sun Dance. The Mandans sometimes went without food or sleep for a few days beforehand; they got a little spaced out. I don't need quite that much preparation. We fasted when we filmed *Dances Sacred and Profane.*

There are several variations of The Sun Dance. One version known as "Man Against Himself" involves literally piercing the chest with holes, and putting in eagle talons or hooks that are attached by a long rope to a tree. And you've vowed that you will not leave the tree or quit the Dance until you have, with your own energy, literally *ripped* your own body free.

The second thing I did was what the Mandans and some of the Oglala Sioux did [a more severe variation

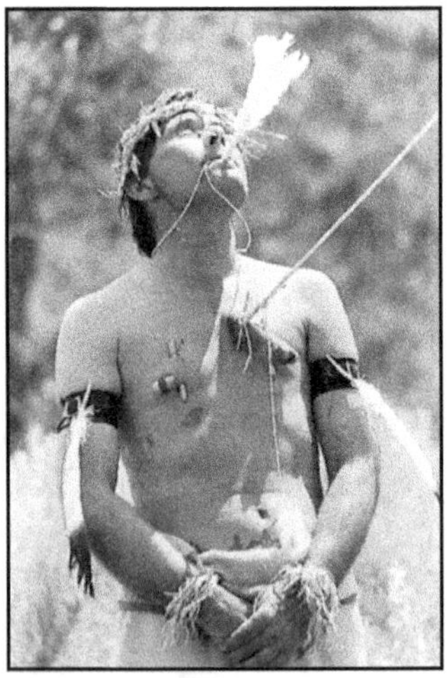

Fakir in 1983 Wyoming Sundance ceremony. Photo: Charles Gatewood.

of the Sun Dance]: O-KEE-PA—hanging by fleshhooks inserted into piercings in the chest for anywhere from 10 to 20 minutes. Jim Ward elevated me up via a rope into a tree, and the object of that was to hang and have an experience—to release those internally generated endorphins and have an ecstasy, an altered state. To go out of the body.

The Mandan myth was this: "A tall man with golden hair and fair skin came down from a high hill and told us that if we were to survive as a people, we must do this in the spring or summer, and that every young man, before he becomes a warrior, must do this: be hung up in a lodge by these piercings in the flesh." This was centuries before the white man showed up, and unfortunately made the Indians predisposed to welcome them into their villages. Now the Mandan were not warriors or wanderers, they lived in cities of big domed houses. They died out from a smallpox epidemic spread by steamboats up the Missouri River.

The most famous corseted lady of all time was Ethel Granger, who had a 13-inch waist. But she was in great health until she died at about the age of 83.

A little aside about the French fur traders who lived in this area and have largely been forgotten: they intermarried with the Indians and didn't try to destroy the indigenous cultures. There are still a lot of descendants of French fur trappers in North and South Dakota; they probably could have gone on for 200 years and never upset anything. But the day people came up the river in steamboats their way of life was doomed.

The oldest photo of the Sun Dance I know of dates from around 1850. It shows a Sioux brave pierced twice in the chest for the ripping flesh, and he also has a very tight band around his waist. He's been fasting for many days, and now he's going for the primal energy; he's going for the altered state to meet the white light or the great white spirit.

■ *V: Tell us all what happened when you and Jim Ward did the Sun Dance.*

■ F: Both of us ripped flesh; it took about four hours to break free. There have been cases where Indians pierced really deep, so they'd take a break and dance, smoke peace pipes, and keep going 24 hours a day for three or four days. There are also cases of people who hung partially suspended from four piercings for four days. That's suspension *not* to rip; a deliberately prolonged ordeal.

Some of the American Indians did physical rituals to have visions. Some of these were just personal visions, some just because it's *fun* to have visions. Some were very illuminating—they made you a better person, and some visions were for the benefit of the community. An example: once the Lakota peoples couldn't find any more buffalo; they had vanished. The whole tribe was starving, so they decided, "We'll have a Sun Dance!" All the powerful men in the tribe volunteered to be pierced and dance for days and nights until one or more had a vision. The vision went something like, "I was dancing the Sun Dance, and something happened to me—I went out of my body and became a hawk and soared over the countryside. And I remembered the hills, and I remembered the streams, and I was led to a certain place where I saw plentiful buffalo." Then the speaker would come out of his vision and tell it to the people, they would all jump on their ponies and ride to that spot and sure enough—there would be buffalo; they would kill the buffalo and the tribe would survive. This was a community use of ritual.

I have an original 1867 book by George Catlin with color lithographs of a Mandan O-KEE-PA Ceremony that was done indoors in a lodge *(O-Kee-Pa: A Religious Ceremony; and other Customs of the Mandans.)*

Catlin's description is vivid:

"An inch or more of flesh on each shoulder, or each breast, was taken up between the thumb and finger by the man who held the knife, and the knife, which had been hacked and notched to make it produce as much pain as possible, was forced through the flesh below the fingers, and was followed by a skewer which the other attendant forced through the wounds (underneath the muscles, to keep them from being torn out), as they were hacked. There were then two cords lowered from the top of the lodge, which were fastened to these skewers, and they immediately began to haul him up. He was thus raised until his body was just suspended from the ground...The fortitude with which every one of them bore this part of the torture surpassed credulity."

I found it in Japan in the Kanda [bookstore area] and they didn't know what it was; it was from some old missionary's trunk. This book is rare as hell; the Smithsonian has one copy under glass in which the lithos are faded and the pages all ripped on the edges and stained. Whereas mine is in mint condition with a leather cover. One illustration shows an Indian suspended by his chest, and another in the back. Catlin lived with the Mandans for about a year.

The Sun Dance was done by the Sioux Indians. However, "Sioux" is a conglomerate name; about 10 different tribes of people were all thrown together and called "Sioux" by the white man. There are no real Sioux; they're all different cultures, different languages,

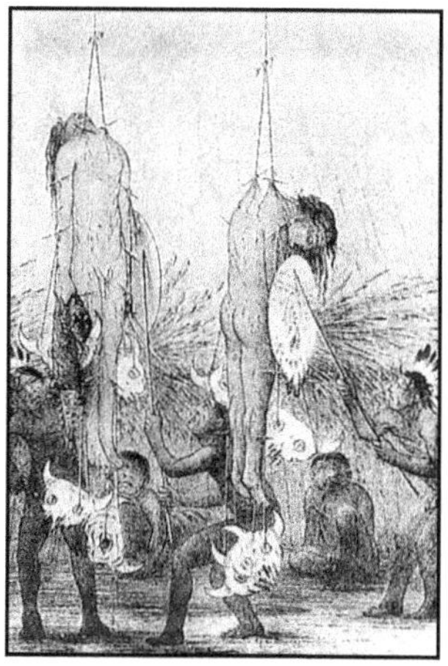

Mandan Warriors suspended from piercings for 20 minutes. From Catlin's 1867 O-Kee-Pa book.

although they're related. For example, the Minatari went to more violent and extreme forms of self-torture than the Mandans ever thought of doing. They would leave the piercings in; put sticks in the holes until they were permanently stretched out.

■ *AJ: How long can you hang?*

■ F: Suspended by the back or the chest with two piercings, the most you can hang is 20 or 30 minutes. Because it's like hanging with a rope around your neck: you'll suffocate because it pulls all your skin and so on up around your windpipe and you'll eventually strangle. So you can't hang too long that way. However, if you hang by multiple piercings horizontally from the back or the chest, you can hang for hours.

■ *AJ: What if you hang from the back?*

■ F: Virtually the same effect.

■ *V: You didn't have any "mystical experiences"?*

■ F: No. The best strange states occur after you actually court them and are kinda expecting something, but you don't know exactly what. If you expect something very specific, nothing will ever happen. You have to go into those kinds of experiments kinda wide open.

■ *AJ: It's funny; it seems you were meant to find this Catlin book, 5000 miles away in Japan.*

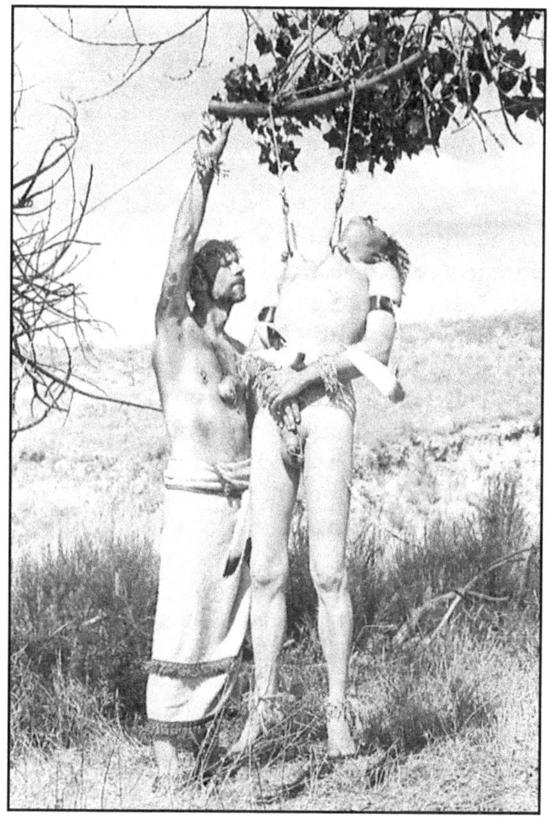

Fakir with Jim Ward. Photo by Charles Gatewood.

■ F: Yup, that's the way life works. The things, the people and the experiences that are needed often appear at the right moment.

Today, a whole part of life seems to be missing for people in modern cultures. Alienation is running amok. There are huge signs and symptoms of massive alienation. Whole groups of people, socially, are alienated. They cannot get closer or in touch with anything, including themselves. Why? What's going on here? Well, there have got to be some remedies and they're going to come from some very strange places. [laughs]

It all comes down to: *it's your body, play with it.* For a long time Western Culture had dictated: don't fuck with the body; it's the temple of God. But finally people are starting to see things a different way.

Times have changed, people have changed. The way I see it is: people *need* these rituals so desperately; that's why piercing and tattooing have blossomed. People need physical ritual, tribalism—they've got to have it, one way or another...

Fakir hangs by fleshhooks doing an Indian O-Kee-Pa ceremony. Photo by Charles Gatewood.

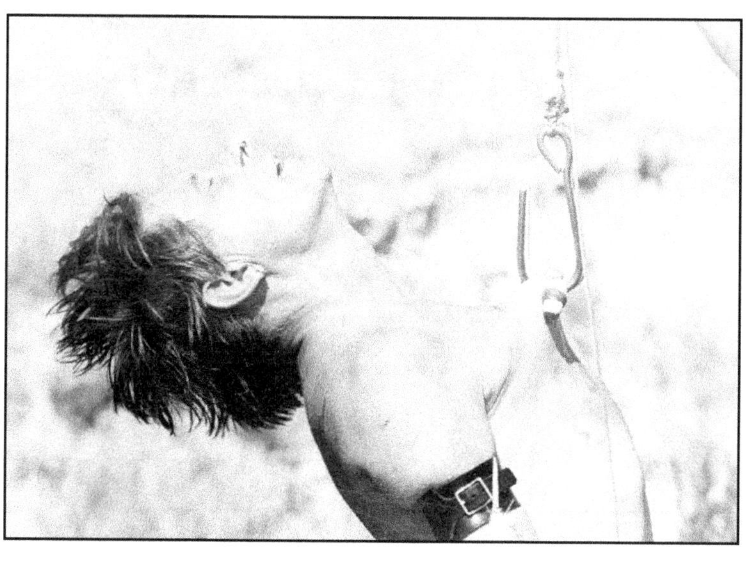

TATTOO MIKE

At an early age Michael Wilson started getting tattooed, progressing to the point where he became featured in Dick Zigun's Coney Island *Side Shows by the Seashore* as "The Illustrated Pain-Proof Man." In this act he lay on a bed of nails while spectators were invited to test the nails and then stand on his body. Michael became friends with several classic old sideshow performers, including Melvin Burkhart (who hammers nails through his nose); Otis Jordan, the armless/legless "Human Cigarette Factory"; and Ruby Rodriguez, aka "Satina, the Snake Woman."

Michael had a featured cameo in Bruce Springsteen's "Tunnel of Love" video, and was the subject of numerous newspaper and magazine articles. 80% of his body tattoos were done by Pat Martynuik of Picture Machine, San Francisco; his head and face tattoos were by New York artists Don Boyle and Fine Line Mike, with additional art by Shadowland Mike. After a distinguished performing career, Michael Wilson died in New York City in the summer of 1996 of natural causes.

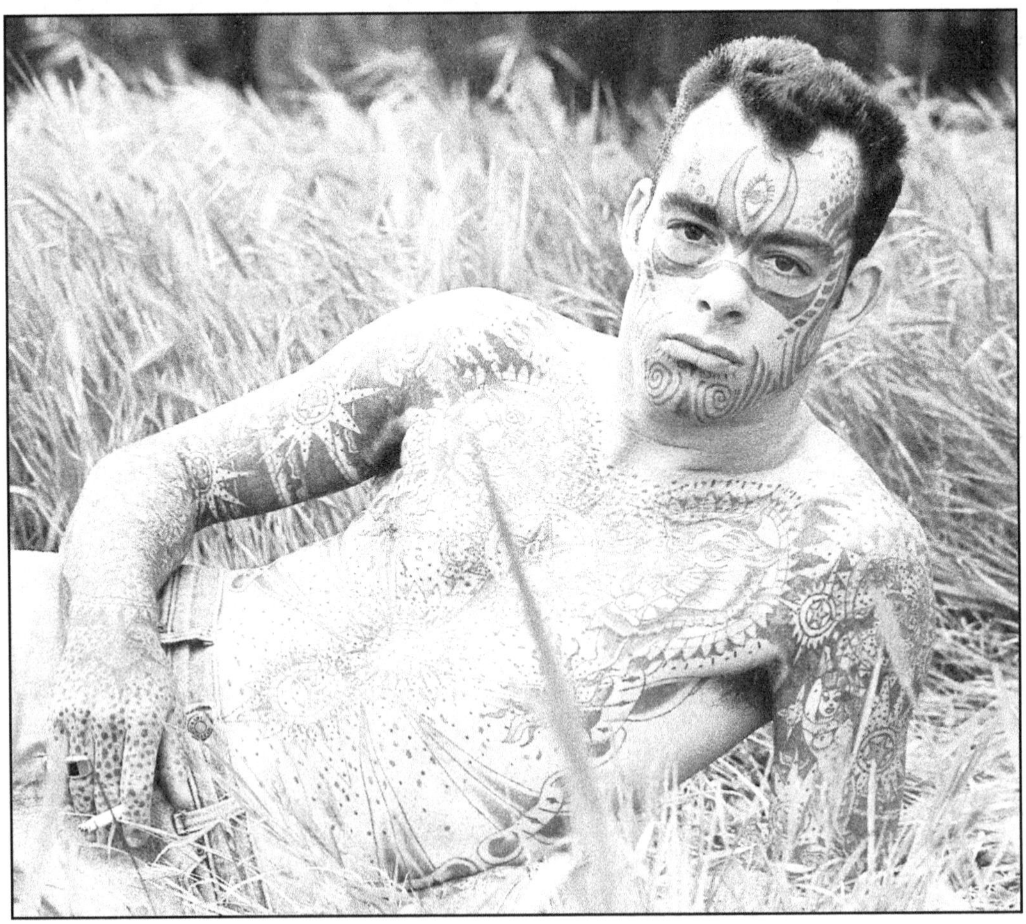

photo by Daniel Nicoletta.

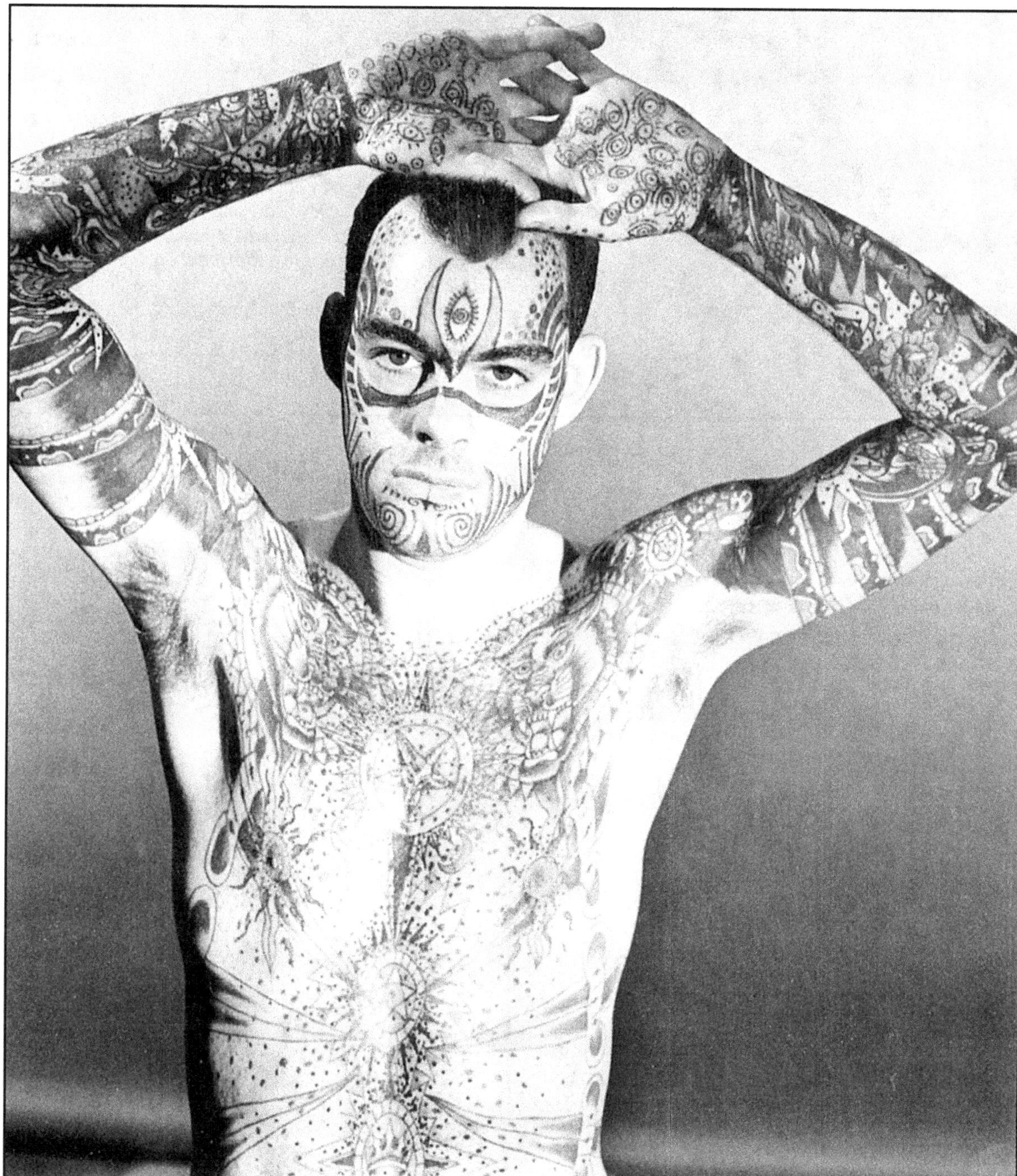

Photo by Daniel Nicoletta.

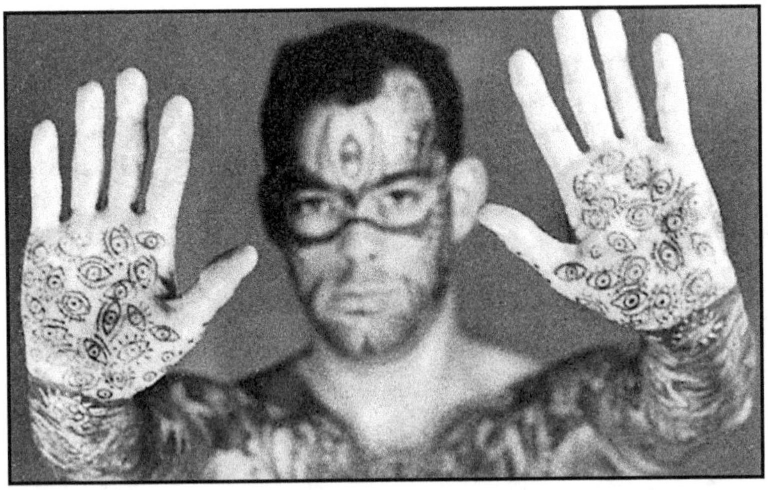

Photo by Daniel Nicoletta.

a kind of theater for myself—people definitely perceive me differently than if I had no visible tattoos. Old women will come up to me and rub my tattoos.

I've never regarded my tattoos as exhibitionistic, even though a lot of people have pointed their finger at me and said that. That was never a conscious consideration; the tattoos are for myself.

The facial tattoos really came about with me doing a lot of homework on tattoos and becoming fascinated, then obsessed by the pictures I saw. My hands, feet and penis had already been tattooed—already those were outside, more or less in public view. I started feeling very *uncomfortable* that my face wasn't tattooed, because the rest of

[Tattoos] signify a possible way of going through the looking glass for me to achieve a whole other frame of reference, and to elicit experiences beyond the "normal" .

■ *ANDREA JUNO: When did you first get tattooed?*
■ MICHAEL WILSON: When I was thirteen. I'd been trying to get into tattoo places before then but I was underage. I kept going and going and finally the tattooist could see I wanted to have it done (and I had the money) so it got done. He put some stars on my shoulder and that started it. They're covered over now.
■ *AJ: What did that mean to you?*
■ MW: Nothing then, but I kept going, building more patterns. Seeing more and more circus photos inspired me. Also, when I was thirteen I was studying a lot of Surrealist art. I saw photos of a stage production by Jean Cocteau starring a heavily tattooed man and this became a *key,* signifying a possible way of going through the looking glass for me to achieve a whole other frame of reference, and to elicit experiences beyond the "normal"...presenting yourself as a signal beacon drawing things to happen to you. In other words: *tattoo as a passage to another life.* However, I've never had an *absolute* philosophical or religious program behind what I was attempting to do. But getting heavily tattooed definitely made interesting things happen to me!
■ *VALE: What does tattooing mean to you now?*
■ MW: To be honest I don't even think about it any longer; I just *do* it. I've gone *this* far with the tattoos I have and I just keep getting more and more. It's like, if you're climbing a very high mountain, you may get to a point where you stop remembering the reasons why you started in the first place. I definitely see it as

Mike at "Bradshaw's Circus of World Curiosities," Dick Zigun's Sideshows by the Seashore, Coney Island. Photo: Dan Nicoletta.

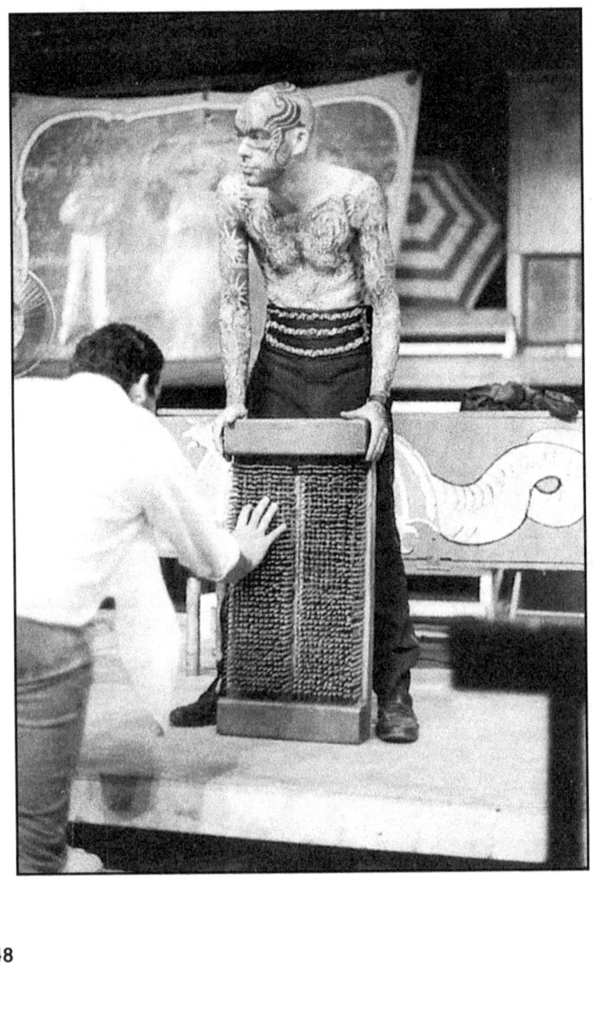

my body *was*—it seemed to make sense to have my face tattooed.

I went to New York to get my face tattooed because nobody in California would do it—there are different codes. I don't think there were any actual *laws*, but nobody would do it, they'd say, "It's too much bother—you'll want your money back and you'll want to have it removed later." So when I heard that in New York tattooing was *outlawed*, a little light bulb went off—I thought, "If it's outlawed, then I can get it done—I can get what I want!"

What I don't like is the obvious. I'm in theater 24 hours a day when I'm in public, and of course you get asked obvious questions over and over again.

■ *AJ: After you got your face tattooed, did the world change?*

■ MW: It changed radically. With my hands tattooed I could still get away with things, but when my face got tattooed I couldn't get away with anything! I was definitely a marked man, and most of the time I liked it, but it does get in the way, such as when I'm looking for work. I like the tattoos themselves—I thought about them carefully and chose the tattoos I wanted. I like meeting people with my tattoos—it's a weird bridge to meeting people; sometimes I'll meet people in kind of an odd way.

But what I don't like is the *obvious*. I'm in theater 24 hours a day when I'm in public, and of course you get asked obvious questions over and over again. Once when I got irritated a friend suggested I make cards with answers on them, because the questions are all exactly the same: "Do they hurt? Do they come off? Do they get in the way? Is this something you'll want 20 years from now?"

I say (and people accept this without question): "I started getting them when I was young." For some reason this works like a charm to shut people up. They perceive a whole line of evolution, instead of, "I was on a drunk last night!"

One thing about getting the tattoos: the more I get, the more I like them. In other words, instead of me regretting them more and more with time, I *like* them more, except for the basics: getting a job and finding a place to live. In Los Angeles, I was looking for a place to live and knocking on doors at the time of the Nightstalker [Richard Ramirez, who in the summer of 1985 went on a murder spree in the Bay Area and Los Angeles, sneaking into homes at night and killing or mutilating the inhabitants. He spray-painted Satanic pentagrams on the walls of some victims, and described himself as a "Satanist"], and all these people thought I was the Daystalker! [laughs] Although obviously I couldn't get away with anything!

My tattoos comprise everything from Samoan to Indian designs—there's a kind of *psychedelia* of different cultures combined. When I'm planning a tattoo I get deeply involved with spiritual and metaphoric implications of the prospective design, but after it's on I forget about it—it's become a part of me. Just like: you probably don't constantly think of the color of your eyes, or your haircut. Unconsciously the tattoos are probably protective in nature, although there's no such conscious dogma.

I used to wear a hat and try to hide my tattoos in public. Now, occasionally I dream that I'm in a public situation and for some reason my hat has been removed ("Ohmigod—where's my hat?") and suddenly the people around me are frozen in mid-step, staring at my tattoos...

MANWOMAN

Canadian artist ManWoman had a dream forty-three years ago that his mission was to rehabilitate the swastika. He has since amassed a museum full of swastika artifacts and cross-cultural documentation, all the while producing an enormous output of paintings, silkscreens and sculpture. Contact him at manwoman@cyberlink.bc.ca, website: manwoman.net. His art can be found at Artrageous Art Gallery 32A 11th Ave, S. Cranbrook, BC Canada (250) 426-4223.

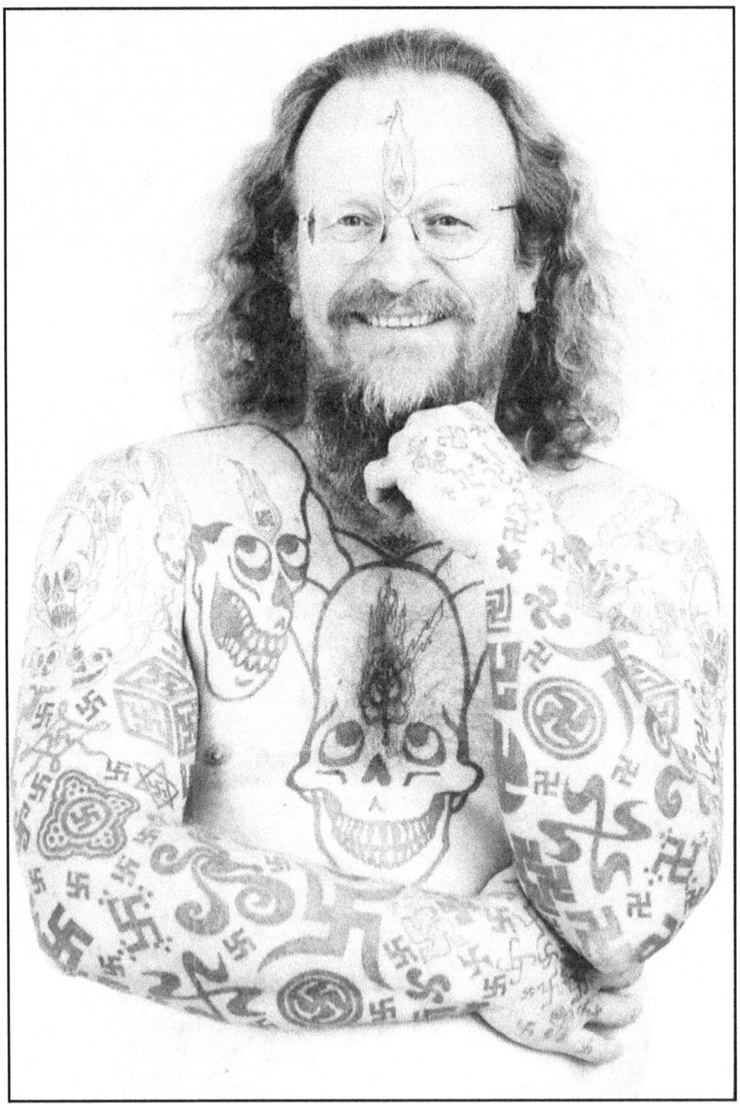

ManWoman 1988. Photo by Brian Clarkson.

■ *VALE: Why did you first get tattooed?*

■ MANWOMAN: My first tattoo came as the result of a dream: I dreamed I had a swastika on my left baby finger. I had never even *thought* of getting a tattoo before. Sure, when I was a teenager some of my friends had got drunk and gotten tattooed with "Death Before Dishonor" or a skull with a dagger through it, but that sort of thing had never appealed to me. But when I started dreaming about the swastika—being told it was a beautiful symbol that had just been misused, *and* being told that I should detoxify it as a life's mission, then I began thinking.

The symbol of the swastika has done nothing in *itself*—it's innocent. It's intrinsically just lines on paper, a graphic design that's found in cultures all over the planet for thousands of years. So it's a question of educating the public about its tremendously complex, multi-cultural past. Learning about the swastika and its history turned my life upside down; my values got shook up like crazy! I spent a lot of time stripping away false education I'd gotten; false attitudes.

■ *V: Can you describe in more detail the dream that said your mission was to rehabilitate the swastika?*

■ MW: Yes. It was a dream in which a very beautiful, spiritual holy man was showing me a glowing symbol which he said was a symbol of god's love. It was a pure white swastika radiating light. I was asking, "But what about the Nazis?" and in reply he reached over and drew this little swastika on my throat and said, "Take this as your sign, and use it as your own symbol, because

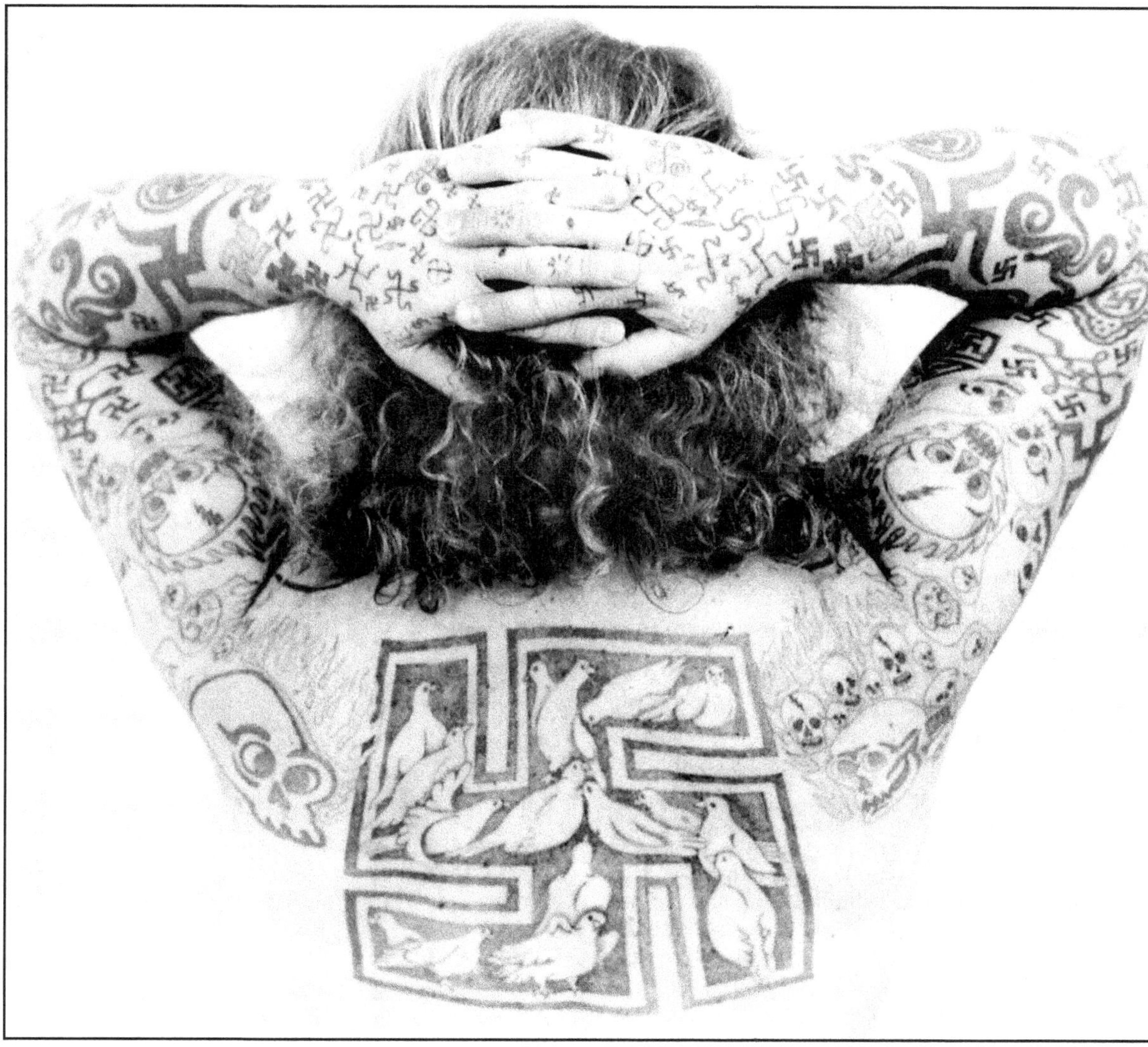

Photo by Brian Clarkson.

it has to be freed from the taint of the Nazis. It is a symbol of the Divine, and you should take it as your task to purify it…or purify people's attitude toward it."

I was sort of choking, because my mother is Polish and we have relatives that were in a concentration camp—they have numbers tattooed on their arms. So I was quite shocked.

Then I had many more dreams about swastikas… dreams where Florence Nightingale had swastikas on her uniform while the Edmonton Symphony Orchestra was applauding, "Yes!" You know how dreams are—getting approval from the Edmonton Symphony Orchestra seemed to be the height of social acceptance.

■ *ANDREA JUNO: What else did the swastika represent to you?*

■ MW: Powerful, divine energy. It's a symbol of the center of the universe, a symbol of being and creativity…representing the inner absolute, the inner light, the energy of that inner experience. So to me the image of the swastika and the image of god are equivalent. Of course, I realize that most people look at the swastika and think of evil, terror, torture—all the brutal, ugly things that can happen to you.

The swastika represents powerful, divine energy. It's a symbol of the center of the universe, a symbol of being and creativity, representing the inner absolute, the inner light, the energy of that inner experience.

■ *AJ: And what do you say to people who object to your swastika tattoos?*

■ MW: I give them the history of it, if they're interested: "Got a minute?" There's been the odd time where people have been upset, but generally, because of my appearance, people will look at me and think, "Holy shit, I better not ask that guy *anything*." Yet if they only knew that I'm really a person who has no interest in fighting or gratuitous violence, only in creativity. People talk about god in terms of Love, Truth and all these ponderous concepts, but what about *creativity?* The people who I think are closest to god are poets and dreamers and writers and artists; people who are being creative are being closer to god.

■ *AJ: So your dreams dictated your tattoos?*

■ MW: The dreams specifically laid out which ones. After I started dreaming I had a swastika on my little finger, I heard about a guy who was using primitive tattoo set-up: a couple needles tied to a broken-off pencil, and india ink. He gave me my first tattoo—the one I'd been dreaming about. I actually never thought I'd get another one, but a few months later I started dreaming I had swastikas *all over* my hands, and that signified creative energy. I found a better tattoo artist, Pat Martynuik, but he wouldn't do it. However, an associate of his, Fat Rick, *would.*

■ *AJ: Are your hands identically tattooed?*

■ MW: Identically. Every time I had one done I had it done on the other hand; they're bilaterally symmetrical. I chose the neo-primitive style because it's solid black, strongly graphic, and I'm a strongly graphic person—I don't like things that are finicky, with lots of little details and preciosity. When I was in art school I did woodcuts; I loved the strength and boldness of that black-and-white style. I'm a blunt person and I don't like pussyfooting around; I like to come right out and say what I think, and if it rattles a few bones—well, what the hell!

I mean, I have tact—you can go overboard with being blunt—but in terms of my personal beliefs and feelings, I don't beat around the bush. I've had a lot of struggles over the years with the swastika and the name "ManWoman" and with tattoos. I feel that what I'm doing is much more worthwhile than just bending to public pressures—to get a job, keep your "friends," or whatever. There are too many people who lose their souls by yielding and bending too much. You know: stick with what you believe in without betraying yourself; be strong *that* way.

Now my arms are completely covered with at least a couple hundred different swastikas that were used in every culture and religion on the face of the earth.

Then I started dreaming I had a flaming third eye tattooed in the middle of my forehead. And in terms of my first marriage that was the straw that broke the camel's back. My wife was really upset when I did my hands, but when it came to my *face*—! I started painting the vaguest outline of this in yellow on my forehead; this was in the late '60s when me and my friends were putting on festivals and happenings, doing body painting and things like that. I went to Fat Rick and told him I wanted a third eye tattooed on my forehead, and he said, "I'll tell you what. If you're still painting it on a year from now, then I'll do it."

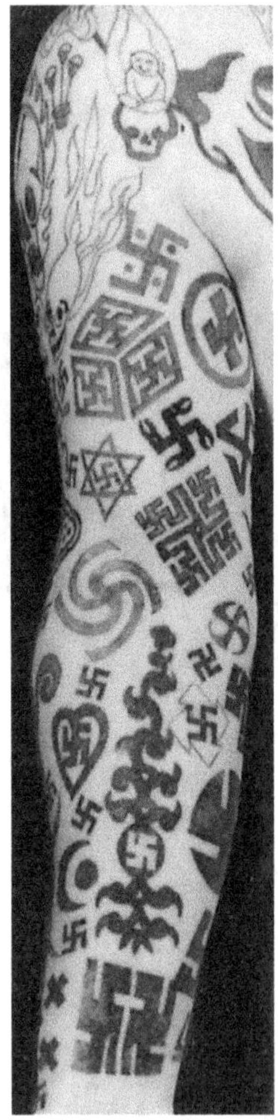

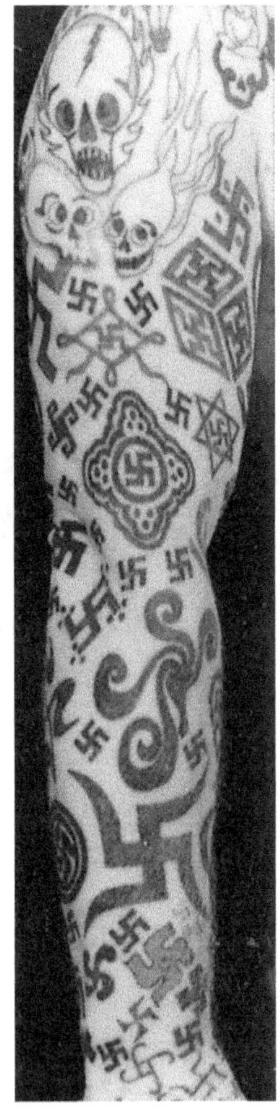

"My arms and hands are identically tattooed. Every time I had one done I had it done on the other hand; they're bilaterally symmetrical." Photos by Brian Clarkson.

A year later he started with just the outline in yellow. Now my wife was really freaking out, but I still wanted to go further, so he did a red outline with a yellow flame, with a little skull outlined in blue in the center of the eye. I had that on for ten years and the reds and yellows were starting to fade. I talked to literally dozens of tattooists before I found someone to redo it in black outline.

One guy who kept urging me to take LSD, but I looked at him and thought, "Who are you to give me advice?" His whole life was falling apart—it didn't make sense!

■ *AJ: What does that symbolize?*

■ MW: The third eye. I also have the heart chakra in the middle of a skull. After that, I started dreaming that my shoulders were covered with skulls, so I got a yoke of almost life-sized, flaming, laughing skulls on my shoulders and chest, with a big one in the middle of my chest. On my back I have another design from my dreams: a swastika filled with doves of peace!

■ *V: What does the skull symbolize to you?*

■ MW: The idea that making friends with death, confronting death, transcending death—death as a transformation rather than real death; death in the sense of: die to the ego and transform yourself. The surrender of the ego. There's a point in the mystical experience where the ego peels off and what's left is just an absolute kind of pure essence. Just prior to that there's a moment of fear because the ego is really threatened, and the ego has to drop off. The mystical experience is like a preview of death—you face it, you go through it and you become eternal, you become everything. You really feel all that stuff about becoming one with the universe, one with god or whatever label you want to attach to it.

As far as my skull tattoos go, I wanted the skulls to look joyful—almost going overboard with being silly. And when I finally did the flame on my face, that was the end; my wife couldn't cope. Because people wouldn't ask *me,* they'd ask *her.* And many of them said, "Your husband's insane."

The skull symbolizes the idea of making friends with death, confronting death, transcending death—death as a transformation rather than real death; death in the sense of: die to the ego and transform yourself.

Whereas my second wife—well, I was *already* tattooed and named ManWoman and wearing swastika and skull tattoos when we met. She choked on it at first, a little bit, but when she decided she liked me enough that was it—even though her father didn't speak to me for five years. But after a while they realize you're human and they might even like you, if they just get beyond the first superficial judgment. In my hometown all these local Christian ladies think I'm some kind of *Satanist* and devil worshipper! And if anybody says a good word about me, they'll say, "*See*—he's already gotten to you!" It's crazy! But I don't bother being negative to them—it's them that are suffering, not me! It all depends on your attitude.

Through the years a lot of people have noticed my tattoos and asked, "Why did you do that?" and I always reply, "Well, I just ran out of canvas one day!" What are you supposed to say? Women will come up and ask, "Did it hurt?" and I never admit that it did, especially if they're looking at me with grimaces of pain. But—it's not as if I think somebody has to get tattooed to become enlightened! Or even to be enriched—but in my case it's certainly part and parcel of my whole pathway, and I love it. Although I didn't do it for this reason, it gives me a certain extra persona or charisma. The people who won't talk to me because of my tattoos are probably people *I* don't want to talk to. And the ones who spot me in a crowd and come running over—sometimes I meet interesting people that way, and that's one of the side benefits.

Having gone my own way and followed my dream, I know that to do anything otherwise is to betray yourself. So I feel strong as a person—not strong in the sense of being physically violent, but I feel I know who I am, and that's really what counts. I feel good about myself and what I'm doing.

■ *V: What's your attitude toward religion?*

■ MW: When my first out-of-body experiences started happening, I was terrified and frightened; I ran away from them. It was difficult to learn how to integrate them into everyday life and somehow deal with other people. All my childhood I'd been raised in the Catholic church and told I was a sinner that had to grovel at the foot of the cross; that I was tainted; that I had Original Sin and was just generally a shit. All of a sudden this god-like embrace happened and I felt, "This can't be happening—I'm unworthy." Now when it comes, I just melt right into it; I'm not fighting it off.

Basically I'm very anti-Christian; I'm anti *all* those old dead religions. I've had people approach me and say, "You know, you can't even be buried in a Jewish cemetery if you have tattoos," and I reply, "You mean I'm *that lucky?*" I don't respect *any* of those old religions—Muslims, Buddhists, whatever. They all boil down to something pretty stifling and ignorant. But I believe in *personal* religion, or whatever you want to call it.

■ *AJ: Why did you change your name to ManWoman?*

■ MW: For three years I had dreamt every night that my name was ManWoman, In my dreams I was both male and female. Sometimes I was twins; one was male and one was female. Sometimes I was half and half; one side was male and the other was female. Sometimes I was wearing women's clothing in the dream but being a man. So there was all this incredible intermixing of male and female things.

Dreams suggest inner principles and really have nothing to do with outer realities so it's not that I was a transvestite or drag queen or transsexual—although in the dreams I was.

In one dream I was walking down the street and all the little children of the block gathered around me and started chanting [singsong], "ManWoman, ManWoman, ManWoman!" In another dream I was on a university campus and this old, authoritarian-type lady looked at me and said, "There's another one of them ManWoman!"—apparently it meant something about rebellion and students. I'd be signing my previous name in a check and it would disintegrate; I couldn't write it, then I'd realize I was writing the wrong name, so I'd write "ManWoman" and it would be perfect.

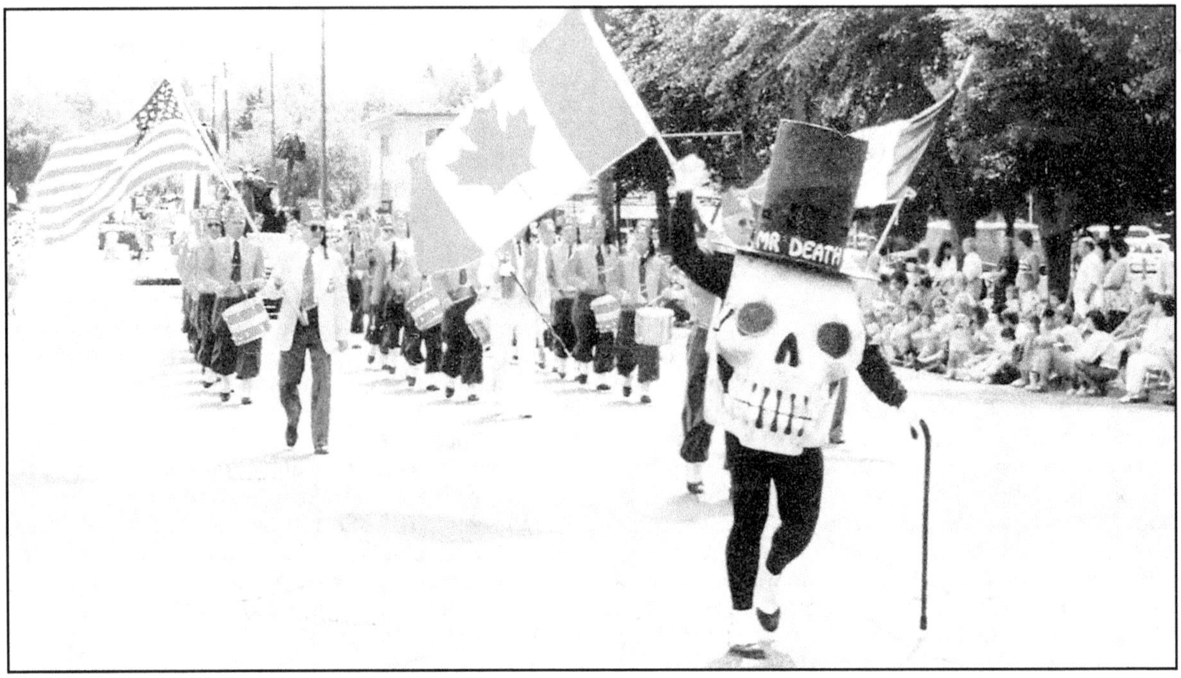

ManWoman dressed as Death in the Cranbrook, B.C. Sam Steele Days Parade, June 23, 1988.

From my experiences, and the idea that in your physical body you may be a male or female but in your spirit you're beyond all that (you're whole, not just a half), I figured I had to change my name. And that's what the name represents, although some people do get the wrong idea—at least *before* they meet me. I could send you hundreds of these dreams—they're all written down. So you could say that the pressure from within to be ManWoman was overwhelming...

Then I had an art show at which I officially said, "This is the work of ManWoman." Trying to get your friends to switch over and start calling you ManWoman was—! [laughs] My first wife to this day has never taken the name on her lips. She got totally freaked out by it. Because she'd married just an art student—we were both art students, and I was a *rebellious* art student, but still relatively normal until all of this started coming up.

Also about this time I started wearing robes—all through the whole hippie period I wore nothing but floor-length robes, some with hoods, but mostly bright yellow—I have a thing about yellow; I never wear *anything* but. I don't own a stitch of clothing that isn't yellow; I slowly phased out everything else. In my dreams I'm always driving yellow vehicles—I have a yellow Dodge Ram van.

■ *AJ: What does yellow mean to you?*

■ MW: It's the color of joy and spiritual energy. Like, red is physical energy; yellow is the intellect and the spiritual energies; the warmth of the sun, and joy and intuition.

■ *AJ: How did your mystical experiences first start? Were you meditating?*

■ MW: I didn't know what the word meditation was, but I was sitting in my front of my canvases for a couple years. I started having visions, and in my visions this Bride started to appear. I found out later that the "bride" metaphor is common in India; the Song of Solomon mentions the bride; the bride symbolizes your own soul seeking the godhead, or union with god. The bride is a common symbol for the longings of the soul. The adoring bride: she bursts up through the clouds into the light.

I'd be sitting meditating and suddenly I would be rushing up into this void (which is really inside myself). My body was still sitting there, but my spirit was just soaring into this kind of inner, heavenly realm, experiencing ecstasy.

■ *V: Did you take any drugs?*

■ MW: None of my visions or union-with-god experiences had anything to do with drugs. In 1967 I smoked a couple of joints with a friend and except for that incident, I didn't touch anything—LSD, peyote, etc. I had friends who smoked grass all the time and barely got a buzz out of it, but I got an extreme reaction. It was like you weren't in control at all; you were in this fog. I felt really disjointed; time broke up and I didn't know whether I had said something or just *thought* I had said something. It was very sensual, whereas a mystical experience is very alive, very aware, totally beyond your body. On marijuana I was brought down into the senses: taste and smell and touch may

For three years I had dreamt every night that my name was ManWoman. In my dreams I was both male and female. So you could say that the pressure from within to be ManWoman was overwhelming.

have been heightened, but I didn't think it was worth the trade-off. So I made a personal decision: *No Drugs.*

Often I would go to a party and people were smoking or taking other drugs, but I didn't care; they had made their decision and I'd made mine. But looking back on it, there's a lot of casualties in the drug thing, and none of it ever leads to ecstasy; none of it ever leads to enlightenment, so it's just as well to have ignored it. There are so many things that pretend to give you ecstasy and enlightenment and they never do, and then you get dependent on them, or there are physical side effects that are negative. I know people who are basically vegetables these days who just took too much LSD or whatever it was, under the wrong circumstances perhaps. Sometimes people say they had peak experiences, but did that have a significant impact on their life—what did it *really* do for them?

There was one guy who kept urging me to take LSD: "Do yourself a favor and take LSD—it's the greatest thing that's ever happened!" I didn't really feel inclined to do that, and he couldn't understand why—I was such a liberal person, such an *experimental* person and all. But I looked at him and thought, "Who are *you* to give me advice?" *His* whole life was falling apart; his marriage was collapsing; he couldn't cope with life and his whole world was tumbling down around him. Yet he was telling me to do the same thing—it didn't make sense! In the end he destroyed his mind completely with drugs; he lost his wife and kids and everything; he just lost it. You'd see him walking around and he looked like a ghost. That's an example of how I felt good about walking on my path and not letting other people interfere.

■ *V: Maybe your dream life provides all the "altered states" you require.*

■ MW: I've had an incredible creative overflow from my dreams and visions, and I have written all my dreams and visions down since 1965 when they first sprang out at me. I've got literally 300 steno pads full of dreams. I write at least one steno pad a month. In a week, probably 5 days out of 7 I'm writing down one dream, two dreams, three. Sometimes I wake up in the middle of the night with a very powerful dream that I know will be forgotten by morning, so I just get up and go downstairs and write it all down, then go back to bed. If my life's work turns out to have some significance, it'll make one hell of a psychological study for the future. Who knows—someone might find something out about creativity just from dissecting the dreams I leave behind.

I met this psychiatrist who was pretending to be a Jungian, and showed him my dreams. He missed the point—he missed the whole exciting, creative point. He didn't see that I was experiencing things beyond the normal that for me were very enriching and creative. All he saw was: I was kind of *sick*. So I thought: he couldn't have been reading the dreams like a Jungian, because a Jungian would have seen that all people are reaching for wholeness, and your dreams really are a balance, compensating and kind of giving you a wholeness. When you're sleeping at night, the dream compensates for all the alienation and stress you're going through in the daytime.

■ *V: How do you work?*

■ MW: I work 9-5 every day, and I work because I know that inspiration is important, but *perspiration* gets the job done. I've met a lot of people who claim they have a fantastic idea, but you never get to see it because they don't write it, make a movie out of it, make music out of it, make art out of it, but "Boy, that marijuana sure makes me feel creative!" I've hand-done over 50 editions of silkscreen prints, and there's 49 prints in each edition. Plus I do a couple dozen paintings, sculptures and other projects each year—I've got literally hundreds of designs for various products and clothing that are all in those dream-books of mine.

■ *AJ: What was the first major turning point in your life?*

■ MW: Well, in the fifties I enrolled at a University in the ROTC, planning to be an officer in the army, because some of my friends were doing it and I thought, "This is a way to get university training for free." I did this for two years, but then one day I kind of woke up and realized, "Holy shit, I'm in the wrong life! I've got the script."

■ *V: What happened?*

■ MW: That summer I had painted a flame job on my father's '49 Ford and was doing other modifications. I had blocks under the axles and I undid the spring, not realizing the jack was swaying. I heard a voice yell, "Get out of there!" and I did a quick roll, and the spring which had been poised right over my chest drove itself 6 inches into the ground with the whole weight of the car on it. I just barely escaped—I got a cut across my nose and had stitches where the spring grazed the back of my head. I also had gravel rash all over my face, but I was alive.

About two months later, I returned to the university and changed my major to architecture, even though what I really wanted was to go to art school. One afternoon I started floating out of my body and went across the bed and floated over to the door. I felt like I was like a lightbulb turned on for the first time—so awake, so aware; my mind or spirit (or whatever) drifted around the room. I saw that the door was closed and thought, "Hmm...I wonder if I could go up!" And whatever you think in that state happens instantly—I went up through the ceiling, and scared myself so bad that I ended up smack back into my body, with cold sweat all over my forehead. But that opened up a whole new future. Right then on the spot I knew I couldn't stay at university; I had to do what I wanted to do. So I enrolled at an art school.

And all these artistic ideas started coming to me. But because I had been raised as a Catholic, I thought, "Gee, this is an experience that saints talk about"—I thought I should become a monk. So I started going to mass every morning. At art school the students called me "Patrick the Pure" or "Patrick the Priest" because I went to mass every morning for the first year I was there. You know how art students are—*very* skeptical.

I went to see this priest—not because I wanted to go groveling back to the Catholic church or anything like that, but I just wanted to say, "Look, this is what's happening to me." I described my experiences and he said, "My son, I'm sorry to tell you this, but you're *insane*. You should go to the nearest mental hospital and turn yourself in!" I said, "But what about St. John of the Cross? What about St. Theresa of Avila? They had these kind of experiences!" "Oh, did they? Well, in that case you'd better come back to the church!" [laughs] He switched in midstream!

After this I moved to the country for 2 years in general solitude and isolation and just worked on my art. Like I said, I would start to feel myself going into a trance when I was sitting in front of my paintings. I felt like a sculpture, very stiff. And at these moments, sometimes when I was sitting in front of a painting or sometimes at night when I was sleeping, I would just explode out of my body into the inner void, and feel this incredible, revving energy going higher and higher, carrying me up.

At first this was quite frightening. Basically you're dropping off your body and your spirit is breaking free, and when you leave the body, that's death. So even though this was like a preview of death, in another way it's a return into the center of being, which is ecstasy. And to be in that center of being without the body awareness is a condition that you can't describe....And it was always totally spontaneous. I didn't know what the hell was happening; it scared the hell out of me. But that experience was to happen fairly regularly for years and years.

■ *V: And you also started incorporating the swastika in your art.*

■ MV: When I was dreaming of the name Man-Woman I was dreaming about the swastika. I started incorporating it into some of my art, and of course that offended a lot of people. I had Jewish friends, too, and they were all quite puzzled as to why I was using it. But now, anybody I personally know likes the swastika because they associate it with me and what *I* say it means: creative energy, good luck, divine power. It's the center of your own being which is the god-being within you. That's what the swastika is all about and has been for thousands of years.

I have literally thousands of pages of documents on swastikas and their origins and migrations. A key historical source is an 1894 Smithsonian Institute yearly report in which Thomas Wilson did an incredible essay on the swastika—that's one of the best.

The Hindus used the swastika for centuries. All the Buddhists used it; they particularly liked the one that faces to the left. All through the Orient it's used both ways: right and left. Actually, *swastika* is the right-facing one, and swavastika is the left-facing one—they're two different words—and the first is considered male and the other female. (Hitler's faced right.) The North American Indians have used it for centuries, in both directions as well.

I started dreaming I had a flaming third eye tattooed in the middle of my forehead. And in terms of my first marriage that was the straw that broke the camel's back. My wife was really upset when I did my hands, but when it came to my face—!

Did you notice that we here in Canada pronounce it Swas-*tee*-ka? The original word was Sanskrit. There are other names, like *flyfoot*. A lot of people do quilts with a swastika pattern and call it the flyfoot pattern, not realizing the derivation. My mother-in-law had a big red quilt with a huge swastika in the center, and she hung it up on the line one day and the neighbors told her, "You know, Margaret, it's time to get rid of that thing," so she chucked it out! [laughs]

Another name is *gammadion*. The Hopis say the symbol represented the migration of the four original tribes; the Scandinavians call it the Hammer of Thor. There's even a steamship line out of Iceland that has the swastika on their boats, with an explanation on their post-cards. In Ireland there's a Swastika Laundry—I have photos of their trucks and buildings. In Germany the word swastika doesn't exist in that language; they use the term "hakkenkreuz," which means hooked or twisted cross. So if you use the word "swastika" in Germany, the people won't understand what you're talking about.

Many people write me letters of thanks, because they loved the symbol of the swastika but hated the stigma associated with it. And a lot of them send me things; one woman sent me an art deco purse from the 1920s made of black cloth with silver beadwork swastikas all around the silver clasp.

I have an incredible collection of artifacts from all over the world that covers thousands of years of history with this symbol being used as a beautiful sign. A lot of it is local North American origin. Many of these were household things. Like, I've got a trivet for an old flat-iron which you heat up on the stove; it has swastikas on the stand. I've got tea towels, tablecloths, Good Luck canning jars, cracker tins, brooches from the Victorian era with imitation rubies; hatpins. There's a branding iron from San Antonio, Texas; a faucet tap; a lot of clothing; a Boy Scout penny that has swastikas on it; a

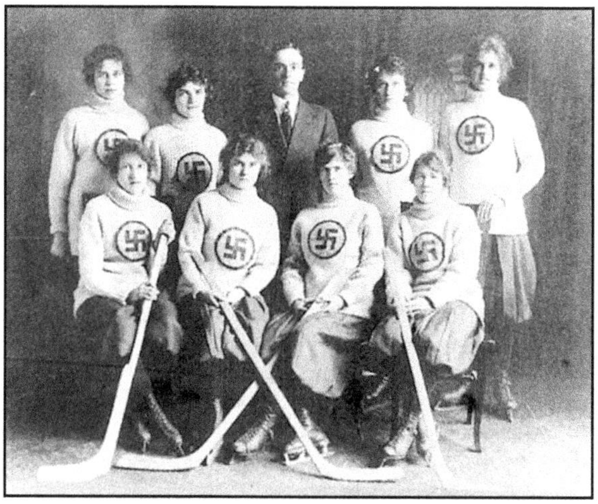

The Edmonton, Alberta, girls' hockey team, circa 1916.

Masonic penny with swastikas; a Coca-Cola watch fob that says "Drink Coca-Cola—5 cents in bottles." The University of New Mexico yearbook used to be called *The Swastika* and it has a swastika on the cover; there was also a Swastika Hotel in New Mexico. The Boy Scouts of Canada and the Boy Scouts of America both have swastika badges; the Canadian one was a badge of thanks given to someone who had done a favor for the Boy Scouts, but who wasn't necessarily a Boy Scout. The American one was a badge of courage; it was called the white swastika, and was earned by staying out overnight by yourself in the woods with no special equipment. For a young boy this was quite a trial.

The Swastika townspeople in Ontario had a baseball team; they have a uniform in their museum from their early days with a big swastika on it. There were two girls' hockey teams; one was the Furney Swastikas, who lived 70 miles down from where I was born; and they were the champs in 1922; I have photos of them. There was a hockey team from Edmonton, Alberta, with big swastikas on their sweaters; I have a photo of them that dates from 1916. I've got a 1908 Simpson/Sears (the Canadian version of Sears) Catalog with swastika bracelets and hatpins advertised.

In the early part of the century there were these girls' clubs all over North America which were founded by *Ladies' Home Journal,* and the symbol was all over their little hope chests, etc. Like I said, the symbol was found on buildings, even ones in San Francisco—they're beautifully done, and you'll notice there's no taint of any Nazism about the sign; the swastikas are very square and even and put together in a very decorative way.

I have pictures of mosaic swastika floors from the University of Manitoba in Winnipeg. The Furney Courthouse has swastika borders all in mosaic. I'm constantly getting sent new material, and we haven't even started talking about the Buddhist swastika which covers the Orient.

When you see swastikas used in such an innocent way—that's what really impresses people. Lyle Tuttle gave me his grandmother's silver brooch bearing a swastika with vines and leaves surrounding it; it was from a Temperance Society. I've got postcards you wouldn't believe, that say, "God Bless You" with a big swastika below. I'm not the kind of person who wants to sit and mother-hen a museum, but I definitely hope my collection goes into some major museum at some point, or at least goes on tour, because it's education.

■ *V: Did you ever try to have a museum show?*

■ MW: Glenboe Museum in Calgary were planning a big show with me. Two of the curators started discovering all these little items in their enormous collection of Canadiana and folk art, like a Charles Russell bandana which had swastikas all over it—he and Frederic Remington are considered the two greatest cowboy artists that ever lived. However, the B'nai Br'ith Society got wind of it and put pressure on the museum to shut it down—which is unfortunate, because it could have been such an amazing and enlightening show.

It's kind of crazy: the historical revisionism that's been done in an effort to destroy all traces of the swastika. In libraries in Germany, a lot of books and old periodicals have had graphics involving the swastika destroyed or defaced! If you buy a plastic model of a Luftwaffe plane, usually the swastikas are removed or blocked out.

An excellent British aviation history journal published a photo of a restored Finnish air force plane. The Finnish air force, from 1918 to 1944, had blue swastikas on their plane—that was their symbol long before the Nazis adopted it. They changed it when the Russians started shooting them down, thinking they were Germans. But this journal, which is mailed all over the world, published a photo of this Finnish plane with the swastika intact, and now it's been banned from Germany! Just for this one swastika. See, Jewish people are sensitive about the swastika, but I think Germans can be almost more sensitive—it's like a guilt trip.

I don't collect any Nazi stuff—none. People have brought me swords and guns and you name it—things I could have resold to a collector for a huge profit, but I just said, "No. Thanks for thinking of me, but no thanks." Because people don't need *that* reinforced; the Nazi use of the swastika was only about 10-20 years, compared to the thousands of years the swastika has been around; it disappears into pre-history.

■ *V: Did you say there was a town called Swastika?*

■ MW: There's a whole town in Canada called Swastika, Ontario. They found a mine there called the Swastika mine in 1911, and the next year they found another mine which they called the Lucky Cross mine (which is just another word for swastika). During WWII the government tried to change the name of the town to Winston (after Churchill), but the people went out at night and tore down all the Winston signs and put the Swastika signs back. A drugstore there put out a little matchbox that said, "Hitler be damned—this is our sign since 1922!" If you talk to almost *anybody* who was born before the war, a lot of people still remember the swastika being used.

So, one of my major efforts in life is to detoxify or repatriate the swastika. No. 1 is my own personal enlightenment, No. 2 is my art, and No. 3 is education concerning the swastika—the fact that it is a beautiful, great symbol. I can't think of a more powerful symbol. I'm sorry for all the Jewish people who are upset about me and my swastikas—I've got Jewish friends. But what can I say—it's a beautiful sign and we need to re-educate people.

I don't collect any Nazi stuff—none. People don't need that reinforced; the Nazi use of the swastika was only about 10-20 years, compared to the thousands of years the swastika has been around.

My basic stance is: I think the swastika itself is innocent; it's innocent of what was done in its name. Museums and institutions that rely on grants have rejected my art; there's only a certain range of what they can do. When they step into an area that'll upset people, they back off. It takes one nutty person to persevere and hang in there, and maybe in the end start a new trend of awareness.

■ *V: So you haven't been unduly persecuted for your swastika convictions?*

■ MW: I'm a pretty big guy, and I have all these tattoos, and a lot of people would probably think twice before they'd come up and hassle me. I know this has saved me many a time. I look like a biker that could take people apart, and if I go into a crowded hot springs, instantly I get room! Although—things are changing.

I was in Fort Worth, Texas—my second wife is a dentist, and we went there for a course she was taking. I was unloading suitcases from the trunk while she went in first, and she came running back and said, "We've got to go in the back way! There's a huge convention of B-17 bomber pilots from WWII in the lobby!" (it was a reunion) But what could I do? I grabbed the suitcases and, wearing a cut-off t-shirt with my arms showing, headed straight through the front door. And by the end of the week we were all friends—these guys were telling me all their old bombing stories. They used to shoot at swastikas, right?

A funny thing happened to me; I met a photographer who was quite taken with my swastikas and everything, and he took a lot of photographs which he placed in a show of tattoo photos in a gallery. The editors of *Outlaw Biker* magazine saw the show and asked him to submit an article on me, but when they received the package they suddenly rejected it because they were "afraid of the controversy it might generate"! I couldn't believe it—with a name like *Outlaw Biker* it seems like they shouldn't be afraid of *anything!*

■ *V: Yes—a lot of people are afraid of taboo information.*

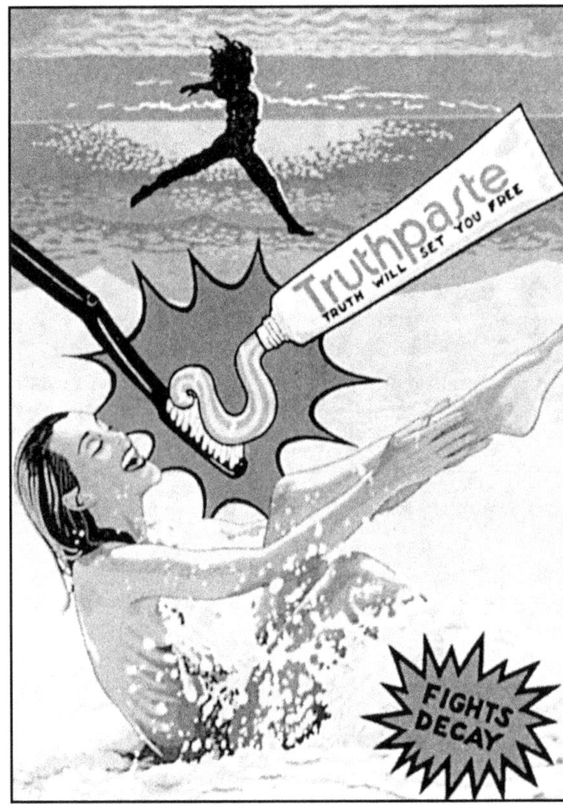

Painting by ManWoman.

People talk about god in terms of Love, Truth and all these ponderous concepts, but what about creativity? The people who I think are closest to god are poets and dreamers and writers and artists.

■ MW: Yet to me the swastika's the most auspicious sign I could think of, and the most universal—more universal than the cross.

It's all over Japan and China; everywhere you'd find a cross here you'll find a swastika there, like on a tombstone or temple or church or bell. It's often in the center of the breast of the Buddha—it's called the immaculate heart of Buddha, which again is another reference to inner being—the divine center of everything. I can't think of a more universal symbol than the swastika—it's used by every culture and religion. And I have proof positive from an old American encyclopedia of Jewish history that it was used as a decorative motif in synagogues!

Now there are two theories. Did the swastika loom up from the collective unconscious, as Jung would say, or did the swastika migrate? I think a little bit of each.

■ *AJ: Tell us about some of the swastikas on your arms.*

■ MW: Sometimes the swastika has curved arms, or

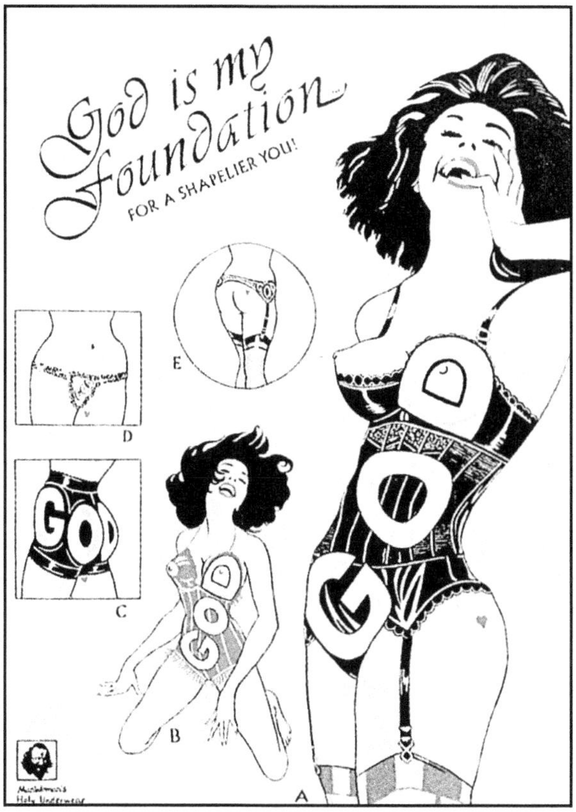

Painting by ManWoman. 45" x 60".

hooked arms, or more than four arms (it might have six arms). Some are hooked in on themselves; some are hooked out and have little feet; some are short—the arms are short, and that's the one that was used by the Hopi Indians. This one with the little scimitar things is from the Islamic region. The one with the spirals on the end is from Africa. The swastika inside the heart was called the Immaculate Heart of Buddha.

The one with the curved arms, crescent moon and dot was from the Jains in India who are total vegetarians; they wear a mask and sweep the street as they go because they don't want to inhale a bug or step on an ant—they don't want to kill *anything* so they kinda take it to extremes. The one of the Star of David with the swastika inside is from India and it's called a *yantra*. A mantra is a sound that provokes this inner divine thing, and a yantra is a graphic symbol that provokes the idea of divinity and divine energy. The one called a *swastikao* has three dots on the end of each of the arms and that one was found on all the gold bars that came out of King Solomon's Mine, so that's a Jewish swastika right there. The one with real sharp little hooks is Mexican; it looks Aztecan. This one's a Cubist swastika. One from India—don't know if those are bird beaks or little pairs of pliers or what.

A lot of the same swastikas can be found not only in Greece but also in China and Japan. One with the dots inside each of the arms is from Tibet. There are so many variations.

One called *God's House* is from Lapland; it's made of three arrow shapes, each pointing a different direction and suggesting that god encompasses all directions. They're like little rooftops, so this was called God's House.

One was from Malta; I met a kid in New York who ran up to me on the street and said, "Oh, have a look at my ring!" It had these curving, comma-like shapes on the swastika and he said that his grandmother was Basque. I later saw this also used on the isle of Malta.

One of my major efforts in life is to detoxify or repatriate the swastika. No. 1 is my own personal enlightenment, No. 2 is my art, and No. 3 is education concerning the swastika—the fact that it is a beautiful, great symbol.

My little smiling swastika with the arms and the legs is next to an octopus from ancient Greece; it's Mycenean.

■ *V: Tell us about the Jewish cross.*

■ MW: The Star of David is actually two interlocked triangles: one pointing up, and one pointing down. The upward-pointing one signifies the earth, and the downward one heaven, just like fire and water; they're opposites. They're interlocked, so basically the Star of David is a symbol of wholeness. The Cross, the vertical and horizontal that intersect, is the intersection of material and spirit. Same with the swastika: it's like a zig and a zag that have overlapped; male and female energies. All that again is similar to the yin-yang where the two cosmic opposites are embracing each other, symbolizing wholeness. All the great religious signs seem to be symbols for wholeness and oneness of spirit and material together.

■ *V: How did you meet the other swastika scholars you know?*

■ MW: Loosely we're the International Friends of the Swastika—something like that. We haven't officially organized; we're individuals who just work together. There are also other people who correspond.

I had heard about the town of Swastika in Ontario, and in 1972 wrote a letter to the Postmaster asking if there was anybody in the town who could tell me about the history of the town or why the name Swastika had been chosen. I wrote twice and didn't get an answer. Finally, I called up the Telephone Company and asked for a phone book which covered Swastika, Ontario—if you pay for it, you can get it. I went through the phone book and sent a letter to everybody—the fire department, the drug store...There was a "Swastika Research Laboratories"—they're a gold assay office, and I got a nice letter from the owner telling me they had a swastika on their sign prior to the war. He suggested I write Carolyn O'Neal, and gave her address.

I wrote her a letter, and she didn't reply for the longest time. Then I got a very hesitant letter: "This is a brief history of how we got the swastika"—very guarded tones. I wrote back and sent xeroxes of almost everything I had, and she couldn't resist. She wrote me back and sent some photos, and I sent her more things. A year after that first letter she wrote, "I don't know why you've bothered with just a housewife in Swastika, Ontario, because I'm a nobody, but this has been the most fabulous year of correspondence I could possibly imagine!" Now we're dear friends. She runs the Kirkland Lake Northern History Museum; Kirkland Lake is a bigger town next to Swastika, which is only 700 people.

About a year later she wrote, "I got a letter from a strange person in Germany, and I'm passing it on to you." It was addressed to the Lord Mayor of Swastika, and came from a little town in Germany. The sender called himself "Guru Svastika." He called himself a "world conscience artist," and his card had four swastikas on it and a photograph of him with a swastika on his forehead above a German inscription, "To be good." I wrote him a letter: "Surprise—you have a brother over here in Canada!" and sent him material, and he sent both me and Carolyn photocopies and photographs of things from his collection.

After two years of correspondence with these two, WHAM! comes another letter to me from Chicago. I had written to the Theosophical Society headquarters in Chicago, because I'd heard they had used the swastika. The actual symbol was a metaphysical conglomeration incorporating a serpent swallowing its tail, a swastika, a Star of David and an Ankh. Five years after my inquiry they sent me a little pamphlet, plus a letter from Douglas Youngblood, "I went to the Theosophical Society pursuing my swastika research, and they gave me your address." It turned out he was writing a whole encyclopedia on the swastika.

■ *V: Did you all meet?*

■ MW: On Easter, 1985 all four of us met at Swastika, Ontario and had a fantastic meeting. Douglas Youngblood brought me a xeroxed volume of his swastika encyclopedia and it practically filled up the trunk of his Toyota. Now I've got *so much* information…

We all had little gifts for one another. A friend of mine had made four stuffed swastikas out of plush, and I gave one in red to Guru Swastika from Germany, one in blue to Carolyn, and one in yellow to Douglas. They had brought swastikas of all shapes and sizes and we traded—it was a real swastika swap meet!

British Columbia Television aired a 10-minute segment on me and my swastika collection on BC-TV News. I got letters from people telling me, "I've got this little trinket left me by my grandmother," and another guy started to correspond with me, but it was too much, so I sent his address to Douglas and they've been corresponding ever since and getting good information trades.

I think this is a nice international effort to teach people about the whole history of the symbol. If you look at a paperback book rack at a drugstore about half the covers have swastikas on them: *Nazis from Outer Space, Nazis from Brazil, Nazis from Anywhere.* When you see that, your blood's supposed to run cold. People say to me, "It's too early. Too many Jewish people have memories; too many German people have memories." But every day now it's being imprinted on everybody as a symbol of everything that's evil and fascist. So I think, "It isn't too early; it's *never* too early to re-educate people about *anything.*"

Think about it—maybe Attila the Hun or Genghis Khan or William the Conqueror had a symbol on a flag when they went out and conquered people, so everybody they conquered hated that symbol, but it's gone out of our consciousness—we don't even remember it. And it could have been a cross, or a Star of David or a crescent moon and stars. There are still people in India who absolutely detest a crescent moon with a little star because it's a symbol of the Muslims who once tried to conquer them.

■ *AJ: It's interesting to contemplate just what will happen to the collective unconscious when a symbol as widespread as the swastika is tainted. The swastika has been around as a primordial, holistic symbol for centuries, so what kind of loss to the unconscious has been brought about when an archetype as important as that gets twisted? The collective symbolic language just becomes poorer—less profound.*

■ MW: I've often thought that if aliens did land, they might have swastikas on their ships and we'd think that they're evil! So we have to teach people that it's a good symbol for the rest of the universe. If you were black and somebody burned a cross on your lawn, how would you feel about the cross? That certainly could prejudice your view of what the cross was all about.

■ *V: Tell us more about your dream notebooks.*

■ MW: My dream book is called *The Book of Astonishment*; it's literally thousands of dreams. And the dreams will go in sequences, as if trying to teach me something. A symbol will recur in dreams for a month or two, and then another symbol will appear and develop, like my dragon motorcycle—every night I would surge on this dragon motorcycle which was like kundalini or your sexual/spiritual energy. And I don't differentiate between the sexual and the spiritual; one takes a physical form and the other doesn't. That's how I got into my whole secret doctrine of the Holy Fuck and the Celestial Screw; the kundalini experience up your spine is your sexual/spiritual energy taken up to higher levels. . . .

One of my key dreams was: I was walking up a ravine, and this gigantic black beast was following me. It was all black and shaggy, with the body of a bear and the head of a bull. I saw up on the bank this shining king in golden armor, and I shouted, "Will you save me from my enemy?" He said, "Yes, I will turn you into a root, and you will grow into a great tree such as the world has never before seen. But first!"—*k-ching!* he drew his sword: "You must be cut up into a thousand pieces and be buried in the ground!" He went *hack, hack, hack*—chopped me up into a thousand pieces and buried me. And for several years after that I dreamt about being cut up, dissected, and roasted on a spit. [laughs] In the dreams I would go into rooms and there would be nothing but cut-up parts of bodies! It was the idea of looking within yourself and understanding all parts of yourself absolutely and totally in order to free yourself from entanglements, prejudices, hang-ups, narrow-minded outlooks, negative thoughts, and in general everything that we need to be free of.

■ *AJ: In alchemy, the first step is putrefaction.*

■ MW: That's right—this is the inner alchemy. So now it seems that the whole inward-looking search through all the entangled workings of my "self" has come to an end, and it's pouring out the other way. It was invisible because the root is underground; but now these roots are full size!

For 20 years I've been underground; it was like the whole art world was shut to me. I seemed to intimidate them; everybody ignored me.

■ *AJ: But that establishment is always locked into the status quo. If you have vision and creativity—*

■ MW: I'll win—I'll just outlive the suckers! People have awakened tremendously since 1965. All that garbage buried in the human psyche for centuries has been bubbling up to the surface; we have to look at it before we can transform and grow to the next stage where we can take universal responsibility for our actions. If we went into Space right now and met other civilizations, we'd just spread diseases. We've got to cure ourselves first before we can go out to that next stage. I'm optimistic about where we're going. Part of it *is* painful—it's like, "Hey, look at this horrible ugly cancerous growth that's inside your own soul"—you better cut that out and get rid of it and grow. The only way is to open it up and unblinkingly examine it...

■ *V: And maybe make fun out of it.*

■ MW: And my dreams are so rich in humor. All of my art pieces come from dreams, like "Hope Soap: sees through dirt!" and "Truthpaste: fights decay!" and "Harmless Boxing Gloves" and "Our Lady of the Immaculate Contraption"—all of those ideas which are really rich in humor are all straight out of dreams. My dreams have this incredible sense of humor.

■ *V: Pop art lifted the taboo against humor in art.*

■ MW: Plus the taboo against humor in religion has been lifted. Religion used to be serious—morbidly serious and grim: sin, despair, hellfire and damnation—all of those things are so non-humorous. But I think humor is one of the greatest divine qualities; after all, life's such an incredible joke! [laughs] I don't know how we'd survive without our sense of humor.

■ *V: That's how we survive.*

■ MW: These are bellycology baby blessings. I've done them on more than 50 women.

■ *AJ: Did they have great births?*

■ MW: Yeah—they have! As a matter of fact, one woman had a child die. She discovered that I did this, and said, "Oh, you've got to bless this child, because my first one died." I did it, it was a perfect child, and then she came back and asked me to do the next one. She moved away, but said, "If I have another child, I'm coming back!" I don't attribute magic to this, but she somehow did.

■ *V: How did you start out doing that?*

■ MW: In the sixties, me and my friends were doing a lot of body painting at communes and solstice celebrations and all that. One day up came a pregnant lady and I painted her, and that's how bellycology started. I've been doing them ever since. The belly button forms a fantastic nose, and women just seem to love it! I had a whole show of about fifty photographs of my bellycology painting in a gallery. They made a postcard and a whole string of women have contacted me; I made one painting just a couple days ago. Women at that stage of pregnancy feel ugly and rejected, and when I do that they brighten right up! It kind of lightens up the whole experience.

ManWoman, Doctor of Bellycology.

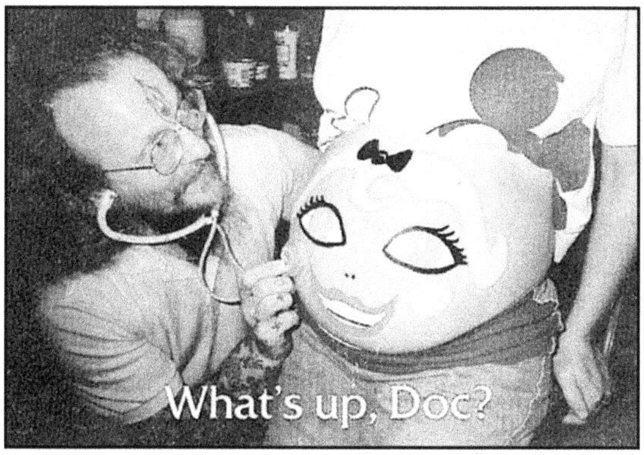

Triplets.

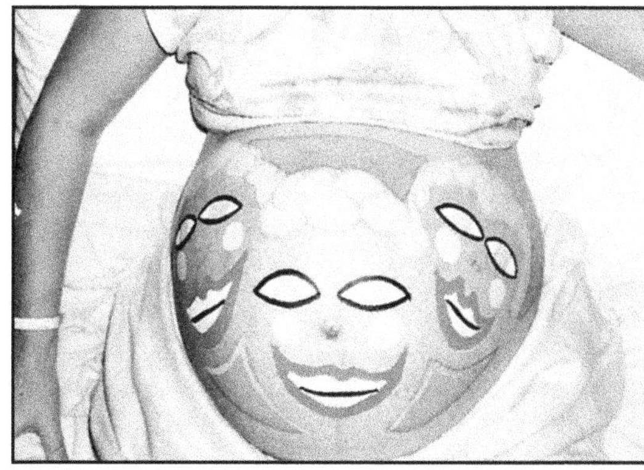

DON ED HARDY

One of the foremost practitioners of the ancient art of tattoo is Don Ed Hardy, a philosopher, historian, painter and innovator who, on a global scale, has greatly advanced the cultural credibility of his profession. As editor of *Tattootime* he chronicled and disseminated little-known mythology, anthropology, history, and photo documentation about tattoos. He also spotlights current innovative trends both in technique and content. His goal: to raise artistic standards and extend the range and complexity of symbolism depicted, while reinvestigating and preserving past traditions.

Currently D. E. Hardy lives, paints, writes and publishes in the Bay Area, administering Hardy Marks Publications (with his wife, writer Francesca Passalacqua) and Tattoo City, 700 Lombard St, San Francisco CA 94133; tel (415) 345-9437; fax (415) 345-1813.

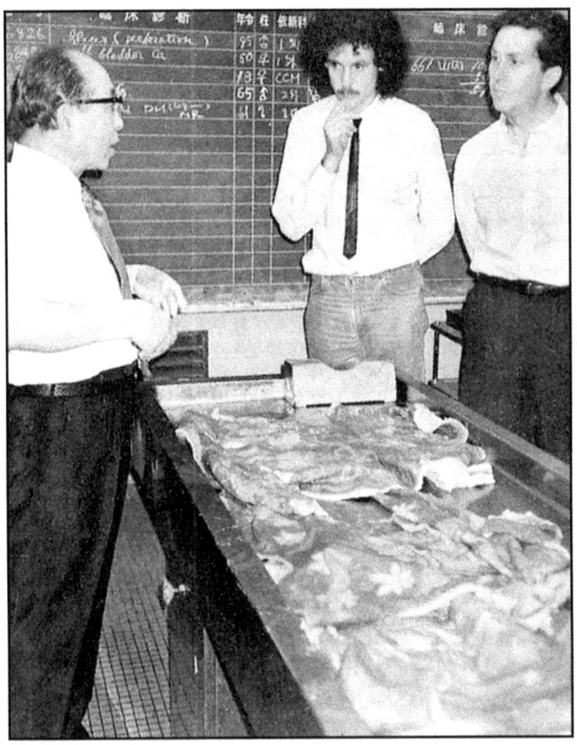

Ed Hardy (far right) with Dr. Fukushi (far left) and tattooist "The Dutchman" (from Vancouver) admiring the collection of more than 100 preserved tattoo skins at the Anatomy Museum of the University of Tokyo Medical School.

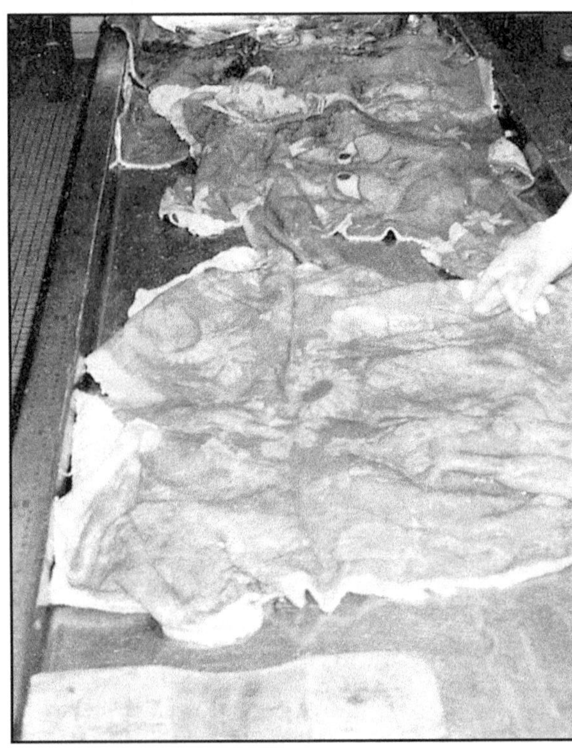

■ *VALE: Even though you're famous for doing large color tattoos, your black "modern primitive" work is some of the best that's been done.*

■ ED HARDY: I came to black tattoo work kinda late. I really like it, but I don't consider myself specifically aligned with that style. However, tattooing oneself is a primitive act; the bottom line is: you're doing this basic, ancient practice.

■ *V: Also, there's a lot lacking in this society, and people feel it—*

■ EH: And that's why a lot of this is happening. Tattooing is still not socially acceptable, and it probably never will be, unless it happens 'way down the line—which is kinda nice! If everybody hads 'em, who'd want 'em? [laughs]

■ *V: There's no college degree called "tattoo artist"; just to become one you had to deviate...Another thing—as people get older, their bodies look better with tattooing on them, than just* plain.

■ EH: They certainly look more *interesting.* Cliff Raven put it so succinctly in the first issue of *Tattootime:* "The perfect tattoo...the one I believe we are all struggling toward...is the one that turned the jackass into the zebra."

Tattoos make the body a more interesting surface; I *like* how they look when they get old—I like the whole *process.* When people first get tattoos they're often obsessed: "How is this going to hold up?" and I say, "It'll hold up the way you will." Because it's on a living organism, it's always in transition. Old tattoos sometimes get really mysterious-looking; the design may soften and blend and sag—I love that look.

It's part of the larger problem of getting people to accept themselves. Part of what's fucked up in this culture is the absolute *denial* of everything having to do with the *aging process* and *death.* That's what I think really kicks people in the head about tattooing: they see it and remember they're going to die, and they don't want to *deal* with that.

A tattoo is an affirmation: you put it on yourself with the knowledge that *this body is yours to have and enjoy while you're here.* You have fun with it, and nobody else can control (supposedly) what you do with it. That's why tattooing is such a big thing in prison: it's an expression of freedom—one of the only expressions of freedom there. They can lock you down, control everything *but:* "I've got my mind, and I can tattoo my body—alter it my way as an act of *personal will."*

■ *ANDREA JUNO: The first thing people say when tattoos are mentioned is: "But you can't get that off!"*

■ EH: The permanence really hits them, and that is linked to mortality. And that's why skull tattoos really *ice* it. Bill Salmon reminded me that we were in Rome at a big tattoo art exhibition, one of the editors of the exhibition catalog was being *very* tolerant. He included photos of crude prison tattoos and genital shots...yet balked at including tattoos of *skulls.* Tattoos always tell you more about the people looking at them, than the person wearing them! [laughs] They're like a geiger counter reading out people's fears...

The perfect tattoo . . . the one we are all struggling toward . . . is the one that turned the jackass into the zebra.

That whole Judeo-Christian belief system imposes an absolutely negative connotation on tattooing. It's a basic human tendency to want to decorate one's body; it's something people have *always* done. Yet this society doesn't provide any place for it, and the cultures that *did* have indigenous tattooing were pretty successfully wiped out by the Christian missionary intrusion covering the world with White Western culture.

Tattooing is basically anti-repressive. I think people's main subconscious motivation is to clarify something *about* themselves *to* themselves, and only

Tattoo by D. Ed Hardy, 1985.

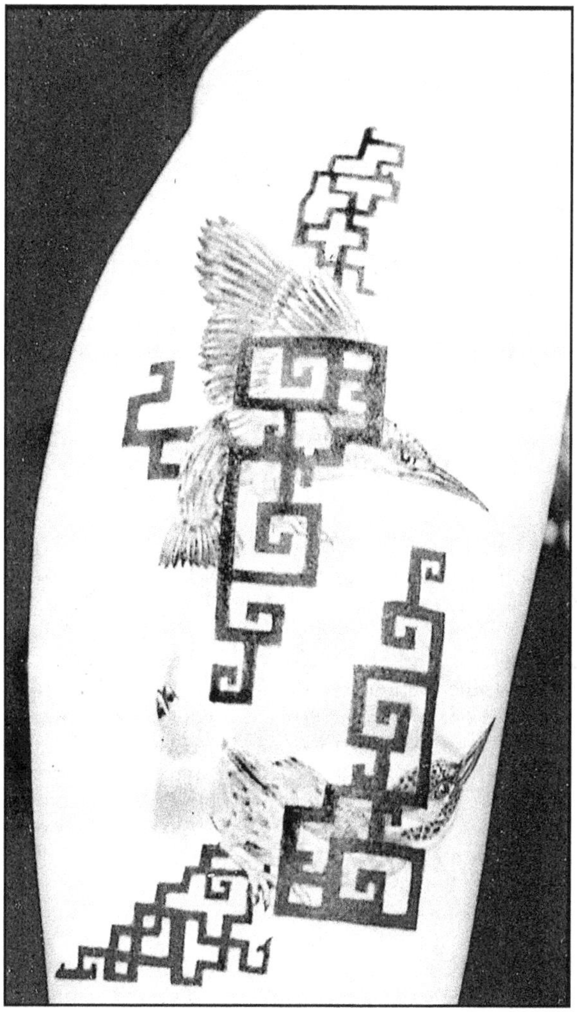

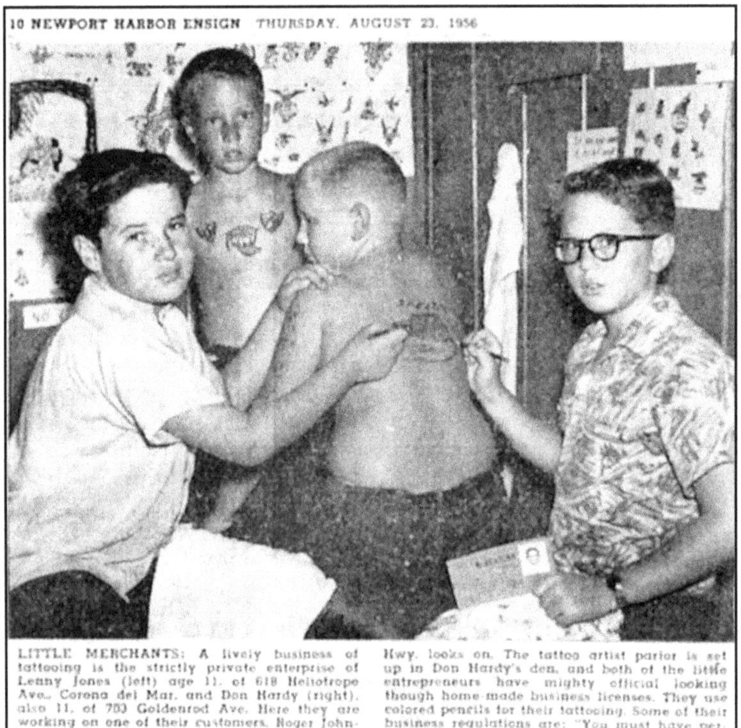

10 NEWPORT HARBOR ENSIGN THURSDAY, AUGUST 23, 1956

LITTLE MERCHANTS: A lively business of tattooing is the strictly private enterprise of Lenny Jones (left) age 11, of 618 Heliotrope Ave., Corona del Mar, and Don Hardy (right), also 11, of 703 Goldenrod Ave. Here they are working on one of their customers, Roger Johnson, 11, of 612 Goldenrod Ave., while another

Hwy. looks on. The tattoo artist parlor is set up in Don Hardy's den, and both of the little entrepreneurs have mighty official looking though home-made business licenses. They use colored pencils for their tattooing. Some of their business regulations are: "You must have permission of your parents" . . . "Ages 9 to 12"

Ed Hardy at age 12—future tattoo artist at work.

incidentally (although it depends on the individual; some humans are peacocks) to show to other people. It's mainly to prove or clarify something they feel about themselves, and nurture that: "Okay well I *am* this"—it's kind of an empowerment on a personal level.

Ultimately it's a real statement of freedom, and I think that's what flips people out. Tattoos throw people a curve in society because there isn't really an acceptable context, especially for all these weird tattoos now. Before they'd go, "Oh—you were in the navy" or "You were drunk"— there's this stock set of responses that *still* go on somewhat, but they were *really* going on when I first started tattooing. Because then the implication was: "I really shouldn't have done this—I was drunk when I got it." and that's a cop-out, to say: "Yes I'm ashamed of it; I've dirtied myself with this." Instead of saying, "I really *like* it; I got it consciously." People still get upset, even though tattooing is a modern usage of a very ancient practice which has yet to be codified in this society.

When I was tattooing in a street shop with a walk-in clientele, learning my chops for the first five or six years, it was mostly sailors—the 18-21-year-old age bracket. Most tattooers thought that was *all* that would ever get tattooed: kids going through their rite of passage of becoming adults, who thought the tattoo went along with that and their military service. But nowadays most of my clients are over 30; a lot of them are in their 40s and even older, and they're people who have thought about it for a long time, and decided to get major work.

I do mainly large tattoos on people who've made a major commitment: "Okay, I'm going to go ahead and *really* alter myself, and get this big design done." And they go to a lot of trouble. Before, a lot of them felt very alone. That's one reason I did *Tattootime:* so people could know that, "Oh there are other people out there like us." It's very important to have support.

■ *AJ: And also remove stigma—that a person bearing a tattoo is some flaky drug-addict, criminal or pervert.*

■ EH: Yes, that implication that if you have a tattoo it means you're completely unstable. I think there *is* a kind of rebellion involved, although this doesn't always manifest itself—a lot of my clients are literally CEOs or boardroom presidents. But if the tattoo does something for them that way, freeing them up so they think, "I am in control of *this* part of my life," and leading them toward a more positive self-image, then that's *good,* and hopefully they'll reflect that out onto the world with the way they deal with people.

So I've always striven to turn tattooing absolutely opposite from the usual belief in the West: that the person's a real asshole, and very anti-social. It doesn't have to mean that at all.

I think the hook tattooing had for me as a kid, was that these guys really were like the Keepers of the Images. They'd have displayed the whole emotional gamut: love and hate and sex and death—all in codified designs that were bold and bright.

■ *V: You've done a lot to elevate the quality of tattooing as an art form.*

■ EH: I've always liked tattooing for many reasons, starting when I was really little. I painted simulated tattoos on kids when I was in grade school. But when I decided to get into it at an art school level, I realized its challenge as a medium: "What if you could draw huge, outrageous tattoos?" To be able to transform somebody *that* much seemed truly spectacular and unexpected—untapped artistic territory.

Nobody was doing really big work; that didn't exist in our society. I had seen a lot of historic photos of people tattooed all over, but always with big sections of tattoo shop flash more or less randomly applied. These people had had to fit their individual psyche into pre-congealed images that were often very out-of-date, because of the generally low level of artistry available.

■ V: *Like tattooing a 19th-century sailing ship on their chest—*

■ EH: But that's okay if people are really *into* that! There are people who are nostalgic and who want that in a very thought-out way...Anyhow, I was thinking, "I'll have to create an entirely new situation." It was like having to make the ink, go out and strip the trees to make the paper to do the painting on, etc.

I knew that after enough years and a few thousand tattoos I could get the technical skill to make machines do things that nobody had done—I *did* that. Now the big problem was: getting people to wear them! I had to create an entire era of trust; a whole milieu to do the work in. Tattooers all over the world had always said, "*My* customers would never get *that!*"

The human interaction was as crucial as the artistry itself—that *trust:* making people feel that you're going to do them *right*, to the best of your ability, as well as essentially function as a conduit for them to realize themselves—the *art part* of themselves. Because if I had a nickel for every time I heard the line, "That's *exactly* what I had in my head"—I love to hear that! Of course, there are certain key forms and inner rhythms that appeal to people and suit the contours of the body. But basically, what I've always been after is: *they're* really doing the tattoo. I've always forced people to give me input, although sure, I've had people come in and say, "Do whatever you want—I just want your work," which is nice for the ego, but that's not truly satisfying. I like that challenge of having to do it *differently* for each person.

Everybody could be an artist—you guys know that—but society's got it so screwed up; they've dampened that whole potential. Art is regarded as: "What a *useless* pursuit!" Little kids who might naturally want to draw or otherwise experiment get told that art is useless, right when they're young and still pretty connected to real gratification; when they don't have that many applied layers of society and experiences in this body. And if it's stamped out of them then, it becomes real hidden somewhere—sometimes it disappears forever. And people get sick—that's why so many people get so screwed up.

I think tattooing can allow these people to backtrack and recoup some long-lost creative expressiveness. I respect that in people who get tattooed, especially the ones who go to the trouble of making a conscious aesthetic *quest*—not just go down and get the first thing they see. Again, it's that one reason I started going public—so people would know: "There are people in the world who can really do something right." Because the first tattoos *I* had—I just went in and got them off the wall, because I wanted them and nobody was offering anything else.

■ V: *It's best that the person chose something that's really* them.

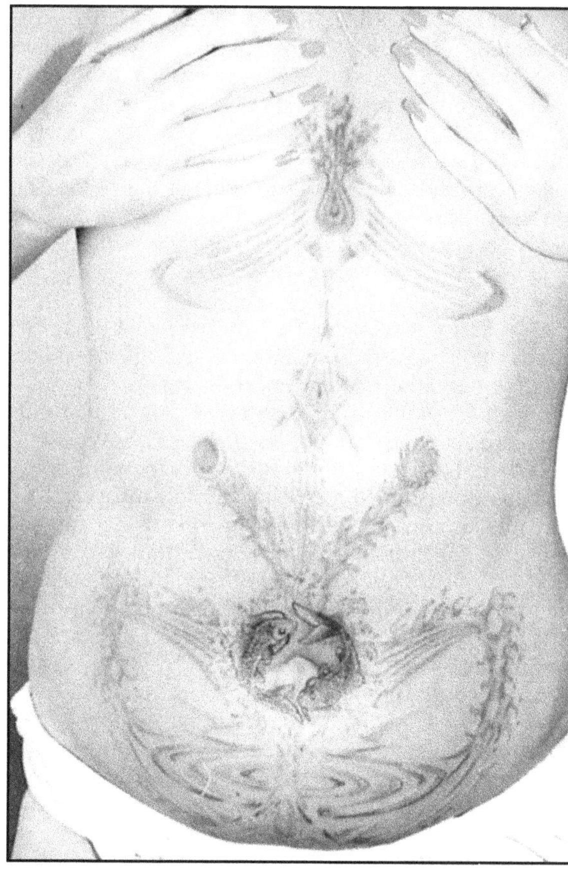

Tattoo by D.E. Hardy, 1987: Water/double Pisces themes—composition based on African female scarification patterns.

■ EH: It is. I can talk volumes about the whole moral responsibility of people doing tattoos, because to me this was the ultimate art form in the world for really forcing you to question what you're doing as an artist: what your motives are, where your ego is involved, and what might be *pure intent* or just *fucked-up strutting.*

If enough people say about your work, "God that's really great!" you could start believing them until—well, there's a carny phrase: you become a sucker for your own game! So you always have to keep that distance: awareness that you obviously should strive to do better, plus the realization that the way you're doing it is not necessarily the *only* way. You have to really put yourself back.

I strive to be technically capable of just about anything. I'll suggest ways to possibly improve someone's idea or bring it closer to what their interior vision is, particularly if it's not that clear. It's always a matter of clarifying; bringing it into focus—trying to be a human camera and taking what they're seeing on the inside and showing them *x* number of possibilities.

It's great seeing people light up to other realms. It's like—if they see tribal work for the first time, they might realize, "Oh, it doesn't have to be a *picture* of something," and then start exploring a whole new area. You never insist, "*This* is the best way to do it." And you can't dogmatically say that tribal work is better, or more "refined" or "pure" than say, big American eagles, because every individual is different. Your goal is to bring all your skills to bear on the particular subject at hand.

■ *AJ: So you function as a kind of therapist; a vehicle to help people channel their unconscious urges to the surface—*

■ EH: And connect them to the rest of humanity, too; to the best parts of themselves. Things kinda fell apart long ago; now, while society is losing *all* its rituals, it still is trying to force on everybody all that old cardboard religious crap nobody believes in anymore.

When I was at art school, abstract expressionism had ended and Minimalism, pure form over content, was fashionable—obviously people were starved for ideas. That whole art school environment was so vapid—it was so hideous and still is, with all that ego and self-analysis and everybody caught up in their own petty little problems. The whole concept of art is *so* important to culture and people's lives, yet so easily diverted and perverted and watered-down.

In 1967 I graduated. Then I started tattooing, and it was like getting a giant shock: "Wow, this really has *power*, it really has *magic;* it has real *balls* to it and a very strong connection to humanity. It's something that people feel really strongly about. *Even* if it might be corny images, people are very sincere about this; there's a genuine emotional connection."

I like the fact that tattooing is *one-on-one*. Not everybody I tattoo has a great aesthetic background or familiarity with world art history—some *do*, and that's great because they bring ideas ideas *in*, but many operate on *pure instinct*. Others actually get into discovering types of art or paintings that will really *mean* something to them, and become incorporated into their tattoo.

■ *V: Kind of an educational process.*

■ EH: They learn, and then hopefully…

■ *AJ: Nowadays the gallery has merged with the department store; you go to a museum and art has become just a commodity for signifying economic status.*

■ EH: Yeah, it's *weird*. Now people are making money with *art!* It's unbelievable. And these young painters are going, "When am I going to hit it rich?!"

■ *V: It's investment, not inspiration. I saw someone on TV saying, "This is for my children's college funds; I'd rather buy this art than Pillsbury stocks."*

■ EH: Exactly.

■ *AJ: I think it'll be hard for tattooing to be tainted by the economics of society. Art is a commodity, whereas tattooing is still rooted in pop culture, like cartoons—you can still actually find creativity there. Tattooing also has roots that are deep—that have spanned thousands of years in different cultures.*

■ EH: It's good for people to realize they're participating in an activity that has *good references*. People ask, "When did this start—in Japan in 1800?" and when you tell them the *Egyptians* did tattooing, it's usually a pleasant surprise. There's a lot of tattooed mummies; the tattoo survived because they mummified the bodies. But it was all connected with rituals: sacred amulet tattooing, symbolic tattooing.

I think the Egyptian tattooing is the oldest. Aside from that singular example of the frozen tattooed Scythian warrior [est. 2,500 years old] found in Russia, the rest of the documentation's all in literature. Cultures like Micronesia and Polynesia have never had a written language, so no one knows how far back it went there. But I think tattooing is pretty much pervasive throughout the world. And the African people who were too dark-skinned did all that scarification.

A tattoo is an affirmation: that this body is yours to have and enjoy while you're here. Nobody else can control what you do with it. That's why tattooing is such a big thing in prison: it's an expression of freedom.

I think it's healthy for people to again feel like they're connecting with humanity—to get out of that frame of reference where the world is just what's been happening since the year they were born, and where they believe what the Church and the State is telling them. That's the best thing about the current information explosion: being able to have access to all these realms of life all over the world; having all kinds of cultural ideas simultaneously available.

I think it's a difficult time for a lot of people, because it's rough to have things shaken up so much, but it's very healthy. It's good to live in a place like San Francisco where there's so much freedom of expression and social mobility, where people can be as strange as they want to be and still function okay. In

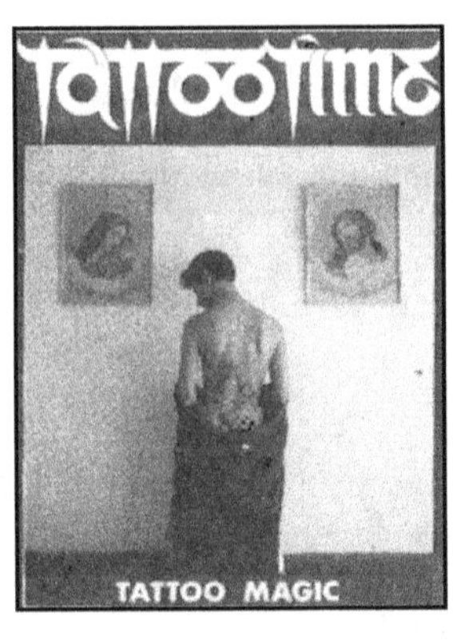

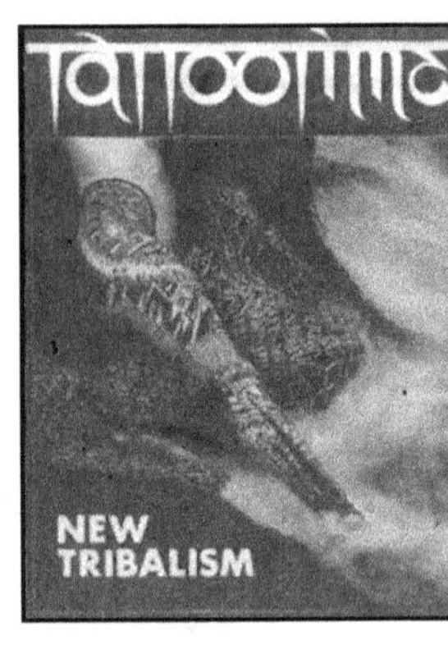

The first two volumes of Tattootime edited by D.E. Hardy.

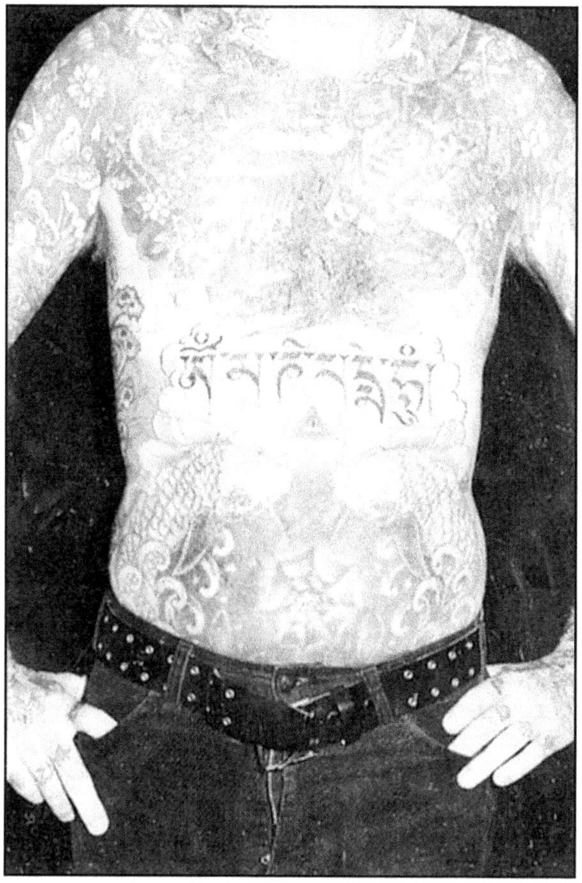

Mantra by D.E. Hardy, 1983. Stomach by Sailor Jerry Collins, 1964. Chest by various artists.

S.F. we live in this weird little vacuum of Bohemian freedom, but—

■ *AJ: All you have to do is wait 10 or 15 years for the ideas to migrate to the small town and then suddenly all these people are going to get tattooed.*

■ EH: And I love that—it's like being in a time machine. In 1967 I went to Vancouver, Canada to start my first tattoo shop. That was my first awareness of time machine living, because I had lived in San Francisco and was raised in Southern California before that, and when I got to Vancouver the people, the look, and the atmosphere were like ten years previously, and I thought, "I know what's going to happen next!" And I did! I felt like—drunk with power; if I'd come in with T-shirts I could have really made money! Just having anticipated the future style and all that…

That happens all over the world, I'm sure. There are certain urban centers that are like power bases where, for whatever reasons, trends get initiated and take force, and then it all trickles down. Just look at all the punk fashion now—ten years ago who would have thought it would take over Chinatown and the business world and the newspaper ads. Well, it's not really acceptable everywhere, but people are more used to seeing it. And because of the media—the instant insatiable TV blitz—people have seen many more tattoos.

People still regard tattooing as a freak activity, but at least they've *seen* it, and they know *somebody*—the guy down the street whose aunt has a tattoo! That's how it'll grow in the culture. In another 50 years it'll be much more pervasive.

■ *V: Your publication of* Tattootime *influenced all these artists, who influence everybody else. At least the* artists *have seen it.*

■ EH: It has; it's had a ripple effect. And that's the way a lot of things happen. I felt it was really important to present tattooing in a straight documentary legitimate high-ticket form—in other words to take it seriously, but also to show a lot of the *raw power* of it, and try to get people to understand—*not* to pretty it up, not to *gentrify* it, but to present it in an articulate format. That had never been done before, and I think that was important.

■ *AJ: "The Thinking Man's Tattoo Magazine."*

■ EH: Right. You picture yourself in a library in a big wing leather chair instead of out on the trash truck. It's funny, because tattoo does span that whole spectrum. The reason I can spend all my life thinking about this, is because tattoo is in fact a medium and you can't really encapsulate it—it's like saying, "Okay, let's talk about *world painting*." Especially now, when it's opening up to such an extent.

I mean, there are still people doing straight Sailor-town tattoos—there'll always be a call for that, but that shouldn't be the *only* work available. There are people doing refined, thought-out work like what I do, and there's all shades in between. And that's good; it was too limited before. To have that basic human impulse *only available in this color,* or filtered through an I.Q. of 85—that's stupid.

■ *V: When I was in Vancouver I talked to an Indian who had Haida or Kwakiutl tattoos—ancestral designs. He was proud of them, and I felt they were really appropriate for* him.

■ EH: I think that was done by the Dutchman—he's done some really elegant work up there. He's also done some really beautiful tattoos on one of the last surviving carvers, who produces unbelievable traditional work in ivory. It's great when you can get people to *re-connect* to their culture—reconnect to something they had 'way back. Most of us grew up in this weird limbo of being *nouveau American,* without a tradition we're linked to, whereas this Northwest Indian was able to reconnect to a tangible cultural heritage.

I have a client with a lot of tribal work (snakes and grid work on his legs which was Samoan-inspired; a fusion of Samoan and Japanese) who wanted this piece which was like a tribute to Sailor Jerry—a big '40s *va-va-voom* tits-and-ass nurse. And he wanted it next to a lot of Tibetan Tantric imagery. For years he had been reluctant to ask me, but finally he did: "You don't think it's too dumb?" I said, "It's great!" Because he

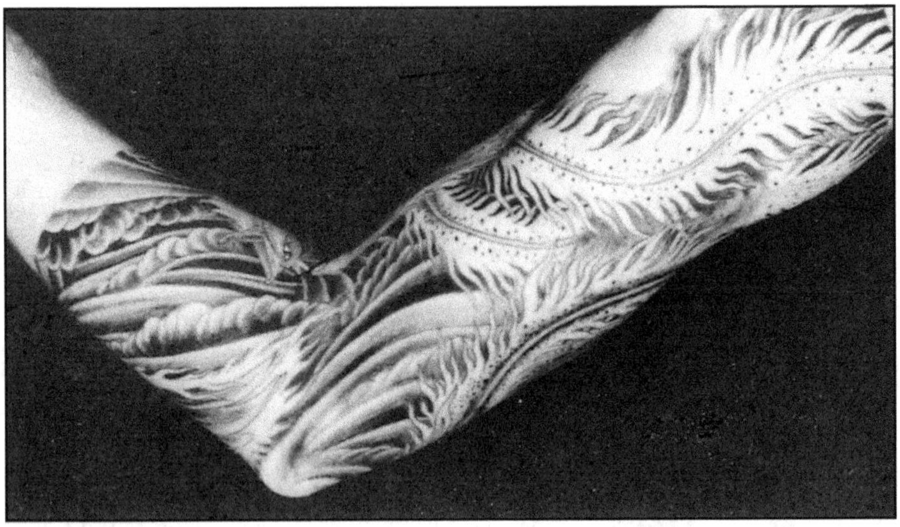

Phoenix, fire and wind by D.E. Hardy, 1987.

had grown up in the '40s and had a great affection for this image.

I put it on him and thought, "This is real *American* tattooing"—having all these cultures floating next to each other. I mean, it's all right if some people want to really ape the Japanese, or whatever, but the most exciting possibility for me as an artist is to do this fusion—be able to make references to different parts of world culture. There'll probably be more and more of that; I suppose that's kind of *post-modernist:* making references to references within the business itself.

I think the hook tattooing had for me as a kid, was that these guys really were like the Keepers of the Images. You'd go into a tattoo shop and they'd have displayed the whole emotional gamut: love and hate and sex and death—all in codified designs that were bold and bright. I thought, "This is so great, because you can reflect any kind of emotion with these."

Another aspect: if you're an artist putting the tattoos on, you can experience them vicariously—I mean, there's a lot of tattoos I'd love to wear if I had room! But by being an artist you can kind of experience that, and go, "Yeah! that's great!" and it walks away. It's a little like living in a house full of your own paintings; you don't have room for them all.

But mainly I like the fact that if people *re-connect* to something, or *find it*...it's like solving the missing link. And by getting the tattoo, they can put it behind them, in a sense. Because for a lot of people, the event of getting the tattoo is the main thing. And it remains as a record of, "Okay, we went over that hurdle," similar to the way it functions in primitive society: as a ritual marker that you've done *this;* therefore you have *this* kind of tattoo. Once you have it, then it's done with.

Perhaps that's what keeps people wanting new tattoos—they think, "Okay, I've settled *that* with myself." Or, "I've codified *that,* made that clear for

myself." Or, "I've codified *that,* made that clear to myself, and I've got that power. Now I'm going to go for *this* one." Maybe that's why people end up getting *covered*—it's hard to stop.

On those super-elegant designs, especially with black work, it's hard to preserve all that negative space. I've done some great work on people which functioned perfectly... yet later they wanted to add *more* work around it. That's up to them, and as an artist you can't just dogmatically say, "But it looks great just the way it is." Because if it means that much to them, then...

There's a lot of tattoos I'd love to wear if I had room!

A tattoo is never *just* what the appearance is, anyway. You can only *really* know about the tattoo by getting to know the person wearing it. Tattoos are indicators, or little vents to their psyche. And I can appreciate a lot of tattoos that might not look so great as tattoos! Knowing the artist who did them, and how it's a reflection of his style, especially if he's a funky old-timer; some of them have great styles that are real primitive—talk about *art brut!* But it's great stuff because it's so much *him*—it's like eccentric tramp art.

Also, a lot of people have tattoos that might not make that much sense, or may not strike you as an art statement, but when you hear their reason for getting it (or you get to know them and see how it reflects them subtly)—well, there's nothing else that quite does that.

■ *V: It's like the tattoo opens a door to another dimension. It's never just the painting, it's the whole setting and the hidden history and the metaphor and the entire range of inter-connections. Nothing has meaning solely* in itself; *the meaning lies in its* relationships. *At best, the painting itself is always just a window to so much more.*

■ EH: Yeah, that's it! That's the whole thing. And the tattoo really should function—it should draw people into you. It's interesting that the people who have the guts to come up to me and say something, usually have a pretty positive, or at least *open,* attitude toward it. The ones who have negative remarks won't say them to your face; they'll say 'em behind your back: "Oh

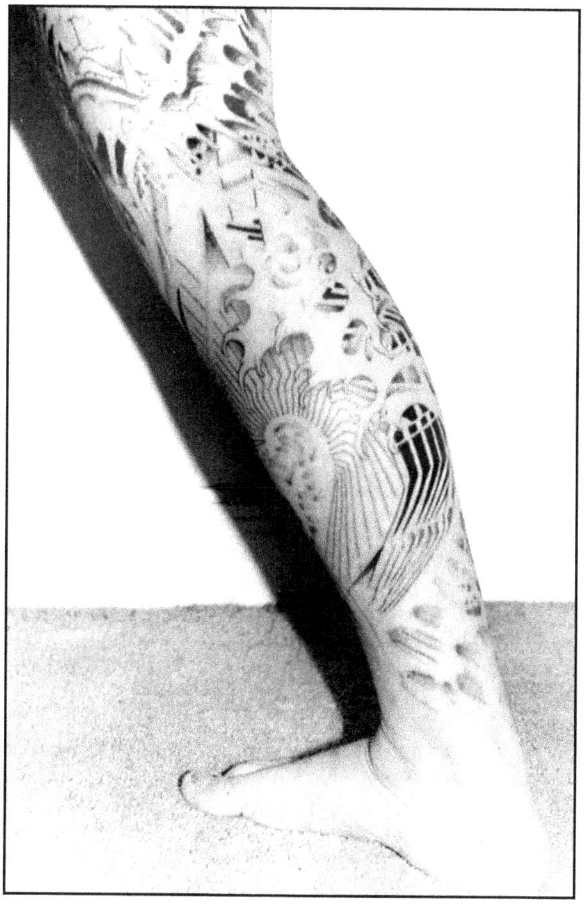

Tattoo by D.E. Hardy, 1986 on Dan Thome.

God, *look* at that guy!" But hopefully, it should draw people *in.*

Remember the old salt with the tattoos telling stories to the grandkids, "Well I got this one in Madagascar..." The tattoo really is just that—the flashcard to the story. Thus it taps into the whole dying *oral tradition;* the whole heritage of story-telling in humanity that's lost now. Gone is that very intense *vibe* of sitting there with somebody and doing all your takes of interacting with them as a physical presence, looking at their skin and re-living what that meant to them.

I love to get old people talking about their tattoos. I love going up to old guys and saying, "Wow, that's a great tattoo—did so-and-so do that?" A lot of the time I can guess where they got it or the circumstances, especially with *Americana,* because it was codified for so long. There were certain sets of designs that were popular, that were drawn a certain way or that incorporated certain errors. Sailor designs—things that would be for a particular Service guy, or a certain style of Black Panther.

When I started tattooing, if I saw a black panther (which is one of the most ubiquitous designs in American tattoo), there were so few people tattooing that I could almost always tell where a person got that. I used to love to spot old people I'd never seen before and go up to them and say "Oh, you got that in Wisconsin about ten years ago." (That's great; like one of those little cheap magic tricks!)

Remember the old salt with the tattoos telling stories to the grandkids, "Well, I got this one in Madagascar . . . " The tattoo really is just that-the flashcard for the story. Thus it taps into that whole dying oral tradition.

A lot of the more soulful tattooers knew the subtleties of rank and service. Like if a certain design had extra elements, it meant that the wearer had done *this* kind of a tour of duty. For many sailors the tattoo became a permanent insignia of their station.

In wartime, tattoos are so popular because of the uncertainty of survival. People are strengthening themselves by using the tattoo as a kind of psychic armor to reinforce their image of themselves. Also, people get melodramatic: "Well, they can identify me even if my head's blown off, because I had this tattoo." In wartime, tattoos are always *really* popular.

■ *V: It's interesting: that connection with death or mortality again.*

■ EH: Sure. And I think those soldiers were feeling they didn't have anything to lose: *"This is it*—we're going off to the front!" Sailor Jerry told me stories about tattooing in wartime in Honolulu where there were tens of thousands of guys streaming through the streets—the tattooers were working day and night. All those recruits were getting the "sign" put on them, in the spirit of "We Who Are About To Die..." and all that.

Marines still go for that. There's a lot of corny melodramatic stuff we used to put on them besides "USMC," like: "This soldier should go to heaven—he's served his time in hell." Those were put on even *before* going there, because that was at the tail end of Vietnam.

■ *V: I can understand why guys in war had their girlfriends' names tattooed—*

■ EH: They're going away to the front thinking about the rats back home who didn't join up and are going to steal their girl! It's that *possession* idea: you get a tattoo of something because you want to possess its qualities. The most blatant and macho example of that were the property stamps: "Property of ..." which were real popular—they started with the bikers in the '60s and really boomed in the '70s. You'd bring your "Old Lady" for a Property stamp right above the crotch or on her butt—anywhere near the "works." You know: "This is mine—don't touch it!"

■ *AJ: In a sense this is all the bathos of our culture—the whole emotional range codified.*

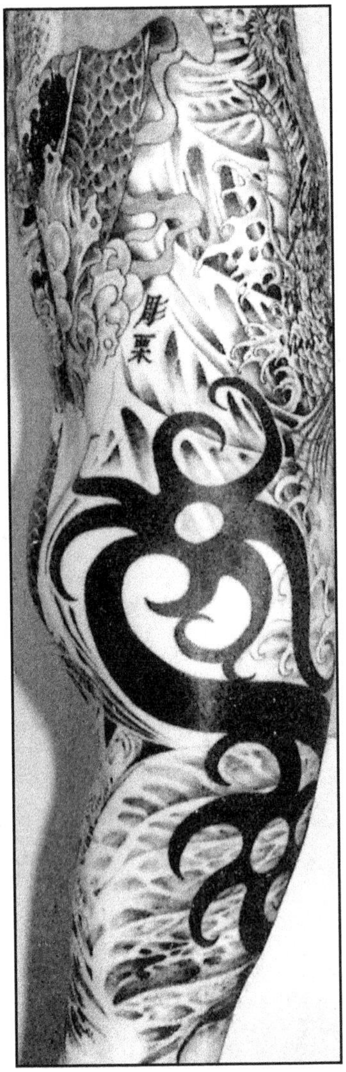

Black curvilinear design by Cliff Raven. Waves & water (rib to leg) by D.E. Hardy, 1986.

■ EH: I love that, and partly because I love the sincerity of it. Tattoos ultimately are *kind* of a corny thing; they're funny and peculiar and immediately transform a person into instant Surrealism. Here's this person with a picture or marks on his skin who's been changed into something else. It's bizarre and it's sorta fun—there's a lot of whimsy to it, plus that *play element*—you know, like kids dressing up and painting themselves up—play in a real *positive* sense. I mean: death is serious enough, so why shouldn't life be more playful? There's *plenty* of time to be serious after you're dead!

But there actually is this absolute seriousness involved with tattoo. And that's what's going to keep it from ever getting totally gentrified, because a lot of people just won't—"God, put something on myself *forever?*" Again, there's that "mortality" issue and the way you feel about the preciousness of your body. I think people who get tattooed see it as a way of making the body *more* precious: it's for yourself.

I was into tattooing when I was a little kid—that was the first art form I was drawn to. But because I wasn't old enough to learn how to do it, I went into custom car painting—we called it "crazy painting" in the '50s. It was grotesqueries; real power images from the culture, but ones that had been *torqued* around. Since then there's been an explosion of imagery. Simultaneously, among people getting tattooed, a kind of confusion has arisen, with the (almost) *glut* of images available now. At tattoo conventions you see people who are caught up in tattooing as a kind of *hip* thing to do, or as a hobby. The same people show up with more and more on them—it's like the tide's coming up higher every year...

When I got a neck tattoo I got it because it was the craziest thing I'd seen. In East L.A. these real badass *vatos* had them, with this real gangster mentality, and to have a tattoo on your neck—*wow!* After I got this in September of '78, I went to a tattoo convention and people were really shocked: "Oh God!"

At the time everyone was really into *not* having the tattoo show, even me, because I've always wanted to enforce being not predictable; I always liked the "psycho-preppie" look—you know, "He's okay and he *sorta* fits in, but something's really *wrong* with this picture." I always found that much more interesting than a predictable slot. And people were going, "*Ed Hardy* got a tattoo on his *neck*."

Some of the old-timers got really volatile; they came up and went, "What'd you do *that* for?" It was like, "We've been trying to keep this under wraps; we've been tying to enforce this..." Everybody used to think it was against the law to tattoo on the hands or face (in some places it is), but mainly it was something tattooers had enforced to keep the *heat* off themselves, and partially to save people from themselves, where kids are too young to know that they might not want a tattoo on the hand—especially in this society.

But then, each year after that, more and more people started showing up with neck tattoos. Then all hell broke loose—people started getting work *everywhere.* But sometimes it's like they're collecting *HO* trains or something: "Well I got more feet of track this year than you did." And they're not taking into account the *whole;* they're doing this because it's a fad—*the thing to do.* I find that kind of upsetting—it's like taking it 'way out the *other* end, where it's *too* popularized among a certain set of people. And they're not being selective about it; they're confused about what images to get, so they try to swallow it *all.*

There's all this imagery available now. It was only a few years ago that people in the tattoo trade got hip to the fact there were books of "source" images from other fields of art, like those great Celtic designs. In the '70s the tattoo crowd discovered Frank Frazetta—the embodiment of the macho dream of America and the rest of the Western World: giant warriors and *va-va-voom* chicks, but in a "barbaric" format, with lots of thongs (the bondage reference). And when people started getting hip to that, it was being *churned* out in the tattoo shops—all these bad versions of it in flesh.

That *kitsch* aspect of tattoo is always interesting. I'm having a lot of trouble with it now; I actually get almost physically sick at the conventions because of having to look at so much badly done imagery that I don't feel is *important* enough to get tattooed with. I almost liked it better when it was simpler—when there were fewer images to deal with. Maybe some of them were out-of-date, but this forced the tattooers to channel themselves into certain *proven* designs.

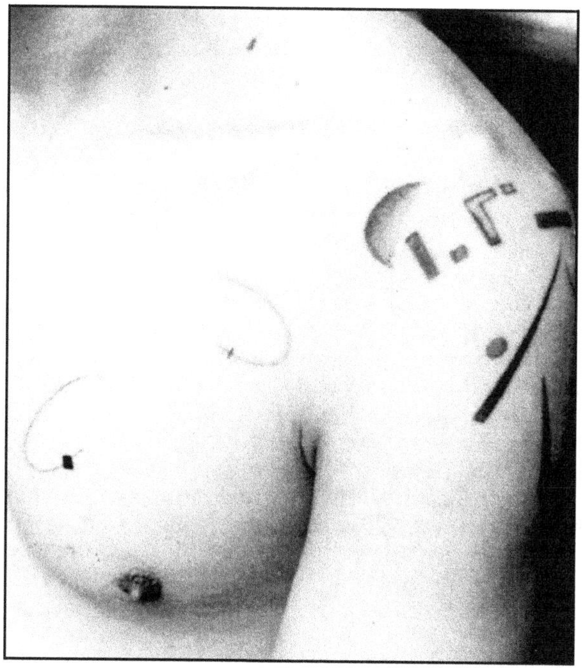

Tattoo by D.E. Hardy from a design by El Lizzitsky, 1986. Natural body moles were incorporated into the design.

It's like the media glut, like MTV, and all the records coming out—who needs more of this crap?! Some 19th century critic wrote, "Who needs more paintings?" It's almost out of hand! So I think there's going to be a swing of the pendulum, and then hopefully there'll just remain a greater awareness and possibility for people to get custom work. The tattooers will be *forced* to do things that are really individualistic. But a lot of tattooing will always be really kitsch.

■ *V: What is kitsch, exactly? When does something cease being pop art or folk art and start being kitsch?*

■ EH: I don't know. It's like: you know it when you see it, but it's hard to say what it is until you have *a* next to *b:* this is not kitsch, but this is. A lot of it has to do with the cultural reference something exists in, because when it gets *too* popular, then things can become really cloying—somehow they make it safer; they take away the real fire of it.

Things often start out as a perfectly good, powerful image that means a lot to somebody, but then it gets *pre-empted.* When it gets embraced by the culture at large, somehow they take the rough edges off and make it more palatable—*cute-ify* it and render it safe.

It's like the current glut of cat things. We all love cats, and there's something that happens in *Krazy Kat* (the epitome of cat cartoon art) that's really *out there* on the zen plane. Whereas Middle America is overrun with cuddly cats and cat stickers on car windows—the Garfield thing. And they're playing off certain qualities that *are* existent in a cat... that do make cats absolutely hypnotic and magic for people for a millenium. But they shade it over into the *pastel* realm.

■ *AJ: Krazy Kat is the real psycho-cat, the essence of the cat that can't be civilized.*

■ EH: Right, and it's *real love* and *real hate,* not that cuddly, cutesy stuff. The same thing with tattoos: I think everybody ought to cultivate positive or pro-humanitarian aspects of themselves and edge away from negative trends, but you don't do that by *ignoring* the negative side or glossing it over—you go *completely through* it so you can come out the other side, and know why the destructive parts are destructive for you. It's like not being scared of a skull design: "*I* can look at this," because then you defuse its horror potential.

Everybody used to think it was against the law to tattoo on the hands or face (in some places it is), but mainly it was something tattooers had enforced to keep the heat off themselves, and partially to save people from themselves.

I've done my share of cute tattoos on people—more, of course, when I was in a walk-in shop. These sailors would come in and (it was always the pattern) look at the wall, and go, "I think I'll get...*this* one!" like they'd just made the greatest discovery in the world, and it was just a schlock image which was—you know, helping me pay my rent and learn how to tattoo. But that used to drive me nuts! Since then I've tried to shy away from kitsch stuff, unless someone's choosing it as a kind of tongue-in-cheek *art ploy.* But unicorns and butterflies?! In the seventies the winged unicorn (the combination Pegasus-unicorn) became like *the* vapid tattoo of the decade. It was like, "God, if I have to do another one of *those*—"

*But...*when somebody chooses something like that, you're on very thin ice, because you don't want to insult their taste. Maybe to them that is a real potent image, and *meaningful.* And that has to do with *cultural* conditioning—maybe that's the only image they can think of that expresses freedom—people like tattoos with wings because it means freedom. And I used to always say, "Well, I don't really *do* those"—it's *okay* to want those, and there are *ways* to do it that isn't just tracing it off a Hallmark card (which is what usually happens). But again, it's that thing of: you have to take each case *individually.* You have to think, "Okay, this *means* something to this person, and they are *sincere* about it." And you can diplomatically suggest, "If you're trying to make yourself different with this and express something really unique, how about doing it *this* way?" But if they really want that image, then *maybe* it's okay for them!

You can't just judge, "What a dumb image!" because they might have some very ennobling reason behind it that has made them more aware of themselves. Yeah, the kitsch element definitely figures in,

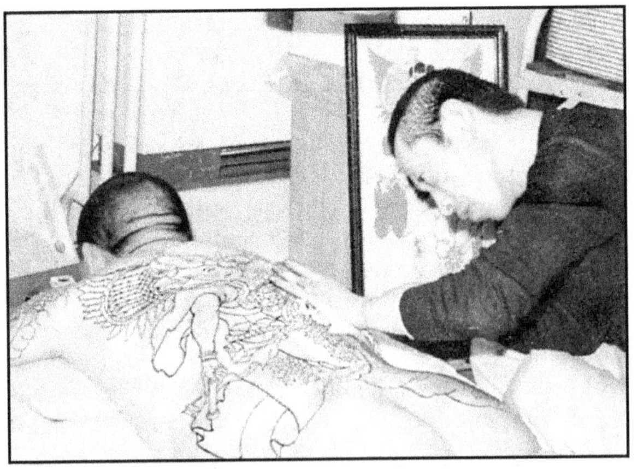

Kazuo Oguri tattooing in Japan, 1972.

and as tattooing becomes more popular to the masses, then mass taste rises—maybe ten years from now they'll get "better" tattoos. That's why they should save some space and not jump ahead! It's not like buying the latest Michael Jackson video. Because then they start coming in and going, "Can you cover this?"

■ *V: Tattoos are not this year's fashion clothes.*

■ EH: That's why I put out a flyer, "Beyond Fashion." People have to understand that there *are* elements of fashion to it, but they're signing up for the long haul. It's important for people to really think about that and basically be more conscious—everybody ought to be more conscious, anyway! And I think tattoos help you—if you let 'em. They're a great tool for that.

■ AJ: Monte Cazazza was talking about his tattoo, which seemed so simple at first, but then yielded more and more meanings. [See Monte Cazazza interview]

■ EH: That's where I think tattoos have such *prime power* for the wearer. People do like to show them off, but it's most powerful and interesting when they're meant for the person. I don't even care if people see 'em.

Proselytizing for tattoos is morally repugnant; I don't think people should push them. But I do think it would be better if the public became more aware: "Oh, that guy has tattoos, *and* there's a whole story behind them." The tattoo probably triggers *interior* reverberations that summon up events. That's the souvenir aspect of it—they get it because *this* happened; they were in a certain place at a certain time, and the world was like this...

When I eventually do a book on my work, it will not only have the picture of the tattoo, but an account of at least the higher points of what this signified, and the process we went through as two people to create it. Because the tattoos are really just a tip-of-the-iceberg; it's the only person they're connected to that's important.

I think a lot of tattoo artists are in grave error because they get caught in a lot of ego-delusion crap about their "great art," plus the control aspect. I've probably tattooed ten thousand people, and it would be cool to see 'em all lined up end-to-end sometime, but that "I am the Shaman" stance—that's completely embarrassing.

■ *AJ: Ideally tattoos should internally spring from a person.*

■ EH: Yes. That's what I had against the piercing scene, because most of the piercing people I was around were always trying to punch holes in people's nipple—just power/control shit. Although—we're all adults, right? If you suddenly realize you're being drawn in to being a partner in a routine you don't really consent to—well, you can leave.

■ *AJ: Of course, the people I know who are pierced did so out of internal motivations—they wanted it.*

■ EH: And there *are* people running around in the tattoo scene saying, "Oh, let me put one on you!" Goodtime Charlie Cartwright told me about when he first worked at the Pike in Long Beach, he had to work with these *morons* just to get to learn how to use the machines. This real slimy, struttin' little guy who was really into like hurting the customers said one night, "You know, I'm just tryin' to think what tattoo I'm going to put on you tonight, Charlie," and Charlie whirled around and went, "Are you kidding? Man, I don't even *like* you—I can barely stand being in the same room with you. Where did you get the idea I would *possibly* want you to tattoo me?" That's a typical example of that whole *branding* mentality: let me rule part of your life and make my mark on you. Of course tattooing is ready-made for that possibility; it's a natural for that SM world...

Tattoo by Kazuo Oguri, 1972.

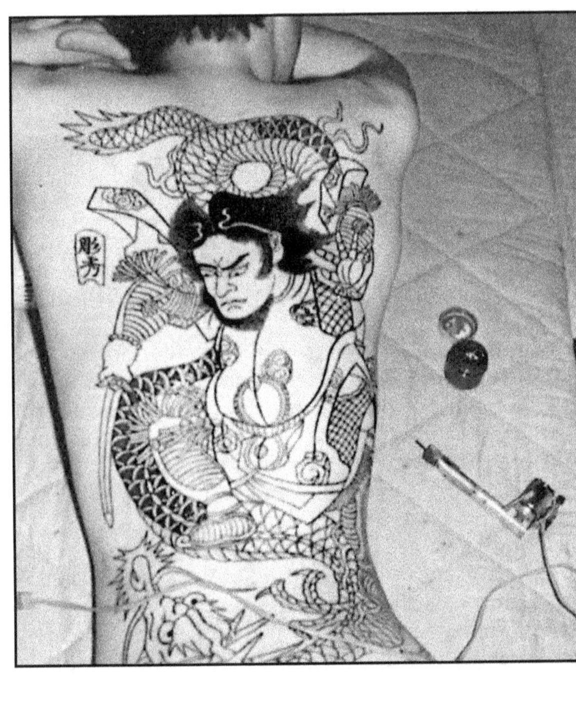

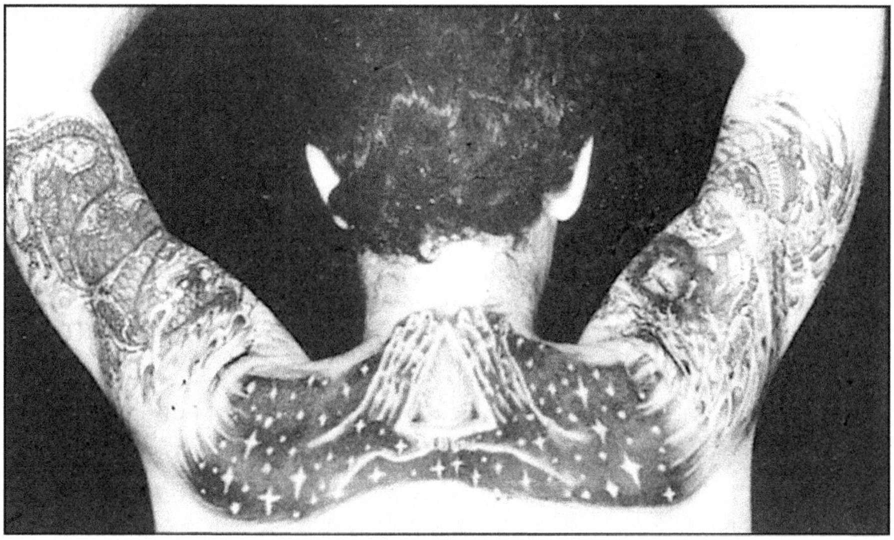

Tattoo by D.E. Hardy from a dream image by the client, 1987.

then..." The *pluses* were evident—you could get tattooed in a quiet, *controlled* environment.

Again, the tattoo is just part of something much bigger. You start out with the tattoo within the tattoo shop, and the other images on the wall, and how that reflects out to society—you have all these boxes within boxes, and it's all pieces of that puzzle. You see the person's tattoo, then see it in the context of where they got it and the kind of person who put it on, and it should all be a smoothly integrated picture—again, all for positive effect.

Again, the ideal is: people *choosing* to get tattooed out of their own volition, and feeling strong about it, not doing it 'cause every kid on the block's doing it, or because they're talked into it, or they're drunk. It should be something that people are actually aware of—not to make it stuffy, but just to *actualize its best potentials*—I guess that's what I'm after. It's not taking the fun out of it, it's making it even *more* fun. It's like, "We've really thought about this leap off the high board, and now we're going to do it." Instead of just being pushed.

■ *AJ: Of course, with you, you're not on the street. People have to* know *about you and* already *be pretty committed.*

■ EH: Yeah. One of the best things about going to Japan was: not only was I able to understand more about Asian culture and imagery, but I found the *context* of tattoo so different from in the West. I went there and worked in this studio in an apartment building; it was all word-of-mouth and it was really hard to get an appointment with this great tattooer, Oguri (Horihide, the first Japanese tattooer I worked with).

I had had these delusions of maybe being a re-born Japanese, and thought I might end up living the rest of my life there. But I realized I didn't fit in; I couldn't "be myself" in that context. But the point is: *that's* when I made my determination to run a private studio. I wanted to set a stage to magnetize people who would get big body tattoos, and create an awareness, an acceptance, interest and consciousness that could allow that. And it's only being fully realized now—more than I thought it would, but it took me *twenty years.*

Anyway, I'd been wondering if this could be done, and in Japan I saw this society where it operated that way for *everybody;* they don't have street tattoo parlors. I thought, "Hey, if people can do that there, and people are *serious* enough about it to seek that out, then..."

But to undergo this super-intense personal experience where you're going to wear it for the rest of your life, yet you have to get it with a bunch of yahoos coming in, going, "God, whaddya doin' *that* for?" or "Look at *this* shit!" or "He's *bleedin'*!" Forget it!

I've also worked in all these bad-ass street scenes. I felt tattooing was genuine folk art that could be expanded into something serious, with finely tuned intent. So I had a lot of romance about that. But after a few years, the romance goes out of seeing that guy pukin' in your doorway.

Although...that's all right if that's what you're after! With tattoos there's a lot of slumming that goes on, on all kinds of levels—psychic or whatever: "Okay, I'm going to identify myself with this renegade, dangerous group." It's kind of like a Genet shot with a lot of people. And if they like it, that's cool...

But again, that shouldn't be the only game available. Tattooing's too great a field; there are too many great possibilities. Some tattooers go, "You're up there, and you guys think you're *better* than us. But I *like* my parlor down here"—hey, that's fine, pal! And I can sit down and tattoo any kind of fuckin' environment; I can tattoo in the worst rathole on earth, and I have.

■ *V: Didn't you work on the back of a truck in Guam?*

■ EH: That was Palau. I've also worked in all these bad-ass street scenes—that was one of the things that interested me about tattooing, because at the time I was reading a lot of William Burroughs; at that stage in art school I was devouring *everything* by him. And again, I was very taken with the whole idea of *power art, rough art.* I was also interested in Dubuffet and a lot of *art brut* painters—that reflected back to my roots doing custom car painting. I felt tattooing was genuine folk art that could be expanded into something serious, with finely tuned intent. So I had a lot of romance about that: "Wow, here I am down in the honky-tonk street..." Plus, in those days I was drinkin' and I liked whoring around and all that, you know. And it *was cool,* but also, after a few years of it—!

■ *V: You were reacting against—*

■ EH: —against the middle class thing. I was raised in Orange County in a super middle class, insulated suburb, so in a way it was natural to want to rebel and be out there with the *raw deal,* with the sex and death and the fear, where you know you *feel* something—you're after that *jolt.*

*But...*after a few years, the romance goes out of seeing that guy pukin' in your doorway. It's like, "Okay, we've taken this course." That reminds me—when I opened Tattoo City in the Mission district, I'd wanted to do all-black tattooing. I had met Good Time Charlie Cartwright and Jack Rudy, and this was the first *new* form of visualization I'd encountered: real pointillist, fine line, all gray shading, with a "realist" approach to doing portraiture.

Previously, I had put out a poster advertising that style of work, and Bob Roberts had come here to work with me. But I thought, "Man, nobody's going to really *get* that work; we have to go down to where people want this"—i.e., to a Chicano neighborhood. So I opened this whole shop just to be able to learn to do that kind of work—to put myself in the stream: "They're bitin' over here," so you go over to *that* part of the fishin' hole.

I set that shop up really cool. There was no graffiti in this town, and I graffitied up the windows. People would come in and say, "You guys are from L.A." They knew we were running that kind of barrio art style. We weren't Chicano but we *liked* all that and it was part of our heritage—being Southern California kind of *bad boys,* you know.

We started doing black-style work and people liked it. Now since 1974, for four years I had been running this appointment-only studio after coming back from Japan, and people had been *thrilled* to have this environment to get tattooed in. It was 1977 when I opened Tattoo City on Mission Street, so I'd been away from the "street" for about four years, and I'd forgotten...

Here's me with my "art" consciousness, and—I used to dig the styles of the Cholos and I was in East L.A. Then you'd realize they're all full of angel dust and they've got weapons on them and you're going, "Oh, god..." It's *romanticization; slumming,* and here I was guilty of that! And the first time I got some real

Tattoos above and next page by D.E. Hardy at the Rome Tattoo Exhibition, 1985.

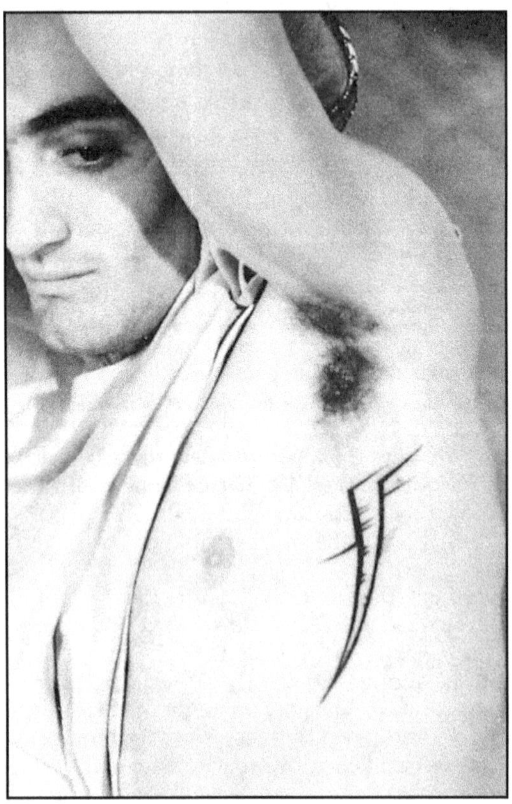

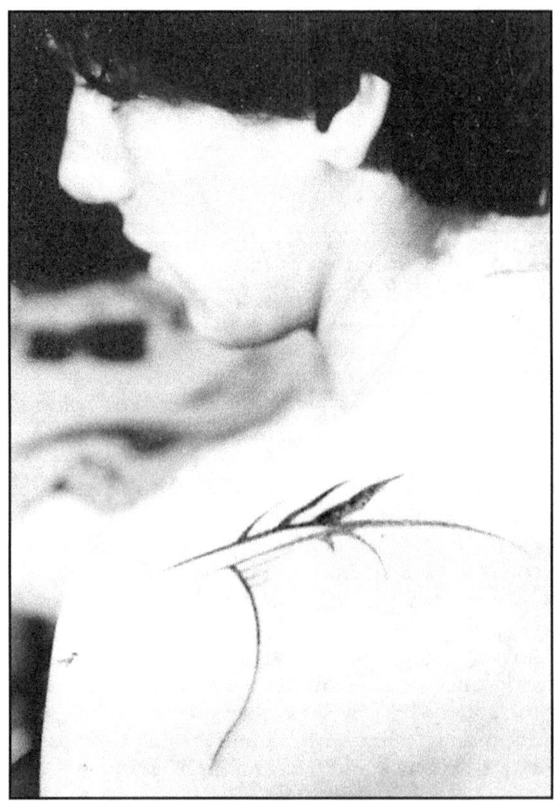

argumentative junky in there and he's going, "*Eighteen dollars* for this?" I thought, "Wait a minute—I've *seen* this movie! I shouldn't be going through this again." It's like, "I have to do *this* to learn the style?" I closed the shop down.

I realized that people who were getting my more custom creations *did* like the possibilities of this black work, so I could incorporate it anyway. Here I'd gone through this whole elaborate scenario—it's a lot of work to build a tattoo shop and open a business on the street, just so you could get some *practice,* right?

But every tattooer who's done time working in a street situation has some great stories, so I think that experience is invaluable—it's really good for your character and good for the reality of what a certain aspect of tattooing is all about. And it takes away the *preciousness* that's afflicting a lot of people in the business today. I fled the "cloying environment of the fine arts" to do tattooing, but I should have seen this coming: by giving tattooing its legitimization and status as fine art, suddenly you're getting into the same old crap!...with these same types of people coming around. I shouldn't have been surprised, but

Things often start out as a perfectly good, powerful image that means a lot to somebody, but then it gets pre-empted. When it gets embraced by the culture-at-large, somehow they take the rough edges off and make it more palatable—cute-ify it and render it safe.

I was rather chagrined to see it. A lot of people in the business who are real pragmatic—you know, products of the old school—just think it stinks to *high heaven...*

I have an ambivalent status among the tattoo community, because I do have my credentials as an old-school tattooer—I'm part of that tradition. But by doing all this chi-chi nouveau kind of work I get: "All that *perfume* shit —what are you guys doing up in those private *ateliers?*" A lot of the people really look down on this, while simultaneously being suspicious—it's like the Wild West where the Dude from back East rides into town: "What the *hell* kind of a shirt is that with frills on it?" And I like being able to swim in *all* waters—it's best to be able to get along anywhere. Again, that's what Burroughs is a past master of.

■ *V: At your recent video shoot you had Hells Angels who were real friendly to you.*

■ EH: Michael Stearns, who produced the video, had kind of a rarefied vision of what tattooing is; he had only been around my studio. I kept saying, "I have lots of different kinds of clients, and friends from all walks of life." Tattooing has that real potential for being a common denominator or a *neutral zone* that all these people can be interested in. It means something different to each one, and they're getting them for a variety of reasons, but at heart they're all kind of after the same thing. When that happens at a tattoo convention, that's the best part of it—

■ *AJ: Against all expectations, and blending the pop, spontaneous parts of the culture with the more thought-out, analytical, symbolic aspects.*

■ EH: I think it's fine that the symbolic and the analytical run rampant with us for awhile, because there's been such a dearth of it in tattoo; it's all been *gut-feeling.* And I think a lot of the old-timers who had greater aspirations became embittered and ended up hating themselves at the end of their lives, because they'd never realized tattooing's great potential. Most of them were really in love with it; they caught a glimpse that it could be *much more,* but were trapped in this time period where it was so limited...where society looked down on it so much.

My Japanese friends are going through something similar; the ones that are more forward-looking. Nakano, who's a great artist and a brilliant guy, and is young enough and modern enough to see what's going on in the world, wants to extend his work. He flips out because we get to do all these wild effects on people, whereas most of his customers want what he considers very boring work. Those beautifully controlled traditional designs they're all wearing—he looks at it like we look at hearts and anchors: "This is the *old* crap, the old days!"

Even with me, I wish I was wearing the kind of work I can do *now*—but you only get *one* skin! And that sorta makes me feel bad, because when I'm surfing in Hawaii and people see my tattoos, I always have to go, "Well this isn't really what *can* be done." But you can't always be the only guy on the block with the hippest thing happening, and besides, when things happen and people become too aware of them, it changes that very thing, and the self-consciousness comes in. It's such a fine edge to always be balancing on.

■ *AJ: You're always straddling this razor-thin edge, striving to never get dogmatized or crystallized in any form...you watch that ego, and hope for something spontaneous and soul-fulfilling. The whole process of this culture is to assimilate and spit out forms as quickly as possible.*

I fled the cloying environment of the fine arts to do tattooing, but I should have seen this coming: by giving tattooing its legitimization and status as a fine art, suddenly you're getting into the same old crap!

EH: It is, and the media is so hungry for anything colorful they can superficially showcase. That's why I started *Tattootime.* One day I was bitching about an article in the newspaper on Lyle Tuttle—it had the same predictable viewpoint, and I knew that wasn't the only stance that tattooing existed in, and Fran [my

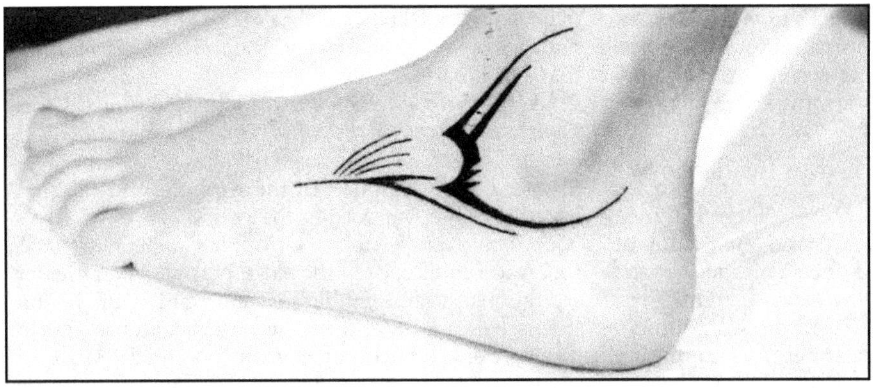

wife] said, "Listen, you're going to have to shut up about this or go public, because how are they going to know unless *you* stand up and say something?"

■ *V: It was necessary to do* Tattootime*—theory and history are very important.*

■ EH: Yes. Being in control of the message—that's what I like best about publishing. You *can* get these embarrassing, worshipful people—they mean well, but they come up with these big Bambi eyes and are quoting statements you made in the past and you have to go, "Wait a minute, pal—I just pulled that out of a hat!" I suppose people are always going to do that, because they're all looking for answers. So you're always supposed to keep 'em guessing.

If only you could somehow break 'em through to that key that allows 'em to let all passing phenomena flow through, and not stop any of it. It's that *stopping of the mind* that fucks people up, where they think, "Okay, this is *it,* period," and don't think anymore.

The media is always using us, or anything interesting, for fodder, and that's why whenever I'm on TV talking about tattooing, I like to make it not quite what they think it's going to be, and leave them going, "What did he say? Wait a minute—" Because they come on real smooth and ingratiating, inviting you to be "the Wild Man of ___," but you're not going to make any point by being predictable and obvious. It's easy to be the "hog-ridin' fool" for the media, but you can project a much more subtle kind of anarchy (or something) with an image and thoughts they don't quite know what to do with.

■ *AJ: They want you to be the square peg that fits into the square hole, because then they can toss you away.*

■ EH: Right; then they've used you up. That's the inevitable process: neutralization. They want to neutralize all this raw power and raw humanity. We're just doing what the Impressionists did in the 19th century, or what anybody did in *any* period where they're breaking out of what the Academy wants you to do: *what's acceptable,* what the *status quo* is. And some status quo art might be terrific, but again, if it's the only game in town and the only sanctioned thing, then you immediately want to look around and go, "Wait, let's do something else."

■ *AJ: Again, tattooing is never going to be that safe.*

■ EH: It's on your body, it's permanent; you have to live with it; and it hurts; and it does have that ritual aspect going through it. Although—I'm not a big *pain encourager;* I tell people, "Hey, get pills from your doctor, if you want." I'm not trumpeting that "rite of passage" thing or fetishizing that *process;* I think it's enough that people decide they're going to go through with it. Because the big hurt you face is: what will change with you and society?

My friend Betsy Berberian and I were talking about people and the way they react to tattoos. (She's got this big black tribal design that Bill Salmon put on her wrist; it's actually an echo of the one Leo put on her leg that we published in the first *Tattootime.*) She said, "When people see these, I don't fit in anywhere, and I know that, but that's okay—it's just part of the thing that you do." And she's got some of the most *personal* set of tattoos I've ever put on anyone, and some of the most sublime. It's being awfully aware that you've got the work and you *are* going to separate yourself from a whole lot of polite society—you're not going to be able to pass anymore, you're not going to just be anonymous; you're taking that stand: "Okay, I'm this, and I'm crazy enough to wear it. I got it done."

By getting that tattoo, Betsy knew that people would never look at her the same, because her work is very evident and *out there*—you really notice it. And she's not your stereotypical, hard-bitten tattoo *dame,* so there's that crazy dichotomy, which is best. I love it when people say, "They don't look like the kind of person who'd have a tattoo."

■ *AJ: Like Jane Handel.*

■ EH: She's got the most completely acclimated look; she's got the most total look of anybody. 'Cause she's very considerate about the whole way she dresses, and her jewelry and everything, and the tattoos fit that exactly. I did this necklace on her the other day that's the most elegant tattoo I've ever done. It's very simple, but somehow the forms really came out.

■ *V: I liked what Richard Tyler said about asking people to record their dreams; trying to get them to delve into their subconscious and background before deciding on a tattoo.*

■ EH: That is really good. You can do that to an extent. The greatest practitioner of that, and the one we don't have around to interview, is Jamie Summers, because that was her whole approach: she was a psychic, and was working with the psychic Helen Palmer in Berkeley.

However...some people *need* a Tweety Bird—that's *right* for them—Tweety Bird's part of their reflection on the world, a little facet of their diamond personality and of their mythology! So whatever's right! [laughs] The work that I do on someone is based on my readout, which is more or less inaccurate, more or less pretentious [!]: the way they dress, the language they use, and personal history: "Where are you from? What's your dad do?" Plus the way they react to other images or photos: I *always* make people look at pictures of my work and tell me about kinds of art they like or kinds of *whatever* they like—if they like the color yellow—whatever.

It hurts and it does have that ritual aspect going through it . . . I'm not a big pain encourager; I tell people, "Hey, get pills from your doctor, if you want." I'm not trumpeting that "rite of passage" thing or fetishizing that process.

And when I have a *chance,* I try to get *more.* Some people have brought back very fruitful ideas, by going out and researching things and matching them to their interior dream states, etc. I think that kind of work is *very* important, and I think it's part of the potential equipage of any tattooer. But again, there are different levels of people and different levels of tattooers. There aren't too many people working that way. Unfortunately, some that are, have gotten so far off the yo-yo being the great prognosticator and putting on the ju-ju robes, that they've failed to develop basic *technique.* And this is an *incredibly* difficult craft; some people are working *way* over their heads. I really believe there is a lot about the *touch;* you can pontificate about the "hand of the artist," but with this it's genuine and palpable.

■ *AJ: And in a sense your energy and your being is going into their bloodstream.*

■ EH: Yes—you're laying your hands on them, running over those acupuncture points, lighting up that nervous system. Zeke Owen said it best—he's one of the great hidden mystics of tattooing, who tattoos Marines back in North Carolina in this godawful little spit section of town that's go-go bars and tattoo parlors. But that's part of his deal that he operates in that zone; he's like a Taoist madman. He said to me on the phone, "When I put on those tattoos, I'm in that little molecule of ink looking out at the world into the eye of everybody who looks at that tattoo...all those thousands of people. So when they look at the bulldog on that Marine's arm, they're getting something *beyond* that whole expression I put into that." Zeke loves working in that absolute structure where you have this bulldog head design you've done literally thousands of times, but the real zen is to impart a unique spirit of life in a flash of the particular moment to that universal form.

I read in *Sacred Calligraphy of the East* that someone scrutinized a number of famous examples of calligraphy under an electron microscope, comparing an original painting to an imitation. It turned out that while the brush strokes *appeared* similar, the actual molecule of ink in the originals done by these great masters 500 years ago vibrated with a lot more energy and spirit.

So there is something about the hand of the artist in the tattoo, that subtly reflects some kind of astral plane.

■ *AJ: The wrong tattoo can be a violation, if somebody just slaps it on a person.*

■ EH: But then again, that's part of—is there a new word for "karma"? As a tattooer, you always have to monitor yourself: "How much of this do I take responsibility for? How much ethical responsibility do I have here? How much do I have to save the person from themselves?" Zeke got really mad at me once in San Diego because I wouldn't do a design on someone—he stormed out, saying, "Hey man, this isn't kindergarten, this isn't like play school, this is a *tattoo shop.*" Because there were certain things that I just wouldn't do, and there are certain things that I *still* won't do; I'll say, "Okay, if you want to get that, it's cool, but

Multi-colored tattoo by D.E. Hardy, 1976.

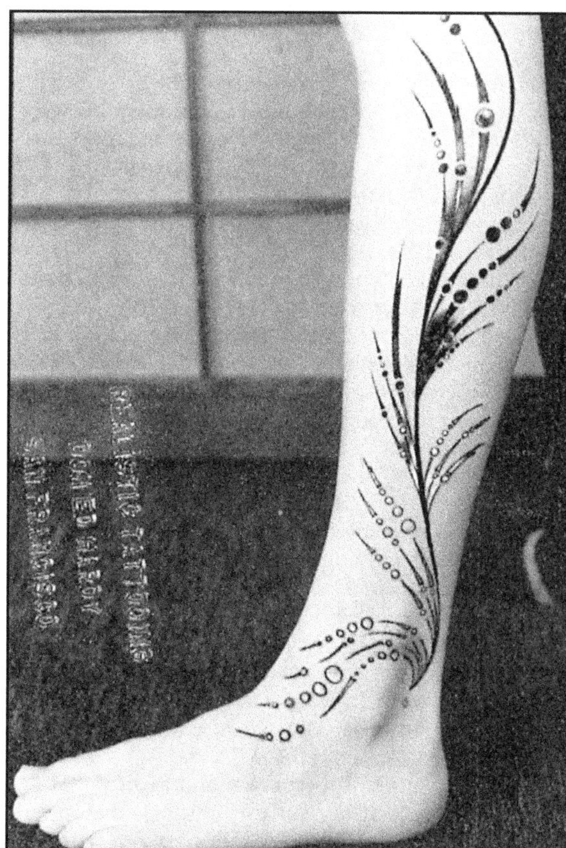

I'm not putting it on you." And sometimes I've just overtly told people: "You *shouldn't get it;* you don't realize you're going to wear this the rest of your life, and it's just going to cause bad feelings to yourself about yourself. It's going to worsen your condition."

■ *V: "Born to Lose."*

■ EH: Yes, all that fuckin' negativity and that whole realm of tattooing that's like self-mutilation. There are people who get into "I'm mad at myself," like this one nut in San Diego who would come in and just want weird marks put on him.

■ *AJ: What else did Zeke say?*

■ EH: He said that it's not always up to us to make a judgment as a tattooer. Again, the difficult part is *reading* people and deciding, "Well, this is okay." Like that person who wanted the '40s pin-up nurse next to his Tibetan Tantric designs—a lot of high-art tattooers are going to see that and just *shit,* which I love. Because they don't understand the implications and the acceptance of a person's history.

We talked earlier about how a lot of tattoos reveal the unexpected: "You see this tattoo and it's *this,* but here's what it really *meant.*" And then you'll look at it differently—like a trick photo where, "Oh yeah, there *is* a clown in the tree." It's like—once you know it, then you never see it the same way.

■ *V: A person's story can totally undercut what might appear to be a lousy tattoo, because it upends the cliched aesthetic exalting form itself.*

■ EH: And you know what it's ultimately for—my feeling is that all these people, especially some who were acting in the heat of the moment, whether they were drunk, or whatever—hey, they're tapping into something that's really important to them, that society has kept repressed. All of a sudden they're in the tattoo shop and they go [bellows], "I'M GONNA GET *THAT* ONE!" and then the rest of their life they marry someone who's a lot like their mother and end up back in Ohio, and they're made to feel servile and fucking *guilty* about that tattoo, and they *shouldn't*—they should, like, *re-connect,* because that was the *one moment* in their life when they burst through into the realm of freedom.

I've seen sailors from Iowa or wherever come in, and the great thing about tattooing these guys is, you can just tell they're lighting up to the possibilities of the world and to being themselves in a real expressive, *dramatic* way—bringing out the *art* part of themselves: "Man, this is part of who I am, not just Sam Snerd, the little guy who can't see well, who's going to go back to the assembly line in Toledo." And that's really cool—it's that empowerment aspect, and maybe those people eventually learn that it's *okay* to have that, and that their tattoo can mean *fond* associations.

Michael Malone and I have always loved going up to old guys in the supermarket and asking, "Wow! Some Tattoo!" and they're usually so shocked at someone giving a *good* reaction to an old Betty Boop design or something. We like to draw them out to make 'em feel more positive about themselves. That's important.

So... sometimes when people just come in and get something slapped on, it's really good—just right for the moment. And it's important for the people to be able to live up to that and stand behind it, and not punk out in later life: "Oh yeah, I shouldn't have done that." Once they have it they oughta just say, "Yeah, great, that's how I got one." Again, it's a record of that event; it's record of that event; it's a record of the night we were on the *Liberty* at Singapore, or whatever.

I do object to a situation where the girlfriend picks out the tattoo—I've thrown *more* people out of the workroom! You let people in and you get that "Significant Other" starting to give their opinions—talk about *control!* You want to get the person *only;* you want to get a very clear reading where they're just themselves; you want to be really neutral and non-threatening.

■ *AJ: It's hard enough to have your own individuality, and it's bad enough that society's always there, but to also have somebody else—*

■ EH: The girlfriend of the week, or whatever—it's like, *give me a break!* I was trying to figure out what it is that makes it *right* about those nights where people do go in and get a tattoo banged on—I mean, that's part of the person's destiny too. As Zeke used to say, "Everybody gets the tattoo they deserve." But that's a little brutal—I guess it holds up if you take the *big view* that somewhere down the line it all links up, but I know so many people who were not given the options—they just didn't have enough information.

Also, people have to choose the tattooer that's right for them. Sometimes when I'm in North Beach I see all these white trash low-gene-pool guys from god knows where that come in to raise hell on Broadway, and I think, "God, I wouldn't want to have to deal with *them* in a tattoo shop." And a lot of those guys *will* get tattooed. But that's just like part of their *destiny,* and the tattooer can only be responsible to a certain extent for elevating the incoming crowds, or whatever.

I love it when people say, "They don't look like the kind of person who'd have a tattoo."

■ *AJ: I like that dualism between "fine art" and "the street," because you don't want to dwell in either extreme.*

■ EH: I want it *all;* the best of all things—that's where freedom really is, otherwise you're locked in. And as Americans we deserve it! [laughs] Because we shouldn't have to be compartmentalize, and in this day and age with all the information we have—knowing everything we do about all the people and styles and preferences in the world, we ought to be able to live a lot of different lives. And I think it's all leading up to something exciting; I wish I knew if it were like this at the end of every other century—

■ *V: Or the end of every other civilization—*

■ EH: Right! [laughs] I get that sense of like, *Minutes To Go!* That's it, it's that freedom, and realizing we're poised on the edge of everything...

BIOGRAPHY

■ EH: I grew up in Corona del Mar, Southern California and got interested in tattooing in the '50s. My best friend's father had a lot of tattoos from his navy career in WWII. I think that about the end of '55 I started drawing; I always had an art interest. Me and my friends started doing tattoos on ourselves, and then drawing them on neighborhood kids—we got a little toy tattoo shop together and started making up sheets of designs. I was living 25 miles south of Long Beach, which had the "Pike" (the Coney Island of the West Coast), so there were a lot of tattoo shops nearby.

We used to ride up to the Pike on the Greyhound bus to check those out, and a tattooer, Bert Grimm, ultimately let us hang out there. I went up there a lot; I'd do little sketches off his flash. I drew a lot of designs—I had about 100 sheets of designs. I also did a lot of tattoos on kids with colored pencils. That was kind of like the basic, firm grounding at the beginning. I looked at anything I could get my hands on about tattooing, and wrote away for all the tattoo suppliers' catalogs advertised in *Popular Mechanics*, etc. At that time there wasn't much literature out; I had a British book that was published around that time in the early fifties. That and the book by George Burchett, *Memoirs of a Tattooist*, were all that was in print.

But after about three years I lost interest. I was too young to learn how to tattoo; nobody would give me an apprenticeship. I got tired of doing it as a little kid's kind of thing, so when I was 13 I switched my interest to custom car painting. I'd still go to the beach and check out all the tattoos; the town I grew up in was like a resort town in the summer so a lot of people flooded down there. There was a nice beach with a big parking lot and concession stands, so I could see a pretty good range of people, including a lot of visitors from all over—you could see a lot of tattoos in the summer. And in the parking lot were all these great cars with custom paint jobs. I got real revved up on the idea of car painting. And I started painting shirts—that's when Big Daddy Ed Roth was just getting his start doing what we used to call crazy paintings: monster images and other wild designs on sweatshirts and T-shirts.

So I kind of gravitated into another kind of extreme imagery. I was hung up on that for a while, then I got into fine arts and went to art school. During art school I rediscovered tattooing. When I was getting out of high school I had done a few paintings with tattoo themes—pop art paintings of arms with tattoos on them, etc. I had done a few collages using my old tattoo flash that I'd had from the fifties. So I'd never completely dropped my tattoo interest; it was sort of sub-surface. But in art school at the San Francisco Art Institute, I did a lecture for a class in 1966 and really thought I should re-examine it—check the tattoo shops and see what was going on. At this point I realized that tattoo was this great undocumented American folk art.

After visiting a number of local tattoo shops I saw that these guys didn't have much finesse on the art end; they had this raw power but no real refinement. At the same time I met Phil Sparrow in Oakland and he showed me a book on Japanese tattooing that had just come out, by Donald Richie. This was the first book published in English on that subject, and I was astounded because I liked Japanese artwork anyway—the whole aesthetic was so different from American art. I began thinking of tattoo as a more refined art form. And Sparrow, the first person I met in tattooing who had an academic background, was a big influence, and he ultimately led me (or I led myself, via his example) into tattooing. I saw that you could be a tattooer and still have an intellectual life; that tattooing could be more than honky-tonk cowboy/sailor stuff.

So I decided to get into tattooing while finishing art school. I did some tattoos on my back porch; I tattooed friends from the Art Institute. I got my undergraduate degree in Printmaking. I also got married to my first wife.

Then my father-in-law bankrolled me, and I opened my first shop, Dragon Tattoo in Vancouver, B.C. I wanted to get out of the Bay Area, travel and see something new and do all my practice work elsewhere. I was there less than a year, then went to Seattle and worked with Zeke Owen for a few months. Then I gravitated down to Southern California and tattooed in San Diego for old Doc Webb. I got to do a lot of repetitive imagery on sailors, which is just what I needed to get the technical end down. After two years at Doc's I was able to get a bankroll together again and open my own shop in San Diego, and ran that for two years.

Zeke Owen said it best. "When I put on those tattoos, I'm in that little molecule of ink looking out at the world into the eye of everybody who looks at that tattoo. So when they look at the bulldog on that Marine's arm, they're getting something beyond. . ."

It was during that period that I started corresponding with Sailor Jerry in Honolulu. He'd always been like the big guru, and I'd wanted to connect with him. After several months of corresponding he agreed to let come over there and spend a week watching him work. I went over there in '69 and we hit it off really well. He became my real guiding light; he was the only one at the time who was doing anything different. He was the best example.

I corresponded with Sailor Jerry on a frequent basis. We exchanged photos and he really shaped my whole aesthetic in tattooing, as far as giving me a tradition and outlook and technical expertise and advice. I tried to marry that with my art school sensibility. I kept studying Japanese art and practicing the Japanese style of tattooing which to me was like the pinnacle; it seemed to be the only viable high-culture form of tattooing in the world at the time. And through Jerry's introduction I began corresponding with a Japanese tattoo artist.

In 1972 this artist, Horihide (Oguri) invited me for a visit, so I closed my shop in San Diego in '73 and moved to Japan with my second wife, Fran, to work in his studio. For 6 months I lived over there working in that traditional environment and realized Japan wasn't the big Mecca—that I wasn't going to just fit in there. I learned a lot about tattooing and about myself, too; I'd had fantasies about being reincarnated Japanese, and discovered that's exactly what they were—fantasies. When I left Japan I felt I was ready to come to San Francisco and open an appointment-only place. In Japan tattooing is very underground; the only way you can get tattooed is by appointment and through an introduction.

So I came back to America and worked in San Diego for a few months to save up some money. Then I came to San Francisco in '74 and opened *Realistic,* the first by-appointment-only tattoo studio in America. It took about a year to get that rolling. I worked by myself from '74 until the beginning of '77, and then met Bob Roberts. I got along really well with him, and felt he was somebody who could handle the level of work I was trying to create here. So we decided to open a shop in the Mission District, Tattoo City.

At this point single-needle, all black work was a very new thing. I had met Jack Rudy and and Goodtime Charlie Cartwright at the first big tattoo convention which was in Reno, January '77. Those guys were doing the first really new work outside the Japanese tradition; they didn't care at all about the Oriental stuff, they were doing this whole style that was based on Chicano art, the jailhouse milieu, and super-realist portraiture and fantasy. Not only the imagery but the whole look of it was very unique. They were doing this monochromatic design; single-needle and stipple work which was all a big change in the tattoo world. Those guys really pioneered that.

Bob Roberts and I opened a shop in the Mission District so we could be closer to people whom we thought would go for that kind of imagery. We brought in a whole series of people to help run the shop: Jamie "La Palma" Summers, even Chuck Eldridge apprenticed with us, too. I had both shops going then.

Then Charlie went through this big religious apocalyptic vision and decided to quit tattooing. I bought his shop in L.A. and had Jack Rudy continue to run it; I wanted to keep the place in business so the style could keep going and developing. But then all kinds of crazy things happened. We had the building bought out from under us by a rival tattooer, so we moved down the street and opened Tattooland where Jack and Freddy Negrete worked. I was bouncing back and forth to L.A. every month, just keeping an eye on things and tattooing there a little bit until finally I sold that property.

In the middle of all that, Bob went off on his own to New York; he had been playing in a band and doing a lot of other things. Jamie went off on her own and developed her whole style, and by 1980 I was back by myself at Realistic—which I really liked; I realized it was nice just to have the place for myself. The next big thing that came along was the Tattoo Expo in '82, and starting *Tattootime.*

This tattoo supplier from back East, Ernie Carafa, knew I was trying to write a book and was looking for a publisher, and he suggested doing a magazine—he funded the first issue of *Tattootime.* Leo Zulueta and I got that together in time to do the Tattoo Expo, which we did in Long Beach on the Queen Mary in '82—that was the first privately funded convention. There'd been other conventions over the years sponsored by Tattoo Clubs, but we tried to do something that was more informational. Instead of just having a bar set up for everybody to get together and get stupid, we had lectures, films, slide shows and videos. People were tattooing and socializing and all that, too, but a whole lot more happened. Some people came over from Japan, and this became a much more international, inspirational kind of event—a lot of people said that. And it got a bigger draw than any previous event; we had about a thousand people there.

■ *V: Who organized that?*

■ EH: Ernie and I and Ed Nolte [T-shirt printer]. I pretty much did the software—got all the people, concepts and lectures together. That event actually changed the tone of all subsequent tattoo conventions. When the National Tattoo Club had their next convention, they had some slide shows. It just took people seeing that, "Oh yeah, we should have more information." There had always been sort of a sense of community, but more like everybody down at the neighborhood bar. Our Expo got people thinking a little more about what they were doing; it gave them a certain pride and maybe a certain direction they hadn't had before.

For one thing, the Expo presented a lot of the new work. There was Leo's whole consciousness—the theme of the first *Tattootime* had been the upsurge of "New Tribalism." I had finished Ron's legs which we used on the cover, and he was there in person and people got exposed to a whole new look. Also, people got a really good look at Japanese work, because I presented a ton of Japanese photos.

One thing that I like about the Asian tradition: you don't give a shit about that notion of "originality," because the point is to copy stuff. There's something great about surrendering part of your ego to a "greater" tradition or stream of expression.

I had sent letters to all the Japanese tattooers I knew (which were 3 or 4), and Oguri was supposed to come and be a guest tattooer, but at the last minute things went wrong with his life and he just disappeared. But thankfully Shimada (publisher of the Japan edition of *Tattootime* and other works on tattoo) came over with all these big photos and a display of Horiyoshi's work. He brought a guy with him who was wearing a big Horiyoshi backpiece, and that was cool—you had more of an international mix.

In '83 Fran and I went back to Japan several times; I worked and studied with Horiyoshi, and that kind of made a big turnaround in my tattoo sensibility. Also, I had started going to England in '79 and tattooing over there; I made trips there in '79, '80, '81 and again in '83.

So we kept doing *Tattootime,* and then in 1983 I met this Italian journalist/producer and his wife who was in television. They wanted to put on a big tattoo expo in Rome and get the government to fund it, which I thought was a big pipe dream, but I said, "Yeah, I'll go along with that. Once you get your money and some concrete plans, let me know." They got back to me in '84—they actually had convinced the Cultural Arts Council of the city of Rome to do this, so late '84 was spent putting all that together. I tried to assemble a team of people from all over the world to represent different styles of tattooing from all these different cultures.

So in March '85 the Ass & the Zebra Show took place for a month. That was probably the biggest public display of tattooing done in a cultural context. About 20,000 people saw it, and we got coverage in virtually every newspaper, magazine, TV, radio station all over Europe and the Middle East. That was pretty neat.

Right after that, Bill Salmon came to work with me at Realistic. Greg Irons had come in and worked about a month and then took off for Asia to get some traveling out of his system before he really settled in here, but he got killed in Bangkok. He and Bill were going to run Realistic, and that's when I got my condo on O'Farrell street to work out of. After Greg died it was pretty much just Bill at the shop. Dan Thome came back into town and worked there; Filip Leu worked there for awhile, and now it's back to just being Bill there.

The last few years I've been thinking about my own work and analyzing my past: the kinds of art that I like in tattooing and the art I was interested in before I started tattooing. I've been trying to withdraw from the public flurry of doing shows—they're great in some ways, but take so much energy that I've felt sort of starved for the time to think about and interiorize my own work more.

The big move that we made to Hawaii about 15 months ago has allowed me to be a little more contemplative about what I'm doing. Basically I'm not run so ragged with the business end. I spend a quarter of my time in San Francisco—just tattoo flat out while I'm here for ten days; then the rest of the time I spend designing the work, thinking about it, and working on more publications. I'm going to do more *Tattootimes* and I've just done a book of dragon flash, which is a way to utilize some of the thousands of images I've collected and invented over the years—get them out and disperse them as material for people to use as designs in their tattoo shops. I never sold flash before, so this is kind of new. So I want to do publications and continue public awareness activities, but also fine-tune my work, too.

Tattoos on Alex Harmon (herself a tattoo artist): Leopard work by Juli Beasley. Skull by D.E. Hardy, 1987.

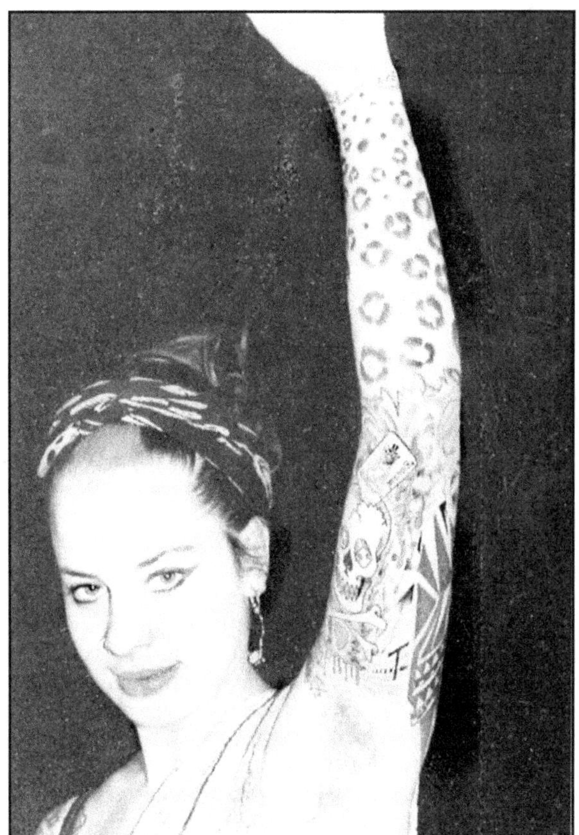

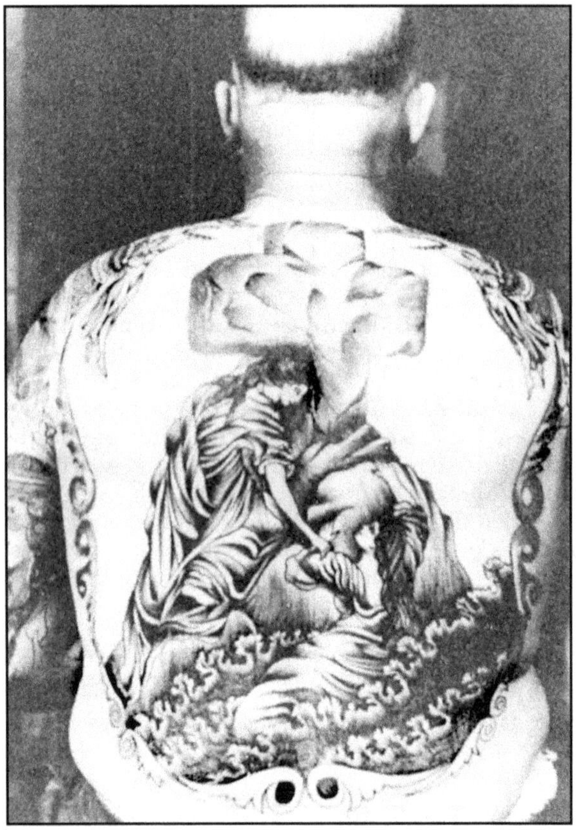

Rock of Ages. American artist, probably Percy Waters 1920's-1930's.

■ *AJ: What kind of work do you want to do now?*

■ EH: The designs I prefer now seem to represent a return to raw primary images. I really liked the Lucky Skull I put on this woman Alex's arm, with a playing card stuck on top and dice for eyes—it's like a take on old Americana tattooing. It's surrounded with shock waves. When I did Betsy's backpiece with the flying colors, I'd just seen this show of Kandinsky's early works. I've been getting into more abstract tattooing of just color fields—work that's still bold but isn't specifically recognizable imagery. I've been taking images and then breaking them up and diffusing them...getting a little Cubist.

When I put that skull on Alex's arm, there were already roses there, so I added some rose petals breaking away and just turning into pure form. There was also some tribal work and I continued lines off that but had it shatter and break apart. Basically I've been going back to my roots and mixing up all those different elements. I've always tried to be versatile, and I know how to do a lot of different styles, so I'm trying to pull those different tricks together and see how it all fits. And having the assertiveness to say to a person, "Let's do it this way"—being more adventuresome, and not taking exactly what was in their mind. I've always tried to do a pictorial representation of what someone was after, but more of a *twist* on it—try to suggest ways an idea could go more toward pure form. This relates to all that tribal work which got popular via Leo, where we were working with pure form that had no content, and wedding that to a contemporary sensibility...

I mean, I really like content. I've always liked pictures with a story. I've always liked symbolic art. I'd like to keep that, but take it more into the realm of pure form, so you'd have both. Yet a tattoo is a collaboration that's dependent—it can't work unless it's a product of both the person and myself—my work is catalyzed by the person being there, and the combination of both of us creates the tattoo. So I'm always very loath to say, "Well, *I'll* do this," and make that decision solely myself.

That's what I'm struggling with now: doing art for fun on my *own:* absolutely non-tattoo related work. I started doing acrylics last year that were out of the top of my head and had nothing to do with tattooing. It's like: I need to do that *about-face;* I need to get back and rediscover what it's like to just do work for yourself, out of absolute selfishness...in the way that you create art that isn't so much for public view. For twenty years I've been tuning myself to respond to somebody else and cater to their needs, and now I want to find out what it's like to just explore what *I* want to do.

Conversely I'm finding that I keep wanting to draw this imagery that's kind of tattoo imagery, but then I think, "Oh no, that's making it a tattoo!" I started working on watercolors that are like tattoo imagery; specifically, this Rock of Ages theme I was nuts about when I was a kid, that has *monolithic magnetism* to me. There's a book called *Megalithomania* about giant magic stones and monuments traced throughout history—it's a fantastic book.

To me, the Rock of Ages always was this mysterious thing. It was one of the tattoo designs I really gravitated toward when I hung out at Bert Grimm's shop in the '50s, and, as we wrote up in *Tattootime #1*, it was one of the great totems of American tattooing. More than just being this Christian icon, it drew on all those Druidic, pagan associations—this strange cross, this great primary form cut out in the middle of the sea. So I want to do some paintings that deal with this theme, just to remind myself, "Well, it's okay to paint this, and not have to think of it as tattooing." It's just art for myself.

Colored Pencil tattoo by D.E. Hardy, Corona del Mar studio, 1956.

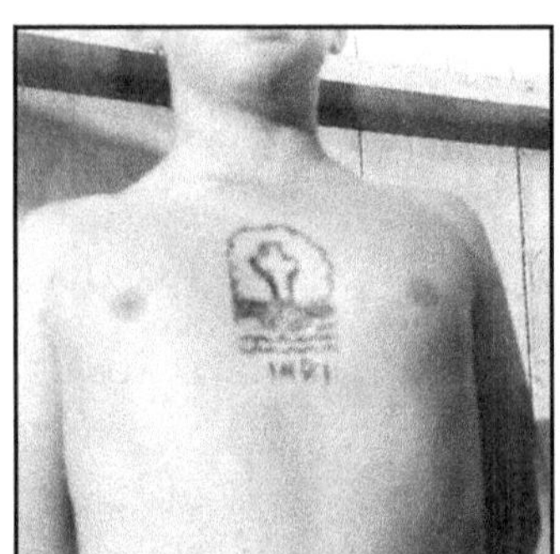

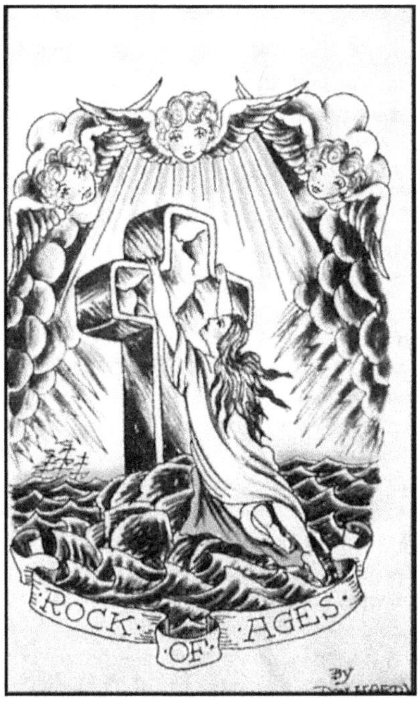

Rock of Ages by D.E. Hardy, 1988.

■ *AJ: This brings up a whole issue. Painting, for its own sake, just confined on a square of canvas, has largely eluded contemporary needs. Very few paintings being produced now are relevant. There are classics by artists such as Bosch or Gustave Moreau or the Surrealists that you go back to all the time, but I can't imagine any contemporary painters surviving as well. I think forms like tattooing or cartooning have an unpretentiousness far more suitable to express current mythology as it is emerging today.*

■ EH: Because "art" has gotten so commodified, so Sotheby-ized. It's so incestuous.

■ *AJ: The history of art has come full circle. Everything has been done, to the point where it's all self-referential—painting for painting's sake—or concerned with form.*

■ *V: Yes, being obsessed with form is like being obsessed with a corpse whose spirit has long since fled. Mistaking the corpse for the person.*

■ EH: And I got caught up in—well, I shouldn't complain about being too busy, but I got to the point where I'd be so busy just drawing images for people that I downplayed developing extreme obsessions that were solely my own. And hey—images go through my head at the rate of a million a day; the stations are always on. But I didn't have the time or energy to draw all the ideas that come. Now I've got a bit more time.

And the tattoo isn't just the tattoo itself, it's also the studio and the people and this whole enormous interconnected context. And the tattoo field was (and still is) so exciting because of being this absolutely untapped medium. I mean, it was like: "Let's create this whole set-up, and notify all those people out in the world about what we're doing." And we did *Tattootime* and it went all over the world. Now you're creating this enormous performance (in the best sense), and it's fantastic and it's dealing with real primary roots—roots that *mean* something to people, that require a commitment from someone.

As far as "art" goes, I'm trying to suss out all that in my head as to the "why." I know I like tattooing because it had a purpose, because I'm a real plodding kind of pragmatic guy. I like having that purpose. And sometimes I feel kind of lost now, sitting down in front of paper and thinking, "Well, I could draw *anything*, but what should I do?" What I should do is give myself a reason to do this. And that reason is: "I want to reflect, and teach things to myself *about* myself, and lead on from there."

The greatest art from the past—*someone* had to be passionate about it. It had to well up from some deep inner reservoirs of thought and feeling, whereas most of the "art" today is so much icing and bullshit. I read a review of this post-Impressionist show by Kenneth Baker. He said that the late 19th century, when these painters were joining groups and putting out manifestoes, was the last time in the world where people really believed that pictures could *change* people and the course of history. Subsequently the whole electronic global media came in, photography came in, and everything changed. The capability of art to move people and to be relevant—have that kind of shock connection—was diffused into other fields or media.

■ *AJ: Only forty years ago when the Surrealists put on a show, it actually created controversy. Now there's no such thing as a controversy in an art gallery, except maybe about how much a Van Gogh fetched at an auction.*

■ EH: Did you see that Julian Schnabel show? What a load of shit! I went to see that just to make myself mad, you know!

■ *AJ: Back to tattooing: not only is it an art form that's relevant, that still has power and shock, but it also is like a performance art form in the sense of having a whole uncertain and kind of "deep" interaction between the conception, the people involved, the actual art process, and subsequent reactions that art will provoke. Whereas I think painting does not have that power.*

■ EH: For art I think the criteria is that it has to be done out of some absolutely profound and desperate urge. Who knows why people do any of this; maybe they're cursed with some ambition, but the art should be the meaning of their lives; they should not be having an eye toward being the new Julian Schnabel.

As far as originality goes, maybe it's all been done, but that kind of thought creates a kind of impotence and fear because you start thinking, "I can't make one line that hasn't been already drawn!" That's one thing that I liked about the Asian tradition: you don't give a shit about that notion of "originality," because the point is to *copy* stuff, right? And in doing that you give yourself up to a sort of *lineage*. So that's kind of what

I liked about traditional tattooing: "Wow, I'll just do these eagles, and Jerry says to shade 'em this way and do the wings that way, and I see why, so I'll do it that way." There's something great about surrendering part of your ego to a "greater" tradition or stream of expression. I'm not saying that's for everybody.

So I just want to do these paintings to solve questions for myself that I think of. Because sometimes in the middle of a tattoo I'll think, "Wow, I could do this effect on paper and not have to go through the considerably more complicated process of finding somebody to get it." A lot of the game is over by the time you've found the person to get the tattoo. And like I said, the tattoo itself is the finalization for both people of a certain process that's been in progress.

I do think that people are going to have to get back to painting or drawing or whatever for *themselves,* and stay away from that whole evil, that whole snare, that whole serpents' nest of the commercial gallery world, with its critical machinery and all the art magazines, because anything creative is being overexposed to death, fast. Most of these painters are only doing it for the few hundred people who go to galleries, and the smaller number who have big bucks and go, "Oh yes, *this* is important, I should buy it." God knows what they're fulfilling when they buy this shit—I mean they're all *gaming* each other.

■ *AJ: I can't recall seeing anything on a canvas or in an art show that has moved me to a new way of thinking. Yet for some reason I find tattoos exciting; a painting that I might find interesting somehow takes on excitement and power when it's on skin. I react and feel something, and I'm not sure why.*

■ EH: Arnold Rubin said tattooing had this incredible power—that it was the only art form in the world today that could really shock. He said, "Well, what else really sets people on their ear? This does it in a way nothing else could. Maybe it's the fact that the people committed themselves; that they went ahead and got that tattoo." That just unhinges people, it strikes them in a real central zone or at the core of their being. Because they're members of society, and the tattoo sets into play all those dominos of what society expects, and what's proper and acceptable and all that...

■ *AJ: The impact is: the tattoo becomes more than the image. And in today's context—well, we live in the age of image overload where we process thousands of photos a month, not to mention TV images. Because of video and film which simulate more of the dream state, our language is being reshaped; it's hard to figure out exactly how, but it's happening, and it may well mean a drastic deterioration of written language and vocabulary, so that nuances of meaning disappear with fine analysis. Thirty years ago you had Walter Benjamin writing about a whole new way of conceptualizing art in the age of mass reproduction brought about by photographic replication. And when a painting is reproduced as a tattoo, it becomes really different—there's a whole new level of what images are, because they're on skin. A new level of animal impact is brought into play.*

To me, the Rock of Ages was this mysterious thing. It was one of the tattoo designs I really gravitated toward, one of the great totems of American tattooing. More than just being this Christian icon, it drew on all those Druidic, pagan associations-this strange cross, this great primary form out in the middle of the sea.

■ EH: To function again, art has to really mean *that much* to the person who painted it—then maybe it connect again. When I got out of high school I was really big on art with a social consciousness, and I think that still has stuck with me somewhat. What I liked about Asian art was: I felt it was working toward some betterment of humanity—but not in a WPA-placard-carrying way. And what I like about tattooing is similar: I can do that one-on-one, trying to do tattoos that are positive and that reinforce something good about the person. Basically all the art I like takes people out to a new plane of thinking, and so betters them.

But with tattooing, there's another aspect that can be a Frankenstein. Sometimes I wonder, "Just what have I spawned by publishing *Tattootime?*" Because you go to the conventions and now there's people jumping on the bandwagon, and there's beginning to be a fair amount of posturing—the same type that goes on in the fine arts world, and there's a lot of just *attitude* rather than conviction. You wonder, "Why are these people getting these tattoos? They should feel *strongly* about it; they should do it for some kind of *reason*—not just because it's the thing to do." I guess I'm sad to see it getting too popular, even though there are attendant good things that come out, such as now there's better work...but there's also a lot of crap.

So now the knife's at the throat: "Well, should we do this?" It's like, "What did you create? Where do we go from here?"

CAPTAIN DON

A survivor of the forgotten era of the traveling circus sideshow, the heavily tattooed Capt. Don Leslie is one of the last active sword-swallowers and fire-eaters. His one-and-a-half hour show consists of sword-swallowing, fire-eating, human blockhead, bed of nails, comedy, jazz of the thirties, rock of the fifties, country & western—all in one act.

Born in Cambridge, Massachusetts, Capt. Don ran away and joined the circus at the age of 14. After working as an animal handler, cage boy and concessionaire, he became initiated into the dangerous discipline of sword-swallowing. (How does he do it? "Very carefully. I've been working for 36 years and every single year a sword-swallower has died.") For the past 35 years he has appeared in thousands of circuses, nightclubs, concerts, and fairs, besides making special presentations to medical organizations and working for companies such as Upjohn testing their stomach pumps and nasogastric tubes. Capt. Don holds the unofficial world's record for throwing the longest flame: forty feet!

Captain Don can be contacted through Henry Goldfield's tattoo studio at 404 Broadway, San Francisco, CA 94133 (415) 433-0558. [NOTE: Captain Don died June 4, 2007 R.I.P.]

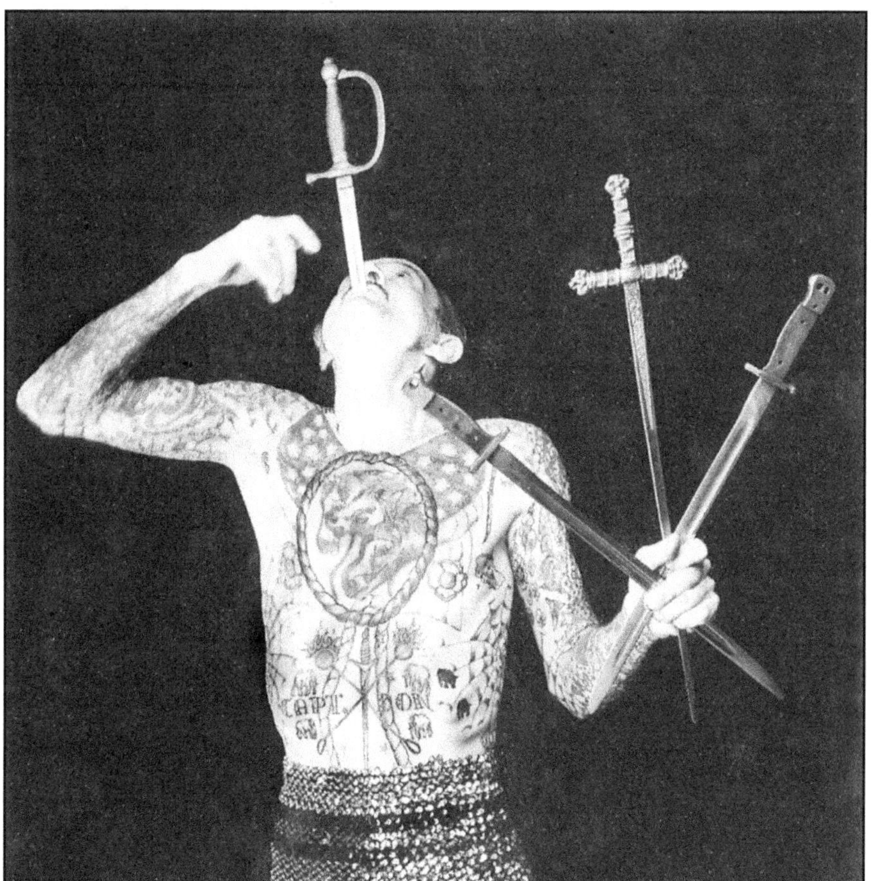

Photo by Bobby Neel Adams.

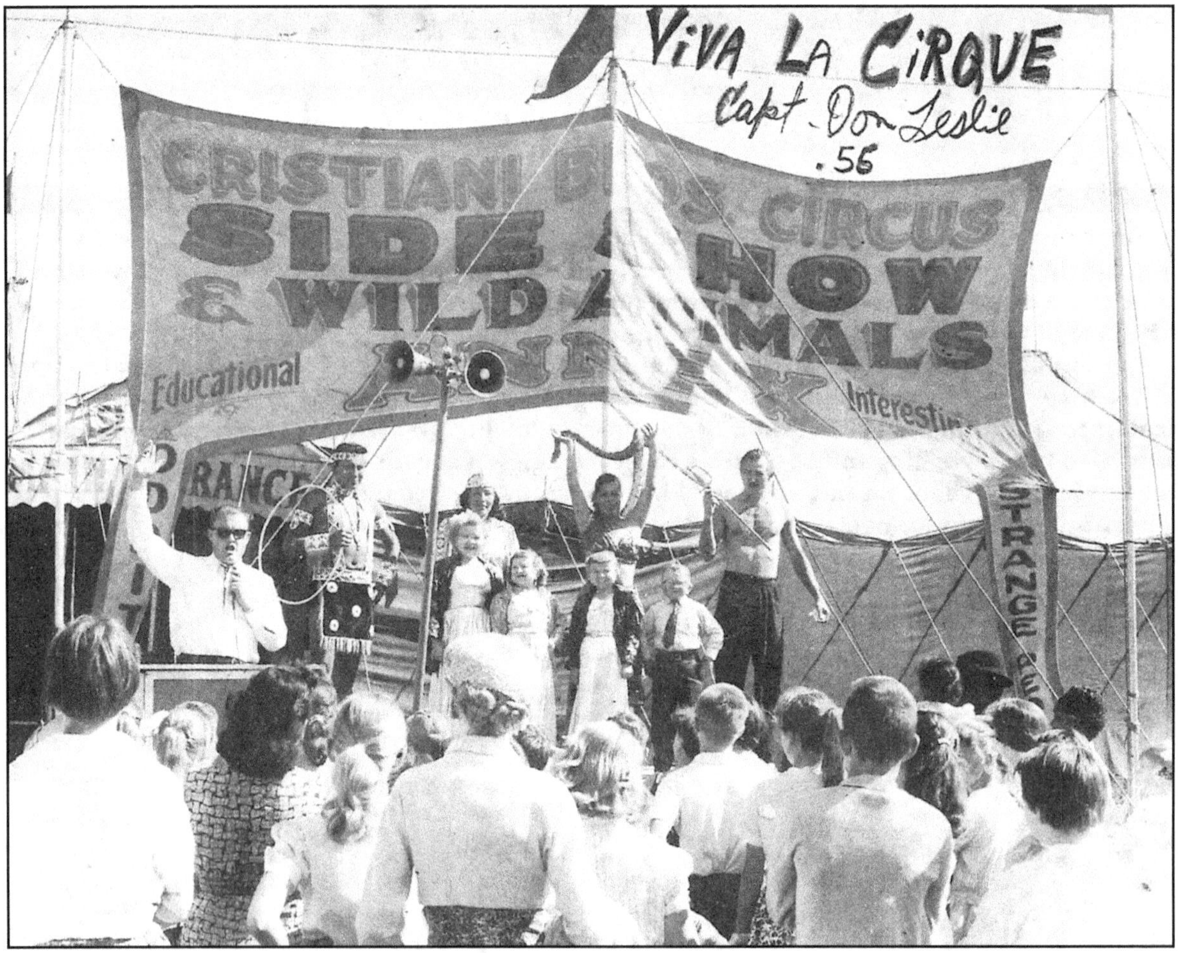

Captain Don (top right) with Cristiani Bros. Circus.

■ *Vale: How long have you worked as a sword-swallower and fire-eater?*

■ CAPTAIN DON LESLIE: For the past 34 years. I can do a show for a Church Ladies Social or a hardcore porno theater; for little children or drunk adults in a nightclub!

Sword-swallowing is deadly dangerous and sword-swallowers die all the time. I've been to five funerals of sword-swallowers since I've been in the business. And most sword-swallowers die while performing onstage.

■ *V: Your specialty is sword swallowing—*

■ CD: Yes, and it's a very thankless act. All countries all over the world know that a magician is a magician and a sword-swallower is a *daredevil,* and that sword-swallowing is deadly dangerous and that sword-swallowers *die* all the time. I've been to five funerals of sword-swallowers since I've been in the business. And most sword-swallowers die while performing onstage. Only the American public thinks you're an illusionist and a magician, and it's hard to get sword-swallowing booked at nightclubs because even agents think that too: "He's just another magician," and magicians are a dime a dozen.

It's hard to explain to an agent that there are only *eleven* sword-swallowers left in the entire United States today. In 1958 I was the youngest, and today I'm the second oldest, and none of us have a student. It's a dying art. So the people who see sword-swallowing now are probably the last generation to see it in this country, unless some Hindus come over, and perform although *they* do it as a religious ceremony.

■ *V: Are any of your family in show biz?*

■ CD: My sister was a stripper for years; she was what we called a bally broad: a girl who handles snakes and entices crowds and does the electric chair.

■ *ANDREA JUNO: The* electric chair?

■ CD: [carny voice] "The young lady will be seated in the electric chair, similar to the one used at Sing Sing penitentiary and other infamous prisons from years

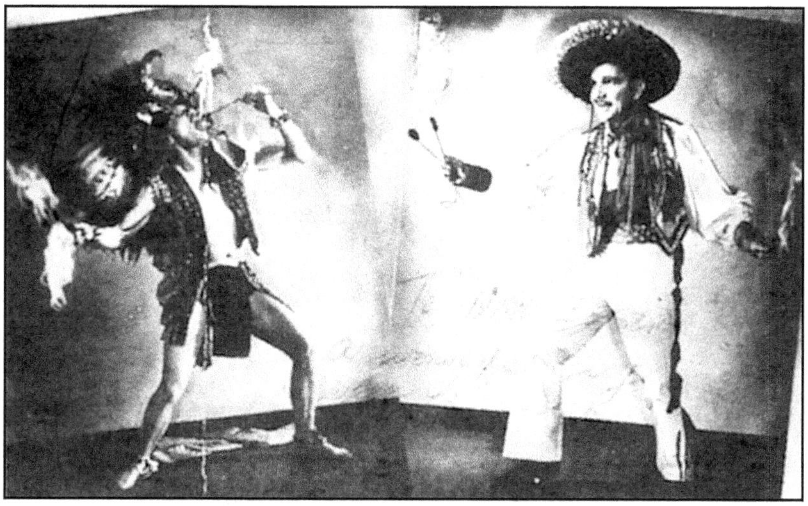

Carlos Leal, fire-eater and sword-swallower, was Capt. Don's first teacher.

ago. They will flip on a switch and charge her up with 25,000 volts of electricity and commence to light gasoline-soaked torches off the flesh of the young lady's body. I will hand her fluorescent tubes and they will glow and flicker right before your very eyes, climaxing her thrilling performance by actually lighting a gasoline soaked torch from one of the most sensitive parts of the young lady's anatomy" . . . her tongue!

■ *AJ: Are any of your children carrying on your tradition?*

■ CD: No, I wouldn't teach 'em nothin'. I find myself a man of 51 years old who's worked for myself all my life, with no insurance, no social security, no medical plan—*nothing*. I just live for the day. If I got sick tomorrow I'd be done for.

■ *V: Hmm . . . could you describe your acts.*

■ CD: I've done the human volcano spittin' fire: that's a gunpowder and gasoline explosion from the mouth. I've swallowed as many as 5 swords at a time, and have been x-rayed with a 26-inch sword in my stomach at Harvard Medical School; this was done for a graduating class of anatomy students. I've also swallowed a 26-inch piece of bracing steel. I can do the human pincushion (7 hatpins through the throat and 3 near the eye) and the human blockhead, where I drive icepicks up my nostrils and shishkebab skewers through the cheeks. I play guitar and piano and sing, too. I've also laid down in broken glass, and worked numerous circuses, boxing matches as the intermission act—I did the Sugar Ray Leonard/Roberto Duran fight.

I've played the Hawaii State Fair, the Boston Centennial, Canada, the old Dave Garroway show (before Jack Parr, Steve Allen and Johnny Carson). I was in a group called the Joy Boys and we did all dirty songs—not filthy, but dirty, plus skits. I also do cocktail lounges, dinner music, country & western, and '50s rock. For a publicity stunt in 1958 I hung upside down from a helicopter in a straitjacket hovering over a field of soldiers.

In my mother's attic are several footlockers of photos, memorabilia and publicity I've received. All that publicity and 50 cents will get you a cup of coffee—but you gotta have the 50 cents! Because the other stuff ain't worth a damn. Publicity's nice, but . . . In the old days you'd get offered a gig, and ask what you'd be paid, and they'd say, "Oh, you're gonna be in the newspaper, and on TV," and when you're young that's okay. But nowadays I want to know how much they're paying—*period*. I've been all through that other stuff.

■ *V: Didn't you record an anti-Christian song?*

■ CD: Everywhere Christianity is found it was brought there with force. Explorers like Captain Cook found these places and on the return trip they always brought Christian missionaries. That's worse than bringing an army—however, they had the armed army to back up the Christian missionaries for those who didn't obey. Just as when Martin Luther King uncovered a lot of black history that wasn't in our school textbooks, so there's a whole history of atrocities that were committed in the name of the Prince of Peace, in Polynesia and so on.

There are only eleven sword-swallowers left in the entire United States today.

■ *AJ: When did you begin your circus life?*

■ CD: I ran away from home at a very early age to get away from a bad situation—everything that goes along with having two alcoholic parents, not knowing that I was carrying the very gene that would express itself later on down the line. I had my last drink on September 5, 1980, but for 26 years previously I stayed drunk 'round the clock. I drank my way through two wives and two sets of kids, in and out of the penitentiary, through several homes and businesses, house trailers, trucks, cars—you name it. Now it's nice to be sober—I wouldn't be alive if I were still drinking.

I first ran away in 1953 and worked the concessions at the Ringling Bros Circus, but was picked up by the juvenile authorities and brought back home. The following year, when I was 16, I ran away and haven't been back since! I was a cage boy, a concessionaire—my first job in the circus was running the pony ride: taking the children on and off the ponies, taking the tickets. Right away I was fascinated by the sword swallower, and said, "That's what I want to do!"

One day I was in the crowd during my break—instead of getting a coke or fries I'd watch the sideshow.

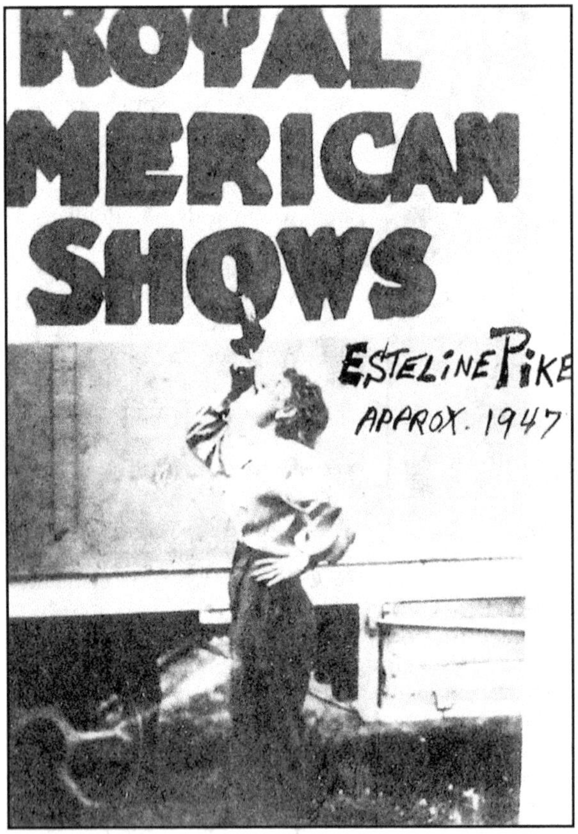

Estelline Pike, the last lady-swallower, now retired in Florida.

And one day after the crowd had dispersed, the sword swallower singled me out: "Boy, come here a minute. Haven't I seen you five days running?" In those days these were called mud shows—you were in a different town every day. "How old are you?" I told him. "Do your parents know where you are?" "No, but I'd sure like to learn how to swallow swords."

This was Carlos Leal, an Argentinian fire-eater and sometime sword swallower, who was probably the best fire eater of the time, but a *very* inferior sword-swallower. I didn't realize it at the time, because I had never seen another sword-swallower before, so I didn't have anything to compare with. There was always trouble: blood on the blade, etc. Anyway, he said, "I'll make a deal with you. If you let me send a telegram to your folks telling them that you're safe and well—I won't tell 'em where you are—then I'll teach you how to swallow swords." He did that, thinking, "This punk kid'll never make me take him up on it," but I did!

In 1956 the Ringling Bros Circus had to fold early in the season, right after Madison Square Gardens—they couldn't keep up the expense. A lot of their employees got spread around the country to different shows. I ended up in the Cristiani Bros Circus with the famous Doll Family of midgets, Johann Peterson the Viking Giant, and Josephine the famous snake charmer from he Ringling Bros Show. Harry Doll did a lot of stuntwork for Spanky McFarlane of the *Our Gang* comedies. In *Freaks* Harry Doll and his sister, Daisy, played the little lovers.

The first time he saw my act he said, "Boy, you make me nervous, and I've been around sword-swallowers all my life" (I was about 17 at the time). He said, "I don't know what the hell you're doing wrong—I can't swallow swords myself, but the way you're doing it ain't right! Next Sunday there's a carnival playing about 80 miles from here, and my good friend Alex Linton from the Ringling Bros Circus (world champion sword swallower listed in the *Guinness Book of World Records;* I was his only student) is there. I'm going to wire him and see if he'll come and visit us and show you a few tips." So had it not been for this favor by Harry Doll, I probably wouldn't be alive today, because Alex Linton came over and stood in the crowd, and that made me even more nervous because the Very Best in the World was in the audience. When I finished, he took me aside and straightened me out.

■ *AJ: What was happening—were you actually cutting yourself?*

■ CD: I was doing a lot of things wrong. When Carlos Leal swallowed a sword he would retch and gag, and even though I had long killed the gag reflex, when I swallowed swords in front of a crowd I would gag and retch anyway because I thought that was part of the *act*—I had nothing else to compare with because I had never seen anyone else! It was grossin' people out. I didn't know you could do it with class and finesse—make it into a very classy act. Basically, Alex Linton showed me six crucial steps, and two moves that must *always* be avoided.

■ *AJ: How did Alex start you off? What did you learn first?*

■ CD: The first thing he showed me was the stance: I had had incorrect posture. He said, "A boxer stands like this; in case he gets hit he has a leg behind him so he can catch his balance. Your good posture is based on this." (I had been standing any ol' way.) He also showed me a few other things I'd rather not go into. [laughs]

■ *AJ: You really insert these swords all the way down. What prevents them from puncturing you?*

■ CD: I don't exceed my capacity and depth. Most swords you buy are 30 inches long, and I cut 'em down to 22 inches. My capacity is 27 or 28 inches sometimes with a full stomach, but I prefer 22" to keep them from resting on the bottom of my stomach.

■ *AJ: Can you feel the sword if it touches the bottom of your stomach?*

■ CD: So well, that when it happens, you'll swear you will never do that again! [laughs]

■ *AJ: How do sword swallowers die?*

■ CD: Mostly trying to do some outlandish feat—they get into competition with each other. Nowadays, the sword-swallowers that are left all know each other

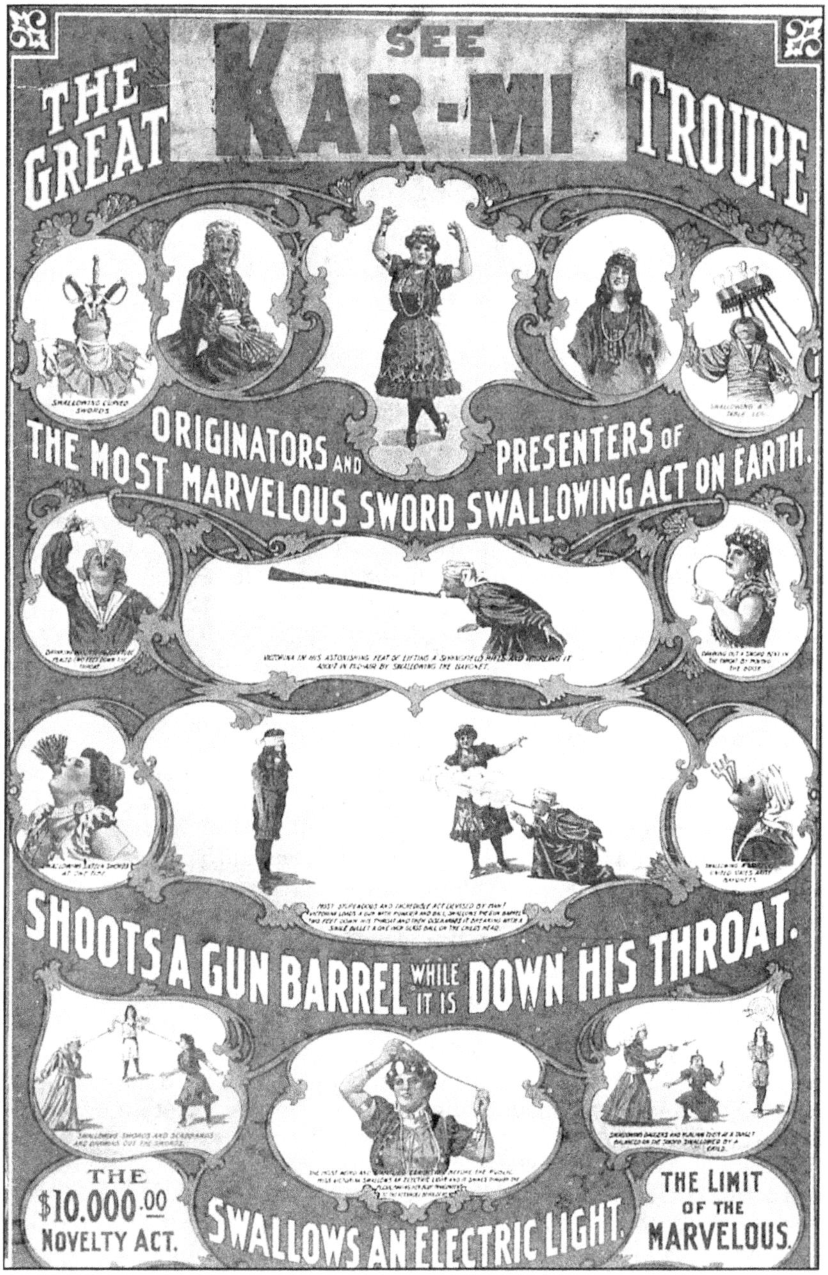

One of the world's greatest sword-swallowers was Kitty Fisher, better known as Miss Victorina, shown here with her husband when they performed as the Kar-mi Troupe around the turn of the century.

personally (or of each other, or through correspondence) and we don't compete; we respect each other's act, because there are some things they can do that I can't, and vice versa. A lot of people think that the major competition would be: who can swallow the longest sword. But that has noting to do with expertise, it has to do with your natural anatomical endowment. I'm 5'10" and can swallow a 27" blade, but Alex Linton was a short pudgy man who could swallow a 30" blade easily, because he had a longer torso. So it's not necessarily true that a guy 6'6" could swallow a longer sword.

The *Guinness Book of World Records* has stopped taking entries for "longest sword" category; it's now multiples: how many swords. Wayne LeSherety is unofficially the world's champion sword swallower; however, the *Guinness Book* had stopped taking entries before he was able to get in there. The last entry was Count Desmond who swallowed 12 swords; however, Wayne has swallowed 16.

Actually, the greatest sword-swallower ever was a woman, Mlle. Clifford, who worked with Barnum & Bailey around the turn of the century. Nobody has ever come close to what she did. For example, she strapped a bayonet to the stock of a high-powered rifle and swallowed the blade, fired the rifle and caught the recoil in her arm so the sword wouldn't stab her inside, or the butt knock her teeth out.

■ *AJ: Wow! . . . How did you train to suppress your gag reflex?*

■ CD: With the finger. You have to keep doing it until the retching stops. When you get to where you can put your whole fist down your throat without your eyes watering, you're ready for swords!

■ *V: How long did training take?*

■ CD: That depends on the individual. I knew a sword-swallower who got the first sword down in about 4 months. I knew others who took over 2 years. I had one down in about 7 months, but to be really relaxed and feeling confident and polished and have an act together with some showmanship, it was at least 11 months before I had a halfway decent act, and many many years before I brought it to where it is today.

■ *AJ: I heard that when you withdrew the sword, you threw it up in the air?*

■ CD: I go through all different routines. I go down on one knee and have someone in the audience retrieve it, and sometimes I slide them down and slide them out easy, and other times I flip them way up in the air and they twirl and then I catch them. It's to make a routine, you know. In order to do a halfway decent sword-swallowing act that's appreciated as entertainment, you've got to be able to do at least 8-12 minutes without repeating something twice.

■ *AJ: Do you practice every day?*

■ CD: No, but if 4-6 days go by, then I run a few up and down to stay in shape.

■ *V: How much did you practice each day when you were learning?*

■ CD: Like I said, it was a long time before I got an act together, because I hadn't seen many sword-swallowers. As the years went by I got more and more opportunities to see people I'd heard about, and I took a little bit from this one and that one and put an act together. In later years, as a few more came into the business, I watched their acts and saw a lot of stuff they took from me!

■ *V: Yes, because it's not just the act, it's the dialogue, the pacing, building the audience up more and more.*

■ CD: Right. Gestures—not necessarily choreography, but you learn how to manipulate crowds without them realizing you're doing it. It's money for you; you've got to get as many people to buy a ticket as possible. Just like with many sales, you open and close a sale, and you can close too early, and you can close too late. There's a natural point that comes where you think, "Okay, it's time to *close right now.*"

Before I go on, when there's an act or two ahead of me, I always get in the wing and look at the crowd, and by them judge how I'm going to gear my act.

■ *V: Are there any living women sword-swallowers?*

■ CD: Mimi Garneau, a nice lady and a good friend of mine, who passed away two years ago—her husband ran a flea circus where the actual insects did tricks, all viewed through a big magnifying glass. Estelle Pike, a terrific sword-swallower, is retired down in Gibsontown, Florida. She's the last lady sword-swallower left, plus the 11 men, as I said. It takes a lot of buckling down, a lot of dedication, and a super-allegiance to a goal: "I'm going to do this, and I'm not going to be defeated. I'm either going to die or do it." And the youth today don't have that kind of discipline—if they can't learn it in five minutes on a video machine, the hell with it!

■ *AJ: Did you ever have any assistants or students?*

■ CD: I had one student, David "Peanuts" Vaughn, that I became close friends with, and thought that he was as fond of me as I was of him! I taught him sword-swallowing and fire-eating, and we had a lot of good times together. One spring the show closed in Sarasota, and usually I went to Key West or Miami and tattooed, or got a C&W band together and played the dive bars, and then in spring went to Winter Quarters and got a job again. This one spring I walked into Winter Quarters and they said, "We can't use you this season because we got him." It was the guy that I'd taught.

■ *V: Obviously that broke up your friendship.*

■ CD: Yeah, I was more hurt than angry—it was pretty sleazy. But then Dave had a pretty bad accident. He was doing a gig at a ski lodge in the Adirondack Mountains in New York, and was in a bar one night among a bunch of rowdies. One drunken guy had bet another a hundred dollars that Dave couldn't swallow the sword. Of course Dave swallowed it, and the guy who lost got so angry that he whirled around and punched him in the stomach while the sword was still *inside.* Immediately the people froze—an immense silence fell over the bar as everyone stared, horrified, as Dave clutched his stomach and then slowly, agonizedly, began working the sword out. When he pulled it out it was covered with blood mixed with a thick, white mucous-like substance. This was snowbound country, and it took a long time for an ambulance to arrive—Dave almost lost his life. He bled internally and all.

■ *V: Did he die soon after?*

■ CD: Miraculously, no. He did die a couple of years later from a collapsed lung, but it didn't happen while sword-swallowing—he was a heavy smoker.

■ *AJ: When did you learn fire-eating?*

■ CD: I learned fire-eating first; I did that before I was a sword-swallower. Let me say that fire-eaters are a dime a dozen; if you're having a party, you can get all you want, plus jugglers and acrobats and strippers and magicians and illusionists and musicians and dancers and singers, too. But you'll wait two years to find a sword-swallower, and I doubt if you'll get one then. I'm the only one that's out here, trying to hustle a buck from the bars. But people don't know what I'm about; they don't know it's a deadly dangerous, death-defying feat. A lot of fire-eaters *are* hurt, but they're still plentiful! A lot of people think it's more dangerous than sword-swallowing, but it isn't.

Actually, the most dangerous act is the human blockhead: a very gross act that's presented as gross as you can. You watch for the queasy ones in the audience and you use them to really get down and dirty. And the reason for that is to sell tickets—you want people walking out of the show onto the midway saying, "There's a guy in there that—I'm telling you, it's disgusting!" That makes people curious—curiosity killed the cat. And that's what you want: you want people to go out there and advertise the show for you.

■ *AJ: What is the human blockhead?*

■ CD: You drive forty-penny spikes, screwdrivers, icepicks, up the nostril to the base of the brain. But there's a routine that goes with it; a monologue that fits it, and a way to work it different with each crowd. It's hard to work it with any class at all. You could present it in a kind of educational way, but it doesn't have the impact if you do it really filthy, down and dirty—*gross.* I never let the press take any photographs of that; I refuse interviews with the press about that act, because it's hard enough already. The human blockhead is something I do and I put myself into that character, but I am not the human blockhead! I become that person to sell tickets and make some money, and hopefully I've entertained the crowd with the sword-swallowing, and they leave the show knowing who I *really* am.

■ *AJ: Do you know Fakir Musafar?*

■ CD: We go 'way back! I have old photos of him; I met him back in the fifties! He used to do magic shows for little kiddies; he's quite a guy. He was in show business for a little while but he got out of it and went into other things. He really does live two lives; Monday-Friday 9-5 he wears that $500 suit and drives the BMW, but the rest of the time . . . He collects dungeon relics—he buys implements from old castles and torture chambers and may someday open a museum with his collection of chains and shackles. He studied a lot of Hindu cults; it must have been pretty hard for him personally all those years, because he had to stay in the closet with almost everything he did, or he'd have been labeled a real weirdo, bordering on deviant. Fakir was the protege of 76-year-old Sailor Sid Diller, who claims to have about a pound and a half of metal piercings in his genitals. He learned a lot about piercing from Sailor Sid.

■ *V: How about the human pincushion act?*

■ CD: I very seldom do the human pincushion act, especially now that AIDS is here. I've made up my mind that it's too much of a hassle keeping the needles sterilized. Before we just used to dip 'em in alcohol to avoid getting hepatitis, but now there are staph and things around that make it too risky.

■ *AJ: They don't seem to leave any scars.*

■ CD: Oh, they do. When you've done a whole season, towards the end after you've been out on the road doing it 25-30 times a day during those fairs, it gets to where you'll bend 5 or 6 pins before you finally get one through because of the scar tissue.

■ *AJ: How do you train to overcome the pain?*

■ CD: There's a little line I use; it's mind over matter: *you don't mind and I don't matter!* Actually, even though that's a corny joke, that's it in a nutshell. People have paid a dollar extra to see the human pincushion. I'm on stage and see 500 faces waiting for me to show them what the man out there said I was going to do. Now you either do it or give them back five hundred dollars. That's what it boils down to: you forget all about pain and all that shit and you just *do* the show.

■ *AJ: So you just transcend the pain?*

■ CD: Pain isn't even a good adjective. And agony certainly isn't, either. It hurts and I guess it's painful in a sense, but it's not that big of a deal. It's nothing like a toothache!

■ *AJ: In the carnival situation, isn't there a real support structure?*

■ CD: Circus people don't like carnival people. And it's only in recent years I've been going with carnivals, because the circuses have dropped their sideshows because there are no more freaks, due to the ACLU and welfare. Years ago there was no welfare; you either stayed in a state hospital all your life or joined a circus sideshow. A lot of them were exploited by these sideshow managers who got really rich off them, but some of them, like Sealo and the Seal Boy (born without hands) got hurt. The ACLU picketed a show that Sealo was on, protesting it was taking advantage of him, etc. Sealo got himself a lawyer and went into court, and his plea was, "All my life I've been self-sufficient. I contribute to society; I support myself; I'm not a burden on society. I pay taxes and social security, and I saved the system a lot of money; otherwise they'd be supporting me in an institution. I resent someone coming along and trying to take that away from me. If these people had their way, I would go to an institution where everything would be done for me, and feel no dignity, no worth at all, and not be able to feel I'm a full citizen and a member of society as a whole." But in spite of that, the ACLU kept pushing, and now all those people get SSI checks, and even if you approach them to go on the road, they're too comfortable.

■ *AJ: Weren't freaks pretty high up in the sideshow hierarchy?*

■ CD: Yes. We never used the word "freaks" ourselves; in our vocabulary they're Very Special People. There were also self-made freaks, like my good friend Sam Alexander, the man with two faces. Actually he had no face at all—he wore a mask. When he was a teenager he worked a hat-check at a speakeasy in Chicago during the gangster era. After hours he and his buddy would go from speakeasy to speakeasy to have drinks after duty. They were walking down a dark alley behind some factories, and there was a 55-gallon drum sitting there. Someone said, "I wonder if there's anything in that barrel? I think I'll find out" (thinking it might be hooch). He lit a match and blew it up and killed the other three, and blew Sam's face completely off! He was the most grotesque attraction in the circus sideshow for years—how he managed, I don't know, but he got through 17 years without letting anybody ever photograph him. No one has any photos of him except a dermatologist. Finally he saved enough money to have his face rebuilt from the skin on the top of his thighs—$260,000! The doctor did a pretty good job.

I've swallowed as many as 5 swords at a time, and have been x-rayed with a 26-inch sword in my stomach at Harvard Medical School.

Another example of a self-made freak is somebody who would tattoo himself all over. Once a lady saw my tattoos and my show and asked, "Why do you mutilate your body? You tattoo your body, you put steel blades down into the vital organs of your body, you burn the mucous membranes and the inside of your mouth with gasoline-soaked torches, and run shishkebab skewers

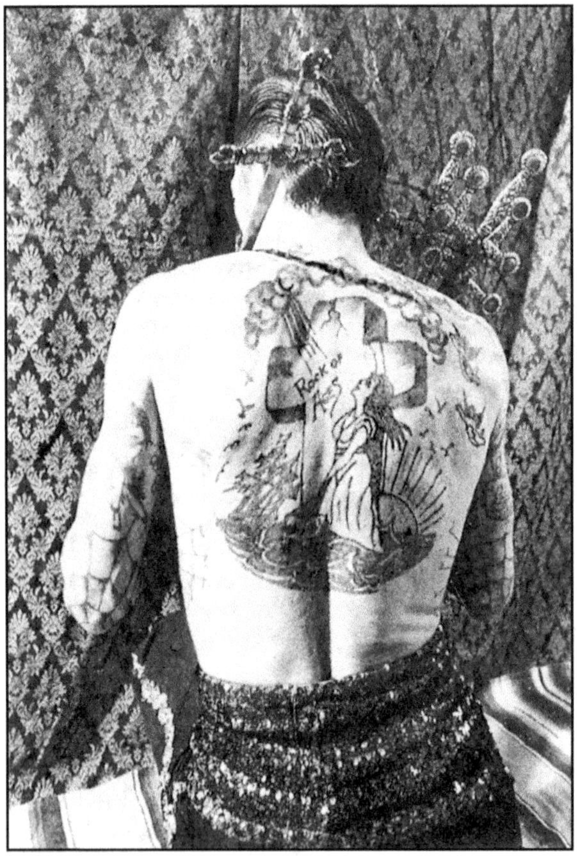

and hatpins all through your body—why?" I said, "Did you buy a ticket to get in here?" She said, "Yes." I said, "That's why—I got your money!"

Anything that you want to see—if you've got the money, somebody will do it for you! You can have somebody killed; you can get sex, drugs—you name it and it's out there if you've got the money.

■ *AJ: But you're not just doing this for the money.*

■ CD: It was a challenge, and I love my audiences, and it's very frustrating knowing that 70% of every audience that faces me thinks I'm doing some kind of an illusion act. I pass the swords out into the audience for them to inspect, and hit them on the floor and do whatever test they can think of, and then they hand them back and I sterilize them and go into my act.

■ *V: Somewhere along the way you also learned tattooing.*

■ CD: I got tattooed to be on exhibition. It used to be that you had the sword-swallower, the fire-eater, the tattooed man and the tattooed lady, the Fat Lady, the midget, the Giant, and other grotesque features. Let me give you an example: in music, you'll get the saxophone player who also plays clarinet, or the trumpet player who plays trombone; the banjo player who also plays guitar, and the piano man who plays organ. So a lot of sword-swallowers learned fire-eating because you pay a sword-swallower *this* salary, and you pay a fire-eater *that* salary, but I'll cut a little bit off each one and do both for this amount—the show saves money that way. So I learned the human pincushion, the human blockhead, the iron tongue (the hook through the tongue), I got myself tattooed—I learned all these acts. The salaries that you'd have to pay individually would amount to a lot of money, but I'd do them all for one lump sum that got me more money and saved them a bundle!

But nowadays sideshow acts are so rare—the "freaks" are gone from the scene and we'll never see them again. The sideshow "marvel" acts are becoming rare because nobody's teaching anybody—not too many people want to learn, and it's just a hassle. One of my sons once begged me to teach him, and I said, "Be a lawyer, a dishwasher, a truck driver, or a bank hold-up man, but don't swallow swords or eat fire—it's too rough, all these years! Yesterday's a canceled check, tomorrow's a promissory note, today's ready cash!"

Extensive tattooing used to be rare; it was pushed into the underground. But even if you make it illegal, it'll still go on—man has a basic need to decorate his body both temporarily and permanently. In the old days, tattooers were paranoid and separated from each other and didn't share secrets and friendships. It was hard to get supplies, and if someone made a discovery, he didn't share it with anyone. But gradually the machines and the art became improved upon, ever since Edison invented the first electric tattoo machine without realizing that he did. Charlie Wagner, the "Professor" of the Bowery in New York, a turn-of-the-century tattooist, improved upon it, and then Capp Coleman of Norfolk, Virginia improved on it, and Bert Grimm, and now Paul Rogers, who brought today's tattoo machine to what it is.

Professor Charles Wagner who tattooed soldiers and sailors during both WWI, WWII, and the Korean War, was also famous for having tattooed more tattooed attractions with road shows than any other individual. Betty Broadbent (heavily tattooed woman whom he worked on) told me that Professor Wagner, besides being a tattoo artist, was quite an eccentric character himself. He liked to wear clothes that were a hundred years out of fashion; many times you could see him wearing a stovepipe hat like Abe Lincoln wore, and button-up shoes and spats. He had a whole attic full of clothes from different eras; one day you'd see him wearing a fez, dressed like an Egyptian; the next day he'd look like Sherlock Holmes. When the circus was in town, you could see a lot of famous circus people come in and out of his shop.

There were tattoo artists in the sideshow because of its rarity—people got their bodies tattooed for that reason. I got tattooed for that reason, too. But then, after I studied what tattooing was all about, and its history, I became more fascinated, and now when I get tattooed, I experience the spiritual part of it—the camaraderie between the person doing the tattoo and yourself. Nowadays, you may want a tattoo from somebody, but they may choose *not* to tattoo you! People like Ed Hardy, the tattooer's tattooist—if you get a tattoo from them, you went to them, but *they* picked *you!* It's not just because they want the money. So that's something more you could feel good about: that a master like that chose to tattoo you!

Did you know the word "stigma" specifically applies to breaking the skin—the word generally applies to anyone strange or unusual. It's from the Greek; the term referred to bodily designs designed to expose something unusual, or the moral status of the signifier. The signs were cut or burned into the body, and advertised that the bearer was a slave, a criminal, or a traitor . . . a blemished person, ritually polluted, to be avoided especially in public places.

■ *V: Who did your backpiece?*

■ CD: Leroy Minugh, who's now the Reverend Leroy Minugh today; a baptist minister in Long Beach, California. He tattooed Steve Allen on NBC TV one time, and he also did Bill Mokrey, the most solidly tattooed person in the world, with all this solid green pigment between the designs. Lyle Tuttle did most of my other tattoos; I met him when I was 18 and he was 22 and he had his first shop. We've been friends for years. I didn't see him from '58 until 1981, but all through the years I'd been reading about him getting famous tattooing Janis Joplin, etc, and he'd been following my career on the East Coast.

That reminds me: circus sideshow people and tattoo artists, because they were part of the same scene for so many years, share a certain sympathy. A lot of the time when a circus sideshow actor was on the road, and had landed in a town broke with no funds and nowhere to go, he went to the local tattoo shop, told him who he was and dropped a few names, and the tattooist would help him—get him a meal, put him up for the night, give him a pack of cigarettes and some spendin' money. Then, when the person landed back on his feet, he'd mail back the money with thanks. And even today, anywhere I go, if I land in a town and the motels are full, I'll call the local tattoo artist, and usually I either know him personally or he knows who I am. And I can stay in the back room of his shop or in his house.

■ *AJ: But you do tattoo, right?*

■ CD: No, I'm not a tattoo artist. I'm a tattoo-ist—that means an applicator. Most people get a tattoo from me as a souvenir because of who I am, like, "I've got to have a Captain Don!" Just like Betty Broadbent tattooed her autograph on me, and my old friend of many years, Lyle Tuttle, did the same. I have a lot of souvenirs from tattooers of the past: "Tatts" Thomas of Chicago, Capt. Al Wriglesworth, Commodore Dick, Sailor West—they're all gone now, but I still carry mementos of them. That's what Ed Hardy does, you know. He's probably been tattooed by a hundred people, and he knows every tattoo he's got—when, where, and what happened that evening or afternoon.

■ *V: When did you meet Ed?*

■ CD: I never heard of him 'til '81; I wasn't around the tattooing scene *per se;* I was around the circus sideshow. But when I came to San Francisco everyone told me . . .

■ *AJ: What's the difference between the circus and the carnival?*

■ CD: A circus is a professional show business; you go to a circus to be entertained. A carnival is a professional robbery; you go to a carnival to get robbed! Let's say you have a little child who can't wait for the circus to come to town, and you've promised to take them if they're good. The day the circus arrives, something comes up and you absolutely can't keep your promise to the child. So you say, "I told you I'd take you but I can't. Here's twenty dollars. Buy yourself a ticket, and you'll have enough for a hot dog and popcorn and a monkey on a stick." The kid does that; he sees the complete performance and buys a few food items and maybe a toy, too.

Then we take the other way around: "If you're good you can go to the carnival when it gets here." Same situation: "Here's twenty dollars. You go there and get a cotton candy and ride the merry-go-round, the ferris wheel and go in the funhouse and get a hot-dog." Now the kid goes there and he isn't six feet within the gate when some shark goes (carny voice), "C'mere, boy! Tell you what I'm gonna do. See these three balls here? Bip-bip-ping!" and in five minutes he's got that twenty dollars! And the kid walks around watching everyone else having fun and eating cotton candy and riding the rides. [laughs] And that shark will sleep well at night—no conscience at all about stripping a little child. So, that's why we didn't like carnival people when we were in the circus.

Carnivals always carried sideshows, and so did circuses. And sideshow people in circuses looked down on those "commoners" in the carnivals. But now, since a lot of circuses have gone broke or have dropped the sideshows because of expense or lack of marvels, the sideshows are almost all gone.

Just like in other subcultures, among circus people there was not only a certain camaraderie but also a vernacular. If someone was an outsider or intruder trying to be "in," as soon as they said a certain word we'd *know.* For example, we never said "truck," we said wagon or rolling stock. And we never said "elephant"—they're *bulls,* whether they're males or females. There's a whole wonderful language that's largely disappeared: "Gaze along the long line of pictorial paintings to the left and to the right, and everything you see pictured, painted, illustrated or advertised up front you will see on the inside absolutely live." (That's enticing a crowd in) Or when the elephants entered the tent (bass voice): "Entering the Big Top now: 84,000 pounds of pachydermic pulchritude!"

■ *AJ: Can you talk about the meaning of early sailor tattoos?*

■ CD: When you see pictures of pirates or old sailors, you often see earrings. One earring symbolized crossing the equator; two earrings meant you'd crossed it twice or more.

Lyle Tuttle says that you'll get a tattoo when the tattoo god tells you to—that may happen or may not. He doesn't mean a real entity, of course, but I know what he means—the desire to be tattooed comes from deep within your psyche—the theologian would call it your spirit.

So—why not get a tattoo if you have the urge? Because you never know . . . Betty Broadbent, the heavily tattooed woman whom Lyle Tuttle brought to his tattoo museum in 1981, sent me a letter which read: "Dear Don, Poor Mimi (Garneau) isn't going to be with us much longer. She's just wasting away to nothing." While I was reading the letter, Betty herself was already dead—she died while the letter was en route to me! And Mimi Garneau went to her funeral! So . . . "Ye know not the hour! I come like a thief in the night, and my sword is swift and my judgment final!"

Man has a primitive instinct to decorate him or herself both temporarily and permanently. We style our coiffure differently; we shave our beards differently; we wear different colored clothes, we wear jewelry, we pierce ourselves. In Africa we do scarification or split-lip Ubangis or make giraffe-neck women; in China we bind the foot so it doesn't mature. We do all kinds of mutilations and modifications, and a lot of that is because a certain social structure decided this is beautiful, or sexy, or has appeal. But most decoration is because "I want you to know who I am." We make a statement in many ways by our decorations; especially we who like to separate ourselves from the populace and be in special groups . . .

Sometimes a tattoo is a message from the soul, and sometimes you know why you got a tattoo and what that means to you. Sometimes it's too close to let anyone else know; it's none of their business. And what you do with your body is your business. Each one of us has one life, and we own our body; nobody else owns our body, and we can do with our body as we will, as long as it doesn't affect our fellows in some way. I can't understand how people get offended because someone got a tattoo—it's not on *you*, it's on *him!* But our parents don't own us; we don't own our children; we are free to do as we will. Life's short so have fun!

All my life I wanted a tattoo on my neck; however, I didn't do it because it would cost me dearly. Over the years I've put on long-sleeved shirts to hide my tattoos in situations where the prejudice would have been detrimental to my progress. Now in this time of life I don't give a shit! I want to do something super-spectacular before I die, so sometime in 1990 I aim to swallow a Ford truck axle right from the chassis—have it lowered into me from an A-frame! And there'll be only the press that I want there—not the *National Enquirer!* And hopefully with the publicity from that (if I live) I'll get some money; it'll be a last-ditch effort to get a little bread before I retire. During the 1890s a sword-swallower swallowed a carriage axle, and in 1916 another sword-swallower swallowed a Ford automobile axle. That hasn't been done since, but someday I'm going to swallow a truck axle!

CAPTAIN DON TATTOOED BY:

Carol Nightingale, Leroy Minugh, Lyle Tuttle, Commodore Dick, Capt Al Wriglesworth, Tatts Thomas, Sailor West, Rocky Antoinelli, Broadway Leo Walters, Suzanne Tuttle, Erno Szabady, Cheri Kitchens, Sailor Cam Cook, Dan Thome, Bill Salmon, Inny Lee.

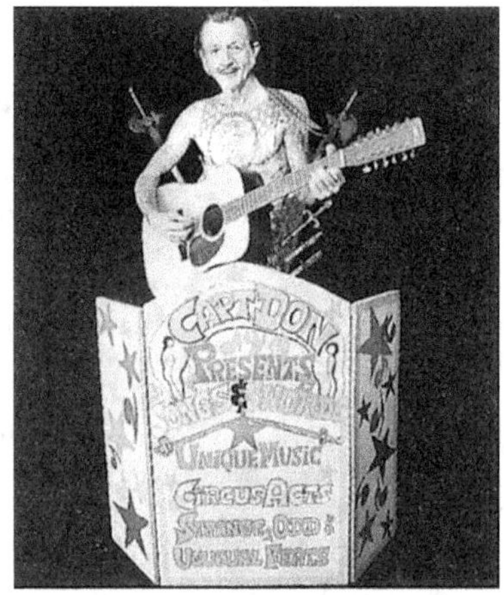

Song by Captain Don Leslie

POLYNESIAN SLAUGHTER

Have you ever noticed when the other fellow doesn't think or act like us,
Some of the rest of us won't even sit beside him on the bus?
We say that he's a little strange and brand him with some hateful made-up name,
Why can't we all be different and still respect each other just the same?
All down through the ages the self-appointed righteous make the rules,
All those in opposition are said to be the evil, heathen fools,
Tattooed people been around for many thousand years,
They've been murdered, scorned, and hated, by politicians and religions out of fear.
In the South Pacific Islands live the Polynesian peoples long ago,
Happy stories were told on their drums as they danced to and fro,
Their tattooed legs and bodies bore the symbols of their honest ties with life,
Every mark and every line told the truth of their history and strife,
And out of the seas' horizon came the ships of the earth's other end,
With a foreign people who thought they had life's answers for all men,
They stepped upon the beaches of the Polynesian people's sacred land,
And in time they tried to kill them, every woman, every child and every man.
These Christian missionaries who forgot about the Golden Rule,
Claimed any Polynesian with a tattoo was a fool,
And not one theologian to this very day wants to preach,
How these tattooed people were slaughtered in the name of the Prince of Peace.

JANE HANDEL

Jane Handel is a photographer, sculptor, collage artist and writer. She's written a hard-boiled novel which in part explores the transsexual and lesbian underground in San Francisco, and is currently producing an autographical novella which will be illustrated by artist Eva Garcia. In this interview she explains the genesis of her tattoos to V. Vale and Andrea Juno.

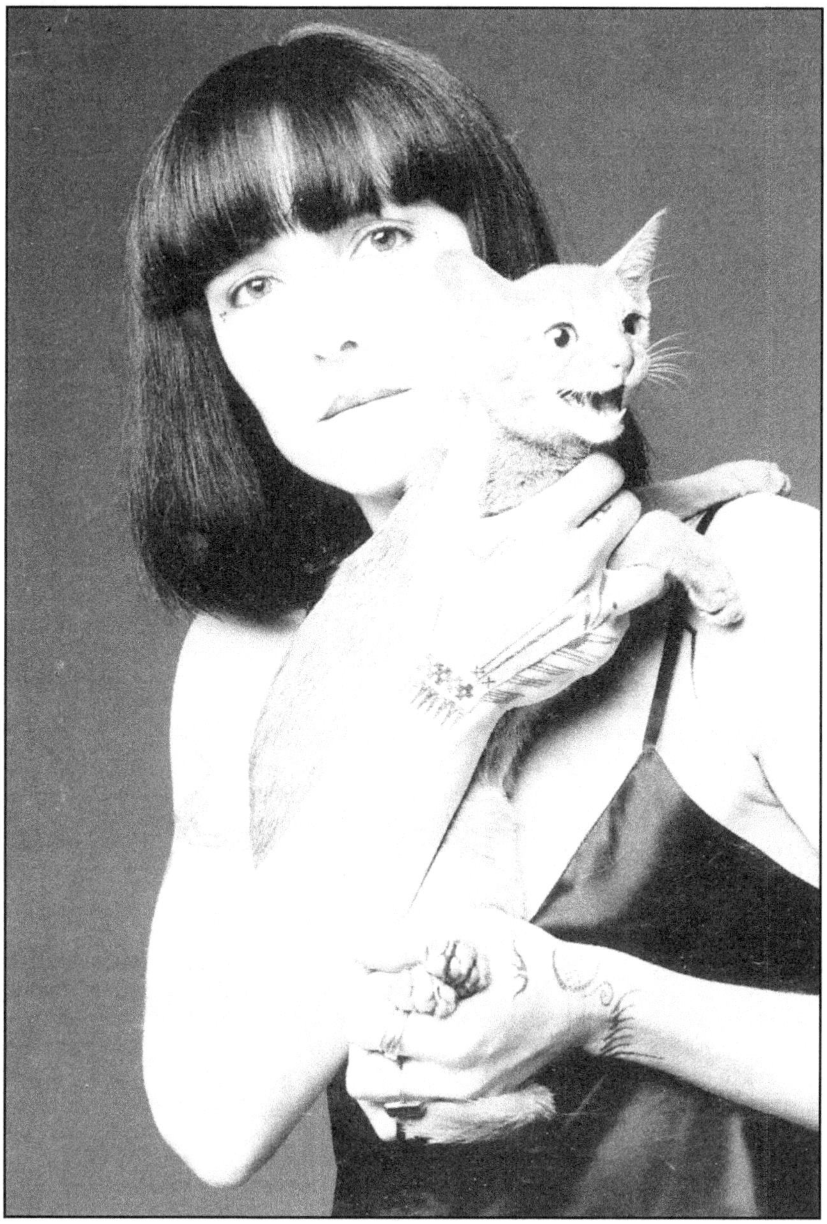

Photo by Bobby Neel Adams.

■ JANE HANDEL: My first tattoo I did *myself* 17 years ago, above the right knee. I was studying Middle Eastern dance (especially North African) and was very interested in body decoration. I tattooed the crescent moon and star—a symbol I really like, which is on the Turkish flag. But I was a little too timid about pricking my skin, and it sort of *came off*—it left a little smudge that wasn't anything. For years I wanted that to be redone, and now I have it on my hand—Ed Hardy did it as a kind of *homage* to my first tattoo . . . .

I wanted work that was inspired by traditional tribal designs, but contemporary, too, and abstract in the sense that it wasn't rigidly symbolic of any religious or cultural references.

■ *VALE: When did you start your recent tattoo work?*
■ JH: In 1980 I saw Ruby Ray's photos of Leo Zulueta in *Re/Search #2*, and was really knocked out. Those stark black geometrical designs were something I had always been attracted to in other cultures, but I had no idea one could get work like that done here. I made inquiries and learned that Ed Hardy was responsible. I'd seen photos of Ed's work in books and had recognized he was a master artist, and when I found out he was able to do *this* kind of work, I got very excited. Plus, he lived in San Francisco, and his studio turned out to be five blocks away!

I wanted work that was inspired by traditional tribal designs, but contemporary, too, and abstract in the sense that it wasn't rigidly symbolic of any religious or cultural references. I wanted something personal, or *personalized*, and certainly decorative or aesthetically pleasing—that's of major importance to me.

I met Ed and trusted him immediately. I knew I could give him a rough *verbal sketch* and he would be able to interpret and enhance it in a way I would find exciting. The first one he did was a cover-up above my right knee. I wanted an abstract lightning bolt-design, kind of a ziggurat, and he made it *unique* in a way I could never have thought of myself.
■ *V: So this tattoo "broke the ice."*
■ JH: Yes, then I started getting one every year. Next was the Ouroboros, the snake on my arm, which is an image I was instinctively very attracted to. That seemed like a much more major commitment on my part—by that time the little one above my knee seemed so paltry in comparison. The Ouroboros is kind of a *totem figure* for me; it's the only design I wanted to be specifically representational.

After that I got the tattoo on my neck, which was inspired by ancient interlocking Celtic designs. In this culture I think the neck is overlooked, in contrast to Japanese culture where the nape of the neck in a woman is considered the most beautiful and erotic zone—that's why when you see Ukiyo-e paintings of women from behind, they have the kimono

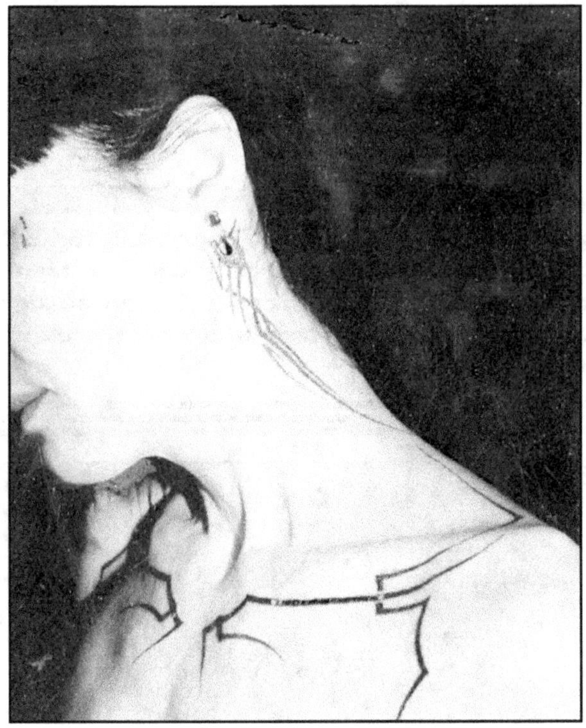

Tattoos and Photo by Ed Hardy.

draped down and the hair up so the back of the neck is exposed. At the time my hair was really short, so the tattoo was much more visible, above the collar line. This was the first time Ed had done anything like that, although interestingly enough Leo got one on his neck shortly afterward.
■ *ANDREA JUNO: Did people react adversely?*
■ JH: Fortunately, I've been able to work at jobs where it didn't matter. By and large the response to all the tattoo work I've had has been overwhelmingly positive, even by seemingly conservative, straight people who invariably comment something like, "It's beautiful!"

I hope I'm working hand-in-hand with Ed trying to upgrade people's concept of tattooing as an art form, so they can see it's something with tremendous potential artistically. So many people have such reactionary ideas as to what it is, and so many people get really junky tattoos because they don't know anything else is available. So they're missing out on all that potential!
■ *V: Many people get tattoos that aren't truly personal.*
■ JH: I gave my tattoos a lot of thought; they're not frivolous or something I'm going to be fickle about. For a long time I've been interested in tribal cultures from all over, and was intrigued by Southeast Island peoples where the women tattooed their hands and forearms.

That was my next progression: my hands, because I wanted to be able to see the tattoos *myself*—everybody else was getting all the pleasure and I couldn't see them! In a number of cultures the hands are a traditional place for women's tattoos, so I felt this was not without precedent—although some people think this is *out there.*

■ *V: For the hands, did you come in with a set of drawings?*

■ JH: No. I knew that I wanted my right hand to be very sharp and geometric; a little more hard-edged and dynamic (I'm right-handed). I wanted the left hand to be rounder and more introspective. So the right would be extroverted and the left introverted—there would be a balance. Ed worked up several sets of drawings, we talked, and he went to work. He put my initials on my hands, too: an "H" on the inside of my right middle finger, and a "J" on my left hand.

It was particularly painful to get the finger tattooed—it was *excruciating.* Tattooing near any *joint* tends to be much more sensitive. That reminds me—I also have a tattoo on my right ankle which Leo put on. Leo is [or was] very slow, and the first time he didn't do it deeply enough; he had to redo it. During the redo I thought I was going to die! I'm not a drug-taker; it's completely against my grain to take anything for the pain, so I just gritted my teeth and tried not to cry! [laughs] Whereas the tattoos on my arm, neck and face didn't hurt at all.

■ *AJ: Did you feel different after you got your hands tattooed?*

■ JH: If anything, I felt more in harmony with the outside world—not necessarily with other people, but I just feel more at peace with the universe. I think it's because the tattoos give me so much pleasure—I love to look at them, and they never cease to amaze me. None of this is related to wanting to be part of some tattoo group or New Tribalism club—I'm basically a very solitary person. . . .

After my hands, next I tattooed my face. I'd always wanted to have a Cholo "tear"—I like the look of it, and it intrinsically signifies kind of a rebellious person. Some people would be horrified that I'd want to "disfigure" my face— they can understand getting a tattoo on the arm or leg, but . . . However, I had had my nose pierced 20 years ago, so the face tattoo didn't seem that extreme. I had worn a ring in my nose for 15 years, but had taken it out five years ago—partly because there started to be so many young punk kids with pierced noses! Plus, it seemed like my face would be too cluttered. The hole has grown over now.

My next progression was my hands, because I wanted to be able to see the tattoos myself—everybody else was getting ·all the pleasure and I couldn't see them! In a number of cultures the hands are a traditional place for women's tattoos.

So first I got three small dots in a triangle next to my right eye—they're supposed to ward off the Evil Eye; I don't know if it's worked for me. Then I added the two tears on the left later.

■ *AJ: Do the tears signify sadness?*

■ JH: Well, I'm a pretty sad person, basically, so it seems appropriate. [laughs] My husband Don told me I couldn't have a Cholo tear because I hadn't been to prison, but this could signify a metaphorical prison! I'm a prisoner of life, or of this body, or whatever.

■ *AJ: Maybe externalizing that feeling takes some of the pressure off, or by bringing it out into the open makes it easier to deal with. Have you been less sad since you had them tattooed?*

■ JH: Oh, yes! In a way, because the tattoos make me happy. Plus, I have this fabulous new cat that makes me happy every day!

■ *AJ: Do you consider your tattoos a source of inspiration?*

■ JH: Always. I've always loved them; I've never grown tired of them; they're a continuing source of pleasure and inspiration to me.

■ *AJ: Do your tattoos have a spiritual or occult significance?*

■ JH: Spiritual in the sense that my goal is one that I think should (ostensibly) be everyone's goal: to become a fully integrated whole person—not fragmented or discordant or out-of-sync with my environment or who I am. Certainly this work has not so much helped me find myself, as accentuated and confirmed who I was already, or who I am in this constantly evolving process. The way you dress or decorate yourself is always a physical manifestation of your identity at that point in time.

But with regard to my tattoos, I'm not practicing any kind of occultism, although it's impossible *not* to think about occult meanings occasionally. But I'm pretty cynical overall, and I just try to take a lot of things, like the "magickal" ability of tattoos, with many grains of salt. If something *works* for somebody, that's fine, but I don't go for a lot of mumbo-jumbo. At the same time I think it's interesting that in some cultures there are various dot patterns tattooed on different parts of the body, like the hands or face. Possibly at one time they were intended for a kind of acupuncture purpose, or other protective reasons—I'm always curious about things like that.

■ *AJ: What's your latest tattoo?*

■ JH: I've just gotten a new one from Ed; a necklace. It's a really spontaneous, flowing design—very unique. I love it!

■ *AJ: You have a fourteen-year-old daughter, right? What does she think of your tattoos?*

■ JH: She used to say (especially when she was going through her preppie phase): "Oh no, mom—not another tattoo!" But now she really likes me the way I am. I think she's finally adjusted!

GENEALOGY OF A TATTOO: THE OUROBOROS

by Jane Handel

The circle, being without end, has from ancient days been a symbol of eternity. In the form of the Ouroboros (a serpent, dragon or fish biting its own tail), "its meaning embraces all cyclic systems (unity, multiplicity, and the return to unity; evolution and involution; birth, growth, decrease, death, etc." (J.E. Cirlot, *A Dictionary of Symbols*) The serpent with its tail in its mouth frequently appears in early Christian remains and has often been associated with Moses' serpent of brass that the Lord commanded to be set upon a pole: "and it shall come to pass that everyone that is bitten when he looketh upon it, shall live."

Wherever nature is revered, the serpent is revered as symbolic of its divine life. Christ is often considered to be an incarnation of the serpent. The basis of this is that the origin of evil coincided with the act of creation itself. The serpent in the Garden of Eden was sent to release entrapped spiritual forces voluntarily and is also often associated with Eve. Many consider the serpent and Eve to be one and the same.

Half of the mythic Ouroboros is dark and half light as in the Chinese Yin-Yang symbol. It is therefore positive and negative, constructive and destructive, active and passive. It is the male and female sexual symbolism; a dual image.

The serpent's ability to slough its skin and so renew youth is interpreted as the mystery of rebirth. It is the lord of the waters; the moon waxing and waning. And, when imagined as biting its tail, it suggests the waters that in all archaic cosmologies surround as well as lie beneath and permeate the floating circular island, Earth.

The Ouroboros was a basic Gnostic emblem that was later taken up by the alchemists who applied it to the processes of their symbolic opus of human destiny.

Finally, because its form is such that it destroys free movement, the cross is the antithesis of the Ouroboros, the serpent or dragon denoting the primeval, anarchic dynamism which preceded the cosmos and the emergence of order.

WHY I GOT TATTOOED by Jane Handel

The process of receiving a permanently engraved talisman on one's body is not only complex and mysterious, but can also be confusing. It changes forever the way we perceive ourselves and, certainly, the way we are perceived by others. On the one hand, it opens or exposes one to the outside world and, on the other, creates a protective barrier or shield against the world. For me, it is both an unequivocal affirmation of who I am, as well as a form of mask-wearing.

It has always been important to me to transcend cultural stereotypes and boundaries in much the same way that I aspire to transcend spiritual and artistic boundaries. For instance, my "tear" is an *homage* to Cholos and rebels in general including myself, rather than an *identification* per se.

I consider myself extremely fortunate to have been the recipient of several remarkable tattoos created by the master artist/shaman, Ed Hardy. Through the application of stylized pictorial images, symbolic tribal designs, or abstract expressionism, Ed casts a magic spell.

Because after receiving a tattoo it is impossible to ever think of ourselves in quite the same way again, our self-image becomes inextricably bound with that of the artist responsible for this permanent alteration. Something totally unique is experienced as one relinquishes one's own body to be used as the artist's canvas. Thus, a connection develops that is profound, erotic, androgynous, and primitive. It is reciprocal and yet we remain, as individuals, solitary and subjective. The relationship we consummate is timeless, but paradoxically, it ends along with the art itself when we do.

WES CHRISTENSEN

Wes Christensen is a painter and writer living in Los Angeles. His work, which has been shown throughout the U.S., is exhibited at the Space Gallery in L.A. For many years he has pursued a scholarly and artistic interest in Maya studies...

A FASHION FOR ECSTASY: ANCIENT MAYA BODY MODIFICATIONS

Text and Illustrations (unless otherwise noted) by:
Wes Christensen

The fate of two sailors shipwrecked off the coast of the Yucatan is one of the Mayan Conquest's more remarkable tales. They were kept in cages to fatten while witnessing the rest of the crew become sacrificial victims and cannibal fare. Spared this grisly fate, one, Geronimo de Aguilar, was rescued by Cortez to become his Maya interpreter. The other, Gonzalo Guerrero: "since he understood the language, went to Chetumal, which is the Salamanca of Yucatan. There a lord named Nachan Can received him and placed him in charge of military affairs; he taught the Indians to fight, showing them how to construct forts and bastions. In this way, as well as by adopting the habits of the natives, he gained a great reputation and they married him to a woman of high rank, by whom he had children; and for this reason he did not try to escape, as Aguilar did. On the contrary, he tattooed his body and let his hair grow, and pierced his ears, so as to wear earrings like the Indians, and it is probable that he became an idolater like them."

The Mixtec historical book, (Codex Nuttal) shows a figure, named "5 Alligator", piercing his ear with a bone awl. The blood from his penitential act is shown flowing out in front of him and "feeding" the sacred bundle (tribal collection of ritual and lineage fetish items) in the sanctuary of a stylized temple.

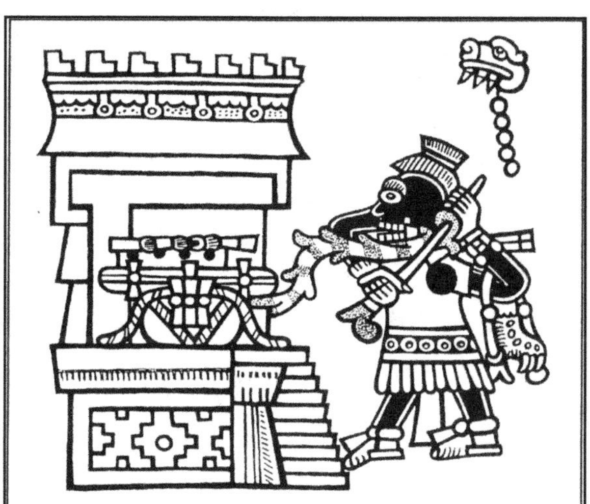

A scene of ritual penis perforation from the Classic era site of El Tajin in Vera Cruz. The penitent is shown with his penis transfixed by a sharp awl. The blood flowing from the wound feeds the figure with the fish hat in the pool of liquid in front of him. (South Ball Court, panel 5, El Tajin, after Michael Edwin Kampen).

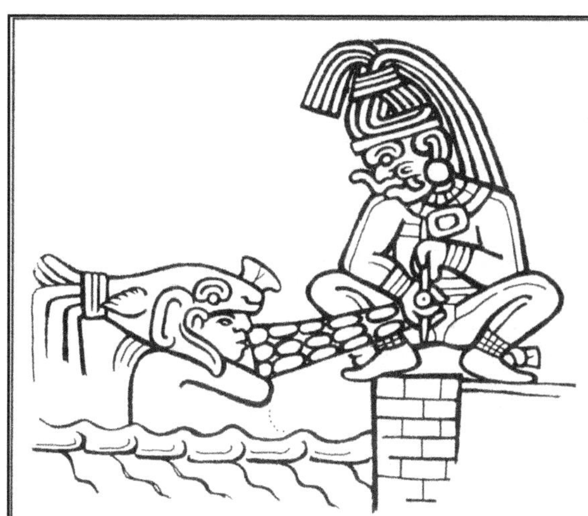

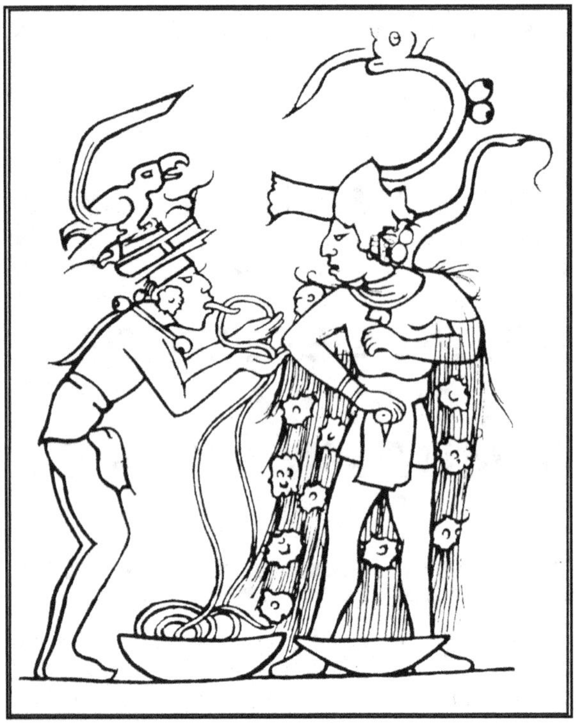

The two figures shown engaging in two forms of auto-sacrifice comes from a Late Classic vase painting. The penitent with the parrot hat pulls a cord through a hole in his tongue, while his companion perforates his penis with a pointed instrument. Genital mutilation is well documented in ethno-historic accounts and referred to in frequent visual metaphors. Frank portrayals such as this, on the other hand, are quite rare. (after Plate 15; Classic Maya Pottery at Dumbarton Oaks, Michael D. Coe, Trustees for Harvard University, Washington, D.C., 1975)

An account of his reply to the offer of rescue is given by Bernal Diaz: "Brother Aguilar, I am married and have three children and the Indians look upon me as a Cacique and captain in wartime—you go, and God be with you, but I have my face tattooed and my ears pierced, what would the Spaniards say should they see me in this guise?" (Alfred M. Tozzer's annotated *Relacion de las Cosas de Yucatan*, by Diego de Landa).

> "It is certainly not true that there is in the mind of man any universal standard of beauty with respect to the human body. It is, however, possible that certain tastes may in the course of time become inherited."
> —Charles Darwin.

> "The consciousness of being perfectly dressed may bestow a peace such as religion cannot give." —Herbert Spencer

Our view of the methods that other cultures use to modify their bodies is often colored by the xenophobia which insulates our own standards of beauty and ugliness. Bound feet and stretched necks have given missionaries sermon fodder and given colonial administrators the excuse to eradicate native practices in the name of Western progress. Even today, we must be careful of such opinions, even though the extreme measures taken by our elite to conform to a near-impossible canon (dictated by *Vogue* Magazine) rivals any aboriginal puberty rite.

We must be careful to remove the bone in our own noses before criticizing another's "duckbill lips." Contemporary cosmetic surgery surpasses any "primitive" society in the scope of persistence of bodily correction. From the puberty rite of orthodontia, to adult hair implants and silicone breast enlargements; from nose jobs and liposuction to the last, final facelift—the ritual surgeon's knife attempts to deliver the "Number 10" figure to those wealthy enough to endure the pain. Should the operating room fail to deliver the "can't pinch an inch" body, there is, for today's devotee, high impact aerobics and bulimia! The ascetic regimens of medieval, cloistered nuns are revived in the death-struggle anorectic teenage girls embrace with the mirror. Their sense of "purity" regained by the loss of their menses, these modern "athletes of God" have different icons now—Balanchine ballerinas and Romanian gymnasts—like them, "never too thin."

"Mortifications of the flesh" has been undertaken in most societies for two primary and interlocking reasons: status and spiritual discipline. To conform to the canon of beauty is to submit to the rules of the society.

The Aztec ruler, Motecuhzoma II, draws blood from his ear. Drawing from a greenstone box thought to have contained personal instruments of penitence. (after Pasztory, Aztec Art).

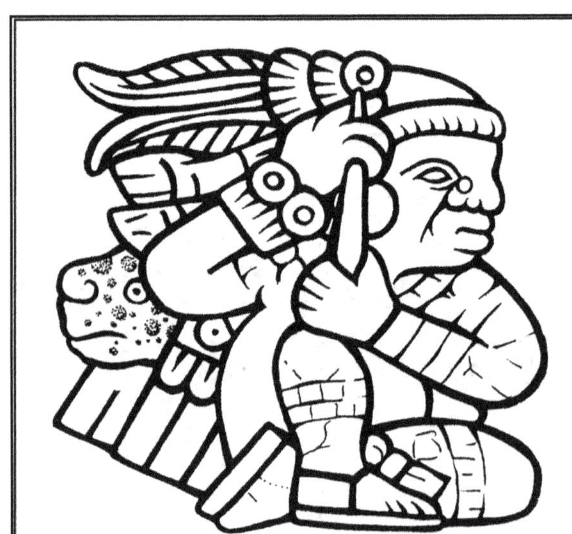

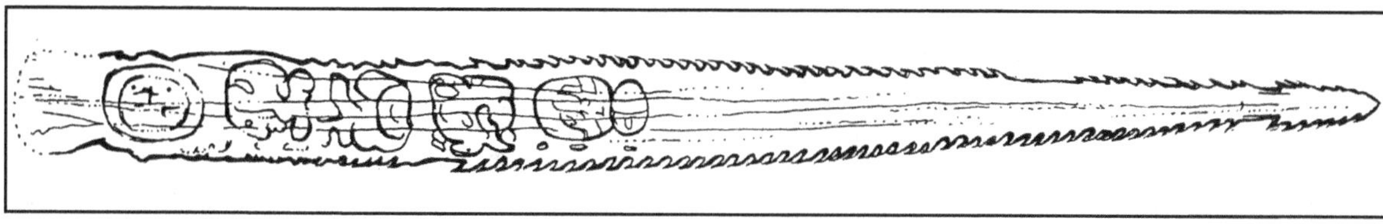

Stingray spines were the most frequent tools used in Mayan bloodletting rituals. "Nature's needle" was found in the pelvic area of buried men—two were crossed over a jade effigy of a ruler's penis in a tomb found at Tikal (drawing of an incised spine after Nicholas Hellmuth).

A sense of belonging comes with the completion of the rites of passage required at puberty, marriage, and other milestones. Rulers have specialized rituals to complete before their authority is accepted—the sword must be drawn from the stone—and maintained (he must always decode "Writing on the Wall"). The second, less palpable, purpose of these rites, sets the practitioner apart from the group by the extent to which he takes the ritual transformation to an extreme. This extreme is seen by society as heroic in its devotion, even mystical if it involves a shared mythos. Less stoic peers stand in awe at the ecstatic transformation of the saint; his suffering endows him with magical, oracular powers—even as it removes him from ordinary social discourse. This revered status is honored and feared, whether the "specialist in the sacred" is a shaman or a psychiatrist.

> "When the children are very young, their heads are soft and can be molded in the shape that you see ours to be, by using two pieces of wood hollowed out in the middle. This custom, given to us by our ancestors by the gods, gives us a noble air, and our heads are thus better adapted to carry burdens." —Torquemeda, quoted by Tozzer

> Among the Thracians, "cuts in the skin signified noble birth; not having them, absence of it." —Herodotus

> "They tattooed their bodies, and the more they do this, the more brave and valiant are they considered, as tattooing is accompanied with great suffering...This work is done a little at a time on account of the extreme pain, and afterward also they were quite sick with it, since the designs festered and matter formed. In spite of all this they made fun of those who were not tattooed." —Diego de Landa

The ancient Maya pursued the dual goals of body modification to an unprecedented degree. In their quest for the perfect facial profile, head deformation was a routine practice, begun in infancy, the forehead shaped in wooden molds into an admired, continuous arc extending back from the (often artificially enlarged) bridge of the nose. Balls of wax were hung between the child's eyes to induce them to cross—a sign of beauty. Male facial hair was stunted by scaling compresses, then plucked out—like female eyebrows. Bodies were painted to indicate status, occupation, as an insect repellant, and for pleasure. Tattoos were acquired over much of the face and body by both men and women. Lips, noses, and earlobes were pierced and decorated with as expensive jewelry as the wearer could afford. The openings in the ears were gradually stretched out to an astonishing degree, judging from excavated examples of jade "ear flares" found in tombs. (The importance of these donut-size ornaments to Maya elite from their earliest expressions is an unexpected aid to the student of Maya sculpture—in a confusing welter of serpentine forms, the large, simple concentric circles of the ear flare helps the novice find the figure amidst the ornament!) Both sexes wore elaborate long hair and enjoyed the variety of fragrances the jungle had to offer. Finally, in perhaps the most grueling procedure, the fashion-conscious Maya filed their teeth to points and inlaid them with precious stones, particularly mirrored pyrites—for the final "close-up" effect.

Contemporary cosmetic surgery surpasses any "primitive" society in the scope and persistence of bodily correction: from the puberty rite of orthodontia, to adult hair implants and silicone breast enlargements; from nose jobs and liposuction to the last, final face-lift.

> "Examined superficially and from the outside, the refinements of ritual can appear pointless."
> —Claude Levi-Strauss

> "The steles of Copan and Quirigua reveal that 'horror vacui' so typical of Maya decoration. The eye must not rest for a moment. The baroque ornamentation overflows, spreads out over the background of the relief, and completely covers every available spot, destroying

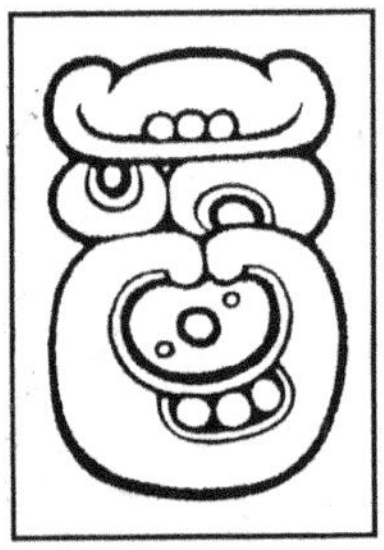

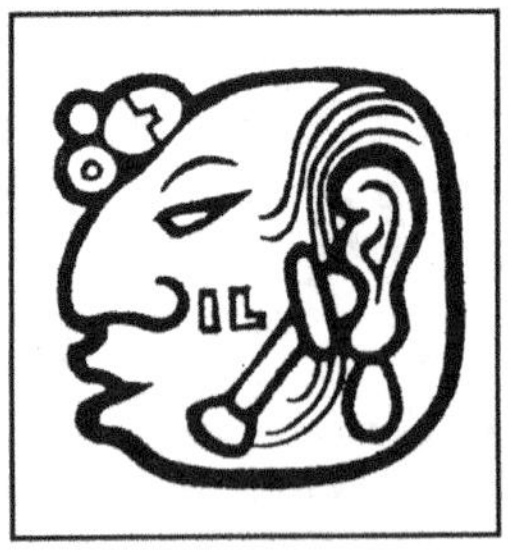

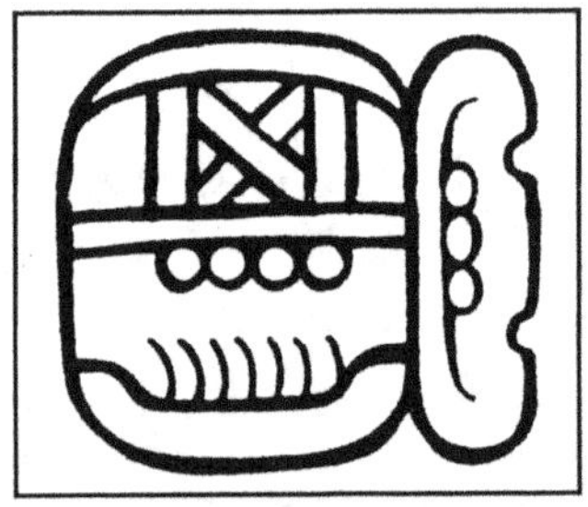

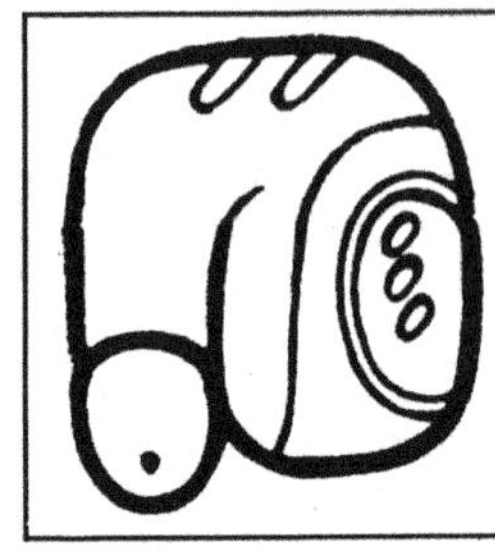

"Na" event: A cluster of phonetic glyphs is found to accompany events involving bloodshed. It is present in phrases describing the self-sacrifice of tongue and penis perforation; as well as in texts describing warfare and the ritual execution of captives. Together the cluster of glyphs reads: "Na-wa-ah." In Tzotzil Maya, "N" means "to know, feel, and remember." It is a root word in phrases describing martyrdom and commemoration of ancestral dead. In Yucatec, "Nah" means "merit, to deserve," in an ancient context, the "Na event" commemorates auto or captive sacrifice to gain public merit and respect." (Schele 1984:7-45).

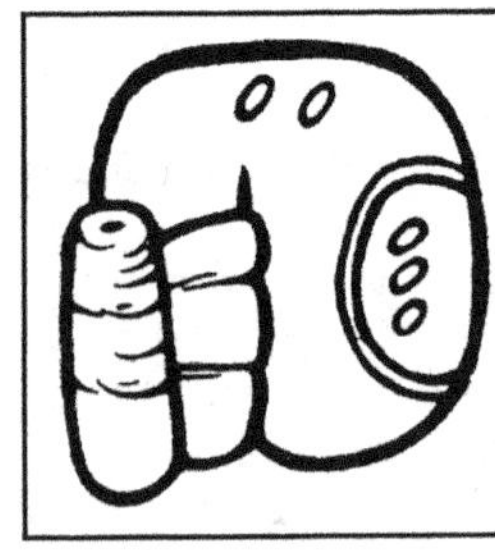

The phonetic "Na" glyph is used as a "postfix" to an ideograph known to mean "Sky," which then is combined with a pictograph of the male genitalia. The resulting "couplet" forms an honorific title that May Lords could claim once they had endured the penis perforation ritual. Another "Sky Penis" title graphically underlines the bloody "Na" event by wrapping the penis with a knotted bandage.

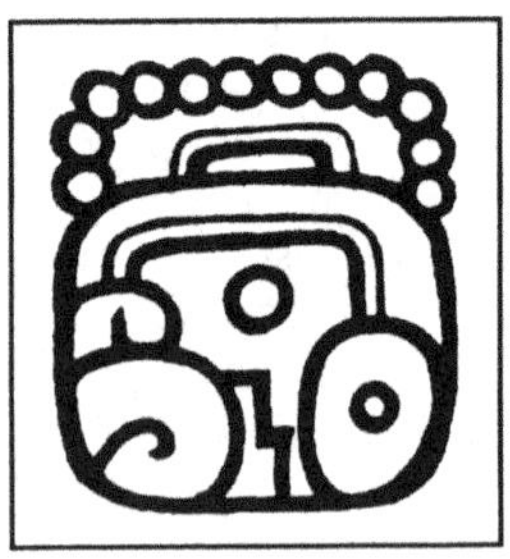

Lines of connected dots are thought to represent the flow of clotted blood. They were previously thought to mean water, or, in the "scattering" gesture, corn kernels. The monkey-faced "God C" is now thought to be the patron, or personification, of blood. His stylized face is shown on the front apron of the Lord's kilt. It is also found on representations of the "world tree".

> the structure of the body. Only the face is left free, an oasis in the jungle of the ornament. Maya art delights in quantity. Tropical proliferation, exuberance of the 'tierra caliente.' The excess of tropical fantasy, tropical sensuality."
> —Paul Westheim

Official Maya portraiture from the "Classic" period reveals no concept of "gilding the lily." The painstakingly sculpted bodies became mere clothes horses for a bewildering plethora of personalized accessory items. Sandals, loincloths, and mantels (for men)—and traditional huipils Maya women wear today—push back in time the justly famous weaving and embroidery techniques one still finds in highland Maya markets. The spectacular headgear of these ancient notables, with their cascades of iridescent feathers, would make Flo Zeigfeld gasp. Portrait sculptures fill every available empty space with items crafted from precious stones—carved and in mosaic—rows of shell tinklers, tropical feather designs using plumes of parrot, macaw, and hummingbird. There were capes of jaguar skins, belts and necklaces hung with shrunken trophy heads, stuffed boa constrictor tails, shark's teeth, and concave obsidian mirrors. Special care was reserved for the scepters, masks, and crowns. The elaborate patterns of human, floral, faunal, and composite grotesque figures that were worked into these "crown jewels" were, in fact, three-dimensional, full-figure hieroglyphic texts. The Bosch-like reptilian or ophidian monsters combined natural and conventionalized forms to create the protective royal totems, the Maya "heraldic devices." The crowns, often built around alligator or jaguar jaws, are too enormous to have been made out of anything heavier than paper-mache on basketry or light wood supports. Towering above this wedding-cake millinery, masses of yard-long Quetzal tail feathers, the Maya equivalent of ermine, rippled in iridescent waves. Amidst the undulating chaos of the Maya ruler's Sunday dress, it can be difficult to find the human figure at all! Like the tangled vegetation that cloaks their ruined cities today, the fully exploded Maya pictorial style looks like so much spaghetti to the uninitiated.

Western notions of beauty once again. Confronted with the tangled web of Maya graphic complexity, and unable to unravel its interior formal logic, the aesthetic jury favors European Classical ideals and interferes with our ability to see. Judgments are passed based on the nudes of Praxiteles; poetic metaphor is dismembered by Cartesian logic. If all we see in Maya art is disorder and superfluity, we are likely to find judgmental comparisons from our own artistic tradition. To call a style Mannerist or Baroque implies an underlying pejorative message. (Imagine a comparison to, say, the decorative arts from the time of Louis XVI without thinking about the Guillotine as well). Western notions of clarity, progress, "universal" ideals such as the Golden Mean, Vitruvian proportions, "le mot juste"—not only are these values absent among the Maya—but, they aren't seen as desirable. To the civilized Mesoamerican Indian, to be succinct is to be simple-mided.

The native rhetorical style admires the orator's ability to expand metaphorically. A truly long list of synonyms is an event to relish. The elaborate puns and double entendres, the use of images with multiple nuances of meaning, careful use of undercurrents of connotations; the expressive force of repetition, the measured meter of endless paired couplets; all these rhetorical devices were evidences of the speaker's profound knowledge of his universe. Any search for meaning in Maya art must begin with this premise: multiplicity of meaning is the only way to approach the shape-shifting face of the natural world. It was a *Weltanschauung* that accepted the logic of contradiction, the beauty of chance, the sadness of pleasure and the necessity for magic. The dynamic of its underlying dualism required the ecstatic discipline of ritual. New notions of the truth, such as the foreign Christ, were absorbed syncretically as yet another natural phenomena. Narrative prose, like 3-point perspective, cannot describe this world. Poetic metaphor is its only logic.

The written language seems to be ideally suited for these communication needs. Its form and syntax invites both visual and aural puns and metaphors combining these senses. The artist/poets of Copan seemed to delight in the use of puns to such a degree that one of their most illustrious rulers was never referred to twice with the same configurations of glyphs. Interlocking with the rhetoric of song, the poetry of visual forms, word and image never separated as they did in the West with the invention of the alphabet. As in Egypt and China, writers needed to draw and artists wrote. Nature was everywhere.

The glyphs could express a word, an idea, a phonetic sound, or function as semantic determinators, modifying meaning depending on their context. Some signs were clearly pictographic, others symbolic abstractions. Some naturalistic forms signified instead a phonetic component. Surprising substitutions for glyphs with known meanings have been carefully demonstrated. These are some of the characteristics of a unique written language which is slowly becoming understood.

A series of synonyms for abstract ideograms consisted of subtle variations of profile portrait-head glyphs. These portraits are thought of as "personalized" substitutions for the main signs they represent. They are differentiated one from another by individualized, significant details "infixed" onto the profile head. A mirror may be in a forehead, death marks on the cheek, a human ear is replaced by that of a jaguar or a shell. Often discrete, these infixed qualities are recognized to change the meaning of similar profile heads completely. In some inscriptions, these "personalized" glyphs become full figures with all the interlocking formal needs and opportunities of both writing and visual art.

As the glyphic texts slowly become understood we should be watchful for meanings underlying the primary intention. The choice of an ideograph with known secondary uses may have been intended to imply both. The visual arrangement may subordinate a usual configuration of signs. In most cases, on public monuments, the primary meanings refer to dates, places and events. They name people, sometimes giving phonetic "spellings" of these characters; the monuments record births and deaths and marriages. They recount battles, count captives and celebrate transfers of political power. They record the ritual sacrifice of captives, and the ritual of the ruler himself. The meaning of the texts is often reflected in, or expanded upon, in the visual record. Many costume details reveal themselves to be Maya versions of our slogan T-shirts—glyphic elements announcing the wearer's name, lineage, rank, and affiliations; they might describe his professional accomplishments, (or pretensions); they might reveal his patron animal spirit guardian or the totem of his clan or military order. The finery assembled for these formal stone memorials was probably not worn much in the tropics. Like the British crown jewels, the regalia was for ceremonial events and tucked away after the official "Snowdon" portrait was snapped.

A great deal of time has been spent analyzing the emblems of authority worn in these official stelae. The series of conventionalized grotesque figures that are scattered throughout many areas of the Maya area are usually referred to as gods.

In their quest for the perfect facial profile, head deformation was a routine practice. Also balls of wax were hung between the child's eyes to induce them to cross—a sign of beauty.

They combine natural features of men and animals, with invented or exaggerated additions. Dance masks and totemic costumes might also signify the lineage branches ascendant in various sites. The emblems might be more generalized indicators of power; perhaps the grotesque composites were simply clusters of signs. Notable among these "personalized" implements are items with prominent awl-like needles, often identified as sting-ray spines, which are often found in tombs of buried Maya rulers in the pelvic area of male skeletons.

Besides the needle-sharp sting-ray spines, excavators also discovered pointed blades of chipped flint and obsidian, awls of animal and human bone, as well as effigies made of precious jade. Their central and specific location in elite burials points to the importance of the

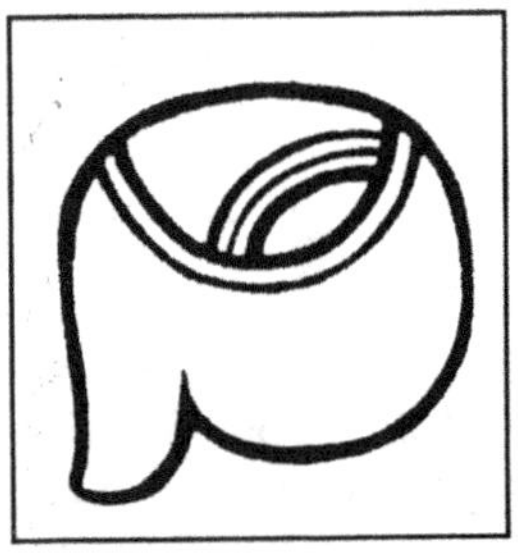

The "lancet" represents the instrument of bloodletting and is shown along with stingray spines and bloody paper blotters in platters used in the rite. The sign may correspond to the phoneme "Ni," meaning "nose, tip, or point." Here the main glyph is "infixed" with the bisecting arcs of the "mirror" glyphs giving the object a quality of "brightness" (polished obsidian).

bloodletting rite of the Maya king. With these sacred tools, he played out a central function of his duty and privilege of rank: by piercing his penis to bring forth the flow of "blue" blood, the Maya believed he sustained and nourished the land and its people.

> "At the end of the Law of Lord 5 Ahau, his flint knife shall descend, his genital organ shall descend. The cord had come forth, the arrow had come forth, in its 15th tun, it would be."
> —*Book of Chilam Balam of Tizimin*

> "Quetzalcoatl did penance, piercing his legs and drawing blood with which he stained and made bloody the maguey spikes...and this custom and order the priests and ministers of the Mexican idols took over as Quetzalcoatl had used it." —Sahagun

> "Ca tu hop-oc-O u-tok-ol; Y-ak-O ti y-e-O ci..." (and then his tongue will begin bleeding, from the point of the maguey...)
> —*Ritual of the Bacabs (Roys, 1965:77)*

The artist/poets of Copan seemed to delight in the use of puns to such a degree that one of their most illustrious rulers was never referred to twice with the same configurations of glyphs.

> The priests making a sign unto them, every one taketh his rasor, and turning their eyes unto the Idoll, they gash and wound their owne tongues, some thrust them through and the most part cut them so that the blood issueth forth in great abundance, all of them."
> —Peter Martyr

> "They offered sacrifices of their own blood: sometimes cutting themselves around in pieces and they left them in this way as a sign. Other times they pierced their cheeks,

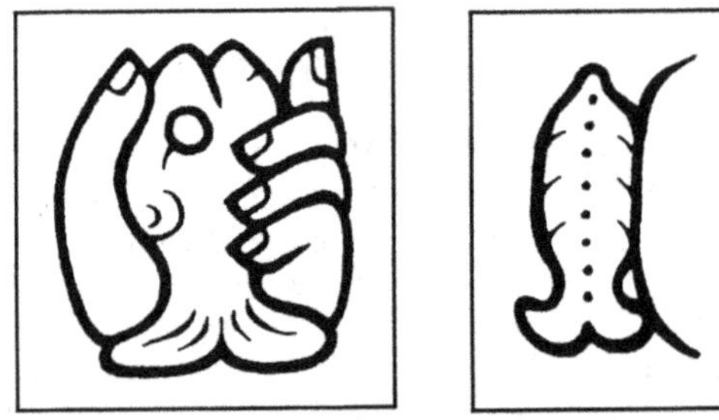

The "hand-grasping-fish," means "to bleed (someone)." Its phonetic value, "Tok," is derived from the word for sardine (small fish: "Ix-Toc"). The glyph occasionally substitutes a stingray spine (often mistaken as a feather) for the fish. The fish is a rebus for "flint" (in Maya, "Tok"). This sonic metaphor is illustrated by the example from Machaquila where the "hand-grasping-fish" glyph is followed by the realistic affix pictograph of an "eccentric flint."

> at others their lower lips. Sometimes they scarify certain parts of their bodies, at others they pierced their tongues in a slanting direction from side to side and passed bits of straw through the holes with horrible suffering; others slit the superfluous part of the virile member leaving it as they did their ears, on account of which the general historian of the Indies was deceived saying that they practiced circumcision. At other times they performed an obscene and painful sacrifice, those who were to make it gathered in the temple whereafter they were placed in a row. Holes

An Olmec shaman produces his "were-jaguar" nagual (alter ego) from the precursor to the Maya "Vision Serpent": his elongated penis. (Oxtotitlan Cave, Guerrero, Mexico; drawing after David C. Grove).

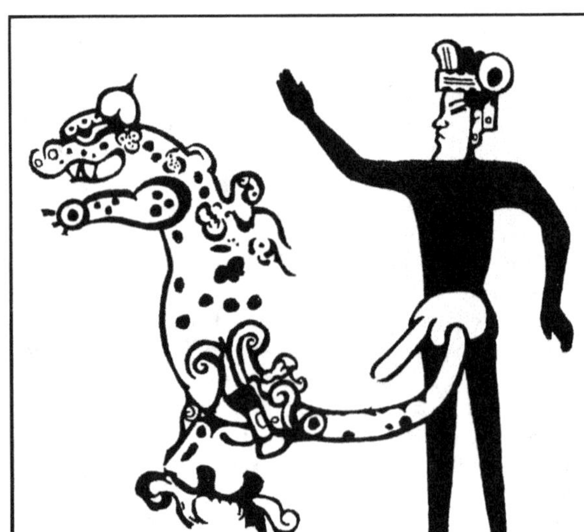

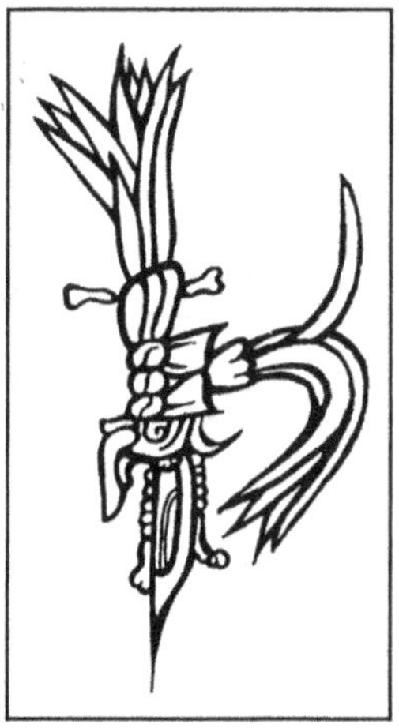

The "perforator god" (identified by David Joralemon) is recognized by the three knotted "bow-ties" (here in profile) topped with feathers, and above a long-nosed, upper jaw of a Maya dragon head. The pointed instrument of sacrifice Is here jeweled and infixed with the "Mirror" glyph, and descends from his serpent head.

were made in the virile member of each one obliquely from side to side and through the holes which they had thus made, they passed the greatest quantity of thread that they could: and all of them being this fastened and strung together, they anointed the idol with the blood which flowed from all these parts; and he who did this the most was considered as the bravest; and their sons from the earliest age began to practice it, and it is a horrible thing to see how inclined they were to this ceremony." —Diego de Landa

"In addition to these extraordinary sacrifices it was very usual, as I have already said, among the Mexicans and Guatemalans (for all had certain sacrifices and rites) to sacrifice to the idols that they found on the roads, anointing the face of the idol with blood they draw from their private parts, according to what others say, so that anyone who passed by an idol and did not offer him any portion of blood drawn there from his own body was not considered devout or good, in the same way that we do reverence when we come upon any cross or image on any journey, for thus that blind people likewise had their shrines and sanctuaries in the fields and roads."
—Tomas Lopez Medel, "Relacion" (1612)

An effigy of Tecpatl (sacrificial knife) is animated by features made of shell and turquoise mosaic (from a cache in the Great Temple of Tenochtitlan, Aztec).

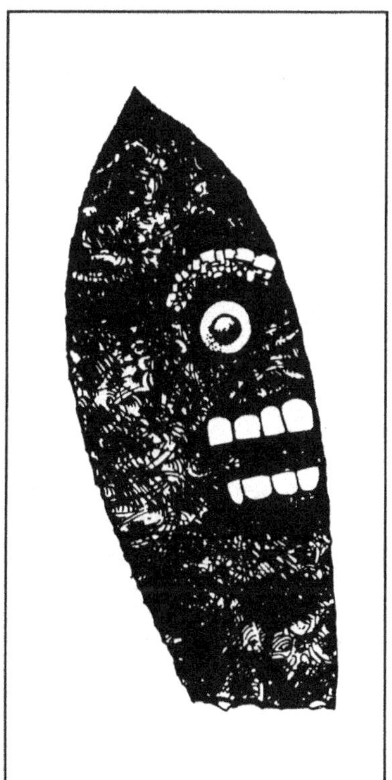

Silhouette of an "eccentric flint" found beneath a monument at Quirigua. It is a masterpiece of flint knapping, with at least one profile featuring a God K-like flare in the forehead (Maya).

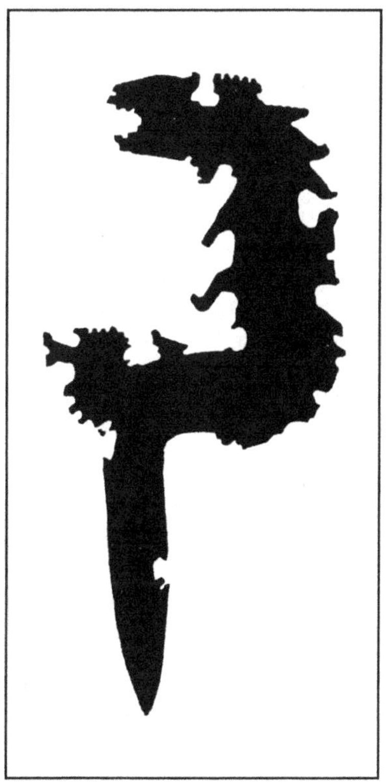

A woman from Palenque presents a ruler with an "eccentric flint" shaped to represent a supernatural, placed on top of a "shield" whose central feature may be the flayed and preserved facial skin of a previous ruler, kept as a fetish.

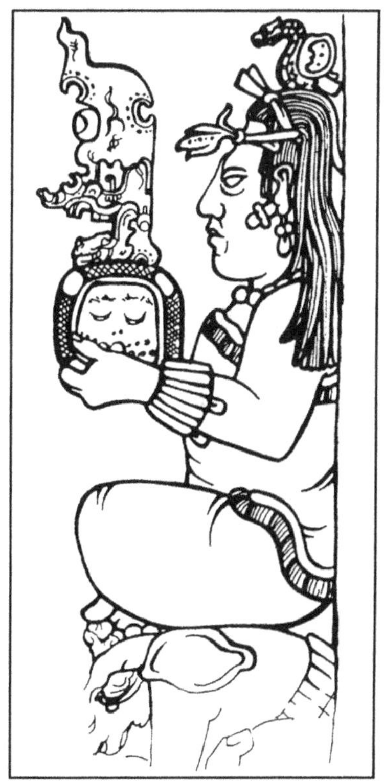

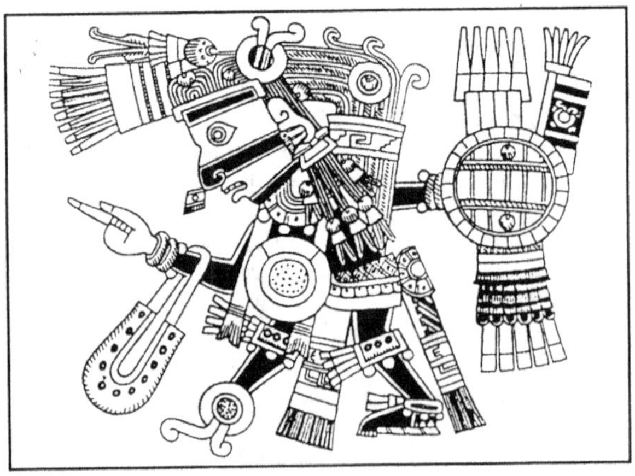

I.

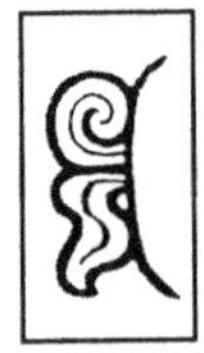

2a.

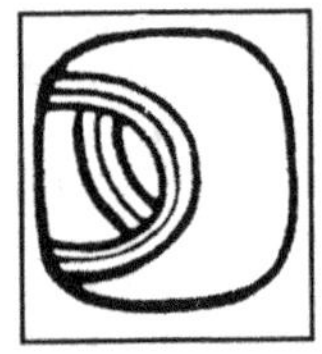

2b.

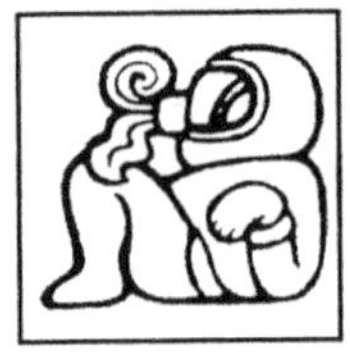

2c.

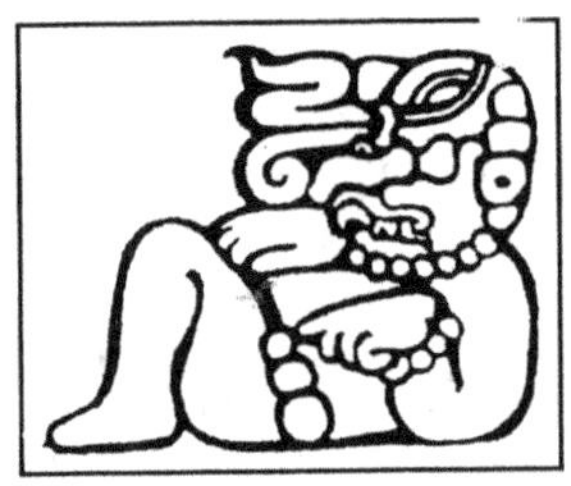

2d.

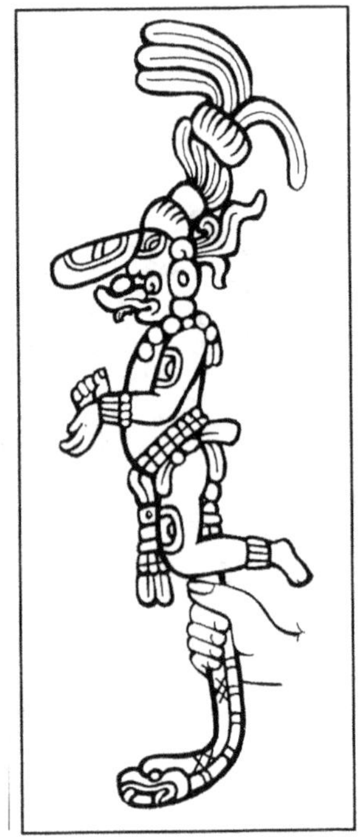

2.

The "Smoking Mirror" (Aztec: Tezcatlipoca, Maya: God K; "Ah Bolon Czacab") was the Shiva of the New World, primordial shaman, trickster, ruler of fate and patron of princes. His Mexican form (I) is recognized by the circular "smoking mirror" which replaced one of his feet and adorns his temple (after the Borgia Codex). His Maya form (2) is often found on the so-called "Manikin Scepter." It is recognized by the composite body which replaces one leg with a serpent, and features a grotesque long-nosed head with either an ax or a smoking tube imbedded in his forehead. The forehead element may be replaced by the hieroglyph of his name: "smoke" (2a) and "mirror/brightness" (2b). This glyph can be used alone. It can replace the head in a full-figured glyph (2c), or it may be "infixed" into the forehead (2d).

The Olmec, Mesoamerica's oldest civilization, provides the earliest, and one of the most graphic illustrations of genital sacrifice. A remarkable mural found inside a cave in the modern Mexican state of Guerrero, shows a crouching jaguar, symbol of the priest-king in later times—emerging from the stylized jaw of a serpent whose body, in turn, reveals itself to be the greatly enlarged penis of a human figure. The obligation of ritual blood sacrifice was one the Maya later shared with the other cultures that inherited Olmec patterns of ceremonialism.

The Nahuatl myth describing the birth of the sun of our current era, provides man with his model and his obligation to repay for this divine self-sacrifice. Nanautzin, the outcast syphilitic god, courageously threw himself on the sacrificial pyre, rising in apotheosis as the "Fifth Sun," Tonahtiuh. Rather than free man from sin and death, as Jesus' death and resurrection did for the Christian west, the effort of the sun's daily battle with death in the underworld of night, called for man to emulate his self-sacrificing example and sustain his life-giving energy with the blood of "ixiplatli": victims who impersonating the god, reenacted the myth, and by the sympathetic magic of their sacrificial death, rejuvenated the world by keeping the sun in motion.

The inauguration of the Azec "Tlatoani" (Speaker) featured the sacrifice of conquered war prisoners, but the ritual culminated in the ruler following the example of the culture hero, Quetzalcoatl; by drawing blood from his penis he completed his right to rule. This central act was understood to mimic the mythic first penance of the "Feathered Serpent" who brought mankind to life by mixing his genital blood with ancestral bones from a previous era. The penitential nature of this new world Prometheus is indicated by the presence of a bone bloodletter in his regalia. In a similar fashion, the Maya "shekinah" is an indispensable feature in any representation of a ruler, either held in one hand, present in the headdress, or, most frequently, attached to the apron covering the king's genitals.

Iconographers have identified a series of forms in sculpture and vase painting that they believe represent "perforators" or "lancets" that have become "personified" power objects, if not deities in themselves. Recognized primarily by a stack of three knotted "bow ties" of cloth or absorbent paper, the blade or spine extends downward from a conventionalized dragon head, itself a simplified serpent upper jaw with human and amphibian attributes. The single front tooth of the young sun god (God 1), humanized as Chac-Xib-Chac, shaped like a shark's tooth has been seen to be a

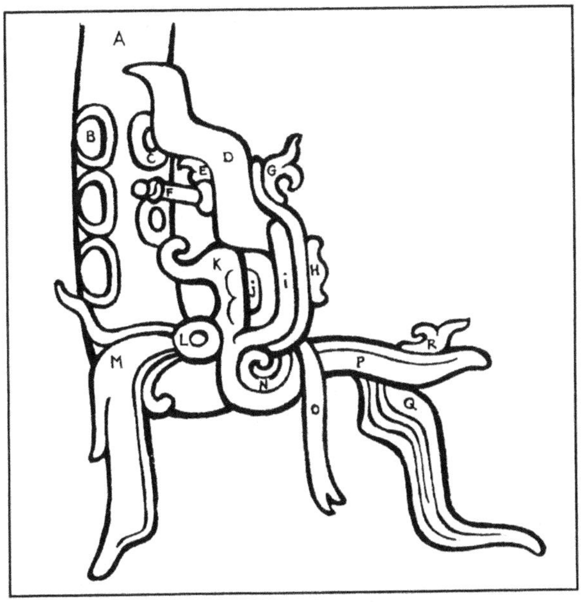

Typical conventionalized Serpent head (after Herbert J. Spinden): A) body; B) belly markings; C) back markings; D) nose; E) nose scroll; F) nose plug (ornament); G) incisor tooth; H) molar tooth; I) jaw; J) eye; K) supraorbital plate; L) ear plug; M) ear ornament; N) curled fang; O) tongue; P) lower jaw; Q) beard; R) incisor tooth. This breakdown of the features of the Maya dragon/serpent was done in 1913, but the terminology is still used, as the details Spinden noticed then are found in one way or other in most representations of this creature.

perforator as well. The "Triadic" emblem of kingship common to the Maya area from earliest times, contains as a central element, the upright spine of the sting-ray. The "personified lancet" is thought to be an avatar of the deified Flint knife, whose cutting edge is yet an aspect of the "Smoking Mirror," patron of princes and ruler of fate.

Known to Mayanists rather prosaically as God K (or God II of the Palenque Triad), he was called "Ah Bolon Dzacab," ("9 of Many Generations") and his association with ruling families in the late Classic period seems to have been popularized by a dynasty at Palenque, which claimed certain congenital deformities as evidence of their divine kinship with this deity. The founder of this ruling family, Pacal, had an inherited clubfoot, which he likened to God K's serpent foot. Like his Mexican equivalent, Tezcatipoca, who was also lame, the missing foot was replaced by the "smoking" obsidian mirror of divination. Likewise, one hieroglyphic name for this personage among the Maya combined the glyphs for smoke and mirror. The connection the mirror has with kingship is stated outright in the Maya dictionary of the Motul dialect; "U nen cab, u nen cah" which describes the priest, chief or governor of the land or village, who is in the mirror in which all the people see themselves.

The Smoking Mirror was patron of Aztec rulers as well, one of his names being: "Master of the Lords of the Earth": (Tlatocateotl). His many names and disguises however reveal his origin as the prototype Amerindian trickster: the shaman/sorcerer who ruled fate, the impartial "blindfolded one," who, walking backwards, was known as the "Enemy of Both Sides." He could bestow power and riches, and just as arbitrarily reduce the famous to misery. His jaguar avatar, "Heart of the Mountain" (Tepeyollotl) was a title shared with Maya rulers and magicians (Balam). As Huemac, he was the mythic adversary of Quetzalcoatl, yet he could, as the self-created "Night Wind," the "Soul of the World," subsume the benevolent, creative features of the Feathered Serpent in a union of dynamic opposites. The poet-king of Texcoco, Nexahualcoyotl, is credited with creating a cult crystallized from these numerous features of Tezcatlipoca. His vision of Tloque Nahuaque ("lord of the far and near") was that of an Immanent divinity which approached the philosophical abstraction of monotheism.

A more frightening aspect, however, was "The Night Ax": here, Tezcatilopa was visualized as a headless man, haunting cross-roads, with a dreadful wound in his chest which kept opening and slamming shut like an ax blow. Taking the form of the cutting edge of a curved obsidian, he was the frost (Itztlacoliuhqui). As the agent of sacrifice he was "Tecpatl" the flint knife. The Maya "personalized" bloodletter and the "eccentric" flint knife were obvious corollaries to these animated fetishes.

The Smoking Mirror in Ah Bolon Dzacab's forehead was frequently replaced by a burning flare, or a smoking tube of tobacco. (The Maya word "tah" meaning both torch and obsidian.) These might be glossed with a yet more ancient symbol: an oblong Olmec "celt: the oblong stone hammer—the oldest and most basic tool, buried in large numbers as ritual fetishes, collected along with other Olmec heirlooms by later cultures, and still considered one of the most characteristic artifacts produced by this ancient culture. Like Thor's hammer, thunderbolts were thought to be heavenly ax blows of the storm gods. Flint and obsidian were thought to be created when lightning struck the earth.

Flint and obsidian were as sacred to the Maya as rain or corn. They alone provided the sharp cutting edge necessary, not only for sacrifice, but for all the chores of everyday life. The ancient, venerated form of the Olmec celt added a pedigree of antiquity to the form of the stone hammer. Nature gave man a needle in the form of the spine of the maguey and the sting-ray. Fetishes fashioned from these powerful materials were animated by their sacrificial usage, releasing and compounding their innate magic, transforming them into the "personifications" of the divine protectors of the ruling Maya lineages, who had, like their ancient Chinese counterparts (according to K.C. Chang), "the monopoly of high shamanism, which enabled the rulers to gain critical access to divine and ancestral wisdom, the basis of their political authority."

> **Genesis 17:6.** And I will make thee exceeding fruitful, and I will make nations of thee, and kings shall come out of thee.
> **17:10.** This is my covenant, which ye shall keep, between me and you and thy seed after thee; Every man child among you shall be circumcised.
> **17:11.** And ye shall circumcise the flesh of your foreskin; and it shall be a token of the covenant betwixt me and you.

> "This is, in truth, your God; this is your support; this is, furthermore, the representation, the memory of your Creator and Maker. Do not give your fire to the tribes until they present offering to Tohil. Ask Tohil what they should give when they come to receive fire."
>
> All the tribes were trembling and shivering with cold... "Will you not have pity on us, we only ask a little of your fire?"... "Well! Are they willing to give their waist and their armpits to suckle? Do they want me to embrace them?" (that is, to deliver up victims to be sacrificed)...And this was the opening of the breasts about which Tohil had spoken; Tohil said then: "Give thanks before setting out; do what is necessary to bleed your ears, prick your elbows, and make your sacrifices, this shall be your thanks to God."
>
> "Very well," they said, and took blood from their ears. And they wept in their chants..."
>
> —*Popul Vuh, Sacred Book of the Quiche Maya.*

> "On Good Friday 1868, (in Chamula), a boy 10 or 11 years old, Domingo Gomez Checheb, was crucified, the blood removed from his body and perfumed with incense."
>
> —Demetrio Soli Morales (on the War of the Castes).

The notion of a deified "penis perforator" certainly seems more bizarre to us in a post-Victorian, post-Freudian era than it did to the Spanish of the 16th century. In an era when men's fashions featured the "codpiece," Montaigne observed that, regarding the penis: "in most parts of the world that part of the body was deified." Apart from the machismo characteristic of the Spanish in worldly affairs, it was a time when spiritual lessons were taught by displaying the nude body of the infant Jesus; when the circumcision of Christ (his "pruning") was the occasion for masses and sermons. St. Catherine of Siena claimed the prepuce of Jesus to be her mystic betrothal ring; this same relic, along with the holy umbilical cord was treasured in the church of St. John Lateran. A sermon, delivered to

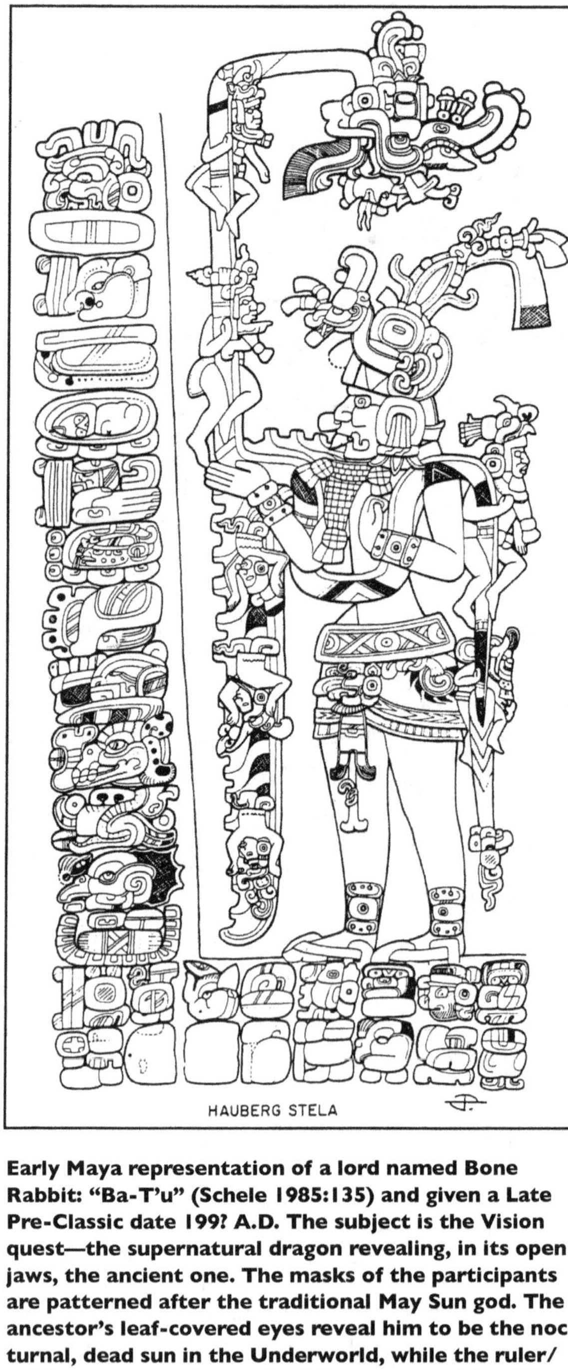

Early Maya representation of a lord named Bone Rabbit: "Ba-T'u" (Schele 1985:135) and given a Late Pre-Classic date 199? A.D. The subject is the Vision quest—the supernatural dragon revealing, in its open jaws, the ancient one. The masks of the participants are patterned after the traditional May Sun god. The ancestor's leaf-covered eyes reveal him to be the nocturnal, dead sun in the Underworld, while the ruler/celebrant wears the mask of the new sun rising. The Vision Serpent here winds around his shoulders and rears up in front of him arching downward over his head. Miniature spirits shinny up the serpent's body (which seems to be made of flint due to the characteristic markings). Three of these Maya leprechauns who have failed the climb fall in a stream of blood, their bodies cut in half. Archaic versions of the "lancet" and "God C" glyphs identify how"Ba-T'u" came to have this vison. (Drawing courtesy of James Porter.)

a Maya "True Man": "Today Our lord began to shed His consecrated blood for us...Today His precious blood flowed. His flesh was cut with a stone knife."

In the same state of mind, we should also look at the imagery presented to the Maya for the first time, without explanation or instruction. Tortured and bound sacrificial victims decorate every Christian church verbal imagery of the redemptive blood of the sacred ordeal, the cannibal sacraments, the death of apotheosis of the victim. The list of attendant martyrs follows this example, enduring the most inventively gruesome deaths, all the while singing and blessing their tormentors like misplaced Iroquois warriors. We understand, of course, that there was only one Crucified Savior, that the sacraments are symbolic, and that the martyrs didn't choose their fate like an Aztec "Ixiptlatli" would.

The native deity impersonator of Xipe totec, "Our Flayed Lord," was believed to quite literally become the God as he died tied to a cross similar to Christ's, tortured like He was, and killed with atlatl darts. A literal communion followed where his divine flesh was eaten, and the skin flayed from his body was worn as the token of the husk of spring corn. When Cortez visited the pilgrimage shrine of the Maya island of Cozumel, he destroyed the idols of the oracle of Ix Chel. Thinking his job was completed by baptizing uncomprehending native worshippers, he left for Mexico after installing a Christian cross. How was he to know that this symbol was equally revered as a schema of the pagan Maya cosmos: the world tree and the cardinal directions? Human sacrifice continued, now on Christian crucifixes. The oracle of the Moon Goddess continued until the 19th century as the oracle of the "Talking Cross." As a voice of class war, and call to return to the ways of the ancestors, the seers of the "War of the Castles" dictated in 1868 the creation of an Indian Christ, and the boy, Domingo Gomez Checheb was crucified in Chamula.

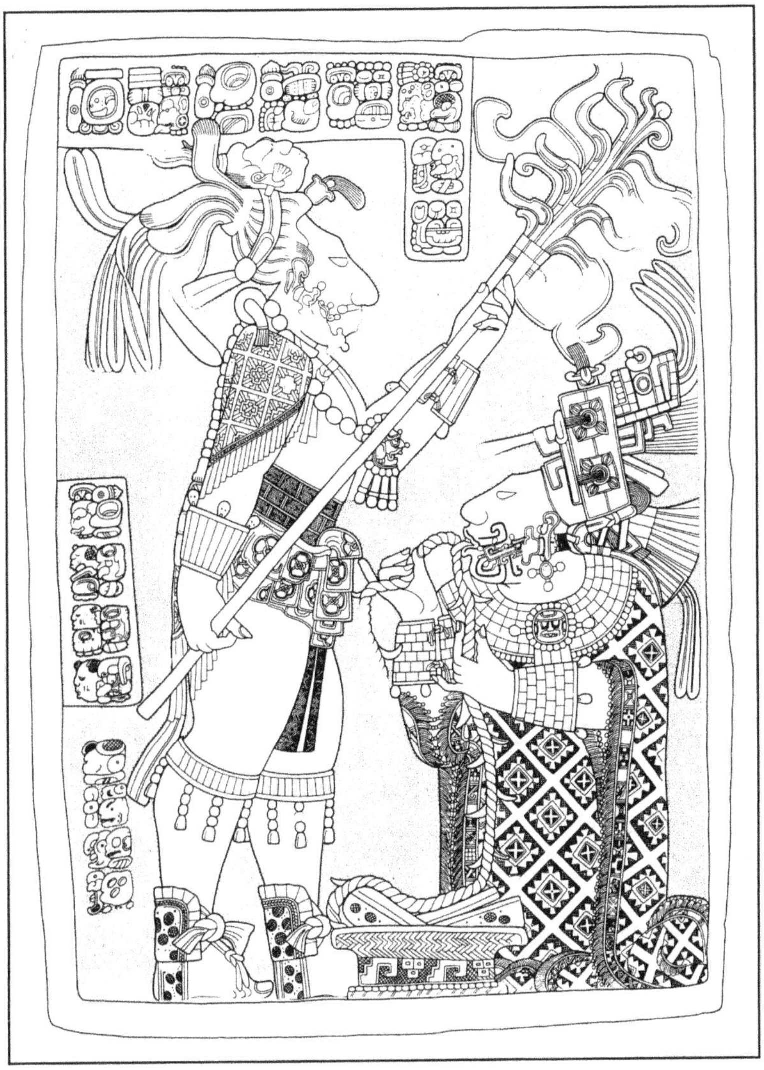

On October 28, 709 A.D., "Shield Jaguar," five days after he assumed the title of Blood Lord of Yaxchilan, performed the bloodletting rite, and is shown here supervising the Tongue-piercing ceremony as it is performed by his principal wife, "Lady Xoc." He wears a shrunken trophy head on his own and carries a staff which resembles the enormous tobacco smoking tubes used by the Warao on the Orinoco today. "Lady Xoc" pulls a cord studded with maguey thorns through a hole in her tongue; the flaming design of her mouth tattoo indicates that she is no stranger to this ordeal. The design of her headdress indicates the type of event her act is a part of; the foreign cult totems—the mask of Tlaloc, the Mexican "lightning hurler," and the Year sign of the reformed calendar—indicates the sort of vision she seeks. (Lintel 24, Drawing by Ian Graham)

Pope Alexander VI, father of both Cesare and Lucrezia Borgia, examined the theological ramifications of such relics, arguing the case, for and against, whether the divine foreskin of Jesus joined the Savior when he ascended into heaven. On another such occasion, the sermon sounded like something one might hear in Yucatan at the same time, apropos the auto-sacrifice of

Within a yet wider scope, Maya religious practices share features, not just with their neighbors but with all aboriginal groups migrating over the Bering Straits from Serbia. The magical nature of war and sacrifice build on these widespread chthonic spiritual assumptions. While it is tempting to view the penis mutilation ritual as some Spanish did—a memory of their past as remnants of Israel's Lost Tribes, the notion is as misleading as comparisons to Christ. Viewed with the much more invasive self-mutilation generally practiced by women, that of pulling spiny cords through holes in the tongue, explanations ought to be sought at more basic levels. The psychological equation of the penis and the tongue needs little reiteration, but both the Oedipal castration fears proposed by Freud for circumcision and Bruno Bettelheim's contrasting notion of "womb-envy" with the "Symbolic Wound" mimicking the magic generative power of the menses, fail to account for the *Weltanschauung* of the New World. If the sacrificial act reflects such primordial longings and fears, it seems concrete anthropological examples such as those Bettelheim finds in Australia or Melanesia ought to emerge. If the wounding of the Male expresses the desire to own the magically fertile menstrual flow by mimicking it, the symbol seems less important than its function of linking the opposing forces of mother/father, sky/earth in one ritual practitioner. This way of looking at the rite is less male dominated as well, as it allows for the pervasive influence of women in the ritual life of shamanistic village life. The tongue sacrifice, then, is the woman sorcerer's rite—a rite in which she symbolically imitates the male to achieve the same equilibrium. The Quiche Maya shaman of today is called Mother/father (Chuch quaja) and this reconciled dualism recalls the original creator god/goddess (Ometeotl/Omecihuatl).

> "The objects of a man's physical environment, such as animals, plants, heavenly bodies and various sorts of natural phenomena are his equals or even his superiors in the possession of skill and intelligence and a will to help or hinder. The individual chooses from these his best friend in the society of nature."
> —H.J. Spinden

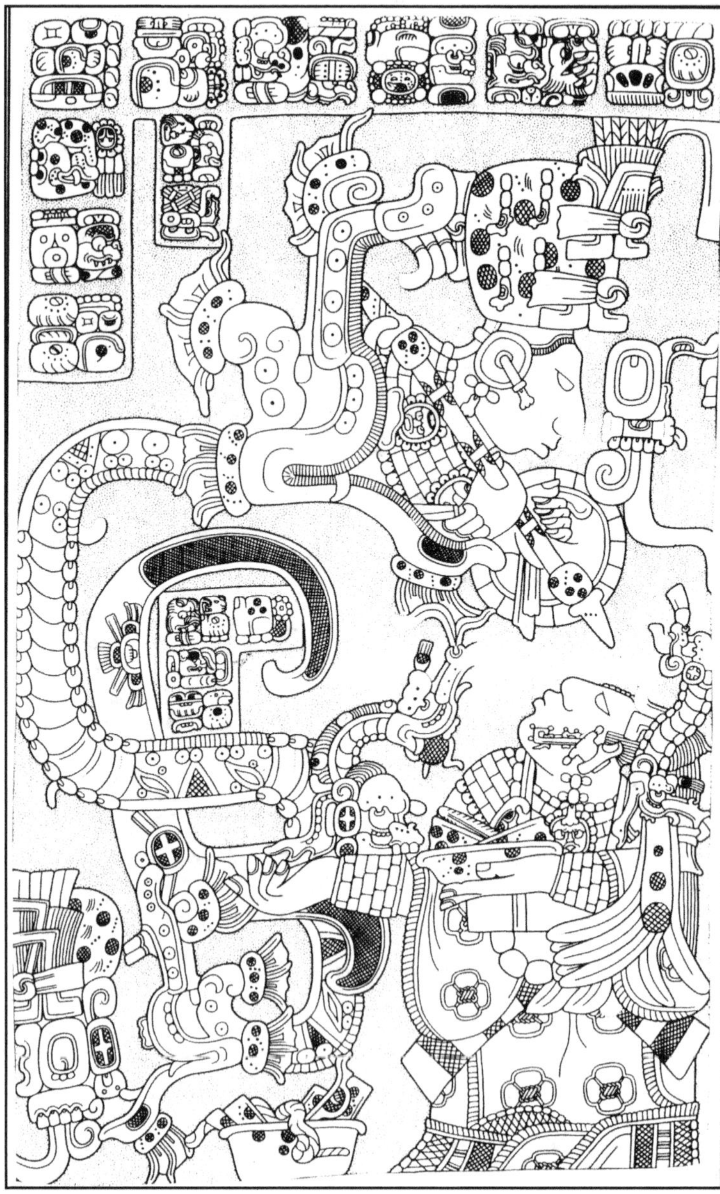

On October 23 681 A.D. on the event of the "Shield Jaguar's" accession to the throne of Yaxchilan, Lady Xoc summons her Vision Serpent, the Tlaloc-Warrior Knight, ancestor-founder of the Order the "Lightning Bolt Hurler," a clan of military-political elite, now ruling Yaxchilan, whose lineage descends from the "Curl Nose and Stormy Sky" dynasty of grand Tikal. For the event she wears and holds the underworld insect with two skeletal heads—the dragon and the human skull; her bloody lancet and cord rests in the offering bowl, fillets of paper soaking up the precious liquid. Another bowl is on the ground, its gathered blood turning to smoke. Amidst the clouds of swirling smoke, her Vision Serpent looms up over her. It opens its monstrous jaws, allowing the ancestral lineage warrior to pose. He brandishes a spear; behind the mask of his knightly patron, the goggle-eyed mask of the Storm bringer. The device that forms his totem also emerges from the nether head of the miraculous reptile. The writing on his scene was written backwards—mirror writing. Is this affectation a metaphor for the transformative nature of Lady Xoc's experience: the world turned inside out? (Lintel 25, Drawing by Ian Graham)

"Je dis qu'il faut etre voyant, se faire voyant. —Le Poete se fait voyant par un long, immense et raisonne dereglement de tous les sens." —Arthur Rimbaud, 15 Mai 1871

"When through intense aggression I wander
in Samsara,
On the luminous light-path of the mirror-like
wisdom,
may the gurus of the sacred lineage go before
me,
help me to cross the bardo's dangerous
pathway,
And bring me to the perfect Buddha State."
—*Tibetan Book of the Dead*

The sophisticated refinements of Maya civilization should not distract us from the basic shamanistic elements upon which its religion was built. While the Maya and their Mexican neighbors are thought to have built political states even empires, warfare was intertwined with religion in a tradition common to Amerindians from Lake Huron to Peru. The priestly hierarchy contained specialists of all sorts from war chiefs and administrators to local herbalists and soothsayers. The shaman was an institution shared by native communities in the arctic, along the Amazon as well as those housed on top of stone pyramids.

This shared world-view knew a magical universe, complete with multi-layered heavens and hells, extending on the surface of the earth in the cardinal directions from a central *axis mundi*, a world-tree—for the Maya it was a giant Ceiba. This universe was peopled by spirits subject to manipulation by "specialists of the sacred," in the person of the shaman. Nature contained no "inanimate" objects. There was no line between the sacred and the profane. Animals as totems, guides, and spirit helpers were man's equal. The shaman could detach his soul from his body and transform into his "nagual," his animal guise. The shaman achieved his powers as oracle and healer through initiatory and periodic trance states. These "archaic techniques of ecstasy" were induced by ritual chants and dances, penitential sacrifice, fasting and purification, as well as a liberal helping of a wide variety of hallucinogenic substances. These techniques allowed the shaman to break the bonds of the flesh; "flay off his skin" was the metaphor, and ascend to the sky or plunge into the infernal regions. The breakthrough to Otherworlds people by Ancestors in the Vision quest, guided and protected by his spirit guardian and alter ego. Returning to the real world, he brought messages and power to manipulate the natural order. The *Popul Vuh* of the Quiche Maya can be seen as a poetic account of such an inner journey to the underworld. The heroes are twins, Hunahpu and Xbalanque, whose adventures elicit the help of animal spirits and a good dose of guile and bravery, in their battle to outwit the Twin Lords of Death. The late retelling of what certainly was a Classic period "Book of the Dead," can be seen by some collectors and scholars painted on the exquisite funerary ceramics dating hundreds of years earlier than the colonial period manuscript of the tale.

"We have drunk Soma; we have become immortal. We have gone to the light; we have found the gods."—*Rig Veda*; VIII; 48:3

"In Vincente Pach's ranch I saw sacrifice. They took a chisel and wooden mallet, placed the one who had to sacrifice himself on a smooth stone slab, took out his penis, and cut it in three parts two finger-breadths (up), the largest in the center, saying at the same time incantations and words I did not understand. The one who was undergoing the operation did not seem to suffer, and did not lose a drop of blood."—Ximenez, among the Manche Chol Maya

"And after that the boys next entered Razor House, the second test of Xibalba. And this is when it was ordained that they be cut clear through with knives. It was intended to be quick, intended that they should die, but they did not die . . ."—*Popul Vuh*

In these bizarre underworld scenes, the hero twins find the deer an important player in the drama. In the extensive network of caves that honeycomb the Maya area, deer remains are frequently linked with evidence of ritual self-sacrifice. Seen by the Maya as entrances to their hell, Xibalba, these caves were powerful places to begin a shaman's Vision Quest, the dark silences conducive to the onset of ecstatic trance states. The reason for the closeness of deer could perhaps be because of the powerful hallucinogenic fungus the animal seemed to "own." Called "Underworld Mushroom" by the Quiche (Xibalba okox) and "Mushroom that makes one lose one's judgment" by the Cakchiquel Maya (K'aizalah okox), the coprophilous fungus, *Stropharia Cubensis*, requires the multiple stomachs of a ruminant to germinate. So the mushroom grew from the droppings of the favored deer, his gift to the shaman. The skins of the *Bufo Marinus* toad also contain a powerful mind-altering substance, and this animal joins the deer in underworld depictions. Highly potent tobacco and nicotine snuff were used as narcotics, and no ritual would even begin without enormous quantities of fermented Balche, a Maya honey mead. Hallucinogens could easily be imported from other regions as other more perishable luxury items were, but this pharmacy lists only those substances immediately at hand. Ritual drunkenness, along with ritual buffoonery, accompanied many a serious ceremony.

Ritual events require a period of preparation, lengthy fasting and sexual abstinence, scalding steam baths, and blood penance. Ritual books of divination were consulted, the propitious calendrical co-ordinates plotted, positions of the moon, planets, especially the baleful Venus were noted. Extended chanting, recitations of past experiences by initiates, careful attention to the refinements of dress, adjustments of masks, rehearsing of dance movements and gestures, the exact ritual movements and recitations practiced. Finally, the numbing rhythms of percussion orchestras, drums, rattles, scraped turtle carapaces, pierced by whistles and conch trumpets. Preliminary animal sacrifices and the burning of clouds of copal incense; lengthy preparations needed to condition the shaman and ready his psychological and physical state for the ordeal to come.

Like the Sun Dance of the Plains Indians, the severe bodily mortifications of the Maya were initiations into a technique of ecstasy the adept shared with Javanese fakirs and East Indian Yogis. Unlike the regular penance of routine bloodletting, the self-mortification techniques required for the Maya Vision Quest were severe: the penis was cut or pierced with cords linked to other participants; the tongue was punctured and long cords or sticks "the size of a thumb" passed through the opening, yet some ethnographic accounts of these rites record no blood and no report of pain. The ordeal of tongue mutilation seems to be specifically adapted to the hallucinations of the trance. The special potency of this organ is a motif the Maya shared with Shamans from the Northwest Coast. Medicine men of the Tlingit, Haida, Kwakiutl practiced tongue mutilation, and greatly valued the magical powers of its blood. Tongue biting is represented in iconography and was described as part of trance-inducing behavior. As with the Maya, the theatrical trappings of attendant ceremonies no doubt increased the tension in the audiences and provided a well-known ritual context for the participant to become immersed in. One description of the climax of a winter "Cannibal Society" ceremony observes, "the celebration terminated with a shocking and distressing show of deliberate self-torment. These men, each with two bayonets run through their sides, between the ribs, walked up and down the room, singing war songs, and exulting in their firmness and triumph over pain."

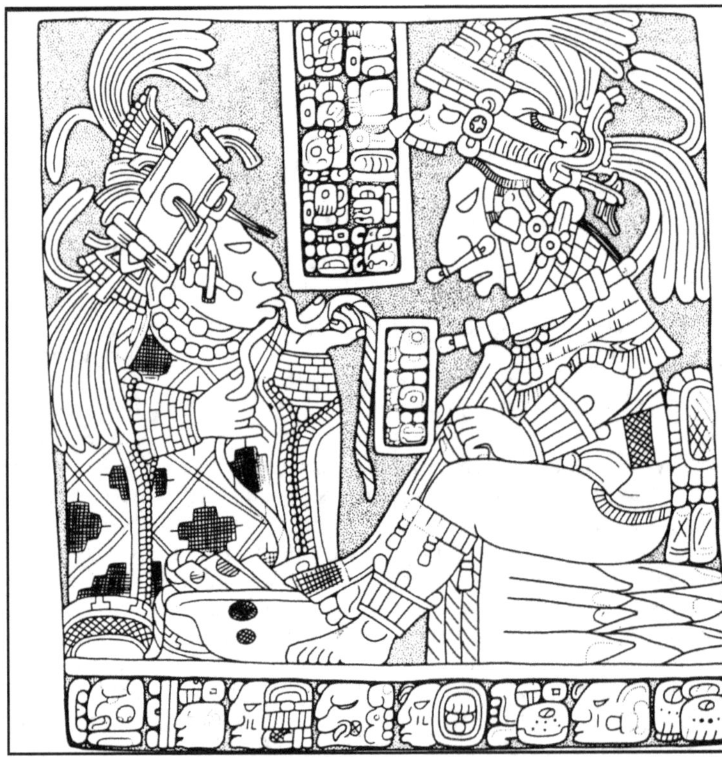

On February 18, 752 A.D., the new lineage Lord of Yaxchilan, "Bird Jaguar" joins his wife Lady Balam-Ix in commemorating the birth of his heir. The couple wear the same Vision clothing as that worn by their predecessor Lady Xoc, indicating they seek to commune with the same ancestral vision. Bird Jaguar wears the Skull/dragon circlet, while his wife wears the Tlaloc war cult turban. She pulls the cord through her tongue while he holds the bloodletter ready in his lap. (Lintel 17, Drawing by Ian Graham)

The phenomenon of self-inflicted "non-hurtful pain" was studied by Dr. Andrew Weil as one of numerous non-chemical ways to induce a trance-like alteration of normal consciousness (the desire for which he finds cross-cultural proven by the near-universal use of intoxicants; he finds this desire innate and equal to the drives of hunger and sex). His study included a personal initiation into an Indian sweat lodge, where, guided by an experienced elder, he avoided serious scalding by temperatures exceeding 200 degrees. To endure this and other ordeals, psychological and physiological conditions normally perceived as painful and damaging to the body, instead produced a "high." As fear was the greatest obstacle to the experience, a preliminary degree of concentration, facilitated by the presence of an experienced veteran guide—someone who had been through the process before and who was unafraid—was essential. Concentration was deepened by the stimulation which emptied the mind of verbal thought so it focused instead on the sensations emanating from the body. The transcendant "high" began during the most intense stimulation and increased after the stimulation is over.

As in other "Believe it or Not" ascetic practices, the body's autonomic nervous system is trained to accept a jolt of energy, normally registered as painful, from the body's periphery to the Central Nervous System, in the process releasing massive electrochemical compounds similar to hallucinogens—indoles related to serotonin (a naturally-occuring brain compound activated by LSD) stimulate secretions of the pineal gland, the body's "Third Eye." While hallucinogens can facilitate the process, they are not necessary to initiate the sequence. These extreme bodily "mortifications" are then another facet of the ecstatic-Shamanistic religious practices brought to the New World by the Paleo-Mesolithic Indians from Siberia.

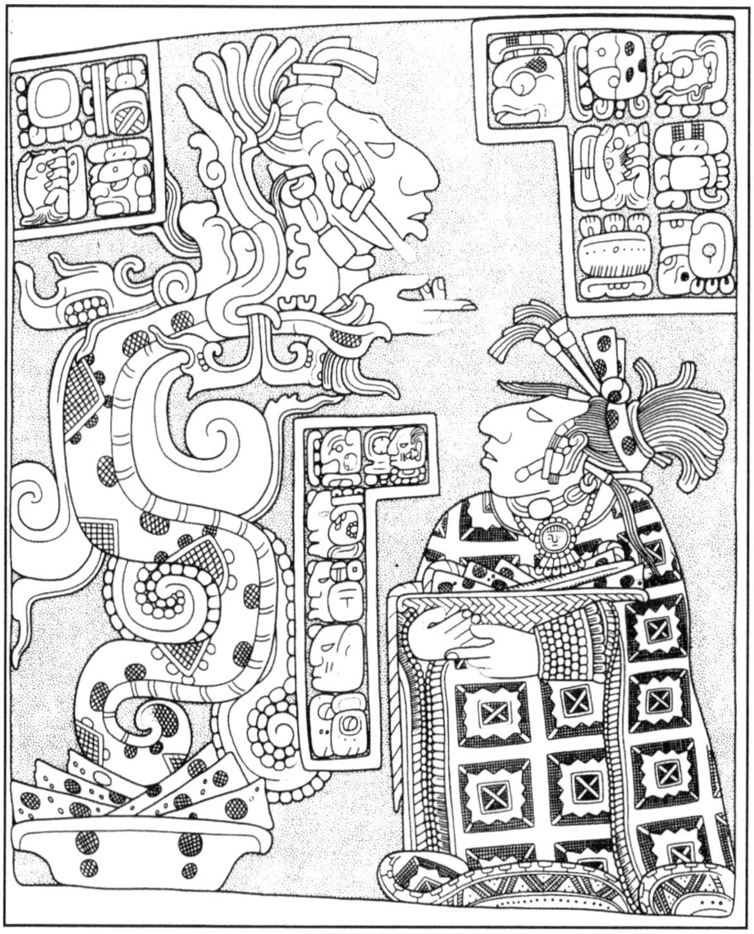

March 28, 755. Lady 6-Tun, secondary wife of Bird Jaguar. A marriage uniting the lineage of Yaxchilan to the (more Maya?) bloodline of IX. The Lady has finished the tongue ritual and is attending to a Vision Quest of another sort. Curling elegantly from her offering dish, this serpent reveals a more benign ancestral image. This is not the fierce Tlaloc Knight who visited her mother-in-law, Lady Xoc. The refined gesture only completes the perfectly shaped profile and careful coiffure. The ancestral gentleman seems to be explaining something; she gives him rapt attention. (Lintel 15, Drawing by Ian Graham)

A series of sculptured lintels from the Late Classic city of Yaxchilan provides a dramatic description of the subjective experience resulting from the Maya Vision Quest.

Just as the visions described by St. Teresa of Avila in her ecstasy are expressed in terms consistent with the Baroque spiritual imagination of the Spanish Counter-Reformation, her Maya counterpart experiences and relates her spiritual experience with imagery she knows. The method she uses to induce the hallucinogenic trance is the tongue ordeal. The women, all consorts of the rulers of Yaxchilan, are shown pulling cords studded with thorns through holes punctured in their tongues. The bloody cords, along with lancets used to open the wounds, are placed in low paper-filled platters. The supernatural conduit of each woman's vision is an elaborate conventionalized "serpent"; a composite, grotesque dragon as uniquely recognizable to the Maya, as Durer's Apocalypse woodcuts were to his German audience of 1500. The Maya adept is no different in this regard than shamans from Alaska to the Amazon. The imagery of each shaman's vision is conditioned by the system of iconography generally accepted in the tribe to which he belonged. The Shaman sees, in his trance, only what he knows.

The serpent certainly had a mythological meaning in Post-Classic times when its bearded, feathered version served as a symbol for the Mexican Quetzalcoatl ("Kukulcan" to the Maya). In earlier Classic times, the serpent form may have had a more generalized meaning. Its frequent addition, in simplified form, to a wide variety of material items argues against a limiting definition of meaning for the form. Instead, it has been suggested that this Maya dragon head functioned much the same for the Maya as the halo did for Western Christian art: designating the item or person it decorates as sacred, filled with power, "mana," something of the sort. The double-headed serpent/dragon likewise may have had some generalized locative meaning the "personification" of the sky, the surface of the earth, the entrance to the underworld. The important feature to notice is the character it holds in its jaws. Like the protective hood of the East Indian cobra, the Maya serpent was a stylistic emblem of the sacred in a more generic sense.

The ubiquitous presence of this conventionalized dragon in Maya art leads one to the conclusion that the natural form on which it was based was seen by these people to be "the ultimate expression of grace." This observation, made by Herbert Spinden in 1913, still seems valid—as does his astute analysis of the way the Maya conventionalized this reptile. The creature, by alternating quick and slow curves, fit any given shape in nature—so too, its tapering parallel lines could fill any design area. Its essential, natural lines combined with an increasingly conventionalized head. Through simplification and repetition of some realistic forms; by modification and elimination of others, and by the addition of forms wholly alien to the natural reptile, a consistent characterization of the form gained widespread and standardized usage. In short, as the form departs from its natural model, it imbues the design of the whole of Maya art with its essential, serpentine character.

If the wounding of the Male expresses the desire to own the magically fertile menstrual flow by mimicking it, the tongue sacrifice, then, is the woman sorcerer's rite.

While Mesoamerica developed refined cultures with many advanced intellectual features, it retained many of its basic animist, totemistic, spiritual and kinship patterns, derived from the ecstatic shamanistic practices upon which its other social structures were built. The supernatural figures appearing in much of Maya art, like that of the Northwest Coast Indians, was characterized by a unique and highly conventionalized stylistic visual language almost wholly given over to what would be considered in our culture as the "pathetic fallacy." That is, ascribing human characteristics to "lower" forms of life (the dog painting of Queen Victoria's favorite painter, Henry Landseer, is a typical example). As these New World cultures viewed nature in relative terms with its creatures equal to man, to treat an animal with disrespect would be to invite the wrath of who knows?—after all, it could be a dangerous sorcerer in his nagual, or animal disguise.

In its role as "Vision Serpent," the Maya dragon served as a conveyance for the penitent's quest, providing the conduit through the continuum of nature and time, through which the speaker communes with the spirits of the ancestors. Floating above the heads of Maya kings in portraits from earliest times, these dragons open their jaws to reveal the forebears who validate the ruler's right to rule. Held in the arms as a ceremonial bar, the ancestors emerging from the opposing heads are replaced by the deities who consecrate rulership itself. From the first representation of the Jaguar Nagual in the Olmec cave, the vision serpent allows the living to commune with the dead, to receive guidance and to validate their legitimacy.

Early spirit guardians took the form of the Nocturnal Sun, the dead ruler like the sun at night in the Underworld. The living descendant wears the mask of the New Sun, just risen, reborn. Here reigns the aesthetic of combat, where death provides room for new life. The spirit guides who appaer to the Yaxchilan women are of a different sort. One sees an elegantly gesturing young lord, whose delicate bearing and beautifully deformed skull bespeaks his aristocratic, conservative Maya lineage. The other phantom is both foreign and bellicose. Wearing regalia associated with the Tlaloc cult of Central Mexico, representing perhaps a knightly order of Storm God warriors, he presents himself in battle array before the lady who wears his emblem in her headdress. What these honored spirits tell their listeners remains a mystery, but the scene can no longer be seen as a mythological account. They are instead concrete depictions of the royal wives' subjective experience of transcendant states with visions brought on by a ritual of self-induced bodily trauma.

The power instruments used to induce these states are presented as deified personifications of the gods who protect the lineage's right to rule. They are displayed as badges of office. The ritual mutilations, so central to Maya social and spiritual life, are signs of the covenant agreed to by an interdependent community. While reminiscent of the covenant demanded of Abraham, the Maya contract exists in a fundamentally different time frame, operating under entirely different conceptions of debt and guilt. Existing in a fluid time of recurrent cycles of death and rebirth, revolving like the seasons under a rotating sky, their universe was a relative one, balanced and influenced by the continual interaction between man and his gods through the sacrificial action of sympathetic magic. The ever-present spirit world was always ready to be experienced by the intrepid shaman, the native specialist in the techniques of ecstasy by which he could travel at will through his evanescent heavens, through his harrowing hells.

ACKNOWLEDGMENTS

The main thesis of this paper derives from ideas presented by Peter T. Furst on the Vision Quest and Maya Auto-Sacrifice published in the proceeding of the Second Palenque Round Table (edited by Merle Greene Robertson, Pre-Columbian Art Research Institute, San Francisco, 1973. This series of studies of Maya art, iconography, and dynastic history has showcased many innovative studies in this specialized field; e.g., at the first meeting David Joralemon identified the "perforation god.")

The recent book *The Blood of Kings*, by Linda Schele and Mary Ellen Miller (1986, Kimbell Art Museum) summarizes most of the information on Maya blood sacrifice. The identification of "Ah Bolon Dzacab" (God K) with Tezcatlipoca was made by Michael D. Coe (*The Maya Scribe and His World*, the Grolier Club, 1973). Translations given here of Maya texts derive mainly from Linda Schele (whose "Workbooks" for the annual Maya Hieroglyphic Writing Workshops are excellent beginner's guides; University of Texas, Austin). Other translations derive from Victoria R. Bricker (*A Grammar of Maya Hieroglyphs*, Tulane, 1986). I would like to thank Donald Hales for pointing out the "Sky Penis" title in the Copan inscriptions illustrated here. Herbert T. Spinden's "conventionalized serpent head" is from the classic 1913 *Study of Maya Art* (Dover, 1975). My drawings of glyphs, as well as the "T" numbers follow designations in the essential Catalog of Maya Hieroglyphs, by J. Eric S. Thompson (Oklahoma, 1962). Landa's *Relacion de las Cosas de Yucatan* edited with notes by Alfred M. Tozzer (Peabody Papers, 1941) is the source for most of the ethnohistoric accounts quoted here. The drawings of the Yaxchilan lintels by Ian Graham are from the *Corpus of Maya Hieroglyphic Inscriptions*, Volume 3, Part 1 (Peabody Museum Press, 1977), President and Fellows of Harvard College. The new drawing of the "Hauberg Stela" is thanks to James Porter.

I am also indebted to the work of many scholars of Mesoamerican art, primarily Tatiana Proskouriakoff, whose 1950 *Study of Classic Maya Sculpture* (Carnegie Institute) remains the best formal analysis. Her student Clemmency C. Coggins' observations on Tikal iconography are used here as are comments on Mesoamerican aesthetics by Esther Pasztgory (*Aztec Art*, Abrams, 1983). All these people are serious scholars and may not approve of the tone of this work, as well as some tangents I take, but in a field that attracts cranks and crackpots, I have limited my sources to academically respected ones.

ANTON LAVEY

Anton Szandor LaVey, author of *The Satanic Bible*, was a "Renaissance man" whose conversation drew from a vast storehouse of occult (in the true sense of "hidden") knowledge and culture: forgotten books, magazines, films, music, artists, power figures and incredible characters. In 1966 he founded the Church of Satan in San Francisco; many of its rituals and exorcisms were essentially under-documented performance art pieces testing the limits of the morality of the day. Besides producing an LP, *The Satanic Mass*, he also authored *The Compleat Witch*, *The Satanic Rituals* and the *Satanic Papers*.

The following was excerpted from a conversation lasting until 4 in the morning, whereupon LaVey played on organ and synthesizers his version of "Je T'aime," which the *Temple of Psychic Youth* had previously recorded, splicing in a recording of LaVey's voice speaking. Present were A. LaVey, Blanche Barton, Genesis and Paula P-Orridge (T.O.P.Y.), and V. Vale.

Anton LaVey is now deceased (heart attack), his possessions and archive scattered to the winds (gone are the bed of nails, the mermaid table, the collection of mint-condition hardboiled paperbacks, the classic midnight-blue Jaguar sedan, the huge "Nightmare Alley" movie poster, and so forth). We shall never see the likes of him again.

■ *VALE: Why do you think there's an upsurge in "modern primitive activity"—piercing, tattooing, scarification?*

■ ANTON LAVEY: I would say the *past* motivation (in contemporary Western society as we know it) for adornment, embellishment, and tattooing, was much more experimental or rite-of-passage. When a man joined the Navy, or got a girlfriend, or was out with his buddies and drunk for the first time . . . doing something that in a peer sense would establish this belonging, a sense of camaraderie.

But *now* it's much more of a solitary choice. The person who proclaims, "I have this particular symbol on me" is trying to say, "You should recognize it because it's important to me." Now it's not necessarily something that's universally understood; it can be much more esoteric.

Today most people don't just go into a tattoo parlor and get the stock tattoos that are displayed on the wall; they have something much more personal in mind. Nowadays there are so damn many people who have an occult or mystical interest (I call them *occultniks*—these magical idiots—they're not very magical, of course) who have this idea that *their* particular symbology or bodily adornment is much more *important* than it actually is!

I've known some heavily tattooed people. One couldn't help but wonder about *how* they were motivated, especially when a guy would go to a tattoo parlor and have this incredible Egyptian deity tattooed on his back, or one on each thigh, and then across his chest have something like the double eagles of the Hapsburgs or a huge symbol of Baphomet across his back! Of course, things like that weren't being done back at the turn of the century, or in the twenties or thirties. Now tattooing involves a much more diverse symbology.

■ *V: Sometimes there's a totemic relation, in that the person believes he derives personal power from the symbol that's tattooed. If the tattoo constantly reminds him of certain goals he's striving toward, then perhaps it actually does give more power. And if a piercing gives someone more sexual pleasure, then that person probably gets more out of life! Besides whatever pleasure that derives from just the adornment in itself. . . .*

I think that if a person feels alienated; if the frequency they're on leads them to that Dark Side instead of the light side—if they didn't happen to be born looking freaky or strange, then activities like getting a tattoo are a way of stigmatizing one's self.

■ LV: You can put the various forms of bodily adornment into classifications. Fakir Musafar has been at his activities for so many, many years: infibulation, nipple piercing, constriction, etc. I saw a lot of *that* sort of

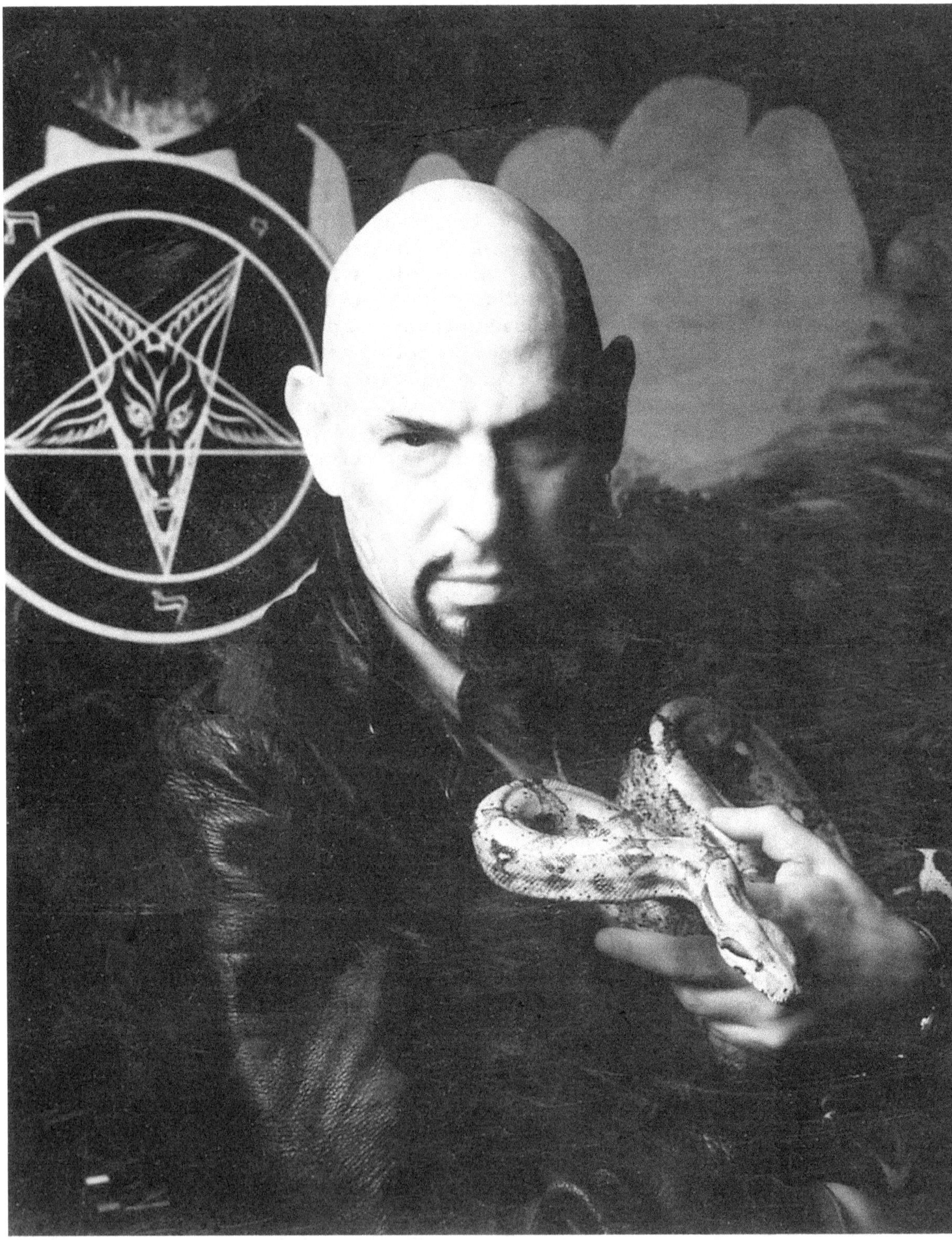

Photo by Bobby Neel Adams.

thing when I was in carnival work [late forties]. At that time tattooed people had to live in almost a twilight world: a society set apart from ordinary society. They were really aliens. Now many supposedly "respectable" people are able to celebrate a secret or fetishistic life. That's a motivating factor that didn't exist so much in the past: the satisfaction of knowing that one is different underneath one's business suit. . . .

In the carnival there's a pecking order: *born* freaks vs. *made* freaks. The people who are *made* freaks have special acts they've learned that enable them to work in the ten-in-one, the Sideshow, as opposed to the people who don't have to do *anything*—they're *born* that way. If a person is freakish enough to start with, probably they will not get tattooed. Born freaks—for example, Frank Lentini who had an extra leg, or the Hilton Sisters, Violet & Daisy (Siamese twins)—I've known them, and Johnny Eck, who had no bottom half of his body. Prince Randian was another one—the human torso. It's not just accidental that these people didn't have any tattoos, because they really were alienated—so different they probably never felt the need to adorn themselves.

I've known plenty of people who have had tattooing and all kinds of modifications to their bodies that I would say are really screwed up!

I think that if a person feels alienated; if the frequency they're on leads them to that Dark Side instead of the light side—if they didn't happen to be *born* looking freaky or strange, then activities like getting a tattoo are a way of *stigmatizing one's self*—I've done that. When I shaved my head, when I took on certain appearances to augment what I already had, I had reasons.

I'm sure that with people who get extensive tattooing, it's often a feeling that, "Well, maybe if I didn't look strange or if I didn't do something strange to my body, and I *did* or *could* blend in, lord *knows* what I might do that might be *really* dangerous!" So it's a *safety valve,* a way of keeping yourself—not on the straight and narrow, certainly, but from maybe being a mass murderer! I really feel that *we who are not as others* (to use Dan Mannix's title) often (whether we know it or not) are inclined to sort of wave a sign and say, "Okay, here I am—keep a good eye on me, because as long as I *am* strange, bizarre, outrageous and different, you people don't have too much to really worry about! But when I start being devoid of anything bizarre, then lord help you!"

That's why I think a lot of people gravitate to modern primitive alterations in their bodies: it's like taking an *antidote* which enables them to co-exist with the workaday world. It's a way of linking themselves with the twilight world or the Dark Side. Some people do this in ways *without* physical change: doing, saying or thinking things that would certainly alienate them from "normals." But that's just another variation.

In other words, people set up a certain stigma that says, "Watch out for me—I am dangerous!"—like the hourglass on the black widow spider's belly. Modern primitive activity serves as a self-alienation device to bring attention to the owner of that particular device, whatever it happens to be. Because a sailor doesn't look at it that way (one of the old-time sailors, that is), he wants to be one of the guys. He wants to be identified *with* a group rather than *outside* of a group.

■ BLANCHE BARTON: The outsiders are taking what *used* to be a method for identification inside a group and using it for "nefarious," invented purposes!—sort of *appropriating* it.

■ *V: Modern primitive activity facilitates stratification in society.*

■ GENESIS P-ORRIDGE: People who dissociate from society by doing it can recognize other people who've dissociated. They don't have to agree on a *philosophy,* but they can see a kinship on a certain level: "There's another person who's chosen to step outside . . . and there's another one." They get reinforcement of *their* decision, too. So it's strange: you step outside to become part of a tribe that's fragmented, that doesn't have a common bonding *except* the mark of being outside of the other society.

■ LV: It's a reversal of what it used to be.

■ BB: But that's what binds us together: the fact that we're outside the majority.

■ LV: Sometimes people that outwardly look the most weird or the most bizarre are, when you get to know them, the most tuned-into the frequency that I'm on. Not always, of course, but often. There's got to be a stratification: tell-tale signs that are little litmus tests by which you can know other people.

■ GPO: Almost like a developing initiation. You think, "That person may be an idiot, but they've still gone through *this* amount of pain, and *this* decision-making; they've still done something irrevocable. Therefore a certain amount of attention can be spared on them, at least."

■ *V: But the speech is always the dead giveaway.*

■ LV: The dead giveaway. We are victims of our speech patterns. And when someone talks like a *prole:* opens their mouth and starts using pop expressions—certain terms, certain phrases—or displays common denominators like knowing all of what's going on on TV, then . . . I'd say the concordance of society is—well, the supermarket checkstand tabloids are the checklists of what the person is supposed to know about if they're going to be one of *them* as opposed to one of *us!*

Also, proficiency at sports: when anyone has a consuming awareness of or interest in spectator sports or in group sporting activities, and it really matters to them, you can't help wondering what frequency their brain is on that obviously yours is not. And certain articles of clothing: I call them *uniforms.*

There are certain uniforms that are just universal, almost like prison garb: they might as well be black-and-white stripes on the old chain gangs! When you see somebody in a jogging suit and running shoes—sweatpants and the whole thing; or a prole cap, T-shirt and stonewashed jeans, you know there's a mind-set there. I think, "Could I feel right wearing that?" I would actually feel impotent, I'd feel uncomfortable, I'd feel vulnerable, I'd feel weak, I would feel I was sapped of any vitality or resourcefulness if I were to look like that. Those clothes would place me in this amorphous mindless grouping that would be enervating; it would deplete my energy. I call them *slave clothes;* any kind of clothes that are worn by impersonal slaves or slaves to "the system."

So you think, "Well, now, these people obviously feel warm and good dressed that way; they feel *right.*" Obviously they're on a different frequency, a different level . . . just like the "occultniks" whose lifestyle and nitpicking, pedantic approach to magic is such that obviously they're not magical—it's all on a cerebral level.

■ BB: They have no conception of intuition—

■ *V: Or that sense of humor!*

■ BB: That's what the litmus test for these occultniks is: if they don't have a sense of humor. If they can't laugh at themselves or get some perspective that way, then it's pointless to talk to them.

■ LV: Yes . . . pretentiousness and pomposity. And I've known plenty of people who have had tattooing and all kinds of modifications to their bodies that I would say are really screwed up! You can't just generalize and say that everyone who goes and gets their foreskin pierced or walks around with clothespins on their nipples all day is where it's at, you know. Because if we're going to be really objective, a lot of people are just plain and simple gluttons for punishment! They simply thrive on pain—which is great if they can get it! (I think self-aware masochism is wonderful, but full-time *unself-aware* masochism is terrible.) And if they get it by being squeezed in a box, or if they get it by getting their anus clamped together, it's all relative. Whatever it is, it's only effective if it's done with a real desire and need, and isn't done to follow the lead of someone else.

■ GPO: Do you think this *Modern Primitives* book is just going to encourage people to emulate and mimic . . . like people becoming junkies to emulate William Burroughs, or people going to prison to emulate Jean Genet?

■ *V: Tattooing and piercing are basically forbidden by the Bible in the book of Leviticus, and most of the world is ruled by Biblical religious beliefs—even Africa now. I want to encourage anything that's a statement against Christianity, because over the past 500 years Christian missionaries systematically destroyed virtually all of the world's diverse cultures, making the world a much less interesting place.*

No other religion—Buddhism, Islam, Confucianism, Paganism—did anywhere near the damage Christianity did. Bishop Landa burnt almost all of the one-of-a-kind Mayan codices—an incalculable historical loss. There have been so many atrocities (like the Inquisition and the Salem witch trials) in the name of Christianity that—it can't be too soon to be rid of that alien belief plague. In fact, aliens from Outer Space could hardly have devised a more crippling weapon against the people of planet Earth than the Christian religion.

The Christian religion, especially Catholicism with its unscientific, suicidally reckless birth control views, is responsible for the major unstated problem in the world today: overpopulation. In less than 25 years the world population has doubled, from 2.5 to over 5 billion. The populations that are breeding the fastest, yet have the fewest resources—Latin America and Africa—are mostly Christian, and usually Catholic.

■ LV: No one addresses that problem anymore: overpopulation. Nobody addresses *a lot of problems* anymore. And you can *feel* the overpopulation—it's oppressive—*very* oppressive.

■ BB: They want to just keep feeding Africa, keep feeding Third World countries, loaning South America billions, keep feeding all the poor. How about inundating all those countries with birth control pills? *No, we can't do that!* People say, "I have the right to keep having children as long as God tells me to keep having children."

That's why I think a lot of people gravitate to modern primitive alterations in their bodies: it's like taking an antidote which enables them to co-exist with the workaday world.

■ *V: The modern primitive trend is a reaction against overpopulation, fueled by so many uninteresting-looking, conforming clones and drones.*

■ LV: There is going to be *stratification:* there has to be, there's no choice. There will be cell systems, small groups or clans; there will be—not communes, but certainly *communities* or environments; insular options for people to move within. I've mapped it out as a series of total environments conducive to the particular lifestyle of the individual who would enter that total environment, very much like an Epcot Center or a Westworld or a Disneyworld, but on a much less commercial level, certainly, where they develop of their own *necessity*—much like Solvang, the Danish community in Southern California.

Let's just say we have a *film noir* city—wouldn't that be great? And when people go in, they have to wear the right clothes, the cars even have to be the right vintage, and the music is the right kind of music. Just like Frontierland—if somebody wants it to be like Cowboys and Indians but on the banks of the Rhine with the Germans and the Russians having their cowboy camps and teepee villages, then that's what it'd be. And that'd be great—*that's* what I'm looking forward to. And them that don't like it can [waves hand] because at least there will be guidelines. And for the people who can have fun or can at least feel comfortable in that kind of environment, then even the weather hopefully can be controlled.

I think that's be wonderful: *total environments.* If a person wants a Gay Nineties environment—fine! They can live in that as long as they wish. A Victorian environment with gaslights—*fine,* but with modern conveniences, and only those which will augment the reality of what *appears* to be authentic. In other words, instead of having to go through striking a flint, the street lamp will be lit automatically, but it'll still look like a real gas lamp, and for all intents and purposes be one.

■ *V: If you set the stage right, somehow you can regenerate a spark of the actual original spirit that might have been present—*

■ LV: You have just touched on the essence of my principle: *you set the stage.* The *approximation:* if it's there, even if it's not authentic—if it just *looks* authentic, it's close enough to evoke that feeling. I've been working on the concept of creating a total environment since 1965, and I know it works. Because you know it may not be actually turning the clock back in time, but if it's *aesthetically* pleasing and does something to make you feel *good,* to make you feel better than you would in this *Land of the Dead,* then it serves a very worthwhile purpose, I think. And you would certainly want to opt for that!

Meanwhile, to survive, I feel the vampire concept is a valid one, in terms of being awake at night and sleeping during the day—having the best, most creative time available; the time when other people are sleeping and not cluttering up the atmosphere—not jamming the frequencies, not dehydrating the ozone layer, so to speak.

■ *V: It's also much quieter at night.*

■ LV: Especially in urban areas where there's a great deal of highly concentrated activity. That's why I've always gravitated to the *opposite*—whatever the opposite may be! Almost as though it were the most natural direction for me to go, shunning the average or the usual or the predictable, very much like I would shun a poison. Because I know that no matter what it is that is immediately grasped upon as the *norm* or the thing that is the positive ionization factor, it's immediately going to be the *wrong* thing for me. So it's almost a cybernetic reflex—I have to almost not analyze it, but simply go with it. If I run towards it or run away from it, that's what makes it *right* or *wrong!* That's a rule of thumb—a mean average, a calculated risk that I'm going in the right direction.

I inherently believe man is a foolish, self-defeating, self-destructive creature who can't stand too much success, too much pleasure—he dies of satisfaction, because his life has outlived the potential for his boredom to override it. So he just can't go on any longer. But with all my "humanitarianism" I still feel there's a chance for improvement—at least a *slight* chance! Although Satan knows we sure need a good thinning-out process. Every time there's a disaster or something goes wrong, I start tallying things up and wondering *not* that it was such a tragedy, but wondering only, "So few? Is that *all?*"

■ *V: As people stratify themselves into small groups or clans, what other standards apply? Certainly not race.*

■ LV: My most elitist, Satanic society dream is of something that's not based on racism, but based on *intelligence* vs. *stupidity*—THAT'S IT! *There are the stupid and there are the intelligent.* There are people who are alive and vital and sensitive and thinking, and there are the people who are the dead, the cloned, the pods that are just *things.* They're the ones that I feel should be put to the flamethrower, regardless of race.

I have to keep an overview of all of these things. Fundamentally, everything translates down to stupidity. That's the great Satanic sin: *stupidity.* That's the cardinal sin.

■ *V: Whether or not you have tattoos or piercings, the bottom line is that purposeful self-evolved intelligence . . . whether or not you've done the most you can with what you have—that's always the goal. If the tattoos or piercings help you evolve, then they've more than justified themselves.*

LEO ZULUETA

For the past decades Leo Zulueta has championed "primitive" all-black tattooing based on traditions of Borneo, Polynesia & Micronesia. His own tattoos are startling, bold designs which integrate perfectly with his body musculature. Leo now works at Spiral Tattoo, 3060 Packard Road, Ann Arbor, MI 48108 (734) 477-5000.

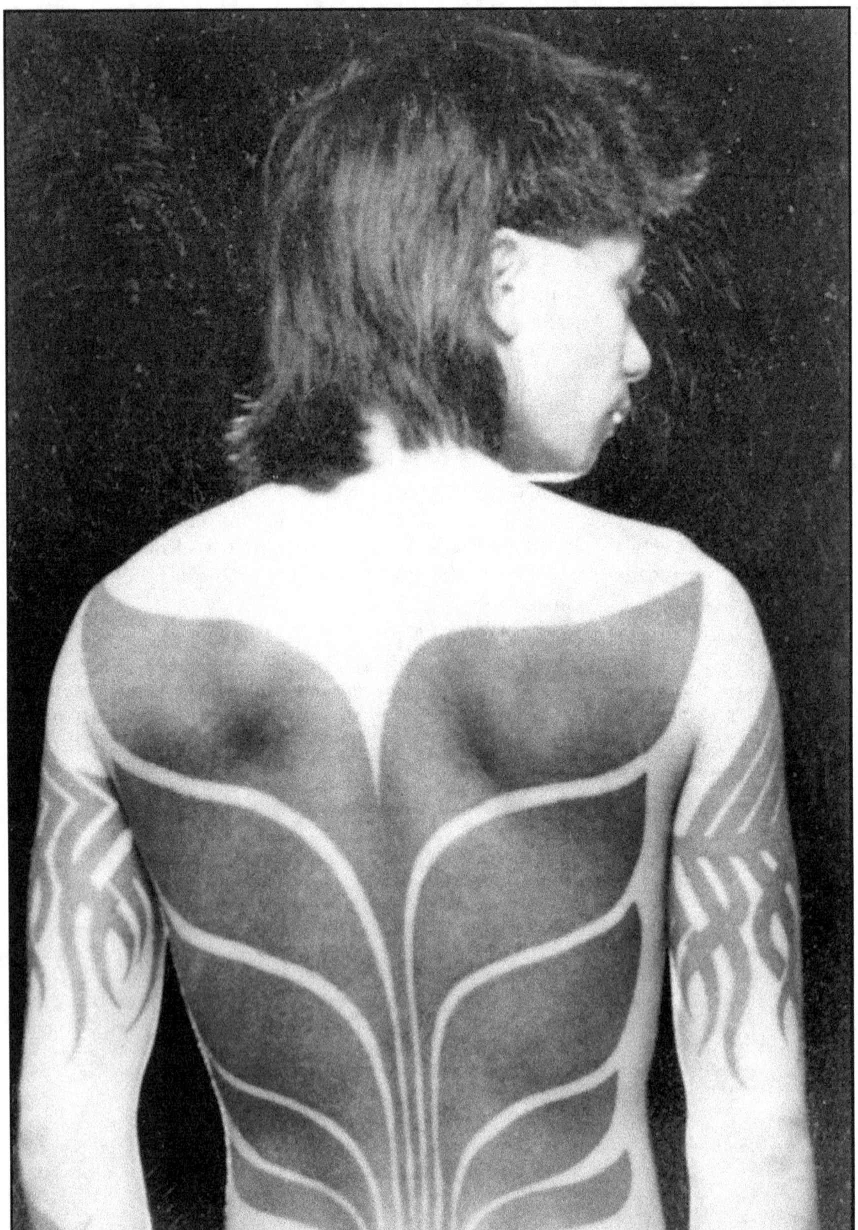

Leo Zulueta's back. Tattoo by Ed Hardy.

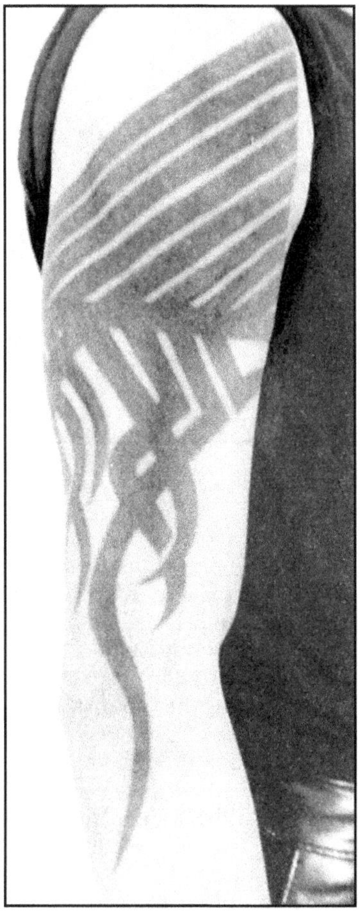

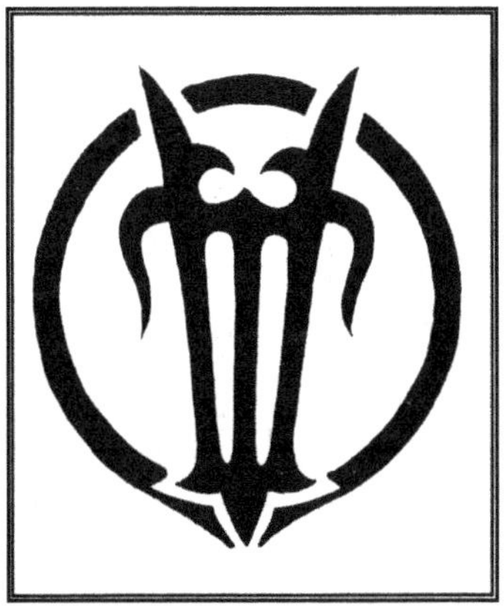

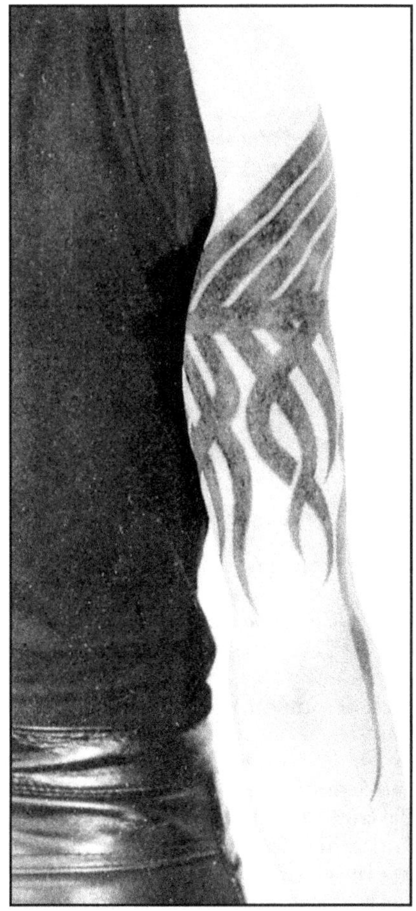

R & L: Leo's arms tattooed and photographed by Ed Hardy.

Center: Logo by Leo Zulueta.

Those tribal designs imply a cosmography and knowledge of the powers inherent in "nature" which those "primitive" peoples knew much more intimately than we did. Their knowledge wasn't written out in encyclopedia form, and we are left with the residue—the symbols of their understanding of the interrelationships, causes and effects in nature.

■ *Vale: You did a lot to popularize primitive black tattoo designs—*

■ Leo Zulueta: Well, yes and no—several people influenced *me*. Ed Hardy was the biggest inspiration—he encouraged me to study tribal designs from Polynesia, Borneo, etc, long before I even started tattooing. However, when I grew up in Hawaii I had a lot of Filipino relatives with tattoos, and I always admired them. The ancient Hawaiians didn't emphasize tattooing as much as the Marquesans or the Samoans or the Micronesians, but nonetheless they did have a very strong tattooing tradition—it just wasn't *quantity*. Hawaii, being the melting pot it is, afforded lots of opportunities to see all kinds of "primitive" tattooing. When I was a kid I always wanted a tattoo, but being in a strict Catholic family I couldn't get one, of course.

■ *V: Weren't you an artist before you began tattooing?*

■ LZ: I studied crafts at San Diego State College from '70-'72, not fine art and drawing—Botticelli really didn't do much for me! A primary interest was American Indian and primitive art: jewelry made from bones, leather clothing, etc. At that point I wanted to go into jewelry and furniture-making. I had drawn all my life but had never sat down and disciplined myself to really *learn* drawing. Then in 1977 punk rock came along and I got swept up into that. I met an artist named Bob Basile and we kind of spurred each other on to make posters. We were hanging out in the scene a lot and it was an easy outlet for our work.

■ *V: When did you get your first tattoo?*

■ LZ: From Mike Malone in Hawaii, 1974, after I left college to play surf bum in Hawaii for a few years. The design was a small heart on my left arm that's still there, next to my tribal work. Then I moved to the Bay Area and worked cutting coins out in San Mateo, doing leatherwork in Sausalito . . . then I got a regular job at an enamel factory in San Francisco. The punk

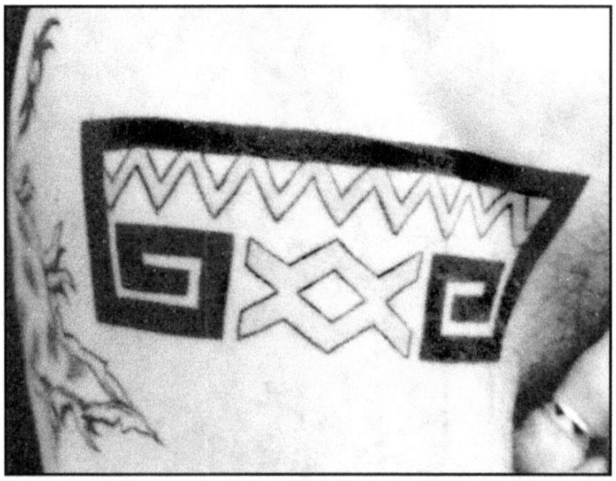

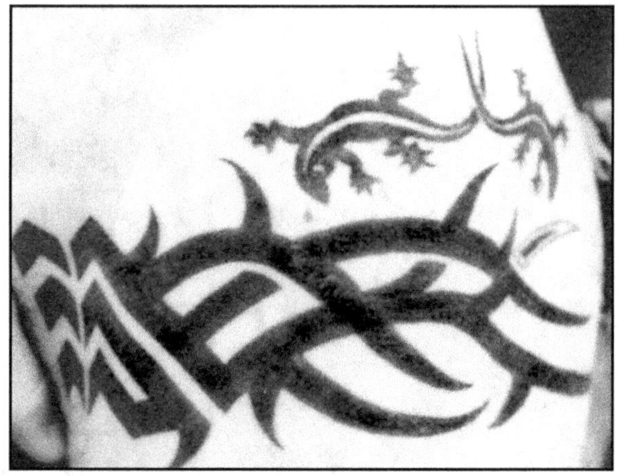

Tattoo by Leo Zulueta on Zapata.

scene began and that's basically when my artwork began to come out.

■ *V: How did you get into tattooing?*

■ LZ: There was a very intelligent article in Francis Ford Coppola's *City* magazine on Ed Hardy and his Realistic Studio. I read it and tracked him down and got a small tattoo from Bob Roberts who was working for Ed, but Ed himself was never around—he was always on the go. Then I went to a tattoo show at the Oakland Museum and actually met Ed there. We had dinner, and from then developed a friendship as well as a business relationship. He planted the seed in my head: "Why don't *you* be a tattooist?" I wasn't ready for quite a few years, but he kept on encouraging me and finally I did it.

I used to hang out at Realistic Studio, looking at Ed's photo albums of tattoos which really knocked me out (and still do). I also spent a lot of time hounding used bookstores and collecting old magazines like *National Geographic* which eventually gave me quite a big source of tribal style tattooing. I made a bigger and bigger scrapbook. Ed kept encouraging me: "This is *great!* There aren't many people doing this, or getting tattoos like this. You should further your studies, and research this as much as you can." That developed into a friendship where we saw each other quite often for dinner.

After a year or two I told Ed I wanted to get a big tribal-style flame on my right arm. He said, "You draw it, bring it to me, and I'll put it on." That was in 1978. Then I got the matching piece on my left arm in early 1981.

■ *V: Who did your large back piece?*

■ LZ: Ed. That was started in '82 and finished in '83 before my departure for L.A. There were about seven sessions. To be honest, it was hard for me to sit for

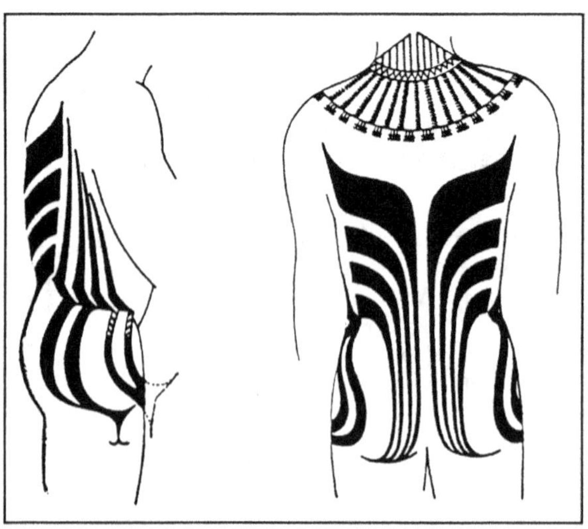

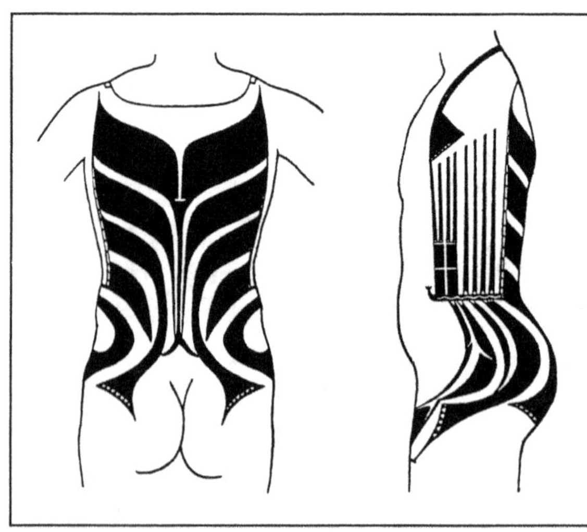

Micronesian body tattoos from an early 1900's article.

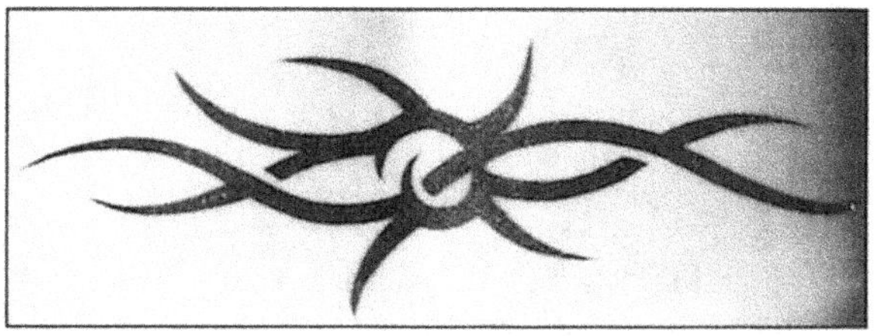

Tattoo by Leo Zulueta.

that; I can't be worked on 8 hours a day for a week straight.

■ *V: It almost looks like you were born with that tattoo—it seems as "appropriate" as the stripes on a tiger—*

■ LZ: The "primitive" style fits the body very well. Over the past ten years I've tried to study as many tattoo styles as I could that weren't traditional American or Japanese. It's hardest to find sources on the Celts or the Picts—supposedly that's why they were called "Picts": because they had pictures tattooed all over them. Putting permanent designs on the body is an impulse that's probably a million years old! And people still have that impulse, even in this technological world.

I would never want to *not* credit people who were very important to me. Back in the mid-seventies in San Francisco I saw a guy who worked in a store in San Francisco called *Hot Flash* who had wild tribal tattoos on both forearms. This was before I had met Bob Roberts, or anything. He told me it was done by Cliff Raven. So Cliff Raven has always been one big inspiration to me—here was someone who was not doing strictly American or Japanese or Chicano-American style work.

Another big influence was Leo Brereton, who was a curator for Lyle Tuttle's Tattoo Museum. Dan Thome (fresh from Micronesia) was also a big inspiration—he won't even use a tattoo machine, because it's not *pure* enough for him. Dan helped me do my own research; in fact he provided me with half of my xerox file of tribal designs. His design sense has been a big influence; I could look at his books for hours!

It seems that lately tribal tattooing has become really popular. I actually think there's quite a bit of spirituality behind a lot of those tribal designs, although it may not be readily apparent. The designs imply a cosmography and knowledge of the powers inherent in "nature" which those "primitive" peoples knew much more intimately than we do. Their knowledge wasn't written out in encyclopedia form, and we are left with the *residue*—the symbols of their understanding of the interrelationships, causes and effects in nature. But symbols work by stimulating correspondences and connections on the part of the viewer (and in the case of tattoos, the wearer); it's a cumulative process which can be educational and thus definitely beneficial . . . even if we never *totally* understand the "original" significance of the symbol or design in question. Who knows—maybe the meaning can appear in a dream!

Arm Tattoos by Leo Zulueta.

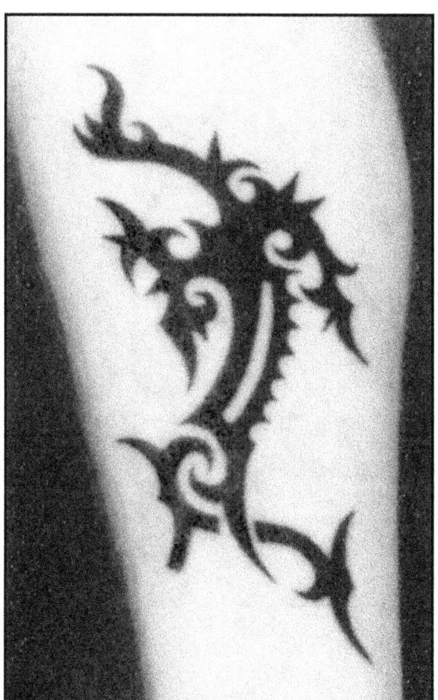

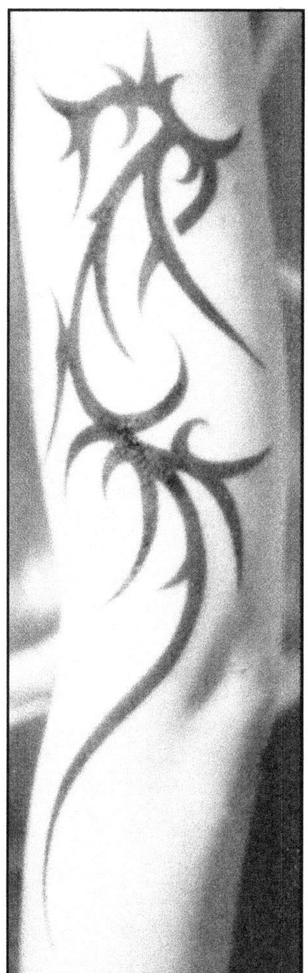

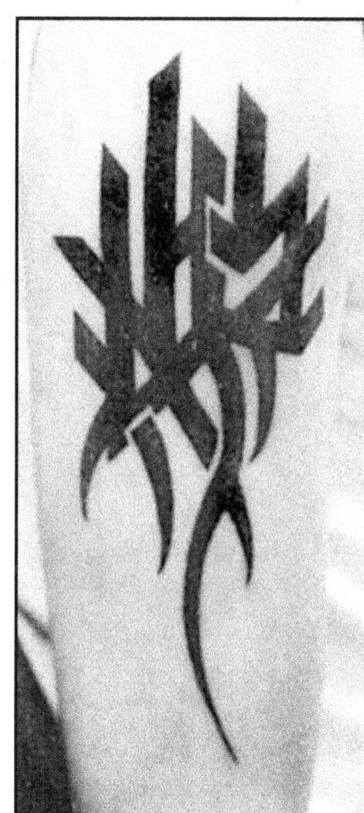

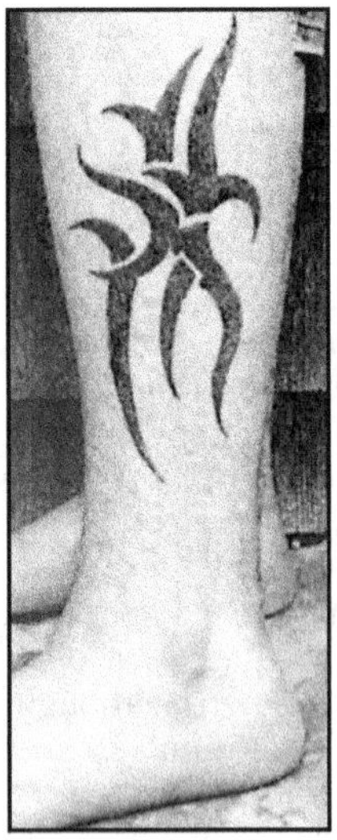

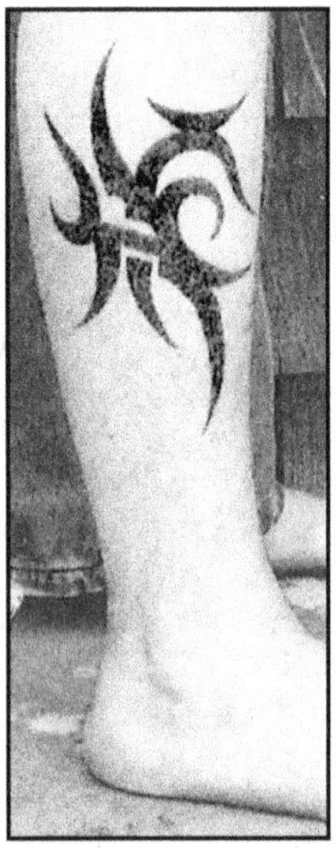

Tattoos by Leo Zulueta.

Also, for the past twenty years now there's been a reaction against "high" art and highbrow culture (pretty paintings that are not that relevant to us today) . . . just as people are sick of looking like (or trying to look like) new clean advertisements; they want something more visceral; they want to break out of the mold. *I* know that the more tattoos I got, the more I felt confirmed in my own path.

A funny thing happened when I went to Mike Malone's studio in Hawaii, right after I'd gotten my large back piece. Three older tattooed Micronesians came into the shop and I talked to them for awhile, and then told them, "Hey, I've got a really neat Micronesian-style tattoo on my back" and whipped off my shirt. Two of them were yawning and turning the other way before I even had my shirt back on—they were *far* more interested in the colored American eagles and naked lady designs on the walls!

What I'm trying to say is: I really am carrying a torch for those ancient designs. But I'm afraid (judging from the reports of Leo Brereton, Dan Thome and others) that those traditions are dying out where they originated; the original peoples have no interest in preserving them—they'd rather have a ghetto blaster and a jeep and a pack of Marlboro cigarettes. The Western encroachment has triumphed; all the old men having "primitive"-style tattoos are dead . . . The last man to have a back piece like mine, who was over 90 years old, passed away a couple years ago. This is why I really feel strongly about preserving those ancient designs: besides being original art, they might contain talismans for the future, or perhaps encode some cryptic knowledge that could be valuable or illuminating in some way—who knows? But if they're not preserved, we'll never know!

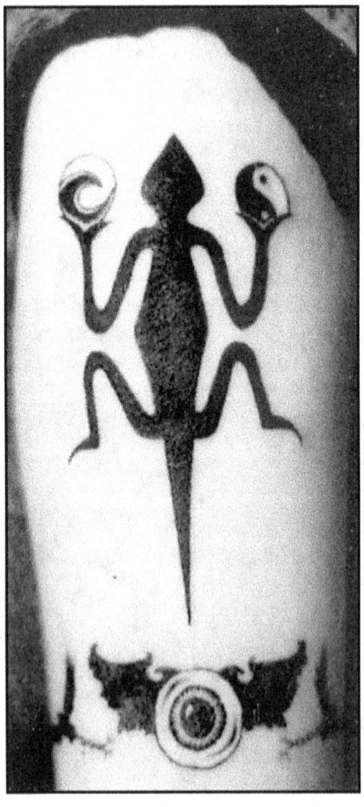

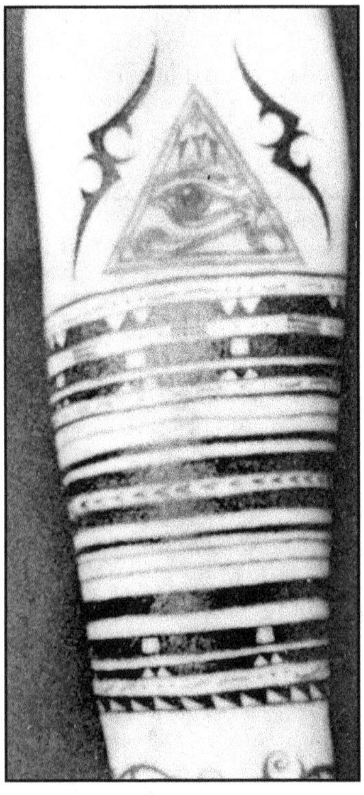

R & L: Tattoos by Leo Zulueta except eye and triangle by Morbella in Amsterdam.

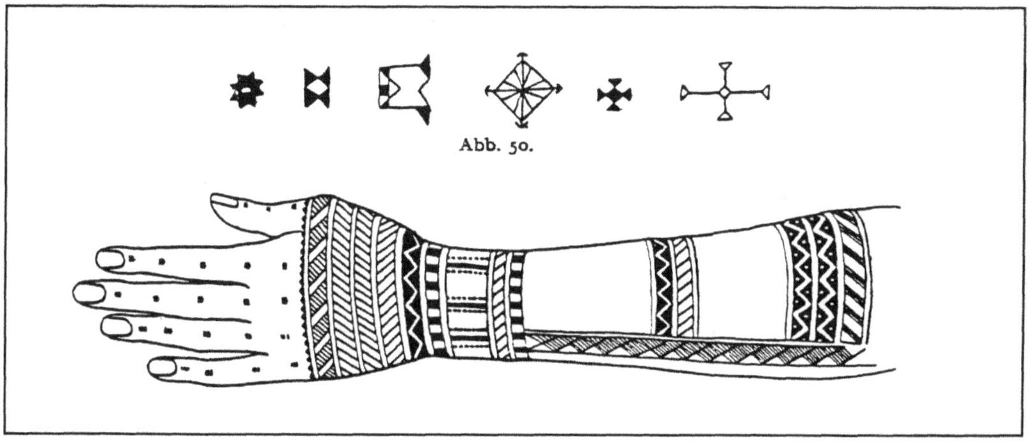

Micronesian arm tattoo.

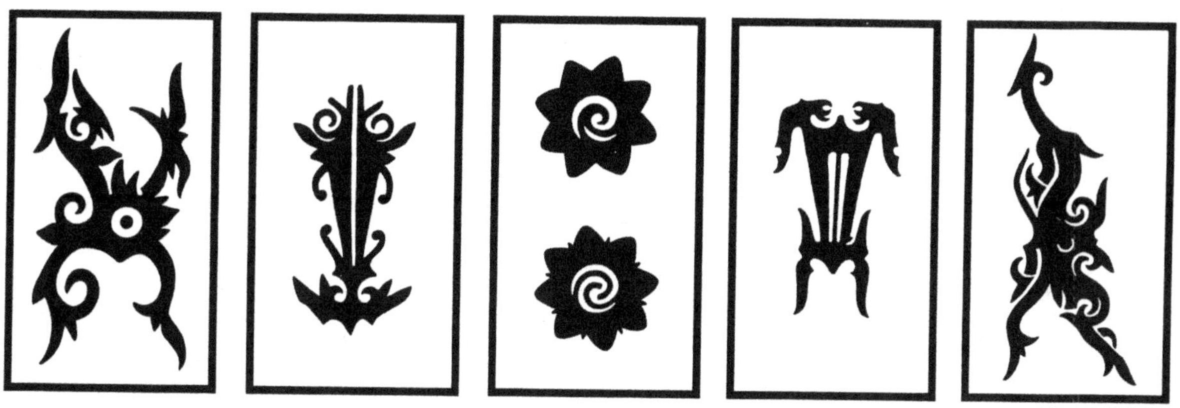

Iban tribal designs by Leo Zulueta.

RAELYN GALLINA

Bay Area body modification pioneer and the "grandmother of piercing," Raelyn Gallina specializes in scarification as an art. Contact her at 1271 Washington Ave #640, San Leandro, CA 94577 (510) 383-1938.

■ RAELYN GALLINA: A lot of men blanch at the thought of *cutting*, which has become an increasing phenomenon in the SM gay community. So far it's mostly women who are into this. These big heavy-duty leathermen often recoil from the thought of cutting, or of blood.

■ *ANDREA JUNO: Do you find that men have a lesser tolerance for pain?*

■ RG: I'm not sure; I haven't had experience with causing men pain in a sexual SM scene. I've heard that men can take more, just because generally men are stronger and have more muscles built up. But the women who can take pain can take a lot, too. I've noticed that men deal with pain differently. Men are more matter-of-fact.

■ *AJ: Let's start from the beginning. You do piercing and scarification to women only?*

■ RG: No, I pierce men from the navel up. I figure I'll pierce what I have in common with people. And being a lesbian, I'm just not that familiar with men's genitals; I would want to bring a greater degree of expertise to my piercing. So I pierce what I am really capable of and well-experienced to do.

■ *AJ: Have you done many piercings?*

■ RG: In the past six years, yes. I used to keep a record and then I just stopped—it was too much. But unlike Jim Ward, I'm a one-woman establishment; I don't have anyone working for me. I've been an artist all my life; a jeweler for fifteen years, and I got into piercing six years ago when I started getting pierced. Women were coming up to me begging me to pierce them, so I started collecting information and experience and now I'm definitely the women's community piercer.

■ *AJ: So what attracted you to piercing in general?*

■ RG: At the time I was into SM quite intensely. In 1984 I went through intense personal grief due to the death of five friends in a year, and that put me through such intense emotional pain that the physical pain couldn't compare. I learned lessons in death, sex and blood sports. And what I found that stuck was the blood sports: basically piercing and cutting.

Piercing can put you into such an altered state, and it's so immediate! Even though a lot of times, especially with play piercings, it's not really painful; it's the psychological mind-fuck that really gets you—the fear. Play piercing means skin-popping with hypodermic tips, and maybe putting little weights on them. They're temporary; you can take them out after you're done playing. This isn't really painful, but like I said it really is a mind-fuck. It sends you out there, plus it gets your endorphins going. I discovered I liked the sensation of being pierced; plus I love piercing other people. It's like I'd been doing it for lifetimes and lifetimes. And when I started making jewelry and manipulating metal, I knew I had done that for lifetimes before.

■ *AJ: So your piercing activities have a spiritual component?*

■ RG: I find that if I sat down and questioned everyone who comes to me for piercing, I'd say 95 out of 100 people will end up saying it's been a spiritual act. I don't even have to do anything special as far as making it a ritual. Just in the way I treat people—basically I *serve* them when I do it. Some people I know pierce and it's like, "Head 'em up, move 'em out!"—it's very expedient. And some people pierce with a sadistic bent, in that maybe they're causing people a little more pain than is necessary. Not me.

I feel I'm in a position of serving someone when I pierce them; I take care of their emotional needs. But I don't see a lot of that happening—also, not everybody wants to deal with that, too. When I'm piercing at a Castro Street Fair, and I'm piercing the gay men—well, a lot of times they're drunk. And sometimes a man will come in and say [abruptly], "Okay, pierce my tit!" and it's done quickly and they don't need much in the way of nurturing. But I find that women or men that let themselves feel more and express more feelings require more nurturing. Some people want to know if it's okay to yell or react, and I let them know that whatever they do is totally appropriate and totally confidential—nobody's going to know. And whatever they go through and however they do it—it's all fine.

If someone nearly faints, they might feel bad, but I try to reassure them: "Whatever it takes is okay." This is their little test of endurance. And a lot of times it becomes a ride of passage for people; it marks a certain time span or a certain event in their lives.

■ *AJ: Give some examples.*

■ RG: At one point I was doing piercings on myself to mark birthdays. I was giving beautification and body

To ask to be cut (not in a violent situation, but in a loving, supportive, trusting situation) and then bleed and then end up with something beautiful can be very empowering.

adornment to myself; that was a nice gift. Piercing started at a time in my life when I was experiencing a lot of death and grief and transformation. For a lot of people it's a rite of transformation, when they go from one state to the next. And it can be as physical as: their nipple was not pierced, and from that moment on it is.

■ *AJ: You have permanent jewelry all over your body?*

■ RG: I have one nipple pierced, a navel pierced, and a labia pierced. I used to have my nostril pierced, but I let that go. I have eight holes in one ear and two stretched holes in my other; I'm stretching them so I can put more massive jewelry in, or eventually, grommets you can see light through. A lot more people are getting into stretching piercings.

■ *AJ: I've always liked what Fakir said: Western society thinks of piercing in terms of letting poisons out, whereas primitive society regards piercing as for letting light in—a more positive view . . . Could you describe your nipple piercing? Where exactly is it?*

■ RG: When the nipple is erect it's just at the base, where the nipple meets the aureole.

■ *AJ: We've heard about a lot of problems with nipple piercings.*

■ RG: Well, I always tell people to call me if they have problems, because I'm invested in their piercings. If they don't "take" or if something flares up, there can be a multitude of reasons. Sometimes they're having an allergic reaction to the metal. Sometimes I use kinesiology to muscle-test them for the different metals or different gemstones. That's a technique chiropractors use: isolating a certain muscle and seeing how strong it is. Chiropractors will touch a certain other muscle to see which ones are weak or strong, and what organs are weak or strong. You can use this approach to see what vitamins you need.

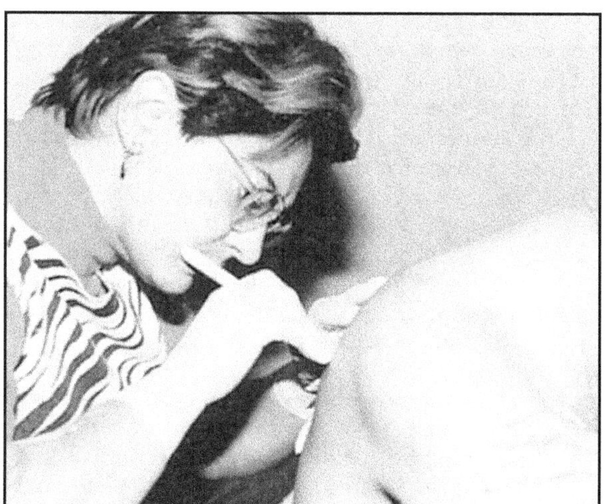

Above: Raelyn making a cutting on client. Right: The finished cutting with red tattoo ink rubbed in. Photos by Myra Fourwinds.

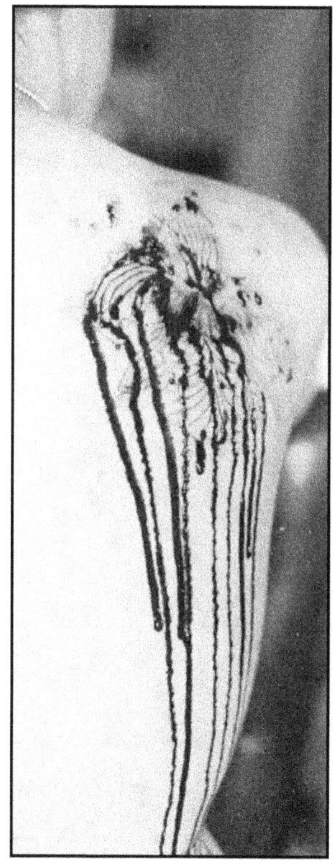

■ *AJ: Show me.*

■ RG: Push your two fingers together. When I say, "Resist!" I'm going to pull them apart. Okay—now we know how strong that muscle is. Next take a little honey and put it under your tongue and let's try again. Okay—honey makes you stronger. Let's try that again with a dairy product—you might have a dairy allergy and if so, you'll be weaker.

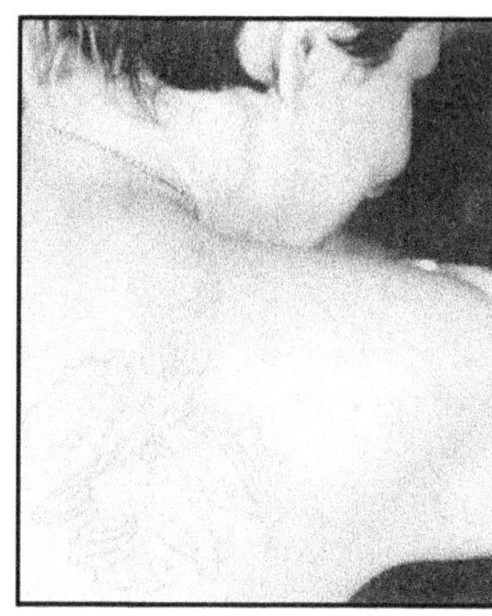

You can test for anything. I'll ask people beforehand, "Do you have any sensitivities or allergies? Do you react to anything in your environment or something you wear?" Because sometimes people will want stainless steel because it's cheaper, but if they're used to wearing gold and they like gold or the color yellow, then chances are gold *will* be better for them to use. And I use 18-carat gold or better for my major piercings. I don't use 14-carat because I don't think it's pure enough. Some people can take silver for certain piercings, like for a lot of women's nostrils. But silver's the most problematic of those three metals.

■ *AJ: How does a nose piercing stay in?*

■ RG: There's a piece of jewelry, originally Indian in design, called a nostril screw. There's a little gemstone, a straight little post only as wide as the nostril is thick, that makes a right-hand turn with a half-curl of metal. You curl it in and pop it down, and on the inside of your nose there's only a flat half-circle of metal. You can pick your nose, blow your nose—*whatever* with it. It stays in and is very comfortable.

Some nose piercings you see are a straight post. But I won't put a straight post in a nose; it'll come out

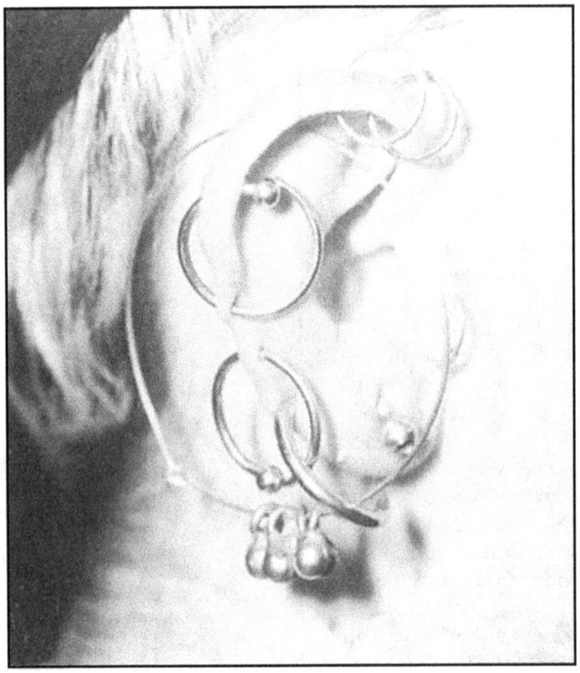

From collection of Charles Gatewood.

too easily. And snot and other stuff collects; you can't clean it. You also can't get inside your nose as well, plus it's easy to have it on too tight . . .

People who pierce noses with a gun—I think that's horrible. You know how tight those backs are when you get your ear done? Can you imagine ripping the back off when it's in your nose? That's terrible. And they're too long and can sometimes go into your septum—not good.

■ *AJ: Back to the nipple piercings; can you explain why they're difficult?*

■ RG: Besides being allergic to metal, you can have reactions to cleaning solutions. Perhaps Betadine or Hibaclens or the peroxide is too strong. Or someone can be allergic to rubbing alcohol. Or they use neosporin too long. So I ask a person to describe their cleaning process; what they're doing morning and evening. And they may end up switching to salt water; lately I've had many people tell me that's the best.

If I question people who say, "I got this rash," or, "My nipple's red and it's secreting," or, "It's oozing," many times I find that if I question them intensely enough, I'll find out they did something stupid. They did not use common sense. So I drill people when they come in. They do sign a release. I give them a handout as to how to clean it and what to use, and tell them to call me. I sit down with them and tell them how to take care, especially with nipples and navels: "Take hot soaking baths in plain water—water is one of the best healers there is. Or sit there in salt water."

■ *AJ: What's the average healing time?*

■ RG: Approximately two months for a woman; maybe less for a man because there aren't any milk ducts there, or if there are, they're so underdeveloped. There's *more* in a woman's breast to get infected. A man's nipple is a much smaller piece of tissue than a woman's. So healing takes maybe about six weeks for a man.

■ *AJ: How about the navel?*

■ RG: I hear there's about a fifty-fifty chance of it being rejected: it will grow out, or just won't heal no matter what you do. I think what will cause a navel to either get infected, stay infected, not heal, or grow out, is *irritation* more than anything. Anyone who wears jeans or pants that cut across the navel—forget it! You have to dress for the occasion—dress for the piercing, and change your wardrobe for a few months.

■ When I got my navel pierced I was living out in the country, and I went around in "sweats" all the time. Whenever I could I just pulled them down so that my navel was exposed to air. You have to really *dedicate* yourself to healing a navel; some people will do it, and for other people it's too much.

■ *AJ: What about labias?*

■ RG: They'll heal *like that!* It takes anywhere from three to fourteen days. The cleansing process is not nearly as complex as for a nipple. They kind of heal themselves, because of the nerves and blood supply.

If I question people who say, "I got this rash," or, "My nipple's red and it's secreting," many times I find that if I question them intensely enough I'll find out they did something stupid.

■ *AJ: What about a clitoris piercing?*

■ RG: Genital tissue heals quickly. Wherever there's a lot of nerves and a large blood supply, especially where the tissue engorges with blood, it's going to heal fast.

Now I haven't done a clitoral piercing because of the nerves. I've done clitoral *hood* piercings—they heal fast and are really beautiful. As of yet I still haven't managed to meet women who've had their clitorises pierced, and talk with them and gather information. I need to research that more.

Among people who've had nipple piercings for awhile, some will say they have more sensation in their nipples, and some will say they have less. So I'm not sure what's really going on. As for the clitoris, there are so many nerves packed into that little 3-5 square centimeters, that putting a large needle through that may cut some of those nerves off, and I would hate to do that!

I heard abut one woman who had it done, and then she couldn't take a step without being totally turned on . . . all the time! She couldn't do anything; it was too much for her. So I don't know. I have mixed feelings about this, just because it's such an intense area. The head of a man's penis has the same amount of nerve endings as a clit, but they're spread out. When they're so compacted, I can't help but think that if you go through it, you're going to *deaden* some.

I have an ad featuring clitoral hood piercing in a magazine, *On Our Backs.* And I'll get calls from women who say, "I want my clit pierced just like the one in the ad." And I'll say, "No no no, that's a *hood* piercing." And they'll say, "Fine!"—they're drawn to it because it's so beautiful. It's a round circle around the hood, and I do it so the bead is right over the clit, occasionally rubbing the clit. Of course, this depends on how the woman is constructed.

■ *AJ: So is there a constant contact?*

■ RG: There might be some, but it's not as intense as having it down further where the bar of the ring pushes against the clit, which is irritating. That's *too* much, too constant. You can have pressure if you want it, but it's not too much to have the ring rest on it. Because a lot of times the clit is tucked up in there.

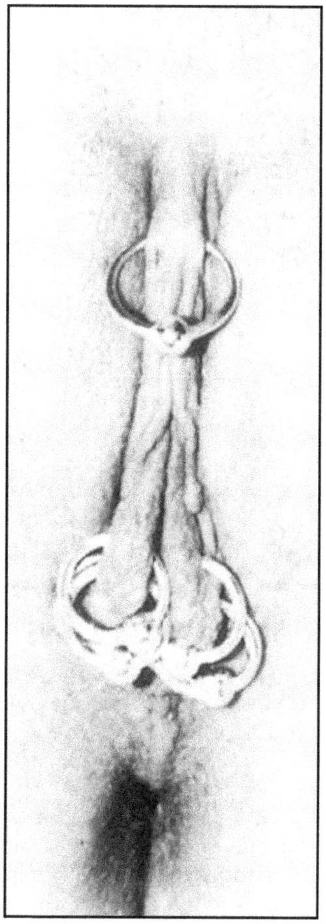

From collection of C. Gatewood.

■ *AJ: And what reports have you gotten?*

■ RG: The girls *love* 'em! Just love 'em. And they heal quickly.

Another thing that can impede healing or cause a piercing to flare up is: emotional stress. For some people, their piercing becomes a pressure valve. And when they're under stress with their job or their relationship or their life in general, their nipple will goop up. Also I've found with a lot of women who call me, "My nipple just flared up out of nowhere!" that a lot of times it's seven to ten days before they bleed. There's that hormonal, chemical change in a woman's body that men don't have, so they watch for that. Or maybe they're sensitive to the amount of dairy they take in, because this is a milk gland—if you take in a mucus, you may give out more mucus.

■ *AJ: So how has your nipple piercing changed things?*

■ RG: It's easier to make my nipple erect. I can feel more, just because of the bar going through, so it's better for me. I think most people have increased sensation and increased pleasure.

A lot of women tell me that their nipples are like their clitoris—they're so sensitive they'd never get them pierced. Sometimes you'll pierce a man behind the nipple into aureole and it'll "grow." It pulls 'em out; it develops the nipple for them—which a lot of men want.

■ *AJ: What about the labia piercing?*

■ RG: That's more like decoration. You can do things like hang a little weight on it, not wear underwear, and go dancing. Then it becomes one of those private pleasures, and you can feel it by the vibration. And the closer you get to the clit, the more sensation. You can play games with the rings.

■ *AJ: Do you ever pierce heterosexual women?*

RG: Yes; I have all kinds of people coming to me, but I'm in the lesbian community, so by word-of-mouth I have a lot of lesbian clientele who only want to be pierced by a woman, particularly a lesbian woman.

■ *AJ: So the genital piercings don't get in the way?*

■ RG: No. I know women who'll attach their nipple rings to their labia rings, or their labia rings to a string in their mouth and they pull on it—it does create more sensation to have them pulled on. The lips are very sensitive. But it's subjective—some women love their labia piercings and play with them all the time, and others don't . . . If there *were* something there, you'd think about it a lot more!

■ *AJ: What other types of piercings can you get?*

■ RG: Septums—I don't do many of those; more men than women get them. I'll get waves of different piercings at a time. Sometimes I'll get a lot of traguses (that little piece of cartilage in the ear) and those heal remarkably easily. You can do it with a gun—shoot it in and then leave it alone. You can clean it but don't mess with it; don't change it too soon into a ring . . .

I'll get a rash of nipples, then labias will be popular for a month or two. Then there'll be a lull. Next I'll get a few nostrils. Multiple earrings are really popular right now, so I'll get women wanting their cartilage pierced all the way up, but with a ring, because it heals a lot quicker and more easily. Plus you can clean it more efficiently—rather than a stud that you shoot in.

■ *AJ: Have you gotten reports from women who've had sex with men who have penis piercings? Is it more pleasurable?*

■ RG: That's all I've heard. But frankly, I've only talked to a few women who have said that to me personally. I've *read* that it's more pleasurable. I've heard that penis piercings will enhance sex for *both* partners—period. But I really haven't sat down and questioned people in depth about this!

■ *AJ: You also make jewelry; do you actually make the studs and jewelry?*

■ RG: I basically do silver and gold work: your basic bead ring, Ouroboroses (snake eating its tail), and other custom work. I get my surgical stainless jewelry elsewhere.

■ *AJ: Have you thought about the "why" behind getting pierced?*

■ RG: For me part of it is past-life re-stimulation. My first major piercing was my navel—I saw it in a *PFIQ*

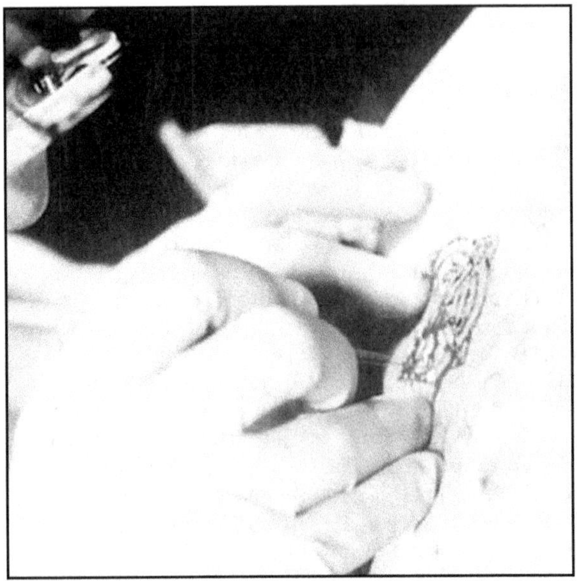

Making the cutting. Photo by Myra Fourwinds.

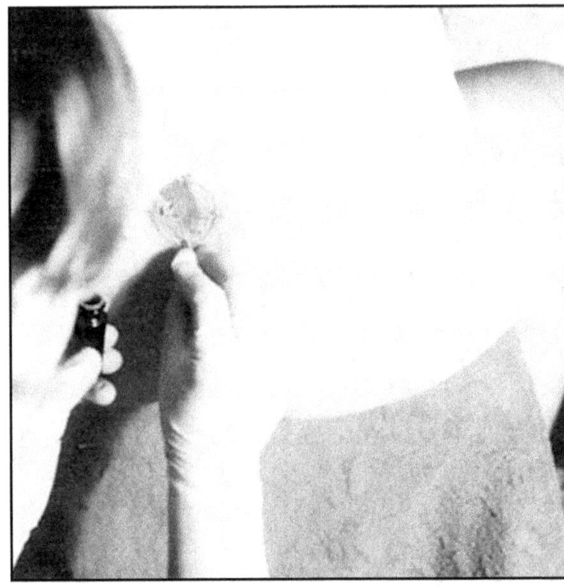

Applying the tattoo ink. Photo by Myra Fourwinds.

(piercing magazine—see Jim Ward article) and it was like *I have to have that now.* So I think something was triggered—who knows from where: ancient Egypt, probably.

I like the way multiple piercings in the ears and on the face look. Another one I was drawn to originally was the labrette (lower lip): I never did it but I thought it looked so beautiful. And as an artist making jewelry—the process of making a piece of jewelry and then placing it in a part of the body where it hasn't been before was exhilarating. Plus the extension of the act of adornment itself: people wear jewelry to beautify their hands or their ears or throats, but this was taking it further: not just adorning the visible body, but the hidden as well—having the entire body participate in the adornment.

■ *AJ: You also do scarification. How did this develop?*

■ RG: I haven't done that the way different African tribes do it for social or sexual reasons; i.e., a woman is available, or a woman has gotten married—rites of passage with a socio-sexual connotation. I haven't done things like make a series of bumps or a pattern of bumps. I prefer having a person bring me an image or picture or object. I transfer that design onto their body and either cut it into their skin and either rub tattoo ink into it or not, depending. Afterwards I'll take a blood rubbing of it. And it can be anything from a large scarab, an orchid, an iris, a bird or different abstract designs or objects that have meaning for the person. I don't do hamburger cuttings—where people just cut randomly. They're not pretty.

I need a double reason: besides doing it to a person and them wanting it done, I need to have something beautiful in mind. In the SM community there can be more random cutting for the powerplay aspect, but I wouldn't do it just for that; I do it to make the design. They end up with something beautiful that they love to wear and enjoy wearing for years or however long it takes to fade.

■ *AJ: The Africans make this permanent by forming a keloid or a scar.*

■ RG: There are different ways: one is by rubbing tattoo ink into it so you'll end up with a line or outline tattoo, but you've been cut. Like the outline of a flower in red or black on the skin.

■ *AJ: How is that different from a tattoo?*

■ RG: Not very different, except in the *way* you got it. A lot of times being cut—the act of being cut and surviving—is a very strengthening and powerful experience for people. Especially for people who've been in abusive situations or have gone through a lot of "stuff" in their lives. To ask to be cut (not in a violent situation, but in a loving, supportive, trusting situation) and then bleed and then end up with something beautiful . . . and then it heals and you have it and you're proud of it—that can be very empowering. It can be a *reclaiming* for a lot of people.

■ *AJ: So this is a semi-ritual?*

■ RG: It can be, depending on what people want. If that's what they want, we'll do it that way.

■ *AJ: Do you do that yourself?*

■ RG: No. Years ago I used to play a little bit with cutting, but I stopped after I went to the phase of not wanting physical pain. My taste for blood remained, but . . .

■ *AJ: Even though I have problems with aspects of SM society, I think that getting into ritual cuttings and pain could possibly reawaken or liberate a whole world of sensation, depending on the individual—especially if they've suffered a lot of repressive conditioning.*

■ RG: It can be an incredibly positive and strengthening experience. It can be a very damaging experience too, depending on the person. Anything that anyone does to

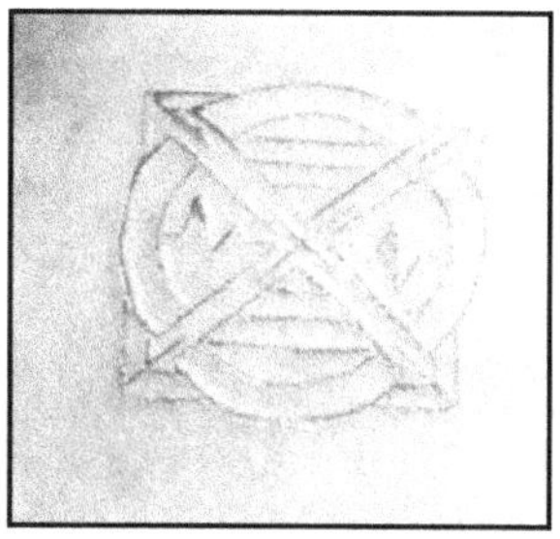

Photo by Myra Four-winds.

such an extreme that it's abusive or compulsive or addictive is bad. Whether that's drugs, drinking, eating or fucking, anything that one does to the extreme where they can't live without it or will do anything to get it, is damaging and self-destructive. There's a very fine line there between safe play and unsafe play—what's healthy and what's not.

■ *AJ: I think that's true of all life. You have to employ real flexibility and intuition to skirt any dogmas, whatever they are.*

Cutting is a high-risk sport because of AIDS. So both piercing and cutting require precautions: you wear gloves, you clean the area thoroughly, and you use a scalpel or needle that has never been used before and will never be used again.

■ RG: Cutting almost always ends up being a very spiritually moving experience for the cuttee: the building up to it, the experience itself, the healing afterwards (it scabs up after a few days). They're not deep cuts by any means. We're talking about mostly white people who do not tend to keloid. If someone wants a permanent cutting and doesn't want ink in it, one thing that can be done is cutting out a little wedge to make a thicker line so the scar tissue has to fill in that little gap, that little wedge cut. Not too many people want that as of yet. Also depending on the grain of the muscle and which way you cut—if it's with the muscle or against it—you'll get thinner or thicker lines. So you have to know how to place 'em and where to put 'em.

Your body will heal things out; it'll just push things out. People with Asian or black blood tend to keloid easier; they react more readily to certain pigments than white people.

■ *AJ: What exactly are blood rubbings?*

■ RG: I have the paper towels with designs made from being pressed over the fresh cutting, so the image in blood is preserved in reverse. For my portfolio, of course! Cutting is a high-risk sport, however, because of AIDS. So both piercing and cutting require precautions: you wear gloves, you clean the area thoroughly, and you use a scalpel or needle that has never been used before and will never be used again.. And you dispose of everything safely, carefully, and efficiently.

■ *AJ: Is AIDS in the lesbian community?*

■ RG: It depends on who's using I-V drugs. As far as sexual transmission—that's very low risk; the lesbian SM community has a grip on safe sex. But people do I-V drugs cut across all sexual and cultural lines. So in any community where you have drug using, you're going to get AIDS.

Lesbians who are in the lowest-risk group—who don't use I-V drugs, or any drugs, period, and who are clean and sober—are starting to use rubbers on their dildoes, and wear rubber gloves. Because this is safe sex. Plus, you don't know whose partner ten-times removed you're fucking, when you're fucking one person.

In any situation, the principle that applies is: when there's danger involved, you have to be careful!

■ *AJ: Could you elaborate more on the ritual possibilities of piercing?*

■ RG: Well, sometimes if somebody wanted it, I'd specifically ritualize a piercing or cutting or whatever for them. But my house has become a sort of temple; people often come in and gasp, "Ohhh . . . it's *nice* in here." So I don't have to do anything specific. But they end up feeling after they've been pierced that it's been a ritual for them. Because those are the feelings that are just *there*, living in my house.

■ *AJ: But you also did the Castro Street Fair.*

■ RG: Yes, and I enjoyed doing that, too. My booth is a pyramid that I can close off totally for privacy. I really do like going out there and being visible for that. Gay men will see my booth and go, "Oh, body piercing! I've been thinking of having my nipple pierced for years but I never knew anyone who did it." And there I am, so they'll do it. They'll be the ones who'll do it on the spur of the moment: "Okay, pierce me up!" They're in and out. So I've enjoyed doing that.

■ *AJ: Among the women you've pierced, are there beginning to be traditions? For example, the sailor tattoo tradition started with—*

■ RG: Ringing was a sailor thing too. Every time a sailor would cross the Equator, they'd get a ring in their ear; there was a piercing ritual that they did.

■ *AJ: But are traditions starting to unfold?*

■ RG: Sometimes women have had a traumatic experience and they'll want to reclaim their sexuality in a way by having a nipple or labia piercing; this becomes a *reclaiming ritual* that helps undo a lot of *shit* from their past. And from that moment forward they can go on. Sometimes that happens.

■ *AJ: That is an interesting aspect about piercing and tattooing: the reclaiming of the body, particularly the sexual parts.*

■ RG: Sometimes you'll have your basic romantic or bonding rituals where people will get their ears pierced together and have the same earring, or they'll both get their nipples pierced, or one will do it as a gift to the other when they become lovers. Those are basic romantic or bonding rituals. Many people in the SM community will get a piercing either on the right or left side, depending on if they're submissive or dominant—so there is that communication significance or meaning there. But whatever the ritual or communicative aspect, what ultimately matters is whether the life of the individual has been enhanced or diminished. It's never going to be up to me make a final judgment on that!

BILL SALMON

Junii & Bill Salmon work at Diamond Club Tattoo Studio at 2113 Van Ness Ave, San Francisco, CA 94109 (415) 776—0539.

■ *VALE: What's been the biggest change in tattooing today?*

■ BILL SALMON: The idea of the tattoo as a full body concept—not just a badge or sticker on the body. At the San Diego Tattoo Convention a few years ago Nakano (Horiyoshi III) got onstage and showed a full body suit done *25 years ago* that looked immaculate; a real example of high standards and quality. So the new ideal is: having the vision comprehensive enough so that whatever specific tattoos you get are just part of a bigger plan. Of course, the Japanese have been doing that for a long time. Their standard images of gods, dragons, tigers, flowers are almost always in the context of the elements: the wind, water, air, fire. And that elemental context: well, that's what American tattooing usually lacks.

Greg Irons was one of the first to take American style tattooing (which he developed out of his comics underground) and incorporate Japanese environment and influence, thus inspiring a lot of stock American tattooists. He left a whole legacy of flash that's already been copped by half of Europe—many people don't even know they're getting an Irons piece. In a short period of time he innovated a very strong, synthesizing style. I worked with him at Realistic just before he died and he always emphasized that the ten years that Ed Hardy worked to elevate tattooing to an appointment-only, custom work procedure—well, that's where we *started*, and we take it from there.

■ *ANDREA JUNO: You basically have a full body suit.*

■ BS: That's how I can relate to people like Nakano or Ed Hardy who are totally dedicated; I can appreciate the patience involved. My own body suit is a collection of work by 48 artists, and kind of an *homage* to them as well. For example, Ed Hardy did a portrait of Lyle Tuttle on me, which Lyle sat for on his 50th birthday. Lyle was the first American man I ever met with a full body suit—he had already *done* it, and I was just getting started with a couple little tattoos. This was back in '74, Lyle was about 42 at the time, and to me he represented a kind of ideal. It was the post-sixties, cosmic, *little tattoo* era, and I got the badges of that time: the mushrooms, the stars—they were part of my history.

There are waves of tattooers and to me they're all part of the same tattoo support system. Lyle is from a different school from me or Hardy, but we're all connected. The professional quality art statement side is what I'm talking about: working against the worldwide belief that tattoos are only for criminals or crazies, and that they're ugly or bad. That's why *Tattootime* was a good vehicle for bringing people back to the "New Tribalism," to show them the tattoo magic and the interconnections with music and art and life and death. You read the text and look at the pictures and—compared to when I started getting tattooed, you're already way ahead!

■ *AJ: How old were you when you first got tattooed?*

■ BS: About 24. I got my first images when I had no education and was naive on a lot of levels. I was working at Columbia Music on Market Street, and just wandered into Lyle Tuttle's tattoo shop nearby on my lunch hour and got a rose—I'd never even seen a tattoo shop before. I didn't get it on my shoulder because I didn't know if I wanted anybody to see it or not; I got it on my hip. Then, it was so exciting—I had my pants down more that week than the entire previous year, showing off my new tattoo to people!

A week later I went in and got a "Saturn" and three stars on my shoulder, because I was always under the influence of that planet. Then, because I'm a Libra, I felt unbalanced. I'd just moved here to California from New York and had never seen a palm tree before, so I got a palm tree on my other shoulder! And because I've been a musician and played guitar since I was six years old, I got some musical notes put on—ten bucks! I had the two musical notes flying over Saturn.

Obviously, I was in the same slot as a lot of Americans who try to get too much, too little, without any larger pattern in mind. Obviously, a person should start out with a small tattoo, but utilize the part-of-the-whole system. To make a long story short, I got a number of tattoos from a lot of different people before I went to Ed Hardy.

I'd heard that Ed was expensive, but by now I was working in a stereo store and making better money. I called him in late '78 and met him in 1979. My left arm was covered with sixty-ish/seventy-ish work, but my right arm was bare. And the work that Ed put on my right arm was the difference between day and night; the difference between Japanese style on the right and American style on the left.

Then I became a full-fledged tattoo collector. I got work from Dean Dennis, Greg Irons—the list goes on and on.

My own body suit is a collection of work by 48 artists, and kind of an homage to them as well.

■ *AJ: So your body itself is a history of tattoo styles.*
■ BS: Many. I'll give you a list of the 47 artists who did work on me, not including myself or my mother, who wrote "Mom" on my knee—*I've got a "Mom" by Mom!* In American tattooing, the Mom tattoo is so traditional, and such an emotional issue. She'd never held a tattoo tool before, but I just handed it to her and told her to do it, and it was easy! I took advantage of the moment—there is a time and place as well as a person from whom to get your tattoo, when the feeling is right—it's kind of a Zen thing. I've had that feeling *many* times, and I knew that if I didn't get it then I'd probably never get it. Kinda like with books—if you see a book you like in a used bookstore and don't get it, by the time you go back for it it'll be gone.

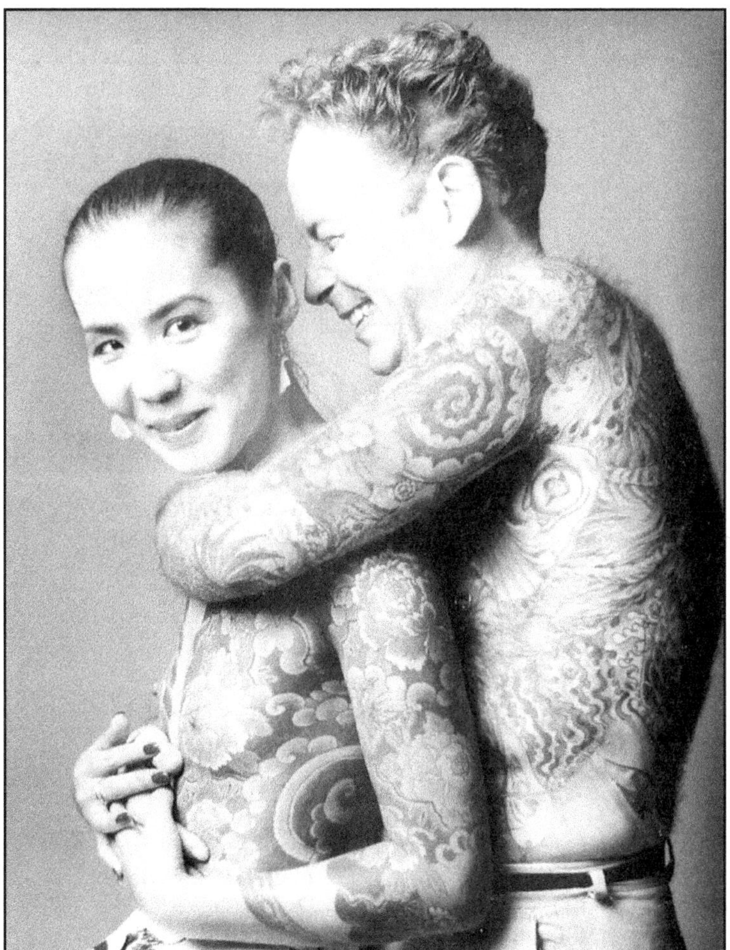

Junko and Bill Salmon. Photo by Bobby Neel Adams.

■ *V: Did you tattoo your mother?*
■ BS: Yes; I've given her two tattoos, a heart and chrysanthemum. There is a whole sentimental side to tattoos: who does them, and when. I was in Rome for a tattoo convention and everyone was getting a piece of Samoan pe'a (traditional geometric pattern) from a Samoan artist who'd attended. I told him to do anything he wanted to do. He knew that I liked diamonds, so he took his hand tool, went tap, tap, tap and put a diamond necklace on this woman on my leg. And in Sweden I got a tattoo of Edna St Vincent-Millay's "burning the candle at both ends." You've got to have your own magic symbols!

A turning point for me, from collector to tattooer, came when I attended the Tattoo Exhibition on the Queen Mary, 1982. By this time I had gotten really zealous about collecting tattoos—I was emulating The Great Omi, in a way, and I rented a booth that was a tribute to the Great Omi and dressed up as him. I realized, *I cannot do work in the straight world anymore.* Ed Hardy suggested, "Start drawing."

I had never drawn before, even in school. I really didn't have any drawing background, but I was good with my hands—I'm an ex-dental technician. I practiced with a half dozen sheets of flash and periodically showed my drawings to Hardy and he was always constructive in a positive way; he would never say, "That sucks." He has a good way of telling you how to get better; he knows you can't run 'til you learn how to walk. I had to practice a lot—nothing was handed to me!

Dean Denis, who started off Greg Irons and Leo Zulueta, was working with Chuck Eldridge and Terry Tweed. A young man named Wade was the apprentice; an unfortunate incident happened and Wade had to leave. That's how I got my start; I learned the basic American style—designs emanating from Sailor Jerry, Greg Irons, Mike Malone, Rollo, Hardy's early flash, and learned the designs that the punk scene wanted, all the way up to H.R. Giger designs. I scraped by with help from neon artist Betsy Berberian while getting unemployment from the stereo store job. It was rough, especially when I was left alone in the shop and was worrying that somebody would come in and want a Jack Rudy single-needle fine line portrait, but I *learned.* Some people were like scum of the earth, trying to run games on you—it was a crazy scene,

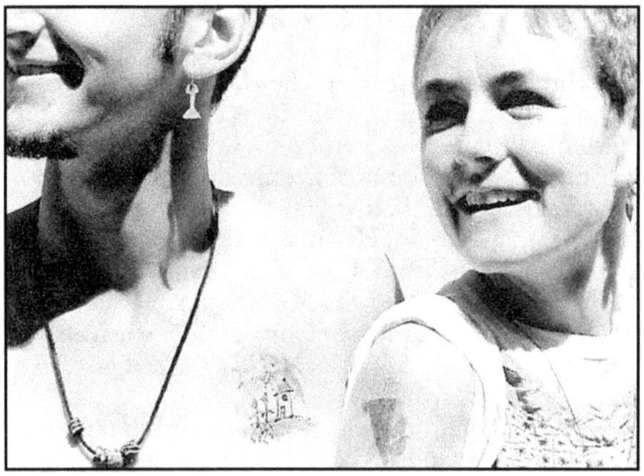

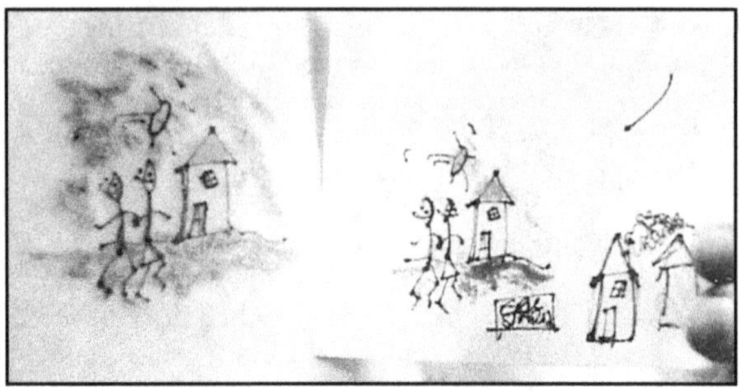

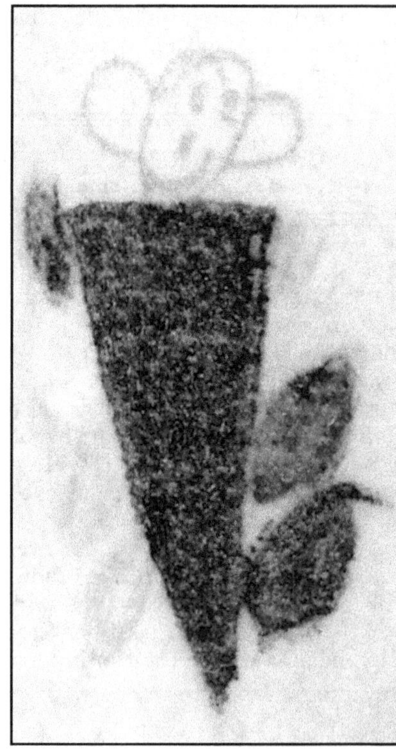

A love tattoo story. Photos by Bill Salmon.

but a street shop is good experience—I *tightened up* a lot!

■ *V: Tell us about one of your favorite tattoos.*

■ BS: Besides the magical, symbolic and decorative aspect of tattooing, I think there's a romantic reverberation as well. A Scottish craftsperson brought me a kid's style drawing of a boy and girl smiling and holding hands in the sunshine, and asked me to tattoo it on him. At the time it was kind of a voodoo charm for conjuring up what he wanted to happen. Later, he referred this Irish schoolteacher to me—she brought in a crayon drawing of an ice cream man that one of her five-year old students had drawn. That was a challenge—to make it look like crayon, but it turned out pretty well. They ended up getting married and going back to Scotland; I went to their wedding just before they left. That was one of my favorite experiences: a tattoo, and a love story, too! [See photos this page]

ARTISTS WHO HAVE TATTOOED BILL SALMON

Pat Martynuik, San Francisco CA
Lyle Tuttle, S.F.
Brian Freeman, S.F.
Leo Brereton, S.F.
D.E. Hardy, Honolulu, Hawaii
Henry Goldfield, S.F.
Sailor Moses, Biloxi, MI
Scott Sterling, Biloxi
Dean Dennis, S.F.
Chuck Eldridge, Berkeley, CA
Greg Irons, S.F.
Jamie "La Palma" Summers, Fairfax, CA
Freddy Negrete, East L.A.
Leo Zulueta, Garden Grove, CA
Mike Brown, East L.A.
Jack Rudy, East L.A.
Dan Thome, S.F.
Maria Yatar, Guam
Filip Leu, Switzerland
Ama Leu, Switzerland
Dieter Zalisz, W. Germany
Pinky Yun, Hong Kong
Horiyoshi III (Yoshihito Nakano), Yokohama
Larry Allen, Anchorage, AK
Doc Forest, Sweden
Hanky Panky, Amsterdam
Dennis Cockell, London
Petelo Suluape, W. Samoa
Tony, Amsterdam
Gippi Rondinella, Rome
Lance McClain, Honolulu
J.J. Turner, Honolulu
Kandi Everett, Honolulu
Inny Lee, S.F. (Goldfield's)
Vyvyn Lazonga, S.F.
Sailor Sam Cook, S.F.
Terry Tweed, Everett, WA
Charlie Cartwright, Modesto, CA
Dave Gibson, S.F.
Zeke Owen, Jacksonville, N.C.
Jonathan Shaw, L.A.
Horitoshi I, Tokyo, Japan
Jane Nembhauser, Austin, TX
Michael De Witz, S.F.
Gary Fink, S.F.
Bob Roberts, Hollywood
Capt. Don Leslie, S.F.
Mom, Troy, N.Y.
Myself, S.F.

SHEREE ROSE

Sheree Rose is a Los Angeles photographer and video artist. Much of her work involves documenting the sexual underground, tattoo and piercing communities. She lived with Bob Flanagan, whose life was celebrated in the independent feature film, "Sick."

■ *ANDREA JUNO: Is a penis piercing very pleasurable to a woman?*

■ SHEREE ROSE: Absolutely. In fact, the *Kama Sutra* recommends that a man have an ampallang, which is a piercing that goes horizontally all the way through the head, and on either side are two little balls. In intercourse you definitely feel it. Also the Prince Albert which is in the front, right through the urethra, is also incredible in intercourse.

■ *AJ: So it really stimulates the inside?*

■ SR: Oh, absolutely. First of all, it's very hard, but because of lubrication it doesn't scrape. It's like a steel dildo—it's incredible! Everyone I know who's experienced it says the same thing. I know several men who are getting the Prince Albert because they hear how pleasurable it is for the woman. It looks good, too!

■ *AJ: I thought that from the woman's viewpoint, the ampallang was best.*

■ SR: Well, one goes this way and the other that way. Basically, you have steel leading the way!

■ *AJ: Is your boyfriend pierced?*

■ SR: When I first met Bob he was already pierced. He also said he was a submissive man, and I asked what that meant. He said, "Well, I want to belong to a woman, and do everything for her. I will be faithful only to her." As a symbol of that his penis had a ring under the head in a piercing called a frenum. I'd never seen a pierced penis before, and it was startling. Once we got together more formally, I discovered I really wanted to explore the idea that he was my complete slave and that I owned him. I thought about how I could modify his body to my pleasure.

One of the things I wanted, and that we talked about, was: as my slave he wasn't allowed to have sex at all unless it was with my permission. That meant no masturbation—he couldn't do anything unless I wanted it, and then only when I wanted it. To that end we tried a lot of different approaches—leather restraints, padlocks, various kinds of strap arrangements, but the penis is really weird—it moves and changes, and none of those methods worked very well. Bob was also very ingenious and could always manage to get free—I call him the Houdini of the SM world.

■ *AJ: What other piercings does Bob have?*

■ SR: Bob has a guiche which is behind the scrotum. So . . . I would put very heavy rings in the guiche and the Prince Albert and tie them both together with a padlock, and keep the key. His nipples are pierced also. We became very friendly with Jim Ward; Bob became his model for piercing demonstrations. Jim would always say, "Rose, when are you going to get a pierce?" I'd always say, "*Me?* Never."

But then more and more people started doing it. It became almost fashionable within this group of people. One night at a meeting I had a nipple pierced in front of almost a hundred people. It felt like a rite of passage, like, "I'm brave enough to do this." The piercing took on a whole different meaning, like it wasn't just for sexual gratification, but was something more serious. Although, piercing is not necessarily permanent—you can take a piercing out and it will heal up quite soon. So in a way, tattooing and branding are much more of a commitment.

■ *AJ: Branding? You mean with a hot iron?*

■ SR: Yes. I know Fakir; I'd seen him do a branding demonstration in the Bay Area. Later, I had a slave I wanted branded, and asked him to come down and do it. We worked on the design, and then in front of an audience of a hundred people my slave was branded, and another person's slave was also branded. That was real intense!

One night at a [SM] meeting I had a nipple pierced in front of almost a hundred people. It felt like a rite of passage, like, "I'm brave enough to do this."

■ *AJ: Did you get branded, too?*

■ SR: No, no! I was the *mistress;* the slaves are the ones that get branded. But that's changing—it used to be only the submissives got pierced or branded. But lately a lot of the tops (dominants) are getting into it as well. I think it's symbolic of the fact that we're living a different lifestyle—that we're part of this underground subculture. That's one way of knowing if you're in it—if you're pierced.

Also, piercing is no longer just for SM people; now there's a *whole lot* of people who are into body piercing. It's amazing how many there are.

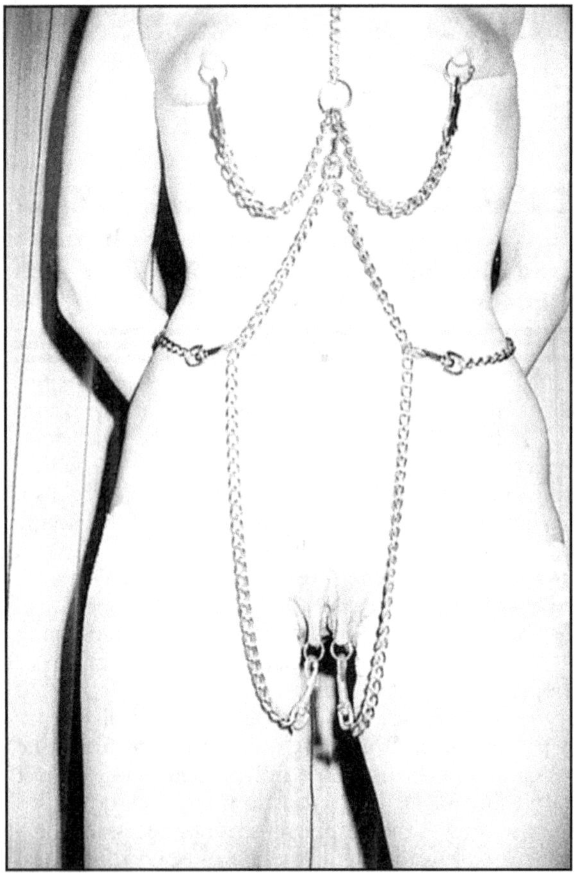

Photo by Sheree Rose.

To me the act of piercing the skin is a very old feeling. You see it in old photographs from all different cultures. In our society, people are petrified at the idea; yet the sensation of actually being pierced is a *rush.* That sensation when the needle goes through—it's hard to explain if you haven't felt it . . .

■ *AJ: Do you feel a sort of—triumph when it finally gets through the other side?*

■ SR: Well . . . there's something about the piercing ritual that makes you want to have people surrounding you. The second time I was pierced was at a private club meeting, at the home of a friend of Jim Ward's who has an incredible number of piercings. Janus, the club I belong to, is not private—anyone interested in SM can belong. But this was the Pierced and Tattooed Club—only for gay men. Because I was friendly with Jim Ward, and everybody else knew Bob, I was invited to one of the meetings. Being the only woman with 20 or 30 mostly nude, tattooed and pierced guys was quite an experience. They were really wonderful with me.

In the living room was a low table where Jim would do the piercing. Everyone would gather around and hold the subject's hand or foot, and when the piercing was over everyone smiled and laughed or clapped. I was scared to do it, but the feeling I got from being there with all these people around me was—I felt I was in some ancient ritual that had been reenacted many, many times. I got another nipple pierced.

Some time later, Bob was working for Jim Ward as an assistant piercer. I decided to get a labial piercing. We invited a few of our friends to a get-together, and Bob pierced my friend Jane and then pierced me—one labia each. *That hurt;* the nipples hadn't hurt as much. There was a flash of searing pain, but then it was over fast. It doesn't hurt afterwards.

■ *AJ: I'm surprised there's even that much feeling. I would have thought the nipples would be more sensitive.*

■ SR: Well, during my first nipple piercing a friend kind of hypnotized me, telling me I wouldn't feel any pain. When I had my labia pierced Bob did it—it was a little different having my slave pierce me. It felt really great, and now I'm thinking of having my clit pierced.

■ *AJ: Let's go back to the nipples. How do the piercings feel now?*

■ SR: Now, it's great! They're constantly erect, and because they're erect you notice them all the time. Bob gave me some beautiful things called nipple shields that would hold the nipple out really far. After a couple of hours of wearing those, the slightest touch would practically send me into orgasms. There are some women who say they can experience orgasms just from having their nipple piercings played with and I can believe that.

The thing about genital piercing is: you feel stimulation there all the time. Those of us who like vibrators find it's incredible because you put the vibrator on the metal and the metal starts vibrating and—it just blows you away.

■ *AJ: Do you feel much sensation from the labia piercing?*

■ SR: I have a barbell in mine, not a ring. I feel it—it's there. It's sort of like a little surprise. It's a very private part of your body that no one (unless they know you intimately) knows you have it. To me female genitalia are really beautiful; what's so amazing is how different everyone's is. I'm doing this series of close-up photographs of pierced female genitals, and no one knows who they are unless they know them *very* intimately.

■ *AJ: Is it a turn-on, too?*

■ SR: Definitely. So few women have genital piercings that those of us who do feel like we're part of a sisterhood. I don't have rings in my labia; submissive women have rings that can be locked by their masters. My piercings are just for myself. Everyone I know who has the clit piercing says it's great.

I know four women—two had it done on the hood. One goes right through the clit horizontally, and one unbelievable piercing goes vertically through the clit—that's in the video I made.

■ *AJ: How did you happen to video a clit piercing?*

■ SR: Jim Ward knew I was doing a video on piercing. I had asked him to let me know if any unusual piercings were requested. He called and said, "Hey, this

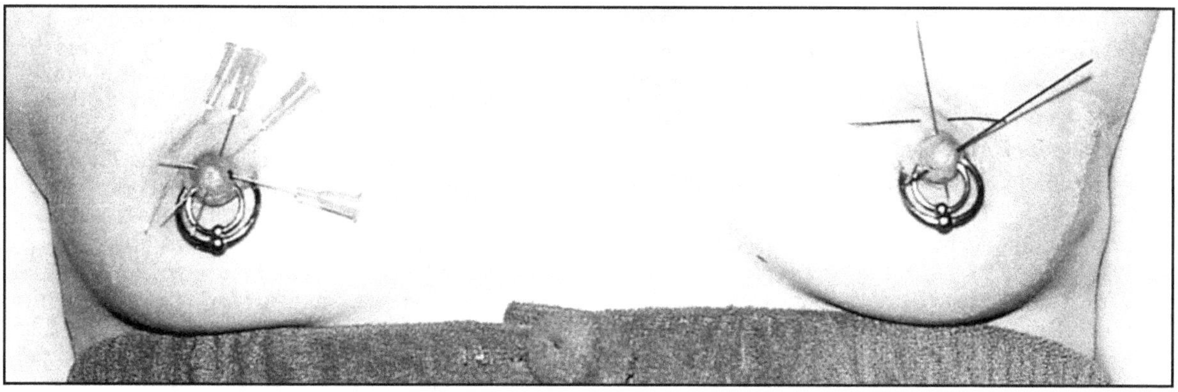

Photo by Sheree Rose.

We were trying to develop a subculture of dominant women and submissive men. completely switched around the social norm. The women were all dominant and fully clothed and the men had to be in the nude.

woman wants to have her clit pierced." I said, "Oh, great! Can I come?" He said, "Yes; I just asked her." So I walk in and this woman is just beautiful; she's blonde, about 25. I've never seen her before. I introduce myself, explain what I'm doing, ask permission to video her. She says, "Fine. No problem."

She takes off her clothes, lays down on the table, spreads her legs—I'm just dying 'cause she's such a hot-looking woman—just gorgeous. They discuss where it was going to be, and she had this vision that she wanted to have it in this one place. She didn't do it for her boyfriend or SM reasons—just because *she* wanted it. Where she got the idea, I don't know.

Of course, Jim, being a gay man, wasn't exactly sure of the placement! Usually you use a clamp on piercings—you mark it, then clamp it to hold it firm... but with a clit you can't—it's too slippery. So he's looking around, figuring where to put it. Finally he makes one little push, but nothing happens yet. Then another push, and you can just *feel* it going right through.

■ *AJ: Where's it going through?*

■ SR: Up, vertically [demonstrates with hands]. At the end she says, "Is that it? I was expecting so much more." Jim asks, "Are you disappointed?"

■ *AJ: She didn't have any anaesthetic?*

■ SR: No. She just did it. Now she loves it.

■ *AJ: What does it feel like? It seems like it would be a sensory overload.*

■ SR: I don't know. I guess you kind of get used to the stimulation. I've heard that the clit piercing is almost constantly stimulating!

■ *AJ: What kind of women have gotten these genital piercings?*

■ SR: As a generalization I would say that the women who get these are usually pretty sexy. A lot of submissive women are very sexy—more so than the dominant ones.

■ *AJ: Sexy—meaning sexually charged or turned on?*

■ SR: Sexy, meaning their masters or mistresses like them to be turned-on all the time. The joke among dominant men is: they prove their manhood by how many orgasms their slave can have. They train them to have lots and lots of orgasms. One woman claims to have had 100 orgasms in ten minutes!

Piercing in the SM subculture is definitely a mark of submission. It's something a slave does to please the master. The act of doing it is the symbolic showing that they do belong to this person.

■ *AJ: What are some of the deeper, underlying reasons why someone chooses to be a slave?*

■ SR: For Bob, I think his sexuality is tuned into submissiveness to women. Where that comes from, I don't know. He gets normal hard-ons; in fact, he's very highly sexed—more so than average. That's true of submissive men—they're much more in tune with their bodies than a dominant or straight man. They're usually less inhibited, too. If you go to an SM party, all the dominant men will have their clothes on, and all the submissive men will be naked.

■ *AJ: What about dominance? What are some of your reasons for being dominant?*

■ SR: For me I got into it out of feminist philosophy. I didn't like being with a man who wanted to boss me around or tell me what to do. I was brought up in an era where you were a virgin until you got married. The husband was the one who did everything; you just stayed home and had babies. I was married for 14 years. I though that maybe I should try somebody else—maybe I'd like it better, and I did! I discovered that I enjoyed sex!

I went through about 50 different guys in the period of a year just to see if I could find somebody I really liked. In my exploration of sex I found that most men couldn't satisfy me. I didn't like the way they touched me; the way they moved their bodies. I would try them once or maybe twice and then never see them

Anytime you're in a relationship with somebody there is a power imbalance. We call SM an erotic exchange of power. It's really based on your sexual needs rather than your personality.

again. I did find one, which showed me I wasn't completely turned-off to sex, but he wasn't psychologically right. After a while I got very discouraged.

When I met Bob and he told me he was submissive, I thought, "Well, this is a new thing to try—let me see how this feels." I liked the idea that he would only sleep with me and nobody else. I liked the idea that I would control his every move—that was sexy. He would clean the house, do the laundry, wash the dishes, do errands—this was all part of the relationship. And he was turned-on all the time. Having someone as your sex slave is a hot thing—it's really fun.

■ *AJ: What's your responsibility to him?*

■ SR: Mainly, I have to make the decisions. I have to let him know what's going on. I found that to be very difficult. It was not a perfect relationship at first; there were a lot of problems, mainly my own insecurities. For a while, in the "scene," we became well-known as a couple and people looked up to us. If we went to a party people would watch us to see what we would do—how we would play—we were considered very heavy. And this got to be a bit of a burden for me.

■ *AJ: Now you could experiment with other people—*

■ SR: Absolutely, and I did. What mainly happened was that I became interested in women: I started having female slaves. I discovered that the turn-on is that they're *submissive* to me—not that they're male or female. I only wanted the truly submissives. A lot of people *say* they are, but then go, "Well, do it to me this way," or, "I only want to do *this*—I won't do *that*." I was more interested in really exploring an alternate lifestyle.

For a while I had an organization called *The Matriarchal Society* and I had a friend in New York who had a group called *The Center for Matriarchal Awareness*. We were trying to develop a subculture of dominant women and submissive men. There were several parties at my house where we completely switched around the social norm. The women were all dominant and fully clothed and the men were only invited if they weren't with a woman. They had to be in the nude. They couldn't sit on furniture, they couldn't eat or drink anything, they had to serve us and were only there to amuse us. If we didn't want them around, we'd dismiss them or have them go out of the room. It wasn't an orgy, it was like a cocktail party, but reversed. It was real interesting just to have that energy going on.

■ *AJ: Like a redressing of historical inequity.*

■ SR: Very much so. That's really why I got into SM.

■ *AJ: Of course, there are those who will say, "Why not try to find equality?" rather than be a woman and then do the same things that men have traditionally always done.*

■ SR: That's fine, except I think most relationships are not equal. Anytime you're in a relationship with somebody there is a power imbalance. We call SM an erotic exchange of power. It's really based on your sexual needs rather than your personality. So a person can be really dominant, but sexually might be very submissive. That's true of a lot of men. The men who are the best submissives have very dominant personalities. They're not wishy-washy. That's a real misconception: that they're wimpy—they're not. The best submissives are very strong—both men and women. They can take control of a lot of things. They know what they want; they're very directive. But sexually they're submissive; they want to completely surrender the control to someone else. That's what turns them on, that's what gives them hard-ons. The thing to remember is that they are voluntarily giving up this control; there's no coercion involved.

■ *AJ: The turn-on of abdicating all responsibility?*

■ SR: Absolutely. If you trust the person you're doing this with and know they're not going to hurt you, it can be very liberating.

Most women tend to be submissive because it's easier in many ways. The dominant person has to be the one who comes up with all the ideas. It's like game playing on an adult level. People in their twenties generally don't understand this;

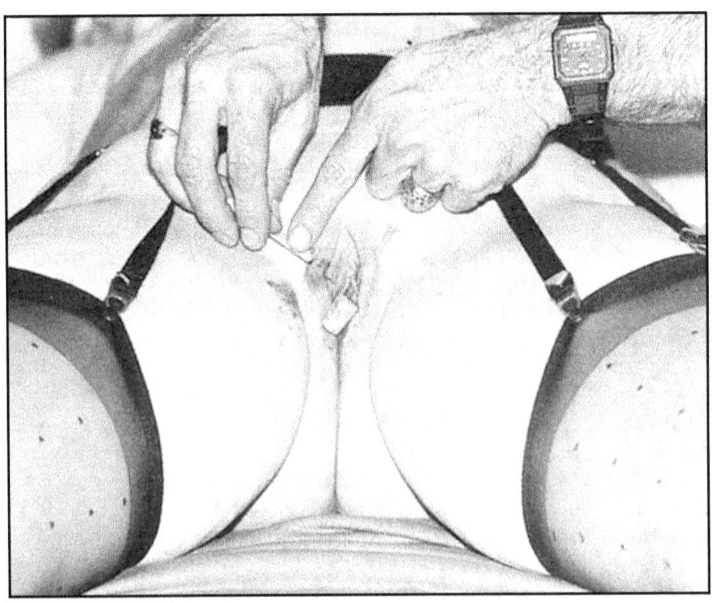

Labia piercing. Photo by Sheree Rose.

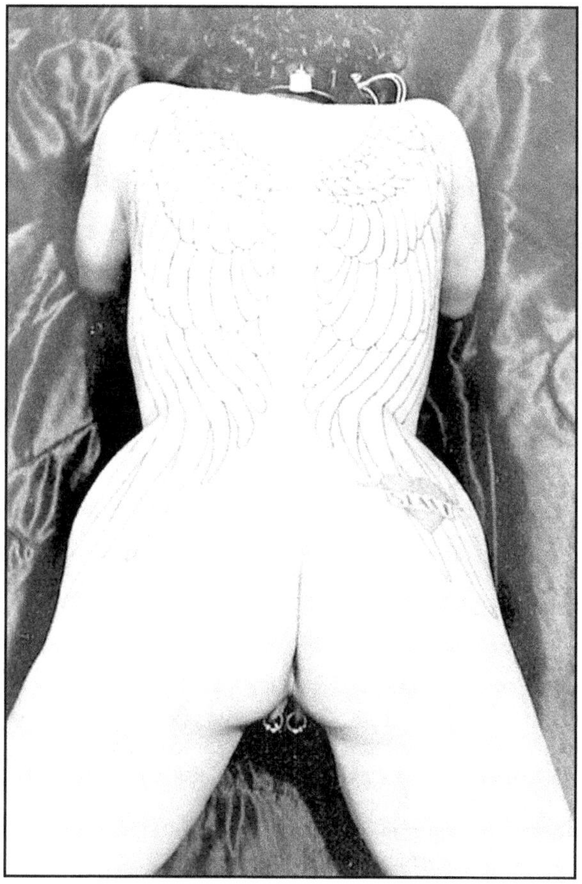

Photo by Sheree Rose.

you first start realizing these things in your thirties and forties. A lot of older people are getting into SM because they've been through *normal* sex (whatever that is), and found it unsatisfying. SM is a higher level of sexuality; it's much more explicit and overt.

I'm going to a party tonight where there will be 20 or 30 people who will have orgasms in front of everyone. The others will stand around and watch or help while someone has an orgasm in some unusual fashion. It's like social sex, but not necessarily intercourse. A lot of SM does not involve intercourse; that very often is saved. With me, for example, even though I have other slaves and do other things with them, I only have intercourse with Bob. I save that for him; it's something special that we do together. A lot of couples are like that: intercourse, actual genital fucking, is only done with your partner, but you're very sexy and you do a lot of other sexual acts with others. At a party you'll see a lot of interesting scenes go on but you won't see penetration, except with dildos. A lot of submissive women will be dominant with another woman at their master's request.

■ *AJ: What's the Janus Society?*

■ SR: It's been going on in San Francisco since 1974 and in Los Angeles since 1982. It's a consensual club involved in SM and B&D and all that. It started because people needed a support group. When we first started in L.A. there were maybe 8 or 10 people; now there's over 400 members. It's going through all kinds of growing pains now. We don't advertise—we're just there if you need us. For me, it's almost getting too big; to the point where it's losing that feeling it had as a family.

■ *AJ: Let's go back to the ritualizations that go with the theme of Modern Primitives, who are trying to recapture some of the lost sense of community, or reawaken lost rites of passage.*

■ SR: There's a new group (of which I am a part) consisting of about 20 committed couples who get together for group piercings or tattoos. There are writers, artists, photographers and we're all sort of coming out. We go out together in public places dressed in our leather, rings, etc.

■ *AJ: There's a certain sense of loss in our society. Do you have any analysis of how this kind of group fulfills that social need?*

■ SR: I think what is common to all the people I'm talking about is: they've always felt like misfits. If they're men, they didn't go on to become lawyers or doctors, they don't have that drive and they felt ashamed for that reason. Money wasn't their overriding concern. They have all these sexual fantasies which of course they're found difficult to fulfill.

The women—if they had a lot of interest in sex at an early age, their parents probably gave them a lot of pressure and didn't understand them. For example, one girl had fantasies about submitting, but no one to talk to about it; no place to go. Most of them really felt alienated from normal society. I was never comfortable being married; here I was, a very typical Encino housewife, wondering, "What am I doing here?" yet having no idea where I belonged. There was no place for me to go.

When I got into feminism after my divorce, I thought, "Well, maybe I'm a lesbian." But I discovered I wasn't a lesbian. I was really pretty despairing of ever finding any place where I would fit in.

When I met Bob, we both felt that no one else in the world does this. I felt very depressed by that. I thought, "I must be *weird*. Why are we doing this? How come nobody else does this?" etc.

We started advertising for another couple, and got one answer. The woman was a professional dominant. I had never met anybody who did it professionally; I had done it privately with Bob, but this woman was saying, "Oh, yeah, I whipped this guy yesterday!" and "Come see my dungeon."

It was wonderful. The one thing about SM people is that they're very open; they talk about their sexuality and what they like to do. That's a really *big* difference, because most people never talk about it, or do so only under veiled circumstances. From this couple we got connected with the Janus Society and other people.

We found all these people who thought they were the *only* ones. The momentum kept picking up until now we have 400 members! Everyone who joins says, "I thought I was so alone. I thought I was nothing. Now I feel like I'm home." It's almost as if we were sent down from Mars all over the world, and now everyone's coming together.

■ *AJ: Do you have any tattoos?*

■ SR: Yes, that's my newest project. The piercing started taking over because I couldn't believe how it felt, what it meant, and that it was so taboo of a subject. That's why I really plugged into it. And a lot of people in the video talk about the fact that they did it as *children;* they pierced themselves for no other reason but that they felt this *need* to do it. What they were responding to are some real primitive feelings.

UCLA Art History Professor Arnold Rubin has written a whole book, *Marks of Civilization,* on people who modify their bodies. He says the Judeo-Christian idea is that the body is a vessel for the spirit, so therefore you can't touch it—it's holy. Before Christianity the body was viewed as something for sensual pleasure; something to play with, to change, with which to experience sensations. That's the way SM people feel.

■ *AJ: So-called "primitive" people used to feel that sensual pleasure was not incompatible with spirituality. They felt the body and sexuality was perhaps also a vehicle for illumination.*

■ SR: Definitely; I would say this is also true for submissive men. Bob gets those feelings, and frequently I need to be alone for awhile. I was married, I raised two children—my daughter just turned 18, I have a son who's 20—and I go out with a group and give lectures on SM at colleges and we blow them away. We're changing a lot of people's minds. They see that we're people—we're not murderers or rapists; we have a higher purpose.

We're interested in the imaginative possibilities of body modifications—the creativity that can be made manifest by pushing the body to its limits.

There is some spirituality involved in this. It's like transcending what the body can feel as pain and turning it into pleasure and then turning it into a spiritual experience. It's not easy to get to that point because you have to forget about the modern world which unfortunately is very much with us. For example, I used to do night bondage with Bob; I'd take him outside, tie him to a pole and he'd be there all night long. Another time I tied him to a bench—these were long-term endurance trials. At one point, a police helicopter flew near and Bob screamed, "Come get me!" because if the police came and saw somebody tied up naked, they'd never understand. It's hard to get sufficient privacy.

I once went to a lesbian SM party in Orange County. The windows were open because it was a very warm night. This one woman was heavy into a "scene"

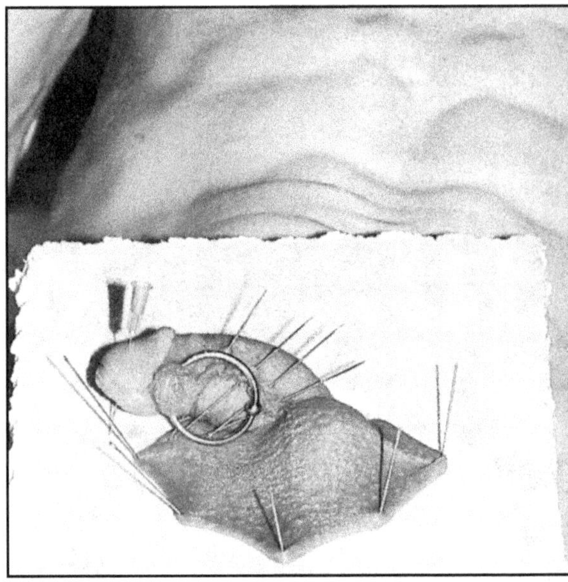

Photo by Sheree Rose.

and her slave was too—the slave was screaming really loud. Everybody was totally fascinated and no one was paying much attention to the noise. Then came a knock on the door—it was the police responding to a neighbor's complaint. The policeman's eyes opened wide as he scanned all these women, "Is everything okay, ladies?" [laughs]

Society really isn't set up to accept this kind of activity, because it requires a lot of time and energy away from society. It's not that you don't want to work, but: your career and getting ahead in the world is no longer your Number One concern. This activity is hedonistic and sybaritic and you want to experience these feelings for long periods of time. Most people experience sex as a half hour (or less): you touch, you fondle, you suck, you fuck, and then you go on to something else. Not so in SM. It's very elongated, very protracted, and some sessions entail hours. It takes a lot of concentration. But you definitely achieve different levels!

■ *AJ: Has the "real" world provided any opportunity where you can indulge your fantasies?*

■ SR: I enjoy the public display of Bob's submission to me. Of course, it's always hard to find places where you can really get away with that. A few years ago, the World Con [a science fiction convention] was held at Anaheim. At the time I had two slaves, Sandy, a female, and Bob. (Sandy was into science fiction.) I dressed as a space mistress, and had my hair all silvered and wore a slinky black dress with chains all over. Sandy wore a little fur bikini with ears and a tail—she was my space kitten. I shaved Bob completely from head to toe—this is a very submissive act, by the way. I painted him green and then painted on gold scales and he was my space lizard. I had a leash on both of them, going to a collar that Sandy wore, and to a chain attached to the rings in Bob's nipples. We walked through this whole convention and must have had a hundred pictures taken of us that night. It was a very high feeling to be able to do that in public.

It *is* true though that the modem world doesn't allow a lot of that. I think they're frightened of it, because people might get turned on to what they can do to their bodies. In fact, some of us think that the government practices non-consensual SM with the citizens.

What we do privately in our SM lives is very consensual—nothing is ever done against somebody's will. The other person may not like something that's done to them, but it's important that they're willing to give this up.

■ *AJ: Back to the tattoos—do you have any?*

■ SR: Yes. I got a small one several years ago as a symbolic act. Being raised Jewish, I was taught that tattoos are very bad—you can't even be buried in an orthodox Jewish cemetery if you have one. But as I got into SM and being dominant, I realized I didn't believe in a male god; I didn't believe in a god that would not let me go to heaven; I didn't believe in a lot more. How do you express that? I expressed that through a tattoo. I was very tentative—it's a very small rose.

I had Bob tattooed with a rose over his chest; the stem of the rose being a whip handle with two thongs. It's a pretty hot tattoo. Other masters often have their slaves tattooed; a common tattoo is the word "SLAVE" placed on the ass.

■ *AJ: What are you working on now?*

■ SR: I'm doing this project called *Under My Skin,* about women and tattoos. Tattoo is one of those big taboos for women, although it's always been something that men could do when they get drunk. But now there are women consciously making a choice and choosing to have a tattoo. I think that's incredible, and I definitely want to get more into tattooing; it's a way that I can feel my own individuality.

When you hear the stories of these women and the reasons they do it, every one is *so* different. It's that individuality that knocks me out. So often society wants everybody to be the same, think the same, do the same, because it's fashionable to buy this record or go to this kind of restaurant. But when you're into your own body there should be none of that. It's really a very personal choice: what you want to do with *your body.* That you don't change for *anybody!*

LYLE TUTTLE

The first tattoo artist in America to gain widespread national media attention was Lyle Tuttle, curator of the Tattoo Art Museum in San Francisco and publisher of the *Tattoo Historian*. In the Sixties Lyle tattooed Janis Joplin (with a heart on the left breast and a floral bracelet on her left wrist), Joan Baez, Peter Fonda and other notables, and the resultant publicity triggered a mini-Renaissance which took tattooing out of the province of bikers and sailors to the middle classes.

Born in Millerton, Iowa in 1931, Lyle received his first tattoo at age fourteen and started tattooing professionally at seventeen. As a U.S. Marine he studied in Japan and Hong Kong, then apprenticed under Bert Grimm. In 1957 he set up his own shop in San Francisco. When the hippie movement happened, he had a brief stint in Hollywood tattooing stars and starlets before the craze for butterflies and flowers died down. While visiting Western Samoa he received his tattoo "initiation" as a Samoan "Maite" or Chief. Over the years Lyle has developed a rationale for his art:

"Winston Churchill's mother, Lady Randolph Churchill, started a fad of dainty tattoos among fashionable women of her set in the 1880s. [She has a small coiled snake around one wrist, usually concealed by a heavy bracelet.] Rosalind Elias of the Metropolitan Opera has her name and Social Security number tattooed on her lower abdomen. Pearl Bailey has a heart on her leg. Sean Connery wears a small skin design on the inside of each arm . . . People are asking for all kinds of religious and mystic symbols too . . . The world of the tattooed is an international subculture. Tattoos have been inscribed on Denmark's King Frederick IX, Czar Nicholas II of Russia . . .

"I think it's caused by all the serious world problems today. People are scared...they're drawing together in clusters and forming cults. Just yesterday a small group had me make a stencil and put identical tattoos on each of them; this happens frequently now. But the real, basic reason for wanting a tattoo can be expressed in one word: atavism. Atavism, the return to a primitive nature, is what it's all about. The tattoo subculture has existed in every civilization, on every continent, from the beginning of history. Tattooing by puncture has been found on Egyptian mummies dating back to 2,000 B.C. And corpora, or painted-on tattoos, date back to the Neanderthal Man."

During a long career, Lyle created tattoos by appointment, published the *Tattoo Historian* and the *Tattoo Calendar Book*, and occasionally lectured—besides crafting silver rings and bracelets. His shop is located at 841 Columbus Ave, San Francisco CA 94133; (415) 775-4991. Lyle is now retired, but the studio is still in operation. This interview took place at the home of Lyle Tuttle and his wife Judy, who is the editor of *Tattoo Historian* and the *Tattoo Calendar Book*.

■ *VALE: What won't you tattoo?*

■ LYLE: Well, the swastika. Although—Charlie Wagner [legendary tattoo artist] told me, "People used to get swastikas tattooed all the time as a good-luck charm. But that Hitler fixed *that!*" Hitler got the idea for the swastika when he was in a jail reading a book by Nietzsche. The book was published by Roland Publishing Co, and bore a drawing of Roland (mythical knight like King Arthur) on his horse with armor on, and there were swastikas on the saddle blanket because it's such an age-old symbol! So he adopted it. I guess if you're in jail and only have one book to read, you sort of absorb everything in it.

■ *V: I just saw an old painting of George Washington, and the border was all rows of Swastikas...How long has tattooing been around?*

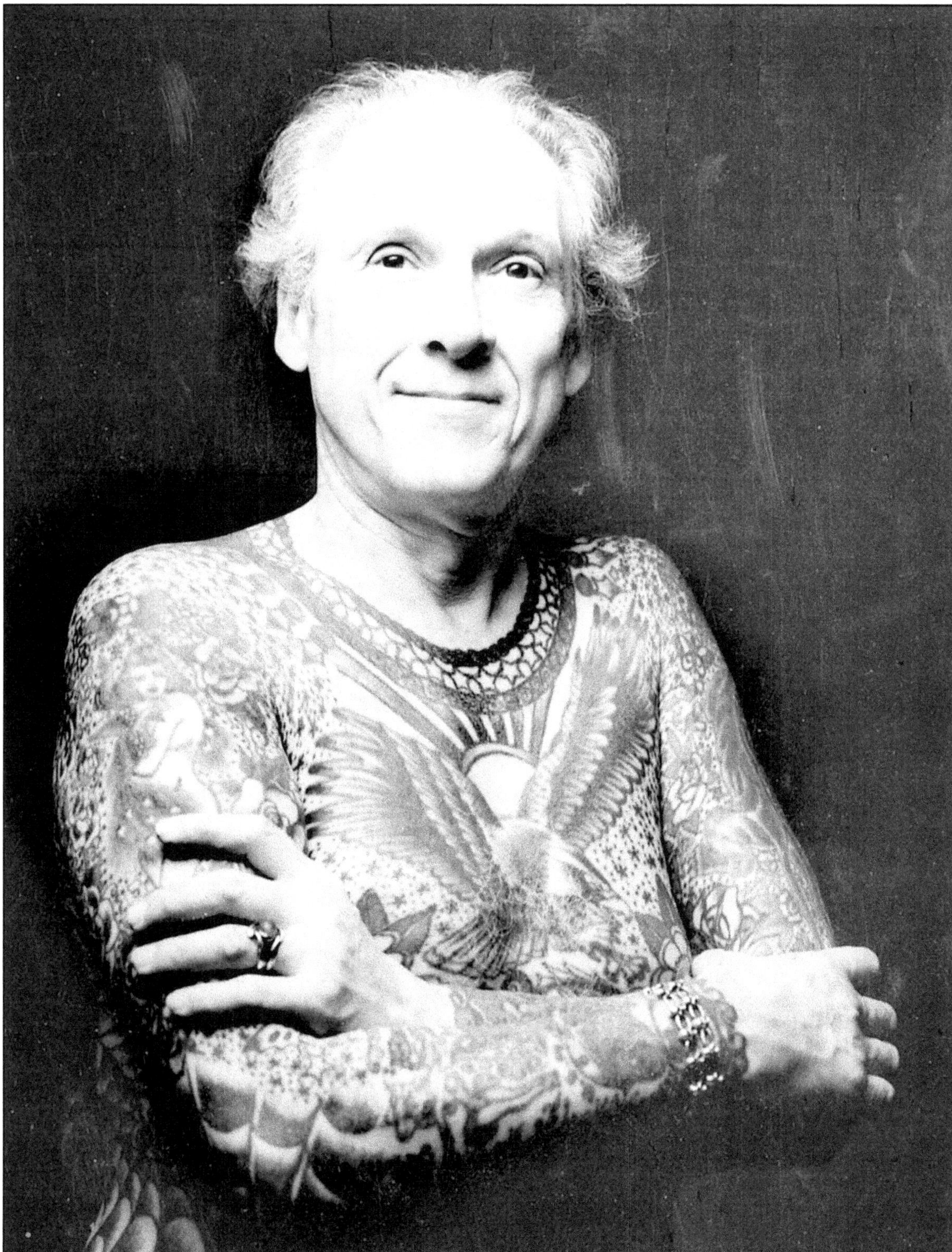

Photo by Bobby Neel Adams.

■ LT: Some of the earliest heavily tattooed peoples were the Picts, a migratory people who roamed throughout Europe a few thousand years ago. On this continent various American Indian tribes tattooed themselves as well as body-painted themselves, particularly before going to war. If you came from a race that wasn't tattooed, and all of a sudden some guy jumped out of the bushes who was tattooed all over, you might be scared!

Tattooing has always been associated with warriors; it's possible that early man figured out that men who were tattooed had a better survival rate from wounds, because a tattoo is a wound—maybe it develops the antibody system...maybe tattoo wounds prepare the warrior for battle wounds. Tattooing: the first inoculation!

In Burma, there's a legend about a king who lost his favorite concubine. Night after night girls were brought to him, and none of them pleased him. One night a beautiful young transvestite was brought to him, and the king, being drunk, was fooled. When he discovered the deception, he cut off the head of the procurer and proclaimed an edict that from now on all men had to be tattooed with "pants"!

Orientals get tattooed for *stories,* while we get tattooed for *memories.* My tattoos are a montage of my life, the tire-patch look: like an inner tube that's been punctured many times and now is covered with patches. When I went to Samoa I was covered from the ankle up to the neck. The one people that kept their pre-Christian tattooing was the Samoans. The men put on a tattoo like a pair of pants.

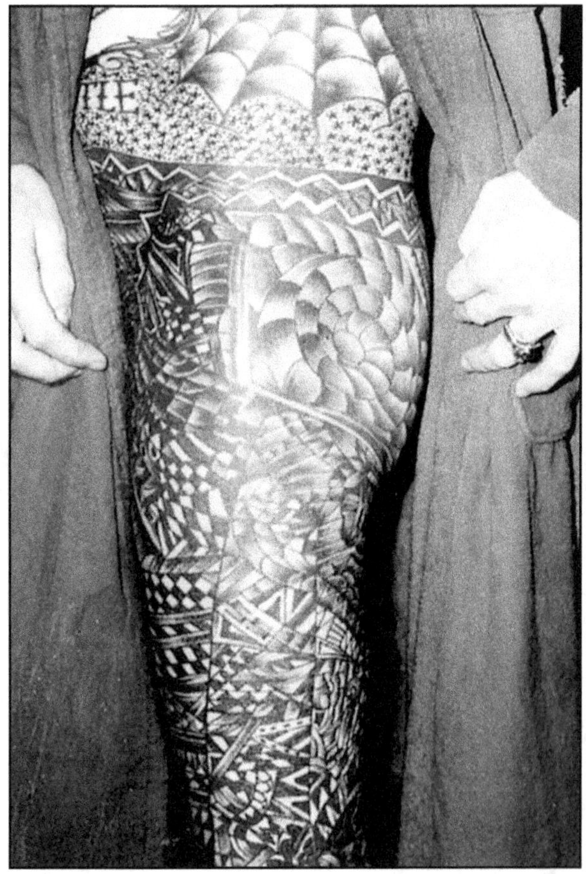

Lyle Tuttle's leg. Photo by Charles Gatewood.

Tattooing has always been associated with warriors; it's possible that early man figured out that men who were tattooed had a better survival rate from wounds, because a tattoo is a wound—maybe it develops the antibody system.

I went to Samoa to get a tattoo because every Samoan I'd met—man, woman or child—was enthralled with tattooing, had an ultra-respect for it. Tattooing was a way of deification in a way. You can be born to a Chief's family, but if you don't have that tattoo, you can't even go into the Chief's chambers and mix kava, and your word means *nothing.* In the old days, if the Chief was thirsty and wanted some coconut milk, the one who went up the tree was an *un*-tattooed man.

It's considered a sin to show your thighs there, so I was running around trying to photograph the old tattoos and it was *impossible,* even though your tattooing is more popular today than in the last hundred years. I finally figured out how to get them to show their tattoos—I would *jerk* all my clothes off and be naked as a jaybird, then they would get caught up in the heat of the situation and show theirs. I visited one village in which every man of age was tattooed; the youngest person was nine years old. And the faster you get it, the more "medicine" it has. To quit a tattoo is the worst thing in the world—you're just *half* of something, because you started and then quit.

It cots a lot of money to get a tattoo there. "Tattoo" comes from the Polynesian; their word for tattooist means "tattoo-builder," because they don't think of it as an art, but construction—they *build* a tattoo. The tradition supposedly came from Tonga—their age-old enemy, in a way and a folktale says that two Samoan women were swimming back with the knowledge, chanting, "Tattoo the women and not the men" when they spotted a giant clam and dived deep for it. After coming up for air they were short of breath and got confused: "Tattoo the men and not the women."

Actually, the women also get tattooed, but with a lighter design, a cross hatch design running from thigh to knee called a *malu*—Margaret Mead got one. I heard that a missionary woman living there also got one, because when she died she wanted to be buried—if you don't have the tattoo they'll take your body out into the jungle and just leave it there.

The word for Samoan male tattoo is also the word for a big fruit-eating bat with a three-foot wingspan. This bat, which is quite rare, has a pretty face like a cat.

The fruit-bat tattoo is a dark triangle with a canoe that goes around each side of the rib cage. When I went to Samoa they tatooed me across the small of my back; I added this "authentic" work to my previous work to "baptize" it; I wanted some of the "real stuff" put on. The Samoans were impressed by my tattoos—they asked, "What island do you own?" Every white men they'd met was either a missionary or a bureaucrat who looked down on their tattoos. To see a white man with more tattoos than their highest chiefs—they loved it! I got treated like royalty—the same thing happened in Japan. It was like going to Disneyland and being the only guest! Also, there was an instant camaraderie with the people.

■ *ANDREA JUNO: Are there professional tattoo artists there?*

■ LT: The tattoo artist is generally a chief, either through heredity or speaking ability; they have a chief's language. But to get anywhere at all you first of all must get a tattoo—you haven't a chance in hell without it. If a young man doesn't want to hoe taro on a plantation all his life, he gets that tattoo to be admitted to the chief's house, where he can mix kava, be delegated responsibilities and rise through the community. Whereas in our half-baked mongrel society, all the basic religions dictate some type of prohibition against tattooing.

I heard a Samoan get asked why he got a tattoo, and he replied, "An old Samoan custom." [laughs]

■ *V: How was your tattoo done?*

■ LT: The chief who was the tattoo artist put it on. The technique varies, but basically it requires a tool like a garden hoe with a wooden handle 12-18" long to *press* the ink into the skin, not vibrated in 3000 times per minute. They used to use human bone. It has a striker made of boar's tusk, sharpened, with a serration in it, and there's only one beach in all of Samoa where they get this elongated coral which they cut down to make the file.

Because of my tattoos, they gave me a chief's name, one they hadn't used since 1909. My name means "safe harbor," "ship's anchor," or "flying fish"—all that. They had a kava ceremony for me with a lot of talk and ritual I really didn't understand. (Kava is a hypnotic—it tastes like chewing on a fresh pine board. I didn't drink enough to affect me.) Then my tattoo got infected and my glands in front swelled up. I went to the LBJ Tropical Hospital in Pago-Pago and queued up with a bunch of Samoans under the palm trees. I filled out the application using my chief's name and when the Samoan nurse saw it, she asked what village it was from, and it was like the equivalent of New York City! She said, "You don't *belong* here," and took me straight to a doctor. Having a chief's name was a real advantage!

SAMOAN NAVEL TATTOO

by Iefata Moe

REPRINTED FROM

LYLE & JUDY TUTTLE'S TATTOO HISTORIAN

There were eight of us in the group: four would quit, one would die and only three of us would make it. As I watched one man getting his pe'a, he suddenly cried out in pain. I had second thoughts but I knew, "This is the one chance I've got and I can't let it go by." Without my parents or family's knowledge, I had gone to Western Samoa to get the traditional body tattoo, the *pe'a*. In the olden days your family had to agree before you get a pe'a, or evil days would fall on your house. I don't believe in superstitions and anyway my family always said *No* every year I asked them.

It was painful but the worst part was when the Tufuga went over the last lines on my lower back that he had tattooed the day before! Lying in bed that night I thought, "Oh god, don't let me end up with just a pe'a mutu" (an unfinished, incomplete body tattoo). "The shame of not being strong enough to finish will last a lifetime."

The *Tufuga*, the man doing the tattooing, told me to kneel down in front of him. I felt a line being drawn across the middle of my back. I looked at the coconut skull full of *lama;* ink made with ashes from the smoke of a kerosene lantern which is mixed with water. The Tufuga pointed to the mats on the floor and I quickly lay down on my stomach. Wham! the *Au* pounds into my skin. The first mark is on my back and the last mark will be on my belly-button five days later.

I glance sideways at the Aus on the mat: different sizes for specific areas of the pe'a. They look like combs but the teeth are filed to sharp points. I wonder if the ancient story is true that they always use the bones from the strongest, bravest chief to make the Au. But these Aus are either shark's teeth or boar's tusks.

The tapping sound of the *Iapalapa* (mallet) pushing the Au into my back is steady and even. He is using the *Au Sogi* to make the wide lines. The smallest one is the *Au Tapulu*. I feel the hands of the two assistants (*Ausolo*) holding me while the third one is stretching my skin and the fourth assistant wipes the blood away with a damp cloth.

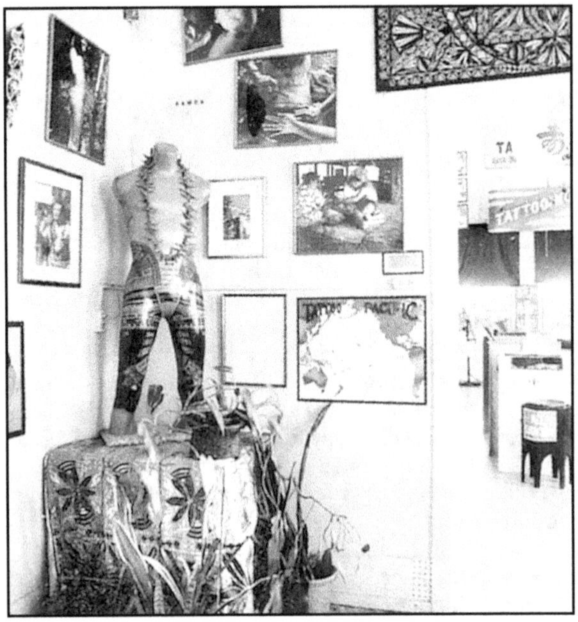

Mannequin of Samoan pe'a tattoo at Lyle Tuttle's tattoo museum.

The tapping suddenly stops. So far so good. At least my lower back is finished. The assistants roll me onto my side; the Tufuga's mallet strikes the Au into my right ribs. Wow—it's really hurting and burning like bee stings! I feel like punching him out.

It's late afternoon and I wonder if I can last much longer. I'm being held down by the assistants when he tattoos my left side. My body jerks because I'm losing physical control, but mentally I don't care anymore. The hands release me and the Tufuga speaks, "Your day is now finished. Go and wash." I took the soap from his hand and walked to the water. It took me hours to wash my back and sides with the soap...stinging and burning...

I walked outside and all of a sudden I heard screams. People were running toward the house and I knew my friend who was next in line to get his bellybutton tattooed was in trouble. I ran back and saw blood all over the mats and saw part of his intestines hanging out of his bellybutton.

The next day I couldn't eat breakfast, lunch or dinner. All I could get down was soda pop. No wonder; that was the day my behind was completely tattooed. It was painful but the worst part was when the Tufuga went over the last lines on my lower back that he had tattooed the day before! Lying in bed that night I thought, "Oh god, don't let me end up with just a pe'a mutu" (an unfinished, incomplete body tattoo). "The shame of not being strong enough to finish will last a lifetime. Just think about the shame and you will make it. *Think about the shame,*" I kept saying and drifted off to sleep.

The morning of the third day I realized I'm beginning to lose weight. Now I'm worried. I still can't eat and I break out in a cold sweat. I gag, leave the food and walk to the Tufuga's place. "This will be a long day," he announced. I lie flat on my back and Ausolo put two pillows under my behind.

He started connecting the back of pe'a to the front part of my body. Every time the Tufuga pounded the Au in my stomach blood would shoot out in spurts. I asked the Ausolo to press my veins as hard as they could to stop the blood from spurting. It was making me sick. At times the Au would hit bone and it felt like they were breaking into pieces. The sound of the mallet striking the Au is a steady, fast beat like a marching band. I wish I was marching by. I wish this custom had died with my ancestors!

The Ausolo pick me up and grin. The front and back designs are connected and it looks like I am wearing shorts. I try to sleep but I can't stop my head from thinking about what the Tufuga will do to me tomorrow on my upper leg...

Day four: left leg begins with the small Au for outlining, which doesn't take long. Afterward he began pounding the area with his mallet, very softly to make it numb. The large areas were covered with the widest Au, the Tapulu and I lost the most blood at this part of the tattooing. Next I was told to sit up and grab my ankle and he began tattooing my knee. I tried to listen to the rhythm of his mallet but all I heard was the sound of hammer hitting bone. The left leg and knee were finished and I crawled into bed immediately. I still couldn't eat and I could hardly drink soda pop anymore but I knew that tomorrow was day five, last day.

He began tattooing my right leg, then the knee. Now it was time for the bellybutton. I began screaming my head off and it took three Ausolo to hold me down. The Tufuga told me to sit up and I knew it was finally over when he kissed me right on the lips and said, "You are now a Soga'imiti," and I cried.

I walked outside and all of a sudden I heard screams. People were running toward the house and I knew my friend who was next in line to get his bellybutton tattooed was in trouble. I ran back and saw blood all over the mats and saw part of his intestines hanging out his bellybutton. I knelt down beside him and he grabbed my hand and asked if he had finally become a Soga'imiti. The Tufuga nodded his head to me; I bent down to my friend and said, "Yes, you are a Soga'imiti." He moaned, tried to speak, then *died* for what he wanted most: a pe'a!

On the sixth day, March 29, 1981, was the ceremony for the three of us who finished. We had to make a flower *ula* (lei) and the string had to be made from a coconut leaf. I wore my best lavalava, the flower lei and went to the village guest house where all the *matais* (chiefs) were waiting. I sat down as best

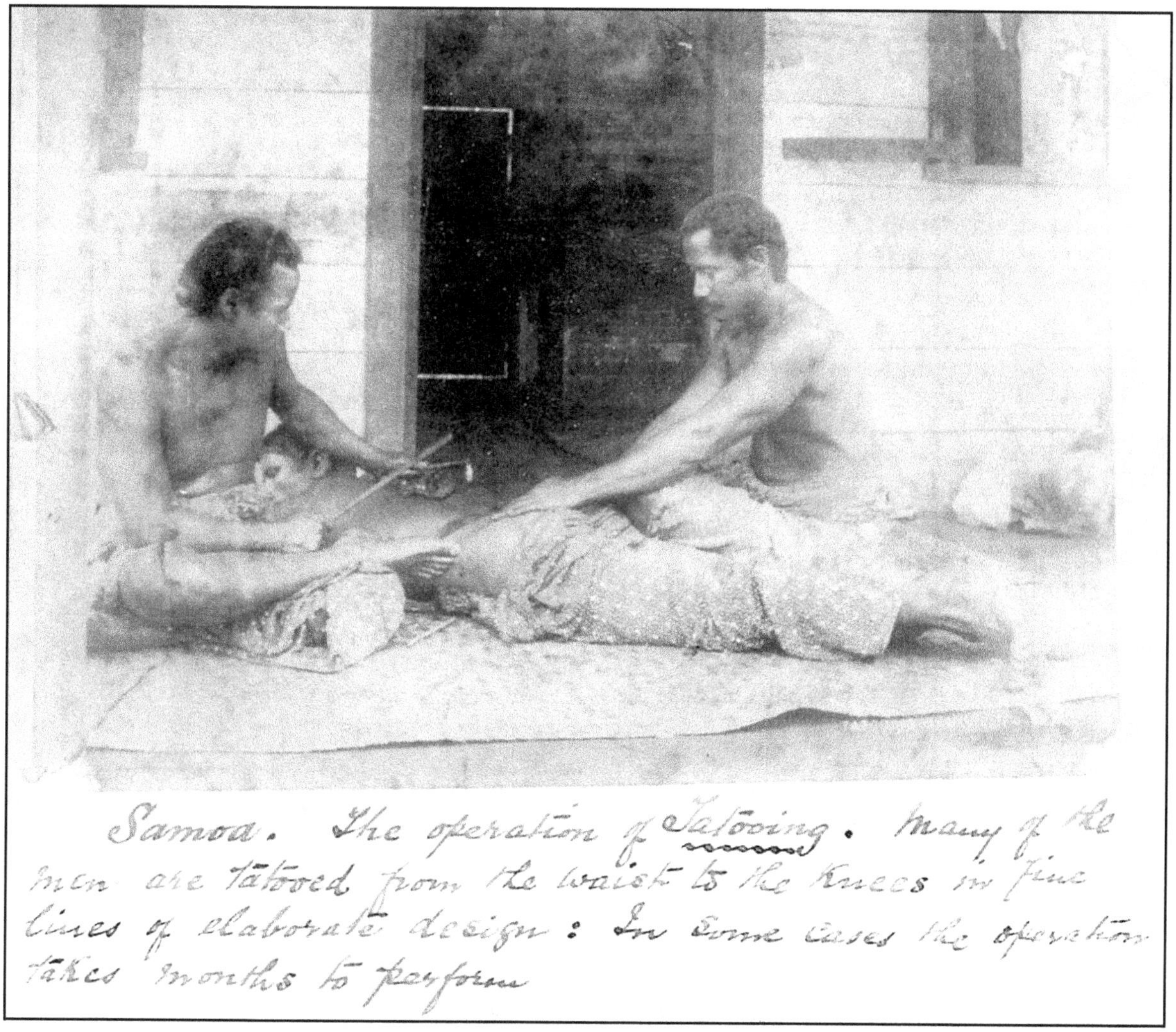

Samoan tattooing. Photo supplied by Hanky Panky from his tattoo museum in Amsterdam.

I could next to the Tufuga. He stood up, asked for the egg and said to me, "This is to make you well fast, feel strong and heal the pe'a." He cracked the egg on top of my head and said, "Stand up." Two men helped me up as the Tufuga covered my whole body with *fagu'u* (Samoan coconut oil). Everyone began singing and—yes, I had to dance. My eyes were so sticky from the egg I couldn't see what I was doing all through the ceremonial dance! Then I walked to the Tufuga and placed everything I had on my body on the ground in front of him. Now I was totally naked in front of the entire village and as the singing began I felt their love.

Getting tattooed cost me two hundred Samoan dollars, two huge kegs of beef and two fine mats which took years to weave. In 1981 that would represent around two thousand U.S. dollars. It took me three weeks to walk normally and three months for my pe'a to heal completely. I forget many times that I am tattooed and I have no regrets. It's the only way for me to show that I am a Samoan—and deep inside I know that *I am Somebody.*

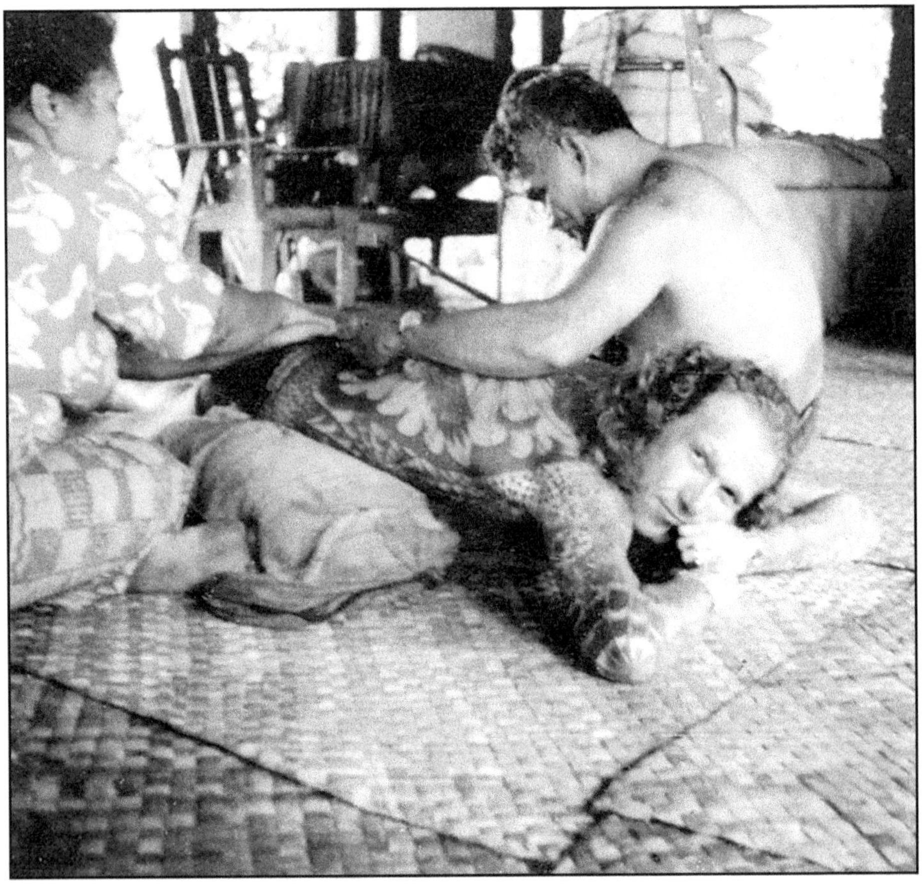

Lyle receiving a tattoo in Samoa.

The Great Omi

by Judy Tuttle
REPRINTED FROM

Lyle & Judy Tuttle's Tattoo Historian

In a country home outside of London, the youngest son of the Ridler family was born in 1892. Raised in an English upper-middle class environment, Horace Ridler enjoyed a privileged life of comfort, security, private schools and a tutor, Joe Green, who was also the groom of his father's string of horses. Mr Green had been a clown during his younger days and spun tales of the circus life to young Horace while teaching him horsemanship along with circus stunts and tricks. This was magic to a young boy—Mr Green had planted a seed in the boy's imagination that in later years would blossom into the creation of the Great Omi.

The privileged life included many trips abroad to Europe and Africa. Horace would seek out the bazaars, fairgrounds, music halls and pageants of the cities and towns he visited, never dreaming that a fairground would become his home.

Showing no interest in pursuing a university education, he decided that the Army would be his career and was commissioned a second lieutenant. A few months later his father died, leaving him a handsome inheritance. He spent his money at a record pace on lavish parties, entertainment, gambling and ill-advised investments. Getting into serious trouble, he was forced to resign his commission.

Soon thereafter the political turmoil in Europe reached its peak and plunged England into war. Ridler was 22 years old when WWI began. He enlisted as a trooper and, due to his outstanding conduct and heroism was decorated for gallantry. By the end of the

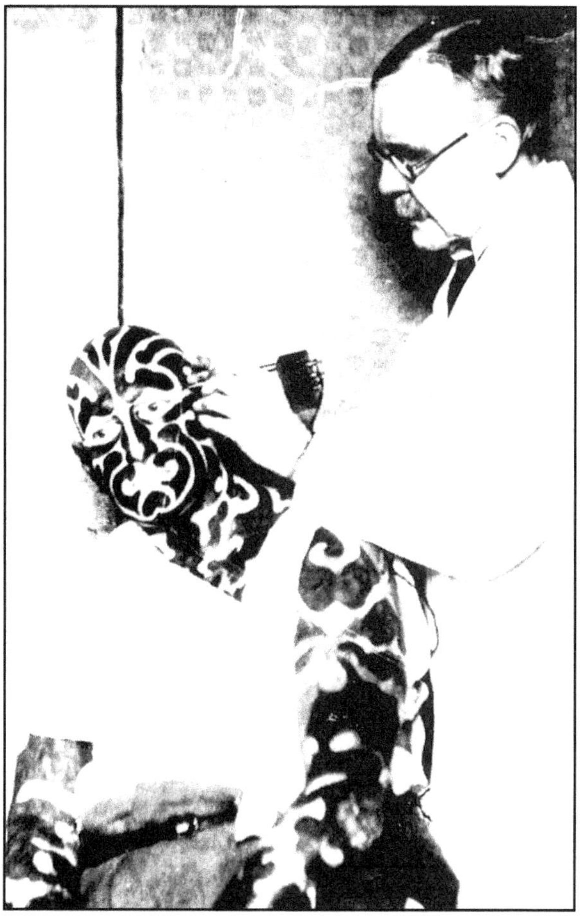

The Great Omi tattooed by George Burchett.

war he was demobilized with the rank of a major with a small pension. But what does a soldier do when the fighting is over? Not much, as Ridler found out.

Having no training in anything else, he faced the odd job, try-your-luck-at-anything type of existence and soon became tired of drifting around. "I was in the unique position of not being able to make ends meet. I was prepared to tackle anything and I always remembered the huge crowds the 'oddities' commanded and I decided to become an act," stated Omi. In 1922 he began to put his plan into action, getting tattooed with 'pictorial' tattoos. He exhibited himself with these crude tattoos in small side shows, barely earning enough to feed himself until the next one. He wasn't spectacular enough, and he knew it.

Ridler was living in Mitcham, a town only a few miles south of London. On May 24, 1934 he wrote asking famed tatooist George Burchett to "completely tattoo me all over."

"I began one of the most difficult tasks I had ever undertaken, to turn a human being into a zebra," Burchett declared. "I had a lot of trouble covering the [earlier] crude tattoos. Omi took more than 150 hours of tattooing. I followed his design of curved stripes about one inch wide which would mask the previous tattoos. He was a tall (six foot), well-built man with a handsome face; cultured and well spoken."

The tattooing began in June and ended during that winter. As soon as the work was finished, Omi had his first well-paid position with Betram Mills at the London Olympia theatre and it was sensational. But after touring England with Betram, there were no more bookings except from a small circus in France. Omi signed the contract and left for France with his wife and stumbled into one hell of a tour.

Returning to England "half dead" and terribly disillusioned, Omi wrote to Burchett explaining why he still couldn't pay him for the tattooing. He knew his act needed to be even more phenomenal, so:

"I had my nose pierced by a veterinarian so I could insert different kinds of ivory tusks. My ear lobes were pierced and stretched until the holes were each about the size of a dollar. Of course I went to a regular dentist to have my teeth filed down into sharp points. I bought brightly colored costumes with jewels all over them and wore long, golden boots."

Wow—did it ever pay off! In 1939 Omi arrived in the U.S. for the World's Fair held at Queens, New York from April 30-October 31, 1939. The theme was the "World of Tomorrow" and various scientific wonders were displayed, including the first appearance of television. Omi and his wife Omette arrived June 6, 1939 on the British ship *Laconia* and stated their

"Omi Over Miami" by Bill Salmon.

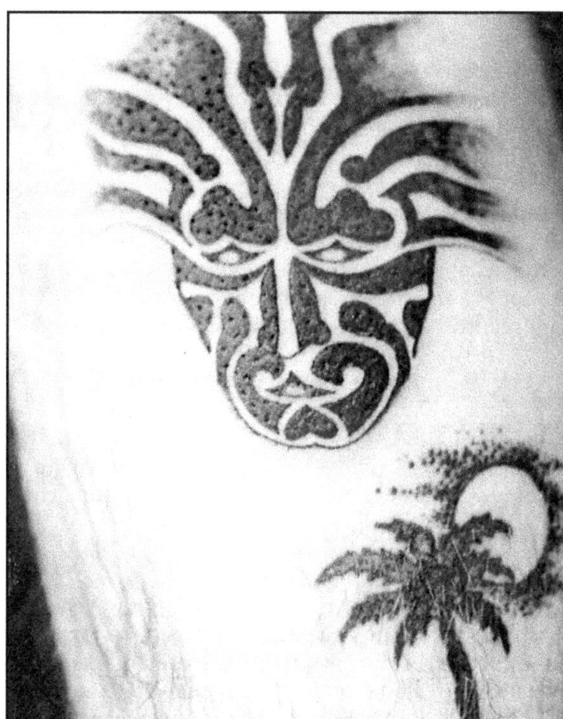

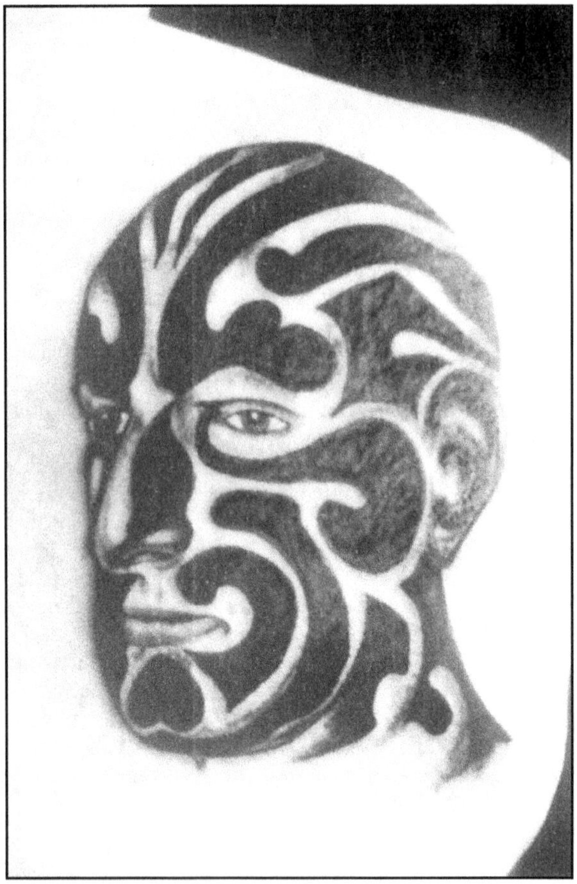

Tattoo and photo by Lal Hardy.

address as the Hotel Claridge in Times Square (*NY Times,* June 7, 1939).

Several evenings later, the couple decided to tour the Times Square area. Omi's face was cut from chin to cheek by an unknown attacker. "I will protest to the British council," declared Omi (*NY Times, NY Mirror* and *NY Herald Tribune,* June 10, 1939). Strangely enough, no photos were taken, so possibly the story of an attack was for publicity. The NY police main records department has no record of the attack ever occurring.

Over 22 million people attended the fair and millions viewed Omi who was appearing at John Hix's Odditorium along with: The Tattooed Venus, Betty Broadbent; Iron Eyelids (he pulled autos with them); Anatomical wonder (heart in the pit of his stomach); and the Fingerless Pianist, Marvello—master of the black-and-whites. Definitely your money's worth of astonishing people for 40 cents!

Immediately after the fair ended Omi went to Ripley's Auditorium Theatre, Broadway, NYC, as the star attraction; so much so that Ripley retained him as one of his "greatest wonders" for six months, the longest time that Ripley ever showed a single artist. Omi appeared over 1,600 times, doing as many as 9 or 10 shows daily.

Omi received a contract from Ringling Bros. Barnum & Bailey and toured the 1940 season, billed as Omi the Zebra Man. Betty Broadbent knew Omi quite well as they did the World's Fair together as well as Ripley's and both were now in Ringling's side show. "I remember Omi as being somewhat of a snob, as if the rest of us were below him, but his manner face to face was that of a charming gent and—boy, was his wife ever jealous!" Understandable when there is a tattooed Venus around. Although...according to Omette, "Whatever people say about Omi, I think he's beautiful. And I can tell you a lot of the girls fall for his barbaric appearance. But I'm not a bit jealous."

Omi may have been somewhat of a snob by this time as he was the star attraction in the side show and he did leave the Ringling Bros. after only one season. But the traveling arrangements were something else. Omi most likely bunked in the musician-freak car outfitted with a 2/3 size mattress, sheets, one blanket, two pillows with cases; changed once a week for which they tipped the car porter 50 cents. The bunk would be up or down depending on seniority and a curtain could be pulled across for privacy. Two toilets with basins were at one end of the railroad car; this for 60-plus people. The water was cold and bathing consisted of a pair of buckets behind a curtain at one end of the side show tent. On the lot the toilet was a little tent with a one hole stool, located in the back of the main tent. On the road was somewhat primitive, to say the least.

Leaving Ringling Bros. for greener pastures, Omi toured New Zealand and Australia in early 1941. Returning to Vancouver for a booking at the beach side show "Happyland" was not up to his expectations: he signed with Bert Lorous Jr.'s "World Fair Freaks" for the dates August 25–September 9, 1941. Being at the top of his career permitted Omi great freedom of choice and a few weeks later he appeared with the Rubin-Cherry show in San Diego.

"I saw Omi in San Diego," remembered Chris Audibert. "He had tusks in his nose and long ear lobe decorations. He was bare to his trunks and bare down to his feet. His total upper body was zebra-striped but his legs had a more conventional type of marking; not zebra-like at all. Omi's monologue was: he had been stranded in New Guinea, captured by the natives and subjected to the tattooing. ("At that time, forty-five years ago, the world didn't know much about New Guinea except that it was a huge primitive island near Australia. So any spiel sounded authentic.") Omi peddled his photo postcards for 25 cents. The show closed the season in Phoenix, Arizona in early 1942 and Omi and his wife began criss-crossing America, playing all the cities and towns along the way.

Omi tried to re-enlist in the British Army though he was well beyond age for active duty and of course the British Consul said he was not acceptable for active service. On May 7, 1945, at General Eisenhower's headquarters in France, Germany signed an unconditional surrender and WWII ended in Europe.

Omi sailed home to a battered England and donated his services, giving free performances for troops and charity organizations. Omi continued to have enormous success in London's Bele Vue and other cities throughout England and Europe. "To become a freak in order to earn a livelihood was a gamble which might not have come off. Fortunately it did and he was one of the most successful and highest paid showmen in both hemispheres." (George Burchett)

The time eventually comes when one should retire gracefully; at the top of one's chosen career. Omi retired as a star instead of a has-been to a small village in Sussex, England, during the 1950s. He lived the remainder of his years in a caravan in the woods near the village. The local people gradually became accustomed to his weekly trips to the post office and the grocery store but, when in town, Omi would cover his head with a hat and scarf to minimize his appearance. "I nearly fell over the counter when Omi first came into the shop" recalled Valerie Brereton. "But really, he's quite a charming old dear. We get on famously."

"Omette dressed up to make me happy. She put white powder on her face, a wig on her head, an old-fashioned clown collar around her neck, frilly blouse and baggy, plaid pants. Now, I let my fingernails grow long and paint them a bright red and wear my beaded costumes." What a couple they must have been, decked out as they strolled along the quiet English country lanes.

During the last years Omi slipped more and more into the world of his fantasies and his stories became more fanciful. "I was the only white member of an Indian cult that worships elephants. I joined the cult when I was stationed in India nearly 20 years ago." (*Weekend Mail*, Sept 20, 1956). That would have been the year Burchett began the tattooing. "I used to make moonlight trips into the jungle to the cult's secret meetings. It was months before they finally admitted me. The rites of the cult are secret but I can tell you the members pride themselves on their barbaric beauty."

The Great Omi died in Sussex, England in 1969. "Underneath it all, I'm really just an ordinary man," said Omi in his last known interview as he thoughtfully touched the ivory tusk in his nose.

Sources: C. Audibert, B. Broadbent correspondence, L. Burchett, *NY Herald Tribune, NY Mirror, NY News, NY Times, Billboard, Amusement Business,* J. Nicol, George Burchett's *Memoirs of a Tattooist*, Tattoo Art Museum.

VAUGHN

Vaughn resides in San Francisco and is trying to establish himself as a tattooist and piercer.

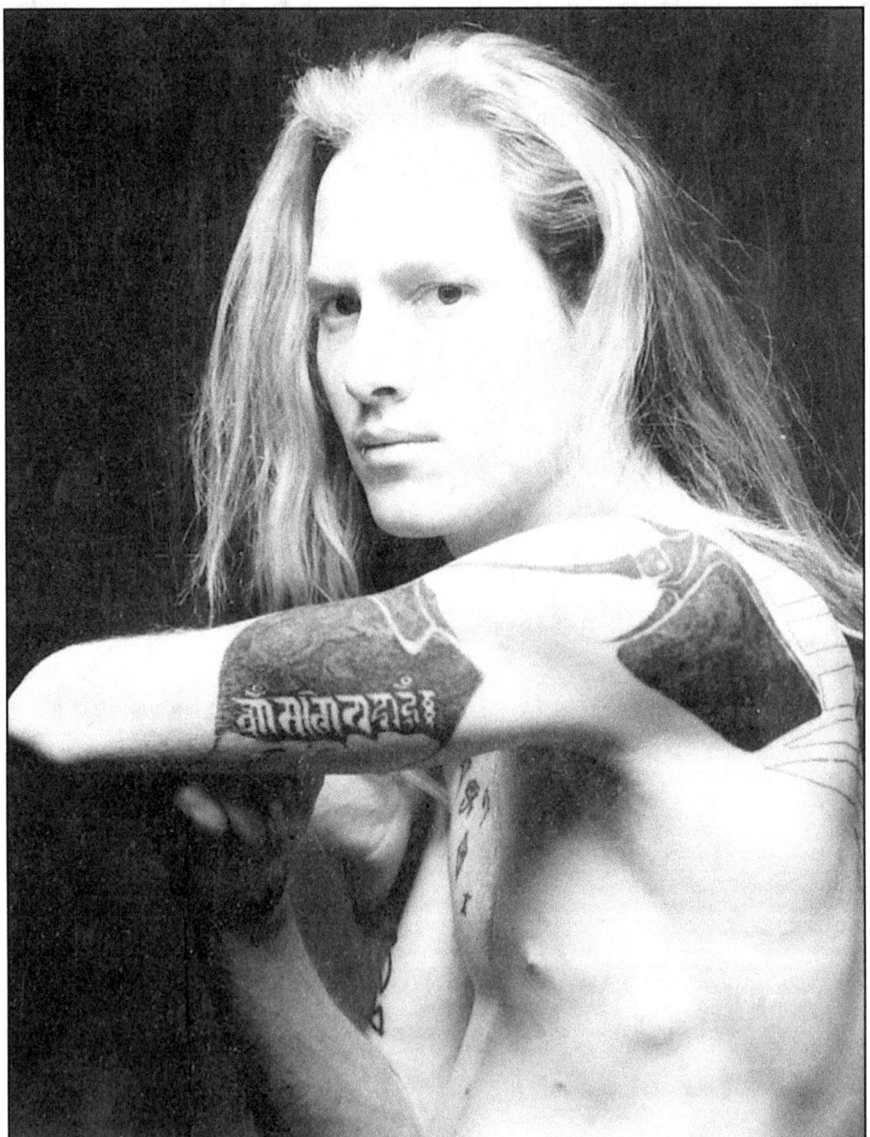

Photo by Bobby Neel Adams.

■ *VALE: How many piercings do you have?*

■ VAUGHN: Besides the one in my lip, just two below the penis. I can't explain to people why I do it. There's a need inside me which I've probably had all my life and have not been aware of, until such time that I discovered there were other people doing this.

■ *V: What tattoos do you have?*

■ VAUGHN: I tattooed Greg Kulz's back so he's doing mine; it's a trade. Greg's was based on bone structures, whereas mine was based on the actual musculature across the back and shoulders. Fred from Erno's shop put on my right arm a tattoo of a Hopi Snake Mound, which is an earthwork approximately 1/4 of a mile long and about six feet high in Hopi Land, as viewed from the air. The dark circle in front represents the Snake Dance cult; the mouth coming around on either side is for protection; the arrow indicates the direction they're traveling; and the two eyes looking back are to protect them from anybody coming up from behind.

I have another tattoo based on abstract bone structures [shows upper left arm]. The letters in back signify *Om Mani Padme Hum*—Hail the Jewel in the Lotus, which is an old Sanskrit chant: the breakthrough (*Om*) of seeing the absolute (*Mani* or jewel) in the relative

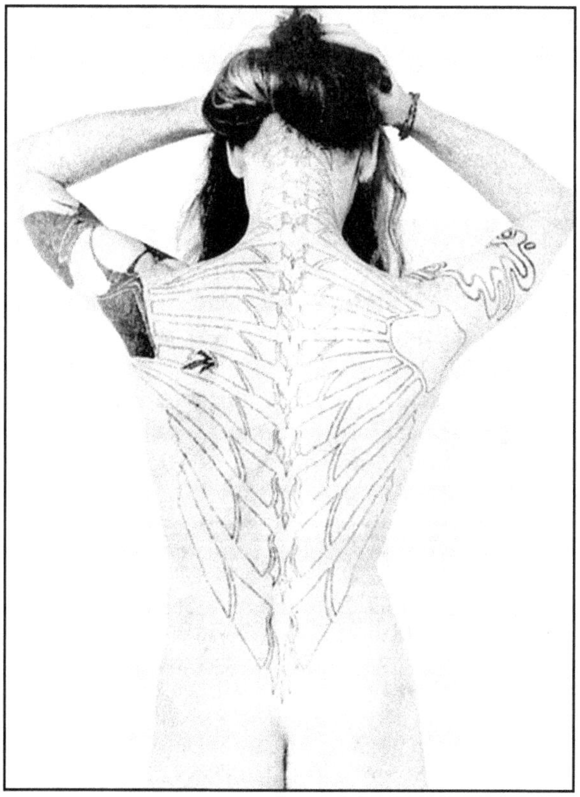

Tattoos by Greg Kulz. Top and bottom photos by Kristine Stephens.

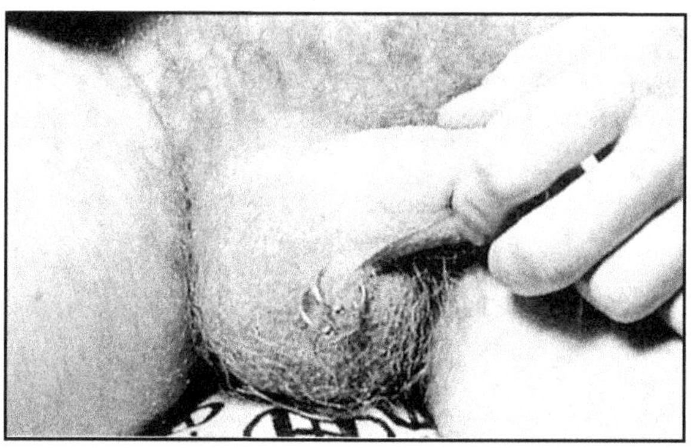

(*Padme* or lotus) beyond individuality, time, and space (*Hum*).

On my chest I have a number of symbols more or less evenly spaced. There's the alchemical symbol for *silver,* the *Eye of Horus,* the *Bass Clef.* Then there's the *Dragon's Eye,* which represents knowledge,

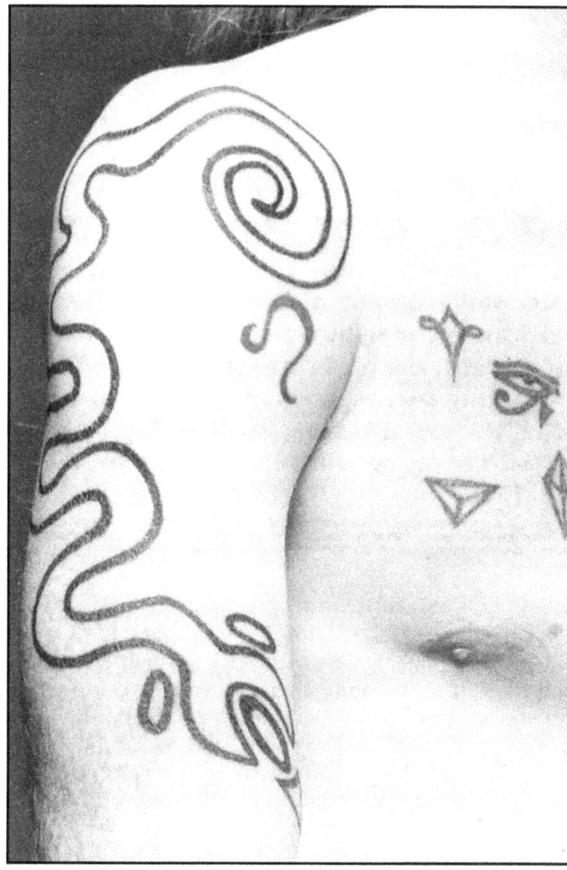

Photo by Bobby Neel Adams.

and the diamond-shaped *Wolf's Eye,* which means strength. They're old German symbols from Ernst Lehner's book, *Signs, Symbols and Signets.* Below is the Chinese symbol for the *Year of the Boar*—my birth year.

The first three tattoos I got were symbols: the Pentagram, the astrological sign of Leo, my birth sign, and a stylized capital "T" plus the Greek letter pi which were the initials of my original name—I still had a need to retain part of my original name: Paul Thorpe. I started using "Vaughn" about 12 years ago, after a dead cartoonist named Vaughn Bode; also, my friend who did my Bass Clef tattoo started calling me Vaughn, and it just stuck. So whenever I sign my name "Vaughn" I also put this symbol behind it. After about 9 years, I came across a book on names and discovered that "Vaughn" originally was a Celtic bastardization of the name "Paul." I was quite shocked!

VYVYN LAZOGNA

At the 1978 St. Paul Tattoo Convention, Vyvyn Lazgona was named "Most Beautifully Tattooed Woman" mainly for three birds of paradise (by Ed Hardy) which sweep downward from her right shoulder around her waist and disappear down her left thigh. When she coughs, the birds flutter.

Starting seventeen years ago in her hometown of Seattle, Vyvyn Lazonga began practicing the art of tattoo, evolving highly original and personalized designs. She can be contacted for an appointment at Vyvyn's, 1526 Western Ave, Seattle WA 98101; tel (206) 622-1535.

■ *VALE: When did you start tattooing?*

■ VYVYN LAZGONA: 1972. I was living in Seattle and was just walking down the street when I discovered the tattooist Danny Danzl. I went into his shop and almost immediately became his protege; for some reason he took a liking to me. I started hanging out there, just watching, and began thinking, "This is really *it!*" Because you can do oil paintings and other kinds of arts and crafts, but to do it permanently on skin was an incomparable *thrill*—you're dealing with something *living* and there's nothing else that can quite equate. This was a street shop, of course. I did all kinds of people—not just servicemen or bikers, but a lot of women and some professional people. I didn't screw up too badly because Danny was always there to help me out.

You can do oil paintings and other kinds of arts and crafts, but to do it permanently on skin was an incomparable thrill—you're dealing with something living and there's nothing else that can quite equate.

Danny gave me my first machine. He took it apart, put it in a paper bag and said, "Take this home and put it together. We'll see how well you do. If it doesn't work, you're in trouble!" I sorta cheated; I had made a diagram of the machine beforehand, so when I got home it wasn't too difficult.

Now previously I hadn't had any art school training. I hadn't really thought, "I'm going to become an artist," I'd just taken art classes in school. By my early twenties I had worked a number of jobs, and when I discovered tattooing it was exciting and a lot more fun than any of the jobs I'd had. It seemed like a unique, viable way to express something unfamiliar to mainstream society. At the time I had a vision: how fabulous it would be to create really unusual art on skin. But it took me more than ten years to be able to do the kind of art I had envisioned.

Danny was from the old school of tattooing, so I guess in the long run that gave me a stronger foundation. But he wasn't totally familiar with a lot of the newer innovative and technological ideas. The first two

Vyvyn Lazonga. Photo by Bobby Neel Adams.

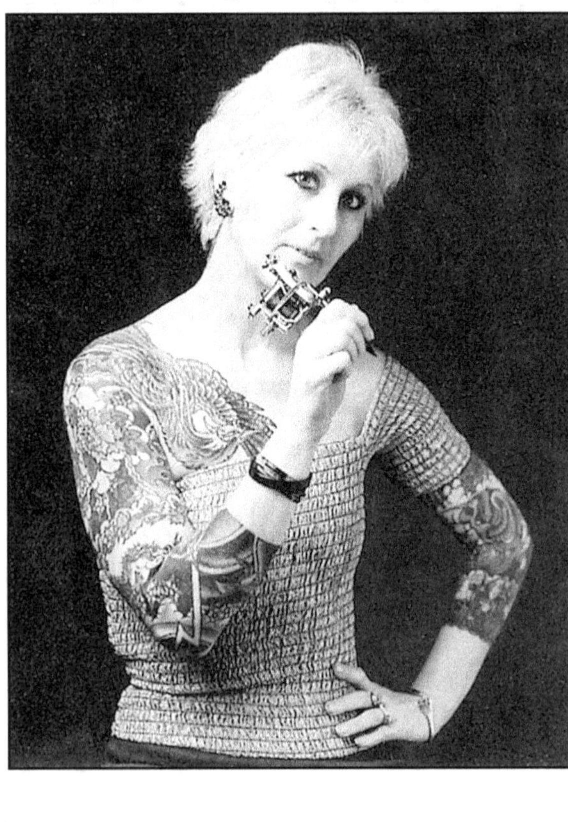

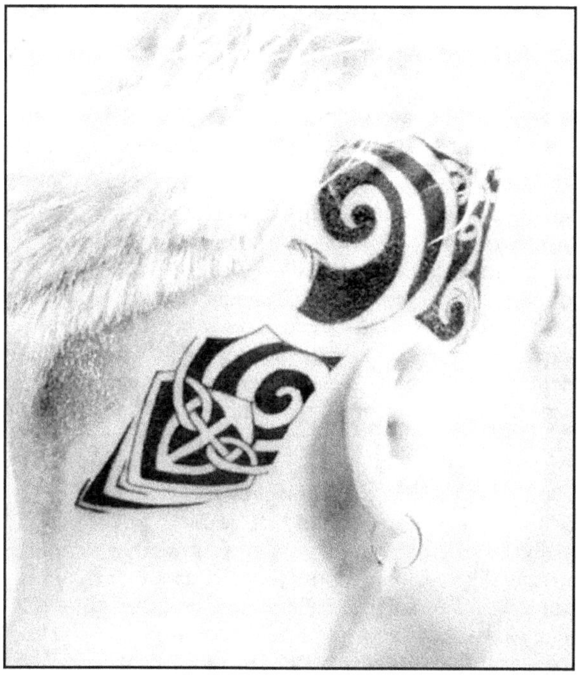

Tattoo by V. Lazonga.

years I spent mostly watching and tattooing myself and my friends, doing regular flash off the walls.

■ *V: Was he from the Sailor Jerry school of tattooing?*

■ VL: No, Sailor Jerry was very radical as far as my teacher was concerned. They were friends and corresponded regularly, and that's how I got to see the new work coming in from the Orient that was filtering through Sailor Jerry to the West Coast. Danny, in a way, idolized Sailor Jerry because Jerry could pull it off and was doing it,

■ *V: What exactly was the "Old Style"?*

■ VL: Tattooing really only became established in America with World War I and II. Back then, before the electric machines were invented, tattooing was very elitist—you could only afford to get tattooed if you went to the Orient or knew someone in England or America who was able to do it by hand. The invention of electric machines began the popularization, and when the war came it became a frantic frenzy, a very trendy thing to do—you weren't *anybody* unless you got tattooed!

For a lot of merchant marine people, getting tattooed was a status symbol showing where they had been and experiences they had been through. Plus, there was an intense spirit of patriotism in the air—the men were going off to war and the tattoo became a really important important symbol for living in the moment, because you never knew when you were going to die. When men came back from the war they mainly had tattoos showing different Service insignia or references to family, sweethearts and places they had been—basically pretty limited designs. The foundation of traditional American-style tattooing was based on decades of building on designs like these.

■ *V: The colors were mainly black and red?'*

■ VL: They never had any good colors. They had black, turquoise green and red, but a lot of times the red wasn't any good—it would cause a lot of problems. That was still true when I first started; colors hadn't yet been developed that were safe and more permanent.

■ *ANDREA JUNO: So you first really became aware of the wider possibilities of tattooing when you saw photos from Sailor Jerry?*

■ VL: Yes. Plus one time some Japanese tourists came in the shop and gave us some photos of Japanese yakuza.

■ *AJ: How was it—learning to be a woman tattooist?*

■ VL: I was pretty young. I think people liked me because I was this innocent thing, you know. So I didn't have any problems. I think my original, primal inspiration was this photograph of an Oriental woman with long black hair who had a dragon tattooed around her body, starting with her ankle and wrapping up around—it was the most gorgeous thing I had ever seen. Visually, I was drawn to this tattoo because it wasn't a mishmash of little designs; it was large, graphic, unified, and done on a beautiful woman. This really inspired me and I began to think of all the beautiful things that could be done. All I needed was to learn how to do it!

■ *AJ: Were you intimidated at first?*

■ VL: Yes; I was scared.

■ *V: What was your first tattoo?*

■ VL: It was really terrible; I got a skull with bat wings on my left arm. This was in Oregon. The guy was really nice, but he was from the Old School; the design was

Tattoo by V. Lazonga.

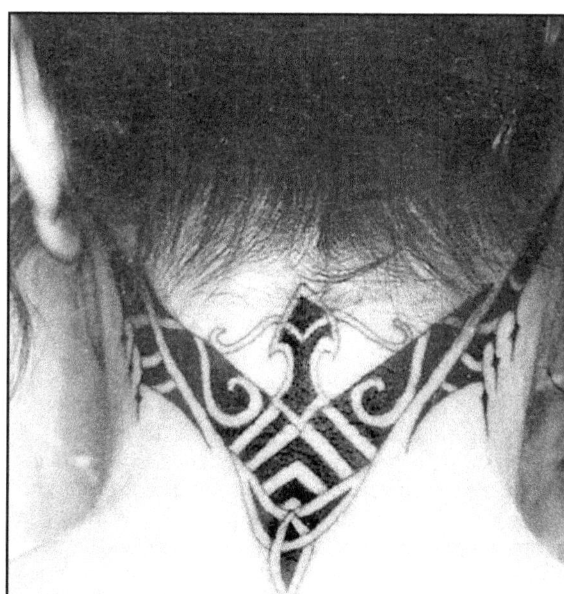

executed beautifully but...it's covered now. At first I was really proud of it; I'd go places and show it to people, but ultimately the imagery was too intense—I couldn't live with it.

■ *V: Why did you choose that image?*

■ VL: They didn't have any choices back then. And I wasn't really a killer macho woman or a biker mama—I lived with the design for a little while, but I quickly discovered its limitations, and I didn't like being limited that way.

When I found Danny Danzl and talked to him about learning tattooing, he was really delighted. What a team! We were an oddball combination, but probably because of that everybody loved us, and we had more than enough work. Becoming a tattoo artist definitely pushed me into another, more unusual world. I became like a symbol of something new; we got a lot of press.

But after seven years, the time came for me to leave. I had been very sheltered, and I knew it was time to get out on my own and start my own business. I still have my studio in Seattle, but since 1984 I've also had one in San Francisco. I work by appointment only, privately, through word of mouth. Previously I ran a studio on Mission Street and had a few hard lessons, but survived—I don't regret it. Now I don't work on any people I don't know, or feel comfortable with.

■ *AJ: How did your personal tattoos evolve?*

■ VL: Throughout the '70s I got my arms done by several artists: Tom Yeomans, Don Nolan, and Ed Hardy who put the three phoenix birds on my torso. When I went to the first tattoo convention I was the only person who had this kind of work [shows award]. The very first tattoo I ever did was on myself—a black crescent moon with a star, on my upper thigh.

Now I feel like they've always been there; they belong there. I can't visualize myself without them. I was rebellious when I was younger, and I guess I did get *carried away,* but I never had any doubts or misgivings about what I was doing. I always felt really strong and powerful about it, and I still do. But I try to keep my arms covered if I'm taking care of business—I sorta wear a *uniform* according to what I'm doing. I want to get my business done quickly and easily, and I don't like having any hindrance or prejudice against me.

■ *V: Why do you think there's such an increase in tattooing and piercing now?*

■ VL: I don't think it's that mysterious. The family unit has never been as torn apart or as small as it is now. And just from the way we live—especially the alienation, there are so many lonely people out there. Getting pierced and tattooed tends to develop a person's awareness of *memory;* the piercings or tattoos become points of reference that reinforce the self and its history. They can function as physical reminders of something very meaningful that happened in the past, and stand alone as a powerful statement of who the person is or is becoming.

Getting pierced and tattooed tends to develop a person's awareness of memory; they function as physical reminders of something very meaningful.

Tattoos can lend strength to a person, like a talisman that's both beautiful and powerful. Going through the whole process of getting pierced and tattooed is like a modern-day ritual that balances out the alienation this technological society has created. Because, all the rituals that have been around for thousands of years—in one or two generations we wiped most of them off the planet! It's all a re-unification awareness of our bodies and spirit—that's how I look at it.

When I tattoo, I feel I'm not only changing someone's skin, but also helping to reinforce their spirit and vision, and it's a lot of responsibility. Also, it affects *me.* I didn't realize this for the first years I worked, but I finally began to realize that I soak up other people's energy—like a sponge. Now that I'm aware of this, I'm more careful and do extra meditation and thought discipline so that I can remain centered and not absorb other people's influence. Fortunately, most of the people who come to me are pretty benign, creative individuals.

■ *V:How many piercings are in your ears?*

■ VL: Ten in my left, and three in my right. It's partly numerological and partly intuitive. After experimenting I had thicker gold hoops made; they worked better than the thin ones. I used to have a nose piercing, too—I got that back in the early '70s. Everything was so radical back then; those were the Golden Years! One day I decided I wanted my nose pierced—not for any particular reason; I just liked the way it looked. So I did it myself with a needle. I guess it was a symbol of freedom, and of new changes and new attitudes. I had something in it for over 10 years.

■ *AJ: Why did you take it out?*

■ VL: When I moved here, I didn't feel very grounded; I didn't know anybody and was feeling very insecure. I figured, "Well, no sense in making it harder for myself," so I tried to become as straight-looking as I could to get situated. But since I've left it out for so long I don't really feel I should put it back in.

■ *V: Didn't you change your name?*

■ VL: My maiden name was Bean, but when I was in school everyone used to tease me. When I got married it changed to Gould. Then everybody in the tattoo world knew me as Lazonga, so I changed it to that. And it was my ex-husband's idea to change my name from Beverly to Vyvyn. I really like Vyvyn (pronounced Viveen) because of its numerological value, and because visually it looks runic, which conjures up memories and feelings of the ancient Celts.

■ *AJ: Do you have any other thoughts on being a woman tattooist?*

■ VL: Well, women are masters of illusion. They always have been with make-up and clothing. A tattoo is just part of the illusion.

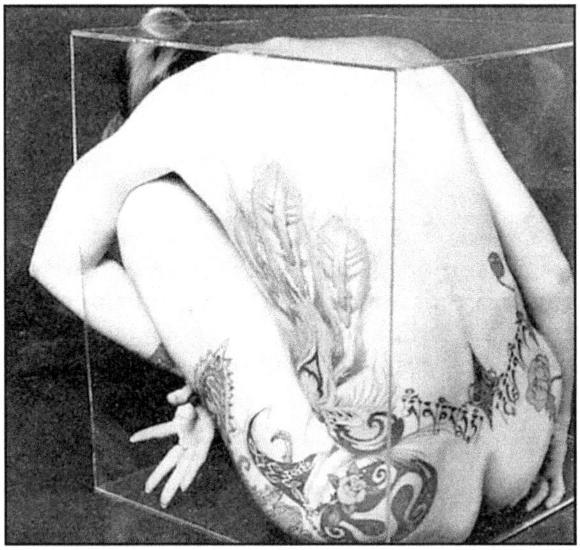

Tattoo by Vyvyn Lazonga. Photo by Skip Williams.

I think that men and women are really conditioned into certain behavioral responses; into very limited ways of looking at the world. And to balance the *animus* and the *anima* within the self is a unique, individualized process which tattooing can help. I don't think there's any undue prejudice against a woman tattooist, only conditioned responses. All I can do is keep my standards as high as I can and try to live true to my vision.

I spend a lot of time alone. A lot of what I've done I've developed alone, studying—I like to read whenever I can. For years I've been reading psychology—all about the human mind and psyche and how to get one's life balanced in this weird unbalanced world. I love looking through visual art books from all over the world, and I think it's best to cross bridges and combine cross-cultural references, rather than just do Samoan or Celtic designs. Being locked into *one* culture is not exciting to me! What's a lot more challenging and fun is to take styles and from different ethnic cultures and combine them to fit the *individual.*

I have a vision that someday women will come more into their own. There's still not that bonding with women that exists between men; the men in my profession tend to do more projects together or share their businesses more. In tattooing in the old days there was quite a prejudice against women, because a lot of times the whores would come in and try to hustle the sailors and other clientele. So a woman in a tattoo parlor became a no-no because all they did was cause trouble. A lot of old timers still think like that.

When I make a decision as to whether or not to accept a client, I have to listen to my intuition. When I had my shop in the Mission District is was a lot different than it is now. I wasn't used to dealing with as many drug addicts and rip-offs. I really learned a lot and it became an invaluable lesson on how to always be aware and strong but still keep my sense of humor and low-key manner. Now that I have a private studio I can get a lot more done and have more fun doing it.

■ *V: Give us an example of how you evolve your designs.*

■ VL: I recently had one client whose animal totem spirit was the cat. So I put a series of stripes on her back, going across her arms, that resemble the stripes of a cat. It was quite striking! Let's see—I put hexagonal snake scales on another client's arm. On another I did these bees: against a pastel yellow honeycomb the bees started out big and got smaller as they retreated to the center of the honeycomb. In the old days a tattoo had to be something; it had to be an emblem or a picture or a cartoon. Now it can be art from different eras or a combination of art from different cultures, or an abstract concept—just as long as it evokes certain emotions and feelings for the client.

Tattooing is just like any other profession: you have to be driven and obsessed and be constantly thinking of new things to do! And because of all my newspaper coverage and other press, I think I was a symbol for other women to become tattooed in a way that's beautiful—in a different, new way that hasn't been done before. Now there's a renaissance going on in tattooing, and the artistic possibilities are limitless; almost anything that can be imagined can be done. My goal is just to keep on experimenting as much as I can!

MONTE CAZAZZA

A founding theoretician of the Industrial Culture movement, Monte Cazazza has continued producing videos (having recently completed a successor to *True Gore*); music (with his band the *Atom Smashers*); media studies (Marshall McLuhan being a perennial favorite); film screenplays; and other project/collaborations with *Psychic Television* and artist Deborah Valentine. Monte Cazazza was interviewed by V.Vale.

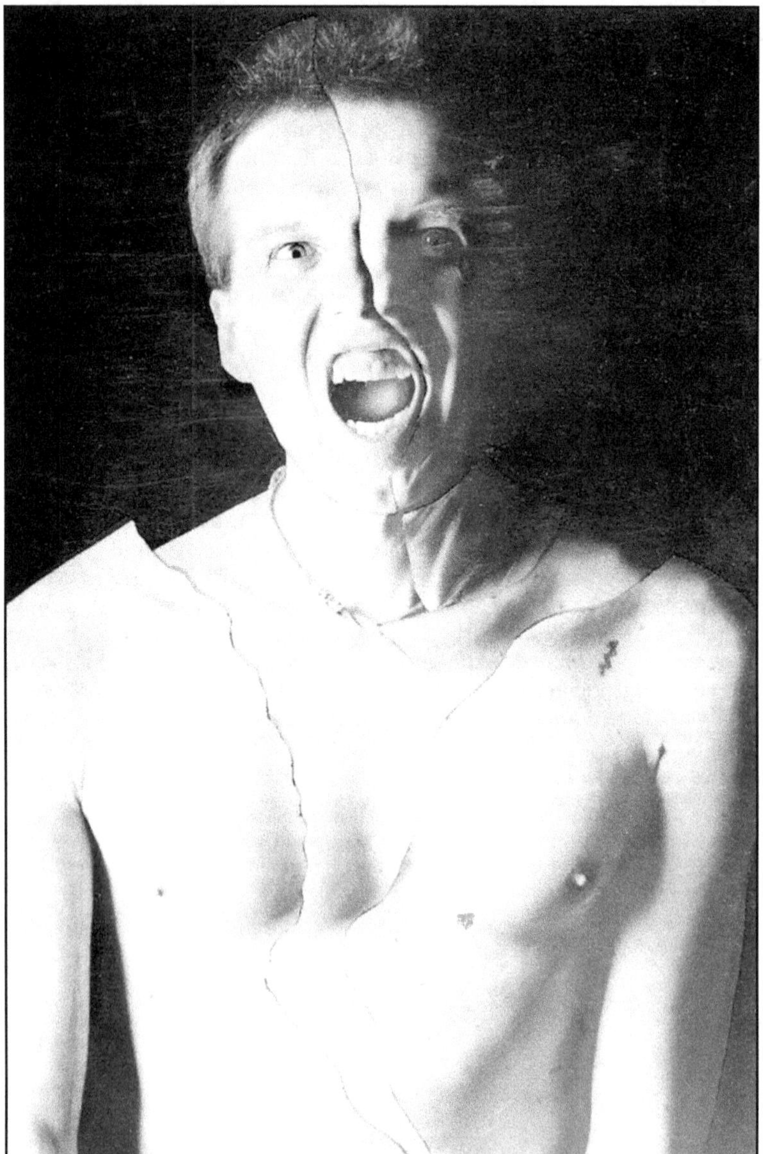

■ *VALE: What new thoughts can you bring to the concept of Modern Primitivism?*

■ MONTE CAZAZZA: Nothing's more primitive than the act of birth, right? But I just read that now it's possible for two men to have a child with a woman, or two women to have a child also. They take half the chromosomes from one man and half from another, then trick the egg cell into accepting the combination. So there's probably already a child like that out there—I don't believe there isn't. Basically, the lid's been put on all the genetic experimentation that's been going on—it's probably far ahead of what's been reported. And this experimentation isn't being done out of the goodness of someone's heart—there's a deep profit motive there somewhere. Something like this is pretty modern, but in a way it's down to the most primitive level. And what's going on today in gene-splicing will probably be considered pretty "primitive" just a decade from now.

■ *V: Or sooner...By the way, aren't you pierced?*

■ MC: I was pierced by Mr Sebastian in London, who has it worked out to a fine art. He's very calm, professional, hygienic and astute—very good at explaining the philosophy, theory and psychological viewpoint behind various kinds of piercings.

Photo and collage by Bobby Neel Adams.

■ *V: There certainly has to be more to it than surface body modification. When Fakir Musafar is hanging from the hooks, he claims he has an ecstatic trance experience. But a cynic might say that's just another "New Age" escape into the infinite subjective...*

■ MC: If someone hangs from hooks, I'm sure they'll have an experience they never had before.

■ *V: Such as fear, pain, vertigo?*

■ MC: I'm not going to define what kind of experience someone's going to have...whether it'll be good or bad. All I can say is: it won't be indifferent!

■ *V: Do you think people should try these experiences?*

■ MC: I think it changes your perception in some way, at least about coping with physical stress. It puts you in a different world than the world you're used to. Why do people tattoo certain symbols on them? Is there a collective unconscious?

I think a lot of people at this time in history have tapped into something primal or basic. Sure there are fakes in every endeavor, but there are also people who are serious astronauts of inner space. Even though some of Fakir Musafar's practices might appear somewhat sensational, you can't say he isn't serious about what he's doing. If you're put in a centrifuge and spun around, and hung upside-down, maybe things do happen—who knows? Obviously these practices have been going on for thousands and thousands of years—why? There has to be some kernel of basic truth there. That's not saying to build your whole life around one practice, but obviously there's something going on.

■ *V: Many societies had a rite of passage that involved the experience of intense pain. The shaman initiations were death-defying, and some didn't make it.*

■ MC: All this is begging the question. Obviously the Number One problem today is *identity*. Identity is nourished by privacy as well as the converse situation of an alliance in action, and both of these are hard to maintain in modern society! Privacy is almost a totally outmoded possibility. If you don't have any identity, you try to re-create your life in such a way that you think you have some. How do you do that? Tattoo some weird design on your stomach—you try to get *more control* over your life.

The problem right now is: you're not supposed to have some kind of weird, unique identity. There are no rites of passage; you become a teenager and your hormones are running rampant and what do you do? There's no one to talk to or anyone who really understands that your situation is shitty, and that you have no rights. So kids give themselves a mohawk or pierce their nose because they're trying to establish some identity for themselves—preferably one their parents don't approve of. Since they don't fit into the status quo, they do something other than what the status quo dictates.

These days who is getting all these tattoos and piercings done to themselves? It isn't just Hell's Angels anymore; it's every social class and age group. And why—what are the underlying psychological dynamics of what is going on? For one thing, these acts change your perceptions; they're something permanent you do to yourself because the rest of the world is totally non-permanent; in a state of flux. Everything's changing all the time...

■ *V: So how did you get the idea to get pierced?*

■ MC: I saw some back issue of *PFIQ* magazine (Piercing Fans International—see Jim Ward article). Then I went to the library and found a few entries on piercing in some anthropology books.

■ *V: But you don't know why you got pierced?*

■ MC: People don't know why they do most of the things they do, do they?

Obviously the Number One problem today is *identity. If you don't have any identity, you try to re-create your life in such a way that you think you have some. How do you do that? Tattoo some weird design on your stomach.*

■ *V: Did you think you'd get more pleasure having sex?*

■ MC: I think that was a consideration. Boredom—I don't know. I had nothing to lose. If it fell off, that would make an even more interesting story! Then I might have fewer problems—my sex life would become much simpler. People who think I'm weird now would have even *more* reason to think I'm weird. I could probably murder people and then go, "Judge, the reason I did all this is because I lost my penis. I had no penis, so I had to do *something*. So I went out and stabbed all those people with an icepick!" People would feel sorry for you...

■ *V: Has anyone ever had to have their penis amputated because of a piercing?*

■ MC: That calls for a computer medical search. I doubt it. If it were done the wrong way it could get infected. But if it did get infected, you'd probably just remove the piercing hardware.

■ *V: Someone said that after you're pierced it's best to wait 60 to 90 days before attempting intercourse.*

■ MC: Mr Sebastian told me to wait at least three weeks, then see how it was healing before attempting to have sex. You have to clean it at least two or three times a day with Betadine, hydrogen peroxide, or salt water. And if you remove the stainless steel plug, the tissue will grow back together, and you'll lose the piercing.

One thing that happened—after being pierced, I was really high for 3 or 4 hours—immediately. It was like taking mescaline—I was *out there*. I could have stayed up for 24 hours. I could see why people go back and get more and more piercings done; I'm sure that has *something* to do with it!

There are people who do non-permanent piercings, you know—they just do the piercing, but don't put anything in...just for the high. I saw an interview with Mr Sebastian in which he talked about a man who

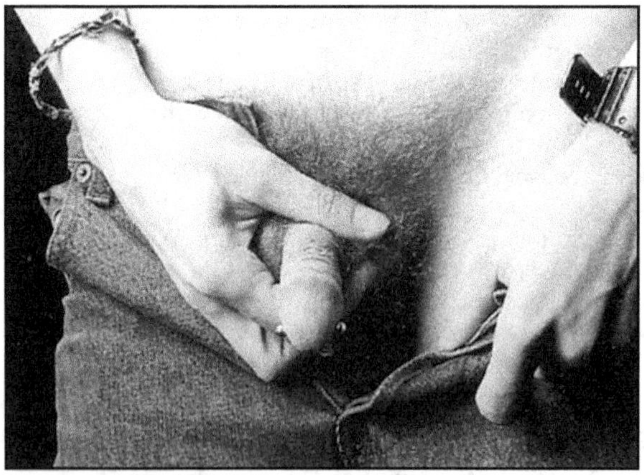

Monte shows his ampallang piercing.

kept coming back, over and over. Finally he had to tell him not to return, because too much *scar tissue* was building up. He told him he had to either get a permanent piercing or have the piercing done in some other part of his body. See, he'd have the piercing done, then remove the plug; it would *sort of* heal up, and he'd return to have another one done!

Masochists are like that, too. Even tattooing is sort of a masochistic process—especially really large tattoos. This kind of activity starts certain receptors firing away in your brain that aren't normally used—your brain gets flooded with endorphins and other chemicals. You're using different synapses and making different connections in different parts of your brain than you normally use—the neurons are firing down different pathways. Many times this provides a stimulus that is interpreted as pleasurable, and therefore, repeatable.

Take neurolinguistic programming. People fall into different types: some are more visually oriented; some more auditory; others more kinaesthetic. Like when Fawn Hall was on TV, she was constantly adjusting her hair and smoothing her clothes—that indicates a kinaesthetic inclination. If you ask someone a question like, "When was the last time you had sex?" and watch their eyes, if their eyes move from right to left they're an auditory person—what's going to come first to mind is what they heard. If they're kinaesthetic, they're going to look down. If they're a visual person, they'll look up. Do you remember being asked a question in school, and you looked up? You were trying to access a visual mode of information retrieval from your memory bank, because that's how you processed the information to begin with.

The best way to make a point with a kinaesthetic person is to reinforce the information with a touch or a probe. If you teach, it's best to use all three modes: 1) write on the blackboard, 2) talk, and 3) use a pointer or move the chair around.

There's a number of books on neurolinguistic programming such as *Frogs Into Princes* by Bandler and Grindler. There are definite ways you process information, and you can train yourself to be more of an auditory, or visual, or kinaesthetic person. If you mention a bad experience to someone, they'll usually look down. Whereas someone who is positive about themselves almost never looks down while they're talking—that's one way you can monitor the drift of the conversation. The more different ways you can process information, the richer your experience of life can be.

For example, let's say the person you were talking to just came back from the beach. If they tell you what they saw, then they're primarily visual. But if they tell you, "The sound of the wind blowing the sand around was thunderous" or "I loved the cries of the seagulls and the crashing of the waves on the shore," then they're an auditory person. You can use this against people, too! It's sort of an unconscious clue or giveaway that previously only salesmen took advantage of, but now it's becoming a lot more consciously recognized.

■ *V: Well, piercing is more in the realm of the kinaesthetic.*

■ MC: Maybe tattooing and piercing have more to do with the *loss* of kinaesthetic experience today. It's perhaps *therapeutic.* People need all the reinforcement they can get! Everybody needs more. If people don't get it; if they get too isolated, they start thinking in strange patterns that don't have a good basis in reality, and that can end up being really destructive.

■ *V: Right now society basically thinks that people who extensively pierce and tattoo themselves are insane. Yet it's happening on an unprecedented scale today all over the planet, and without a lot of mass media advertising, either.*

■ MC: Maybe this has something to do with morphogenetic theory. Lyall Watson gave the example of a group of monkeys on an island who were trained to wash sweet potatoes before they ate them. Lo and behold, on an island totally isolated from the first, monkeys were washing their sweet potatoes too! Eventually this spread to more and more islands all over the world. How? Perhaps through some kind of *psychic transmission,* like a type of microwave that has yet to be discovered. Did you know that the slang term for microwaves is "black magic"? The people who work with them don't even know *why* they work, just that they *do.* So...nobody really knows why so many people are getting tattooed and pierced now, but it's happening and it's observable.

■ *V: Well, doctors don't even know why aspirin works, just that it does...Back to piercing; you've had a penis piercing now for several years. Are you still constantly aware of it, or have you mostly blocked off that awareness by now?*

■ MC: No, it's still there. Even if you've worn an earring for years, you'll still pick at it. In the same way, a genital piercing will periodically give you a pleasure jab now and then. That's another reason for people to want one—it's an innocent, free pleasure that you don't have to pay any money for! Once you've paid for the initial piercing (or if someone did it for free, so much the better), you can keep deriving pleasure from it for the rest of your life!

■ *V: So do you think the piercing increased the range and intensity of sensation?*

■ MC: You'll have to ask my wife, Deborah! It's possibly done more for her than it does for me. The Prince Albert usually does more for the male, but the ampallang usually does more for the female. I asked Paula P-Orridge who's tried them all, and she gave me her views—namely, that the ampallang was the best for her. For the man, it changes things in a really strange way. It somewhat dislocates *your* sensation, but I noticed, especially when I first had it, that it made me more sensitive to the *other* person.

■ *V: It didn't increase your ability to delay orgasm?*

■ MC: I think if you got a Prince Albert, it might—Genesis said that. The main thing I noticed was: it made me more receptive toward the other person. Put another way: the females found it quite interesting (and I tried it with several people). The more fun the other person has, the more fun you're going to have!

But you're not supposed to have fun these days. You're supposed to work hard and suffer. J.G. Ballard's idea of the crystal world is coming true, but in a different way—everything in our society is based on crystals—radio waves, computers. Your digital watch has a crystal in it. Why are so many people wearing crystals? A quartz crystal has piezo-electric qualities—if you squeeze it, it emits electricity. I read in an article that soon there'll be superconductors that function at room temperatures. Let's say you had a crystal hooked up to the right superconductor that worked at room temperature—if you squeezed it you could power your whole house! A breakthrough in superconductivity could change the whole electronics technology, because you'll no longer have to overcome resistance—that'll be a thing of the past. Everything will work completely differently; a lot less power will get a lot more done.

I read in an article in *Scientific American* recently about an experiment in which nerve cells were grown together with silicon cells toward the goal of producing some kind of living instrument.

Genetics and electronics are merging, so maybe someday the kind of increased sensations you get from a piercing will be enhanced a thousandfold through some kind of nerve cell amplification. Then you can incorporate advantages of robotic or android technology into your body while maintaining your human "identity." Maybe you'll have a computer that's actually alive and thinks on some level—you'll have to go to the market and buy it something to eat!

The same issue of *Scientific American* had an article on an experiment where a tobacco plant was crossed with the gene from a firefly, so that the plant glowed in the dark! Imagine doing something similar with a person: a human that glows in the dark? Who knows what kind of people will be walking around a hundred years from now; it might be like that scene in *Star Wars* where all these different species are standing around drinking in an intergalactic bar—the only *good* scene in that movie! All kinds of weird recombinants will be possible—people who can live underwater, etc. That's why they want to do all that gene mapping. And if you can *think* of something, you can bet someone somewhere is going to try it. Look at the weird germ warfare experiments that have been uncovered by the Freedom of Information Act.

The dark side of gene manipulations has probably already affected us: the AIDS virus. A bit more experimentation and you can tailor the strains to be more susceptible to American Indians, or Chinese, or Japanese or Black people. Of course, things like that sometimes happen as stupid mistakes; then it gets out of control and the people involved try to cover things up. Certainly if there *were* some kind of accident, nobody's going to admit they did it!

People have more trouble with nipple piercing than anything else. You could probably put a piercing through your brain and have less trouble!

■ *V: So Monte, when did you get pierced?*

■ MC: January, 1985

■ *V: Have you had any infections?*

■ MC: Sometimes, a little bit. I have a film of my own piercing being done—it looks excruciatingly painful, but it's not—it's funny! It's more the psychology of the thing that upsets people. Why do people get upset? It's not necessarily because of what's happening, but because you're tapping some area of psychological vulnerability, some territory that's not understood.

We did a show in Chicago where I showed the most horrible slides, films and videos from my collection, and people were just *stunned*—they didn't know what hit them. Yet all I showed were just graphics, images, dots on a screen. In Sweden I did a great show including SXXX-80 (a short film on VD and its consequences, directed by Monte Cazazza & Tana Emmolo) and people couldn't handle the scene of a live leech crawling on a vagina, although the leech didn't really *do* anything or injure the girl involved.

■ *V: Can you think of any ways piercing might help someone in the real world?*

■ MC: Sleazy [of *Coil*] told me that after he got his penis piercing he'd occasionally have these high-powered business meetings with record company executives. He thought it was funny that he was sitting with them, and if they *only* had X-ray vision and could see his piercings, they would have had a fit—they probably *never* would have had *anything* to do with him. But he knew it was there, and it provided a constant resource of irony and distancing.

■ *V: Didn't Sleazy have a lot of trouble with his nipple piercings?*

MC: People have more trouble with nipple piercing than anything else. You could probably put a piercing through your *brain* and have less trouble! It seems to me that women have less trouble with nipple piercings than men. I've known lots of people who've lost their nipple piercings; they would constantly get infected, and they finally gave up. Also, I think your attitude at the time of piercing has something to do with it: it's best to "Be Relaxed." Isn't that the whole thing about everything? In any activity, the more relaxed you are the better you can perform. (Although there's something to be said for adrenalin tension or adrenalin flooding. Actually, when you're more relaxed you can probably get more adrenalin going.)

As far as my penis piercing goes, all I can say is, "That's what happened to me; that was my experience." If someone else does it, that may not happen to them—they may have a *horrible* experience! It's like: one person likes to ride a roller-coaster and has a great time. Someone else may get on and puke as soon as it's over. It's the same ride, but the effect is completely different.

I read this book in which the author said that what separates people from animals is: people have another layer of brain. Then he drew this analogy I liked: if you have a flat plane, and it starts to rain, all these patterns will form. In a way your brain is this flat plane: all these stimuli and experiences happen to you, some of which is under your control (and a lot of which isn't), and it's all like rain falling—all these patterns are forming and synapses are firing, and different people will perceive and form different patterns given the *same* information. People are always looking for patterns to try to make sense out of phenomena. Some people think more linearly or vertically (A-B-C-D-E), and some people think more laterally (A-Q-E-M-B).

I would really love to enter the top genetics laboratories and see what's actually going on, because what's reported is just the tip of the iceberg. That's just what's *released,* so you know there's all kinds of weird top-secret activity going on. They're like mad scientists—they get these grants, and who knows what's going on in some laboratory, somewhere?

Certain kinds of science-fiction seems to always happen. Writers like J.G. Ballard who intermesh all this data—what they write has a really bad habit of coming true! They're just picking up on what's truly going on, sitting in a nice, quiet room, thinking—they're just picking up on these thoughts from somewhere else.

A lot of key discoveries have been made while looking for *something else!* People discover things almost by accident because they didn't have a narrow, fixed goal; they discover something because they're able to recognize it: "Wow—look at that penicillin eating up bacteria. We can *use* this!" But Fleming's goal wasn't to discover penicillin. And that's the difference between someone who is more of a linear or vertical thinker and one who's more of a lateral thinker. It's like: you can *skip* steps and go from A to G; *then* go back and fill in BCDEF. More likely you're just doing experiments for the hell of it and because you're interested in whatever you'll find. We need more *pure science,* without restrictive prior patterns and models. That's why kids at certain ages can *say* things or make observations that are brilliant, because society hasn't imposed a lot of patterns on them yet.

■ *V: Monte, do you have any tattoos?*

■ MC: I have one that's like "13"; a "1" through a "3." Thirteen has a lot of different meanings, numerologically. This number kept coming up and I figured it had something to do with me—why, I didn't know. I just kept seeing the number. Judas is the thirteenth apostle—but without him Christ wouldn't have been crucified, and His blood would not be able to *save* you poor sinners out there! So Judas actually did you a great favor—he should be a saint! And if Christ hadn't been a martyr, he wouldn't have been heard of today.

Anyways, thirteen is a combination of 1 and 3 but numerologically adds up to 4 which is the number of completion, the number of the Four Winds, the four states of matter, etc. I didn't want it to be instantly recognizable, so because of the way I drew it, it ended up looking like a snake on a pole (although that wasn't the original intention). It's the symbol of Mercury (actually, the caduceus is *two* snakes on a pole) which is the god of communication—the god of television, or tell-a-vision! (The questions is, *whose* vision?) In Britain, if you visit the Home Office Building where the government communications are headquartered, there's a symbol of Mercury above the door.

I'm interested in communication—what do symbols mean? Symbols are used to condense down massive amounts of experience so you can instantly perceive them. So when you see a building with two snakes on a pole, you know that it's a medical building. Why do doctors use that symbol?

The snake supposedly has the most *ki* of any animal, because it only has one path for the *ki* to flow—a snake doesn't have arms or legs. Martial artists and acupuncturists would define *ki* as an inner force, or inner energy. In a snake the *ki* is never impeded—maybe that's why more people are into reptiles these days; it's part of an unconscious urge that later becomes conscious.

Reptiles are symbols in different cultures: in Christian culture they're identified with evil, Satan the Tempter—the bad guy. But even though they're the bad guy, they're still a giant force; if you look at it from a Christian point of view that force got Adam and Eve tossed out of Garden of Eden, and here we are now. And that's the only force that's ever opposed God, and God *lost.* I don't necessarily believe in the Devil, but looking at it from a symbolic viewpoint, that was the only force opposed to the "good" force which now means sentimentality and hypocrisy—not "good".

You're never going to see tons of TV commercials for snake food—you're not going to see Purina

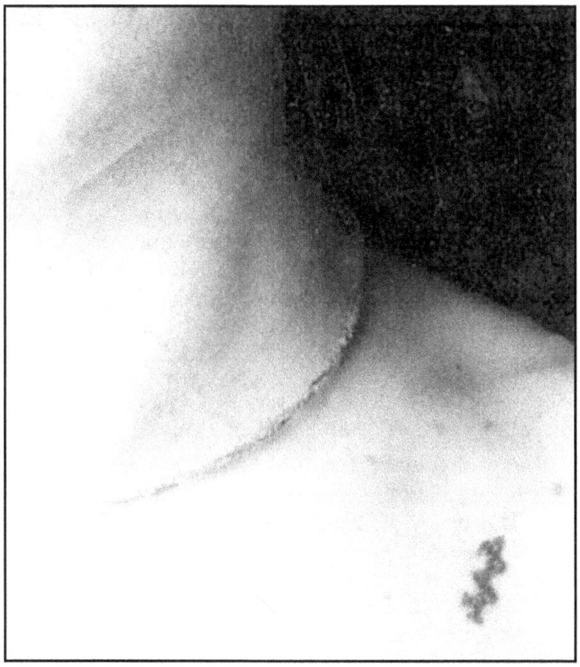

Monte's tattoo.

snake food! The keeping of reptiles has to do, at the least, with a defiance of dominant pet-keeping values, or because people are looking at a different aspect of things—I don't want to say the *Dark Side,* because every day is light and dark; people have added all this baggage to certain words for very mercenary reasons.

First of all, with dogs and cats you can project neuroses onto them, but reptiles...? It's easiest with dogs, but people have crazy cats, too—although usually the cat will run away, they're not gluttons for punishment! Whereas a dog will usually stay for its chow bowl. You *can* constantly keep abusing a snake until it won't like you and will bite you, but it doesn't take neuroses as internally as, say, a dog will.

So in Christianity the snake is the symbol of evil, whereas in Hindu or Yogic culture it's the symbol of power and energy because the snake is related to the human spine. There's the Tantric idea of kundalini, of sex energy.

There's not much money spent on dedicated sexual research. You think of Masters & Johnson or the *Hite Report*, but the amount of people and the amount of money spent is really quite insignificant. Yet it's one of the most basic forms of human activity. If sex had been researched more, probably half the pornography industry would be out of business, or different, because one reason pornography is so popular is because not that much is taught about sex.

■ *V: Even though most people recoil at the idea of genital piercing, they're intrigued by the idea that piercing can increase sexual pleasure. Perhaps piercing a certain location functions similarly to acupuncture.*

■ MC: I've seen acupuncturists burn certain points with moxa in order to insure their patient stays healthy. That whole idea that R.O. Tyler [tattoo philosopher/ artist documented in *Tattootime #2*] was talking about: applying the tattoos at certain points, at certain times, and with certain medicines, depending on the individual's make-up and background—in a way that's a very sophisticated methodology which may or may not work, or may only work on certain people. But we're not going to see the government funding research on this, because what if something like that *does* work? It would put half the medical profession out of business! You're talking big bucks, baby!

You always see these studies in which people are given placebos, and the placebos work. Why haven't there been serious studies about *what* is actually making them work? Why is a placebo working? I'd love to get a grant studying all these people who had some disease, and then took a placebo, and it worked on them. Because *something* happened. Was it in their mind? Just the physical act of taking something—there's some mechanism there that's working. "Psychological suggestibility"—the big drug companies aren't going to make very big profits on *that!*

■ *V: Perhaps "increased sexual enhancement" from the ampallang might be the placebo effect.*

■ MC: Sure! It could be that, too, but *something* is still occurring! And it's more interesting to pursue why is this working. Just the piercing act itself might cause some kind of psychological breakthrough for some people.

It's like: when perspective in painting first occurred, there was a giant psychological breakthrough—it was the first time people started to see things in perspective. The Renaissance was about *seeing the world in a different way,* so the earth was no longer the center of the universe. The Catholic Church burned all these martyrs because they had a vested interest in keeping perspective the way it was, but they couldn't stop it.

■ *V: It's amazing that despite all the space exploration and planetary mapping, churches still exist and collect money with their notion of God up there in heaven and the Devil down there in hell—*

■ MC: Schizo-knowledge. A lot of people still say art is non-functional, but that's a bunch of rubbish—it's just as functional as business; in fact somebody just paid $53 million for a Van Gogh, and if that's not business...Without perspective, where would science be now—nowhere! One things leads to another; one things builds on another. Probably the idea of the zero in mathematics came from some Arab Sufi religious trance state—the idea of nothingness. And without the zero, we'd be nowhere! Of course, some people say we're nowhere now, and I might agree with them.

■ *V: Do you think getting your tattoo changed your life?*

■ MC: I don't know. People always try and make dramatic claims which most of the time is a bunch of *bunk.* I don't think change really happens in that kind of startling way; I think it's much more subtle, and *maybe* over a long period of time it *later* becomes dramatic. So I'm not making any claims for any of these activities; I'm not a piercing salesman; I'm not a tattoo salesman. I know people who've wanted to have tattoos removed, so I understand the consequences of these activities—once you do them, they're kind of *permanent.* Although, sometimes doing something on the spur of the moment isn't a bad idea, either—it depends on the person.

There was a time when I wanted a tattoo of a tarantula on my back. In prison there's a spot on the back where prisoners often put tattoos—it's where your heart is, but from behind. Supposedly this functions as magical protection against being stabbed in the back. *Magic*—sometimes it works, sometimes it doesn't—just like anything else in the world. And the problem is when people get so confused that they invest too much time and energy in thinking something is going to work 100% of the time, because *nothing* works all of the time—in fact from my experience things *don't* work most of the time. Take a computer—sometimes it works, sometimes it crashes; sometimes it's a pleasure, sometimes it's a pain. So don't go overboard!

■ *V: And you don't regret your penis piercing?*

■ MC: Mine broke for some reason soon after I got it—which is really rare. Gen said I must have been *doing something* [laughs] but I wasn't—it just broke. I went back the next day and got a replacement—very important, because it'll heal up really fast if the post is removed. There's defective merchandise everywhere—*caveat emptor!*

Sometimes even people who get their ears pierced get infections right away. But if that happens, you have to make a concentrated effort to take care of the problem. Sometimes when people get sick they don't take basic care of themselves; they can be lazy and not vigilant enough. Any piercing takes awhile before it all heals up, although it's not that dangerous.

Again, I'm not advocating getting pierced, because sometimes people go overboard and invest too much importance in all these things. I'm not saying they're unimportant—maybe they are *very* important! But people get sidetracked—you have to keep things in some kind of perspective. You can't lose sight of the big picture; these may be just minor signposts along the way. If you think getting a thousand piercings is going to make you a better person, that's not necessarily so. Or, that if you get these tattoos, it's going to make you a better person. If you're a *shit,* then you're a shit and that's the way you'll *stay*—unless you decide to do something about it yourself.

Now, making the decision and then deciding to put certain efforts into something...maybe the piercing or tattoo is just a *souvenir* of doing something far more significant in your life. And I'm more of a generalist type of person—I don't want to devote my life to piercing or tattooing; there are other things I want to do. Don't get too close-minded no matter what the subject; there are people with lots of tattoos who are just creeps!

Piercings or tattoos are no big deal; they're not going to turn you into a member of the Super Race, no matter what people think. And they've certainly been done before throughout history. But one thing: they're a great investment—pay for it once and it's yours *forever.* No one can take it away from you, unless they cut a big slab of your flesh out!

■ *V: You mentioned a film of your piercing?*

■ MC: My main motivation in getting pierced wasn't so I could film it, but I thought, "Oh, it'll be great to have a record of it!" And it turned out great. I'm going to edit it, put it on videotape and use it for one of my shows. But I didn't do it just to film it. Just like I wouldn't get a huge back tattoo just to document getting one, although...Imagine that Van Gogh painting that just sold for $53 million dollars—if you had that one on your back, you'd own it forever and if it was worth $53 million dollars no one could ever take it away! It'll be awhile before Sothebys starts auctioning off tattoo skins...

■ *V: Have you done any scarification?*

■ MC: No, although one of the most intense events I've ever witnessed was the scarification of a girl named Sonia. Believe me, people had a great time. I sort of held onto Sonia and talked to her while it was being some, but boy—that was *tough,* I never saw anything like that! What a tough woman, *I* almost fainted watching it happen, and I've seen all kinds of stuff when I was an ambulance driver! Sonia had her mind *set* pretty well. I thought, "They should do this in the Marines—there wouldn't be many people joining up! The Marine Corps builds men—scarification builds women!" That whole thing was a *tough go.*

■ *V: There are so many possibilities for integrating pleasureful experiences and primal self-expression from "primitive" societies into our "modern" world.*

■ MC: There is such a dichotomy between "modern" and "primitive." It's like the world really is now—there are primitive places and modern places existing at the same time. McLuhn talked about the global village—that doesn't make sense, it's a paradox, just like "modern primitive" is a paradox. As to where things are going, what's important and what isn't...nobody can perceive what is going to come out of all this.

One of the most intense events I've ever witnessed was the scarification of a girl. Believe me, people had a great time.

■ *V: In summary, I can think of three reasons why people might pierce or otherwise modify their bodies: 1) visual aesthetic 2) sexual pleasure 3) sense of apartness—*

■ MC: Add: *revolt ... boredom ... reinforcement of identity.* After all, what do you hear the most? "DON'T. NO. YOU CAN'T. YOU SHOULDN'T." Think about when you were at school: "Don't do this. Don't do that." By the time you're six years old you've heard "Don't" ten thousand times! Language and your mind are interconnected; the words you use, how you speak, what you talk about, your approach—what you say is a mirror of your psychology. So I think that anything that promotes a stronger personal identity is good—I mean a *real* personal identity, not just some strange group identity which people can use to hide themselves behind, like Hare Krishnas.

■ *V: Some people may have just one area of deviancy, like being members of a corset society, but in other cultural areas they can be disappointingly middle-class.*

■ MC: Because *that* keeps them safe—that enables them, like a pressure cooker, to vent off steam. In my neighborhood I see a lot of leather guys—macho-looking gays in black leather outfits—but then I go to the bank and see them working behind the counter! Essentially they're supporting the people who are against them. Of course, you have to survive, and a lot of times you have to work for people you don't want to. But it's better to set up your own situation and not be beholden to *anyone*. It's a mean world...

BIBLIOGRAPHY

PIERCING: PFIQ (*Piercing Fans International Quarterly;* write PO Box 69811, Los Angeles CA 90069 for info).

TATTOOS: *Tattootime*. Available by mail from RE/Search.

NEUROLINGUISTIC PROGRAMMING: *Frogs into Princes: Reframing Trance-Formations,* by Richard Bandler & John Grinder.

MORPHOGENETIC THEORY: Lyall Watson's books. Rupert Sheldrake's *New Science of Life*. *The Third Mind* by William S. Burroughs & Brion Gysin.

FICTION: *The Crystal World* by J.G. Ballard.

SYMBOLISM: *Masonic, Hermetic, Qabbalistic and Rosicrucian Symbolical Philosophy* by Manly P. Hall.

SEX: *Sexual Secrets* by Nik Douglas & Penny Slinger. *Caught Looking* from Real Comet Press, Seattle, WA.

MAGAZINE: *Scientific American,* Jan. 1987 pp. 61-62.

PS: I would like to acknowledge the following people who got me interested in some of the above subjects: Deborah Nagle, Genesis P-Orridge, Mr Sebastian, Manly Palmer Hall.

DAN THOME

Dan Thome is a former Merchant Seaman who lived in Micronesia and learned to tattoo traditional native designs using hand tools. Currently involved in researching the fast-disappearing tattoo history of Oceania, Dan divides his time between San Francisco and Micronesia. Interview with Dan Thome by V.Vale and A.Juno. Also present was Dan's wife, Maria Yatar (herself a tattoo artist), and tattooist Bill Salmon.

■ *VALE: How did you get into tattooing?*

■ DAN THOME: I was a Merchant Seaman and for years traveled all over the world. Of course, I saw a lot of different tattoos, but they were mostly the "Mom" and "Anchor" ones. I didn't get truly interested until I went to Japan and entered some public bathhouses. For the first time I saw some of those large, full body suits the *Yakuza* have. They were amazing—so colorful and richly detailed.

A bit later, I went to Micronesia to live. I had been there before, but this time I decided to stay for awhile. I had always been attracted to the beauty of the place; the climate was perfect, and the life there seemed a lot simpler and more basic—somehow more genuine. I also became fascinated with the geometric, stark black tattoo designs that were obviously dying out fast. There are only a few old people left who are extensively tattooed, yet each island had developed an indigenous style; you used to be able to tell one islander from another by the designs he was wearing. And I felt that maybe I could learn how to do that style of tattooing and perhaps help them preserve their tattoo traditions and history. To make a long story short, I slowed down and became pretty integrated into the Micronesian way of life. Their situation had once been like Paradise.

■ *ANDREA JUNO: How did you make the leap from appreciating to actually doing tattoos?*

■ DT: Well, I had tried to find out about tattooing in Japan, but that's impossible—you have to have an introduction. Then in the 'States I saw some work by Cliff Raven, and started looking for him. It took awhile, but I finally found him and he put a black, tribal-style design on my leg. And from spending a lot of time getting tattooed, I couldn't help but learn. I also met Lyle Tuttle, and then Ed Hardy, who influenced me a *great* deal.

I was always interested in hand tattooing—the hand tool itself is so simple, yet so sophisticated. A machine can produce finer detail, but the hand tool has a primal quality that really appeals to me. I started to make my own; then Ed Hardy gave me some tools that had belonged to Kazue Oguri, a pretty famous tattoo artist in Japan.

By this point I was living in Micronesia, and wanted to tattoo those people. However, in the tropics you can't use machine techniques that cause bleeding, because if a tattoo gets infected, they have no medicine to put on it. You've got to introduce that pigment very slowly and very gently, because they dive and fish in the water a lot. So I turned to a picking style, where there's almost no blood released, just lymph.

However, this is painstakingly slow, and some people can't understand it, especially if they've been tattooed by a machine which is so fast—*zip* and you've got a line. With a hand tool you build up a line with a series of dots. I must admit that I haven't been tattooing for 25 years like some Japanese artists who've become quite fast with a hand tool. However, their technique can be deeper because they've got medicine, hot baths, and a relatively hygienic environment. Whereas in Micronesia, you get one shot at a person, and you don't want them to turn up with an infection saying, "Hey, that white guy gave me a tattoo, and look at this mess it turned into."

■ *V: You had to develop a low-impact technique—*

■ DT: Yes. I use stainless tell entomologist's pins, which I store in oil. To sterilize them I burn the tips

Dan Thome (far right) in Ontang, Java, 1987. Photo by Tim Rock.

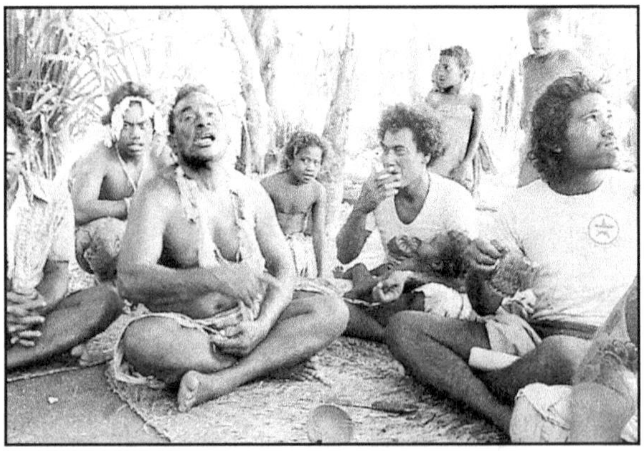

with a lighter until they're red hot. It's a matter of trying to keep the tools clean, wiping them down with alcohol as best you can, because you're really limited to supplies, bandages, and antibiotic ointment when you're out there in the atolls. You're lucky if you can get toilet paper to wipe with—and I don't mean your ass.

■ *AJ: The hand tattoos take quite a long time?*

■ DT: I used to think, "Micronesian tattoos take Micronesian time." But when you go into a tattoo studio the time frame changes *anyway*—the outside world is held at bay, and tattoo becomes the focus. People just can't come in and say, "Hey, I have to be out of here in two hours, but I want to you to finish a tattoo."

■ *BILL SALMON:* The time is totally irrelevant; the adage "Whatever it takes to get the job done" really applies. And *skin* can be very different.

■ DT: One reason I use primarily black is because photo-chemical reaction is prominent in some tattoo colors—I don't want to put color on someone who then has some kind of sun reaction. There's 90,000 people in Micronesia, but the word travels fast—they call it the Coconut Telegraph. You have to constantly be aware of your *invasion of culture.* Everything varies from one island group to another; different language, laws of the clan, laws of class and craft, and there's just a myriad of things that can go wrong for a foreigner in that culture; a million "little" mistakes you can make. You've got to walk very carefully.

But what I like about tattoo is: it seems to really transcend those cultural and linguistic barriers, especially with the old folks. They see this work; they know it's not exactly the same as theirs, but they know what the person went through to get it. They know this person is not a dabbler. They know this person is not just coming in with a camera and a tape recorder to take something from them. And being tattooed—that's fine, but if you're tattooing, that's even more, because suddenly you assume something like a traditional role in the community. And some of these islands are in fact Stone Age cultures to this day—well, maybe they use a steel adz to chop out their canoes, but...

The Micronesians say tattooing was not so much a trial of passage as a work of love—a sharing kind of activity; sometimes a lover's game. The missionaries didn't even realize that there's a legacy of pubic tattooing amongst the women of Micronesia. They could put dresses on them and cover their breasts, but they still didn't know what was going on the pubic area, and the ones that found out weren't about to tell: "Hey, this woman's got this magical fruit bat design on her crotch."

So the legacy of the pubic tattoo still survives. Christianity only reached Micronesia in the late fifties, so a lot of old magic is still there, such as *breadfruit magic:* in times of drought and famine, there are people who have been known to put fruit on the trees. The person who told me about this is now a staunch Catholic, but it's a case of *masked gods*—he's still paying obeisance to the old gods, but in a different way.

According to his story, there was a period of famine right after World War II when the Japanese had

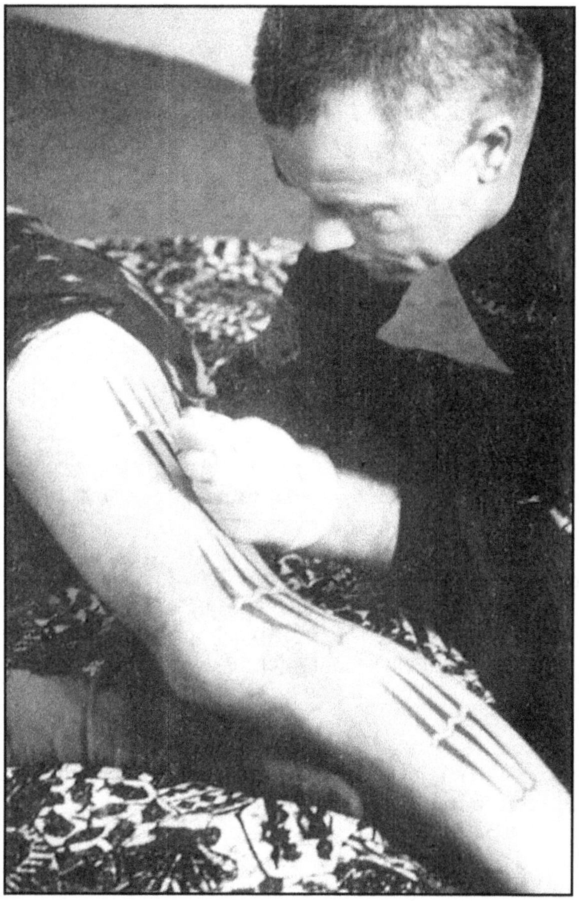

Dan tattooing the Micronesian symbol of the dolphin. Photo by Charles Gatewood.

left. Everybody was hungry; the kids were crying. Now in Micronesia every tree, plant, speck of earth, whatever, belongs to a clan—there might not be any fences, but everybody knows which tree belongs to whom. Suddenly this old guy said, "You people are crazy. On the other side of the island, so-and-so's tree is just *filled* with breadfruit—they're ready to fall on the ground, they're so ripe." Now breadfruit ripen a little at a time; they don't ripen all at once like mangos do. But this tree was completely loaded with ripe fruit (an impossibility), so the people were able to survive. That's one of their legends about breadfruit magic.

Of course, maybe this was the result of a freak of nature; maybe a storm changed the tree's growth cycle. However, this old guy was the one who *saw it,* and the people went and the fruit was *there.*

On the island of Satawal, there's no reef or sheltered lagoon, so the inhabitants have to go deep sea fishing. For over 2000 years they've been carving canoes out of breadfruit logs, and despite no written language they've developed an incredible ability to navigate, and to pass on their knowledge to each generation.

During the '76 bicentennial, the Hawaiians built a double-hulled canoe and wanted to sail it traditionally,

You used to be able to tell one islander from another by the [tattoo] designs he was wearing. I felt that maybe I could learn how to do that style of tattooing and perhaps help them preserve their tattoo traditions and history.

without Western navigational instruments, to Tahiti. But they didn't have any navigators left, so they flew one of the last surviving ones from the Yap airport (Micronesia) to Honolulu, put him in a canoe 2500 miles out of his range, and he sailed it directly to Tahiti.

■ *V: How was this done?*

■ DT: This was accomplished through a series of mnemonic chants which the navigator had learned from his forefathers, from the time he was a small boy. And through observing rising stars, sea birds, ocean swells, wave configurations, cross-currents—a complex, multi-dimensional synthesis of thought—he could find his island group, without any "scientific" instruments, and despite storms. He put all these variables into his human computer, and with the readout, accomplished the goal of getting from point A to B.

Of course, I don't feel good about this lasting. This particular navigator is an exceptional man; he's doing everything he can to see that his knowledge is passed on, but...

These people are living out of time. For example, they depend on sea turtles not only for adding protein to their diet, but for implements—ornaments, spoons, jewelry. But the Taiwanese, Japanese and Korean fishing trawlers are illegally wiping them out. They also harvest taro root, and have survived for thousands of years in an ecologically sound manner utilizing the materials available. But who knows how long this way of life can continue? Because the outside is pressing in.

You're starting to see ghetto blasters there, and electric guitars, and virtually any other manifestation of Western Culture you can imagine. But on the other hand, when those batteries are dead, so what? They just turn it off and strum the two string guitar they've got—maybe it was a six string guitar once, but now they've only got two strings, so that's what they play.

■ *AJ: You were talking about the lover's tattoo—*

■ DT: Well, in the old days, if a man had a crush on a young girl, he and his buddy might kidnap her and take her to the bush, hold her down, spread her legs and tattoo this fruit bat on her. Or it might be a little more ritualized and a woman tattooist might do it. In the Yap archipelago, if some men saw a desirable young girl on another island, they might get a war party together and kidnap her. They'd bring her back and install her into the men's house; in other words, her job was to service the men. And they tattooed her with a special identifying motif. When she had outlived her usefulness, they would take her back as a queen to her own island.

Of course, when they originally kidnapped her there would be war, but when they took her back she was welcomed, because she had been so desirable that other men would come from another place and kidnap her. She would be returned with mats, trade beads, and all kinds of gifts, and would have a higher status than when she left.

In Micronesia tattooing is not something that's feared—*thousands of your ancestors have gone through it, and so can you.* The people just lay there and it's very matter of fact; they don't squirm around or talk. Tattooing in Samoa, on the other hand, is a bit more intensive. It takes three days in a row, and even if a man's big and strong—well, when he leaves, he's not big and strong, I tell you. They tattoo from the middle of the back down to the knees, and it's heavy, solid work. It's done when a man is about twenty—strong enough to endure the process, and is part of the puberty ritual.

The Micronesians say tattooing was not so much a trial of passage as a work of love—a sharing kind of activity; sometimes a lover's game.

In Samoa you have to pay for tattoos, so to have one you have to be of a certain class to begin with. Your status would be elevated, and people would regard you with more respect—which is the way it is in Micronesia, too. I've been trying to get a perspective as to how the diffusion of tattoo took place, but in the absence of written documentation it's difficult. Being extensively tattooed has helped me gain people's confidence, but...

■ *V: Would you say the symbol systems are based upon nearby animal life?*

■ DT: Yes, nature representations. And their great navigational ability implies that their minds worked in a geometric fashion. In their art there's lots of triangles—a symbol which, curiously enough, is rarely found in nature. Triangulation is very important; not only for navigation, but for the design of their sails.

■ *AJ: Is there a connection between tattoo and their cosmogony?*

■ DT: Tattooing is connected to magic, medicine, and healing—it's therapeutic tattooing, if you will. In North Africa there's a belief that arthritic pain is alleviated by the placement of tattoos on painful joints. That's probably related to acupuncture in the sense of energies being released and channelled.

■ *AJ: DId you ever talk to specific shamans?*

■ DT: In Micronesia they don't exactly call someone a "shaman." But if someone's sick, they might call in a certain person with a reputation as a healer—relation, clan, etc have a lot to do with that, too.

One of my best experiences was when I met a man and showed him a drawing of his great-grandfather that he'd never seen before—he recognized him because of the *name.* In the early 1990s some German ethnographers had done drawings of tattooed Micronesians from photographs, because their film hadn't been sensitive enough to clearly capture the tattoos on dark skin. Anyway, I showed him a book containing these drawings and when he saw his great-grandfather, he got really excited. The last people to wear his great-grandfather's tattoo had died more than a year earlier, and he said to me, "I want this design to live; I don't want it to die." So I put this exact traditional design on his back, and he was the nephew of the high chief of the island. When I applied the tattoo, the chief and a few older men were there, saying, "Well, *this* should be this way, and *that* should be that way." It was a real honor to have been able to do that—a great, strange experience.

■ *V: How do you get paid for tattooing there?*

■ DT: By trade—fresh fish, a place to stay, lava-lavas (which are wraps), sleeping mats, fruit—whatever people have. When I'm on a small island, I don't really set a price. If somebody comes around and wants a tattoo, I tattoo them, and next morning there might be a basket outside the door with five coconuts in it. Or I might find two pineapples, or a stalk of bananas, or some taro roots. Then, when you're getting ready to leave the island, these people come around with all this stuff to give you—it's all trade and barter, really. They would rather do that than use money, any day.

■ *AJ: What about their own tattooists?*

■ DT: There are very few left; in Micronesia that link was broken. When the missionaries came in, the first people they focused on getting rid of were the tattooists, who were often the story-tellers. And once the tattooing stopped, the stories stopped.

■ *V: So in the same way that they copied the designs of their ancestors, you do.*

■ DT: Yes. I try to encourage that kind of preservation, but I also do work that's kind of an evolution of those designs, too. Just as each village and each island were different, so each tattooist was different. So tattooing was naturally a constantly changing process.

■ *AJ: How does it feel when you come to America and tattoo? What are the points of connection? You're adopting very ancient feelings and traditions—*

■ DT: You have to respect those designs—what they are and where they came from, and the people who wore them for hundreds or thousands of years. There is that *tradition*. Whereas in the West—well, our own tattoo tradition only goes back a few hundred years, and then you're with sailors aboard Captain Cook's ships in the Pacific, who are the ones who re-introduced tattooing to Europe.

■ *AJ: What do you mean?*

■ DT: The Druids, the Scythians, the Picts and a lot of the tribes of Europe were tattooed, 'way back in pre-history. In 1947 the Russians discovered a tomb containing the frozen body of a 2000-year-old Scythian warrior whose arms and legs were covered with tattoos. I think tattooing goes in cycles; it appears in one part of the world and dies out in another, but I don't think it's ever really stopped.

■ *AJ: You're doing tattooing the old way, today. What kind of reaction do you get?*

■ DT: There's something about doing hand tattooing that makes you feel pretty directly linked to ancient tattooing. I feel I started late and have a long way to go with it, particularly compared to the Japanese masters. But at least I'm making it available in America, and even making it available in the islands. Because a lot of the young Micronesians—well, they're kind of in a time warp. Instead of wanting traditional tattoos, they want brightly colored anchors and naked ladies like they see on sailors. But I think someday they'll be re-examining their roots and reviving the traditional tattoos. And as long as those old designs are documented, they're going to be available for future generations. In terms of cultural diversity, Micronesia covers about the area of the United States, so tattoo styles are vastly different from one island group to another. Documenting all these differences could be quite a project, but I've started!

In America I do a little bit of everything. I can't do the same things that Bill Salmon or Ed Hardy can do with a machine, but people who want my style of work choose me (or is it vice versa)? I don't want to feel that I'm *locked in* to that Oceanic style exclusively, although I love it. I work mostly in black; sometimes I apply a little bit of red for accents. I do think *somebody* should be preserving the tradition of the hand tool—it's kind of "back to the roots."

■ *AJ: I think a lot more people want black tribal tattoos now.*

■ DT: I think the rise in "Modern Primitivism" is because those simple stark designs appeal to the sensibilities of people living in a bland, homogenous, yet complicated (in kind of a meaningless way) world. People are looking for ways to set themselves apart. They no longer feel linked to thousands of years of evolution; they feel they were *born yesterday* with no tradition or history or values that make sense, and they want something to re-connect them to the *primal selves* they've lost touch with, or *never knew*.

It also comes down to something like *fun*. There's a wide range of tattoo available; there are as many different styles and range as there are people doing it. Well, *not quite*—there are *innovators* who do exquisite work, and a lot of second-rate *imitators*. It's an emerging art form. I don't think there are a lot of fine art tattooists, but they're the ones who will give the inspiration to others. It goes back to something Cliff Raven said, simply: "We want to enhance the body." That's the main goal: to *improve* the body, if you will—make it interesting. Naked bodies without any marks on them on them are pretty boring.

■ *V: In Micronesia, could you tattoo with native pigments?*

■ DT: Yes, you could use lampblack—invert a can over a kerosene lantern, turn up the wick, and the smoke builds up in the bottom of the can. Scrape it out, add a little bit of water, and that's india ink. The Micronesians also collected smoke from burning tree resin—that's lampblack, too. But I usually carry *Pelikan* black ink because then I don't have to grind anything.

■ *V: Do you think tattoos can enhance personal powers and abilities?*

■ DT: I think people identify with certain images, and sometimes the images can become a part of them, or

The dolphin tattoo is a shark talisman: whenever there are dolphins, there are no sharks, so if they're in the water with dolphins tattooed on their legs, then . . .

certainly charge or energize them, at least occasionally. Whatever power that image possesses will affect them, at least in a subtle if not a sledge-hammer way. You take an image that's old, old, old and put it on your body and it *changes* you—I don't know *how*, but it can make you different from the way you were before. And that has to enhance you in some way, toward the overall goal of self-development—good or bad!

If it's a positive image—something you feel good about after it's complete—regardless of whether you have your clothes on or not, *you* know it's there, and it's your own little source of satisfaction. You enter into that world which is your *own* as opposed to the outside: "Other people don't know about it, it's *my* secret. *I* can choose whether to show it or keep it secret."

For me, tattooing has focused my life. As an artist I looked for years for a medium. I was never happy and satisfied with just pen and ink; I knew there was a more multi-dimensional medium out there that people were involved with. Somehow I knew cameras were involved (which they are; it's important for me to document the work I've done). When I found tattooing it really gave me a focus.

Tattooing is a visual form of communication, a statement, and an art with its own ethics. I don't tattoo anything I don't want to; I have to feel good about it, or I don't do it.

■ *V: I think almost any tattoo immediately reminds you of time and thus death.*

■ DT: I agree; it does strengthen your awareness of death; the fact, the reality, of your own impeding mortality. The first thing Cliff Raven said when he started a big shoulder piece on me, was "Don't get hit by a car!" Suddenly I realized my interdependency in a collaborative piece of art-making. I realized my symbiotic relationship with this person who I was now related to in some way.

■ *V: What are some other Micronesian tattoo symbols?*

■ DT: The *Pleiades*, which relates to navigation. The *dolphin,* which is a shark talisman: whenever there are dolphins, there aren't any sharks, so if they're in the water with dolphins tattooed on their legs, then... This design can't be too closed or too static; it has to somehow show the kind of movement a dolphin makes. Dolphins occasionally save swimmers from drowning. Recent studies have shown that a dolphin can in fact "see" the lung cavities and know a human is an air-breathing creature; the lung cavity doesn't have the denseness that the rest of the body has. I read an article in *Oceans* magazine saying that in ancient Greece, man first learned to swim by imitating dolphins in the water.

The original tattooing tools lent themselves to rectilinear designs, so most of the artwork was based on common design elements like crosses, zig-zags, and triangles. One clan might adopt a cross design because they were potters, whereas a clan of fisherman might have a zig-zag design.

When the missionaries brought sewing needles, then the Micronesian could do curvilinear designs. They could tie together a group of needles with some thread and work more freely than when they worked with a straight comb that was difficult to turn.

They used the *frigate bird* as a good-luck symbol. It was a sign or omen of land because the frigate bird will never spend the night at sea...they knew that if they followed that bird they'd reach land before nightfall. Sometimes they'd take a bird with them as a pet, and if there was a storm or they lost their point of reference, they'd turn the bird loose—of course the bird knew where to go!

■ MARIA YATAR: Another common symbol is the *vulvic* shape, one of the oldest symbols of mankind—it's in cave painting and is a sign of fertility and wholeness. As Dan said earlier, a lot of older women on the outer islands still have pubic tattoos (which they don't show to anybody). These could be a lover's tattoo, done by a man on a lover, or done by a local male or female tattoo artist. A lot of tattoos were put on by tattooists who used incantations and secret words, who even tattooed secret words on people's forearms or other parts of the body. And often the people who wore them didn't know the stories behind them, only the tattooist did.

I've seen probably ten different styles of pubic tattoos. Some women's tattoos are just for their husbands. Normally women had pre-marital tattoos after menstruation (which showed they were ready for marriage) and these became developed and quite elaborate. Some designs started with the hands first (puberty) and worked up to the forearms (marriageability), then the legs (maturity).

I talked to a woman with a pubic tattoo who was in her eighties, and asked her why her tattoo was so dark. She said that after every birth it was redone. I asked why, and she pulled my hand to feel her belly and it was very hard—*scarified.* She had had *fourteen* children, and the tattoo had supported her lower belly and kept it from sagging, like a *keloid girdle.* She was very proud of it.

In Palau, we found that the *women* were the ones who were elaborately tattooed, whereas in Yap it was the *men.* And often while the designs seemed similar, the reasons for them and the stories could be so different. Perhaps they once came from the same boat but settled on different islands, and in isolation developed different dreams and myths.

■ DT: In Micronesians have a saying: "When you're tattooed, your *bones* are tattooed." Maybe someday that's all that will remain of the human race; all the dreams, myths and buildings will have vanished, leaving only bones, a few bearing tattoo marks to show that the people who lived on this planet also once did *art*...

HANKY PANKY

The foremost tattooist in Amsterdam is Hanky Panky, whose Tattoo Museum of Amsterdam is located at Oudezijds Achterburgwal 130, 1012 DT, Amsterdam, Neth. (tel 31-20-625-1565; fax 31-20-620-4634). Henk has traveled widely, collecting for his museum which is filled with rare posters and photos, classic tattoo books, old tattoo tools, a skull collection including a silver skull from Nepal, a tattooed head (replica), and his own black-and-white charts showing the derivation of basic tattoo motifs (many reproduced below). At the time of the interview he had just finished reading Flaubert's *Bouvard and Pecuchet*.

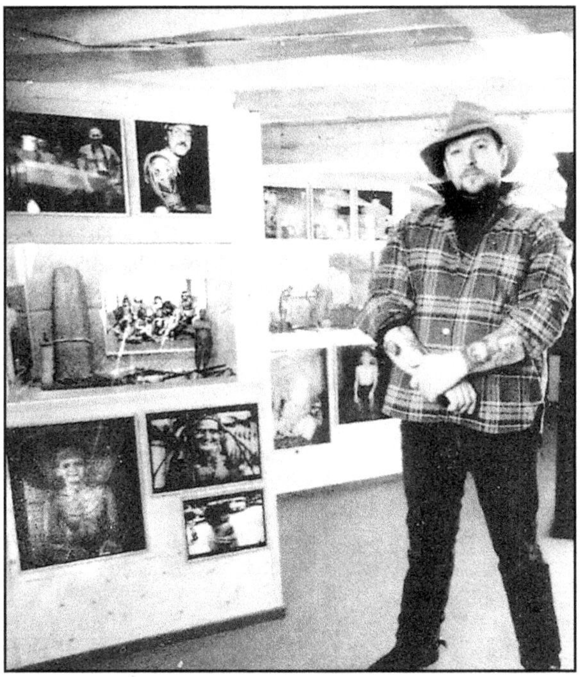

Hanky Panky in his tattoo shop/museum. Photo by Patricia Steur.

■ *VALE: Tell us about the state of tattooing in Holland.*

■ HANKY PANKY: When I started my tattoo shop ten years ago there were only about 5 tattooers in Holland; now there's about 195. Holland is very bad now when it comes to the health situation—not in terms of AIDS; AIDS is a bunch of bullshit as far as tattooing goes; you don't have to worry too much about that.

■ *ANDREA JUNO: But you wear gloves!*

■ HP: I wear gloves mainly because hepatitis is a much bigger worry. But the thing is, now there are lots of people working out of their shithouse, and they don't work the way it should be done. So we're starting a Dutch Tattooers Union of responsible professionals, to get rid of the dirtbags! There are only 2 ways to get rid of them: 1) the old Mafia trick: break their bones, but you can't do that anymore. So the only other way is by the quality of your work in terms of clean healthy work habits—there'll be union rules. So we get all the people filling in their application forms, then we're going to check them out and see who can be a member and who can't. Maybe we'll end up with 25 people!

We're going to launch an advertising campaign to tell people about the union. We'll work the way Pinky Yun works, which is: a guy across the street opened up a tattoo shop. He didn't go over and throw a firebomb in, he bought the place and told the guy to get out! In the old days people would throw firebombs. There are Japanese stories of people's hands getting hacked off.

All those old tribal tattoos constituted a language, With the Maori, different parts of the lace told different stories—you could tell a man's role in the tribal society just by looking at him.

■ *AJ: Were you born in Amsterdam?*

■ HP: No, I was born and raised in a real small place out of town in Holland. Now here in Amsterdam I have a nice house, a nice and busy shop, and my own boat which I ride to work. My wife, Patricia Steur, has a photo studio on the ground floor. She shoots a lot of album covers.

■ *V: Where did you get all your tattoo memorabilia and books?*

■ HP: I bought some of it from Bill Skuse, who was Lester Skuse's son. Bill had all these books and all of a sudden he wanted to get rid of all this great stuff from his old man, signed by these old guys, because they were always sending books and photos to each other—here's an old Lyle Tuttle photo [shows Lyle as a striking young man]. I got it all. So...what are you after?

■ *V: Our projects always try to focus on philosophy.*

■ HP: Every different guy who gets tattooed has a different philosophy. Why do people get one? Each person has his own reason, the same as the design. As for the more tribal designs, lately I've been doing a lot more black work. It took a couple years to teach people—they went through *Tattootime #1* ("New Tribalism") and now they're really going for it. What I do is: I mix the old tattoo designs. I'll draw a Viking and entangle him in a whole Borneo motif. Or if I cover a bad tattoo with a tribal piece, I might add skulls, or a tribal skull with stitched-up eyes, or an engraved skull and filed teeth—there are *no limits* now because we are *not primitives*—we can mix whatever we want! I saw a beautiful piece by Bob Roberts in which he mixed up Samoan work with old-time Maori spirals. We can do that now!

■ *V: PostModern.*

■ HP: Yes, we have no limits. Now, all these old tribal tattoos constituted a language. With the Maori, different parts of the face told different stories—you could tell a man's role in the tribal society just by looking at him. In our society, it would be like Oliver North standing with all his medals—you could see what he'd done, where he'd gone...It could mean what he'd been born into; that he was the son of the Chief. You could see he was married, or an astrologer—things like that. In other societies the markings might tell something about the person's medical history.

I was in Egypt recently and found all these old tattoos that were done by tribes living around oases. The female face tattoos were exactly the same as the female Maori tattoos! The lips were blue with the little design on the chin—exactly the same! And they would tattoo little lines near the eyes to improve the eyesight, which was similar to what happened in the Pacific, and for the same reason. There is an enormous link between those areas. Dan Thome and I were going through a lot of books trying to find correspondences.

You can find a scarification in central Africa of a lizard backpiece, and then find the same design in Papua, New Guinea, but it's *tattooed*. And it's the same goddam lizard with all the same little details. I think there's a migration of people other than what the anthropologists have speculated. If someone looks specifically for tattooing and scarification, they might come up with a completely different explanation of how the world was settled.

Dan and I discovered a few amazing things. I remember I found a plate in the British Museum which is from the island of Rhodes, 800 years before Christ. It bore a "winged god" with tattoos on his legs. These were exactly the same tattoos that the Alfuren, an old head-hunting tribe, uses in Ceram...and they were exactly the same symbols used on the island of Yap for a navigator. These were 20,000 kilometers apart; the people probably never heard of each other, but the symbol survived.

■ *AJ: Hey, you've got a photo of Andy Warhol!*

■ HP: Patricia made that photo when we met him in New York. He was going to make a tattoo design for us to do, but he never lived long enough to do it. I taught Keith Haring how to tattoo and he made his first tattoo and we made bloodprints out of it. Now let's go through my charts. Hanging these "primitive" designs up in the shop has been good; the kids see them and then start asking for them.

Each of these charts that I drew represents a survey of the design elements in primitive tattooing from a geographical area. There are only 2 or 3 areas lacking because I can't find enough information, such as the Aborigines from the Formosa Ami area. I did find some books in the library filled with old photographs, but the detail was lacking—all the fine lines merged together to look like one solid black stripe, but they ain't. Same thing with the Ainu: there are books with photographs, but they just don't show enough close-up detail. And the Ainu were all pretty much covered up, because Hokkaido is a cold island.

For anthropologists the Ainu (Japan) are probably the biggest question mark in the world—nobody really knows where they came from. They have beards and blue eyes and their language is of indeterminate origin, although there are theories they are connected to aboriginal and Tasmanian people. The aborigine has nothing to do with being a negro; they have a full-grown beard, thin lips, but a broad nose. It must be all that inbreeding during evolution. There are signs that they've been around for 40,000 years, but they've found signs that are 70,000 years old, which for mankind is a long time. Then they're in that border area where they can't do these carbon-dating tests.

PHILIPPINO TATTOOING

Here's a chart of Philippino tattooing. Most of it's dead now, but in the Kalinga area you can still find female tattooing. In 1980 Patricia and I went over there. The Kalingas live in Northern Luzon in the mountain provinces. Marcos wanted to build a dam there, and all the tribes united with the N.P.A. to fight the government. (The N.P.A. means New People's Army; they're not communists—there ain't no Communists! They're just freedom fighters, and the only people in the world who will give them support are Communists. That's why we call them Communists. If the U.S. Government supported them, they would not be communists but would still be fighting Marcos.) But, we couldn't get in that area; that was forbidden because there was an inter-tribal war going on—Marcos had divided them by sending in Ranger troops who would chop off a head and then spread a rumor that an opposing tribe did it, so all these tribes were fighting again.

But if you come from the other side of the world, you go: "Fuck Marcos; we're going in there anyway!" So at six o'clock in the morning we sneaked in there and managed to find some tattoo; we got some nice photographs from that area. The tattoos were all built out of little symbols, like frigate birds which are in Yap

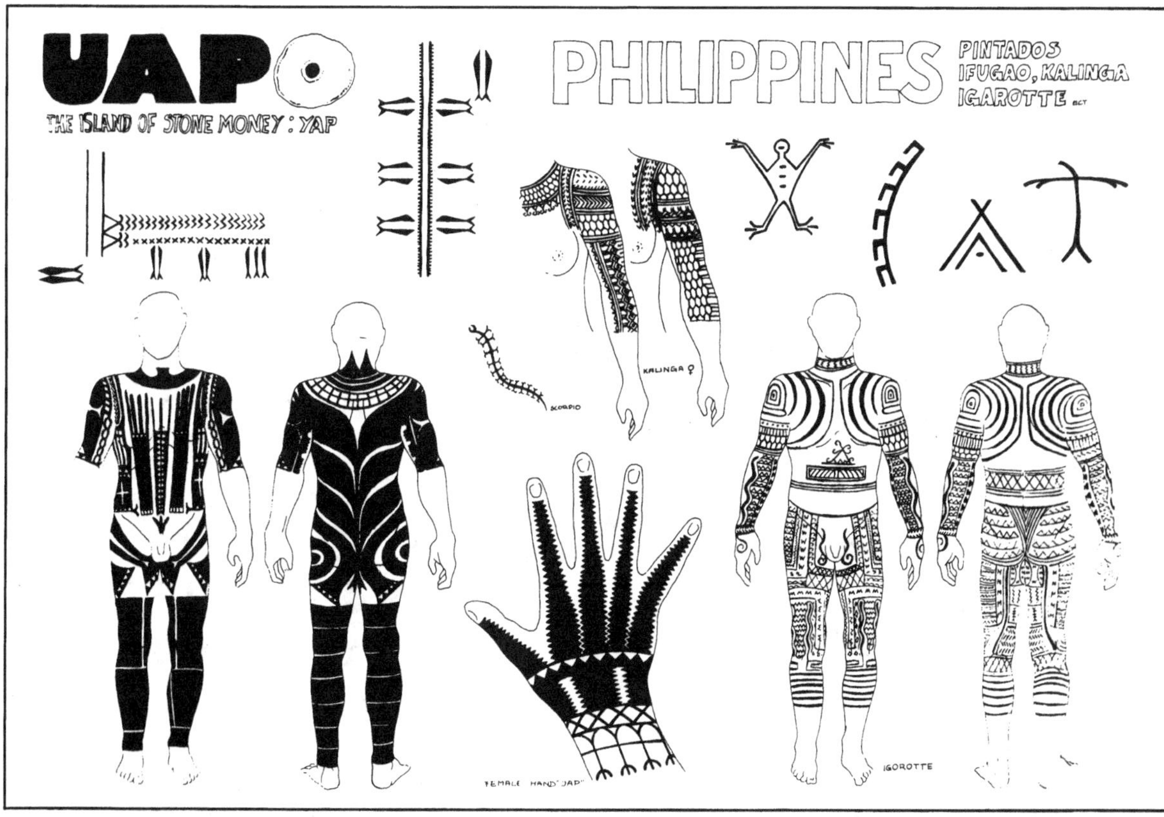

The natives had gotten used to living off the American luxuries so they thought they would lure the big silver birds back by building mock airplanes out of brush and sticks, and clearing the old landing strips. They tattooed airplanes and American and Japanese symbols.

and also in Eskimo tattooing. We had no problem at all. They believed I was a headhunting chief from some great tribe—a very brave man, because of my tattoos.

■ *AJ: Can you tell us who gets tattooed and why?*

■ HP: Most of the females get tattooed—it's a matter of: you're no good without one, or you don't look pretty without one. The men used to get tattoos for long trips, or bravery, similar to Borneo. You would also get one when you became a man. And they would add them on, like medals, to tell something about the person: this person went on a 14-day trip to such-and-such a country, and killed 2 enemies. Some designs represented the animal life around them, like centipedes or birds. Girls can get tattooed after their first menstruation.

In Bontoc I ran into a photo shop of a man called Masfere. He was an early photographer who took this wooden camera into the mountains and took pictures of the Kalinga people around the 1920s. In the Philippines I also found an old blind man who had been the regional tattooist there, or so I was told. But I think that in general, rather than there being a tattoo "artist" of exalted stature like in Samoa, the people did a lot of tattooing just for fun, like kids tattooing each other in this Borneo photo I have. Because the technique is pretty obvious; all you have to do is get a bird's bone, sharpen it up and start sticking the ink under the skin. Just as we have jail tattoos, they had similar tattoos. And right now those people might get an airplane tattooed, because they see them flying overhead.

On those islands where they had cargo cults, the inhabitants had been in the Stone Age until the Japanese came in and occupied them on their way towards invading Australia. Then the Americans came in and drove the Japanese out, bringing with them in their big silver airplanes things like chocolate, chewing gum, tinned meat, and filter cigarettes. When the war ended the Americans abruptly left. The natives had gotten used to living off the American luxuries; so they didn't have to work on their own land or fish anymore, so they thought they would lure the big silver birds back by building mock airplanes out of brush and sticks, and clearing the old landing strips. They tattooed airplanes and American and Japanese symbols.

Dan Thome told me that on the island of Yap a lot of the inhabitants wanted him to tattoo the red Japanese rising sun with radiating rays on their lower arms, because that was a symbol they really liked on the planes that first landed there.

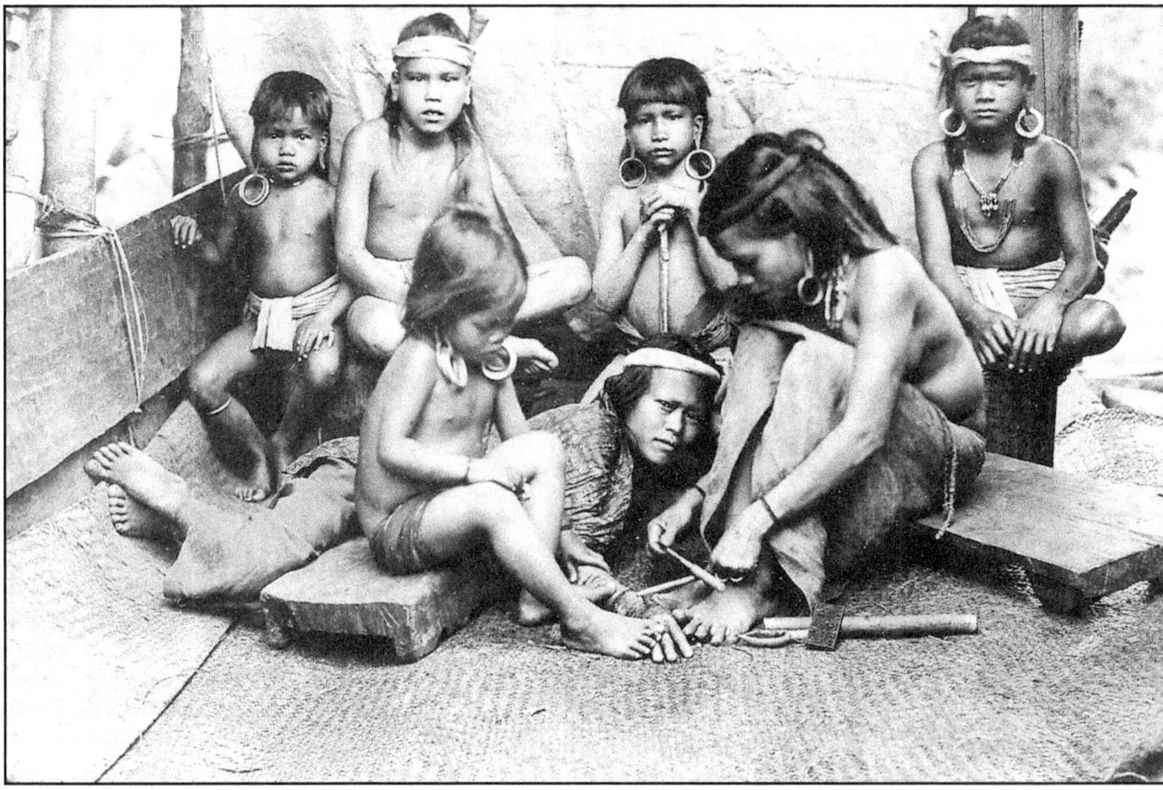

Young Borneo girls tattooing each other. Photo courtesy VIDOC (Visuele Documentatie), Koninklijk Instituut voor de Tropen, Amsterdam)

MARQUESANS

Of course, the bloody ultimate tattoos were done by the Marquesans. We looked around, but none of us ever found anyone with the original face tattoos; all we could find were photos and illustrations. But that was the most radical tattooing ever! Also, it was asymmetric. We always have that urge for making things symmetrical. Most people get a second tattoo because they look in the mirror and feel out-of-balance; they see a little tattoo on one upper arm so they get another tattoo on the other side, exact same spot. The body is built symmetrically; it takes a lot of artistic courage to get rid of that compulsion for symmetry.

■ *AJ: Where are the Marquesans?*

■ HP: Micronesia. That's the area where they fuck up the world with atom bomb tests: Bikini Atoll, the Marshall Islands...

SCARIFICATION

I found an arm scar pattern in Nigeria which was identical to some Alfuren tattoo designs. They probably had meanings, but I think a lot of them had medical purposes. In her book *The Last of the Nuba* Leni Riefenstahl talked about the women who get little coffee bean scarification patterns. She thought this was an early form of vaccination; by making these little wounds you would build up your immune system... make a better healing system. And in those tribes childbirth is so important—you would not save up for your old age, but would have many kids who would take care of you when you were an old man or woman. Childbirth produces little wounds, and these would heal faster if your healing system was stronger.

Sometimes, especially in the Upper Volta, scars were made when the kid was six days old. This little pink baby would have its face cut up by one of the headmen of the tribe—we don't have that in our society. The closest thing I heard about involved Les Skuse; he was tattooed by his old man when he was five years old. His father was afraid he might lose his son in the bombing during the Second World War; he wanted to be able to ask, "Has anybody seen a kid with "Popeye" tattooed on his arm?"

Scarification involves recognition as well as puberty rites. Every tribe had different initiation practices. Germans used to get dueling scars; in the early sixties about 50% of the Reichstag had a scar on their face—like a badge of honor. Remember the famous Baader-Meinhof murder of the industrialist Hans Schleyer?—he had the *mensur* on his face. The only time this was forbidden was during Hitler's era—Hitler didn't like intellectuals or students because he himself was neither. It still

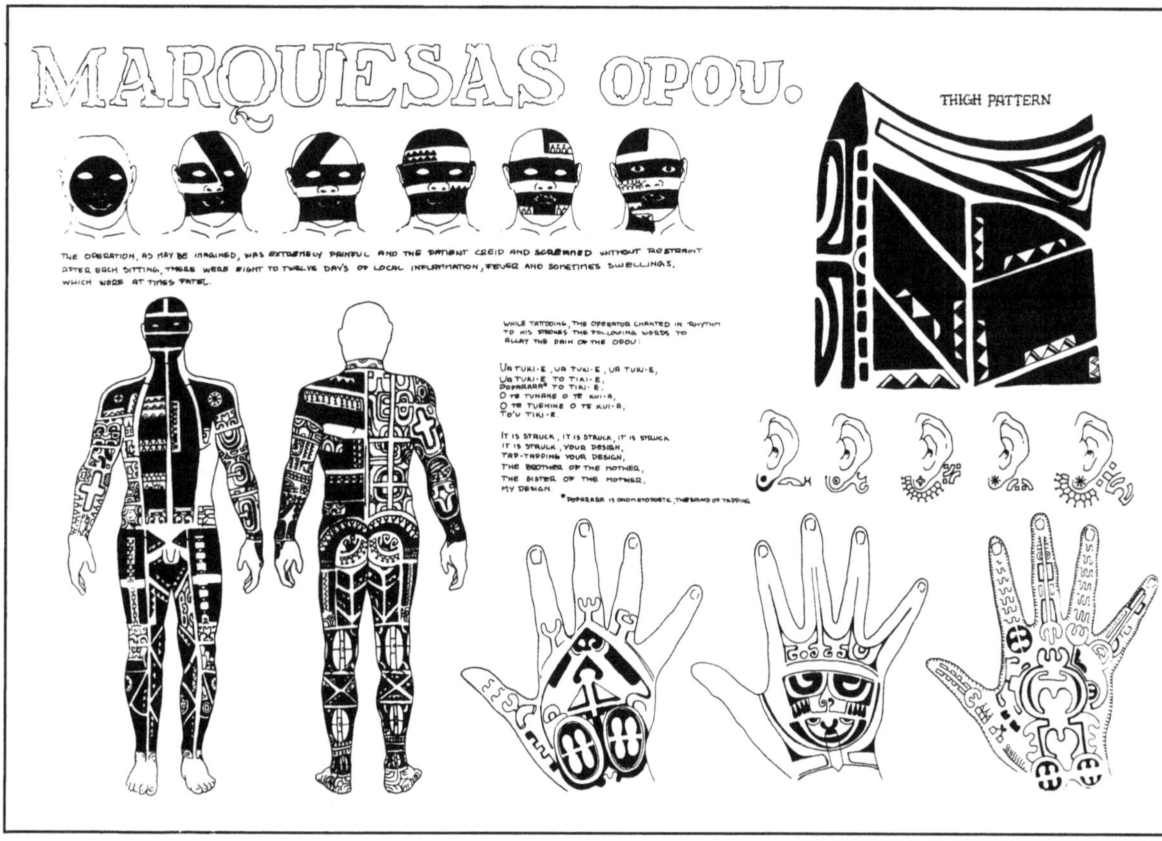

goes on; some people think it's an extreme right-wing practice, but it's not. I went to Heidelberg, and found even socialistic student movements still make the *mensur.* In Europe this is the only scarification we know of in Western society.

This usually happens as a kind of initiation into a student society. On the same day you get a leather patch on the shoulder, glasses to protect the eyes, and if the sword is one meter 50 centimeters long, they stand about one meter 48 centimeters apart and the duel begins. The swords are up in the air, and when the sword comes down, perhaps one sword causes a wound. If the wound will cause a good enough scar, it's over. but if not, then, "Give him another blow!"

ESKIMO & NORTH AMERICAN TATTOOING

They have the y-shaped frigate bird motif as well as chin tattooing. I don't know why most of these tattoos are done on the hands, chin and face. Perhaps it's because whenever you communicate, that's what you look at. There's a theory that this [chin] is the flood-line. All over the world there are flood myths in almost every society—Brazilian, Indian, Samoa, Mayan, etc—they all have a great flood myth. You could stand in the water up to this line and your nose could still be breathing; this line was like a remembrance of that flood line. Egyptian, Maori, Ainu, Formosan, Brazilian women all have this tattoo.

CHRISTIAN COPTIC TATTOOS

These were 400 years old or more, made in Italy. Pilgrims got tattoos as a badge of their pilgrimage. It would take 3 months to walk to Santiago (Italy, Spain, Israel), and you would come back with the Santiago cross tattooed. Knights like Richard the Lionhearted went on a crusade and came back with a tattoo showing they'd been to Jerusalem. Most got a cross tattooed on their arm, but some came back with a cross tattooed on their forehead. In the Coptic area, the tattoo showed you were not a Muslim, because that's mostly Muslim territory there. Coptic women in Egypt still have that little cross on their hand.

■ *AJ: What about Christian prohibitions against tattooing?*

■ HP: The Coptic church has nothing to do with Roman Catholicism or Protestantism. The prohibition came after Alexander the Great. With Jews it's different; when they were leaving Egypt they were probably all tattooed just like any other Berber tribe of sheep and goat-raising nomads, but Moses forbade it, even though, if they get to heaven, they'll probably see that "God" has a big tattoo on his chest!

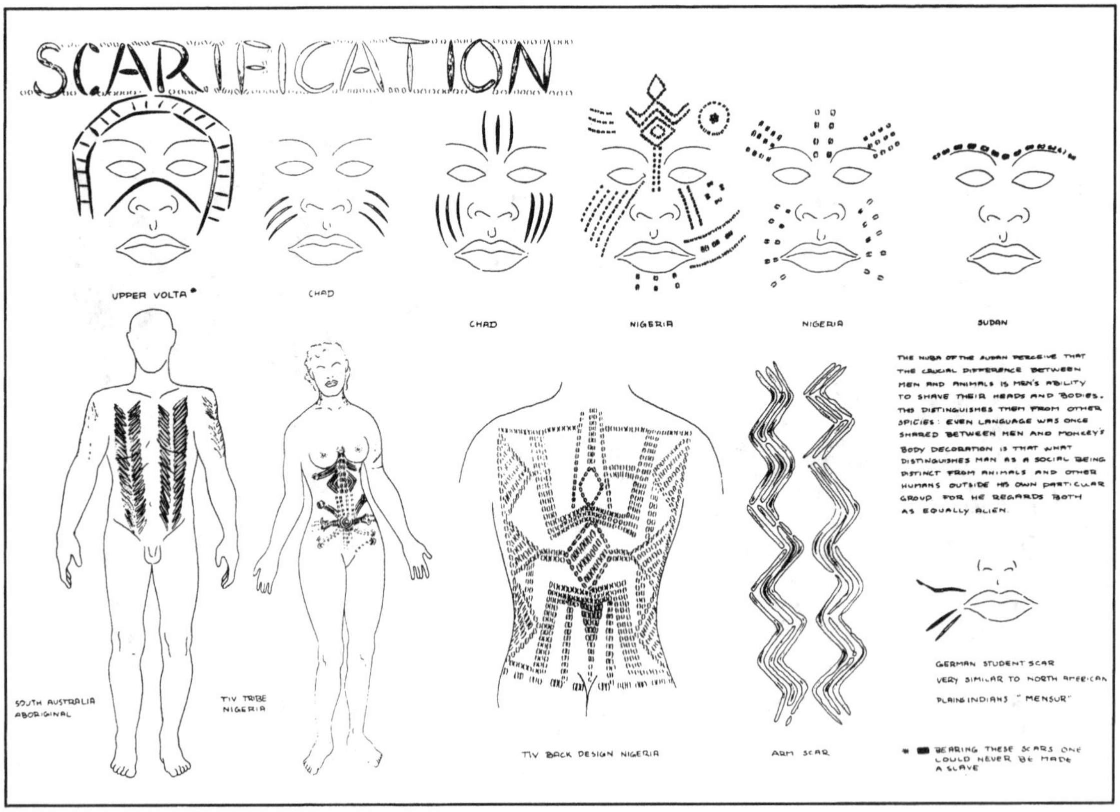
SCARIFICATION
UPPER VOLTA *
CHAD
CHAD
NIGERIA
NIGERIA
SUDAN
THE NUBA OF THE SUDAN PERCEIVE THAT THE CRUCIAL DIFFERENCE BETWEEN MEN AND ANIMALS IS MEN'S ABILITY TO SHAVE THEIR HEADS AND BODIES. THIS DISTINGUISHES THEM FROM OTHER SPICIES: EVEN LANGUAGE WAS ONCE SHARED BETWEEN MEN AND MONKEY'S BODY DECORATION IS THAT WHAT DISTINGUISHES MAN AS A SOCIAL BEING DISTINCT FROM ANIMALS AND OTHER HUMANS OUTSIDE HIS OWN PARTICULAR GROUP FOR HE REGARDS BOTH AS EQUALLY ALIEN.
GERMAN STUDENT SCAR
VERY SIMILAR TO NORTH AMERICAN PLAINS INDIANS "MENSUR"
SOUTH AUSTRALIA ABORIGINAL
TIV TRIBE NIGERIA
TIV BACK DESIGN NIGERIA
ARM SCAR
* BEARING THESE SCARS ONE COULD NEVER BE MADE A SLAVE

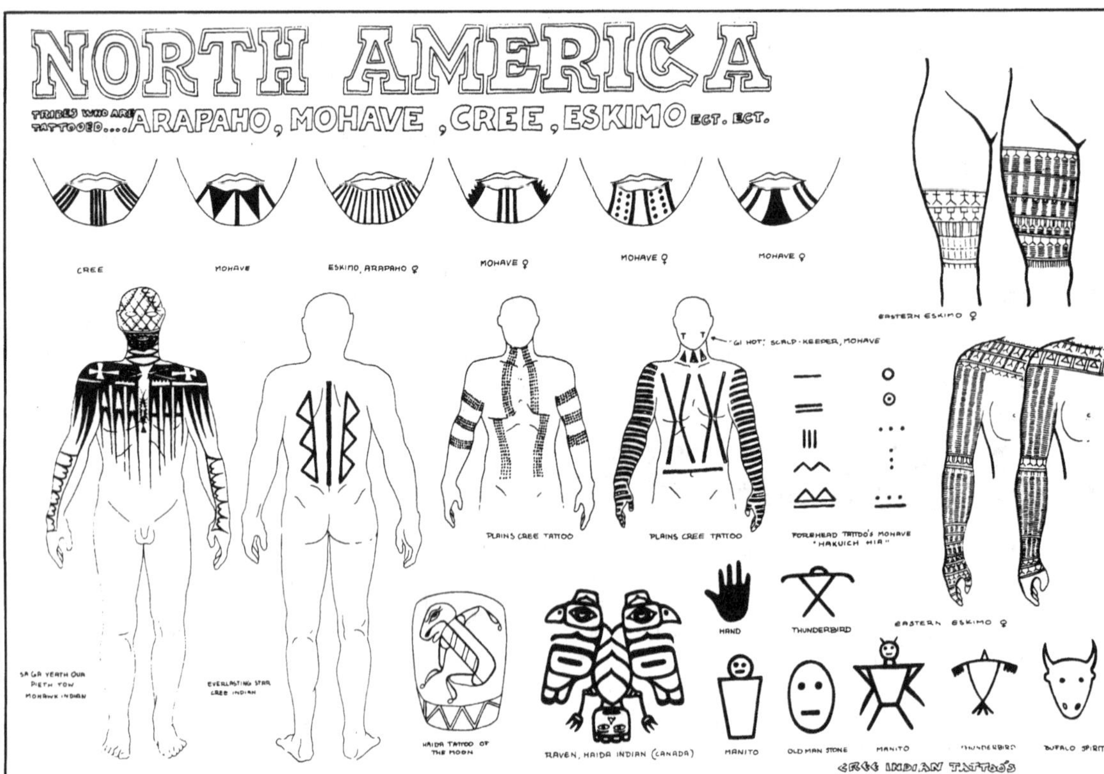
NORTH AMERICA
TRIBES WHO ARE TATTOOED.... ARAPAHO, MOHAVE, CREE, ESKIMO ECT. ECT.
CREE
MOHAVE
ESKIMO, ARAPAHO ♀
MOHAVE ♀
MOHAVE ♀
MOHAVE ♀
EASTERN ESKIMO ♀
"GI HOT" SCALP-KEEPER, MOHAVE
PLAINS CREE TATTOO
PLAINS CREE TATTOO
FOREHEAD TATTOO'S MOHAVE "HAKUICH HIA"
SA GA YEATH QUA PIETH TOW MOHAWK INDIAN
EVERLASTING STAR CREE INDIAN
HAIDA TATTOO OF THE MOON
RAVEN, HAIDA INDIAN (CANADA)
HAND
THUNDERBIRD
EASTERN ESKIMO ♀
MANITO
OLD MAN STONE
MANITO
THUNDERBIRD
BUFALO SPIRIT
CREE INDIAN TATTOO'S

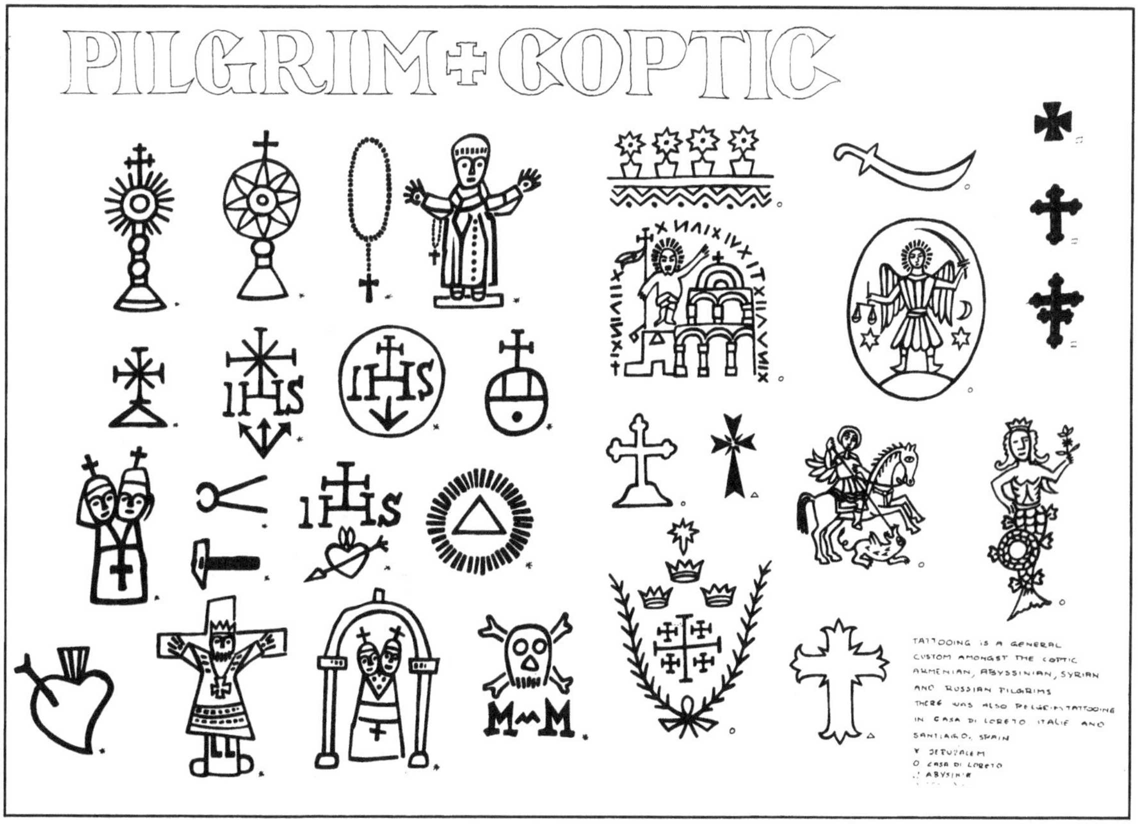
PILGRIM + COPTIC
IHS
IHS
IHS
M M
TATTOOING IS A GENERAL
CUSTOM AMONGST THE COPTIC
ARMENIAN, ABYSSINIAN, SYRIAN
AND RUSSIAN PILGRIMS
THERE WAS ALSO PELGRIM TATTOOING
IN CASA DI LORETO ITALIE AND
SANTIAGO, SPAIN
¥ JERUSALEM
O CASA DI LORETO
ABYSINIE

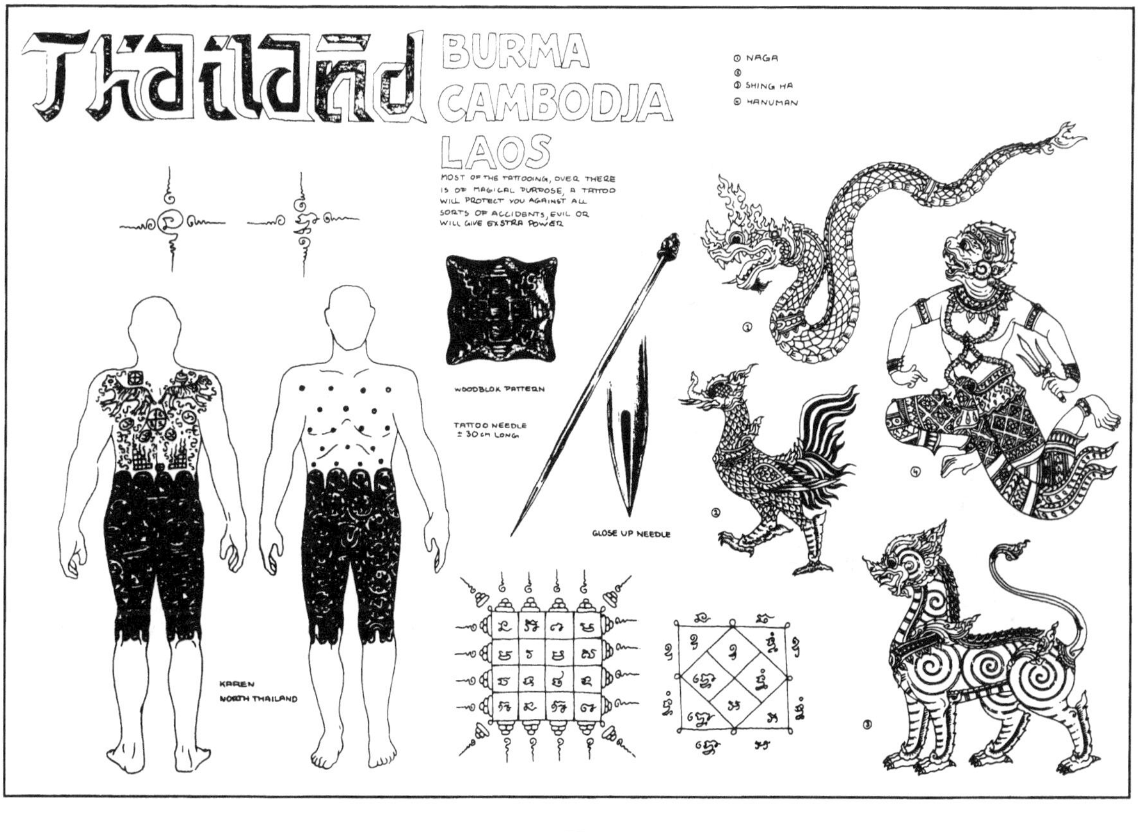
Thailand
BURMA
CAMBODJA
LAOS
MOST OF THE TATTOOING, OVER THERE
IS OF MAGICAL PURPOSE, A TATTOO
WILL PROTECT YOU AGAINST ALL
SORTS OF ACCIDENTS, EVIL OR
WILL GIVE EXSTRA POWER
① NAGA
②
③ SHING HA
④ HANUMAN
WOODBLOK PATTERN
TATTOO NEEDLE
± 30 CM LONG
CLOSE UP NEEDLE
KAREN
NORTH THAILAND

SOUTHEAST ASIA

This area is probably the most heavily tattooed in the world. Almost everybody has a tattoo in Burma, Thailand, Laos. If people don't want it done in ink they have it done with a sacred oil, but they all go to the tattoo artist and have it stamped in their back. Sometimes people believed their tattoos would protect them. The Khmer Rouge in their camps are almost always tattooed for protection against bullets, snake bite, etc. If it doesn't work, then you had bad luck! They also wore little Buddhas for protection, but the fisherman who can't wear those (because they get entangled in the nets) get them tattooed. Rich people of course don't get tattooed; they like to speak English to you and don't even speak their native language; all over, Third World countries have that problem. If somebody's rich, he wants to behave like a man of the world. In the Philippines they say, "Oh no, we don't eat dog!" [laughs] But the native will say, "Dog very good—number one!" That's the bullshit about it.

■ *V: Did you visit Southeast Asia?*

■ HP: Yes. We went to see the *Karen* freedom fighters who beat the shit out of the Burmese with flintlocks. They have a Samoan type of tattooed shorts. In Thailand itself the only people I could find who were tattooing were Buddhist monks. Their tattoo shop had six or seven guys working there all day long. A guy comes in, and he's like bowing and presenting gifts like a bottle of whisky, a couple of packs of cigarettes and some flowers, and hidden in the flowers is the money for the tattoo, because it's like the old Samurai code: you don't touch any money. When the customer's gone they put the money away, because they all like color TV as well! The tattoos go with prayers there. I got two of them in Bangkok. One protects me against dog bites, and the lizard is for fertility, because that's a big thing in societies where they don't have life insurance. Well, they may have gold in their mouths, and when they're 60 or 70 they start pulling the gold out. Greg Irons had a protective tattoo done but it didn't help him much!

■ *V: Tell us a little about your trip there.*

■ HP: I went with Patricia. The Karen is at the Burmese border which is in the Golden Triangle which is a pretty wild area—there are no laws there. You walk right through the poppy fields; there's opium all over the damn place. They're trying to sell you opium, and when you walk the whole day if you take two or three pipes you have a good night's rest. It's a couple of days walking over there—it always is if you want to go see some primitive tattooing. It could be on boats, elephants, motorcycles, walking shoes—*anything*, just as long as you get there!

■ *V: When did you go there?*

■ HP: I went a couple of times to Thailand. The first time I was on this island, and I went out with a translator to see the guy and he said, "Yeah, I can make the

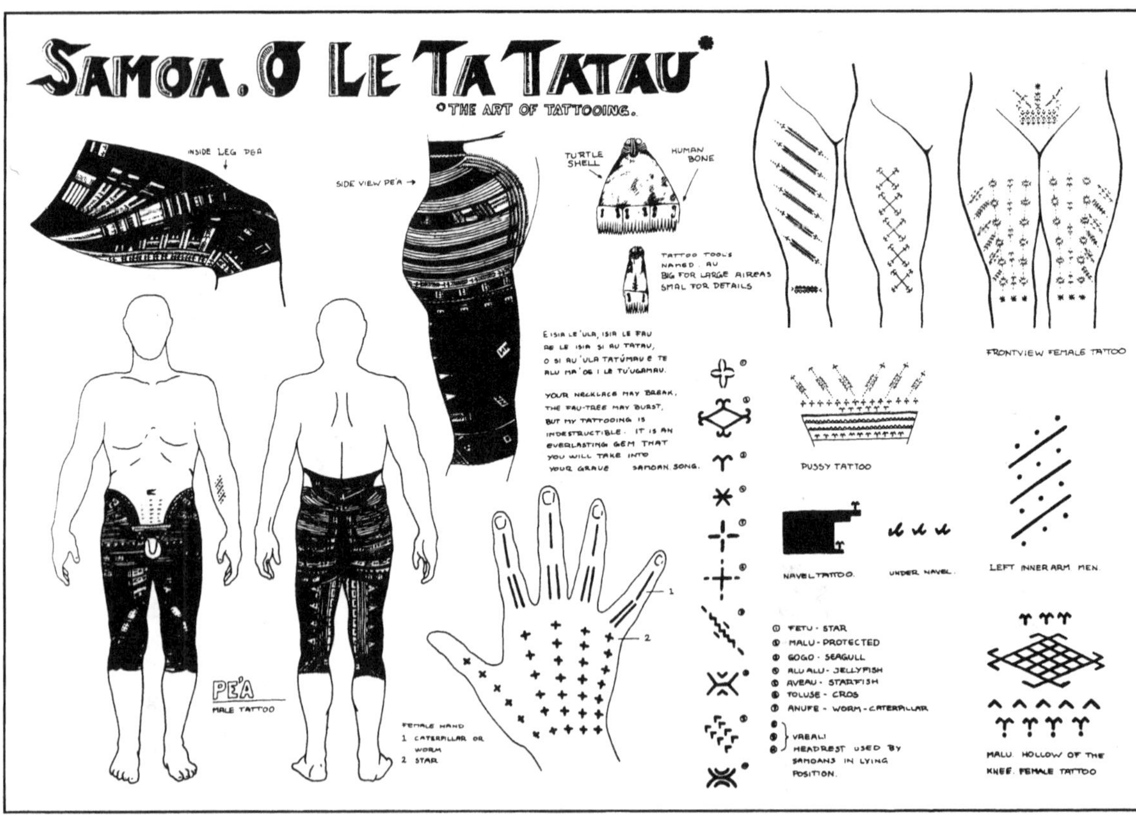

When we went there I had to go in long-sleeved, because they were killing Indonesians at that moment by death squads. They'd just gotten rid of all the criminals, and how does a criminal look? A criminal has tattoos. So they were finding all these stiffs floating in the river with tattoos.

tattoo!" I said, "Let me see the tool"—I wanted to see what he was working with, because they use these long tools about half a meter long—just a little metal pipe, and they cut it in the front and file it into two points and bend the points together. It had a little opening. But this guy gets back in his hut and starts fooling around and comes back with an old piece of umbrella with the handle still attached. I didn't know much about native tattooing, but I thought, "Nobody's going to fuck around on my arm with an old umbrella!" Then I went to a second one, and saw that it was actually the same thing, only he had at least cut off the handle. When you have a big tool you can move it pretty fast; a big move at the top makes a delicate move at the base. You can actually work pretty accurately.

■ *V: I watched Nakano use a long tool and he was fast.*

■ HP: I had a tattoo done in the Philippines by hand and the guy made a big snake around my leg and it took him 2-1/2 hours. I did a similar tattoo with a machine on a guy from New Zealand and it took me 3-1/2 hours. The funny thing is: he had one tool he would do everything with. The tool had 16 needles, of which 13 were at a 15 degree angle, and the other 3 were on the other side, facing at an angle in. He would use the 3 to make the more detailed work, then just flip the tool to use the 13 to do the shading. It was all with the same tool.

SAMOA

Everybody knows everything about Samoa! All these little symbols: there's the y-shaped frigate bird again, the star, the jellyfish, the seagull—lots of the symbols have to do with the sea. This one symbol represents a headrest, similar to what the Egyptians or the Japanese use as a pillow.

In Yap the men would sometimes kidnap a woman and tattoo her. On Yap the women were not particularly tattooed. But there was always one woman who was used in the man-house near the sea on the beach with the canoes. They would have a hooker in there and everybody would use her until somebody would marry her. Nobody would look down on her or anything, but she would be tattooed.

HAWAII—TAHITI

Kandi Everett is doing some work on Hawaiian guys that's fantastic, doing traditional designs. They had a tongue tattoo which was done out of mourning; somebody would die and a person would tattoo their tongue. But most of the designs had to do with navigation or the sea which was their main life.

NEW ZEALAND

See how the face is divided: your temples tell your rank or position in life. Cheekbones: the lines of your rank; where you came from, who your father was. Four: that would tell if you were married or for the second or third time. Five: your signature, your work; maybe the tribe you came from or your family group, rank or social status. Mana: power, prestige, words which generally come from the gods, like wearing a crucifix. Lots of the sub-Moluccans in Holland are from the *Kakayan,* a secret society of head hunters in Ceram; there are probably still some old guys here who have the tattoos. Ceram is close to Papua, New Guinea, and Timor. When you look at this, this is exactly the same as that star done on female Samoans; that stuff has to do with each other. Like the Naga in the North of India; the Mentawi Islands—it's pretty wild there. I was there in 1985.

When the Dutch left Indonesia in the fifties, the new government said, "All right, no more of the spirit religion here. We want you to become either Muslims or Christians—no other religions anymore. We're going to become a modern society." And how do you become a modern society—wearing Western clothes even though it's hot as hell, and building skyscrapers? In these real remote places, the only places in the world where tattooing survived, because they were so remote, because no assholes could go there (not even us; we don't even belong there). I have my tools with me, and what they want you to make is like our stuff; they don't want traditional designs. I'll make modern designs for them; you can't blame them.

When we went there I had to run around to all these offices to get stamps from this guy and that guy, and I had to go in long-sleeved, because they were killing Indonesians at that moment by death squads. They'd just gotten rid of all the criminals, and how does a criminal look? A criminal has tattoos. So they were finding all these stiffs floating in the river with tattoos. I'd seen people there who used just about anything they could lay their hands on to get rid of the tattoos, like battery acid; people were burning them out. The Mentawi Islands are like 3 islands: the top island is in front of the Sumatra coast. There's Nias, and Nias used to have tattoo, but it died out already. Below is Siberut, and Siberut was impossible to get in; they didn't want to let you in because they didn't want you to see real Indonesian people who are running around bare-assed, because that's not how a modern Indonesian looks like—he's supposed to wear a Western suit. So they don't like you to go and take pictures there!

We had to go to an island called Sipora, which is pretty fucked-up already. You had to go up-river to get to the little villages. We arrived at one little village

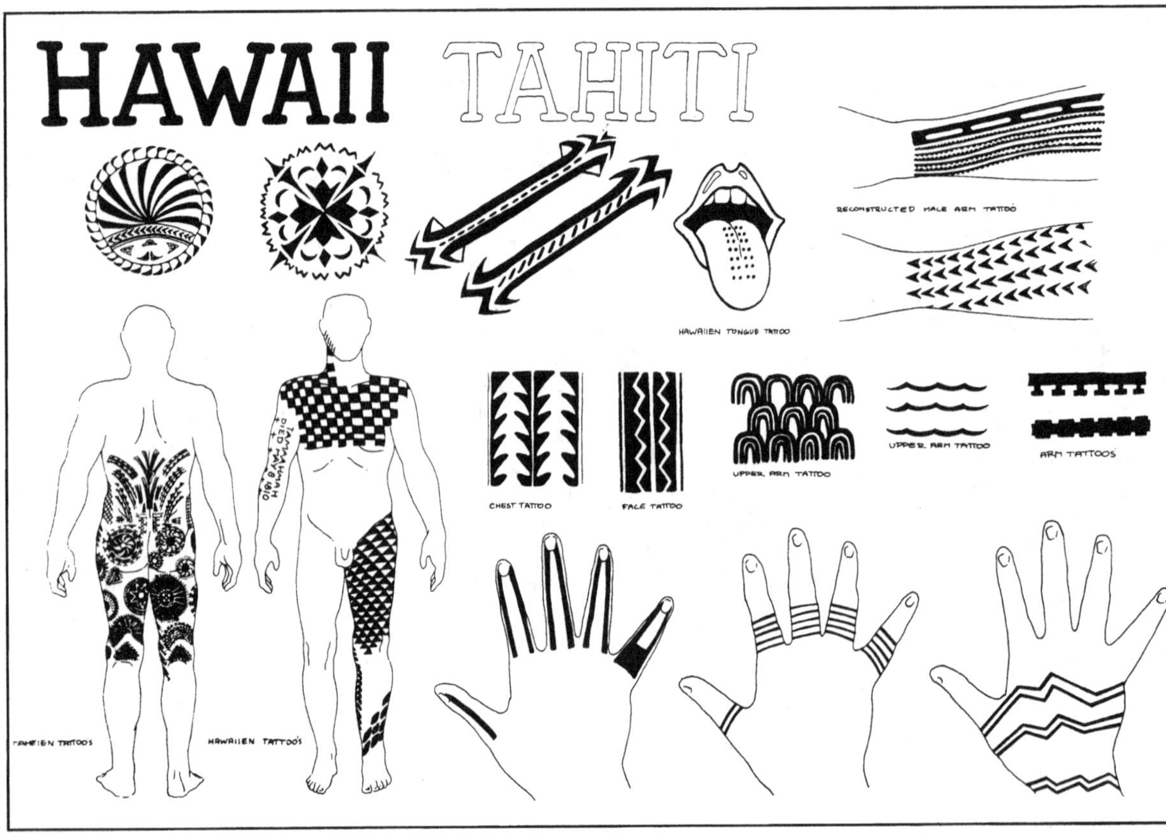

We arrived at one little village on a Sunday and everybody was in church, and their German fucked-up church service lasts four hours! They were all singing, but the funny thing was, the guy conducting the service had facial tattoos and his teeth were filed!

on a Sunday and everybody was in church, and their German fucked-up church service lasts four hours! They were all singing, but the funny thing was, the guy conducting the service had facial tattoos and his teeth were filed! It was really strange to see him inflicting this extreme German Protestant ceremony on the people. But tattooing is officially forbidden there; they don't want you to tattoo anymore.

MELANESIA

Tattooing is still happening here because it's so remote. There's all these little islands; this is where Dan Thome went. It got influenced by the cargo cult thing. Here you are on a little island, nothing is happening for thousands and thousands of years, and all of a sudden the Japs pull in completely armed, rebuilding the whole island, making airstrips, bunkers, because they were on their way to Australia. By the time you get used to the Japs, all of a sudden these big warships from the U.S. are pulling up and the U.S. Marines are running all over the island in an enormous war, because there were heavy battles on these islands: the Solomon Islands, etc. And they were flying in all this food and everything: chocolate, chewing gum, canned tuna and peaches, and all of a sudden they had to go back to the Stone Age again! The only thing they had was the remembrance of these guys who once came in these big birds, and whatever was left behind: old tanks and old planes, rusting away. The natives made all these mock airplanes out of old wood and bamboo to get them back again; they made big airstrips, praying to bring back the big bird who will bring the canned tuna, chocolate, chewing gum and filter cigarettes again.

JAVA

On this island tattoo is for women. Same again, this represents fishes, a frog, a bird. I never went there; it's on my list! When you really start digging into this stuff, you don't want to go on vacation anymore. I can't go and sit somewhere on the beach for a week; if I'm going to go somewhere, I have to see tattooing. So if there is tattooing, I'll go there; my wife Patricia can go sit on the beach and I'll be running around town seeing if I can find something.

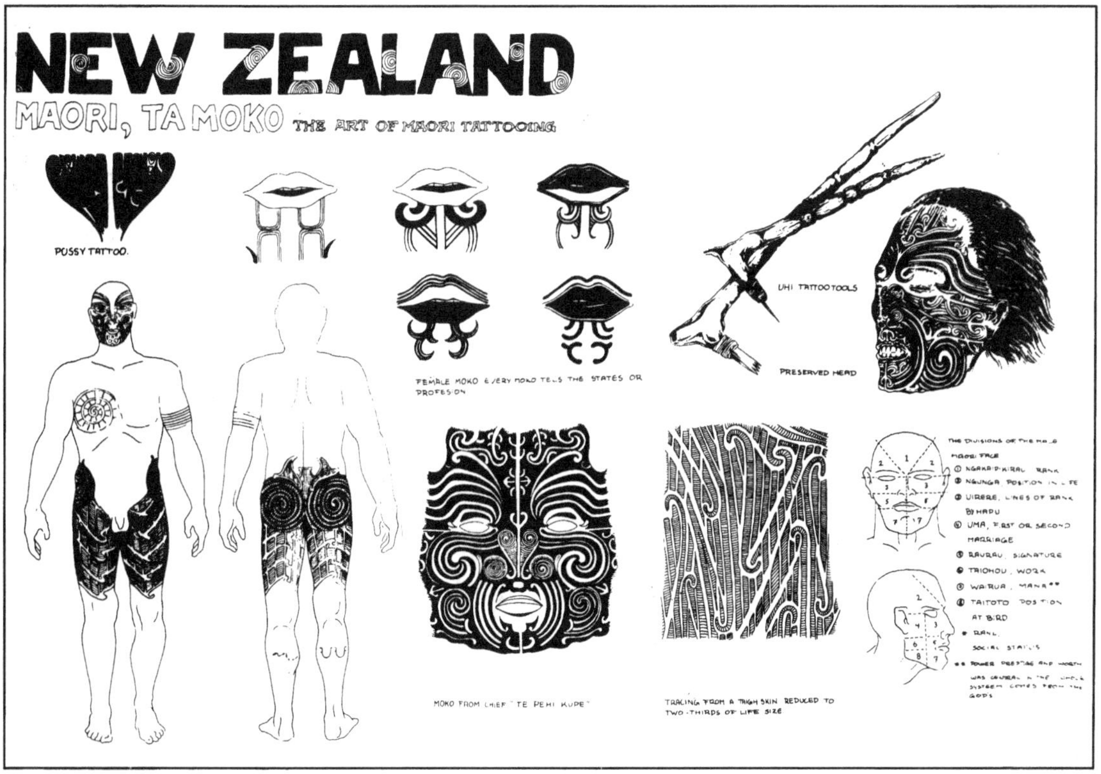
NEW ZEALAND
MAORI, TA MOKO THE ART OF MAORI TATTOOING
PUSSY TATTOO.
UHI TATTOO TOOLS
PRESERVED HEAD
FEMALE MOKO EVERY MOKO TELLS THE STATES OR PROFESION
MOKO FROM CHIEF "TE PEHI KUPE"
TRACING FROM A THIGH SKIN REDUCED TO TWO-THIRDS OF LIFE SIZE
THE DIVISIONS OF THE MALE MAORI FACE
① NGAKAIPIKIRAU RANK
② NGUNGA POSITION IN LIFE
③ UIRERE, LINES OF RANK BY HAPU
④ UMA, FIRST OR SECOND MARRIAGE
⑤ RAURAU, SIGNATURE
⑥ TAIOHOU, WORK
⑦ WAIRUA, MANA**
⑧ TAITOTO POSITION AT BIRD
* RANK SOCIAL STATUS
** POWER PRESTIGE AND WORTH WAS CENTRAL IN THE WHOLE SYSTEEM COMES FROM THE GOD'S

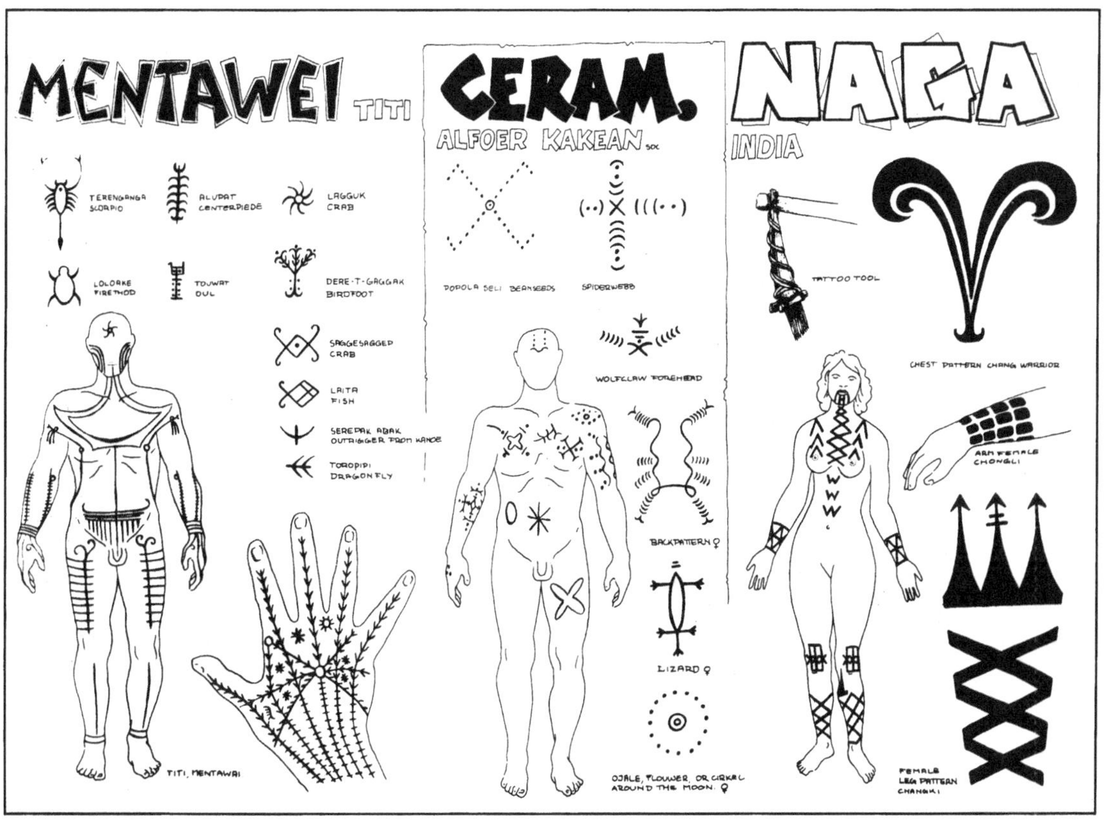
MENTAWEI TITI
TERENGANGA SCORPIO
ALUPAT CENTERPIEDE
LAGGUK CRAB
LOLOAKE FIRETHOD
TOUWAT DUL
DERE-T-GAGGAK BIRDFOOT
SAGGESAGGED CRAB
LAITA FISH
SEREPAK ABAK OUTRIGGER FROM KANOE
TOROPIPI DRAGONFLY
TITI, MENTAWAI
CERAM.
ALFOER KAKEAN SOC
POPOLA SELI BEANSEEDS
SPIDERWEBB
WOLFCLAW FOREHEAD
BACKPATTERN ♀
LIZARD ♀
OJALE, FLOWER, OR CIRKEL AROUND THE MOON. ♀
NAGA
INDIA
TATTOO TOOL
CHEST PATTERN CHANG WARRIOR
ARM FEMALE CHONGLI
FEMALE LEG PATTERN CHANGKI

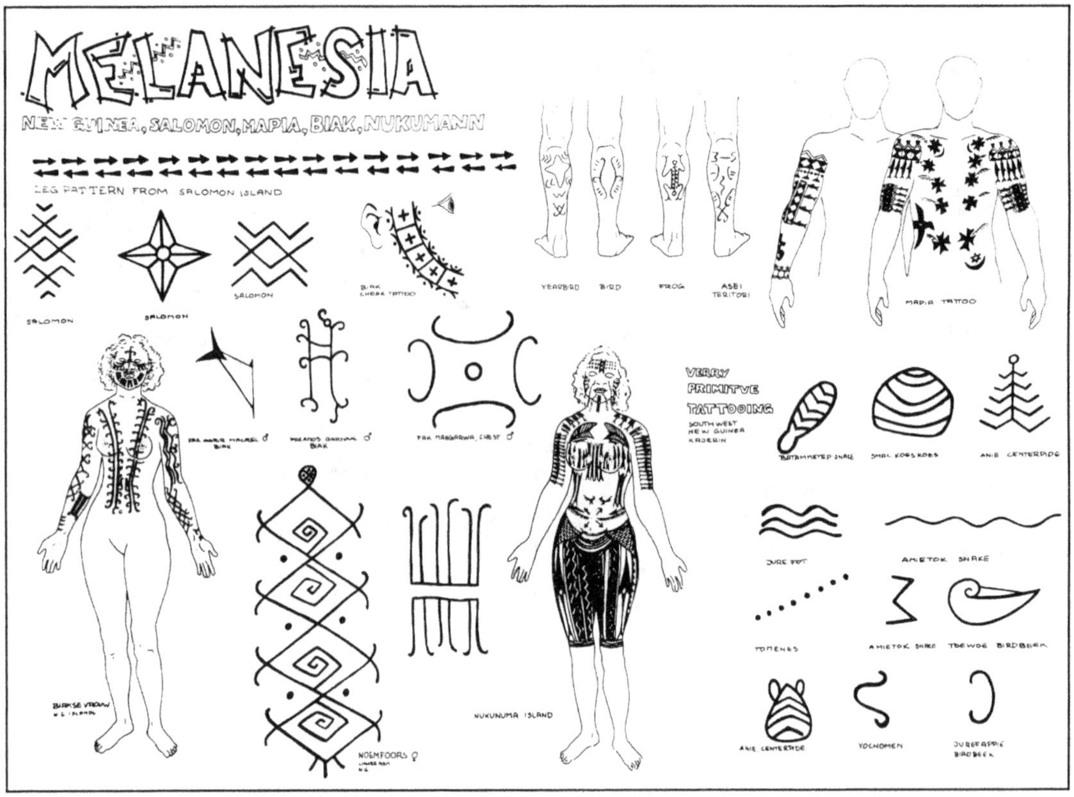

■ *AJ: Does she take photographs with you?*
■ HP: Yes, she always goes along and takes pictures.

BORNEO

Now Borneo we all know a lot about, thanks to Leo Zulueta. Leo did a lot for that primitive style. All of a sudden every self-respecting punk has a Borneo tattoo nowadays. In just a few years there's probably more people running around *outside* Borneo with Borneo tattoos than inside. But you know, there is always hope—Samoans living outside Samoa send their kids now to Samoa to get their *pe'a* done.

Most kids who just graduate from school don't know where Western civilization came from—they all think that it's Greece or Rome. Most of our medicine was based on Arab medicine men who would use tattoos. There's still a connection between rheumatism and tattoos—Arabs still use it, and in the Pacific they still use it. There are similar cases where the cure used to be a tattoo. The Micronesians used them, and the Berbers used them. To me I think Berber tattooing is probably the oldest tattooing there is. Again, it's not easy to find out much about this; you can find some of the stuff in Morocco, but not much. Lyle Tuttle has a beautiful book on Berber tattooing which is done by the University of Beirut; I think they only printed 160 copies or so, and the copies in Beirut have been gone for a long, long time! That's the damn shame with that war. If only it could be just a good fist fight by the border, then..

■ *V: That was the idea behind the Olympics, to sublimate the war urge. But it didn't work, we still have the wars.*
■ HP: Now they're fighting over the Olympics!
■ *AJ: So what percentage of your clientele want New Tribal designs?*
■ HP: I don't know. I do a lot of them. Especially because of a couple of books that showed it, like *Tattootime.* And it was actually something new going on in tattooing. In Western-style tattooing, for years people were making the same old shit; eagles, anchors, and all of a sudden all these punk kids wanted all this tribal stuff. So many books in the last ten years have been published on tattooing; ten years ago to find a book on tattooing was—well, you would find one or two books a year; from 1859, 1920, 1950. It was very hard to find *anything* on it. Now there's a book coming out every year—five or six a year, maybe. And of course all these books were covering the new tribalism, the new thing. So all these kids are seeing the new thing, and that's what they want. The Borneo scorpion is probably the equivalent of the Black Panther of ten years ago—that's the design you're making all the time now!
■ *V: I didn't realize it had become that popular.*
■ HP: Well, the Italians and all these people want that stuff. I have a big Italian clientele. They come to Amsterdam, sleep in the Central Station, but they got like $200 in their pocket for a tattoo. That's what they come to Amsterdam for: to smoke hashish and get tattooed.
■ *AJ: Do you get upper class or professional people in?*

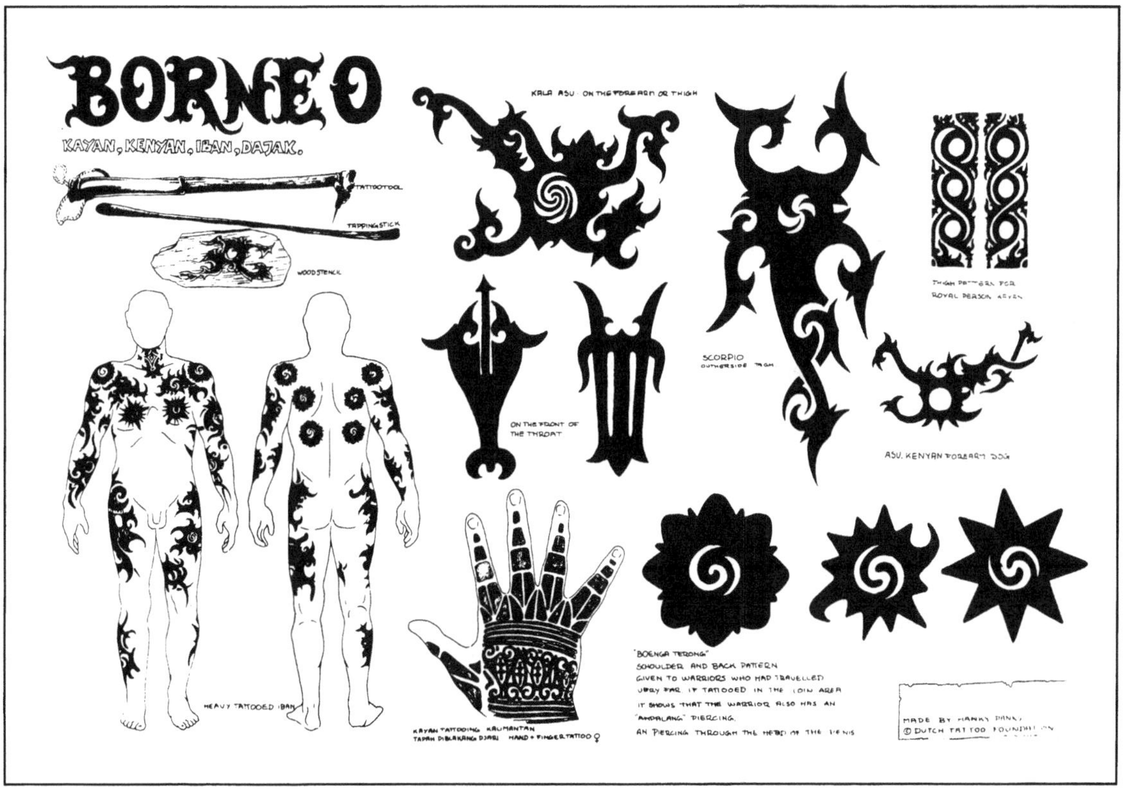

■ HP: It's not like in the States. In the States you go to a convention and see all these older men, decent gentlemen, although they're mostly the gay section, eh? Well the gay section is different: they go for the old macho shit. What they want is the black panther because they want to look like a goddamn truck driver—that's the big trip. So they have an eagle on one side and a black panther on the other, and that's how you look macho. If people get a little more into tattoo, then they're going to see other things and maybe read books and then they're going to come up wanting newer, or different, tattoos.

■ *V: How did you become a tattoo artist?*

■ HP: I was a photographer for a long time for a magazine here in Holland. I did a couple of features on tattooing and became more and more interested in it and started collecting anything I could lay my hands on—business cards, photos, books, and I started correspondence with all these people. All of a sudden I had this tattoo machine in my collection, and another old tattoo machine, and then I had to do this big article on the Dutch Hells Angels for the magazine. And they knew me, they said, "Yeah, you the tattoo guy?" I said, "Yeah, yeah."

■ *V: You'd already been tattooing?*

■ HP: I wasn't tattooing then, but they went, "Well, why don't you make a tattoo on us?" So I put my first tattoo on a Hells Angel—that's one of the best ways to start, because you've got a critical client. You *don't* want to fuck up with him!

I have this theory that you shouldn't tattoo your own wife, just like a surgeon won't cut his own kids.

■ *AJ: Were you an artist, though?*

■ HP: I used to draw as a kid, sure. Most of us used to draw. I think you can get away with not being able to be a good drawer, as long as you are a decent copier or craftsman. A lot of us are craftsmen. Someone like Ed Hardy is an exceptional artist; he can draw the whole scene and anything else you can imagine. But most of the tattoo artists nowadays—they call themselves artists, but they probably couldn't draw anything at all; they have to work from a stencil. That doesn't really matter; if you're a good craftsman, you can still execute the damn thing very well. The only difference is like: when you know a bit about how to draw, and a bit about anatomy, then you're able to put the right shadings on the right place, so when you draw a Viking (or something like that), the guy has the muscles on the right places. Because some of that stuff looks so flat. That's why all these guys jumped on Frank Frazetta—all of a sudden you've got these guys with beards and swords and—also that Boris Vallejo, with his gnomes and elves—I hate that shit! I don't like romantic type of tattoos. So don't come and see me for an elf or a fucking butterfly or unicorn. But heavy black and skulls—you're my man!

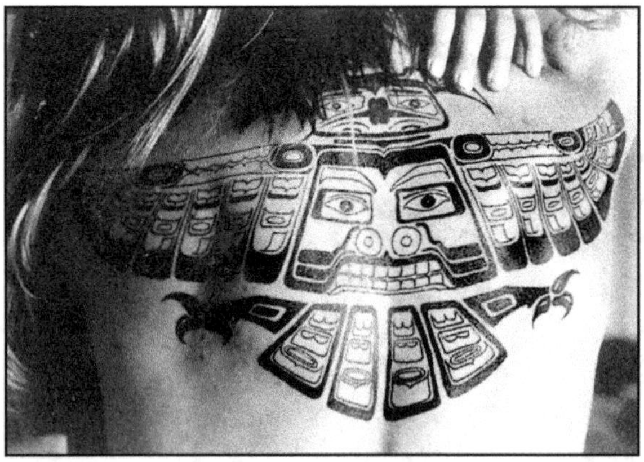

A tattoo by Hanky Panky on a member of Red Hot Chili Peppers. Photo by Patricia Steur.

When you really start digging into this stuff, you don't want to go on vacation anymore. I can't go and sit somewhere on the beach for a week; if I'm going to go somewhere, I have to see tattooing.

I always think tattoos are for subculture...Modern day warriors. I like tattoos when they belong to a certain clan. I like the Hells Angel tattoos, or the punk tattoos, which belong to a certain group, which is actually the same thing: the new tribes. And I like them to be bold and strong and black. No fancy coloring. Maybe it's because as a kid I used to make just pen and pencil drawings; I would never get into any color stuff. I still like to make 'em black, and with a bold outline, like five-needle outline—that's a strong outline. So that when a guy's standing across the street you can see what type of tattoo he has and what he represents, and it doesn't look like he just fell into the mud. Whereas some of that fine-line water-shading, if somebody stands across the street they think, "What the fuck's going on with him?" I mean, the guy has black arms, and when you get closer you see it's all that pointillist realism—very well done, but I don't know how this stuff will look in ten years...

Also, those tribal tattoos were developments. They probably developed almost the same way that modern art developed; out of something which is pretty realistic into something more abstract; a symbol, and the symbol would represent the old sketching. Because these people were not stupid; they could draw a scorpion realistically; that was no problem to them. But they adjusted the technique. And to me, all that photo-realist fine-line crap has nothing to do with tattooing. A tattoo should be a *strong*, recognizable thing. I mean, here you are in the goddam bushes and some guy's coming from that way, and you are over here, and he's ten meters away, and if you recognize him from his tattoo, you go, "Yeah! You're from the friendly tribe!" otherwise you throw your spear into his chest or shoot a dart in him. I mean—that was pretty important! You need symbols—strong symbols which will stand on their own and tell immediately something about the guy.

■ *AJ: Who did your tattoos?*

■ HP: Bob Roberts. And Ed Hardy—Ed did the roll of film on my arm. Lots of different people—I collect them. Morbella, who used to work for me, is a bullfighter in Mexico now—she did the skulls. She's having her first fight soon, I think. There's a Dutch saying, "Whatever she has in mind, she doesn't have in her asshole!" I mean whatever she focuses on, that's what she does. She's real critical about her work. Even the last tattoo she made, she still didn't like it after awhile; she wanted to improve and improve and do it different, which is a very good attitude when it comes to tattooing, because most of these artists are very happy with whatever they're doing—too happy, you know? "Oh, I'm such a good drawer, and I'm such a fine artist!" which in art, don't exist, a least in real art. The greatest painters were cutting up their paintings, because they didn't believe in them anymore. And she was a good drawer when she came in, with this big pile of flash drawn up already. So I thought, "Well, that's the one."

■ *AJ: But then she just became a bullfighter?*

■ HP: All of a sudden she wants to become a bullfighter, and that's what she's doing now. She's training every day. I hear she bought a couple of bulls. She'll be the first heavily tattooed female bullfighter in Mexico! I think she's doing well, because normally that's not something you can pick up quick. It's something your father arranges for you, and it's not just killing a bull, it's this whole dance with all this history behind every movement. If you just go in there and slaughter the bull, they will slaughter you! There has to be certain gracious movements.

■ *V: Why don't you give us a brief summary of your tattoo odysseys around the world, especially your encounters with hand tattooers?*

Hanky Panky at work.

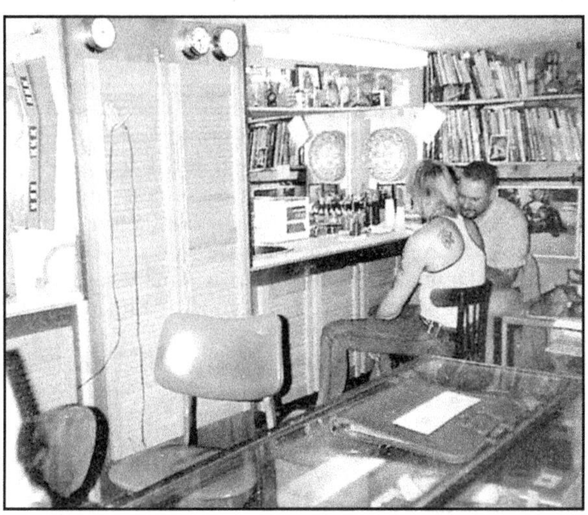

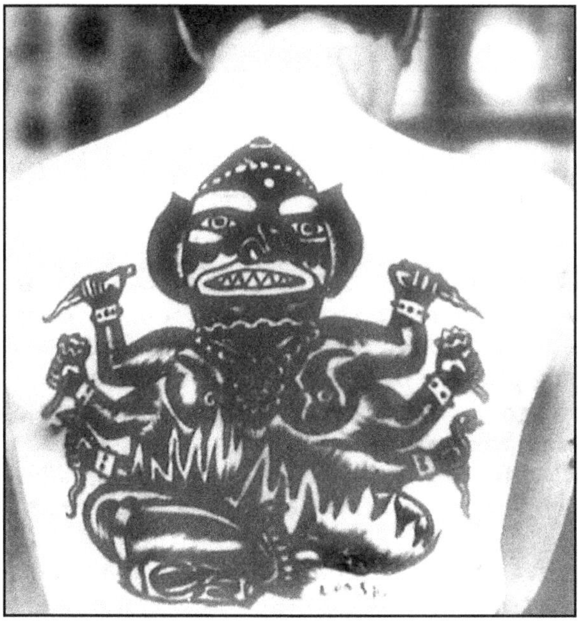

Tattoo by Les Skuse. Courtesy of Hanky Panky.

■ HP: Well, it looks like a big thing but it ain't. You're in this country and all of a sudden the guy who's selling flowers in the bar behind the hookers in Bangkok has a couple of tattoos, and it's the old hand style. Hands and feet are the language: "Me" "You" "Go" "You take me tomorrow" and the next day you're in this place, the guy makes tattoos, you're looking around, and you're trying to communicate with the guy who don't speak anything but Thai, and you speak bar talk-Thai. And you can maybe order a beer and call a taxi and say, "Thank you," and this is very hilarious and they like that because you speak Thai, and you get a tattoo. I got this one tattoo and I kept asking the guy, "Well, what does it mean?" He kept saying, "Yah, very good, number one! Very good! and I finally said, "Oh, okay, never mind—who gives a fuck! Let's just put the thing on!"
■ *V: Tell us a little about Les Skuse.*
■ HP: In those days you had Sailor Jerry, Les Skuse, Christian Warlich, Ole Hansen, Tattoo Peter—these were guys who were connected with each other. They would write letters to each other and tell each other about techniques. Skuse was from Bristol. For the first time these guys would go see each other. Before that you had to go on a boat, and it would be a 3 or 4 week trip, but now you could fly. The world became smaller and smaller so all these guys started seeing each other. Most of these designs you can trace back to one guy. A sailor's grave and the Hawaiian girls are all from Sailor Jerry and Christian Warlich; it all boils down to 2 or 3 great artists around the world.
■ *V: Pinky Yun?*
■ HP: He's not really one of the old ones, but Pinky—you still see a lot of Western traditional tattoos with a little Mt. Fuji in the back. It was Pinky who started doing that, and a lot of people began copying that.

I put my first tattoo on a Hells Angel—that's one of the best ways to start because you've got a critical client. You don't want to fuck up with him!

And then it became normal to have a Mt. Fuji in the back of a geisha girl. Sailor Jerry did that, too.
■ *V: This is the forties, fifties?*
■ HP: Yeah, before that they probably did a bit of letter-writing. Les Skuse actually went to the States to a tattoo convention in the fifties (I think '56). They would have a tattoo convention at somebody's house in the garden like with 20 guys and they would all have no shirt on and the whole neighborhood would be peeking out of the windows wondering what was going on. There would be beer drinking and maybe a bit of barbecue or whatever. That's probably how all these clubs started, like the Bristol Tattoo Club, a pretty well-known tattoo society in England. There's an old picture of Huck Spaulding as a skinny young man coming over to have a look, and Paul Rogers who's still a young man.
■ *V: It'd be neat to have a flow chart showing who influenced who.*
■ HP: That's an awful lot of work!
■ *AJ: Was Les Skuse one of the first to get into New Tribalism?*
■ HP: I don't know; I just found these photos and I thought, "Jesus Christ, what's happening here?" I mean, that was a wild tattoo on the girl. He wasn't a great drawer; I've got stuff on him that shows exactly how he worked. If he had a *Tarzan* comic book from those days and Tarzan was holding Jane because he'd just dragged her away from a real wild tribe that were going to eat her or boil her; if he was walking with this unconscious Jane he would take that drawing and trace the whole girl and change Tarzan into the devil with two wings and have a tattoo design! That's how he was working. He probably got this one out of a *Tarzan* comic book.

I went to the lowlands of Nepal called terai (low-lying jungle) which is closer to the Indian border. One of the things you can do there is to go and watch rhinoceroses from an elephant. I'm sitting on an elephant and all these people are laughing and sort of giggling. Later, somebody told me, "Well, they all think you're gay, because you've got tattoos, and here only the females get tattooed." [laughs]
■ *AJ: Is your wife tattooed?*
■ HP: She has three tattoos; two from Dan Thome.
■ *AJ: Any from you?*
■ HP: No. I have this theory that you shouldn't tattoo your own wife, just like a surgeon won't cut his own kids. If you start tattooing your own wife, you'll probably get so carried away that she's going to be, like, completely tattooed in no time, so it's better for her to get one from this guy, and one from that guy. Dan put two tattoos on Patricia, and Bob Roberts put one on her, but...you want to stay away from tattooing your old lady!

CHARLIE CARTWRIGHT

Originally from Wichita, Kansas, Charlie Cartwright started tattooing as a teenager over 25 years ago. After an apprenticeship in Long Beach, he opened up Goodtime Charlie's Tattooland in East Los Angeles in 1973. He was a pioneer of fine-line, single-needle tattooing in the freehand style, first tracing the design on the skin with a blue Bic pen. The technique is slower than with the conventional tattoo gun which uses as many as five needles, but the artistry can be far more detailed. As he put it, "If you're sacrificing quality for the sake of speed, then your motives are all wrong as far as I'm concerned. I don't care how many's waiting—they can just *wait*."

Charlie returned to Wichita for awhile, but moved back to California to restart his End of the Trail Tattoo Studio at 520 McHenry, Modesto, CA 95354 (209-524-9936). Interview by V. Vale.

■ *VALE: Why do you think people get tattooed?*

■ CHARLIE CARTWRIGHT: I would think the primary reason for being tattooed in today's society is: it's an attempt to present yourself as an *individual.* And in the mere attempt to express your individuality, you're probably, by the subject matter, following after tradition!

■ *V: Do you mean the tradition of the "rugged American individualist"?*

I personally think everyone should be tattooed simply for the experience itself; to just be in touch with primal origins. People should do it for experience's sake only, if nothing else!

■ CC: No, I mean the traditional subject matter of tattooing. People like the skinheads and the punks get off into more tribal-origin activities than the general public, but I think in spite of the fact that most people do tattoo themselves to express individuality, they fall back into the same old trap, because they'll get something that their brother had or their dad had, and therefore they're just carrying on the tradition, so to speak. People may do it just to be a "rebel" of sorts, but I don't find that *that* many of them are extremely different! It seems to amount to: the more things change, the more they stay the same…

I do think some people do it strictly for identification purposes, especially if it's just a one-time thing. But I suspect there's a narcissistic streak in each one of us that is tattooed: just to see and be seen. And while all of this may seem like Vanity of Vanities, I personally think that everyone *should* be tattooed simply for the experience itself; to just be in touch with primal origins. People should do it for experience's sake only, if nothing else! There could be anything from religious reasons to the exhibitionistic drive, but for whatever reasons people do get tattooed, I feel not enough of them do! And I don't know what we can do to change it.

Only a certain percentage of people are ever going to be tattooed, for any number of reasons, and I think it's a shame. But I know it's still considered a taboo with the world in general—the Western world.

Oddly enough, nearly all cultures have tattooed *except* the Western world, and I think that's crazy in itself. Virtually all the American Indian tribes prior to 1750 were really into tattooing. Then the missionary

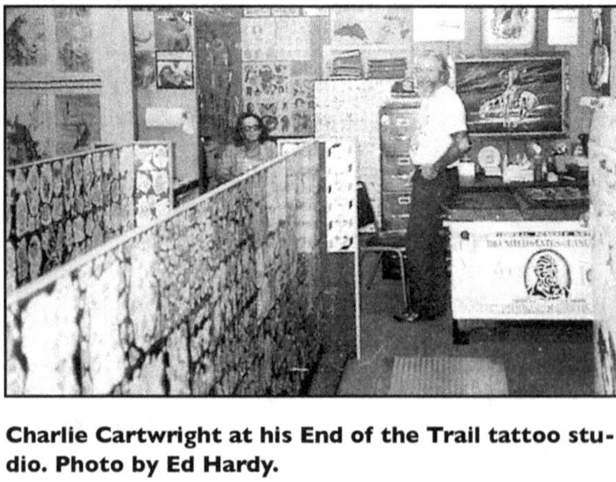

Charlie Cartwright at his End of the Trail tattoo studio. Photo by Ed Hardy.

efforts of the White Man stamped that out as being "pagan," etc. But then—here it comes again, back across the waters from Europe on the sailors who start the revival all over again. The Red Man must think we're *nuts!* They're probably thinking, "You guys told us to cut it out, and now, because you're doing it in a little bit different fashion, it's okay!"

I really appreciate the American Indians' ideas which were quite simplistic in their application, but they still accented the body so intriguingly. Ideally, I'm almost above pictures now; I've reverted back to the primal. I'm back to just appreciating the marks—the patterns or the geometric shapes.

■ *V: You mentioned narcissism—a pejorative term in this society, but that's probably due to Christian guilt. A certain amount of pride in one's self is beneficial.*

■ CC: Yeah, people primp with hair, clothing, make-up and whatever they can think of. My own philosophy of tattooing in a nutshell is: *I believe in decorating your teepee while you're living in it.* After all, people paint their cars, houses, and everything else!

■ *V: The teepee covering the soul.*

■ CC: The natural body is such a temporal thing—why *wouldn't* you? It's not eternal in itself. So I just advocate being decorated while you're around; you've got such few years to really make an impact in this world. Not that the visual appearance is going to be the salvation of anyone's soul, but I do think that for whatever reasons people choose to decorate themselves, they should just by all means do so.

And it could be the copycat syndrome. [laughs] In just the rock world itself, any of these stars or entertainers who get a tattoo must instigate *thousands* of other tattoos being gotten by the general public, simply because of their admiration for that person. And virtually every tattoo magazine that is produced and hits the stands—whether it be good, bad or ugly work that's in it—*someone* identifies with it and just has to have that particular picture put on them. So you've got the motivation of *visual appeal*—because of the subject matter or the location or whatever. And the public may not have seen that particular design before, but now that they've been exposed to it, it's the big brainstorm: "Hey, that's ME!"

■ *V: What do you favor now? Black work—work that's been inspired by anthropology books?*

■ CC: Well, that's my personal preference, although I don't get a chance to do much of that. I'm learning to appreciate more and more the simplicity of the primal mind.

■ *V: What do you mean by "primal"?*

■ CC: Well, going back to the roots or the basics of the primitive peoples—their ideas about the markings and patterns and symbols they would put on people. Just recently I read a book produced in 1883 by the U.S. Govt. Bureau of American Indian Ethnology. It contained a study of tattooing practices among the American natives, and described a Northwest Indian in his early forties who had circular bands of black roughly 1/2" to 5/8" of an inch wide circling his entire right arm and his entire right leg, with an equal amount of flesh between each black band. And starting in the middle of the chest to the middle of the back, also only on the right side, were those same black bands that just went from the center point in the front to the center point in the back. I suppose that when his arm was hanging down, the bands lined up with each other.

I thought, "WOW! This guy was cool." Because he had a dark side and a light side, and had a perfect balance between the "natural" flesh and the "artistic" black. I thought, "If I could do it all over again, I'd be tattooed that way." Maybe not with the black bands; I'd probably have a lightning pattern, with flesh and black lightning so you'd look totally electric! It would be so radical—a powerful look, coming in at a diagonal from above, perhaps, with both arms the same way. So when I read this study, I thought, "This man was on top of things over a hundred years ago!" We think we invent *cool* every day, but these people were in touch with things every bit as cool as we could *ever* imagine.

■ *V: And who knows what's been lost.*

■ CC: Right, They were in touch with—well, we can call them *powers of darkness*, or whatever we imagine to be offbeat. But their thoughts were so spiritual in so many ways that I think they might have been more in touch with reality than we are.

■ *V: Or with what really matters in life.*

■ CC: Yeah. And we might think of it as being quite *Satanic*, when in reality it was just being *spiritual* in all things. We tend to group a lot of things together (that don't quite line up) with our idea of Christianity,

Tattoo by Charlie Cartwright.

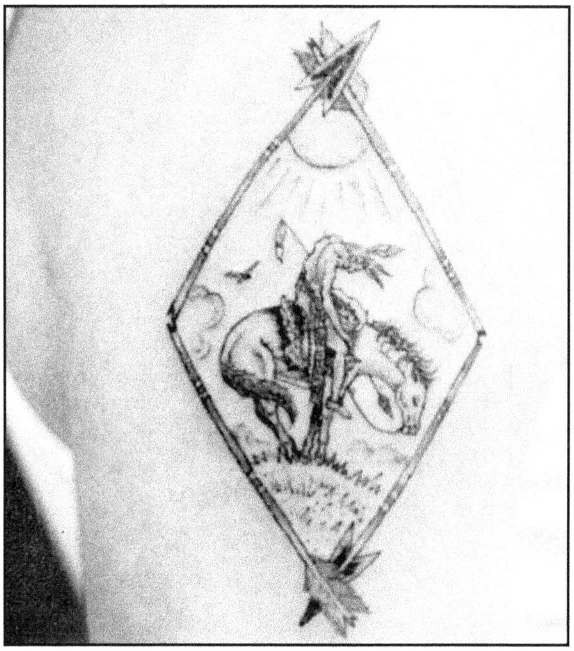

and other things we consider as "The Other Side" or from the "Other Realm" we call *Satanic* or Witchcraft or *evil,* period. And in our attempt to be "spiritual" we're probably as far away from that as we could be. Whereas those "primitive" peoples just accepted things in a more beautiful, simple manner; they didn't really struggle with all these Puritanical values and other guilt-baggage. We don't give them credit for having much on the ball, but I think they probably had more on the ball than we do, when you get down to the bottom line in lots of ways: the simplicities of life. I was always amazed and fascinated with them. The way they decorated themselves probably did have religious connotations, or was done for protection or to enhance bravery, or for a host of other reasons.

■ *V: Are there any other tattoos that strongly impressed you?*

■ CC: Well, that's the only one that hit me *recently.* I was impressed with the Wichita Indians—the women were more tattooed than the men, done pretty much from the waist up (they were all bare-breasted, of course), and wore circular designs accenting their breasts. And very much like the Pacific Northwest and Alaskan Indians, tattooed their chins—well, the New Zealand Maoris did that, as well as the Ainus. So, the Wichita women accented their lips and chin with tattooing, as well as their upper torso with very *nifty-looking* dot-dash patterns and other designs. I've heard that the word "Wichita" originally meant "Tattooed People," but I've also heard that it meant "Dwellers in Grass Lodges," so who really knows? Probably some Wichitan that's 300 years old really knows the truth!

■ *V: Do you think they also used tattooing in the souvenir function: to help them remember peak experiences or events?*

■ CC: Some of the Plains Indians painted their robes to commemorate historical events in their lives, and I'm sure they did it on their own personal hides as well. I think Ed Hardy said that with our tattoos, we all wear little pictures that were once inside on the outside. And in spite of any efforts to deny this, I think this is true.

I think you can tell a lot about a person just by reading their skin. They may be trying to present themselves as something they're not, but that's still showing a side of them. The skinny little wimpy guy who gets a big ferocious hideous killer creature on him really wants to be that. Whether or not we produce tattoos with a realistic approach, they're still a fantasy. I'm convinced that's probably the most appealing aspect of the tattoo: you can have anything you want there, literally. You can tell lies (if you want to) on your skin; fake everybody out (or try to fake 'em out). You can either be a man or wish you were a man! [laughs] And maybe you can project something so huge and universal and visionary that it takes the rest of your life to live up to it. But that's all you got left, any way!

GREG KULZ

Greg Kulz is a San Francisco-based tattoo artist currently working at Erno's Studio, 252 Fillmore St, SF 94117; tel (415) 861-9206. Interview by V. Vale.

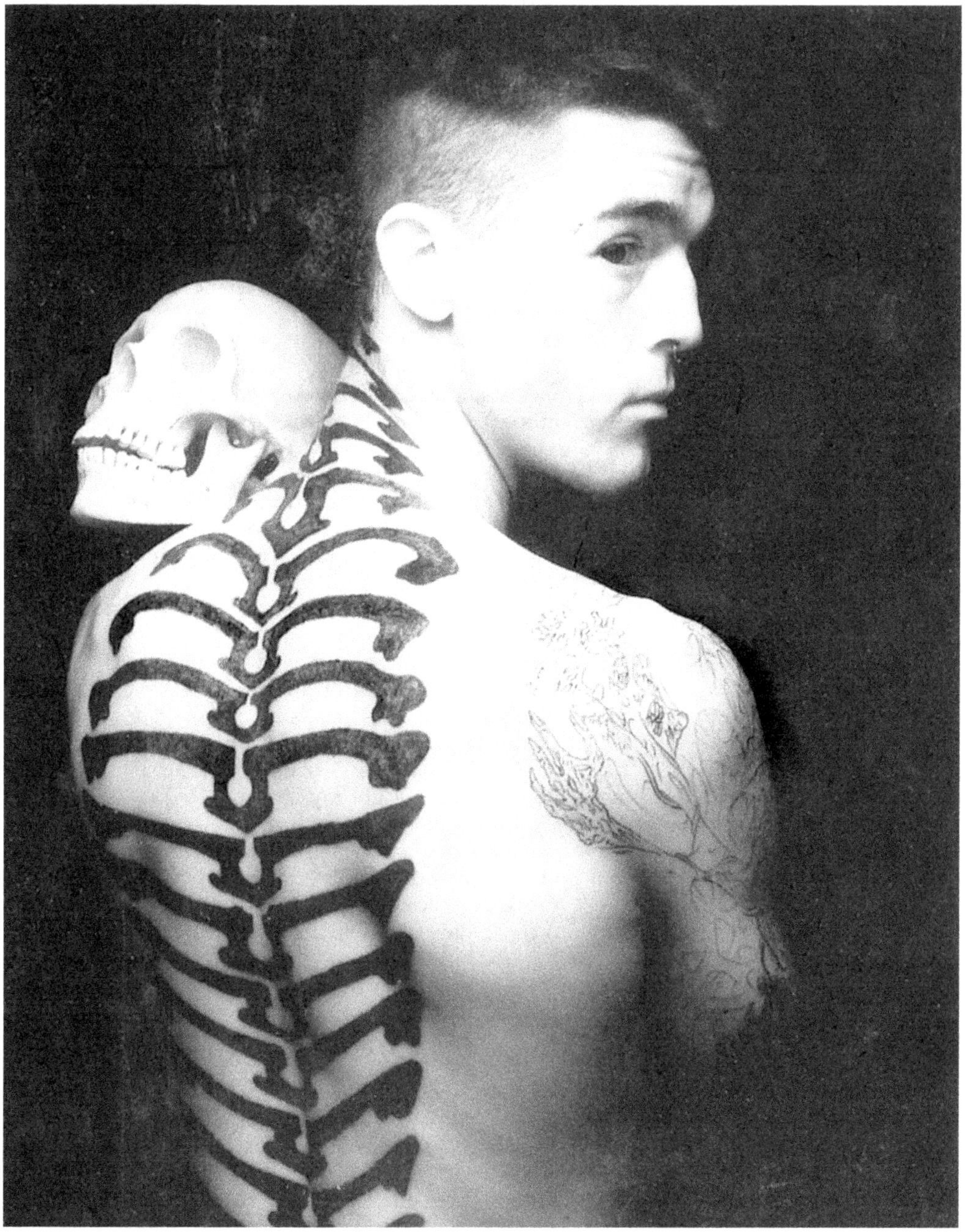

Photo by Bobby Neel Adams.

■ *VALE: Where do you think the impulse for body alternation comes from?*

■ GREG KULZ: People want to *have control* over their body. Even if you can't control the external environment, you can start by controlling your *internal* environment. You can get a permanent mark or marks that no one else has a say in *at all.* Then these modifications can start affecting your external environment, because people look at them and react—even if they throw rocks!

Tattooing is a visual expression and tends to spring more from an intuitive process then a carefully rationalized one. Some people come in with only the vaguest of ideas, so my job as a tattooist is to be like a *lens*—take unfocused feelings and desires and produce a concise design that will make them happy. Since I have an art background—my father is a painter; I went to art school and read fairly widely—I can offer a pretty broad perspective as to the portrayal of different ideal.

Recently I started doing fingernail tattoos—they were first done in the '60s. Technically this could be called tattooing, because it's done with a tattoo gun; in a way it's like scrimshaw. If someone doesn't want to commit to a tattoo, they can start with this—it lasts about as long as a haircut! It's just like working on skin except I'm not breaking any surface. To chisel it into the nail I just turn the speed 'way down. The trick is to produce a tiny design that's imaginative.

■ *V: Your skull designs worked well.*

■ GK: The way I shaded them filled up the fingernail space in kind of a satisfying, credible way. That's the way tattooing in general should work!

People want to have control over their body. Even if you can't control the external environment, you can start by controlling your internal environment.

■ *V: Why did you start tattooing?*

■ GK: I was always interested in getting visual ideas across. I worked as a painter, sculptor, and cartoonist. But there was always a third party responsible for getting your ideas to the people who will see them. This third part—galleries, publishers, people who take accounting classes—don't necessarily have your best interests at heart. Ten percent of people alive today have never been in an art gallery, but everyone's seen a tattoo.

Plus, tattooing is more *personal.* In an art gallery there's an uptight atmosphere—you're trying not to spill your drink, or trying to pick up some girl, and there are people watching to make sure you don't get too close to a painting or touch a sculpture. But art isn't really like something in a fishbowl that you put in a tower—it's all around you; you interact with it and it's part of things.

■ *V: Since Duchamp the concept of "art" has been blown wide-open. I recently saw Captain Don swallow swords and that certainly qualifies—*

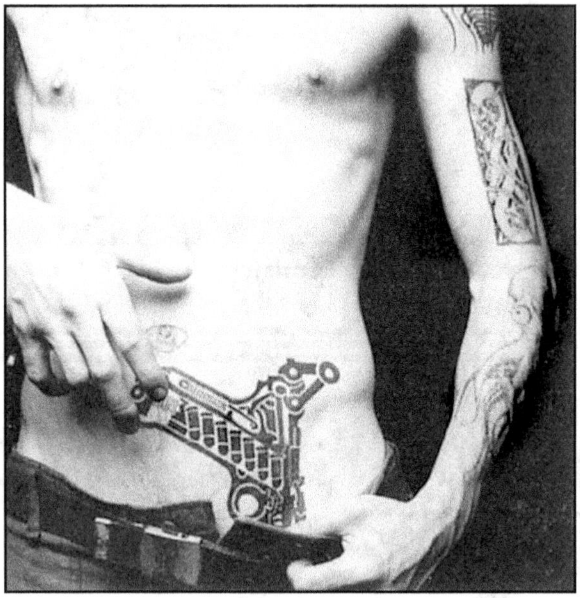

Photo by Bobby Neel Adams

■ GK: Captain Don has an act he calls the "sword sandwich."

■ *V: What's that?*

■ GK: He swallows two swords at once...then pulls them out and they're covered with white tracheal mucus. He'll ask, "You know what that is, don't you? That's the mayonnaise!"

■ *V: What a character.*

■ GK: Yeah, he's definitely on the cutting edge...People would probably rather look at other people than anything else. My tattoos have a more limited audience than a painting in a museum, but they're viewed with much more care and intimacy—they *emote;* they're alive and breathing and they talk back!

■ *V: So how did you start out?*

■ GK: Well, the tattoo business doesn't exactly welcome newcomers—there's an excess of people working, and most of them are terrible and have personality disorders—not to say that I *don't,* but I try to keep mine in check. I got my first tattoo when I was 18; I did it myself: a "666" in a circle on my shin. (I don't like fake Satanic heavy metal bands, however.) Then I did my punk rock tattoo: a safety pin going through the knee, because my pants would always be ripped there. I did it because I had a desire to be tattooed, but had little funds.

I had been drawing for awhile and had basic graphic skills when Ed Hardy lent me my first real tattoo tool. He was giving a lecture on the history of Japanese art at the SF Art Institute, and my friend Bill, who has a lot of my first tattoo attempts (Celtic designs, a man with a briefcase, a combination atom bomb/yin-yang symbol on the back of his head, etc) was in the class. These were hand tattoos done with my early home-made rigs: basically a pencil with needles stuck in the eraser, plus india ink. After this lecture Bill and I went to see Ed, and I made an appointment to get a tattoo from him which (with Ed's busy schedule) meant waiting a year. During that year I worked really hard. After I got tattooed, Ed gave me the tool.

The design Ed did was on my right forearm: it's basically some distilling pipes and tubettes, with a breathing bag (like in surgery) which I can pump up so it looks like it's breathing. [demonstrates] Ed showed me basic sterilization; told me to power my rig with a car battery, and warned me not to "dilute the market." The quality of the machine he lent me was of course far better than one from, say, an ad in *Easy Rider*...I've done that, and I've learned! But the best machines are ones you make yourself, because you know exactly what you want. However, my energies have been directed more towards the designs and graphics themselves rather than tinkering with machines...A tattoo machine is pretty simple, just like a violin! [laughs] A 77-year-old tattoo artist named Paul Rogers said he's still experimenting, trying to improve his tattoo machines.

Previously, I experimented making other rigs using a record player motor or motors from tape recorders, a Bic pen, and an "E" string from a guitar. Even if you only have a primitive rig, if your concept and drawing is together, you can do a lot—I did this Celtic piece [from the *Book of Kells*] on my left bicep using primitive hand tools. The edge is framed by the vein along my arm.

■ *V: I like tattoos that take advantage of body topography—*

■ GK: Like this: [whirls right arm furiously, then shows forearm where the veins stand out and articulate the design itself in *3-D!*] I have a large skeletal back design now, but earlier I had a smaller "bone" design on the back of my neck. I went out dancing the night I got it, because I was really "psyched-up," and my sweat irritated the fresh tattoo and got it very infected [distressed look]: "Oh god, my *tattoo!*" I had to have it redone.

A painting isn't just a two-dimensional surface with a funnel attached to your eyes; it's the whole room, the air you're breathing, and the creepy people next to you making pretentious comments. Equally, the tattoo isn't just a decal on my back, but it does certain things.

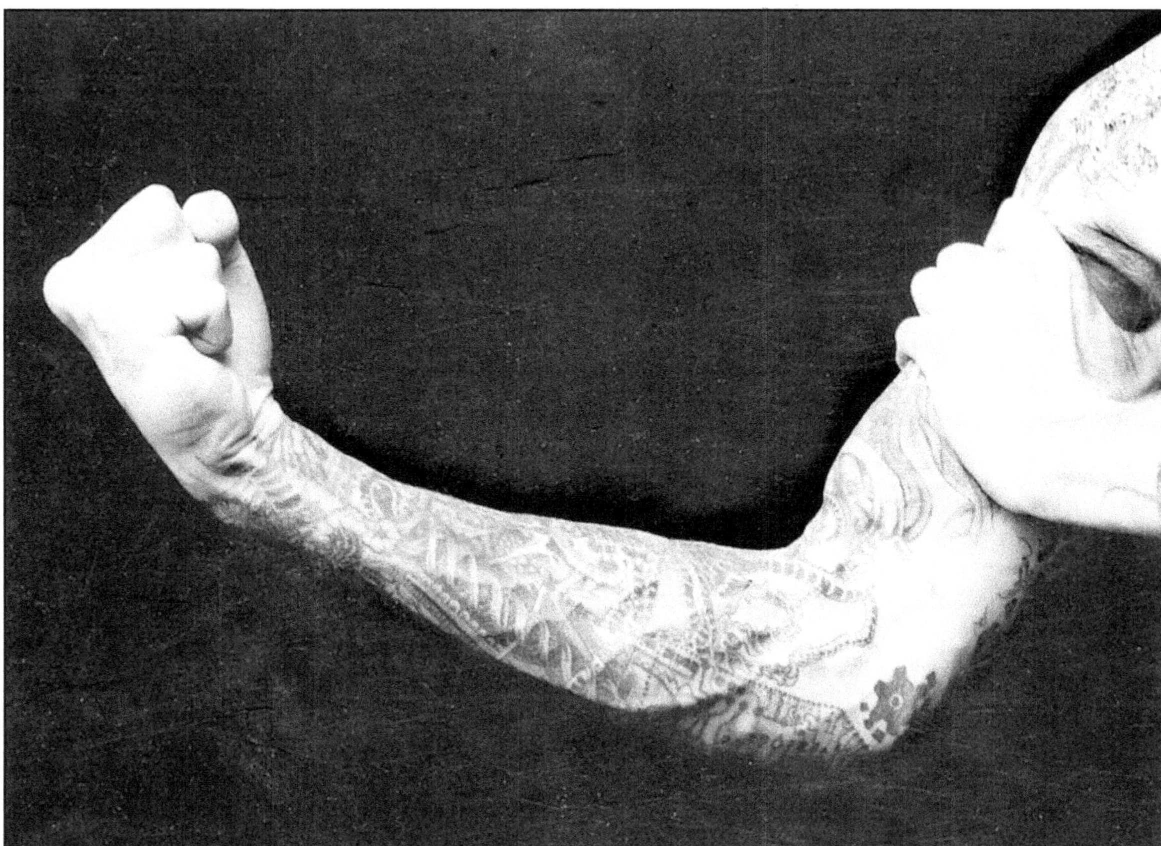

Greg Kulz's arm. Photo by Bobby Neel Adams.

So, even though you might not feel like it, after you get a tattoo it's best to take it easy, stay out of the sun, and avoid getting anything on the tattoo. Sweat contains salt, toxins, uric acid…and if you take in weird drugs and shitty foods, that'll come out of your skin and affect your tattoo—you can get a staph infection. And if the design's in a place that bends, it'll be harder to heal.

■ *V: I have nothing against "flash" books, but isn't the idea for everyone to get a tattoo that's never been in the world before?*

■ GK: Absolutely—that's what I would prefer. My flash books are more just examples of what's possible, so people can see it and say, "Well I don't like that; I want something more like this."

■ *V: A lot of people are now collecting things like animal bones and skulls, minerals and crystals, reptiles and arachnids, besides getting piercings and "primitive"-style tattoos. I think a lot of the inspiration came from movies like* Mad Max II *and* The Hills Have Eyes. *Now you can go into upscale stores and buy bone sculptures just like in* The Texas Chainsaw Massacre *[1973] and charge them to your* Visa *card!*

■ GK: Probably it all stems from the same urge you had as a kid when you played with frogs or kept spiders in a jar. People are going for the *extreme experience*—whatever's accepted becomes boring, so you have to have something new. Eventually even dead things will seem tame, so people will have live animals tied on them—

■ *V: Like that fad in the '50s for going around with a chameleon chained to your sweater. In Mexico you can still buy live beetles inlaid with semi-precious stones which you can wear like jewelry.*

■ GK: One nice thing about getting a tattoo of bones is—it will never become dated or invalid. I must admit, I find Americans who get traditional Japanese full body suits a little strange. They're beautiful, and I've been inspired by them, but the imagery isn't totally valid for my mythology. My history of tattooing is more from the graphic style in comic books and horror movies, which is what I grew up with.

I did a squid on a girl's instep with the tentacles reaching down to each of her toes, so when she wiggled her toes the squid would come to life.

The *context* is important. A painting isn't just a two-dimensional surface with a funnel attached to your eyes; it's the whole room, the air you're breathing, and the creepy people next to you making pretentious comments. Equally, the tattoo isn't just a decal on my back, but it *does* certain things. When I was designing a zebra pattern on my friend Hilary Cross's leg, I tried to follow the musculature so that when she bent her leg, the design twisted out to look like a nautilus. I strive for *enhancement,* rather than just imposing some random overlay.

If I'm dealing with an arm, I like to deal with the *circumference,* not just design a flat surface. I guess eventually you'll get traveling teams of yogis who, when they contort and stand on their heads, will form a mural…

I did a squid on a girl's instep with the tentacles reaching down to each of her toes, so when she wiggled her toes the squid would come to life. It's definitely important to see designs in perspective, figuring in movement and musculature. From my study in karate I'm acquiring a rudimentary knowledge of meridians, and I do try to keep acupuncture points in mind, to some degree. Once when I had bronchitis I was getting a tattoo at my lung meridian, and it went away! I tattooed a person who was studying acupuncture, and he asked for a Mayan dragon spiraling out from a point on his leg that he wanted to strengthen. I think there's a lot of potential in that idea. It's well known that when people get tattooed, their endorphins start flowing…

■ *V: Have you tattooed any faces?*

■ GK: I've tattooed quite a few heads, although I try to avoid the "novelty" effects. One of the nicer facial tattoos I saw was in a video by Charles Gatewood; it was a black tribal sperm as an eyebrow. Let's see—I did a bullet hole, with blood dripping out, on the head of a skinhead named Beau—that bothered a lot of people. I also tattooed "Don't Fuckin' Touch Me" on the back of his shoulder, and one block right away after I did it, he got stabbed by some wino. Life is full of irony—I saw an article in *Easy Rider* on tattoos and death which showed a photo of "Hot Stuff" next to a 3rd degree burn, and "Live to Ride" on a dead biker—part of it's ground away from a road burn…

I tattooed a guy named Crazy Horse with a skull on his head, with two teeth going down his forehead, and tubes and snakes going around his ears. Then I started the outline of a monster on his neck holding on to each one of his sterno-mastoids and biting onto his adam's apple, but unfortunately he disappeared before I could finish it.

■ *V: Do head tattoos hurt more than other ones?*

■ GK: I don't think so. In general, tattooing is stressful and it's best to be in good health before you have it done. Probably one of out of twenty people feel woozy when they first get a tattoo—usually it's just shock caused by anxiety. They break out into a cold sweat, their eyes get glassy, and they feel nauseous. If you're not careful, they may throw up. I've learned to recognize the early warning signs—generally people just get over it, get their tattoo and they're fine. Some people build up a lot of anxiety beforehand: "Can I take it? Don't want him to think I'm a wimp!" Then it happens, and it's not so bad, and they relax…

■ *V: Why did you get pierced?*

■ GK: I'd seen *National Geographic* magazines growing up, but when I saw Dan Thome's ear piercings, I decided to get one—I liked the idea of one large hole in the ear. I used to have a Mohawk and a *lot* of earrings,

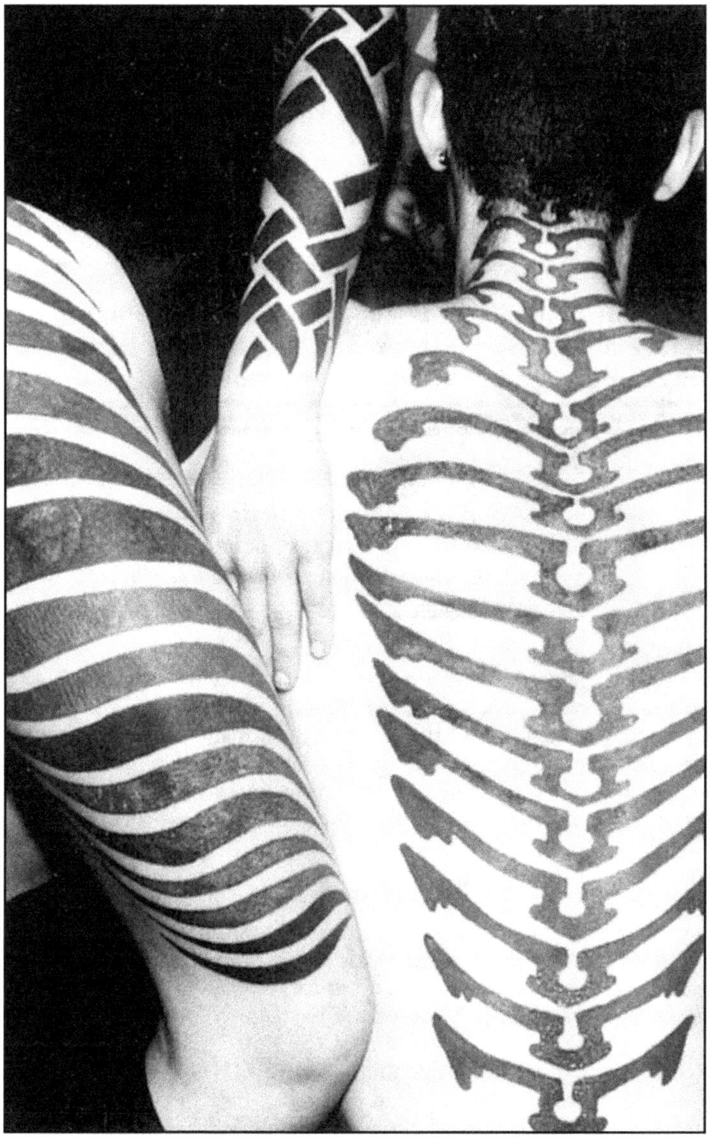

Hilary Cross and Greg Kulz. Photo by Charles Gatewood.

but I do karate and they got in the way, so I got rid of 'em. I saw a book on the people of Papau, New Guinea who all had cowbones and pieces of grass though their nose, and the book said these kept away evil spirits. I never liked evil spirits too much, so I figured I'd get a nose ring. I put crushed ice on my nose, stuck a carrot up one nostril (I couldn't fit a potato), put a safety pin through the thin part of the septum, avoiding the cartilage, and it worked!

■ *V: There's a lot more girls getting tattooed now.*

■ GK: It's now able to be seen as a decorative art, rather than a macho *brand* ("I withstood it!"). And more artistic people are involved who can produce subtler, more ingenious designs. Social stigmas are disintegrating—the influence of Christianity is waning as it becomes more and more obviously *absurd* to more people. All those outdated, rigid cultural prohibitions are dissolving into dust...

HEATHER **M**CDONALD

Heather McDonald is a photographer and designer of post-'60s dress creations in paper and plastic (see her article in *Pop Void #1* edited by Jim Morton). She lived in Japan for several years as a denizen of the yakuza underworld. Interview by V. Vale.

■ *VALE: Tell us about the yakuza.*

■ HEATHER McDONALD: They're the Japanese mafia, who often have beautiful tattoos all over their bodies. Supposedly that originated as a means of guarding against would-be infiltrators or informers. Generally parts of their fingers are missing, because over the years they chop them off, knuckle by knuckle, for various transgressions committed. They have to do this in front of their boss, and show no pain.

Men who have been in the yakuza often go to prison for various reasons—these are the lower class that take the fall for their boss. And in prison they do these penile implants—take a pearl and insert it under the skin of their penis for every year they've been in jail. They carve down a chopstick or toothbrush to a very sharp point, split the skin open about 1/4" wide (anywhere from about 1/2" below the head to about 1/2" above the base), lift the skin up and away, insert the pearl, and then bandage it so the skin heals over and the area resembles a really big wart! I'd say each wart was about 1/3" in diameter.

■ *V: Do you know how these customs got started?*

■ HM: I wish I knew! They're really into self-mutilation as a sign of humility and sacrifice. I had a yakuza boyfriend who had 13 pearls in there, and they weren't real small pearls either, they were at least 1/4" in diameter, bigger than a good-sized wart. They went all around—360 degrees around the penis. Mine didn't have any special patterns, but conceivably they could arrange them in their yakuza crest or something.

■ *V: Did the pearls provide a better gripping surface?*

■ HM: Maybe they made it a little bigger, with these lumps all around, but it's kinda *uneven*, you know. You can definitely feel the "warts," but whether it's a plus or not depends on whether you like bumpy rubbers! So they *can* be felt, but I don't think they really make a tremendous difference. From a woman's point of view it's kinda hokey—a kind of silly *machismo*.

■ *V: What was it like: being around the yakuza?*

■ HM: The lower echelons are the colorful ones; they wear the white ties and black shirts and big white

In prison the yakuza do these penile implants-take a pearl and insert it under the skin of their penis for every year they've been in jail.

shoes—the real gangster look. They have the full body suit tattoos with big dragons on the back from neck to ankle, and the tight curly permanent hairdo—oddly enough, the big Buddha at Kamakura also has one. They're really into shooting up speed—they shoot it in their finger before they cut if off. So they're kinda paranoid—you don't even *blink* the wrong way around them.

It might sound glamorous: having a gangster boyfriend, but I thought they were some of the most boring people in the world—they don't have any *culture*. They have no interest in art, or anything at all, except gambling. A lot of them are just country bumpkins that had no way out of their life except to become a yakuza, and they might have even been social outcasts from the group that evolved to take away corpses and cut up leather—part of the underclass in Japan that you never hear about because they're still considered unmentionable. In Japan, it's against Buddhism to eat meat, but people *want* to eat meat and wear leather. They evolved this underclass to slaughter animals and take all the flak for it, so the rest of the society could congratulate themselves on their Buddhist practices! However, the *bosses* are not underclass—they have a lot of right-wing government connections, and reportedly operate on an international level, importing girls from Korea and the Philippines for their nightclubs.

Japan has very strict social registers—they have detective agencies just to check up on people's backgrounds if they apply for a job or want to get married. They have family registers that go *way* back, and you can disown your children just by taking their names off. I think a lot of these men had no choice but to become yakuza.

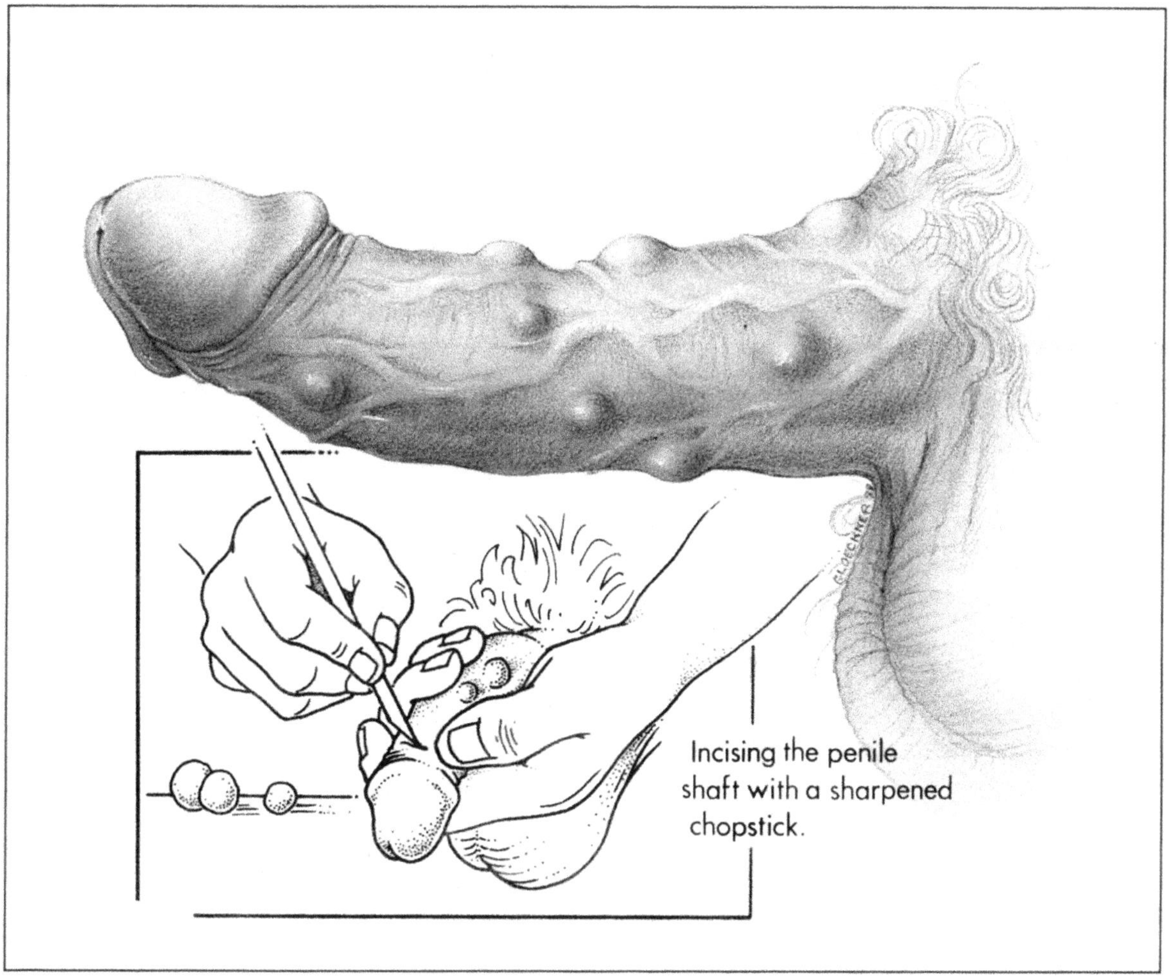

Illustration by Phoebe Gloeckner.

DAVID LEVI STRAUSS

David Levi Strauss is a poet, editor, and freelance critic working in New York. In this essay he examines the history and meaning of the words "modern" and "primitive."

Modern Primitives

by:

David Levi Strauss

The conjugation of these two words—"modern" and "primitive"—is an affront to one of the most basic assumptions of Western Civilization—the assumption of Progress.

It is a savage irony that the English word was actually first used by the Christian Church, to refer to its own "pure" beginnings: "y' primityve churche of Christ."

"Modern" is from the Latin *modernus,* "belonging to the present mode," extended from *mod-us,* "a measure." or *modo,* "just now." Modern has meant "now" since 1500. Jonathan Swift was railing against "modernism" in 1697, against "The corruption of English by those Scribblers, who send us over their trash in Prose & Verse, with abominable curtailings and quaint *modernisms.*" In *A Tale of a Tub* (1704), he wrote, "That his (Mr. Wotton's) Brain hath undergone an unlucky shake; which even his Brother *Modernists* themselves, like Ungrates, do whisper so loud, that it reaches up to the very Garret I am now writing in." The whisper became a roar in the 20th century, and continues as a persistent, indefinable echo. Who was it that said, "Everyone gets the modernisms they deserve"?

"Primitive" means "first": "of or belonging to the first age, period or stage; pertaining to early times; earliest, original." It is a savage irony (in light of later developments) that English word was actually first used by the Christian Church, to refer to its own "pure" beginnings: "y' primityve churche of Christ." In 1628 the word was used in its sense of "original as opposed to derivative, primary as opposed to secondary; esp. said of that from which something else is derived; radical."

It was not really until the beginning of our own century, the century now rushing towards its end, that the term "primitive" began to be used pejoratively, to refer to the appearance and practices of people living outside Western culture. "Primitive" became synonymous with "barbarian," a term which originally meant "anyone not Greek or Roman," and then warped into an evaluative definition as "uncivilized," "crude," "cruel," etc. Other terms that underwent this transformation include "savage" (literally "of the woods") and "native" (literally "native"). It's been said that the word primitive is "probably the first word in which our modern historical sense finds expression."

It was really not until the beginning of our own century that the term "primitive" began to be used pejoratively.

Western Civilization is built on the Ideology of Progress, whereby "mankind is envisaged as having begun its history in ignorance, squalor and fear, and thereafter having risen slowly and continuously to ever-higher levels in the arts and sciences, in its command of environment, and in knowledge generally." (quotation from *The Blackwell Encyclopedia of Political Thought*)

Francis Bacon first used the word "progress" (and "progressive") in the modern sense at the beginning of the 17th century, in the same *Essays* in which he made the distinction between "ancient" and "modern." The idea itself is not strictly modern, but has its roots in the beginnings of Western Civilization, in ancient Greek and Roman and especially early Christian thought. Protagorus, Plato, Zeno, Lucretius and Seneca all wrote of the ascent of humanity from primitivism to ever greater knowledge, sophistication, and *goodness.* Augustine wrapped it up another notch and handed it to Leibniz,

Kant, Hegel, Compte and Karl Marx, but it was when the idea of Progress was wedded to colonialism and to modern imperialism that the Ideology of Progress became a world-class Control mechanism. This ideology posits one unitary and progressive "human race," and a single time frame for "development" for everyone on the planet, with some declared "advanced" and some behind, "underdeveloped." Cultural differences are redefined as differences in "stages of development," with the most developed, most highly evolved culture to be that of Western Europe and Euro-America. The Ideology of Progress has been a blueprint for world-wide destruction of cultural diversity, for historical revisionism, and for eventual world domination by a relatively small "civilized" group.

civilization 1. A condition of human society marked by an advanced stage of development in the arts and sciences and by corresponding social, political, and cultural complexity. 2. Those nations or peoples regarded as having arrived at this stage.

civilize To bring out of a primitive or savage state; educate or enlighten; refine.

It is likely that when the humans first began to make meaningful marks, they made these marks on the surface closest to hand—their own skins—before marking on rocks or other surfaces. So the marking of the human body may well be the definitive *primitive* social act, the first articulation.

Although research in this area is only beginning to be accepted as valid inquiry within academia (see *Marks of Civilization: Artistic Transformations of the Human Body,* Arnold Rubin, ed., 1988), body marking appears to have happened early and often all over the world, even in the West. The Picts and Britons certainly tattooed themselves (in fact, the world "Briton" probably derives from a Breton word meaning "painted in various colors"), as did the Thracians, Dacians and Mosynoechians. Tattoo is one form of body art that actually rewards melanin deficiency.

It is primarily in the Judeo-Christian context that body marking is judged to be transgressive. The Law comes from *Leviticus* 19:28: "You shall not make any cuttings in your flesh on account of the dead or tattoo any marks upon you." This is preceded by injunctions against planting two different kinds of seeds together in one field or trimming your beard, and specific penalties for noncompliance. The death penalty is mandatory for acts of homosexuality, bestiality, incest, adultery, and magic: "A man or a woman who is a medium or a wizard shall be put to death; they shall be stoned with stones, their blood shall be upon them."

In other traditions, permanent and temporary body manipulations are often sacred or magical, and always social. The unmarked body is a raw, inarticulate, mute body. It is only when the body acquires the "marks of civilization" that it begins to communicate and becomes an active part of the social body.

While modern irreversible body manipulation (plastic surgery) tries to hide its traces, to look "natural," traditional techniques make the traces visible, "cultural." Visible traces have come to be taken in Western societies to be signs of deviance, marginality and perversion. With Freud, "...the sphere of primitivism grew to include both children's art and that of psychopaths, that is, the products of the unconscious, the purely instinctual, common to children, madmen, and savages." Western body art is socially stigmatic.

Herodotus used the Greek word [to stick] to refer to Thracian tattooing, and also the word [stigma] to refer to tattoos and brands "showing that the persons so branded were devoted to the service of the temple," but this word was later used primarily to refer to the branding of criminals and slaves. The Nazis tattooed concentration camp detainees, and William F. Buckley recently called for the tattooing of anyone with AIDS. In his book on body marking, Arnold Rubin quotes the Austrian modernist architect Adolf Loos, from a 1908 essay entitled "Ornament and Crime":

The unmarked body is a raw, inarticulate, mute body. It is only when the body acquires the "marks of civilization" that it begins to communicate and becomes an active part of the social body.

"The Papuan tattoos his skin, his boat, his rudder, his oars; in short, everything he can get his hands on. He is no criminal. The modern man who tattoos himself is a criminal or a degenerate. There are prisons in which eighty per cent of the prisoners are tattooed. Tattooed men who are not behind bars are either latent criminals or degenerate aristocrats. If someone who is tattooed dies in freedom, then he does so a few years before he would have committed murder."

Within the Ideology of Progress, cultural diversity is regressive and must be "developed" into homogeneity or, failing that, simply be locked up or snuffed out. As this continues, a vast range of particular, necessary information and knowledge is being lost. The increasing exploration (in one's own body and mind) of these lost "primitive" practices and techniques looks beyond the Ideology of Progress to a possible, syncretic future. That this heresy is gaining momentum now, at the fin de millennium, signals a shift in terms from *progress* to *survival.*

JIM WARD

A pioneer of body play and an early body piercer, Jim Ward designed an early line of piercing jewelry which he proceeded to rigorously field-test, constantly implementing modifications until he was satisfied. In the film *Dances Sacred and Profane* Jim made a guest appearance as Fakir Musafar's collaborator in a ritual. But perhaps his primary cultural contribution was the editing and publishing of *Piercing Fans International Quarterly (PFIQ)*, a glossy, photo-illustrated historical/instructional quarterly that was published until recently. The entire gamut of body piercing (and then some) was explained in clearly written text, diagrams and photographs, both black-and-white and color. Subjects were chosen from around the world, with a particular emphasis on pioneering women involved in piercing and tattoo. Back issues of *PFIQ* are now highly sought after. Jim Ward was interviewed by V. Vale at the Bay Area home of Fakir Musafar.

■ *ANDREA JUNO: When did you first start piercing your body?*

■ JIM WARD: 1968. I was 27, living in New York and had just discovered the leather community. I remember reading an article in *Gentleman's Quarterly* about a man in the Navy who in his many travels had gotten some piercings. I found this *very* interesting; it started me thinking, and I developed a strong fantasy that I wanted to pierce my nipples. Finally I did it, but it was only temporary—I didn't leave anything in. But then I met a man who did have pierced nipples, and realized there was a precedent—that I could make my fantasy more permanent. Shortly after, I re-pierced my nipples, and I've worn something in them ever since.

One of my best customers has over 200 piercings and if you saw him on the street you'd just think he was somebody's grandfather.

■ *VALE: When did you get your first cock piercing?*

■ JW: I moved to Denver, Colorado in the fall of '68—a short-lived love affair lured me there. I stayed there for five years and worked as a picture framer. I did a couple of experimental cock piercings (frenum), but didn't know enough about where to put them, so they healed out. It wasn't until I moved to California that I acquired my other piercings.

■ *AJ: How many piercings do you have?*

■ JW: 13. I don't wear jewelry in most of them. I have a tragus and two ear piercings, a septum and two on the nipples. In the cock I wear the Prince Albert in the frenum all the time; I keep a piece of cord in my guiche. I have about 6 more cock piercings that I don't

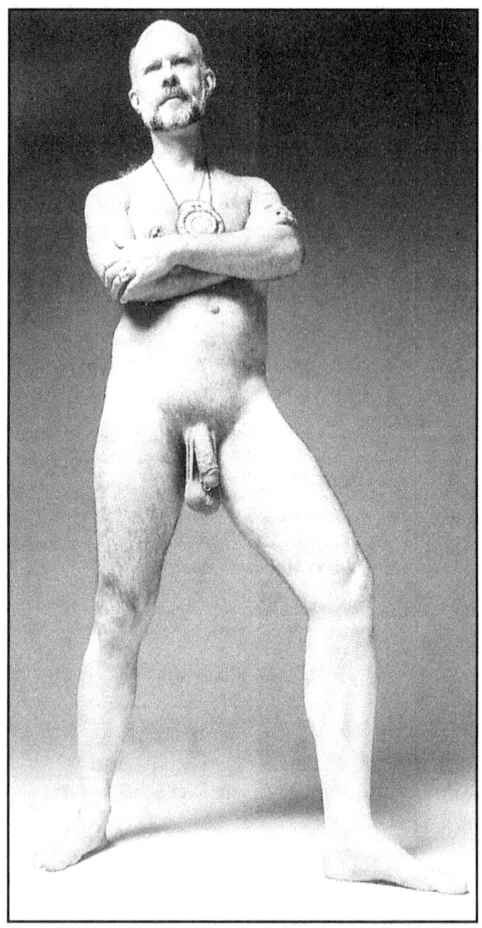

Photo by Bobby Neel Adams.

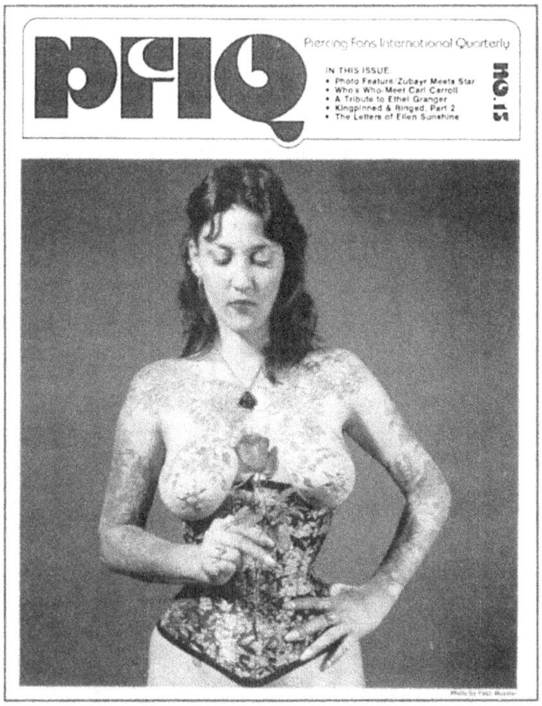

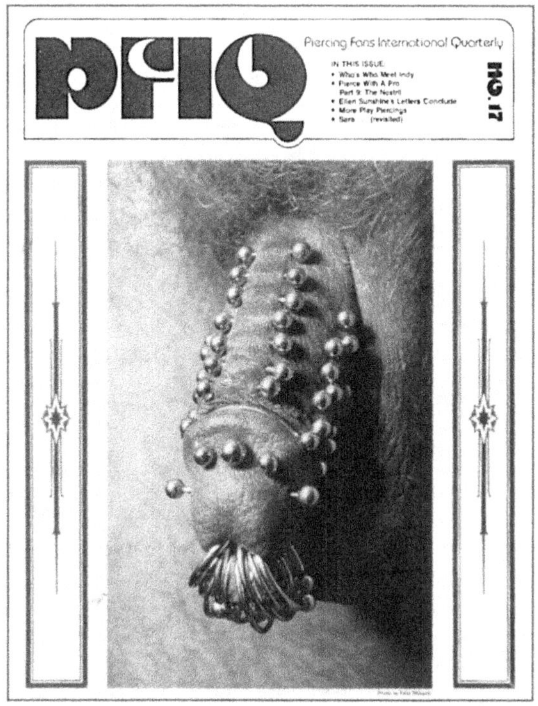

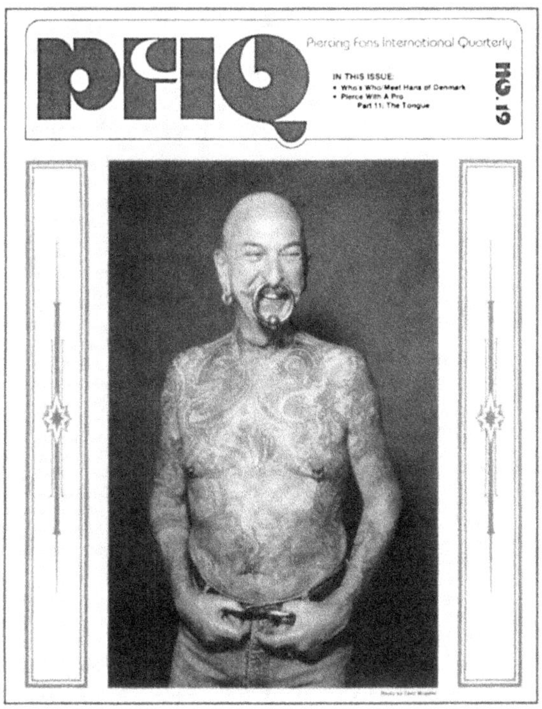

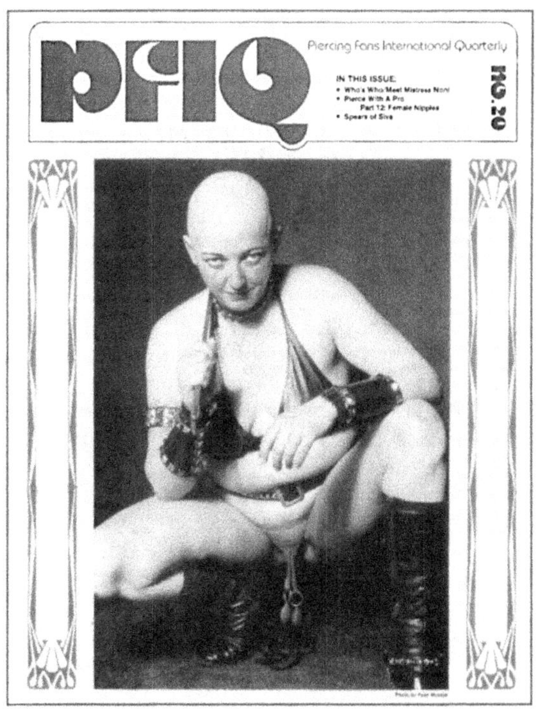

wear anything in, because they didn't work out. The holes are still there, but…

■ *V: What do you mean: "they didn't work out"?*

■ JW: I guess the symmetry didn't work out. For example, I had two dydoes. One of those rejected and healed out, so I took the jewelry out of the other one because the balance was thrown off.

■ *AJ: It seems that proper piercing technique is important—you really have to know what you are doing.*

■ JW: Yes, *placement* is very important.

■ AJ: *Let's talk about* Piercing Fans International Quarterly*—when did* PFIQ *start?*

■ JW: Well, let's back up a little bit and talk about Gauntlet; which was *PFIQ*'s parent. Gauntlet is the business I work from; Gauntlet makes and sells the proper jewelry for piercing. The magazine grew out of that.

When I first moved to Los Angeles in 1973, I met a man named Doug Malloy. He was about 50, and had been involved with piercing for about 30 years! We immediately developed a friendship. At that time I had met somebody who wanted me to pierce his nipples, so I called Doug up and said, "What kind of jewelry do you have? Can you give me some ideas on how to go about this?" At this point I had pierced a couple of people before, but my technique wasn't too great.

Doug said he had some jewelry that he would sell to me for $50, at cost. I starting thinking, "Hey, I should be spending this $50 to buy tools and metals, and make the jewelry myself, and be one step ahead of the game." That's what I did.

Not long after that, Doug suggested I start a business making jewelry specifically for piercings; he thought there was a market for it. I thought, "What the hell—what have I got to lose?" I could do it on a part-time basis and fill mail orders right out of my house. Doug advanced me a little money and that's how I started Gauntlet.

■ *AJ: And obviously it took off.*

■ FAKIR: Much to everyone's surprise. People would ask, "You make money selling *dick rings*?"

■ *V: You first set up a shop, right?*

■ JW: I first set up a shop to make and sell piercing jewelry. Doug taught me how to do piercings, and then I started inventing technical modifications that worked better. I worked out of my house for the first three years.

■ *AJ: How did you advertise? Word of mouth?*

■ JW: That, plus Doug had met quite a few people over the years; he had a mailing list of about 100 people. I sent out a catalogue and got some feedback.

■ F: Why don't you tell us about some of the collaborative projects you did?

■ JW: Doug and I did this flyer called "Body Piercing in Brief." It had drawings of the different piercings and a write-up of the history (the history according to Doug Malloy, that is) of each one. I do question the authenticity of some of that information! Correspondence started flowing in—people asking questions: "How do I put it in? How do I do this piercing? How do I meet other people who are interested in this?" We soon realized we would have to provide this information in the form of a magazine. That's how *PFI Quarterly* was born. We included a classified ad section for subscribers so they could meet others.

■ *V: You'd never done a magazine before. How'd you learn?*

■ JW: I knew a printer in San Francisco and he showed me how it was done. The next issue I was able to do myself, except for the typesetting. It was too impractical to have the magazine printed in S.F., so I had to find a printer closer to home. I had problems with several printers who became real intimidated by the material. The last one printed it all right, but the bindery would only bind it at night when all the women had gone home! Of course, I don't think it's a printer's right to censor, but…

■ *AJ: What kind of people come to you to get pierced?*

■ JW: All kinds—from hardcore leather people, SM practitioners, punk-type kids—there's no stereotype. One of my best customers has over 200 piercings and if you saw him on the street you'd just think he was somebody's grandfather—you'd never in a million years guess! We also get a lot of women. Again, they just run the gamut.

■ *V: Would you say the women who come in are usually under a man's influence?*

■ JM: You can't pigeonhole people that way. I won't pierce a woman who's obviously just coming in because her husband or boyfriend wants it—to me that's a violation; a subtle form of rape, and I won't be party to that. I only like to pierce people who *want* to be pierced. If you don't want it—forget it!

■ *V: What are the primary reasons for being pierced?*

■ JW: The most fundamental reason is aesthetic: it looks nice. The second reason is magical or medicinal. There was a time when men had their left ear pierced because of a belief that illness was caused by a demon crawling into your left ear. If you wore this shiny ring there, the demons were less likely to enter. And grandmothers would say that if you pierced your ears it would improve your eyesight.

Then there are the sexual reasons, which may be divided into two sides: piercings 1) to prevent sex, and 2) to enhance it. The first is called infibulation: Greeks and Romans commonly did this to prevent their male slaves from fucking around. The foreskin would be pierced and a lock called a *fibulum* inserted. In a lot of Middle Eastern countries this was done with women: the labia were pierced, and a lock was inserted to ensure "faithfulness."

But 90% of modern people do genital piercings to enhance their enjoyment of sex. This is the primary reason, and was *my* primary reason—it definitely takes sex up a higher octave! I found that after being pierced, my nipples felt really good—much better than before! In Borneo, even today, it's very common for a Dayak to have the head of his penis pierced by an *ampallang*—a pin inserted straight through the head, with little knobs on either end. This is *demanded* by the women, who reportedly will reject a man if he doesn't have one, or bypass one man in favor of another whose ampallang is larger. I imagine the man's personality still plays a major role, though!

■ *AJ: What guides your editorial policy at* PFIQ*? Is there something you wouldn't include?*

■ JW: I'm pretty open. As far as censorship goes, I probably eliminate material that is not related to piercing. People write in and say we should have articles on tattoo, or castration, or other types of body modifications. No! This is a piercing magazine, and that's our prime focus. If there are some tattoos in there or a lady in a corset, great. But I do not want to get into castration. And you'd be amazed at the number of people who have this as a fantasy.

■ *AJ: To have their balls cut off, or the whole thing?*

■ JW: It varies. I don't know how much is fantasy and how much is in fact reality, and I don't know that I want to know! I do know that is a real good way to get into trouble. And with the political climate being what it is, I have been advised by an attorney to tone down certain aspects such as play piercings.

I won't pierce a woman who's obviously just coming in because her husband or boyfriend wants it—to me that's a violation; a subtle form of rape, and I won't be party to that.

■ *V: What's that?*
■ JW: Temporary piercings just for the feel of the needle.
■ *AJ: Why would that be any more controversial than permanent piercings?*
■ JW: Because then you're talking about SM, which is very taboo right now. The argument for permanent piercing is: this is a body art form with a lot of historical precedents; it is not pornographic or purely sexual. But play piercing from an SM point of view is a real touchy area right now.
■ *AJ: How do you feel about being censored by societal pressures?*
■ JW: I don't like it. I don't like externally imposed restrictions limiting what I print, but I have to be realistic: I want to stay in business. I don't feel that the magazine is watered down just because I eliminate some of the heavier content; I feel it still has a strong impact. My number one concern is that the magazine continue, even if it doesn't contain some of the more controversial material. The climate will change; in time the pendulum will swing back the other way—maybe!
■ *AJ: How do feminists view piercings?*
■ JW: A guy who works for me has a girlfriend who is bisexual. She came back from a feminist gathering and said there were many piercings among the women there. I know a lesbian in the San Francisco area who does piercings. And I don't feel that piercing is anti-female; I don't think there's anything sexist about it. There are situations with a couple where the male is dominant and the female submissive, but there are plenty of reversals of that—it all balances out! However, within the SM culture there is often a sense of ownership. A submissive will be pierced—that's like a love token that shows a sense of commitment to the dominant partner. This reflects a ritual of ownership.

Now, one thing we lack in our culture is a rite of passage: going from being a child to being an adult, or going from being single to being married. In primitive societies piercing is frequently part of the puberty rite: a young man or woman becomes an adult member of the community by undergoing a process which includes being pierced.

Again, my main fascination with piercing is the sexual component, because I find piercings feel so good—at least the ones that I wear regularly.

■ *V: What do the cock piercings do for you? Do they stimulate you?*
■ JW: They just feel so incredible. When you have that piece of metal moving around in your tissue, you get more sensations. It just makes a good thing better!
■ *AJ: Do you ever do clitoral piercings?*
■ JW: If the woman's got enough of a clitoris to pierce, I'll pierce it. I've even pierced some that are very difficult. It's not one of my favorite piercings to do; it's one of the hardest to do if the woman is not well developed. Most women don't have very large clitorises.
■ F: The one that was in here yesterday sure did!
■ JW: That one was a piece of cake!
■ *AJ: How do you do piercings? Do you use a piercing gun?*
■ JW: A gun works well in the ear. We've modified a type of ear-piercing gun to pierce the nostril, and we use it to pierce the tragus as well. The rest we do by hand. It's just—the market isn't there to spend the money to research & develop a gun to be used for body and genital piercings.
■ *AJ: Do you think you'd want one, or do you enjoy doing it by hand?*
■ JW: Doing it by hand works great! I've developed a technique that for all intents and purposes is fast, and possibly more accurate. I break down hand piercing

Jim Ward participating in Fakir's sundance ceremony. Photo by Charles Gatewood.

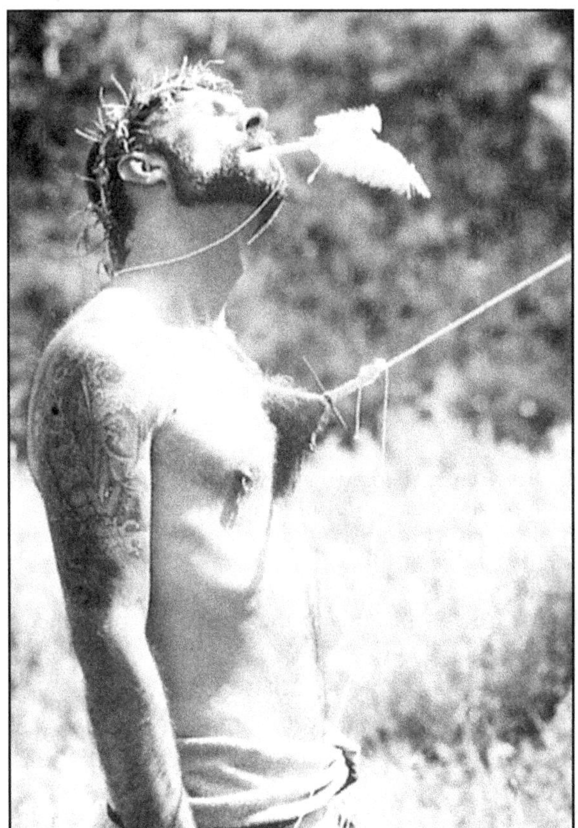

The most fundamental reason is aesthetic: it looks nice. The second reason is magical or medicinal.

into two categories: those that can be clamped, and those that can't. You mark a dot where you want the openings to be, put a clamp on, and pierce through—nipples and a lot of other piercings are done this way. There are a few piercings you can't clamp. The ampallang, for instance, goes right though the head of the penis, and I don't like to use the clamp because I find I don't get very accurate results; it can end up lopsided! So...I put the dot in place and get my needle on one side and see where I want it to come out on the other side, and then I can feel as I'm piercing where the needle's going, so that it comes out on target!

■ *AJ: Are there any dangers involved in piercing?*

■ JW: Any time you break the skin there's obviously a danger of some sort. You could end up with some real disasters if the person doing the piercing is very sloppy, doesn't know what he or she is doing, uses equipment that isn't clean, or is piercing a part of the body that shouldn't be pierced.

■ *AJ: What's a part of the body that shouldn't be pierced?*

■ JW: I don't advise piercing through the shaft of the penis; I think that's very dangerous and risky. You've got major nerve bundles and blood vessels there. The penis is like a tree; you've got a trunk and as you go from the base upward it begins to branch out. There are all these little branches and twigs as you get to the head. If you pierce at the top and you damage a little twig, the person hasn't sustained any serious damage. But if you pierce down through the shaft itself there's a risk of doing damage to the nerves, or causing a really serious bleeding problem. That's why we don't do it.

■ *AJ: In light of that, wouldn't clitoral piercing involve the same danger—of losing sensation forever?*

■ JW: Unfortunately, I have very little information about clit piercing. As far as historical precedents go, there's not much written documentation. Now, I always ascertain how committed the person is, who wants the piercing. The feedback I've gotten has been very positive; the women who have them love them. I've been in the business for over 10 years and I haven't done more than half a dozen clit piercings. Some of the women, I lost touch with, but I asked all of them to please let me know how they liked it.

■ *AJ: What's the historical precedent? Isn't the purpose to get rid of sexual feeling?*

■ F: Oh no! Not with clitoral piercing.

■ JW: You're thinking of the clitoridectomy, where the clitoris is cut off.

■ F: And occlusion, where they sew them up afterward—that's quite severe. In terms of both enhancement and negation, India has a couple of precedents. For example, certain groups use fine gold wire to sew up the women to keep them chaste.

■ *AJ: Does anyone in India do enhancement with clitoral piercing?*

■ F: Well...the clitoral piercing definitely is an enhancement; it creates and amplifies sensation. I know one woman who has a clit hood piercing; a little rod with vibrating parts that she puts on with a little clip and then she just vibrates the hell out of that whole area. The ring comes down and is always vibrating on her clit. But she is very exposed and has a large clit so it could be pierced, and I think she probably will do it.

■ *V: Have you ever met Mr Sebastian of London?*

■ JW: Oh yes, several times.

■ *V: I just wondered if you ever had a piercing clinic talk amongst yourselves, to discuss improvements, new techniques—*

■ *AJ: —talk shop.*

■ JW: Well, as it turns out, Mr Sebastian learned most of what he knows from the same man that I learned from, Doug Malloy.

■ *AJ: So you're the sons of Doug Malloy.*

■ F: In a way. I met Mr Sebastian in Hollywood through Doug, because he had sent money to Alan (Mr Sebastian) to come here for a visit. I think they got in touch through Bill Skuse in England, who sells photo sets of pierced and tattooed people which he got from Bernard Kobel of Clearwater, Florida. Some early photos of me are in there, and have been circulating for years!

■ JW: Anyway, not long after that meeting I started my business. Doug and I went to Europe for a tattoo convention and we spent about a week in London and were on very good terns with Alan (Mr Sebastian). We went to Amsterdam for a tattoo convention.

■ *V: But was there anything in your conversations with Mr Sebastian that might interest us?*

■ JW: Well, I interviewed him for an early issue of *PFIQ*. You know, I met Fakir through Doug, because he knew *everybody* in the piercing world and a lot of people in the tattoo world. There's a lot of overlap, but there are some people in the tattoo community who turn up their noses at piercing!

■ *V: Yes; we discovered that—much to our surprise!*

■ *AJ: So you live totally on your piercing?*

■ JW: Yes, I was working part-time in the picture framing business when I started Gauntlet in November '75 and the following March I had a fight with my boss at the framing place and got fired. I've supported myself with Gauntlet ever since.

■ *AJ: Is the business growing?*

■ JW: Yes. We wondered how AIDS would affect the business, but as near as I can see it hasn't. Once again, if the needles are clean, it's not a hazardous procedure, otherwise you could be in serious trouble! A lot of people are really out to lunch in this respect.

■ *V: Tell us about a particularly memorable body modification.*

■ F: Once I *branded* someone on my kitchen table. It was meaningful to both; they had been planning this for 5 years. This was an obstetrical doctor and his wife.

■ *AJ: Who got branded? Both of them?*

■ F: No, the woman got branded. But—I've heard of other cases where the man got branded.

90% of modern people do genital piercings to enhance their enjoyment of sex. It definitely takes sex up a higher octave.

■ *AJ: Isn't this usually part of a submission ritual?*
■ F: A lot of times. Hey, I'd like a brand—that'd look really neat! I could have a brand on my head, right here! Some people have a sub-mutilatory urge—that's prime territory.
■ *AJ: Well, it depends. I think some of these people don't have very evolved philosophies.*
■ F: But some of them do, surprisingly.
■ *V: Fakir, you mentioned Bernard Kobel. Is he still in business?*
■ F: No, he died years ago. Bill Skuse (London tattooist) got all his negatives; I think he went to Florida and got them when Bernard was ill and dying. These were the most amazing photographs: tattooed ladies, contortionists, three-legged people, every kind of Circus Side Show star. I collected all of these 'way back when I was very young. Since I was poor, I would make deals with him, like: I'd send him some *original* photos (of me) if he'd send me his photos of contortionist women! That's how I got my collection.
■ *V: So Skuse has all these pictures.*
■ F: Almost all of the photos in the Kobel collection are private snapshots that just wound up there. He provided mimeographed lists, like: tattooed lady photos, such-and-such a circus, with a date, etc. You would just take your chances and get one. The prints were only 50 cents.
■ JW: And some of them were the umpteenth generation!
■ F: Right. Copies of copies of copies. Kobel had an ancient 5x7" view camera, so all the pictures are 5x7". In his heyday, you could go to Wall Street or other places in New York and buy war surplus contact printing paper really cheap, in rolls. That's what he used. He copied everything, no matter what size, on a 5x7" negative—sometimes you'd have a little image on a great big piece of paper. He'd pull the images as they were ordered and contact print them on this war surplus paper. That went on for years and years and years.

He either knew somebody, or was himself a freak show man in the carnivals. There was no other access or source where you can get a good collection of pictures of freaks. So he collected all the pictures and snapshots he could find from his friends in the circus and carnival business, and complies them into lists categorized by subject: giants, hairy women, hermaphrodites—
■ JW: —and tattooed people.
■ F: Tattooed ladies. Then an interest in tattoos started to develop.
■ JW: There are quite a few photos from Kobel's collection in Spider Webb's book, *Pushing Ink,* and some have shown up in *PFIQ.*
■ F: Some of these are very rare and precious. There's even a picture of *me* in Spider's book—he didn't know it was me.
■ JW: Yeah, you're billed as a tattooed lady! It's a photo of your foot.
■ F: Yes, it was that foot right there! [points to foot] Nobody else in the world has a tattoo on the bottom of their foot like that.
■ JW: You had a hell of a time getting it to take, didn't you?
■ F: No, I had no trouble at all. I sat in a yoga position for about a hour until my legs went completely numb. Then I took my little 3-needle handmade rig with the sewing needles and thread and some India ink, and pushed the needles in really deep because I knew it wouldn't stay if I didn't. This was a very tender and difficult place to tattoo. My foot was totally numb from sitting in the yoga position.
■ JW: What did you do for a week while it healed?
■ F: I was sore. I did that when I was in the army one weekend when I was very bored.
■ *AJ: Does that symbol mean anything?*
■ F: It's a Middle Eastern design, although I didn't find that out until later. I just did it by intuition; I didn't have any guide. I just doodled on a piece of paper until I thought, "That's it—that's the one!" It turned out to be a powerful Middle Eastern symbol, a modification of a protective "bug." If you examine the *Africa Adorned* book you'll see that symbol repeatedly among the Bedouin people.
■ *V: Have you ever had any problems piercing a person?*
■ JW: If a person comes in and says, "I want this piercing," and I think they're serious, then that's what I'm going to do. So if you're sitting on my table and you start screaming or yelling after I've started, I still am going to make sure that I get the needle all the way through. If you decide you don't want it *later,* that's *your* business; *I'm* going to finish what I've started. Although...I can count on one hand the number of people who've screamed.
■ F: Sometimes they scream bloody murder and cry, and make a big put-on, and when it's all over, they laugh!

There are a lot of *odd* people who love piercing, like this little chicken farmer in Petaluma who comes back in every 6 months for another piercing. There are people who'll do this for *years!*
■ JW: I understand his wife hates it. I guess they haven't had sex in years, so—
■ F: "If you aren't going to use it for that, I'll use it for something else—I'll put gold jewelry in it!" I guess his genitals have assumed a new *plumage* function which is now an end in itself. Since he doesn't have to attract the opposite sex for reproduction purposes, he can at least pay homage to his former glory! I think his piercings have given him a much higher morale, besides a lot of pleasure. I'm sure his chickens are a lot happier, too!

G. & P. P-ORRIDGE

Genesis and Paula P-Orridge were known for their music and video projects under the names *Psychic Television* and *The Temple of Psychic Youth.* Previously, Genesis had been a prime innovator in the Industrial Culture Movement, producing dozens of albums as part of the groundbreaking quartet, Throbbing Gristle, as well as releasing recordings by SPK and others on the Industrial Records label. In the following interview Genesis and Paula reveal motivations and philosophical imperatives for their tattooing, piercing and scarification explorations. Interview by V. Vale in San Francisco.

■ *VALE: How do you account for the upsurge in "modern primitive" activity—piercing, tattooing, etc?*

■ GENESIS P-ORRIDGE: Sometimes people who can't express something in words express it in a more symbolic way, without words. Because words exist in a parallel world of their own, in a way, with complex laws which are still imperfectly understood. Many people don't have a mastery of words; words affect people in ways they don't understand. For example, even doing an interview, I think I've become more aware that there is always a Third Mind present, as Brion Gysin wrote about. Thinking is important, doing is important, casual conversation and explanation and justification *ad hoc* are important—but so laborious to put down on paper. So some people opt for a more symbolic means of expression.

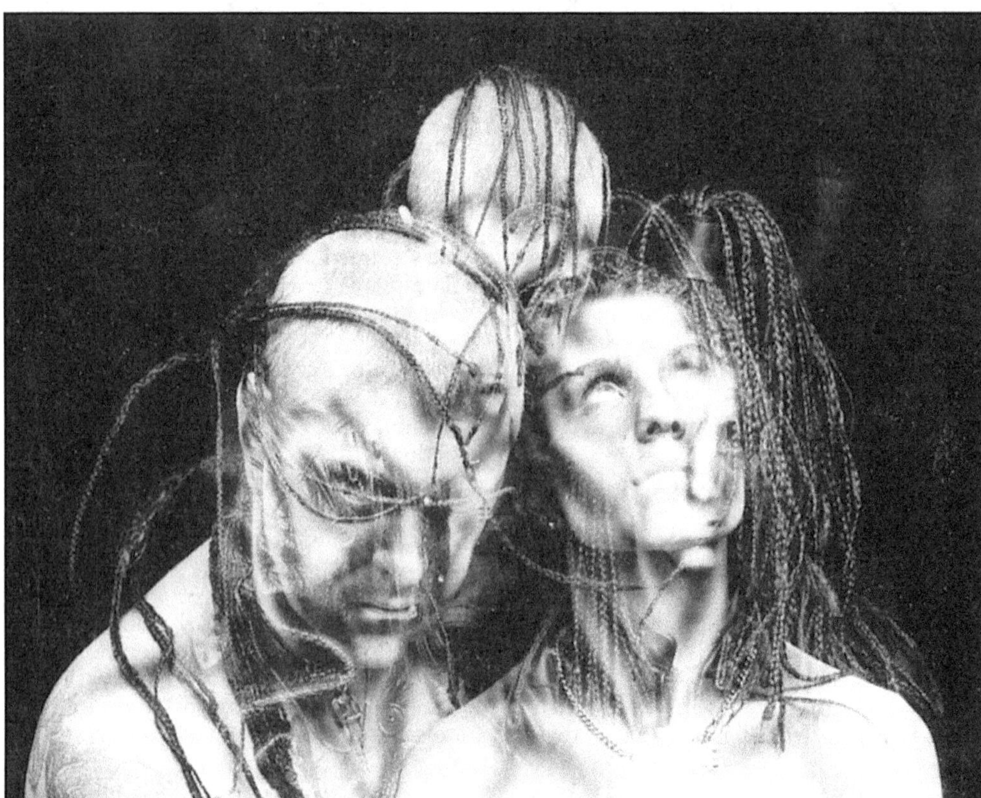

Photo by Bobby Neel Adams. Make-up and styling by Peter MxCandless.

■ *V: What was your first tattoo?*

■ GPO: It was on the top of my left wrist: a "3" with 3 horizontal lines through it, like the 3 horizontal lines on our psychic cross symbol. It was done in 1971 by a man called King Arthur who worked down by the docks in a once busy port in Yorkshire. He was what we called a *scratcher;* the general term in Britain for a tattooist who does not consider what he's doing either as an art or skill, or even has an interest in making things perfect.

Scratchers only use transfers, and do things like "Mom" and "Dad" and "Love" and "Hate" on the knuckles, and always use thick needles so it's fast. They usually only do drunken sailors and the criminal elements, or the macho boys who just want to have a tattoo, and aren't interested in the aesthetic value. So they handle the unsavory end of tattooing, or the purely monetary get-by-each-weekend tattooing—you get them in markets or fairgrounds, navy ports or near army barracks. In Britain they're the Old Guard of tattoos, who do it as a living and that's *it*—without pride in their work, particularly.

Things have changed a lot in Britain through the advent of books on tattooing, tattooing becoming more of a fashion accessory for some people, and the documentation in *Tattootime*. England also has a kind of fanzine, *Tattoo International,* but it's only black-and-white. Published by the Tattoo Club of Great Britain, it tells you who's a good tattooist, who's not, and who died, etc. In summary, all the input from various sources made people take another look.

I don't know when it happened, but at a certain point tattooists like Mr Sebastian and Dennis Cockell started to make tattooing into a higher art; well before the majority of people discovered this quality was possible. Perhaps the work on pop stars like the *Stray Cats* played a part; because of wider media coverage, people saw what a tattoo could really be.

Actually, Mr Sebastian was a bit different, in that he had been (and has stayed) very exclusive and reclusive. Originally he tattooed only gay people, in Earls Court, and it was through Sleazy that I met him. He used to teach art in a school for children between the ages of 11-16, and did etchings and engravings—he's a very skilled draftsman. But his actual, certainly semi-sexual, fetish was piercing and tattooing on himself. So eventually he left his teaching job and went into tattooing full time. He does very fine work with the thinnest needles, and takes a long time to do tattoos—he's probably the slowest one in England.

I think tattooing as an art or skill in which to have your own pride in, and see as something very valid both visually as well as financially, started more in the USA and came over to Europe. In Europe it was primarily a lower-class activity; in fact there's still a lot of the older generation who consider anyone with a tattoo to be either a criminal or almost semi-human... to them it's sort of "scum" people who have tattoos, and pierced ears as well.

When he was out on bail, all three of us decided to get a small tattoo so that when he was in prison (where they take your individual character away), we would all have what we called our telephone, and every time each of us looked at this mark we would think of the others, and he wouldn't feel alone.

When my mother first saw my pierced ear she said it made her feel physically sick, and I had to take it out. So I asked, "Do you feel physically sick when you look at the Queen?" She said, "No—what's that got to do with it?" I said, "All the Royal Family females have pierced ears." She said, "That's *ridiculous!*" and I said, "How do you think those amazing very expensive diamond earrings suspend themselves?" She found that very hard to compute...but did accept the truth of it. She said, "That's different—they're the Royal Family!"

■ *V: Why did you get that first tattoo? What did it mean?*

Photo by Sheree Rose.

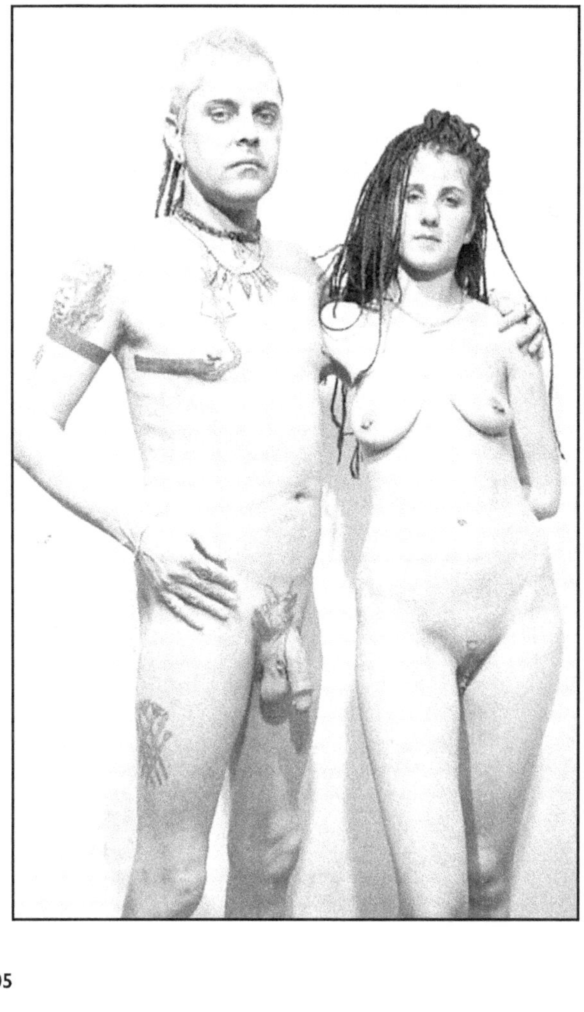

■ GPO: I was living in Yorkshire, and already doing the beginnings of *Coum Transmissions'* performance art and experimental street theater. There were three of us who were close friends: Cosey and I and the Very Reverend Lelli Maul. He was a burglar, but only would burgle policemen's houses and churches—his favorite activity was breaking into churches, putting on the priest's robes, then having photographs taken of him lying on the altar. Eventually, through being informed upon, he was caught by the police and sentenced to prison.

When he was out on bail, all three of us decided to get a small tattoo so that when he was in prison (where they take all your jewelry away, and your hair, and basically all your own individual character), we would all have what we called our *telephone,* and every time each of us looked at this mark we would think of the others, and he wouldn't feel alone, he would feel in contact with us and we with him. And he could actually use it to concentrate on, almost as a psychic telephone—as a glyph for concentrating on not being inside but being outside the prison, in times of stress or depression. Basically, this came out of the realization that he was going to have his whole personality stripped away and become a number, so we decided we'd become numbers too, and make those numbers powerful so we'd negate the magic they were putting on him by turning it around. They'd given him a prison number, but he could think, "No, they don't know my real number. I know my *real* number."

And so each of us designed a tattoo based on what we felt was our favorite or lucky number. I chose 3; Lelli has one which was a complex drawing of 16—it was 2 4's made into a grid (4x4=16). And Cosey's was a small 4 that looked like a camping chair. It was put into a shape of an exact square; it didn't look like a 4, but more like a rune. And they were each on the same wrist in the same position.

The funny thing was, we were still at that point a bit naïve about tattoos, and particularly scratchers who would just do things as quickly as they could. We went in and drew what we wanted, but hadn't drawn it the actual *size* we wanted. I was first. He started to draw mine straightaway without tracing it onto my wrist, and it was 3 *times* bigger than I wanted! I didn't have time to blurt out, "No, I want it smaller!" because by then he'd done too much! So it ended up a lot larger than I initially expected.

But I've now adopted that wrist as my *tattoo diary.* I've added things at particular moments, and can specifically tell people what each mark is, when it happened, and what it represents or reminds me of. I've sacrificed my left wrist to lists of moments in time that are significant to me.

■ *V: So you have a summary of peak moments of illumination or experience all in one little area?*

■ GPO: Right; a band about two inches wide around the left wrist. Eventually I assume it will get more or less filled in completely with signs and symbols. There are only 8 at the moment: 8 really peak personal moments.

Genesis's wrist. Photo by Christine Alicino.

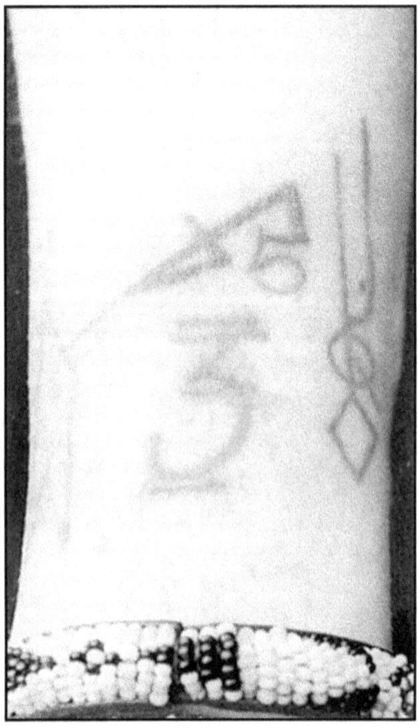

Genesis's wrist scars. Photo by Christine Alicino.

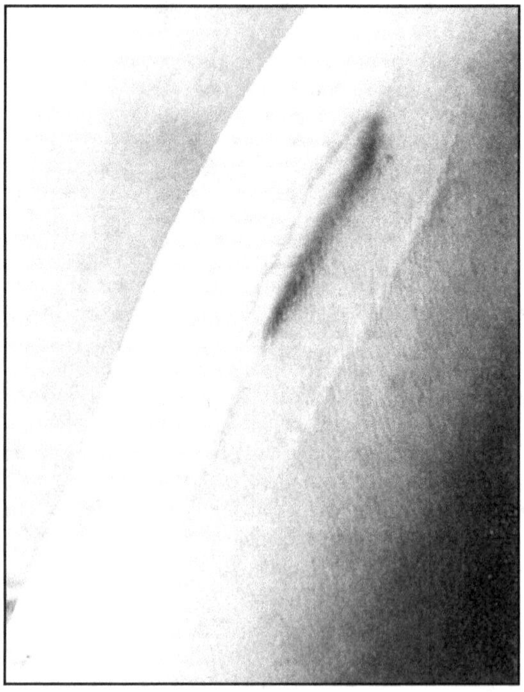

They look runic. The 3-sided red triangle with one dot in the center and 3 dots in a triangular shape over each face, was an adaptation of the Tibetan symbol which is a circle with a dot in the center and four groups of three dots outside which are the 12 steps towards enlightenment. There's my lucky number 3 (the 9 dots plus the 3 lines of the triangle), so that was to symbolize the permanent attempt to reach "enlightenment," whatever that may be. And then when I met Paula I had radiating yellow light put from the center dot outward, coming behind all the triangular shape and the 3. The dots around the triangle also make one larger triangle of dots as well, but pointing in the opposite direction, so it's quite nice geometry.

Then there's the magical sigil of the moon above that, which is a strange sort of elongated "4" shape for when Caresse was conceived, and then the tone under that becomes a 5 for the day she was born. And then on the right, if you look up the arm, is the Icelandic complex rune for my name, Genesis, and on the left hand side is the complex rune for Paula—these were done when we had an original pagan marriage ceremony in Iceland performed by the only living descendant of the original Viking priest who's still alive there, living in a hut in the wilderness in sub-zero temperatures. He's now the high priest of the Old Religion which is now recognized by the Icelandic government again. He married us under the statue of Thor which is in the picture on the front of our LP, *Live in Reykjavik.*

I've now adopted that wrist as my tattoo diary. I've sacrificed my left wrist to lists of moments in time that are significant to me.

Then the complex rune of Paula's is filled in fully with orange, which is for when Jeunesse was born. And there's a line through the complex rune and that joins the tip of the sigil for Caresse, so that the two children are linked through Paula. If you go round to the underside of the wrist, there's Hebrew which says "Psychic TV," which may sound corny, but I like the way it looks. And it turned out afterwards that when somebody analyzed it for me (I don't know in which system), numerologically it signified "666" which I thought was amusing!

■ *V: Why did you choose Hebrew?*

■ GPO: I just liked the way Hebrew looked. And after I found out it could mean 666—that's what made me think it's the right tattoo to get, because it's funny and a nice little joke. The other thing that's amusing is that after that we moved to our hideaway which is in a very heavy Hasidic Jewish community in London, every time I put my left hand out for change with the palm up, they see this tattoo in Hebrew and try and read it, and get confused. Because the concept of Psychic Television is almost impossible for them to take in. Also, a tattoo is not one of their culturally accepted practices, yet because of the language they find it interesting and feel reassured. The overall effect is: they're rather curious and pleasant; they want to try and find out why I've got it and what it is; am I Jewish, and things like that. So I have some good conversations.

■ *V: How did you come to know that 3 was your number?*

■ GPO: I really don't know. It provided a feeling of comfort. The only logical explanation I can think of is: my birthday's on the 22nd of February, which is 222, which is 3 2s. And if you multiply 222 by 3 you get 666. And so you get the 2 and 3 and you get the 6, and a 6 upside down is 9, which is 3 3s, so it was always very geometric. At a very early age I was aware of it being 666 before I was aware of what 666 was pretended to be by certain aspects of our rather decayed culture.

Genesis's wrist. Tattoo by Mr. Sebastian. Photo by Andrew Rawling.

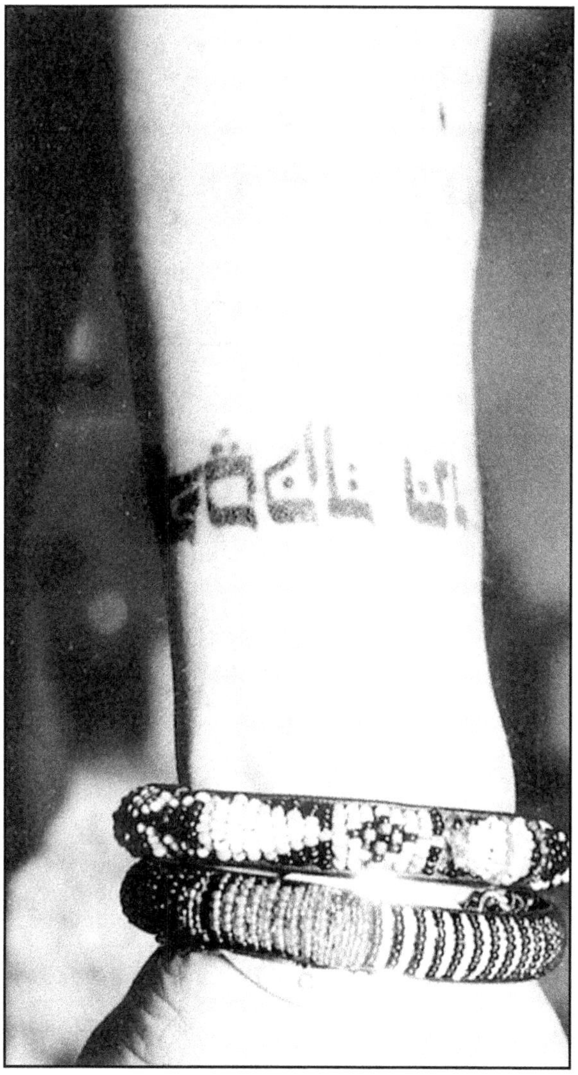

■ *V: What does 666 mean to you?*

■ GPO: Actually, we've done some research into that with Z'ev, who's much better at cabalistic and numerological matters than I am. He broke down the Mark of the Beast cabalistically; he took 666 and discovered it means soma or somatic: the body, but also the magic mushroom or the drug. And he thinks the Mark of the Beast was actually the mark on the mushrooms that were psychedelic; the mark identifying which mushrooms a shaman could use for further progression. In other words, it's knowledge again, like the apple in the Garden of Eden. Which makes a lot more sense to me, partly because I would prefer to believe that version of the story anyway, being the perverse anti-Christian that I am, and also because it seems to make more sense!

■ *V: Do you notice any other correspondences linked with the number 3?*

■ GPO: Like the fact that my penis is 3" long? [laughs] Actually, not on that day-to-day level. 23 happens like that all the time, but 3 is more my internal code. 23 drives me nuts—it's everywhere all the time; somebody'll call and say, "I just arrived at my hotel and guess which room I got—23!" [yawns] That one's everywhere, it's getting ludicrous. Don't know what it's trying to tell us, but it's bloody persistent. Burroughs was one who introduced me to 23—I have him to thank for it.

I've got five rings in my labia—all from different lovers. They're not exactly trophies—more like love talismans.

■ *V: Getting back to the evolution of your tattoos—what was next?*

■ GPO: I had no great interest in getting tattoos for their own sake. After the first one I didn't get any more for awhile; I didn't think anyone could do good tattoos because I hadn't seen any. So it was written off out of lack of information—I didn't have the information to be able to take it further, or the option to choose to.

This was back in *Coum Transmissions,* where I did have an interest in *body marking.* I went into scarification. As the performances got more extreme (and I don't mean in terms of audience response but in terms of my attempts to find limits in myself), pain became involved, and constriction, and risk, and that in itself inevitably led to the inclusion of markings—i.e., from sharp things being present, and in conditions where I could deliberately fall or lean or tread upon them. Instinctively, without pre-planning, I started to do cuts—scrape my body with sharp nails (not razor blades; to me, that didn't feel ritualistic enough; it had to be a dagger or nail or implement—not something clean and neat, but something which was dramatic and difficult and somewhat intimidating to *me.*) I've still got hundreds of pale residual scars all over my chest and arms; my left forearm and chest are almost all second skin. (Since I'm right-handed, they tend to be more on my left forearm and chest.) And that's never stopped—I still do that regularly a few times a month.

■ *V: But you don't do that in your private life?*

■ GPO: Those were in art performances, whereas now it's in private rituals. But I've also scarified a lot of other people since. Mr Sebastian very kindly suggests I'm the only person he knows who's an expert in scarification merely with a knife. I've learned all about the upper forearm and the inner thigh and what all the different parts of the body do when they're slit, because I've done them more or less everywhere (always with people's consent—they've always asked first). I'm putting a spiral of 2-inch cuts from the top of one girl's thigh spiraling all the way down to her ankle. These are cuts with a ritual knife that I only use for scarring people; I don't use it for anything else.

■ *V: What kind of knife is it?*

■ GPO: It's a punch dagger, oddly enough; an all-steel one like you see advertised in *Soldier of Fortune.* Although it's not particularly exciting to look at, it's the one that's done probably a hundred people or more. Depending on whether you believe objects can retain any energy from how they're used, it has a lot of power in it. It's always present in every ritual I do, whether I use it or not. But I have a rule: I don't do a ritual without letting blood in myself. I have to make at least one cut on myself, and it had to be a cut that will scar, no matter how small.

It was getting so messy that I decided to start doing them in bands around my arm. Over the years I'll have rings of them like bracelets, which are far more aesthetically interesting than loads of random cuts everywhere! So I've formalized the application of them, unless there's a *reason* to do something at random.

■ *V: So the scarification began more or less accidentally in* Coum Transmissions?

I remember hearing voices saying, "There's no pulse or heartbeat—what are we going to do?" And I started to project out of my body, but I only got about a foot above myself.

■ GPO: It was just an instinctive extension of what I was doing; I was pushing myself to the point of being declared *dead.* At the last *Coum Transmissions* action in Antwerp, I got into a strange mood, a trance-like state—which is what I used to try and reach anyways. And in the performance I drank about half a bottle of whisky, which at the time was a test; I didn't actually drink, so drinking any alcohol at all was a shock to my system. I weighed about 94 pounds; I was very thin in those days. So the performance began with me already in a trance-like state, and I presume the whisky hit me with a shock. I started speaking in tongues—the only time that's ever happened to me, and also the

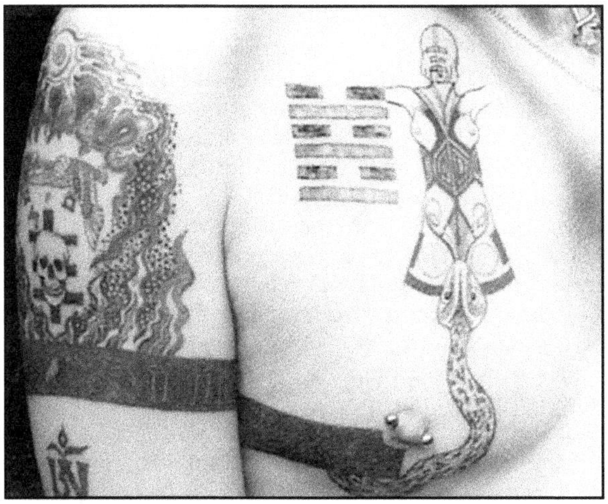

Genesis's chest tattoo by Mr. Sebastian. Photo by Christine Alicino.

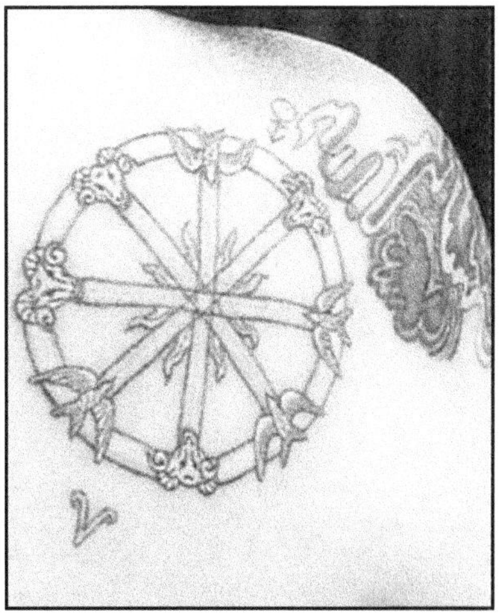

Genesis's back tattoo by Mr. Sebastian. Photo by Christine Alicino.

only time in a *Coum Transmissions* performance that I did a spoken diatribe—it was normally never done with words but with action.

I started cutting a swastika shape into my chest about 9" square with a rusty nail; then I turned it into a Union Jack (the British flag), and then just scratched and cut all over the place. I'd also been eating these twigs I'd found outside in the mud in a building site, and it turned out they were poisonous. The combination of everything: the rusty nail I'd found, the whisky, and the branches made me very ill, and I started to vomit and dehydrate. I was rushed to the university hospital and by the time they got there they couldn't find a pulse. I had astral projections. You know the stories about near-death experiences—well, I had one!

I remember hearing voices saying, "There's no pulse or heatbeat—what are we going to do?" And I started to project out of my body, but I only got about a foot above myself (I didn't feel at all panicked or bothered; I could see everything just as normal). Suddenly I snapped back into my body and was there again, alive—I think the doctors must have given me a big shot of adrenalin. I lost about another 18 pounds in 2 days; I was very ill. But this did not put me off scarification—only rusty nails and poison! I was bedridden for a couple days, and then had to get back to England feeling still really awful. So that's how scarification developed. Besides the swastika, I didn't start doing *formal* cuts until the Temple of Psychic Youth in '81/'82.

In 1981, just before we came to America for the last TG concert, Paula and I decided to live together (as opposed to just being good friends and lovers). And for what we laughingly called my "engagement ring," I got my right ear pierced with one of Mr Sebastian's surgical steel piercing rings with the ball on (they're thicker than the ones sold by Gauntlet in Los Angeles). Paula got an iris tattooed on her foot; in one of the leaves a "23" is subtly included.

That's when we started getting into tattooing again; we'd just met Mr Sebastian through Sleazy, and in a way that was it—we were *hooked*. Because he was so good, so amazing to be with and talk to, and his work was a revelation; I just went, "Wow!"—it's like: a myriad of possibilities flies into your head. You know what's possible, and you know anything's possible, and you also know how and where to go to get what's possible. And that means you're suddenly free to do what you want; to let your mind's desires go where they will. That was a very important connection—it wouldn't have happened without Mr Sebastian.

■ *V: Now your tattoos are on the way to being symbolic markers of peak experiences.*

■ GPO: Although if you talked to the average squatty soldier with several tattoos, he'd probably be able to remember where he got them done and possibly what they were for at the time. So apart from the masculinity motive, which in the early days accounted for a lot of tattooing (in Western European culture; not in a lot of other places), there is the making of a lot of basic things like Mom and Dad or a girlfriend, or having been to a certain war zone, or a regiment.

I think my tattoos were more like a private diary—an extension of the basic usage, but differing from the norm—more particularized and focused. I asked Mr Sebastian to copy certain scratches in a style that looked more like a prison tattoo, as if I'd done it myself, because the marks signified a personal journey where the aesthetic didn't matter; the reasons *behind* the marks were all-important. We were talking about self-empowerment, but I do everything in that way, or try to.

■ *V: What did the iris on Paula signify?*

■ GPO: The first lesbian girlfriend Paula had was called Iris; it was her first sexual encounter ever. She actually got the tattoo done across her only scar, which was from a mosquito bite when she was in Grenada,

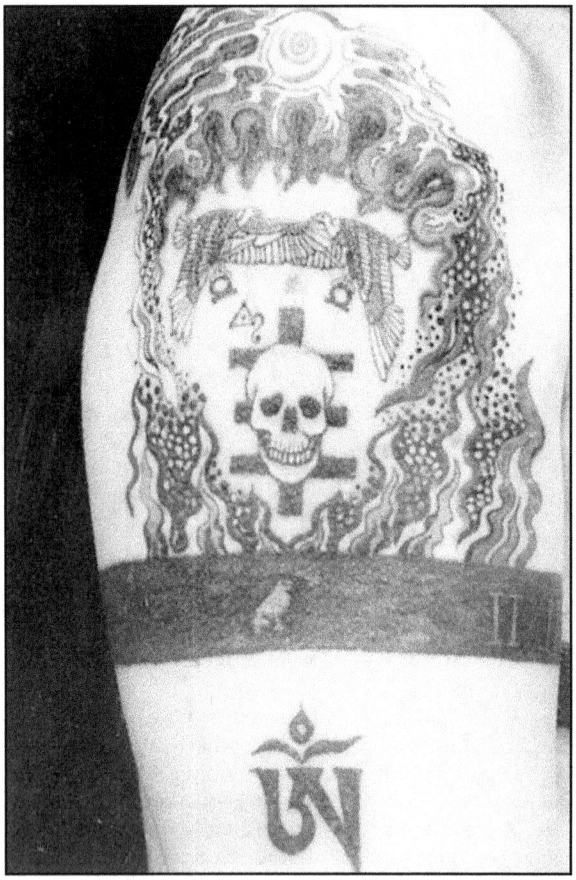

Genesis's arm tattoo by Mr. Sebastian. Photo by Christine Alicino.

in the West Indies, helping the revolution which later on the U.S. squashed. And that was one of her most vivid socio-political memories—that mosquito scar, which reminds her also of going away from Britain so far away for the first time in her life—she was about 15 at the time. So these were 2 key events combined in a private design which other people would just see as a "pretty tattoo."

■ *V: And Mr Sebastian opened up this world—*

■ GPO: Immediately it was as if all these ideas which had been lying dormant sprang to life, upon finding someone who could actually execute them. I couldn't do them myself; I could do the scars myself but not the tattoos. Although, with his help I have done some labial piercings. Because of the scarifications, I'm not sqeamish, so I don't hesitate—you need to know what skin does when things happen to it, and you need to be very confident.

■ *V: Back to the scarification origins in Coum Transmissions; you were testing yourself, trying to transcend the fear and threat that pain presents to most people.*

■ GPO: And even that death presents, too. In a lot of Shamanistic cultures like Tibetan or American Indian cultures, you have the idea of the *small death,* which is basically: in High Magic people talk about having to cross the abyss. In certain forms of High Yoga people talk about the total loss of ego, and so do people like Timothy Leary, and in other cultures like Tibet it's referred to as the small death. And the overall universal fact, whether you go to aboriginal cultures or New Guinea headhunters, or the Dogon tribe in Mali, is: basically, for all intents and purposes, you literally *die.* And it's called the small death because you come back.

That small death is essential to the true measurement of and control of ego and personality and one's actual nature...learning its irrelevance and relativity. You get things in proportion; you have this basic simplification about things: that it's all a matter of ratio, and that in any given moment in time, whether it's a second or a year, one has all the warring factions within one's self—all the emotions, everything, the totality of one's self, whether it's eating, shitting, or philosophy, or sex, or anything that's ever happened to you or is happening on any level—all those things are obviously in different ratios to each other; there's the whole, and then there's the ratio of all the bits. And it's a technique for putting the ego into proportion, in ratio with everything else.

I've met genuine masochists and they're usually rather dull. I'm interested in heightened awareness—not exactly trance states, but altered states in the true sense.

It also teaches you the truth of the meaning of the words "transient" and "mortal." I think that until you know what mortal and transient really mean, you cannot understand what *time* means. And if you don't understand what time means, then your motivation and your intention are diffused, because you don't understand that even if you *do* manage to live 50, 60, or 70 years, that's really not much. Therefore, any second of any minute which is wasted is lost forever, and cannot be reclaimed, and that's a tragedy. So you're left with two results from that: 1) that time is the most precious commodity the human being has, because it is irreplaceable, and 2) we all do die—that's a fact—no bullshit, no life after death, no hiding away, no camouflaging it—we *die.* End. No bullshit. The End.

■ *V: And from there one must discipline oneself and concentrate to accomplish the work which is really you.*

■ GPO: It helps you make the decisions as to how to apply yourself, and what work is actually of value.

■ *V: Yes, because at any given point there are a lot of possibilities that you or I could be doing. You do believe in trying to live a long life?*

■ GPO: Oh yes! That's why I pace it now. I have no desire to waste time by dying! No romantic idea of: "He died at the age of twenty-five." I could have died earlier, and it wouldn't have been romantic or anything—just a miscalculation. And it would have been just reckless; not any big deal.

■ *V: How do you rationalize the accusation that these are just masochistic or perverted activities? That you've merely just twisted your sensations around so you're now experiencing pain as pleasure?*

■ GPO: I've met genuine masochists and they're usually rather dull, because they don't give you any intellectual explanation at all, nor are they interested in one. We know the writer Terence Sellers and she can tell endless anecdotes of unawakened ritualization and masochism which is just not interesting in the least. I'm interested in *heightened awareness*, and I'm interested in learning more and more about—not just myself, but what is possible through the achievement of—not exactly trance states, but altered states in the true sense.

There's a re-balance into a zone of perfection; intuitive leaps, philosophical clarity through rituals which may or may not include pain. I don't always include pain. There are days when I can do a great big scar and I don't feel a thing; and another day I do a little on and it bloody *hurts*. There's no common denominator or ongoing level of tolerance—that's what I find so interesting, and that's why I like semi-improvised rituals, because you find you suddenly go to another spot which you never expected and couldn't pre-plan. But from the fact of doing cumulative rituals, if you didn't have the discipline of doing rituals reasonably regularly, you'd just never discover those new places you get to or those new tolerances, or even the fact that suddenly it *does* hurt again; I can't just tolerate pain *to order*. And I find that's interesting, and that I learn a helluva lot about behavior; it churns up the brain in a way that even I never expected...

I know that my overall psychic or neurological abilities have increased and are increasing—the ability to instantly know something quite revelatory about a person, for example. This has happened to other people who have followed the same route, and they can't give you a rational or logical explanation either. Except: we believe there's a quality of the body or the brain or the personality which has just been left untapped in our culture, but which is commonplace in so-called primitive cultures. And I think that's where you do get this "modern primitive" link. I think a lot of other people recognize the symbols of that, if not all of the techniques, and I find that very encouraging: in the flourishing of tattooing, piercing, and body modifications. It's the tip of the *possibility iceberg*.

■ *V: Why do you always inflict a cut on yourself every time you do a ritual?*

■ GPO: I use the cut as a *symbolic key*. For a start, in traditional magic, blood is seen as something you should keep from other people, because it's supposed to empower them over you. So we negate that concept by collectively storing all those bodily things like hair, sperm, menstrual blood, human blood, and saliva, into our own archive. In theory we say we make ourselves vulnerable because we trust each other, and because you're only hurt by what you're scared of.

I use the cut as a symbolic key. For a start, in traditional magic, blood is seen as something you should keep from other people, because it's supposed to empower them over you. So we negate that concept by collectively storing all those bodily things like hair, sperm, menstrual blood, human blood, and saliva, into our own archive.

■ *V: It seems more logical that you'd have to do a mutual exchange rather than a one-way flow into your archive.*

■ GPO: Well, we do with the people involved. I don't have a great format in advance for all rituals, but I've found, just through my own experience, that it's useful to have certain thresholds that I always cross, whether I feel "in the mood" or not, and bloodletting is one of them. And I always incorporate it into what we call the sigil paper. We start with a piece of paper or card or piece of wood, and we decorate it or add things to it, and it becomes an object, a collage or assemblage if you like, during the duration of the ritual. And that is imbued with the energies or powers released during the ritual, and also is a glyph of the motive behind the ritual afterwards; a reminder, like a tattoo.

The idea is that it goes into your subconscious, just like a symbol would—a cross or a circle—and lodges there; it's just a complex glyph, and it's incomprehensible and indecipherable to anyone who was not present. But in your subconscious it triggers the entire memory like a videotape each time you visualize it or see it. And therefore it re-motivates the intention without you having to make any conscious decision. Basically, I have these stored on the wall so every time I wake up in the morning I see a wall full of a year's very intense

Paula's foot tattoo (Iris) by Mr. Sebastian. Bamboo tattoo by Mr. Sebastian and Genesis. Photo by Andrew Rawling.

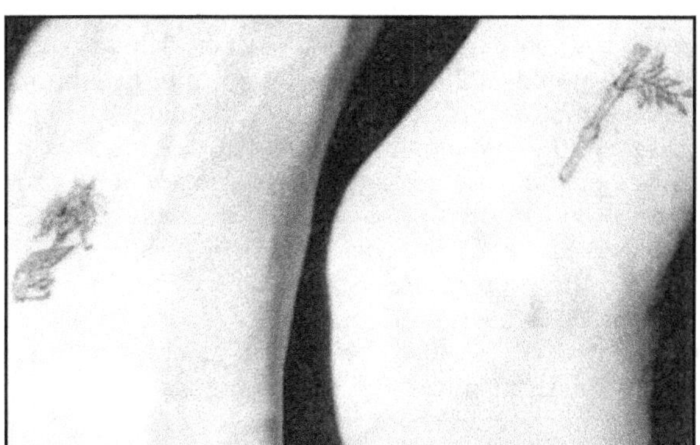

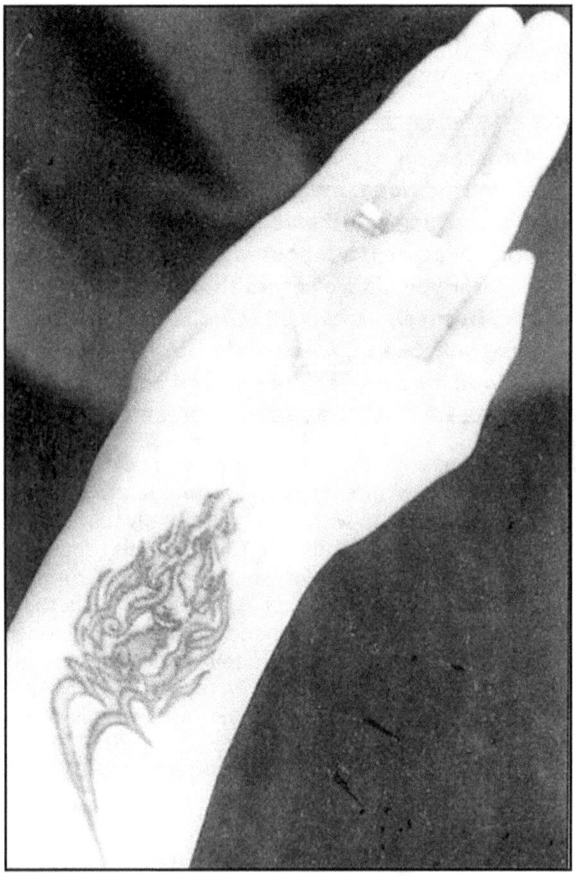

Paula's wrist tattoo by Mr. Sebastian. Photo by Christine Alicino.

work, and it's like a photograph—it goes *flash* into the unconscious, because you're in the dream state when you wake up. So it reminds the brain each morning of all the things we're trying to direct our energy at.

■ *V: Would you say that every time you do a ritual you have a consciously articulated intention?*

■ GPO: You can do that. If you want to help somebody concentrate, you start out with that written on the piece of paper in some way, whether intelligible to somebody else, or an image, picture, photograph, object which makes you think of concentration, or that symbolize concentration to you—it could be a computer, it could just be a polaroid of a finished book because you want to concentrate on finishing a book. And then, the whole point of the ritualizing is that you go farther and farther into the intuitive state, until you don't even necessarily *know* why you're assembling things in a particular order or putting a picture of another thing next to the first one. Or why you're writing a phrase or a word on there. The idea is to become *not-self-conscious.* And there's a lot of cross-cultural verification that this is the basic technique.

Or course, you can always start out thinking, "I just want to find out what my balance is today," or, "I feel confused—let's see why," or, "Let's see what there is." You start out trying to make yourself blank, and you have a piece of blank paper. And you just move about, and start to put things together. You have to make your room feel "right": strip it down, put everything away; think, lie, or talk, or look through books at random, or pick out words at random, or look at tarot cards, tape things and play them back at random—*anything* that makes you *open to your own unconscious.* And, as with any discipline or ritual: the cumulative result of doing things over long periods of time can be remarkable.

At the beginning it may seem rather dull because you're still looking at yourself, you're still being "objective" and standing outside. Then one day you suddenly get a surprise! And my feelings on anything like that are: even if you don't get *beyond,* it's interesting and fun to do, and if something *else* happens to you it's a luxury on top. For me and Paula it's become a way of life, because it reinforces so much that we value and are stimulated by. It takes us further all the time.

■ *V: Everybody's subconscious is an incredible treasure trove of images, synesthetic pleasure recollections, and other data—if only your conscious could access just a bit of it. So the rituals are a conscious way to gain access?*

■ GPO: We believe so. We feel, from our practical experience, that is definitely the case. And that in itself is a very useful tool. It does not descry or negate any of the other ones from the computer, and all of the other things we've always done. It's just another useful access tool to more information. Which is all I'm interested in.

I found it by accident through *Coum Transmissions*—I didn't *plan* it. But then one day there you are: "Hey! That's interesting!" And I sat back and waited a year or so before I did any more rituals, just trying to figure out and compute what was going on before, that I'd been unaware of. I had to decipher and analyze the "bull in the china shop" syndrome that was *Coum Transmissions.* Then I thought, "Well, I've got at least enough of a picture of what I thought had happened in the process, to try and recapture the process and thereby the results." Ever since, I've been working on improving that and focusing it and delineating it further. Because I find it very useful—if it weren't useful I'd stop doing it. So it's not masochism and it's not sadism, it's functional, and as long as it remains functional more than 50% of the time, I'll be interested. Once it becomes less cost-effective, I'll do something else.

Paula and I function as a symbiotic team when we do rituals, and that is the Third Mind—the results we get are definitely the Third Mind. We become fused as an androgynous being, or as we call it, a *Pandrogynous* being: P for Power, Potency, and also for the Positive aspects of being blended male-female. Also because it then makes it Pan, and Pan is also a good concept. Pandrogyny is one of my on-going investigations, and the other one is the idea that we're not an occult group, we're an *occulture*. Because my interest is culture, but I approach it through occult means, if you like.

■ *V: There has so be investigation and extrapolation on the part of the individual. And you have to learn, re-learn and un-learn every day to ensure that nothing ever becomes codified into a belief or a dogma.*

■ GPO: I've always been allergic to dog-mas! Life is exciting and frustrating all at once. Each little discovery you make only makes you realize how much more remains to be uncovered. It's endless...

■ *V: Paula, what's the evolution of your tattoos?*

■ PAULA P-ORRIDGE: My first tattoo was on my foot because I didn't want it to be very obvious. It was an iris to cover up a big scar from a mosquito bite that went septic.

■ *V: Where did you get the mosquito bite?*

■ PPO: In Grenada, the West Indies, 1980. Gary, the President of Grenada, had been getting a lot of money from the U.S. to turn the country into another Salvador, yet there were no hospitals or schools—just one school for the rich people. Basically he was a real fascist. A revolution started by the New Jewel movement threw Gary out. I was working with a youth project in Hackney, London, and part of our group went over there as part of the New Jewel movement to help build a school. I lived in a little hut by the sea with some other people.

Grenada is a very small island. There's an American medical school on the beach, St. George's. If you travel inwards towards the mountains you suddenly encounter one street full of large, grand estates owned by very suspicious people—probably criminals that fled America. There's an undercurrent of dubious things going on—that's probably why America supported Gary.

After the New Jewel movement got in, a man named Bishop took over and things got better. Schools and hospitals were being built and people were getting their lives back. But American and Britain both refused to give them financial backing, so they were forced to turn to Cuba. About three years later Bishop was mysteriously murdered—beheaded, and the Americans went in and bombed everywhere, giving the excuse that the American medical school was about to be attacked by Cuba, which was a lot of nonsense.

■ *ANDREA JUNO: So the mosquito bite scar had a lot of meaning to you?*

■ PPO: Yes, it's a reminder of an important period of my life. I was taken from my culture and put into another very easy-going, different way of life. I was there about six weeks.

■ *AJ: So your parents didn't mind you going there at the age of 17?*

■ PPO: No. I'd been working and saving money since the age of 12; I paid my own airfare (it was a special half-fare deal). My mum and dad were divorced, so if I wanted to do something I'd tell one parent I was staying with the other, and vice versa. So for years I'd managed to do what I wanted.

■ *AJ: Describe the tattoo.*

■ PPO: It's an iris with a "23" integrated into the leaves—you can't see it clearly, and it was done by Mr Sebastian. The first girlfriend I had was named Iris, and "23" was my birthday. After I met Genesis and learned about the theory of 23, I didn't just *accept* it—I'm quite skeptical. However, 23 is this mysterious number. It takes 23 seconds for the blood to go around the body; there are 23 chromosomes in the body. Arthur Koestler wrote an unpublished manuscript on the number 23. The last book I looked at, which was on crystals, I opened right up to chapter 23! The next day I got in a taxi and it came to 2 pounds 30. I went into a shop and bought some things and it came to 2-23. Today I bought an orange juice and the expiration date on the container was the 23rd. All these silly correspondences, but it goes on and on.

With any discipline or ritual: the cumulative result of doing things over long periods of time can be remarkable.

■ *AJ: What does 23 mean to you personally?*

■ PPO: Just an acknowledgement that it crops up so often that it's beyond synchronicity or coincidence. It doesn't mean good or bad; I'm just aware that it crops up a lot. I don't rule my life by it. But if I picked a number like 19, I wonder how many times *that* would crop up?

■ GPO: Did you know that the first group of Jewish immigrants to America numbered 23? People send us articles all the time that link "23" to scientific theories or significant events; "23" crops up far beyond the statistical law of averages.

■ *AJ: Cabalistically it's a very powerful number; it's a prime number.*

■ GPO: We accept the fact that it's one of the phenomena that has reverberative potency. Our easy explanation is that we just use it as the acceptance of a random chance principle within everything. It's the intersecting point, or the reminder of that, for us, because it appears a very clear one, and we're not the only people to notice that. A dwarf actor in England was recently on TV displaying his scrapbook of news clippings and other references, all having to do with the number 23.

■ *V: As far as I know it all started with W.S. Burroughs noticing how often 23 cropped up in his scrapbook of news clippings. Paula, what was your next tattoo?*

■ PPO: This flame/frog design on my wrist, which was done after my first child, Caresse, was born. She was born breech—her bum first, and she had a strange shape, like a frog. So we called her "Froggie" as a nickname. A friend figured out her numerological number, and it was the same as the Egyptian goddess *Heqet,* who is portrayed as a frog. The number 23 in Tibetan adds up to 5, and she was born on the 5th of August.

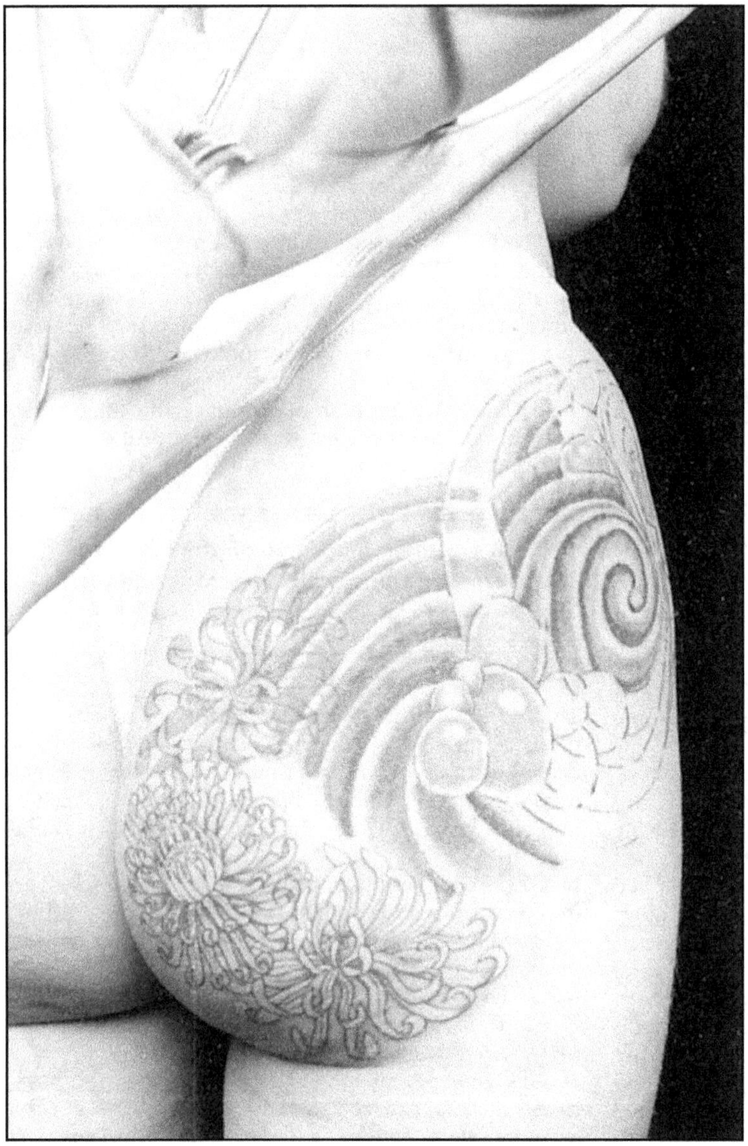

Paula. Tattoo by Mr. Sebastian. Photo by Christine Alicino.

Basically this tattoo is the story of Caresse's birth. The crescent moon symbolized the *Moonchild,* which was the first Crowley book I read. And the five pointed star—I just liked the design.

The third tattoo is the same that Gen has: the 3, triangle, with the yellow emanating from the center, symbolizing our meeting and growing together from 7 years ago until now. Although I first noticed Gen when I was about 6 or 7, about 19 years ago, when I came out of school and he was walking by. Doesn't time fly?

I have a tattoo of two snakes entwined on my shoulder, which is like the symbol of infinity. At the time we had Isabella Constrictor-or-Not—I like all animals, including reptiles. Above are two Egyptian vultures—death and mortality sort of sitting there keeping an eye on everything.

■ *V: What is your attitude towards death?*

■ PPO: When you die you're just a piece of meat. [laughs] I don't believe that when you die your spirit wanders off somewhere. I just think you die and that's it. I don't have any theories to content me that when I die everything will be fine and I'll drift off to some heaven and see all my pals.

■ GPO: I've been dead 3 times and I know what it's like—there's nothing! [laughs] Absolutely nothing, and do not kid yourself. It's the end: blank, black, gone, not even a mini-thought for a second. And these people who've had all these white light experiences, all they've done is projected, while they're not totally dead, what they want or expect (preferably what they want): white robes and tunnels. It's all just wish-fulfillment, that's all. Whereas if it's me, my wish-fulfillment is that it's *nothing!* I'm a cynic even in death.

■ PPO: Although I believe that when you die that's it, you're dead, *finito,* I think Eastern cultures have a healthier attitude toward death than Western cultures. We're very afraid of death; in a sense it's because a lot of things are built on the ego: who am I and what I do. "I can't just die; I can't just not exist anymore." With Eastern cultures I like the way they carry it through: you can really get into designing your death bed, your death chamber. In certain countries you have an effigy of yourself after you die. I think that's better: you can get into that role of being dead. Even for myself, I think, "Okay, when I'm dead, I'm dead. But I still might like this nice effigy to represent me!"

When you die you're just a piece of meat. I don't have any theories to content me that when I die everything will be fine and I'll drift off to some heaven and see all my pals.

■ GPO: Or be remembered with a great big orgy or celebration or anything you like.

■ PPO: Before, the Chinese used to really get into that, with huge funerals burning paper money and paper replicas of everything.

■ *V: They still do that in Malaysia.*

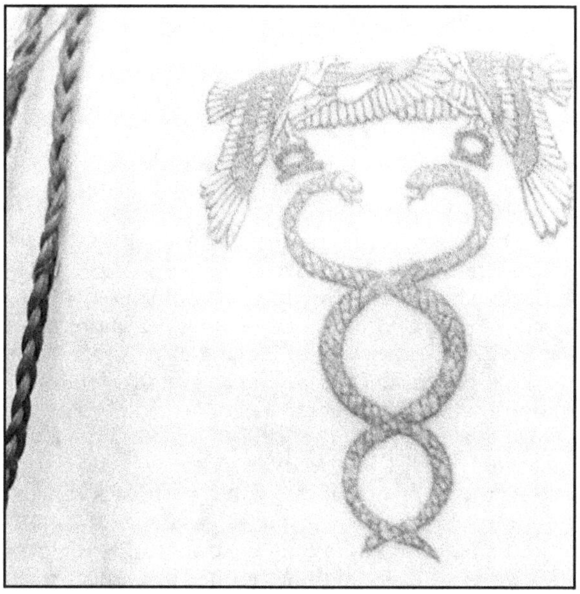

Paula. Tattoo by Mr. Sebastian. Photo by Christine Alicino.

■ GPO: You should start a company: Design Your Death, or Designer Death—

■ *AJ: —Make death a creative act.*

■ GPO: I think rich people today should enact obscenely huge follies to commemorate their deaths. Maybe there should be a law that instead of inheritance, every penny left has to be spent on your death celebration. So, the Gettys would have to pay for a party for the whole of humanity! Not only would that be the greatest ego trip they'd ever had, but it would also wipe out all their money in one fell swoop! That'd be much more fun! People would think, "Hey, he's going to die soon—we're going to have a really good time!"

■ *AJ: Or like the Egyptians, maybe they could leave some really great monuments behind.*

■ GPO: They could find islands in the Pacific and build huge 5000-foot monuments—make the planet far more exciting.

■ *V: I love those huge mausoleums and fantastic monuments designed in the 1700s by Claude-Nicolas Ledoux, Etienne-Louis Boullée, and Jean-Jacques Lequeu—drawings of huge cenotaphs just waiting for a patron to build them.*

■ GPO: People who are financially underprivileged could get into being part of an ongoing amazing catacomb that was decorated with their remains.

■ *V: The Paris catacombs are truly amazing—what an idea to have actually realized.*

■ GPO: That's what I was thinking of. There's one in Rome, full of mummified monks hanging off the walls, as well as thousands of bones decorated in all manner of decorative arrangements. I sneaked some illegal photos when I was there; did a few quick snapshots from the waist.

■ *AJ: Paula, do you have any more tattoos?*

■ PPO: I have a tattoo inside my inner labia: a rune of Gen's name. And no, it didn't hurt! I got it in celebration of our Icelandic wedding. The last tattoo I got was a tattoo in *white:* a psychic cross on my upper arm.

■ *AJ: That's incredible—that white design. Why'd you do it in white?*

■ PPO: Because I wanted it to be quite subtle, really.

■ GPO: Also because it's unusual. Plus the one on your entire right buttock, which you always forget!

■ PPO: That one isn't quite finished yet. It's based on a Japanese watercolor design; the spiral fits with the buttock quite well—I like the way it flows. Unfortunately, Mr Sebastian didn't do that, although he did the flowers. A guy called Brent is the only one in England who can do the Japanese watercolors; I think he has special airbrush needles.

■ GPO: You also have a tattoo on either side of your other leg—you forgot! The tiny bamboo shoot.

■ PPO: Right. Then Gen did a little tattoo; he borrowed Mr Sebastian's tool. There was no smudging.

■ *AJ: What does bamboo symbolize to you?*

■ PPO: Well, it grows pretty quick! It means growth and grace. And I like pandas—I'm really into pandas. The flowers on my bum don't really mean anything; I just wanted something nice and flowing around the edges there.

Tattoos are very addictive—once you get one, then you want another. It can be quite hard to say No.

■ GPO: Piercings *and* tattoos! I think everyone we know who's gotten a tattoo almost immediately has wanted another one. They have the *urge.*

■ *V: And we want to know why.*

■ GPO: Surprisingly, the same applies to piercings. Our friend Cheryl was deliberately not interested—she knew that everyone around us ended up getting pierced, so she wasn't going to. Which was fair enough—quite sensible; she was trying to have a clear, objective view of it all. But eventually she did get both her inner labia pierced. We saw her a few days ago and she said, "I've decided I want four more!" So she has succumbed to the urge as well.

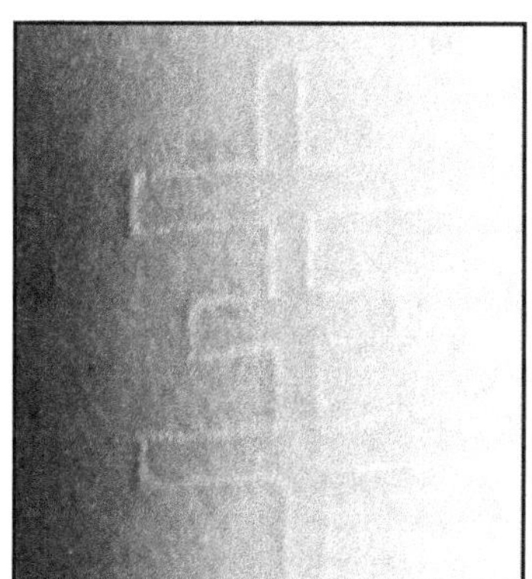

Paula. White tattoo. Photo by Christine Alicino.

■ *V: So how did you first get the idea to be pierced? You met Mr Sebastian and then it started to happen.*

■ PPO: I first had my ears pierced when I was six, my mum took me to the jewelers. The second holes I did

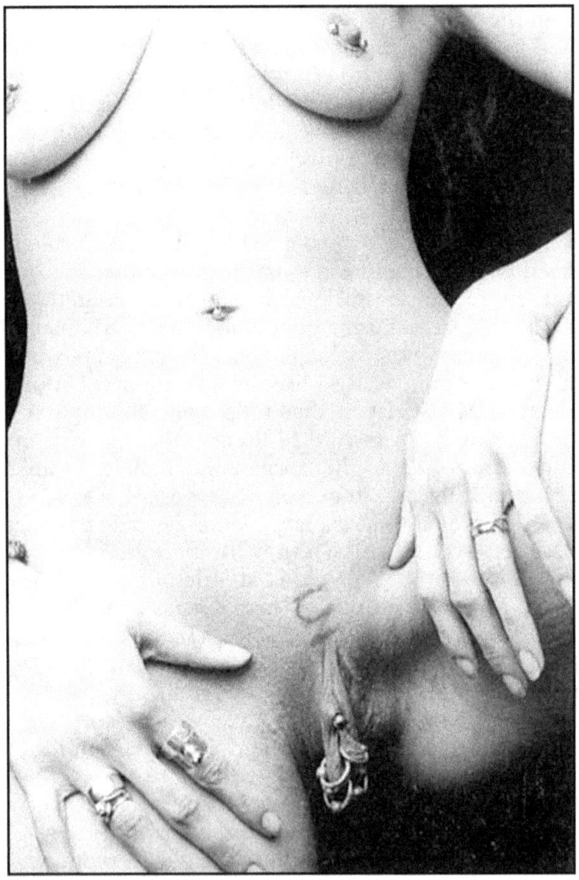

Paula. Piercings by Mr. Sebastian. Photo by Christine Alicino.

myself when I was about twelve. I got a cork and some ice and pierced it and it was fine; it healed up quite well. After I had Caresse, when I was 19, I had my labia pierced. Then I went back a year later and had 3 more rings put in, for a total of 2 on each side. Now I have 3 on one side and 2 on the other; I have 2 rings through one hole. Then I have a clit piercing as well.

■ *AJ: You do? Through the hood, or—*

■ PPO: Through the clit. I had that done at the same time as my labia. I had my nipples pierced too; I had that done after I had Jeunesse, nearly 3 years ago. I had my navel pierced in the summer of '86, and it wasn't fair because I was saying to people, "I really want to have my navel pierced," and all these people that I knew said, "Yeah, yeah!" and got *their* navels pierced, and I was really getting envious because I couldn't—I was pregnant. And they were having these nice rings put in and I couldn't; I was thinking, "You bastards!" [laughs]

■ GPO: What about the "notches on your gun"—the rings on your labia? Where did they come from?

■ PPO: The actual rings were originally Prince Albert rings—P.A. for short; piercing slang! I've got five rings in my labia—all of them from different lovers. They're not exactly trophies—more like love talismans.

■ GPO: Quite unique as a collection—I doubt if anyone else in the world has one like this! The actual, original 5 rings that were put through 5 people's cocks, are now all in her labia. She's got 2 in 1 hole, because she ran out of holes.

■ *AJ: Couldn't you have more holes put in?*

■ PPO: I suppose so, but then it wouldn't stop!

■ *V: Are they for pleasure?*

■ PPO: They're mainly aesthetic, I wouldn't say they make anything more sensitive.

■ GPO: They did when you got the first one. When piercings are *fresh,* the sexual excitation is more pronounced. The other way of looking at it is that your threshold of sensitivity is heightened so that you simply don't notice it anymore.

I personally feel the latter is true. I had an ampallang which I removed for a time. The hole had become too tight so that I couldn't put it back in. For about a year, I didn't have the ampallang and I really noticed a reduction in orgasm intensity and sensitivity, although previously I'd thought I had just gotten *used* to it—the effect had died away. But without it I realized how much it had increased sexual sensitivity, even *after* you've become accustomed to it.

■ *V: Another pierced man we spoke to said that since the piercing his orgasms are reached more quickly and in fact, it is difficult to have sex for as long as when he was unpierced. Do you find this to be true?*

■ GPO: That may be. It's more of a conscious effort to control the orgasm now. But, I'm not a "marathon man"—you know: the longer you have sex, the better, anymore than I think that the hugest cock makes the best sex. The conjunctions that make for good sex are many and varied, thank goodness. But certainly, the orgasms that I *do* have are *wonderfully better!*

■ *AJ: Tell us more about the clit piercing.*

■ PPO: It didn't hurt at all when it was done.

■ *AJ: What about later on with it in you all the time?*

■ PPO: It's quite nice. I think that there's always an underlying feeling, because it is a muscle. It's especially sensitive initially. It's definitely more worth having than any of the other piercings, sexually. Whereas some of the piercings, like the navel, are purely aesthetic.

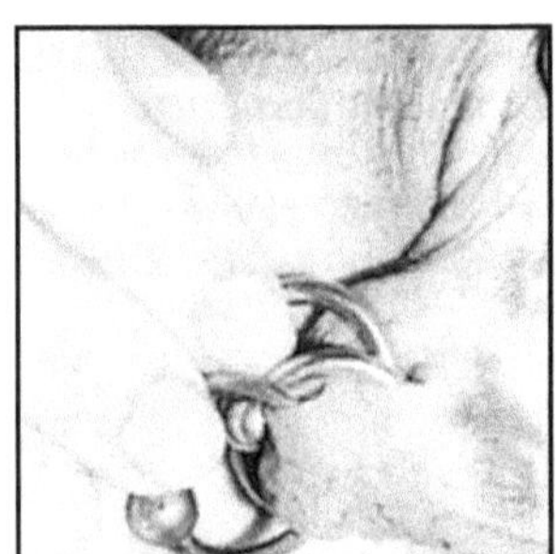

Paula's inner labia tattoo of a rune of Genesis's name. Piercings and tattoos by Mr. Sebastian. Photo by Andrew Rawling.

■ *V: How about the nipple piercings?*

■ PPO: Yes, they do make my nipples more sensitive. Mine were quite sensitive anyway. They took the longest to heal.

■ *AJ: How long?*

■ PPO: It takes some people over a year.

■ GPO: They often can get sore again, even after they've healed. The clit piercing was incredible.

It didn't need to heal. It was all right the same day. She was able to masturbate –

■ *V: It didn't bleed, did it?*

■ GPO: Didn't bleed, wasn't bruised, it was healed instantly.

■ *AJ: You're the third person I've talked to with a clit piercing and they all loved it.*

■ *V: Do you think you could have dispensed with the labial ones?*

■ PPO: Possibly, but then I wouldn't have a place for my Prince Albert trophies!

■ *V: You could wear them as rings.*

■ GPO: That's not as interesting. Symbolically, the idea of them being there –

■ *V: Yes, as a reverse chattel symbol. That's kind of nice.*

■ GPO: *I* think so, despite the fact it means you've been unfaithful to me at least four times! [laughs]

■ *V: When you first met Mr Sebastian, did you have any resistance to the idea of genital piercing?*

■ GPO: When Paula had the iris tattooed, she got me an engagement ring which was the first ring in my ear—my first piercing! Sleazy had just had his foreskin pierced on both sides. He was very proud of it, as people usually are. It took me about a year to actually decide to get a Prince Albert. It wasn't so much resistance, as letting information sink in and have time to think about what I *really* wanted, instead of being impulsive which is my way.

■ *V: You didn't worry about a risk factor?*

■ GPO: Not once I decided to get it done. I've always been interested in the investigation of sexuality and pushing my own thresholds, so once I was given this information (which even then was quite unknown except in the gay underground), it was inevitable that it would appeal to me.

■ *V: How does the Prince Albert work?*

■ GPO: The Prince Albert works because it's going through all the nerve endings. So every time you thrust or move, the ring is twisting around in the hole stimulating the urethra and also sending every vibration of movement through the flesh where all the nerve endings are. It's like being stroked and nipped.

■ *V: It doesn't hurt, ever?*

■ GPO: It took four days for me to heal enough to fuck, and one day to be able to masturbate. It stung once when I had it pierced—a little.

■ *V: I meant later on, like a year later?*

■ GPO: No. Only at first. I was told to wait ten days by Mr Sebastian.

■ *V: I heard 90 days.*

■ GPO: Well, he told me ten 'cause he knows what I'm like. He usually says sixty days, but I waited four [laughs] 'cause I can't stand the idea of waiting so long! It was nice, too—only a slight headache afterwards. While I was fucking it was brilliant—really amazing. The first wank I had the day after the pierce was done shot right over my head and all over the wall like rockets going off—like a ridiculous exaggerated porno. You get pink spunk because of the blood, which is quite weird.

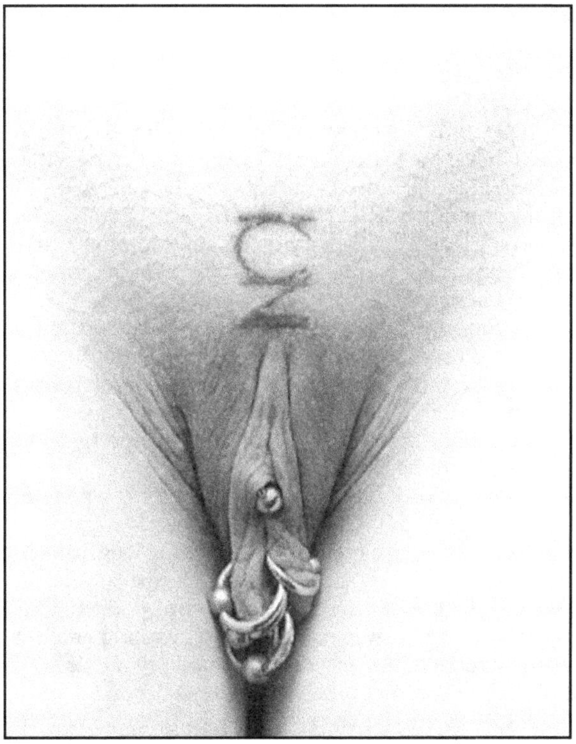

Paula. Piercings by Mr. Sebastian. Photo by Christine Alicino.

I didn't do it to prove I can stand pain—I know I can if I want to. I did it because I wanted the effect, not to prove I was butch. Of course Paula has gone through childbirth which is pretty tough.

■ *V: Paula, you had your children without anaesthesia?*

■ PPO: Yes, and both at home. No drugs at all.

■ *V: Did you use the Lamaze method, or what?*

■ PPO: Just had it! We did have a midwife.

■ *V: I always thought that women should squat when they give birth—*

■ PPO: That's mainly what I did, but I was in labor for 3 days and it was a breech birth, which is of course more difficult. To prepare, I just looked at other people and thought, "Thousands of other women and cultures have had babies, and have worked out birthing methods. No one taught the American Indian or the African women how to give birth, and *they* squat, so it seemed right to go *with* gravity instead of against it (which is the traditional Western way of giving birth). You don't lie down when you're going to the toilet.

■ GPO: In the end, to get the baby out we had to jump up and down. She was stuck!

■ PPO: I had two people on each side supporting me. We'd sort of go, "One-two-three" and then I'd drop to the ground, stopping at the last moment.

■ *V: I've never heard of that before!*

■ GPO: I don't think anyone had! But it seemed logical.

■ *V: It obviously worked, because the baby came out and was born alive.*
■ GPO: And very healthy.
■ PPO: She was a bit blue at first.
■ GPO: She was undiagnosed breech. The birth would have been far more traumatic in a hospital, because once diagnosed, Paula would have been given a Caesarian, regardless. If we'd been in the presence of doctors, they probably would've panicked (since they didn't expect the breech) and jumped to the unnecessary surgery. Whereas we all just thought, "Well, what's the most logical thing to do to get the baby out? Jump up and down!" We also gave her a little tug because she was stuck at the shoulders. It took 3 days of labor. Tough girl!
■ PPO: My second baby, Jeunesse, was pretty easy. She just came right out.
■ *V: Genesis, do you have any other piercings besides the Prince Albert?*
■ GPO: My next piercing was the ampallang. I liked the idea that the majority of the piercing is concealed, with just the ball at each side. I thought it looked visually interesting. It was nice that it was subtle and yet more extreme in that it went *right through* the flesh.
■ *V: Through the urethra, too.*
■ GPO: Yes. If you're crafty, you can hook the P.A. ring around the ampallang inside the urethra so that they pull on each other so that you get an internal action going on.
■ *AJ: Do you do that sometimes?*
■ GPO: I can't now, because the ring I've got is too thick. It's the thickest one Mr Sebastian has ever put in. It takes two full-grown men to undo the ring. I can't take it out at all.
■ *AJ: That's what you had, two full-grown men?*
■ GPO: Even then we could only just do it. We've got it on video at home, the struggle. It was crazy.
■ *V: You tried to remove it once?*
■ GPO: Well, to put it in took two people. When I went back to have the ampallang put in, he wanted to take the ring out. It was a real struggle getting it out and getting it back in. A six foot-two biker type and Mr Sebastian were both *exhausted* from just undoing this ring.
■ *AJ: What's the difference in feeling between the ampallang and the Prince Albert?*
■ GPO: The ampallang is more effective, but the two together are a good combination. I would recommend that everyone get both if you're going to bother.
■ *AJ: Does it affect urination?*
■ GPO: The exit hole for the Prince Albert is underneath, so with that jet and the other one heading forward, you're bound to miss. Now I always sit down to piss. All men should sit, anyways, because there are so many sloppy, lazy pissers around that the toilet stinks and is very unpleasant. I think all men should be *brought up* to sit on toilets!
■ *V: An interesting idea.*
■ GPO: Our office toilet is disgusting because people are so lazy and pathetic. It's so arrogant to assume you can piss on the floor, or the seat and not bother to clean it or worry about the stench. I find it a very unpleasant masculine trait.
■ *AJ: Especially for women who have to come in and sit on the same seat.*
■ *V: What about this report from Borneo that women there prefer and sometimes even demand larger ampallangs?*
■ GPO: I have a *very large* ampallang. Mr Sebastian had it made especially for me.
■ *V: "I've got a larger ampallang than you."*
■ GPO: I might be wrong, but I get the impression that Mr Sebastian rather enjoys my search for the extreme, like having the extra thick Prince Albert ring and then getting this ampallang with ball bearings of solid surgical steel on each side. They weigh a lot.
■ *AJ: Why steel and not silver?*
■ GPO: Silver tarnishes. You could have gold. I prefer the silver color anyways. I didn't bring the "over the top" jewelry along with me; you can't wear it very long anyway. They start tearing the skin—they're so heavy.
■ *AJ: You put them in for special occasions?*
■ GPO: Right. Most females I've had sex with since having piercings have been able to notice the difference, and feel the piercings to an extent. Only one complained that it hurt. Another didn't feel it.
■ *AJ: Do you feel the difference?*
■ PPO: *Definitely.* The ampallang was more pronounced than the Prince Albert.
■ *AJ: How does it feel?*
■ PPO: It just feels like there's something else there. You can feel it rubbing on the cervix.
■ *AJ: Maybe they should mount the ampallang the other way, too.*
■ GPO: She did experiment with that on one of her lovers. She got him to get the piercing that way specifically to see what it was like.
■ *AJ: And what happened?*
■ PPO: I didn't think it was as good, actually.
■ GPO: Poor boy! [laughter] All that trouble and she didn't like it. Sideways it tends to rub on the sides so it's like being fingered and fucked at the same time.

Another variant is a reverse Prince Albert. Instead of going underneath, it goes out and over the top. Mr Sebastian says he finds it very sensitizing to his cock. That would work because it would be on top of the edge.

There are also dydoes [see page ***], but they tend to grow out more than the other piercings. One tore out during sex, perhaps due to impatience!

Does it affect urination? The exit hole for the Prince Albert is underneath, so with that jet and the other one heading forward, you're bound to miss. Now I always sit down to piss. All men should sit, anyway.

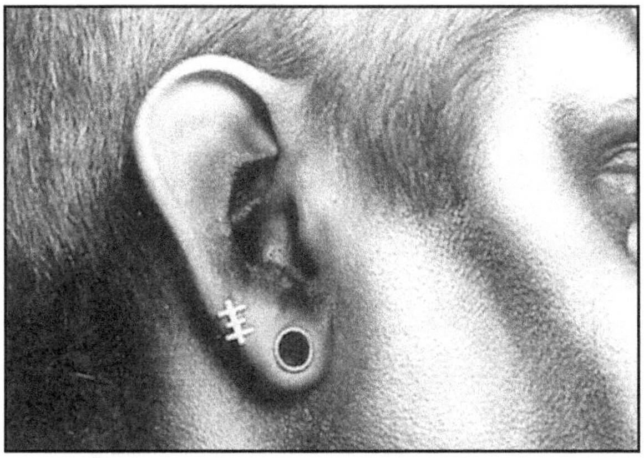

Genesis's ear piercings by Mr. Sebastian. Photo by Christine Alicino.

Most females I've had sex with since having piercings have been able to notice the difference, and feel the piercings to an extent. Only one complained that it hurt. Another didn't feel it.

I have three piercings in the scrotum which I got more for decorative purposes and for Paula to enjoy, but have found them to be quite enjoyable during masturbation, too. They have stimulated that area and jiggle about so it's quite pleasant.

■ *AJ: Is there any danger in piercing the scrotum?*

■ GPO: I didn't have any problems at all. In the sixties there were all these experiments with making a small hole and putting a straw in and blowing up the scrotum like a balloon. Then you fuck—it's supposed to give you this amazing orgasm.

■ *V: Who would do that?*

■ GPO: Lots of people. There's a whole article on this in a magazine, with a lot of debate in the letters section about the pros and cons. It tuned out that—I didn't read of anyone actually dying, but there was a potential danger of an embolism: an air bubble getting into the bloodstream, which put people off, but it was a big craze at one point. Free-loving hippies looking for the ultimate trip, *wherever* it may be. [laughter]

There was also trepanning, where you drilled into your head to release pressure from the pineal gland, causing a permanent high. Quite a few people did that.

■ *V: They did? What happened?*

■ GPO: Apparently it worked, but the effect gradually wore off in about two years. I guess scar tissue covered it up eventually. Nearly all of these things have origins in ancient cultures and have been tried and tested in so-called primitive societies for thousands of years. Incidentally, I have my nipples pierced.

■ *AJ: Did that make a difference?*

■ GPO: Yes! My nipples were a *dead zone* before they got pierced. Then they became a whole new discovery. It was nice—like being *female* as well. I used to like Paula to suck on them and play with them. So I discovered nipples, which was good—two more erogenous zones added.

But that piercing took the longest to heal and was the most painful by far. It was the only one I was tempted not to bother with, because it was such a drag sometimes. It would seem okay and then suddenly get sore again.

■ *AJ: Do you still have them in?*

■ GPO: Yes. There was a good pleasure zone increase and I hate to be defeated! I think you've got to firmly decide you want to do it and have a positive attitude. You can't be trepidant or you'll convince yourself that the pain is bigger than it is, or that the inconvenience is too much. Some people have more pain than others. You get one or two people who are very negative.

I knew of a woman who had her clitoris pierced by Mr Sebastian and then complained that it hadn't worked and was too sore. She took it out a week after that. She couldn't understand why it wasn't healing quickly, and she blamed him. He was quite upset and couldn't understand what the problem was. He felt he had failed: "This doesn't normally happen." Scratching his head…feeling really guilty. We discovered much later that the reason it hadn't worked was because she was breaking in young horses every day! On a brand new clitoris pierce! So you have to be sensible.

■ *V: Have you talked with other people who've been pierced?*

■ GPO: A lot of people who've met us have gotten pierced, not because we've sold it to them: "You should do this," although we *would* say, "This certainly feels good." But we let people know that it exists as a possibility, just like how we found out. Suddenly they know it can be done. They know someone who's done it and say it's nice and they know where to go to have it done. We know about fifty people who have been pierced, and *not one* of them would go back to not being pierced. It's definitely considered by everyone to be a step to another dimension or plane of improvement.

None of these people were dissatisfied before. They didn't think sex was boring; they were people who were into sexuality anyway and were interested and curious. They didn't rush into it, either. It was pondered for a while. And it probably became almost a private challenge: Can you deal with your own conditioning and your own prejudice, when in fact you shouldn't have any, because you've never been told about it before?

■ *V: Fear of pain.*

■ GPO: I think it's something else: *the preciousness of genitals* which we've been taught.

■ *V: It is that. But I know someone with an old ear piercing that to this day has never healed properly.*

■ GPO: I think people have to be sensible and take all these things into account. If they've had trouble with an ear piercing and they don't heal quickly, then

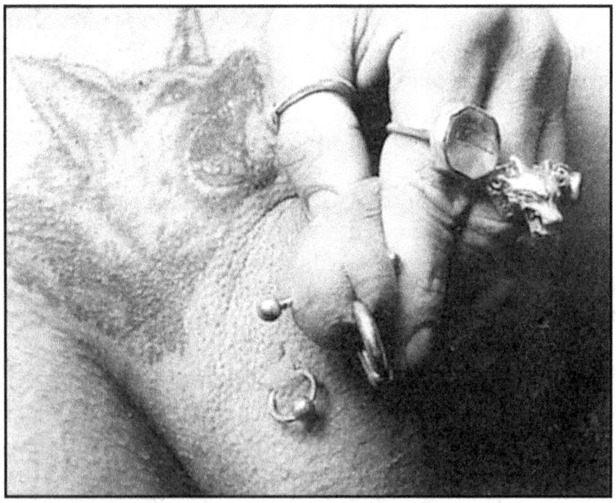

Piercings by Mr. Sebastian. Photo by Christine Alicino.

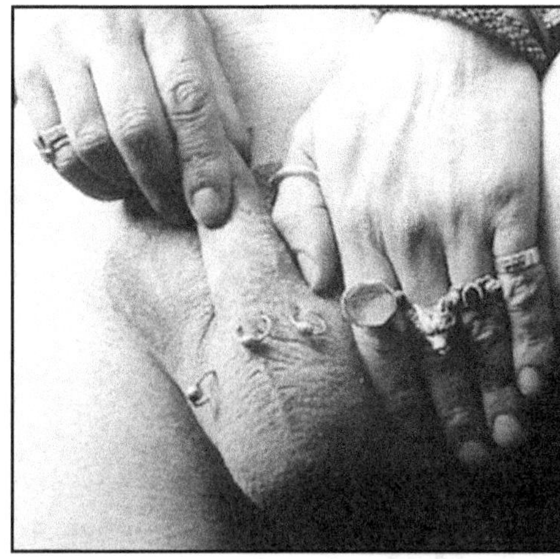

Piercings by Mr. Sebastian. Photo by Christine Alicino.

maybe they shouldn't have more piercings. They're only going to go moaning to everyone…

People have very different ways of dealing with pain and healing. Some people really make a theatrical meal out of it—others keep it to themselves. It's also very mood-sensitive. Like I said, I've been at Mr Sebastian's and have been daydreaming while being tattooed, and other days as soon as he gets near me it's agony 'cause I'm in the wrong mood. You rarely know in advance if you're going to be oversensitive, so you just have to deal with the bad days if you really want to accomplish something.

■ *V: Paula, do you know any other women with a clitoris piercing?*

■ PPO: Only one.

■ GPO: Our friend Sandra did. She liked it, but she had a little accident…

My nipples were a dead zone before they got pierced. Then they became a whole new discovery. It was nice—like being female as well. I used to like Paula to suck on them and play with them. So I discovered nipples, which was good—two more erogenous zones added.

■ *V: Let's hear about it!*

■ GPO: I don't know exactly how it happened, but somehow she caught the ring in her finger and tore the clitoris—not a *lot*, but enough to make the hole larger, which she found aesthetically displeasing. Eventually she took the ring out. That's the only "disaster" I've ever heard of. She was quite neurotic too, so it gave her an excuse not to bother. Or perhaps she was getting pressure from her boyfriend—I don't really know, but it didn't seem like we got the whole story.

■ *AJ: When it healed up, was it like it was before?*

■ GPO: Oh yeah, I checked it out. Worked perfectly!

■ *AJ: That's what a lot of people want to know: that if for some reason they don't like it, they can just let it grow back.*

■ GPO: With Paula, there was a big, noticeable difference right away. She went home and masturbated—

■ *AJ: That night?*

■ GPO: Immediately.

■ *AJ: So it didn't hurt at all?*

■ GPO: Not at all. We were both really surprised. Surprisingly, clits are very much like the heads of cock in that they heal very quickly.

■ *AJ: Fakir said that the reason the cock heals so quickly is because of all the blood vessels. Ears don't heal quickly because of the lack of blood vessels.*

■ *V: What about ball weights?*

■ GPO: That's one of Mr Sebastian's innovations, I believe.

■ *V: I think a lot of gay people do that, though.*

■ GPO: These particular ones he has specially made. They are solid steel and at least an inch deep with a hole in the center. They look a bit like a car part and are polished really smooth. The idea is to pull your scrotum through first as far as you can and then with your thumb you pop one testicle through the hole first. It's quite tight so you have to push it. You get this achy feeling as it goes through. Then you do the same with the other. Then you let the weight settle onto the two testicles. They weigh maybe a pound.

■ *AJ: What do they feel like?*

■ GPO: Once it's on it feels like having your balls licked and sucked and being played with by someone's hand.

■ *V: While you're having sex?*

■ GPO: Or while you're walking along.

■ *V: I suppose if you're having sex it'd be best to do it "doggy style."*

■ GPO: It seems to be better that way, because the weight can bang against the pussy if you do it face to face—that's the disadvantage. It's really nice if you're masturbating or being masturbated, because of the pulling sensation. If someone pulls up on your cock, this weight pulls down on your balls so you get this incredible interplay of up-and-down. You tend to have a semi hard-on all the time when you wear them. It's good. I put them on every once in a while when the mood takes me. If you wear them regularly it stretches the scrotum skin. As the skin is very elastic it will stretch considerably and you can then put on two weights which I can do. Mr Sebastian has photos of a guy who has fourteen. His testicles are actually by his knee. From there on up it's just steel!

■ *V: Isn't that a little impractical?*

■ GPO: He can't keep putting them on and off. Actually, he had one accident where he fell over and injured one of his balls which started to swell. He could feel the testicle swelling up, and very bravely managed to get all the weights off before the ball swelled too much. I'm sure he had paranoid visions of testicular amputation—not to mention the difficulty of explaining that at the hospital! He did recover, but through the healing time his scrotum tissue shrank back up so he had to re-stretch them again.

There is another technique we heard of, which is to use the weights to stretch out and get maybe 3 or 4 on—then you use a leather band in place of the weights. With this on you can actually fuck people with your balls. The leather is like the cock shaft, and the balls like the head. You can fuck two people at the same time...or one person both in their pussy and anus at the same time. Which raises interesting visions. By the way, this has been done!

■ *V: You have a rather large ear piercing.*

■ GPO: Yes, I was at Mr Sebastian's one day and noticed that he had rivets just for ears. I liked the idea, and asked him how to stretch the ear pierce. I thought you would put more and more weight on it, but he said that would tend to tear the hole instead of enlarging it. The best way is to keep putting larger and larger rings through.

■ *V: Does it hurt?*

■ GPO: The first few rings hurt a little, but then the discomfort goes away and you can enlarge the earhole tremendously if you desire. I had a large rivet especially made. I like it because it's subtle and radical at the same time. It's extreme, and yet people don't notice it; I like the ambivalence of it. When people *do* notice it they react *very* strongly and are often really disgusted. They find the size of it horrifying. I think it's because they link it to what they think of as "primitive" culture and they draw back from it even more.

■ *V: Do you have more thoughts on why people are motivated to do these "modern primitive" activities?*

■ *AJ: Or why this culture is opposed to "primitive cultures"?*

■ GPO: I don't think they *are* primitive; I think they're sophisticated. They integrate all the different aspects of life and psychology and don't separate dance and celebration; don't separate so-called "mental illness" but celebrate it when it occurs (which is rare) as the divine gift of the "seer" or the court jester or the shaman who is part of the village tribal community. Dreams are regarded as valid daytime experiences. I think that's a very sophisticated attitude—the integration of things as opposed to the disintegration—

■ *V:—and the alienation.*

■ GPO: Take childbirth as an example. In Britain there was actually a period of time when the medical community declared that there was no such thing as natural childbirth, that having a baby without drugs and not being in a hospital was unnatural! It was insane to hear this but they were serious. That same kind of perverted hypocrisy and blindness is prevalent in people's sexual conceptions of what is or is not possible.

I think that in tribal situations, even though they do ultimately develop sexual rules and regulation, they've also experimented with far more variety and are prepared to accept initiation rites, and what we would consider to be taboo activities. They see tattoos, marking, piercings as being a natural, on-going part of one's life.

■ *V: I like the idea of mutual aid; Kropotkin wrote a book on this idea. Associations with other loners, based on shared interests and affinities, and a recognition that this affiliation and exchange of information facilitates mutual survival.*

■ GPO: Like having a very loose club to belong to, where you don't have to join the club to belong to the club.

■ *V: But all this just belies a certain lack, namely: how few people alive today are capable of conversing on an astounding range of subjects; of being poets and philosophers and historians all at once. Very few people get the opportunity to be exposed to a truly rich conversation.*

■ GPO: Brion Gysin was like that. Mr Sebastian's like that; he's sixty. The people who are capable of that seem to be from that generation.

■ *V: The last Renaissance men who've read really widely, can remember what they read, synthesize data and come up with new conclusions right before your eyes, are almost gone from the planet. All the political "leaders" and media stars are just talking heads reading teleprompters—ad agency creations.*

■ *AJ: How do you view the integration of your body modification?*

■ GPO: I think that what people are doing now is relearning the idea of having a total lifestyle. They're searching as we certainly all have been (since Sartre) for identity—to affirm *existence*. We don't believe in an afterlife or God or gods, so how do we affirm our existence while we're here? How do we feel we are alive? How do we measure being alive? How do you *know* you're alive? Well, one of the times you feel most alive is when you're scared stupid, or you're in pain, or at the moment of orgasm when you transcend your normality—then your level of sensory input is radically altered.

Fight, flight and ecstasy are the three things. Those are all combined in piercings and tattoos and the marking of your passage through life and the idea of it being a visual, permanent library of experiences that cannot be taken from you except by death. You can be locked in prison, stripped of your hair, clothes, jewelry, friends, everything, but you can look at your arm and there's your tattoo and all the meaning it has for you.

I think if you're honest, there is also the enjoyment of being separated from the despicable *norm.* I remember giggling and feeling an amused, almost *smugness* going up the escalator after having the first Prince Albert piercing done...thinking how invisible it was to everyone else, yet how much it would shock them if only they knew. I enjoyed that mysterious separation from the everyday. It's childish in a way, but you can't deny it. It wasn't a prime motive, but it was something that I did experience at the time—feeling mischievous, almost, but glad not to be like all the people passing by with their briefcases looking miserable, who probably have sex twice a year in the dark and feel paranoid about it.

People have become aware that you can go further than nose and ear piercings, and that it's pleasurable and tribal and it's secret. You either tell people or otherwise the only people who discover it are people you're intimate with. So it's symbolic of intimate trust; being part of a circle of people who have a mutual trust and understanding of something that's largely non-verbal. It has many reverberations psychologically, most of them positive. Although there's always the "I can get more than you" brigade. [laughter]

Fight, flight and ecstasy are the three things. Those are all combined in piercings and tattoos and the marking of your passage through life and the idea of it being a visual, permanent library of experiences that cannot be taken from you except by death.

■ PPO: We do rituals every day that we take for granted. For example: as a woman, I enjoy the daily ritual of putting on my make-up on, but most people don't ever think about where this came from. Really, it originated from putting masks on your face for different rituals, for different seasons or festivals, or to define the tribe you're part of. And for beauty.

There is an irony in that the very people who have pierced ears, and who put their make-up on every day, are often the ones who will label people as "uncivilized" for being in tribes and putting on masks and having piercings...yet of course what *they're* doing is something that has passed through the culture—they're using the *remains* of it. They don't realize the connections between themselves and these so-called "primitive" peoples. Yet maybe having a flashy car parallels a shaman having a fancy headdress. Although...most people can't express themselves the way they would like to.

■ GPO: They don't put the content into the symbol anymore.

■ PPO: People's materialistic possessions are often just a compensation for their deep-rooted lack of true self-expression. A bright shiny new car conceals an essentially empty person sitting inside.

■ *V: They're just modern day fetish objects, horribly designed and mass produced, without the original magical significance. Like charms made for the tourist industry.*

■ *AJ: The symbolism is usually the money and alienated status attached to or implied by ownership of the car. A ring that doesn't cost anything but has a direct symbolism and integration into yourself has a greater true personal value compared with a mass-produced car with a far-removed link to the society's value system of money and status.*

■ PPO: Although some people with snazzy cars have very deep-rooted feelings for them. The cars are their creative expression.

■ GPO: Or rather: they get manipulated into this being their creative expression. That's one thing we've always been fascinated by: what motivates people. Are they following deep-rooted impulses or are they conditioned? It's obvious: the lack of understanding of themselves most people have; the lack of self-analysis.

■ *V: That's what advertising preys upon: people's lack of understanding of their very own desires or motivations.*

■ GPO: At Mr Sebastian's I met a very nice middle-aged American businessman in a suit and tie. We talked and it turned out he'd just been tattooed in San Francisco with a full body suit that took a couple of weeks to complete! He took his clothes off to show me and it was *everything*—cock, nipples—the lot! The tattoo extended up to his neck and his wrists so he could look totally normal the rest of the time. I blurted out, "But suppose you want another tattoo in the future? What will you do?" He looked a little disappointed by the thought. I felt really *mean* because I'd sown the seed of doubt only 2 weeks after he'd finished it! It confirmed what I thought for myself: that it's better doing it a little at a time so the thrill remains.

■ *AJ: It can be an evolution and can serve as a marking of time and growth.*

■ GPO: The Romans found the Britons covered in *wode* (tattoos). The heritage of the pagan Britons was to be heavily tattooed, but of course we're not told of our tribal, integrated, celebratory culture in school. The history has been stolen and turned into a perversion called Christianity.

■ PPO: I think many people don't know what their culture was, or is, so they may well be regaining and redefining their culture. How can an experience be labeled "primitive" if you've never experienced it? I think people are finally learning not to take anybody else's word for anything ever again.

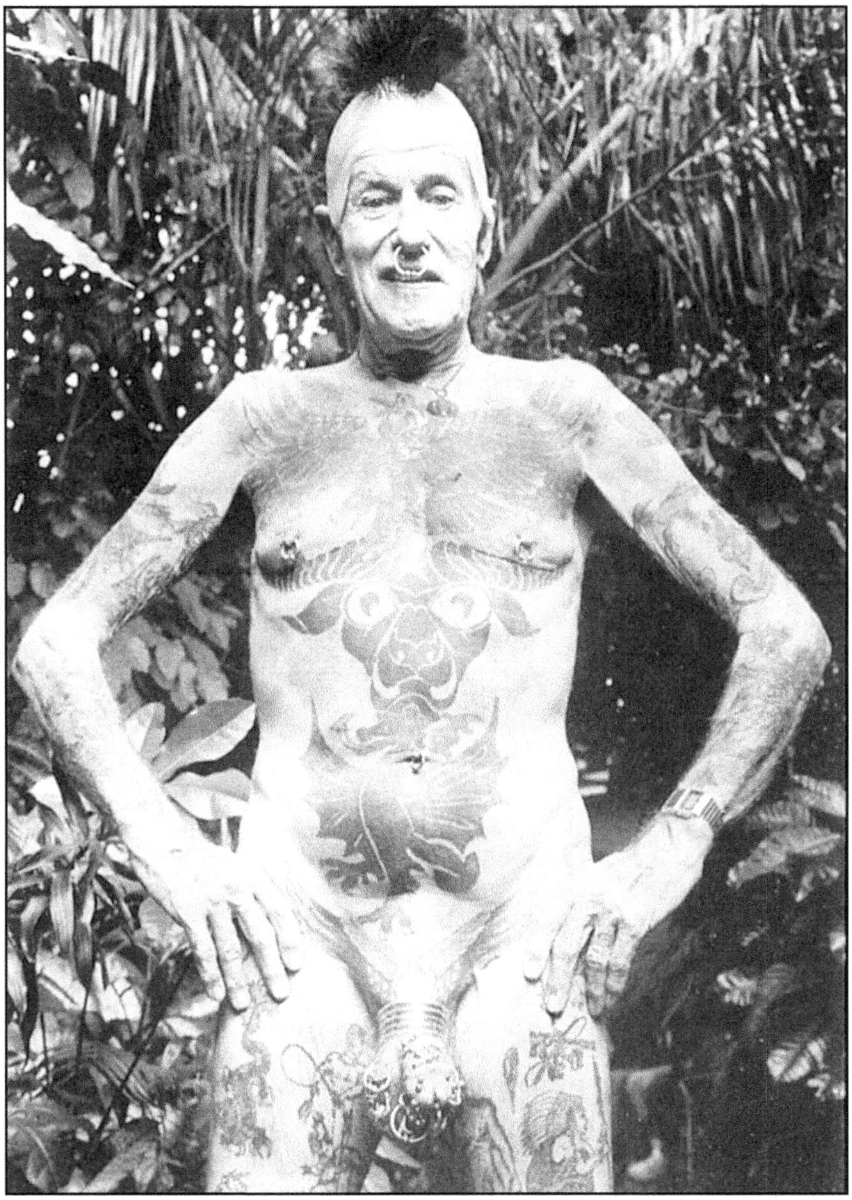

Sailor Sid Diller, tattoo artist and piercing fancier, Ft. Lauderdale, Florida. Photo by Charles Gatewood.

[laughter] That sums up the mentality very well.

■ *V: Will you get more and more piercings for the rest of your life?*

■ GPO: I'd like to, but unfortunately there's not enough places to pierce where it changes the situation in a positive way. If I had six cocks I'd day, "Yeah."

■ *V: Sailor Sid has over fifty piercings in his penis—*

■ GPO:—and I think they all give him pleasure. He was into this way before it was publicized. But the sad thing is that people don't have the subtlety to see that he is no different than the person who has one piercing. Instead, there's this challenge, "Sailor Sid's got 50—I'll get 100!" That's our consumer competing society's banality of vision being applied to something, without any understanding or sensitivity whatsoever. People just show themselves up by trying to compete or emulate something for its own sake. They'll probably regret it later, because it can't possibly have any great lasting effect on them—there's no *reason* for it. That's like deciding to amputate your arm because someone who's really intelligent only has one arm.

Sailor Sid's case was an investigation of what's possible, just like the guy who can turn his cock inside out who was featured in *PFIQ.* These things start out as a question and for private, deep-rooted reasons are explored. I think it's easy to differentiate between genuine explorers like Sailor Sid and people who do things because they're arrogant or want to dare or duel others.

People have such a limited vision—they think that *difference* means *intelligence,* and that by being different you are radical in yourself and challenging society. But most of the techniques people use are consumer-materialist techniques. They actually give *credence* to the very thing they're rejecting.

You have to look at yourself very deeply all the time. If your interests and actions are considered to be

■ *V: There are people who get tattoos and get pierced mainly to shock, not out of any deeper motivations.*

■ GPO: I've seen skinheads who get face tattoos mainly to shock and alienate anyone who looks at them. If you do look at them they threaten, "What are you looking at?" when it's quite obvious you're looking at someone with a great big spider and FUCK YOU OI! tattooed crudely all over their face! That reminds me—we heard about this skinhead who went to a "scratcher" to have "OI!" tattooed on his forehead. However, it was misdone, so for the rest of his life people will ask him, "Why do you have OIL tattooed on your forehead?"

bizarre by most people, then all the better. But to set out to *just* be different for its own sake is to actually surrender to the easiest path of all, which is to be superficial. We've all met people who look weird, but the moment they open their mouth they show themselves to be banal. And the most ordinary-looking, quiet, sedate people can turn out to be incredibly obsessed with something and *truly* fascinating—yet they don't see themselves as strange. That's the trick: you should feel *completely normal* within yourself.

■ *V: Being "different" evolves out of the pursuit and development of obsessive interests which are internal to yourself.*

■ GPO: I wonder what will happen in 30 years to all the people who are getting tattoos now. Will it still be relevant to them? With someone like Mr Sebastian, you cannot imagine him any other way than how he is. He's a polite, charming, totally integrated gentlemen who's always a bit shocked when people suggest that he's different or an outsider. That's a common factor with interesting people: they do not feel abnormal.

■ *V: Can you talk about the pagan heritage of your country?*

■ GPO: There was an idea that the United Kingdom be called the WISE Islands: W for Wales, I for Ireland, S for Scotland, and E for England. This would serve to remind the population that they have a natural geographic unity and that their original history is pagan. The old religion was called *wicca,* which means "wise."

Wicca was like the "street" version of the druids who were the high priests of wicca. Wicca is an anthropologically "natural" religion in that the spring, summer and winter equinoxes and the moon, fertility/healing relationship with the earth and environment were fundamental. Man was viewed as another animal on the planet integrating observation and survival, much like the American Indians or the Aborigines. Every being has a common heritage: they're forced to be on the planet for a certain span of life, so they should relate to each other as mortal and vulnerable.

In England, when the Romans arrived, the Brits were heavily tattooed. There was a time when people everywhere had the same urges and the same ways of relating to their environment and their situations—they needed to have an understanding of the elements and the seasons just to survive. Certain marks identified their area, tribe or family or their spiritual understanding of things. Now what we've got is an imposed colonialized pseudo-religion. The royal family aren't even English—they're German and Greek, yet they're the head of state and church. I find that very ironic.

The overall aristocracy of Britain has been built from invading forces and that's why the pagan religions have been erased so effectively in Britain. At the peak of the Middle Ages anyone who even hinted they were interested in wicca was tortured, maimed and murdered. It wasn't until the 1960s that the witchcraft laws were repealed. Incredible that it's only been 20 years since it was legal to express an interest in your own original roots.

Even now you cannot legally have a pagan burial or a pagan death. You must have your body cremated in a Christianized church. You don't have to have a totally Christian ceremony, but you can't be buried anywhere you want—it has to be in a government-approved Christian cemetery. To do otherwise is illegal. If you say, "I want to be buried in my friends' back garden" and they do it, they'll be prosecuted.

We've been trying to set up a loose charity to lobby Parliament for the right to a pagan death. Muslims, Jews, Sikhs are all allowed to express their ethnic identities, yet the English cannot have an English death. Most haven't realized there's a difference.

Since the sixties, Stonehenge has been a focus for alternative or underground society. Summer equinox festivals were held there for many years until last year when The Convoy was ambushed by the police.

Surprisingly, clits are very much like the heads of cocks in that they heal very quickly.

■ *V: What's that?*

■ GPO: A loose association of people which had been developing over the years and at the time of last year's festival numbered perhaps 300 vehicles, hence the name. People lived in their trucks, cars and vans. They shared a philosophy and lived outside the normal system.

There's a law that if you settle the same site for a certain number of years, you get the eternal right to use that site. It turns out that this would have been the last year needed for The Convoy to gain that right at a certain site, but they were stopped by hundreds of police. Their homes were destroyed with no legal precedent.

The powers that be then set up an organization called *English Heritage,* which was then given all the sacred historic sites in Britain, and which just happened to be owned by the Free Masons. I mean the Free Masons who are descended from the Knights Templars, not your suburban freemasonry.

Take Glastonbury Tor—it's hollow—there are caves, labyrinths and underground rivers. There is one entrance to the underworld, but it's covered in a huge concrete slab that's locked. Only the high lodge of the Free Masons has the right and the means to open it. Once a year (the specific day remains a mystery) they go in and practice ancient ceremonies. Nobody knows who they are. Why do they want to have power over all those ancient sites?

All the key sites have restricted access now—Stonehenge has a cyclone fence around it. If you drive near these sites, especially at the equinox or solstice, you will be stopped—at the very least. Some sites have electric fences, security guards and dogs all year round.

During the Harmonic Convergence at Glastonbury Tor, there were riot police everywhere, even though it was a totally peaceful meeting and celebration.

I think if you're honest, there is also the enjoyment of being separated from the despicable norm. I remember giggling and feeling an amused, almost smugness going up the escalator after having the first Prince Albert piercing done... thinking how invisible it was to everyone else, yet how much it would shock them if they only knew.

All we're taught about early European history is that the Gauls, Picts, and the Goths were war-like savages, just down from the trees, and it was a good thing the Romans came in and "civilized" them. We're always given the impression that there weren't many of them, and they were primitive and uncivilized. Yet recently thousands and thousands of stone circles, villages and sites have been uncovered. There's no question that there were sizable populations in these Stone Age villages, and that the culture was far more developed than we've been led to believe. It also appears that these Stone Age peoples originated in Britain and migrated outward towards Europe and Crete. This population was wiped out by the Romans and it was genocide, just like everywhere else. The American Indians were wiped out in a similar style.

So there was a massive, ancient civilization in Britain that was just discounted, destroyed and erased from history. I guess it makes sense—why should Britain be different from anywhere else? I always thought it was odd that England supposedly had no early civilization, and yet there were all these monuments that archaeologists still to this day can't figure out. Geometrically and astronomically these places are very complex. We were told that the people responsible were primitive, whereas in Egypt and South America the monument builders were sophisticated!

The stones in Stonehenge came from Wales. Just to *build* Stonehenge required a huge organizational plan; it was a feat that perhaps took a couple of generations—or maybe a hundred years—to complete. A civilization that could get its people to focus long enough on such a great task for such a sustained period of time is not savage.

■ *V: What about the druids now?*

■ GPO: The authorities don't mind the ones who are *decorative* getting together once a year. They're probably serious in their own way, but...Some of them *are* diligently researching the old history, legends and culture—a difficult cask. The only other people who have access to this information are the Free Masons, and *they're* not telling; in fact, the way they behave leads one to believe that these sites really do possess special powers beyond logic. They don't want anyone messing with it—they don't want Pandora's box opened. I'm convinced that it's worth pursuing a connection back with those sites, because symbolically at least those sites are a key to re-establishing some genuine relationship with our past history that could lead to a quite different society in the future.

Our society is doomed to break and fragment into tribal situations, eventually. If we start investigating our tribal heritage, and appreciating it and embracing it, we have a chance of balanced survival when that happens. When money disappears we will have to start collaborating again; streets and villages or blocks in a town will become tribal units. Barter will become the exchange again.

Money *will* disappear; its whole enormous, stupid, cosmetic facade will eventually be revealed for what it is: a myth sustained by very dangerous, deluded people...people who are addicted to control for its own sake, but who no longer remember the word *control.* It's like a marksman with a machine gun who's been convinced it's a lollipop. They don't know who or what they are or what they're dealing with, yet they're at the top. They continue dealing for its own sake. They've lost touch with reality.

There are forces on this planet which they're dabbling with in a way that no one understands. No one understands the implications or repercussions of the greedy actions which led, for example, to the destruction of the ozone layer.

So the whole condescending notion of "primitive society"—bullshit! They're sophisticated—very clever. Every thing is integrated, supple, natural—

■ *V: —ideally, yes.*

■ GPO: Those role models arc worth consideration. It doesn't mean you can't have computers or tape recorders, but you use them with a larger perception or overview. You try to consider all the results and reverberations and effects and side-effects.

■ PPO: Like a computer programmer you try to find the most elegant solution to a problem: the one with the fewest number of steps.

■ *V: Like the water wheel in China which is totally non-polluting.*

■ GPO: Exactly. That's why it's really important to learn from these so-called primitive peoples—it has nothing to do with being hippy-dippy or New Age. The issue is *survival.*

MISCELLANEOUS

SCARIFICATION

ROBIN BOUTILIER

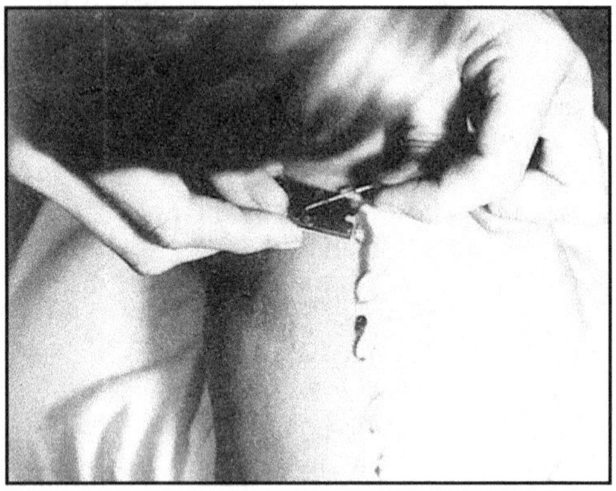
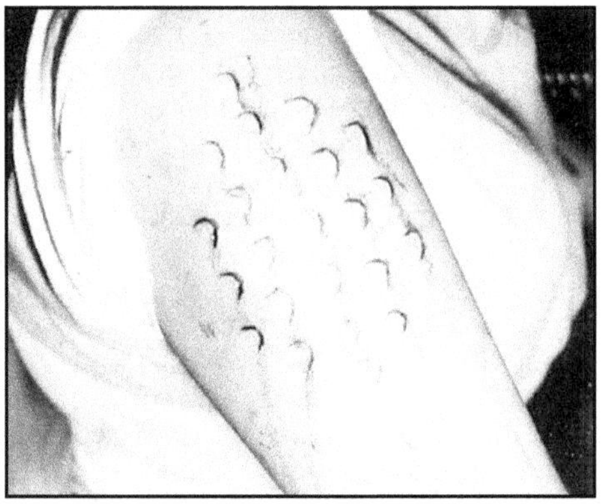
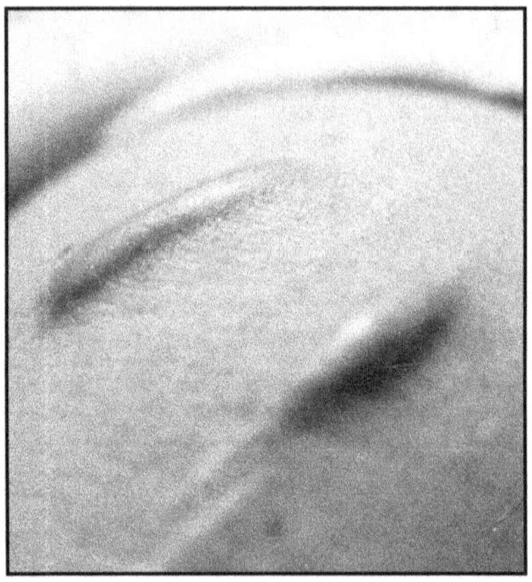
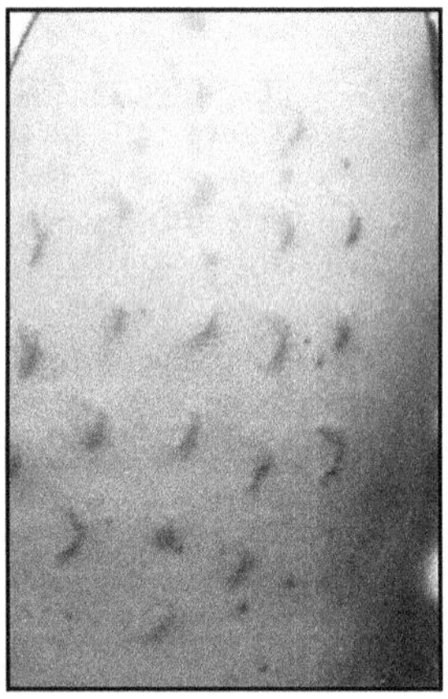

For some time I've been fascinated with more permanent forms of adornment: tattooing, piercing and above all, scarification. Several years ago I found a few old issues of *PFIQ* [piercing magazine—see Jim Ward, this issue]. The idea of body piercing was so instantly appealing that I got three piercings shortly after that.

My first scarification I did myself two years ago on my left shoulder—three fairly deep gashes which left beautiful raised scars. Shortly after these healed I noticed the scar tissue had taken on a pleasurable, sensual quality—I had acquired an unexpected new erogenous zone!

Later I decided that I would add more scars in an organized fashion to the other arm, with help from a friend. At first we tried to pull the skin up with tweezers, cutting with a scalpel, but discovered this didn't work as well as using a fishhook to pull the skin up, then cutting with a new razor blade. Next we deepened many of the cuts. After many of the scars had scabbed over, I began methodically pulling out the scabs, stimulating more and more regenerative tissue growth. After a few weeks I could feel the raised pattens taking shape. —Robin Boutilier. Cutting by Jeph Jerman. Photos by Lance Barton.

ASHLEIGH

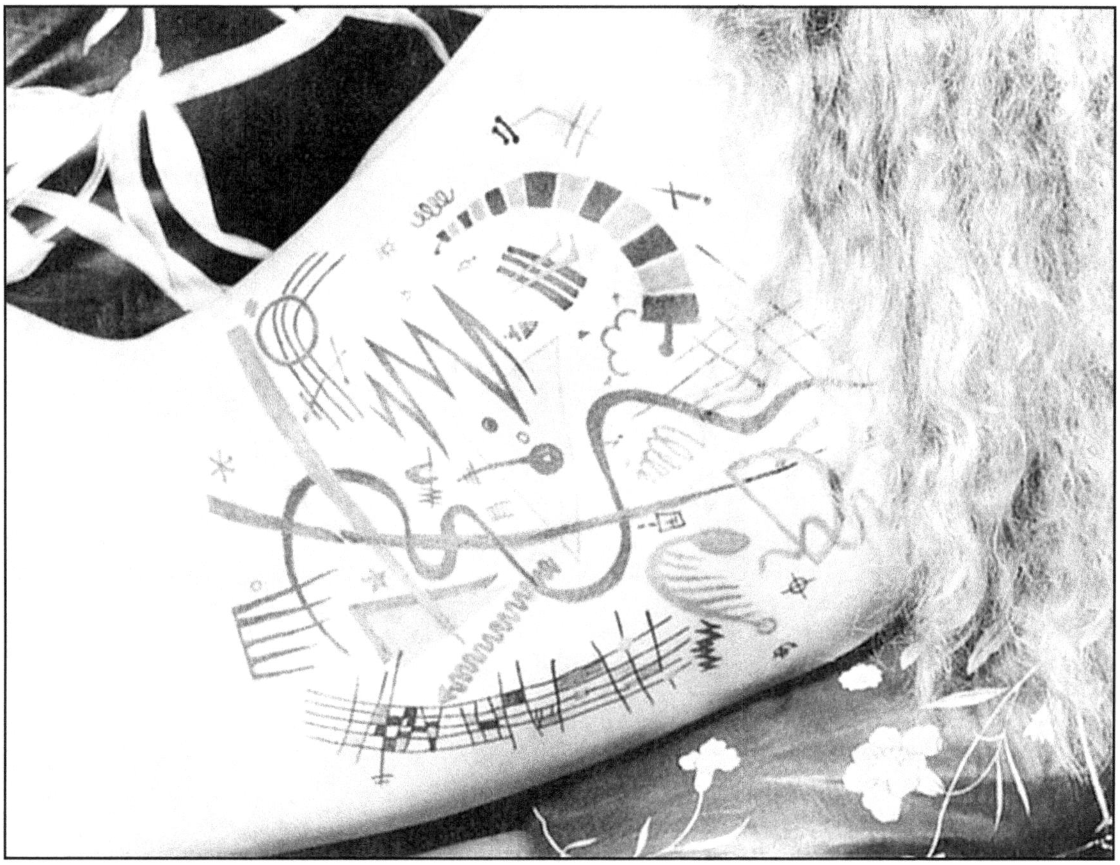

I remember admiring my father's old navy tattoos. He had three: a faded skunk named "Stinky" on his right forearm; a red and black heart with the name "Diane" tattooed across it in a banner; and my favorite, a woman's face and shoulders—she was wearing a cocked sailor's hat. When I was growing up I would often trace the outer, faded edges in total awe of these permanent "cartoons" on my father's skin.

Nine years ago I moved to Seattle from a small town, and to celebrate the change I got a tattoo as a symbol of my freedom. One of my first tattoos was a collaboration with Vyvyn (Madam) Lazonga: a wave of musical notes.

In 1985, my husband Louie and I got engagement tattoos of a rat on both of our right shoulders.

In 1987, Sailor Cam Cook (Seattle Tattoo Emporium) applied my Kandinsky-based design to my back. It took eight 2-hour sessions. The finished tattoo is in full-color, complete with fluorescent pink, orange, red, yellow, blue, etc inks.
—Ashleigh Raffloer. Photos by Louie Raffloer.

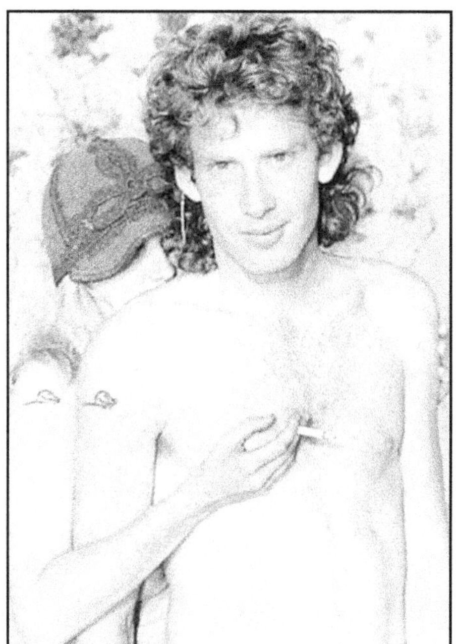

THAILAND

PHOTOS BY CHRIS SULLIVAN

During a trip to Phuhet and Trang, Thailand, Chris Sullivan snapped the two top right photos of window displays in a photo processing store. The two bottom photos he purchased from the store—photographer unknown. Note the bicycle and rifle hanging from various piercings.

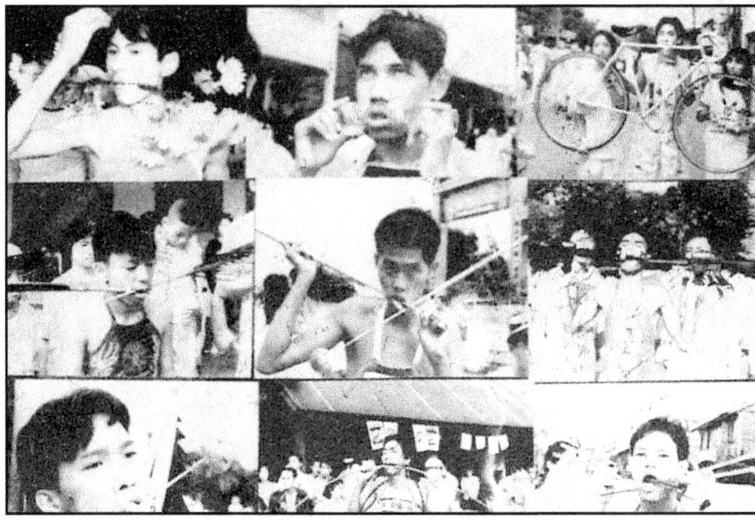

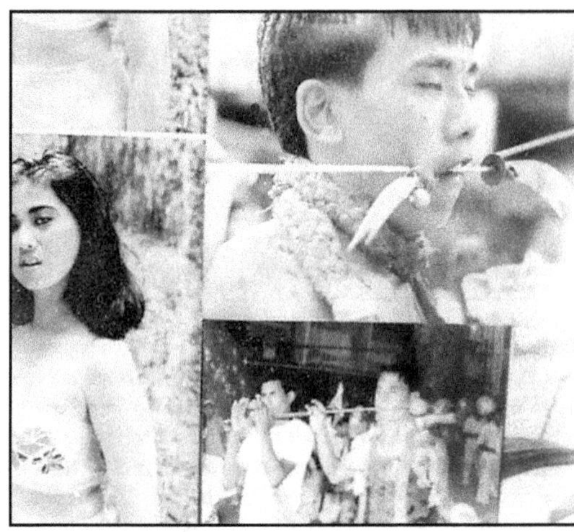

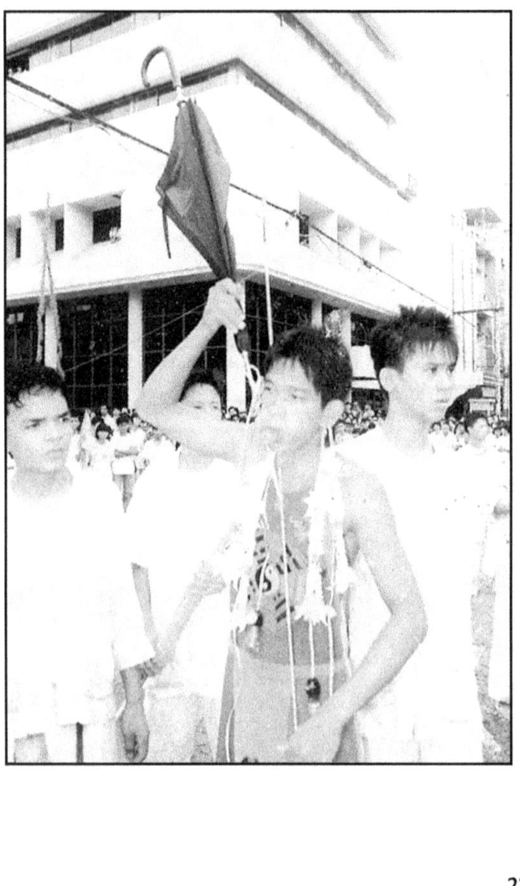

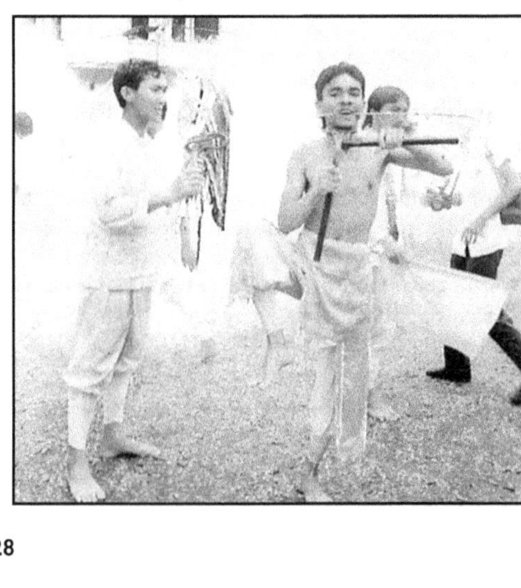

TATTOO FAMILY

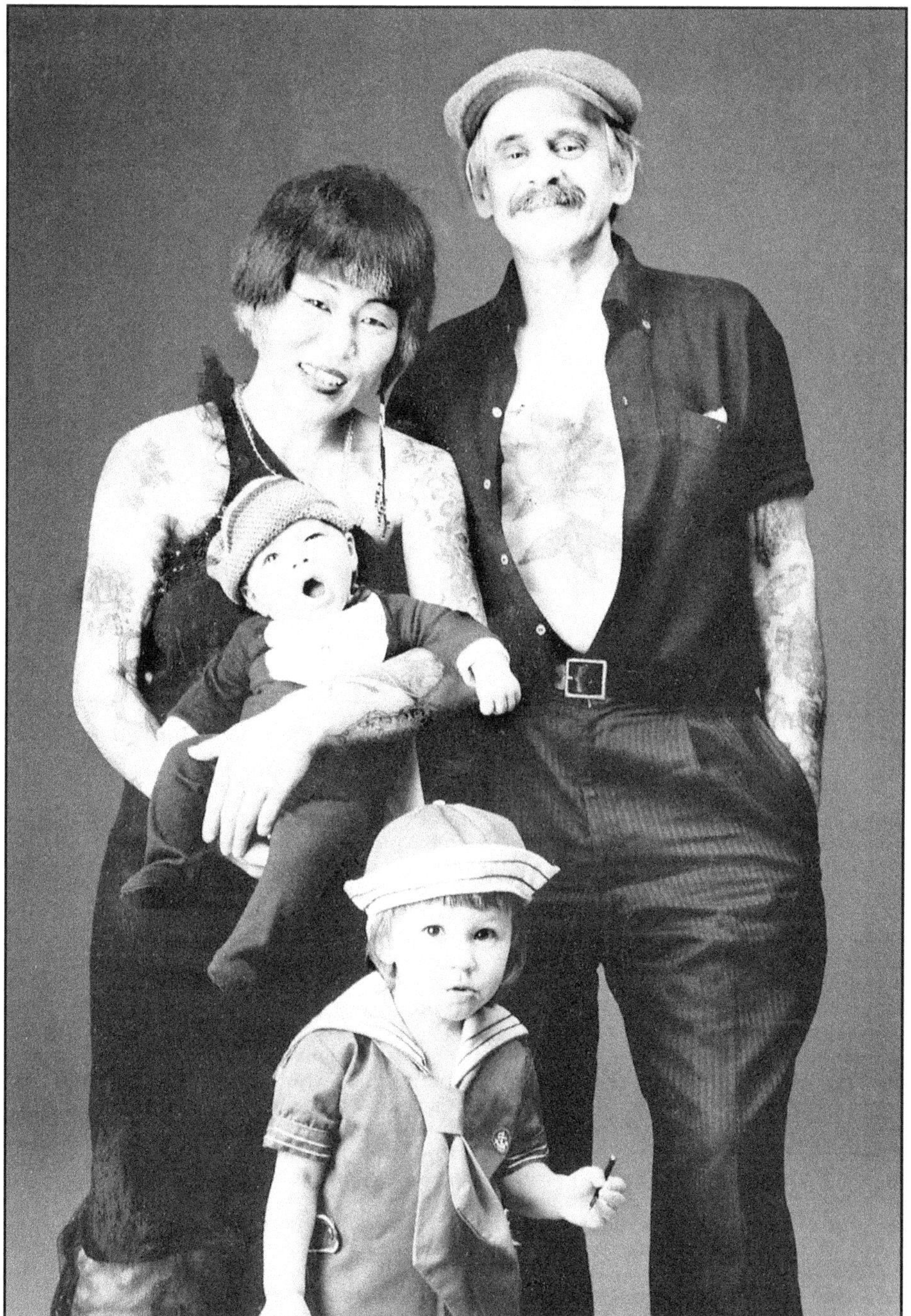

San Francisco Tattooists Inny Lee (originally from Korea; her mother tattooed herself as part of a long tradition of women's rite-of-passage tattooing), Henry Goldfield, and their children Leif and Lydia (named after "Lydia, the Tattooed Lady" from a Marx Bros movie. Note pen in Lydia's left hand and imitation tattoos she applied to her right forearm). Reportedly Leif's first spoken words were, "Tat-too, tat-too." Photo by Bobby Neel Adams.

KAREN MEADOWS

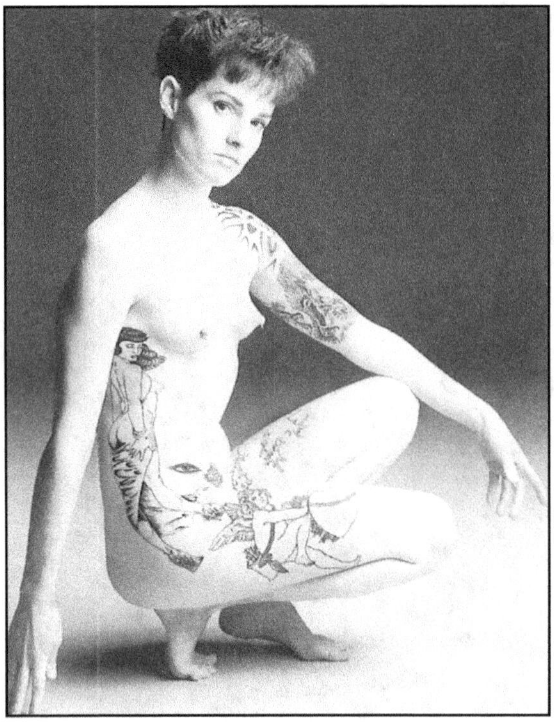 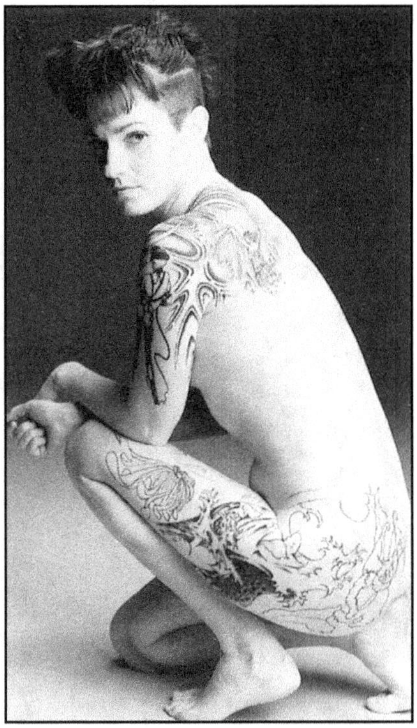

Photos by Bobby Neel Adams.

When I was growing up I would often hear references to my great-great-great-great-grandfather, Horace Holden, who had allegedly been shipwrecked in the South Pacific in 1832, captured by the "natives" and forcibly tattooed. But I didn't start actively researching his story until four years ago, when I got my first tattoo. I had thought about getting a tattoo for five years, but had hesitated because I knew I was prone to rash decisions. So I resolved to get one, and only one, tattoo, and that would be *it*. I got that first tattoo and was in the chair for four hours and 45 minutes...and at the end—immediately I wanted another one!

When I met Chuck Eldridge of the Tattoo Archive, I happened to mention my great-great grandfather, and he said, "He's famous!"—he already knew about him. Since then I've uncovered photos of him (although no photos of his tattoos yet), and discovered that my distant ancestor had been written about in more than a dozen books; for example J.C.Meredith's *The Tattooed Man*:

"One day Holden was told, 'Tugutarie says Yarri is angry with your white skin. It is obscene. We must tattoo you like Tobi men.' There was no choice. While two men held Holden to the ground, Parabua took a sharp stick and scratched a design on his chest. Then selecting an instrument like a tiny rake, with fishbones for teeth, he dipped it into a dye brewed from callophyllum berries, and holding it an inch above the flesh struck it repeatedly with a stick of wood in such a way as to drive the ink deep under the skin, even to the bone of his ribs. For Holden the worst of the nightmare was the way the onlookers laughed whenever the pain grew too intense for him to bear in silence.

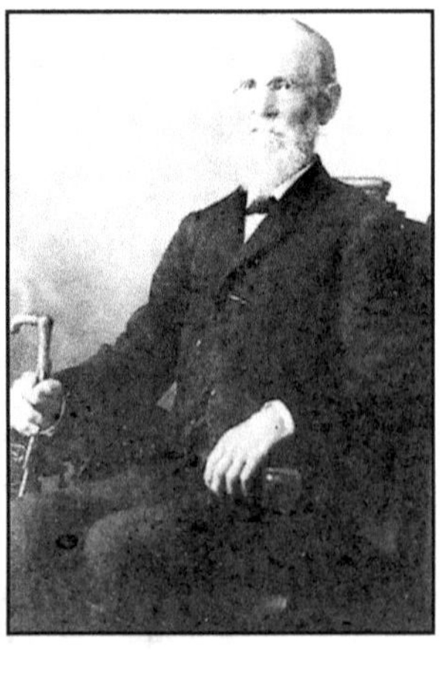

"These sessions were repeated again and again, as successive portions of his body were covered with various occult designs. No part of him was exempt. However, when only his face remained to be tattooed, he told Parabua that he would die resisting...and Parabua, rather than risk losing a valuable piece of property, relented."

In the past four years I've gotten quite a few tattoos (from Sailor Cam Cook, Bob Roberts, Bill Salmon and Chuck Eldridge) and I plan to get a lot more. My only rationale is: It must be in my blood! I also got my nipples pierced, and even though it took them a year to heal, I don't care—I'd never give them up. I hope to find out what designs my great-grandfather had, and get at least one of them put on...then see what happens...—Karen Meadows

TATTOOS

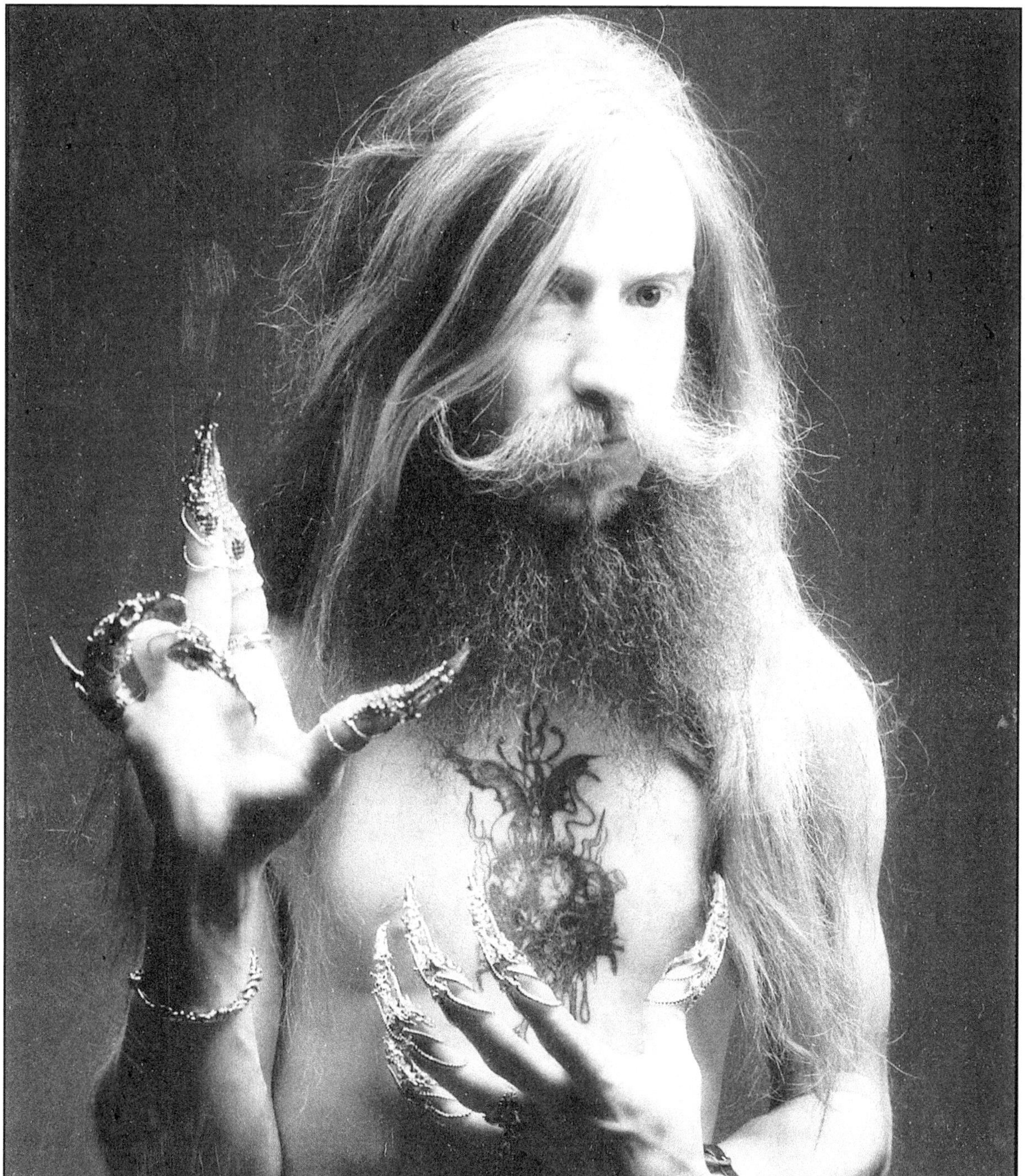

Axel, NYC jewelry maker with tattoo of open heart surgery that he did himself at age 17 with tattoo equipment borrowed from a passing carnival. Photo by Bobby Neel Adams.

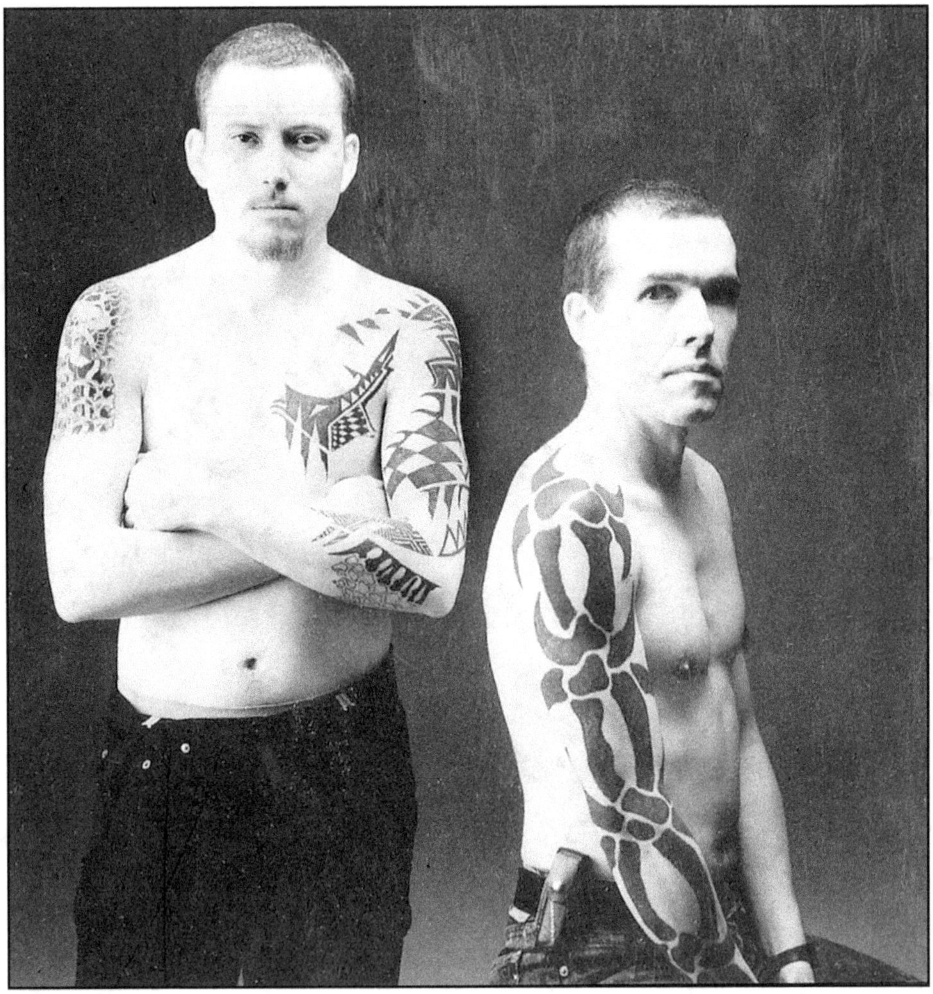

Tattoos by Greg Kulz and Fred Corbin. Photo by Bobby Neel Adams.

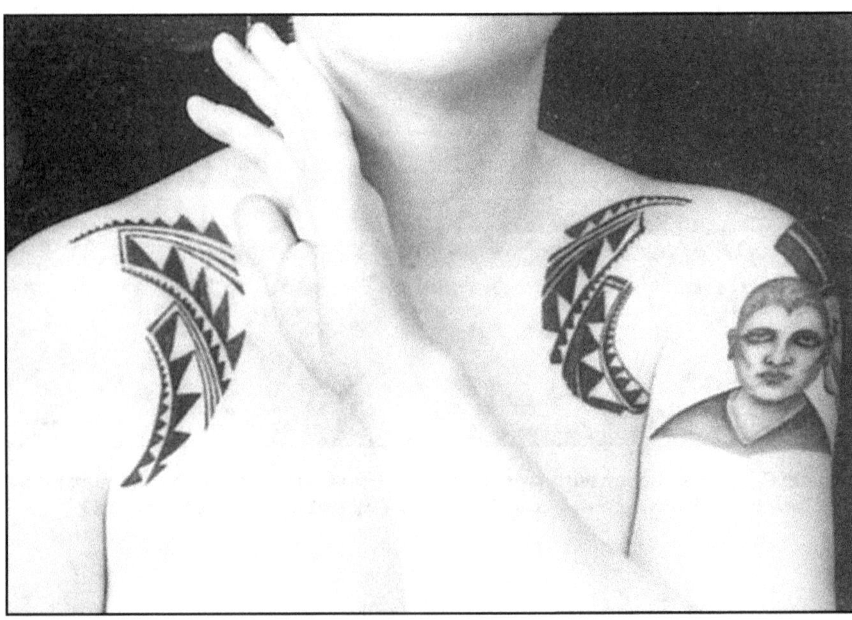

Collarbone tattoo by Bill Salmon. Photo by Bobby Neel Adams.

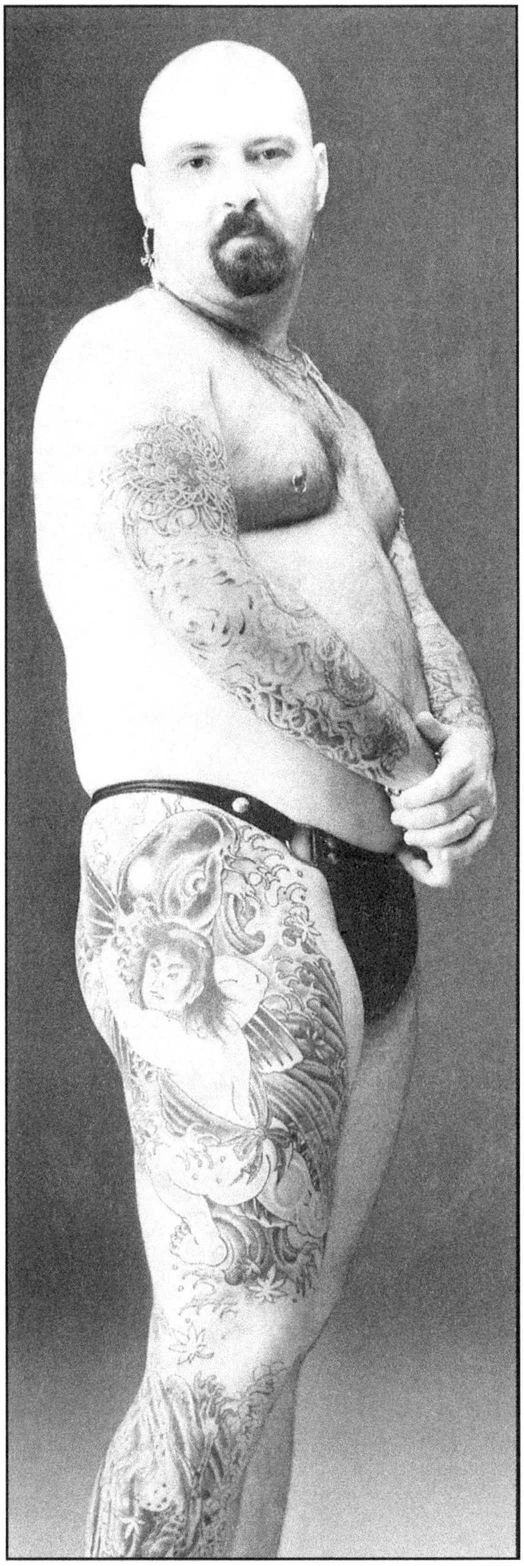

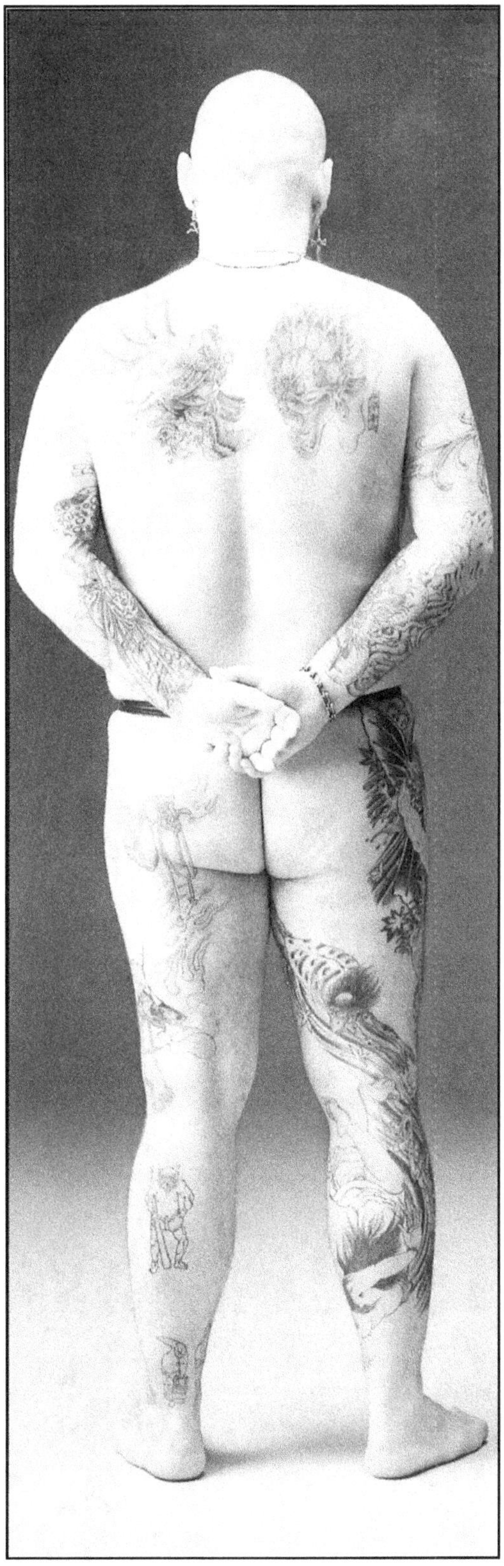

Tattoos by Ed Hardy and various artists. Photos by Bobby Neel Adams.

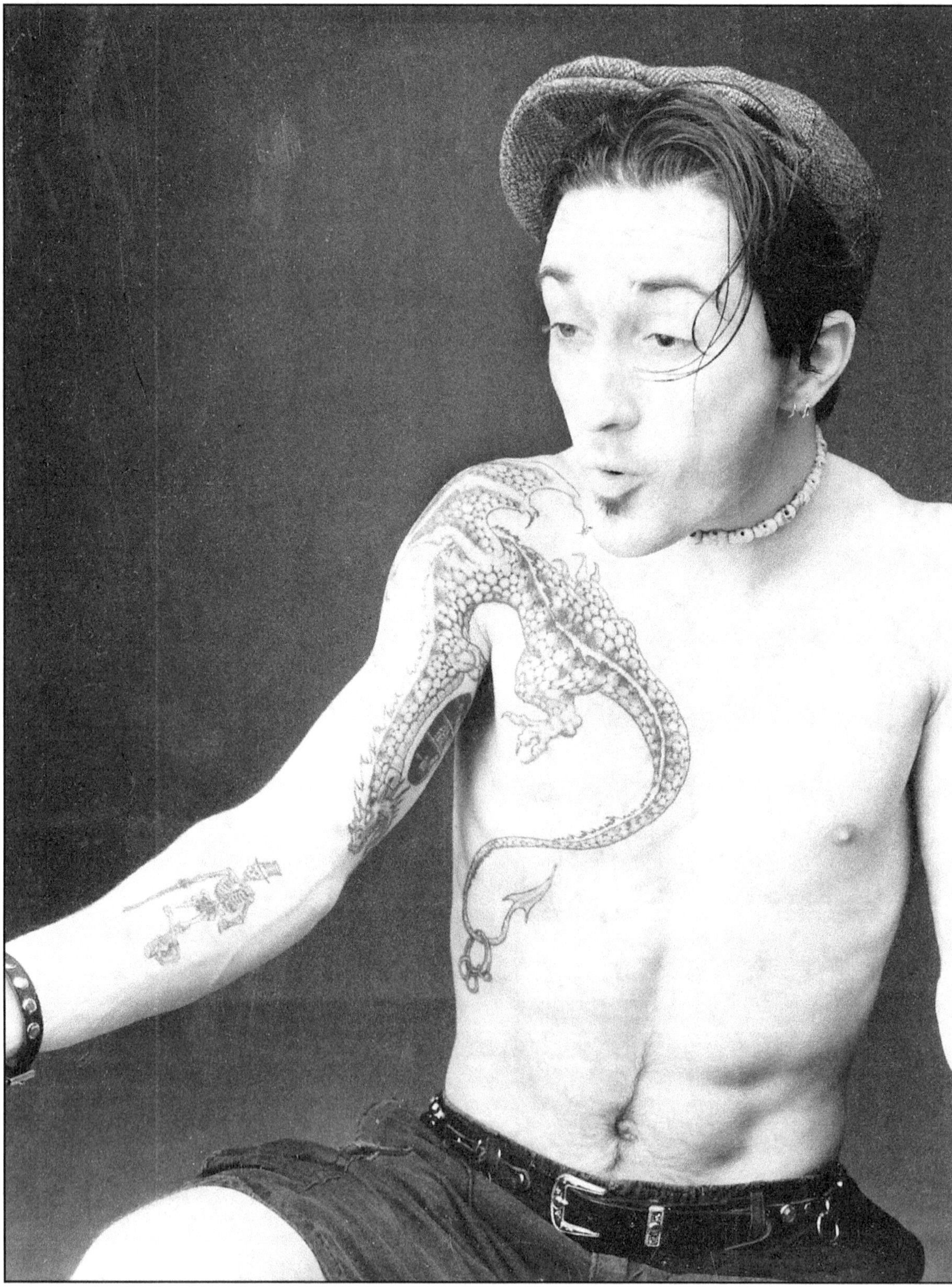

Tattoos by Greg Kulz and Henry Goldfield. Photo by Bobby Neel Adams.

QUOTATIONS

For some half-dozen millennia now, philosophers have pointed to "man's animal instincts" as the source of our woes...Let's examine the characteristics that set civilized man apart from the animals, who operate only on instinct. Human mothers not infrequently abandon the new-born baby in garbage cans, bash its brains out for crying, or let it die of neglect because it interferes with their party-going. No other higher mammal displays this trait. Nazis, during the early '40s, tortured fellow human beings for amusement. They followed an old custom of civilized Man, as recorded in Roman days, and through the Middle Ages. No animal is ever guilty of such peculiarly human acts as raping, then murdering and mutilating the female of his own species...It is time we stopped blaming the most characteristically human acts on "animal instincts," and started examining "civilization." There is most assuredly something about civilization that warps men's minds. And it's been around for a long, long time...

—Editorial, *Astounding Science Fiction*, July '51

My body is that part of the world which my thoughts can change. Even *imaginary* illnesses can develop into real ones. In the rest of the world, my hypotheses cannot change the order of things.

—Lichtenberg, *The Lichtenberg Reader*

All of the Britons colored themselves with woad, which produces a blue coloration...in this manner they are frightful to look upon in battle.

—Caesar, *The Gallic Wars*

According to the official autopsy report, the bullet which began the First World War penetrated through the head of a snake tattooed on Archduke Franz Ferdinand's body when he was assassinated in Sarajevo.

—Dr Stephan Oettermann, "An Art as Old as Humanity"

[Among the Nubans] a young girl receives an initial set of scars (from the navel to the breasts) when her breasts first start to appear. Other more extensive scars are cut (now covering the entire torso) on initial menses, and a final set covering the back, the back of the legs, arms and neck, are cut after a woman weans her first child. This last set of scars signals sexual availability again after a long postpartum sexual restriction while the infant is nursed. The final set is regarded as a beauty necessity, and if a husband refuses to pay for the scarring specialist, a woman may seek a lover who will do so, and her first marriage will end. The scars arc regarded as sexually pleasurable to her lovers.

—James Faris, "Southeast Nuba," in Arnold Rubin's *Marks of Civilization*

[Among the Thompson Indians] the common method of tattooing was with needle and thread. The thread was blackened with powdered charcoal and drawn underneath the skin. Fine needles made of bone or cactus spines were used for making dots. The figures were drawn on the skin with wetted charcoal and pricked over with cactus or other thorns. These were tied in small bunches, generally with their points close together and of equal length. Needles, porcupine quills, and sharp bones were also used... As a rule the first marks were made just after puberty. Persons of about equal age tattooed each other, particularly companions and comrades. Girls tattooed girls, and boys boys. There were no specialists in the art among either sex. The marking was done more or less in secrecy. No special medicines were applied to the parts, either before or after the operation...

Adolescents tattooed marks on themselves partly as a record of their ceremonies and partly to insure good luck and health. Some marks represented objects connected with their ceremonies...others represented objects of a mysterious nature seen during their training, such as mountains, stars, the moon, etc. Still others were representative of dreams or visions. In a few cases the picture of the guardian spirit may have been tattooed also. Others were symbols of their desires.

—James Teit, *Tattooing & Face & Body Painting of the Thompson Indians, British Colombia*

When the real is no longer what it used to be, nostalgia assumes its full meaning. There is a proliferation of myths of origin and signs of reality; of second-hand truth, objectivity and authenticity...

—Baudrillard, *Simulations*

We live and feel as much dreaming as waking and are the one as much as the other. It is one of the superiorities of man that he dreams and knows it. We have hardly made the right use of this yet. Dreaming is a life which, combined with the rest of us, makes up what we call human life. Dreams gradually merge into our waking; we cannot say where man's waking state begins.

—Lichtenberg

Burton was to note with some dismay John Speke's [famous hunter] taste for eating the embryos of the pregnant female animals he killed. The African natives would find the practice appalling. Speke never admitted to it in his writing, but referred to it obliquely as follows: "On once shooting a pregnant Kudu doe, I directed my native huntsman, a married man, to dissect her womb and expose the embryo; but he shrank from the work with horror, fearing lest the sight of the kid, striking his mind, should have an influence on his wife's future bearing..."

—From Fawn Brodie's *The Devil Drives: A Life of Sir Richard Burton*

It is the misunderstanding of the Earth, the forgetting of the star on which he lives, that has made for man an existence at the mercy of the merchandise he produces, the largest part of which is devoted to death.

—Georges Bataille

It seems that our own world is condemned to mass-produced cosmetics, wigs and other beauty aids, and that our body decoration will never again be dictated to by social needs, aesthetic ideals or religious beliefs, but by Fashion.

—Robert Brain, *The Decorated Body*

It is always a question of proving the real by the imaginary, proving truth by scandal, proving the law by transgression...every form of power, every situation speaks of itself by denial, in order to attempt to escape, by simulation of death, its real agony.

—Baudrillard, *Ibid*

A man with a scar or strong, damaged face may often be judged more attractive than one with unmarked features...German university students slashed their faces in der Mensur (students' duel) and poured wine into the wounds to provoke exaggerated scarring—evidence of their strength and manliness.

—Robert Brain, *The Decorated*

Every image, every media message...is a test.

—Jean Baudrillard

Poetry alone, which denies and destroys the limitations of things, can return us to this absence of limitations.

—Bataille

In the late Middle Ages there was a gradual awakening of the senses, with the eyes becoming increasingly active. In the middle of the 14th century...many women suddenly wore 'such low necklines that you could see nearly half their breasts', and among the upper classes in the same century, Queen Isabella of Bavaria introduced the 'garments of the grand neckline', where the dress was open to the navel. This fashion eventually led to the application of rouge to freely displayed nipples, those 'little apples of paradise', to placing diamond-studded rings or small caps on them, even to piercing them and passing gold chains through them decorated with diamonds, possibly to demonstrate the youthful resilience of the bosom.

—Hans Peter Duerr, *Dreamtime*

As late as the end of the17th century a French countess wrote about high-class Spanish ladies: "Among them it is a point of beauty not to have any bosom, and they take precautions early so that it will not develop. As soon as the breasts begin to appear, they place small lead plates over them, and they wrap themselves as one would swaddle a child. One has to admit that they accomplish their goal, having breasts no thicker than a sheet of paper."

—Duerr, *Ibid*

When you see them with their hair on their shoulders flying in the wind, then in this gorgeous ornament of their hair they appear so beautiful that when the sun shines through it is as if through a cloud, the radiance is indescribable and gives off blazing lightning; this is how enchantment comes from their eyes which are just as dangerous in love as in witchcraft.

—Basque judge presiding over witchcraft trials, 1609, quoted in Duerr, *Dreamtime*

Ainu women tattoo bluish-black marks around the mouth to resemble mustaches. Tattooing is a painful process and is accomplished little by little. The center of the upper lip is done first, then the lower, and this is extended from time to time till it reaches almost to the ears. Gashes are cut in the flesh and soot, scraped from a kettle hung over a birch-bark fire, is rubbed in to give the bluish-black color. The women tattoo their arms, also, to frighten away the demons of disease. They learned this custom for the sister of Aioina, their culture hero, who came down from the sky with her brother and told them that the wives of all the supernatural beings were decorated in this way. Now, they say, when the demons come and find the Ainu women tattooed, they mistake them for immortals and flee.

—M.C. Cole & F.C. Cole, *The Story of Man*

In Samoa there is a legend that tattooing was introduced there by the *goddesses of tattooing*. They swam to Samoa from Fiji, singing on the way their divine message: "Tattoo the women but not the men." With constant repetition the message became confused and twisted. When the goddesses finally arrived on the Samoan shore they found themselves singing just the reverse, and so, says the legend, the tattoo became the *undeserved prerogative* of the men and not the women.

—Albert Parry, *Tattoo*

Open eyes are tattooed on American sailors' lids or around their nipples because the sailors believe that such tattoos will keep watch for them when they are tired or asleep. (Some Americans returning from Japan bring with them pictures of bats tattooed on their bodies. In Japan, bats, as nocturnal animals, are tattooed for better eyesight.) I am also told of a few cases where a pair of ship's propellers, or twin screws, were tattooed on the sailors' buttocks.

The claim is that such designs enhance the dexterity of a man's movement on deck and shore. Some sailors and shore-mechanics go in for hinges tattooed on their arms, on each side of the elbow. This, they say, gives their arms more swing and strength.

—Albert Parry, *Tattoo*

I've never been frightened of anything in my whole life. And you know why? Because I wish I were dead...I wish I'd never been born...and if you wish that then there's nothing left for you to be afraid about. There's only hatred to live for; there's only pleasure in that.

—Lan Wright, *The Pictures of Pavanne*

Human affairs are like a chess game: only those who do not take it seriously can be called good players.

—Hung Tzu-ch'eng

Diverse reasons for tattooing: 1) To camouflage an unclothed body when hunting. 2) To secure a place in heaven. 3) To ensure an easy passage through difficult phases in life, such as puberty and pregnancy. 4) To prevent disease and injury and acquire fertility. 5) To propitiate malignant spirits at time of death. 6) To acquire special characteristics through totemism and ancestor worship. 7) To acquire the special respect of the community to allow the individual to climb the social ladder... 8) To terrorize the enemy on the field of battle. 9) To make the body sexually interesting. 10) To express sentiment (patriotism, love, friendship, anti-authoritarianism). 11) To register incidents of personal interest, places visited, etc. 12) To achieve personal or group identity (primitive tribes, gangs, sailors). 13) To make money (circus sideshows) 14) To register important medical data, e.g. blood group.

—R.W.B. Scutt & C. Gotch, *Art, Sex & Symbol*

Even before I emerged from childhood, I seem to have experienced deeply at heart that paradoxical feeling which was to dominate me all through the first part of my life: that of living in a world without any possible escape...I felt repugnance, mingled with wrath and indignation, towards people whom I saw settled comfortably in this world. How could they not be conscious of their captivity?

—Victor Serge, *Memoirs of a Revolutionary*

What does he do? He finds out the place of all the world most of promise for him. Then he deliberately sets himself down to prepare for the task. He finds in patience just how is his strength, and what are his powers. He studies new tongues. He learns new social life, new environments of old ways, the politics, the law, the finance, the science, the habits of a new land and a new people who have come to be since he was...What more may he not do when the greater world of thought is open to him? He that can smile at death as we know it; who can flourish in the midst of diseases that kill off whole peoples...

—Bram Stoker, *Dracula*

Youth subculture forms in the space between surveillance and the evasion of surveillance—it translates the fact of being under scrutiny into the pleasure of being watched... If teenagers possess little else, they at least own their own bodies. If power can be exercised nowhere else, it can at least be exercised here. The body can be decorated and enhanced like a cherished object. It can be cut up and "cooked" like a piece of meat. Self-mutilation is just the darker side of narcissism. The body becomes the baseline, the place where the buck stops. To wear a mohican or to have your face tattooed is to burn most of your bridges. In the current economic climate, when employers can afford to pick and choose, such gestures are a public disavowal of the will to queue for work.

—Dick Hebdige, "Hiding in the Light" from *TEN.8*

Girls have begun playing with themselves in public: parodying the conventional iconography of fallen womanhood—the vamp, the tart, the slut, the waif, the sadistic maitresse, the victim-in-bondage. These girls interrupt the image-flow. They play back images of women as icons, women as the Furies of classical mythology. They make the SM matrix strange. They skirt round the voyeurism issue, flirt with masculine curiosity but refuse to submit to the masterful gaze. These girls turn being looked at into an aggressive act.

—Hebdige, *Ibid*

Many years ago I used to see, strolling about St. James's Park, a huge hairy gentleman, with a bludgeon in his hand, and clothed with a bear's skin to which the head and paws were attached. He wore a pair of gigantic shoes, about a foot broad at the toes, made out of thick cowhide with the hair on, and on his head was a tall rimless cowhide hat shaped like an inverted flowerpot. His bodily covering was, however, the most extraordinary: the outer garment resembled a very large mattress in size and shape, with the ticking made of innumerable pieces of raw hide sewn together. It was about a foot in thickness and stuffed with sticks, stones, hard lumps of clay, rams' horns, bleached bones, and other hard heavy objects; it was fastened round him with straps of hide, and reached nearly to the ground. He had weighted the heavy stick used to support his steps with a great ball at the end, also with a large circular bell-shaped object surrounding the middle...In a strange language (there was no person learned enough in the country to understand it) he would make a long speech or prayer in a clear ringing voice...From the sound of certain oft-recurring expressions in his recitations, we children called him "Con stair Lo-vair"; perhaps some clever pundit will be able to tell me what these words mean—the only fragment saved of the hermit's mysterious language...When closely questioned or otherwise interfered with, a terrible wrath would disfigure his countenance and kindle his eyes with demoniac fire; and in sharp ringing tones, that wounded like strokes, he would pour forth a torrent of words in his unknown language...for upwards of twenty years after I as a small child made his acquaintance he continued faithfully pursuing his dreary rounds, exposed to cold and rain in winter and to the more trying heats of summer, until at last he was discovered lying dead on the plain, wasted by old age and famine to a mere skeleton, and even in death still crushed down with that awful burden he had carried for so many years...

—W.H. Hudson, *Far Away and Long Ago*

Secret societies abound in Polynesia; males are admitted to these at the end of a novitiate, with long ceremonies comprising dances, music, acting and scenes representing the history of the gods. Tattoo-marks arc the visible evidences of alliance with the god of the tribe; it is rare among women, but obligatory for men. The patterns often represent totem animals. Belief in the common origin of men and animals is further manifested in talcs of metamorphosis; in Borneo men can transform themselves into tigers, and become tiger-bogeys.

—Salomon Reinach, *Orpheus*

Mana is the principle of magic; it is the latent power in a person, a thing, even in a word. He who can evoke this energy and make it serve his ends is a clever man. In modern language, this means that there are reserves of force everywhere and that we should use them for our needs...

—Reinach, *Orpheus*

I am one of those who consider the superfluous essential: my love for things and people is in inverse proportion to their utility.

—Theophile Gautier

Art must serve some essential purpose and not be an idle amusement.

—Chernyshevski

Who wishes to be creative, must first destroy and smash accepted values.

—Nietzsche

Art cannot change the world, but it can contribute to changing the consciousness and drives of the men and women who could change the world.

—Herbert Marcuse

Human life is an experience to be carried as far as possible.

—Georges Bataille, *Theory of Religion*

That witches existed in Britain from early times is undeniable. Members of a surviving Somersetshire coven still carry small blue tattoos in woad pricked below a particular finger joint, which stands for a letter in the pre-Christian Celtic alphabet. They call themselves 'Druids', worship a neolithic British god, and meet at cross-quarterly days—Candlemas, May Eve, Lammas and Halloween—in a Druidic stone circle. Druids are chosen, after puberty, for certain natural powers of intuition and diagnosis, second sight, and thought control.

—Robert Graves, *Daily Telegraph Magazine*, 21 May 1965

In all ages, far back into pre-history, we find human being have painted and adorned themselves.

—H.G.Wells, The Work, *Wealth & Happiness of Mankind*

Fashion is out of date the moment it is generally recognizable.

—John Hadfield, *The Saturday Book #26*

The Spartan custom of displaying young girls naked is highly praised, and in the island of Chios it is delightful just to walk to the gymnasia and running tracks to see the young men wrestling naked with the young girls who are also naked.

—Athenaeus

Ecstasy of some kind there certainly is, and the fact of nakedness seems to enable people to establish contact with that whole level of existence which is immune to logic, resists verbalization and proceeds by methods completely unfamiliar to the intellect.

—Bernard Denvir, "The Social History of Nudism"

The final aim of Natural Science is to discover the motions underlying all changes, and the *motive forces* thereof; that is, to resolve itself into Mechanics.

—Helmholtz, 1869 lecture

The higher thought originates as meditation upon death. Every religion, every scientific investigation, every philosophy, proceeds from it. Every great symbolism attaches its form-language to the cult of the dead, the forms of disposal of the dead, the adornment of the graves of the dead.

—Oswald Spengler, *The Decline of the West*

Insanity is the exception in individuals. In groups, parries, people, and ties, it is the rule.

—Nietzsche

A great man, did you say? All I see is the actor creating his own ideal image.

—Nietzsche

Fortune does not change men; it unmasks them.

There are no oaths that make so many perjurers as the vows of love.

Prejudice is the reason of fools.

—Voltaire

Experience is a keen knife that hurts, while it extracts the cataract that blinds. All my misfortunes come of having thought too well of my fellows.

—Rousseau

First you dream, then you die.

—Cornell Woolrich

Let thy speech be short, comprehending much in few words.

—Ecclesiastes

To the true cynic nothing is ever revealed.

—Oscar Wilde

Give a man a mask and he will tell the truth.

—Oscar Wilde

One must be a work of art, or wear a work of art.

—Oscar Wilde

Civilization displays that face which bears the double imprint of sterile blood and ruins forever dead.

—Octave Mirbeau, *Torture Garden*

It would be a good thing to buy books if one could also buy the time in which to read them; but generally the purchase of a book is mistaken for the acquisition of its contents.

—Schopenhauer, *ibid*

In order to have original, uncommon and perhaps even immortal thoughts, it is enough to estrange oneself so fully from the world of things for a few moments, that the most ordinary objects and events appear quite new and unfamiliar. In this way their true nature is disclosed.

—Schopenhauer, *On Genius*

All the wit in the world is lost upon him who has none.

—La Bruyere

Very long and pendulous labia minora are considered particularly attractive in women. They are deliberately produced and cultivated from early childhood by manipulations performed by elderly men who have become impotent. These manipulations are continued till the approach of puberty. At the same time and as part of the same training, the clitoris is not only subjected to prolonged friction, but also to suction, and a certain large kind of ant (native to the islands) is applied to this region in order that its sting may produce a brief but acute and not unpleasant stimulation.

—Ploss & Bartels, *Femina Libido Sexualis*

Probably the favorite and most frequent method of treating, adorning or "improving" the mons veneris is by the removal of the hair.

—Ploss & Bartels, *Ibid*

The custom of tattooing the visible portions of the external genitalia: so far as we are aware, this is only done on certain South Sea Islands...Kubary described the tattooing process as very prolonged: it starts when the girl is between seven and eight years old. At about 12 the hips and lower abdomen are dealt with. The adornment of the genitalia is so intricate and careful that both the labia majora and the vaginal orifice arc tattooed...Tattooing is the sign of maturity and membership of the community of women. It is, therefore, performed in company and forms one of the chief items of the festivities.

—Ploss & Bartels, *Ibid*

Genius may be defined as an eminently clear consciousness of things in general...

—Schopenhauer, *On Genius*

Body markings have been used to ward off evil for centuries.

—Unknown

We found that if we added minute amounts of certain antibiotics (really just traces) to animal feeds, the addition brought the critters to market months ahead of normally-fed animals...It was logical to suspect that it might work in newborn humans, too...

—James Blish, *At Death's End,* 1954

All symbols—and here I mean primarily graphic symbols, though it applies to others as well—operate in a manner similar to that of a mnemonic device or a post-hypnotic command. They serve as catalysts for particular responses in the audience. We see a swastika, for instance, and think of nazis, war, and tyranny. This in spite of the fact that the swastika in and of itself means nothing. It is neutral. But we have been mass-programmed...to respond to the symbol in a certain way...Because we respond to common symbols in common ways, all of us are under a form of mass hypnosis. To be aware of the process is to wake a bit from the trance, to pause a moment before barking at the sound of the bell.

—Thomas Wiloch, "Codes and Chaos," *Photostatic* #32

The average child watches television more than 30 hours a week and has watched more than 200,000 commercials by the time s/he graduates from high school...By the time a young person finishes high school, s/he will have spent more time watching television (15,000 hrs or more) than sitting in a classroom (11,000 hrs)...By the age of 14, a devoted viewer will have witnessed 11,000 TV murders...

—*Society for Elimination of TV Newsletter #26*

The worst possible hazard in my profession [sword-swallowing]: a simple cold...If it ain't too bad you're able to breathe even when you've got eighteen or twenty inches of steel down your gullet. But the big problem is a cough. And a sneeze is even worse. That can *really* kill you.

—Louise Chavanne quoted in Arthur Lewis's *Carnival*

I'd say Delno Fritz was the most superlative performer in the whole world...He tied a pistol on the handle of the twenty-eight-inch blade and fastened a steel ball to the tip. Then he'd take a blank cartridge and load it with powder very carefully...He'd throw back his head, put the blade in his mouth and fire the shot. The cotton wad in the cartridge would hit the ball to drive it forward. It was a real wow! [But he] got careless in Keokuk and put just a little bit too much powder in the pistol. The wad drove the steel ball right through his stomach. By the time they got him to the hospital he was already dead. Too bad! It was a great act.

—Louise Chavanne, *Ibid*

There are four basic principles in Bozo [insulting Clown act]...Number one is *Attention;* without that you have no tip. Number two is *Interest;* that's when the insults start and the tip listens. Number three is *Desire;* the mark's anxiety to punish his taunter. And Number four is *Action;* that's when the mark parts with his cash.

—Biggie Moran quoted in Arthur Lewis's *Carnival*

When somebody offers you something for nothing don't walk—run to the nearest exit.

—Morris Hannum quoted in Arthur Lewis's *Carnival*

A 'glommin' geek...There've been damn few of 'em in show biz...He really ate it; not pretended to and then spit it out like an ordinary geek...Veronica was a wonderful entertainer...In the course of one evening she'd bite off and swallow a half-dozen heads from live chickens and three or four field mice whole and maybe a garter snake or two. Half the marks'd throw up just watchin'...

—Lou Pease quoted in Arthur Lewis's *Carnival*

Nature must be expressed in symbols; nature is known through symbols which are themselves a construction upon experience, a product of mind, an artifice or conventional product, therefore the reverse of natural.

—Mary Douglas, *Natural Symbols*

Each person treats his body as an image of society

—Mary Douglas

The human body is always treated as an image of society and there can be no natural way of considering the body that does not involve at the same time a social dimension. Interest in its apertures depends on the preoccupation with social exits and entrances, escape routes and invasions. If there is no concern to preserve social boundaries, I would not expect to find concern with bodily boundaries. The relation of head to feet, of brain and sexual organs, of mouth and anus are commonly treated so that they express the relevant patterns of hierarchy. Consequently I now advance the hypothesis that bodily control is an expression of social control...the same drive that seeks harmoniously to relate the experience of physical and social, must affect ideology.

—Mary Douglas, *Natural Symbols*

The primary use of language is to affirm and embellish the social structure which rests upon *unchallengeable* metaphysical assumptions... As speech sheds its social harness, it becomes a very specialized, independent tool of thought.

—Mary Douglas, *Natural Symbols*

Poetry has an aim: absolute human liberation.

—Malcolm de Chazal

Analogy: the spontaneous, extralucid, rebellious rapport which establishes itself, under certain conditions, between one thing and another...

—Andre Breton, *Signe Ascendant*

Poetry, in contrast to other modes of thought, remains relatively free of the influence of the *reality principle* and thus opens more easily on the chances of what *can be...*

—Franklin Rosemont, "The Crisis of the Imagination," *Arsenal #2*

The *desirable society* is perhaps one in which things and animals have a function which somehow relieves the pressure of man against man.

—Joseph Jablonski, "Notes on the Revolution of Witchcraft"

He who most resembles the dead is the most reluctant to die.

—La Fontaine

In the eyes of primitive man violence is always the cause of death. It may have acted through magical means, but someone is always responsible, someone is always a murderer.

—Georges Bataille, *Erotism*

The transgression does not deny the taboo but transcends it and completes it.

—Bataille, *Erotism*

The main function of all taboos is to combat violence.

—Bataille, *Erotism*

"As soon as the effort at rational comprehension ends in contradiction, the practice of intellectual scatology requires the excretion of inassimilable elements," which is another way of stating vulgarly that a burst of laughter is the only imaginable and definitively terminal result—and not the means—of philosophical speculation.

—Bataille, *Visions of Excess*

Myth remains at the disposal of one who cannot be satisfied by art, science or politics...A community that does not carry out the ritual possession of its myths possesses only a truth in decline...Myth is in solidarity with *total* existence, of which it is the tangible expression.

—Bataille, *Visions of Excess*

[Circumcision] was practiced by the ancient Egyptians as far back as the Fourth Dynasty, or 3000 B.C., and probably long before that. The ceremony is clearly portrayed on a temple at Thebes...The belief sometimes expressed, that circumcision removes or at least considerably reduces the risks of venereal infection, is authoritatively stated to be without any foundation in fact. One more possible explanation is perhaps the most likely. That is that circumcision is to be regarded as a ritual tribal mark or badge...Analogous with male circumcision is that of females, by which is usually meant the removal of the clitoris...Various reasons have been advanced for it. One is that it is intended to reduce the sexual sensitivity of the woman, so as to make her more submissive to the rule of one man, her husband. Another is that it is to match the male mutilation with a female one... We are on much firmer ground when we recognize that it is an initiation ceremony, through which a girl becomes a full member of the tribe, just as her brother is made a full member by the corresponding rite of male circumcision.

—E. Royston Pike, *The Strange Ways of Mankind*

White man's flesh does not taste so good as colored man's. This was the decided opinion of the cannibals of the South Sea Islands, who had the opportunity of tasting both...Cannibalism among the Fijians, is one of their institutions...Human bodies were sometimes eaten in connection with the building of a temple or a canoe, or on the launching of a large canoe...No one who is thoroughly acquainted with the Fijians can say that there is not a large number who esteem such food as a delicacy, giving it a decided preference above all other. The heart, the thigh, and the arm above the elbow are considered the greatest dainties. The head is the least esteemed.

—Pike, *The Strange Ways of Mankind*

Not one great country can be named, from the polar regions in the north to New Zealand in the south, in which the aborigines do not tattoo themselves.

—Charles Darwin

I have often admired the markings of a chief's legs, when I have seen a coconut tree correctly and distinctly drawn, its roots spreading at the heel, its elastic stalk pencilled as it were along the tendons, and its waving plume gracefully spread out on the broad part of the calf. Sometimes a couple of stems would be twined up from the heel, and divided on the calf, each bearing a plume of leaves. The ornaments round the ankle, and upon the instep make them often appear as though they wore the elegant Eastern sandal. The sides of the legs are sometimes tattooed from the ankle upward; which gives the appearance of wearing pants with ornamented seams. In the lower part of the back, a number of straight, waved, or zigzag lines, rise in the direction of the spine, and branch off regularly towards the shoulders. But, of the upper part of the body, the chest is the most tattooed. Every variety of figure is to be seen here. Coconut and breadfruit trees, with convolvulus wreaths hanging round them, boys gathering fruit, men engaged in battle, in the manual exercise, triumphing over a fallen foe; or, as I have frequently seen it, they are represented as carrying a human sacrifice to the temple. Every kind of animal—goats, dogs, fowls, and fish—may at times be seen on this part of the body; muskets, swords, pistols, clubs, spears, and other weapons of war, are also stamped upon their arms and chests. They are not all crowded upon the same person, but each one makes a selection according to his fancy. I have frequently thought that the tattooing on a man's person might serve as an index to his disposition and his character...The arms were frequently marked with circles, their fingers with rings, and their wrists with bracelets.

—William Ellis, after a visit to Tahiti, 1825

He was considered by his countrymen a perfect master in the art of tattooing...I was astonished to see with what boldness and precision Aranghie drew his designs upon the skin, and what beautiful ornaments he produced; no rule and compasses could be more exact than the lines and circles he formed...Indeed, so highly were his works esteemed, that I have seen many of his drawings exhibited after death. A neighbor of mine very lately killed a chief who had been tattooed by Aranghie; and, appreciating the artist's work so highly, he skinned the chieftain's thighs, and covered his cartouche-box with it.

—Augustus Earle, *Narrative of a Nine Months' Residence in New Zealand in 1827*

In an unforgettable ceremonial manner, he is taken from the camp and scenes of his irresponsible early years. He becomes the subject of a series of rites...He 'dies' to the former life of childhood and of ignorance of esoteric knowledge, and 'rises' or is 'reborn' to a new life. The latter is not merely adult life, for which he has meanwhile been disciplined and instructed; it is much more: it is a life of knowledge and power. At the end of the ritual journey, with its trials, loneliness, 'death', revelations and rejoicing, he can say: "Whereas previously I was blind to the significance of the seasons, of natural species, of heavenly bodies and of man himself, now I begin to see; and whereas before I did not understand the secret of life, now I begin to know."

—A.P. Elkins, *Aboriginal Men of High Degree*, 1946

I mistrust visions come by in the easy way—by swallowing something. The real insight, the real ecstasy does not come from this. Instant light by flicking on a switch, instant coffee, instant TV dinners, instant visions through pills, plants or mushrooms—that's what I want to get away from.

—*Lame Deer, Seeker of Visions*

The sacred pipes have not been shown to the people for some years now. In the summer of 1969 we Sioux medicine men thought that the time had come to open up these bundles. But when word got around and there were rumors of TV crews coming in, offering us money for "exclusive rights" as they called it, we changed our minds. We returned the bundles to their hiding places.

—*Lame Deer, Seeker of Visions*

Most of us have tattoos on our wrists—not like the tattoos of your sailors—daggers, hearts and nude girls—but just a name, a few letters or designs. The Owl Woman who guards the road to the spirit lodges looks at these tattoos and lets us pass. They are like a passport. Many Indians believe that if you don't have these signs on your body, that *Ghost Woman* won't let you through but will throw you over a cliff. In that case you have to roam the earth endlessly as a ghost. Maybe it's not so bad being a ghost. But as you see, I have my arms tattooed.

—*Lame Deer, Seeker of Visions*

There are thousands hacking at the branches of evil, to one who is striking at the roots.

—Thoreau

All you have to do is act like them [normal people], and they can't tell the difference. You just talk with them about the dull things they're interested in, and they eat it up. It's no trick at all to imitate them...

—J.A. Meyer, "Brick Wall," *Astounding Science Fiction,* Sept 1951

A person can't be creative and conformist at the same time.

—*Ibid*

It's the curse of our society that we have to fit into a rigid pattern to belong...There's no room for imagination and creativity in our society, except in art and literature—dead ends!

—*Ibid*

After you once get past the retarded infantilism that the rest of these people are immersed in, you see how empty things are. Once you've grown up, there's no going back—you're alone from then on.

—*Ibid*

The most extravagant reproductive effort I could find was that of the sea hare (a species of large sea slug) which was once observed to lay 478 million eggs during eighteen weeks and which, being bi-sexual, often engages successfully in triple copulation.

—Armand Denis, *Taboo*

Images have become our true sex object, the object of our desire...It is this promiscuity and the ubiquity of images, this *viral contamination* of things by images, which are the fatal characteristics of our culture. And this knows no bounds, because...images cannot be prevented from proliferating indefinitely.

—Jean Baudrillard, *The Ecstasy of Communication*

You have to paint things black if you want to make future possibilities more vivid.

—Michel Foucault, *Impulse,* Winter '89

Only by the negation does one arrive at the affirmation.

—R.A. Schwaller de Lubicz

Even making love involves power relations, charged with eroticism. That hasn't been studied much. There's so much pleasure in giving orders; there's also pleasure in taking them. This pleasure of power—well, there's a topic for study.

—Foucault, *Ibid*

Whoever seriously thinks that superhuman beings have ever given our race information as to the aim of its existence and that of the world, is still in his childhood. There is no other revelation than the thoughts of the wise...Still, instead of trusting what their own minds tell them, men have as a rule a weakness for trusting others...And in view of the enormous intellectual inequality between man and man, it is easy to see that the thoughts of one mind might appear a revelation to another!

—Schopenhauer, "The Christian System"

Essentially man is a "questioning" of nature; nature itself is the essential—the basic given—in every response to a questioning.

—Georges Bataille, *Guilty*

Let him go on asking—his strength lies in asking questions.

—Maori proverb

To sec that thought in its very nature is dialectical, and that as understanding, it must call into contradiction—the negative of itself—will form one of the main lessons of logic...As a matter of fact, thinking is always the negation of what we have immediately before us.

—Hegel

While Intelligence merely proposes to take the world as it is, Will takes steps to make the world what it ought to be.

—Hegel

Nothing belongs to you more properly than your dreams: nothing is more thoroughly your own work. Subject, form, sector, spectator, you yourself are all these and everything is yourself in those comedies.

—Nietzsche

Sleep is the domain of unrestricted thought. The dream is the thought freed and consequently the pure self. If you want to know if you are brave at heart and truly brave, if you arc a coward, or if you are kind or wicked, pay attention to what you do in your dreams. You have there the most precious and surest text you could consult concerning yourself. Nevertheless, you pretend you are not responsible for your dreams.

—Emile Faguet, *On Reading Nietzsche*

To me *knowledge* is a world of dangers and victories, where heroic sentiments also have their place for dancing and playing. *Life is a means to knowledge.*
—Nietzsche

He who goes before gathers treasures; he who lags behind looks for them in vain.
—Maori proverb

If you solve the problem of the *nature and origin of language,* we can explain the rest: what culture is, and how it made its appearance; what art is and what technological skills, law, philosophy and religion are...All we know is that all the peoples of the world, all mankind in its most ancient and humble manifestations, has been endowed with articulate speech...We start off with language as a given element.
—*Conversations with Claude Levi-Strauss*

...The pre-condition of that totalization of knowledge utilization of past experience that we feel, more or less intuitively, to have been the source of our civilization...is writing. It is certain that a people can only take advantage of previous acquisitions in so far as these have been made permanent in writing. Writing had to be invented so that the knowledge, the experiments, the happy or unhappy experiences of each generation could accumulate... in order to improve techniques and achieve fresh progress... We know that [the invention of writing] occurred some three or four thousand years before the birth of Christ... immediately after what is called the "neolithic revolution"—the discovery of those civilized skills which still form the basis of our lives: agriculture, the domestication of animals, pottery-making, weaving—a whole range of processes which were to allow human beings to stop living from day to day...
—Claude Levi-Strauss, *Ibid*

It has often been pointed out that domestic animals are not just wild species which have become domesticated; they are wild species which have been completely transformed by man, and this transformation, which was the necessary pre-condition of man's ability to use them, must have occupied long periods of time and called for great persistence and prolonged and concentrated experimentation.
—Levi-Strauss

You may see dead persons walking towards you, and you will hear their bones rattle. If you hear and see these things without fear, you will never be frightened of anything. These dead people will not show themselves to you again, because your psychic force is now strong.You are now powerful because you have seen these dead people.
—Australian shaman quoted in Mircia Eliade's *Shamanism*

"Like to keep abreast of titillating new products?" reads the PR release, which went on to describe hand-crafted, *non-piercing* nipple rings designed to "enhance a lady's profile." The modest wearer might prefer simple silver bands, which start at $26.50, while the more extravagant customer can bejewel herself with diamond-encrusted nipple rings—yours for $10,000.
—shopping tip from *New York Woman,* March '89

Throughout the country [India] are found old prostitutes who sell little bells of gold, silver and bronze. The women hold great store with them for when they are sewn into the skin of the man's member they cause a swelling of tremendous length of the entire genital parts. Hence they claim their males have greater endurance and give them far greater pleasure than we poor Europeans. It is true that when there are a number of natives about, the woman will invariably choose the one with a titillating member. As soon as the boys reach puberty they rush to have the bells sewn into their members, and constantly change them for larger sizes as they grow up.
—Paolo Mantegazza, *Sexual Relations of Mankind*

[The ampallang:] the operation is performed only on adults. The skin is forced back, the penis is placed between two small planks of bamboo and for ten days it is covered with rags dipped in cold water. Then the glans is perforated with a sharp bamboo needle; a feather, dipped in oil, is placed in the wound until it heals. Wet compresses are used all the while.When the Dayaks travel and work they carry a feather in this canal. As soon as they grow desirous, they pull the feather out and replace it with the ampallang. The ampallang is a little rod of copper, silver or gold, four centimeters long and two millimeters thick. At one end of this rod is a round ball or pear-formed object made of metal; at the other end a second ball is placed as soon as the ampallang is affixed. The whole apparatus is, when ready, five centimeters long and five millimeters thick...Von Graffin has seen one Dayak who had *two* ampallangs, one behind the other! The perforation was always horizontal and above the urethra...The women of the Dayaks say the embrace without this ornament is like rice, but with it, it tastes like rice spiced with salt.
—Mantegazza, *Sexual Relations of Mankind*

The will is rather a special way of *thinking;* thinking translating itself into existence, thinking as the urge to give itself existence.
—*Hegel's Philosophy of Right*

The strangest secret is: you are what you think!
—Earl Nightingale

The only difference between tattooed people and non-tattooed people is: tattooed people don't care if you're not tattooed.
—Cheri

[Among the Arunta of Central Australia] The second stage of the boy's initiation, the circumcision rite, may occur any time after he has reached puberty...Two men are chosen to perform the operation, and they work as a team, one holding the subject and helping while the other uses the stone knife. The blood is caught in a shield and taken to the women's camp; there the elder sisters of the boy and of his mother rub the blood over their breasts and foreheads. The flesh is given to a younger brother to swallow, in the belief that it will cause him to grow tall and strong...

A month or so later he undergoes his second operation, known to surgery as subincision...With a stone knife, the urethral canal is slit open from underneath in a deep, full length cut...The boy's blood flows into a shield, and if the pain is more than he can endure, he urinates into embers and allows the steam to rise, which is said to give some relief. The parts that have never been cut never return to normal, and after this ceremony the men always squat to urinate. Drastic though it is, the operation does not render the men incapable of having children...One such operation might seem enough for anyone, but older men usually come forward a second or even a third time and ask the surgeon to re-do the Arilta operation more thoroughly.

—Edward Weyer Jr, *Primitive Peoples Today*

Unmarried [Ainu] men and women enjoy considerable sexual freedom. Many Ainu girls, with their fine teeth and sparkling brown or hazel eyes, are quite attractive. They can also be coquettish. A girl may take the initiative, and she loses no feminine pride by proposing. It is not unknown for the visitor among them to find himself the object of amorous advances. The Ainus show affection not by kissing but by *biting,* and one traveler describes how one of the girls began gently biting his fingers; presently she extended her affections to his arm, and then his shoulder, and finally put her arms around his shoulders and bit his cheek.

[Upon marriage] the [Ainu] husband now completes the wife's mouth tattooing, the beginning of which has somewhat the significance of an engagement ring among us. In olden times, the completed design may have had the purpose of labeling a woman as the husband's property...Black obsidian knives were formerly used in the tattooing process. The designs are applied by gashing the skin, rubbing in soot, and wiping the wound with a cloth dipped in a decoction of bark.

—Edward Weyer Jr, *Ibid*

[Among the Ainu, tattooing] begins at the age of five, when some of the sufferers are yet unweaned. I saw the operation performed on a dear little bright girl this morning. A woman took a large knife with a sharp edge, and rapidly cut several horizontal lines on the upper lip, following closely the curve of the very pretty mouth, and before the slight bleeding had ceased carefully rubbed in some of the shiny soot which collects on the mat above the fire. In two or three days the scarred lip will be washed with the decoction of the bark of a tree to fix the pattern, and give it that blue look which makes many people mistake it for a daub of paint. The pattern on the lips is deepened and widened every year up to the time of marriage, and the circles on the arms are extended in a similar way.

—Isabella Bird, *Unbeaten Tracks in Japan*

I could not persuade myself that the men and women I met were not also another, still passably human, Beast People, animals half-wrought into the outward image of human souls; and that they would presently begin to revert, to show first this bestial mark and then that...

—H.G.Wells, *The Island of Dr. Moreau*

I look about me at my fellow men. And I go in fear. I see faces keen and bright, others dull or dangerous, others unsteady, insincere; none that have the calm authority of a reasonable soul. I feel as though the animal was surging up through them...I know this is an illusion, that these seeming men and women about me are indeed men and women, perfectly reasonable creatures, full of human desires and tender solicitude, emancipated from instinct...

—H.G.Wells, *Ibid*

I would go out into the streets, and prowling women would mew after me; furtive craving men glance jealously at me; weary pale workers go coughing by me, with tired eyes and eager paces like wounded deer dripping blood; old people, bent and dull, pass murmuring to themselves; and all unheeding a ragged tail of gibing children...Particularly nauseous were the blank expressionless faces of people in trains and omnibuses; they seemed no more my fellow-creatures than dead bodies would be...I have withdrawn myself from the confusion of cities and multitudes, and spend my days surrounded by wise books—bright windows in this life of ours lit by the shining souls of men.

—H.G.Wells, *Ibid*

Each animal in a given area shares more or less the same "environment," but given the different life style of each type of animal, each will possess a specific environment of its own. There are as many spaces and times as are contained in and determined by the individual's functional circle—each individual dwells on its own "island of the senses."

—taken from Von Uexkull's *Theoretical Biology*

[Among the Egyptians] If a cat dies in a private house by a natural death, all the inmates of the houses shave their eyebrows; on the death of a dog they shave the head and the whole of the body.

—Herodotus, "The Egyptians and Their Cats"

It is a well-known fact that primitives, even members of communities which are already somewhat advanced, regard artificial likenesses, whether painted, carved, or sculptured, as real, as well as the individual they depict... If primitives view the pictured resemblance differently from ourselves, it is because they view the original otherwise also...The *objective* features are neither the only ones nor the most important; most frequently, they are but the symbols or instruments of occult forces and mystic powers such as every being, especially a living being, can display...If their perceptions of the originals ceased to be mystic, their images would also lose their mystic properties. They would no longer appear to be alive, but would be what they are to our minds—merely *material reproductions.*

—Lucien Levy-Bruhl, *What the Natives Think*

Primitives regard their names as something concrete and real, and frequently sacred...The Indian regards his name not as a mere label, bur as a distinct part of his personality, just as much are his eyes or his teeth, and believes that injury will result as surely from the malicious handling of his name as from a wound inflicted on any part of his physical organism...At the beginning of a fresh epoch in his life—at his initiation, for instance—an individual receives a new name, and it is the same when he is admitted to a secret society. A name is never a matter of indifference; it implies a whole series of relationships between the man who bears it and the source whence it is derived.

—Lucien Levy-Bruhl, *Ibid*

As for the primitive, I hark back to it because we are still primitive. How many thousands of years of culture, think you, have rubbed and polished at our raw edges? One probably; at the best, no more than two. And that takes us back to screaming savagery, when, gross of body and deed, we drank blood from the skulls of our enemies, and hailed as highest paradise the orgies and carnage of Valhalla.

—Jack London

I believe that life is a mess. It is like yeast, a ferment, a thing that moves and may move for a minute, an hour, a year, or a hundred years, but that in the end will cease to move. The big eat the little that they may continue to move; the strong eat the weak that they may retain their strength. The lucky eat the most and move the longest.

—Jack London, *The Sea Wolf*

The characteristic property of an inventive art is that it bears no resemblance to art as it is generally recognized and in consequence—and this all the more so as it is more inventive—that it does not seem like art at all.

—Jean Dubuffet

Throughout history there have always been forms of art alien to established culture and which *ipso facto* have been neglected and finally lost without trace.

—Roger Cardinal, *Outsider Art*

All avant-garde revolutions in art turn into history: the slap in the face of culture given by Dada has now been framed and hung on the museum wall.

—Roger Cardinal, *Ibid*

The philistine habit of using the concept "sick" to *minimize* and *disparage* draws a veil across a reality which we are by no means in a position to interpret...because we arc entangled in restricted categories of appreciation and in a framework of ideas which still binds us, while we feel it loosening in favor of one which is more extensive, more free, more mobile.

—Karl Jaspers, *Strindberg & Van Gogh*, 1922

An alternative art exists. It crops up in all the places where Art is considered to have no place...Raw creation is hard to stomach: it is unfamiliar, uncanny, even savage and coarse. But it is never degenerate or watered-down. For creation that is truly inventive, that genuinely stimulates passion, will be creation springing directly from the original sources of emotion and not something tapped from the cultural reservoir...Art that thrusts us into emotional and intellectual situations beyond our normal grasp, serving us explanations of reality—our reality?—in a language that is unprecedented and a-historical...will threaten the reliability of our readymade postures and expose the wobbly props of our petrified heritage.

—Roger Cardinal, *Outsider Art*

I deny that there are beautiful colors and ugly colours, beautiful shapes and others that are not. I am convinced that any object, any place without distinction can become a *key of enchantment* for the mind according to the way one looks at it and the associations of ideas to which one links it.

—Jean Dubuffet

Any evaluation of the work of art must take account not of its "plastic" beauty but of its greater or lesser capacity to *stimulate the mind.*

—Roger Cardinal, *Outsider Art*

While I personally get tremendous pleasure and satisfaction from my stretched piercings and from doing my self-torture rites, I don't want anyone to get the idea that that's the only way to go. Piercing doesn't have to involve a whole lot of pain, and it doesn't have to be a matter of one-inch plugs or nothing. A well placed piercing with a 14, even a 16 gauge piece of jewelry in it, can give you an enormous amount of pleasure. The important thing is to give yourself the freedom to explore the outer limits of your own sexuality. You don't have to be a fakir to do that.

—Fakir Musafar, *PFIQ #3*

In my training courses, I put a lot of emphasis on Hatha Yoga. It is MUST for everybody. They must become slim and extremely limber first, before it is possible to safely explore the other six categories of Body Training. Being well-conditioned by Hatha Yoga brings new dimensions to heavy-duty bondage and similar activities—or even to straight sex for that matter!

—Fakir Musafar

Once you have a tattoo, there is something more than what it appears on the surface. All it is is a drawing on you, but it's something that can't be stolen from you. It gives you a sense of permanence. Maybe that's why people who are in creative fields or who have been soldiers—in a life that is really topsy-turvy and volatile—get them, because it gives you a sense of stability. If every Joe Shmoe with a business suit had one, it would take something out of it. Having one for me is kind of like: *rebel with a job.*

—John Lafia, film director (*The Blue Iguana*)

From dreams to reality is a long way.
—Ferdinand Cheval

Brothers, I entreat you, *remain faithful to the earth;* place no faith in those that speak to you of supra-terrestrial hopes. They are condemners of life, moribund and poisoned men themselves...Remain faithful to earth with all the force of your virtue. Let your generous love and your knowledge serve the *meaning of the earth.*
—Nietzsche

Our certain duty is to develop ourselves, to expand ourselves wholly in all our potentialities; it is to succeed in becoming fully what we feel ourselves to be. What we want is to *become ourselves.* Nothing that is should be suppressed; nothing is superfluous.
—Nietzsche

The first duty of man is to be artificial.
—Oscar Wilde

'Truth' never set anyone free. It is only doubt which will bring mental emancipation.
—Anton LaVey quoted in Arthur Lyons' *Satan Wants You*

Dangerously must we live!
—Nietzsche

Life such as *I* conceive it may quite possibly be that of the 'savage,' and may only be realized fully or brilliantly in the 'natural state' or in that primitive state, with its loosely organized societies that is sometimes referred to as the natural state. In the end, it is the social invention itself that stands against me.
—Nietzsche

The body is like a sentence that can be broken down into separate parts, so that its true contents can be put together again in an endless series of anagrams.
—Jacques Lacan

We must love truth for itself, to such an extent that we do not love it for ourselves but *against ourselves.* We must ever contradict ourselves; we must always welcome the opposite of our thought and scrutinize what worth this opposite may have...Every day you must make war also against yourself.
—Nietzsche

The two perpetual hostilities of Christianity: hostility to *life* and hostility to *art.* In the Christian doctrine one finds eternally the hatred of the world, the anathema to the *passions,* the dread of *beauty* and *pleasure,* a 'future beyond' which was invented the better to disparage the present, a *desire of death* and rest until the 'sabbath of the sabbaths.' Religion, metaphysics and all dreams of the supernatural are therefore auxiliaries of death, enemies of life and beauty, and betrayals and degradations of the human race.
—Nietzsche

Nearly everywhere the missionaries went they attempted to impose their own conceptions of the physical body on the people they encountered. They discovered that to prohibit the 'natives' from carrying out their ritual practices, such as *body decoration,* was a necessary step in demolishing the structure of their traditional beliefs.
—Victoria Ebin, *The Body Decorated*

This tattooing had been the work of a departed prophet and seer of his island, who by those hieroglyphic marks, had written out on his body a complete theory of the heavens and the earth, and a mystical treatise on the art of attaining truth, so that Queequeg in his own proper person was a riddle to unfold; a wondrous work in one volume; but whose mysteries not even himself could read, though his own live heart beat against them; and these mysteries were therefore destined in the end to molder away with the living parchment whereon they were inscribed, and so be unsolved to the last.
—Hermann Melville, *Moby Dick*

The Nuba of the Sudan perceive that the crucial difference between men and animals lies in men's ability to shave their heads and bodies and to make their skins smooth. This capacity distinguishes them from every other species: even language was once shared between men and monkeys.
—Victoria Ebin, *The Body Decorated*

In New Guinea the Roro people, who tattoo themselves extensively, describe the un-tattooed person as 'raw', comparing him to uncooked meat...The Roro see the tattooed man as 'cooked meat', transformed by a human process and thus given a social identity. Therein lies the distinction between a social being and a biological entity.
—Victoria Ebin, *Ibid*

Two billion people, three billion, even five billion could be supported by the planet by progressive lowering of the standard of living. When the population reaches eight billion, however, semi-starvation becomes the norm. A radical change had to take place in Man's culture...
—Isaac Asimov, *The Caves of Steel,* 1953

They were savages, the only savages of the 24th century; descendants of a research team of scientists that had been lost and marooned in the asteroid belt two centuries before when their ship had failed...Practicing a barbaric travesty of the scientific method they remembered from their forebears, they called themselves The Scientific People...Checks, chin, nose and eyelids were hideously tattooed like an ancient Maori mask.
—Alfred Bester, *The Stars My Destination*

In his Freak Factory...there, for enormous fees and no questions asked, Baker created monstrosities for the entertainment business, and refashioned skin, muscle, and bone for the underworld...The basement floor of the factory contained Baker's zoo of anatomical curiosities, natural freaks and monsters bought, and/or abducted. Baker, like the rest of his world, was passionately devoted to these creatures and spent long hours with them, drinking in the spectacle of their distortions the way other men saturated themselves with the beauty of art...

—Alfred Bester, *ibid*

They skidded around a corner into a shrieking mob of post-operative patients: bird men with fluttering wings, mermaids dragging themselves along the floor like seals, hermaphrodites, giants, pygmies, two-headed twins, centaurs, and a mewling sphinx...[then there was] a ward filled with temporal freaks: subjects with accelerated time sense, darting about the ward with the lightning rapidity of hummingbirds and emitting piercing bat like squeals.

—Alfred Bester, *The Stars My Destination*

Fun, fantasy, confusion and catastrophe.

—*Ibid*

The accumulation of knowledge is a different thing from the capacity to use it, and there are many who claim that in this respect man is already a degenerate creature. One has only to look at his mental inertia, his destructive wars, his blind subservience to religion, his stupid politics, his dead resistance to changing his way of living, to wonder if he has reached his own blind alley...

—Homer W Smith, *Kamongo*

I haven't succeeded in leaving my memory behind me—not a sound, not a trace, not one deed...

F.M. Dostoevsky, *The Idiot*

You are all awfully fond of external beauty and seemliness, and that's all you care for—that's true, isn't it?

Dostoevsky, *The Idiot*

We are nothing more than a moving row of Magic Shadow Shapes that come and go round this Sun-illumined lantern, held in midnight by the Master of the Show.

—Omar Khayyam

Japanese cabaret artist Miss Ongawa inserts the tail of a living snake into her nostril and regurgitates it through her mouth. As a climax to her act, Miss Ongawa eats the snake alive...An Indian performer inserts the snake head-first into his nostril. He then pulls the four-foot long living reptile out through his mouth to complete the act.

—Ramona & Desmond Morris, *Men & Snakes*

Permanent adornments—those involving some form of body mutilation—are more typical of rigid societies, where allegiance to the group is of massive importance... These are badges that can never be taken off, and that sets their owners apart from all other groups until the day they die. Frequently the application of the decoration is performed at a special ceremony, a tribal initiation, with the initiate suffering great pain in the process. This pain is an important part of the bonding—a physical horror that binds him even tighter to those who share it with him... The very intensity of the experience helps to widen the gulf between him and those who have not shared it.

—Desmond Harris, *Manwatching*

Mind control comes when you have total control of communication in an environment; when you have manipulation inside the group, such as constant self-criticism and confessing; and manipulation of individual guilt.

—Dr Robert J. Lifton

I cannot help thinking about someone like Howard Hughes—one of the richest men in the world who died of neglect and lack of proper medical attention. Or John Paul Getty, a billionaire who refused to pay a ransom for his own grandson and kept payphones in his mansions... Surely living for oneself, amassing individual wealth or fighting to stay on top of the pack is no way to live. Your personality and your worth become defined by what you own rather than by what you are...Life without principle is devoid of meaning. We have tasted life based on principle and now have no desire to ever live otherwise again. You do not know what happiness is until you have lived up to your highest.

—Rev. Jim Jones

A large number of valuable herbs, roots, barks, leaves and flowers grow within the immediate reach of those who may be unfortunate enough to need them to heal their ailments. Every person's physical organization is his own, and he has a right to understand it, and most especially hygiene and Nature's remedies that will relieve and heal all afflictions, or at least a great many of them...Knowledge is power, and he who seeks it is wise; he who neglects it does so to his own sorrow and detriment. Hippocrates, who is admitted by the medical profession to be the father of medicine, says, "All men ought to be acquainted with the medical art."

—J.I. Lighthall, *The Indian Folk Medicine Guide*

...What modern man has made of love: to convert the human body into a machine, even if it is a machine that produces symbols, is worse than degradation. Eroticism lives on the frontiers between the sacred and the blasphemous. The body is erotic because it is sacred. The two categories are inseparable: if the body is mere sex and animal impulse, eroticism is transformed into a monotonous process of reproduction...

—Octavio Paz, *Marcel Duchamp*

Despite the fact that they are made of materials more lasting than our bodies, machines grow older more rapidly than we do. They are inventions and manufactured objects; our bodies are re-productions, re-creations.

Machines wear out and after a time one model replaces another; bodies grow old and die, but the body has been the same from the appearance of man on the earth until now. The body is immortal because it is mortal; this is the secret of its permanent fascination—the secret of sexuality as much as of eroticism.

—Octavio Paz, *ibid*

Language is the most perfect instrument for producing meanings and at the same time for destroying them.

—Octavio Paz, *ibid*

Duchamp was one of the first to denounce the ruinous character of modern mechanical activity. Machines are great producers of waste, and the refuse they leave increases in geometric proportion to their productive capacity. To prove the point, all one needs to do is to walk through any of our cities and breathe its polluted atmosphere. Machines are agents of destruction and it follows from this that the only mechanical devices that inspire Duchamp are those that function in an unpredictable manner—*the antimachines.* These apparatuses are the equivalent of the puns: the unusual ways in which they work nullify them as machines. Their relation to utility is the same as that of delay to movement; they are without sense or meaning. They are machines that distill criticism of themselves.

—Octavio Paz, *ibid*

Metaphors and similes are of great value, insofar as they explain an unknown relation by a known one...The growth of ideas rests, at bottom, upon similes; because ideas arise by a process of combining the similarities and neglecting the differences between things...

—Schopenhauer, *On Some Forms of Literature*

I always had trouble with vaginal orgasms until I tried a dick with an ampallang. But look what happened from sucking it: I had to get two gold crowns—the ampallang cracked my back teeth!

—Deborah Valentine

Cynicism had run out and flippancy had never been more than a temporary shield. So now the people fled to the drug of pretense, identifying themselves with another life and another time and place—at the movie theater or on the television screen...For so long as you were someone else, you need not be yourself, vulnerable and afraid.

—Clifford Simak, *Ring Around the Sun,* 1952

Reading is not an end in itself but a means to an end.

—A. Hitler

Orthodoxy is the death of intelligence.

—Bertrand Russell

The dead look terribly dead when they're dead.

—Somerset Maugham, *The Razor's Edge*

Another essential factor in *control* is to conceal from the controlled the actual intentions of the controllers.

—W.S. Burroughs, "The Limits of Control"

Be regular and orderly in your life, so that you may be violent and original in your work.

—Flaubert

Speak, so that I may *see* you.

—Socrates

A major way in which advertising creates sales is by causing us to 'remember' a product below the level of awareness.

—Silva Mind Control Method

[A young doe and a wise old deer arguing about Man:] "They say that some time He'll come to live with us and be as gentle as we are. He'll play with us then and the whole forest will be happy, and we'll be friends with Him."..."*Friends* with Him! He's murdered us ever since we can remember, everyone of us, our sisters, our mothers, our brothers! Ever since we came into the world He's given us no peace, but has killed us wherever we showed our heads. And now we're going to be friends with Him! What nonsense!"

—Felix Salten, *BAMBI*

When Trevor-Roper claims that Africa has no history, he means that Africa has no history that *he can use.* Those people who *could* write—the scribes and priests of Egypt, Babylonia or China—were rarely disposed to record the attitudes of those they taxed, subordinated and mystified. Writing itself was initially used to keep tax, census and other administrative records; it was, in short, an instrument for the recording of official historians, written by bureaucrats. The oral tradition, the ceremony, the round of daily life...did not depend on writing, nor did they need to be reflected in writing.

—Stanley Diamond, *In Search of the Primitive*

Writing was one of the original mysteries of civilization, and it reduced the complexities of experience to the written word. Moreover, writing provides the ruling classes with an ideological instrument of incalculable power. The word of God becomes an invincible law, mediated by priests; therefore, respond the Iroquois, confronting the European, "Scripture was written by the Devil."

—Stanley Diamond, *Ibid*

With the advent of writing, symbols became explicit; they lost a certain richness. Man's word was no longer an endless exploration of reality, but a sign that could be used against him...For writing splits consciousness in two ways—it becomes more authoritative than talking, thus degrading the meaning of speech and eroding oral tradition; and it makes it possible to use words for the political manipulation and control of others. Written signs supplant memory; an official, fixed and permanent version of events can be made. If it is written, in early civilizations, it is bound to be true.

—Stanley Diamond, *Ibid*

History, then, has always been written by the conqueror; the majority of people have traditionally remained silent, and this is still largely the case. It is the civilized upper classes who, conceiving their positions as determined by God, talent or technology, create the facts of history and the deterministic theories which justify both the facts and their own pre-eminence.

—Stanley Diamond, *Ibid*

When the executive speaks, words emerge from his lips not unlike *mechanical tools* which, having established contact with those spoken to, make them go through their paces. Such words are brief, as precise as possible, and thoroughly impersonal.

—Alexander Goldenweiser, *Robots or Gods*

It is not piranhas, however, that are the most feared of the fishes that inhabit river systems in tropical South America. Even more dreaded are tiny catfishes...eel-like in appearance and about the size of a thin lead pencil. Candirus are bloodsuckers that for the most part belong to the genus *Vandellia*. They have the peculiar habit of entering the human genital opening, of either male or female, and worming their way up into the urethra where they erect prickly spines on their gill covers, thus embedding themselves within the body of their human host...The chief danger to humans is that the candiru will reach the bladder and lodge there while its victim dies in agony. Once a candiru has wriggled up into the urethra, the situation becomes so critical that many a male victim has slashed off his penis, preferring life with impaired sexual ability to a painful death.

—Edward R. Ricciuti, *Killers of the Seas*

The average Nama male is an expert hunter, a keen observer of nature, a craftsman who can make a kit bag of tools and weapons, a herder who knows the habits and needs of cattle, a direct participant in a variety of tribal rituals and ceremonies, and he is likely to be well-versed in the legends, tales and proverbs of his people (a similar list could be drawn up for the Nama female). The average primitive, relative to his social environment and the level of science and technology achieved, is more accomplished, in the literal sense of the term, than are most civilized individuals. He participates more fully and directly in the cultural possibilities open to him, not as a consumer and not vicariously but as an actively engaged, complete person.

—Stanley Diamond, *In Search of the Primitive*

All our inventions have endowed material forces with intellectual life, and degraded human life into a material force.

—Marx

In the white way of doing things, the family is nor so important. The police and soldiers take care of protecting you, the courts give you justice, the Post Office carries messages for you, the school teaches you. Everything is taken care of, even your children if you should die, but with us the family must do all that...With us the family was everything. Now it is nothing. We are getting like the white people, and it is bad for the old people. We had no old people's home like you. The old people were important. They were wise. Your old people must be fools.

—E. Adamson Hoebel, *Man in the Primitive World*

The primitive attitude towards the stranger is not a reflection of the latter's nonexistence as a human being, but of his *lack of status as a social person*. It follows that some way must be found to incorporate the stranger into a recognized system of statuses before one is able to relate to him specifically...The point is that in primitive society a person must be socially located and named before his human potential is converted into a cultural identity.

—Stanley Diamond, *In Search of the Primitive*

By considering the whole sphere of so-called primitive culture as a play-sphere we pave the way to a more direct and more general understanding...than any meticulous psychological or sociological analysis would allow... Primitive...ritual is thus sacred play, indispensable for the well-being of the community, fecund of cosmic insight and social development.

—Johan Huizinga, *Homo Ludens*

It was regarded as an evidence of bravery for a man to go into battle carrying no weapon that would do any harm at a distance.

—George Bird Grinnell

Lower down in the history of culture, the word and the idea are found sticking together with a tenacity very different from their weak adhesion in our minds, and there is to be seen a tendency to grasp at the word as though it were the object it stands for, and to hold that to be able to speak of a thing gives a sort of possession of it, in a way that we can scarcely realize.

—Edward B.Tylor, *An Introduction to the Study of Man and Civilization*

The Eskimos say, "Let the person who wants a vision hang himself by his neck. When his face turns purple, take him down and have him describe what he's seen."

—quoted in Jerome Rothenberg's *Shaking the Pumpkin*

Do not love your neighbor as you love those of your own house. Only if you are wicked will you love other people's children more than you do your own.

—Winnebago saying

In machine-based societies, the machine has incorporated the demands of the civil power or of the market, and the whole life of society, of all classes and grades, must adjust to its rhythms. Time becomes lineal, secularized, "precious"; it is reduced to an extension in space that must be filled up, and *sacred time* disappears...The secretary must adjust to the speed of her electric typewriter, the factory worker to the line or lathe; even the schoolboy to the precise periodization of his day and to the watch on his wrist; the person "at leisure" to a mechanized domestic environment and the flow of efficiently scheduled entertainment. The machines seem to run us, crystallizing in their mechanical or electronic pulses the means of our desires. The collapse of time to an extension in space, calibrated by machines, has bowdlerized our natural and human rhythms and helped dissociate us from ourselves... So faithful and exact are the machines as servants that they seem an alien force, persuading us at every turn to fulfill our intentions which we have built into them and which they represent—in much the same way that the perfect body servant routinizes and, finally, trivializes his master.

—Diamond, *In Search of the Primitive,* 1974

There must be in everything a certain spirit, a view which like a soul directs the whole.

—G.C. Lichtenberg

Nearly every notorious disaster brings out anecdotes to the effect that somebody foresaw it.

—L. Sprague de Camp

Dick Hyland was tattooed from head to foot with the names of 600 friends and celebrities.

—Ripley's Believe It or Not

Wealth is the hidden side of speed and speed the hidden side of wealth...He who has the speed has the power.

—Virilio/Lotringer, *Pure War*

One always says that the primary freedom is freedom of movement.True, but not freedom of speed. When you go too fast you are entirely stripped of yourself, you become totally alienated.

There can be a dictatorship of movement...We pass from freedom of movement to tyranny of movement... Modern war has already moved from space into time.

—Virilio/Lotringer, *Pure War*

What is the pleasure in taking the Concorde if it's only to return at the same instant, or in the few hours that follow, to the point of departure? There's a mystery in that, a riddle of displacement that fascinates me. I think it's a form of desire for inertia, desire for ubiquity, instantaneousness—a will to reduce the world to a single place, a single identity.

—Virilio/Lotringer, *Ibid*

The first casualty of war is truth.

—Rudyard Kipling

Nothing puts a greater obstacle in the way of the progress of knowledge than thinking that one knows what one does not yet know. The enthusiastic inventors of hypotheses usually fall victim to this mistake.

—Lichtenberg

If, as in certain cases of "invasion of privacy," someone should use speed to go beyond [the boundaries of my consciousness], I am *conditioned.* This in fact is what is called subliminal advertising and, of course, propaganda directed at entire populations. You see an image of which you arc not at all conscious. It imposes itself on you without your being able to detect it, because *it goes too fast.*

—Virilio/Lotringer, *Pure War*

The savage bows down to idols of wood and stone; the civilized man to idols of flesh and blood.

—G.B. Shaw, *Man & Superman*

He who slays a king and he who dies for him are alike idolaters.

—G.B. Shaw, *Ibid*

The unconscious self is the real genius. Your breathing goes wrong the moment your conscious self meddles with it.

—G.B. Shaw, *Ibid*

I used to go to tattoo parlors in San Diego just to watch people. Once I saw this guy come in who'd made up his mind to get a tattoo. He was a big tough guy wearing a muscle t-shirt, accompanied by his girlfriend, a Farrah Fawcett valley-girl type. He was looking at all the designs on the wall, and pointed to this big mean panther and tapped on it, "I want *that* one; what do you think?" His girlfriend was looking at it this way and that, but she'd had her eye on this goofy-looking design of Tweety Bird—a little bird body with a great big head cocked to one side, rolling its eyes and looking kinda cute and perky. She put her hand on his arm and said (pleading voice), "Oh no—Tweety Bird would be so cute! I wish you'd get *that!*" I went away, played some games in the arcade, then came back later and sure enough, here was this guy getting Tweety Bird tattooed on his arm! [laughs] Something that's going to mark this guy for the *rest of his life*—he'd wanted a big mean panther, and walked off with Tweety Bird instead! Just to please this girl he probably broke up with two months later.

—from a conversation with a pierced and tattooed person.

Being tattooed has opened up a whole new way of life for me. I now have a whole circle of interesting friends.

—Miss Cindy Ray, *The Story of a Tattooed Girl*

As far as unusual tattoos are concerned, I have tattooed a couple of hundred penises in my lifetime. I have put everything on them from eyeballs on the head to barber poles going around them. I have also tattooed plenty inside vaginas, mostly guys' names. Sure, some guys get off on it. I had a cat who wanted me to tattoo a dot on his cock. He asked the price and I told him it would cost him $10 and $20 if he came and, sure enough, he came. In a year's time he must have had me put 100 dots on his cock. It's a heavy place to get tattooed—it hurts. I know, because I have about seven tattoos on my own. Women really seem to dig them. Like they'll say, "Wow, man, you've got that tattoo clear up inside me."

—Jack Armstrong, quoted in Albert Morse's *The Tattooists*

Tattoos have distinct anti-authority appeal. The origin of this appeal might be traced to the early Christian proscription of tattooing and the resulting European laws against the practice. Whatever the source, tattooing today has an aura of the *forbidden* about it. Second, tattooing may have inherent appeal due to the pain involved in the operation and the permanency of the design; thus tattooing is restricted to the *brave and dedicated*. Third, and most important: in some circumstances, people are deprived of the opportunity to acquire and display the ordinary means of identifying and presenting the self. Although all three factors are obviously related it is the final one, that of deprivation of the opportunity to acquire and display the usual and desirable means of self-identification, that we see as most basic to an understanding of tattooing

—Edger & Dingman, "Tattooing and Identity," from *International Journal of Social Psychiatry,* 1963

The woman who wanted a butterfly tattooed down alongside her port of entry...she asked for a swallow-tailed butterfly right down there, with one tail going down each side of it. You know you have to stretch the skin tight to get the needle in...Well, I couldn't get hold of her right down there. I pulled and struggled for awhile and then I looked at her and said, "You'll really have to excuse me, but this is the only way I can do it." And with that I inserted two fingers and pushed out. That way I got it finished.

—Phil Sparrow, *The Tattoo Jungle*

[Having roamed the earth to discover he may be the last man left alive after a deadly purple cloud circled the globe, the narrator relates:] Surely I am hardly any longer a Western, "modern" mind, but a primitive, Eastern one...Whether this is a result of my own personality, of old acquainted with Eastern notions, or whether, perhaps, it is the natural accident to any soul emancipated from trammels, I do not know; but I seem to have gone right back to the beginnings, to resemblance with man in his first, simple, gaudy conditions: my hair, as I sit here, already hanging an oiled string down my back; my beard sweeping scented in two opening whisks to my ribs...My ankles—my ten fingers—my wrists—are heavy with gold and silver ornaments; and in my ears, which, with considerable pain, I bored three days since, are two needle-splinters, to prepare the holes for rings.

—M.P. Shiel, *The Purple Cloud,* 1930

Normality is what cuts off your sixth finger and your tail.

—tentatively-a-convenience

The bourgeois regarded the Dadaist as a dissolute monster, a revolutionary villain, a barbarous Asiatic, plotting against his bells, his safe deposits, his honors list. The Dadaist thought up tricks to rob the bourgeois of his sleep...The Dadaist gave the bourgeois a sense of confusion and distant, yet mighty rumbling, so that his bells began to buzz, his safes frowned, and his honors list broke out in spots.

—Hans Arp

Passionately committed to causing scandals—it's a reason to live!

—Phillipe Soupault

The desire to pierce myself has always been in part for political reasons—the politics of deviance. Earlier in my life as an art student, the Dada movement had a profound impact on my life. It helped me realize the ridiculous sensitivities that the "establishment" suffered from, which in turn kept that "establishment" from progressing. My piercings are my weapon, to struggle against the authoritarian/conformist tendencies of America which attempt to dissuade the populace from individual initiative and diversity.

—Zapata

Here we find a most conclusive argument for the truth that man is essentially a spiritual being. Matter cannot observe, reflect, remember, compare, reason, understand, and love. It has no voluntary power. Consequently the human body cannot perform one of its functions, after man has left it, though its organization remains perfect. The eye cannot see, the ear hear, the brain think. Matter can perform material offices only. It follows, therefore, of necessity, that it must be some other substance that is the subject of mental and distinctly human qualities, and that substance must be spiritual...all those qualities which distinguish man from the plant and animal, and are properly human, are due to his spiritual nature; or in other words, they are activities of a spiritual organization.

—Rev. Chauncey Giles, *The Nature of Spirit, and of Man as a Spiritual Being,* 1928

So far as our observation extends, distinctness and individuality of form, fineness and complexity of organization, increase with every step of progress.

—Giles, *Ibid*

We have no evidence that any material form can long retain its organization. Matter in itself is dead, passive, has no form of its own, and, by the action of general laws, constantly tends to its original chaotic state...The human form is perpetually maintained, because the soul seizes the new materials and casts them into her own image. The body is always dying and ever being born.

—Rev. Chauncey Giles, *Ibid*

In this world every one has two characters, a real and an apparent one. A bad man can appear to be very good. He can be very polite. He can assume all the airs of virtue and innocence; be kind and attentive to others...Every one can conceal his real feelings. He can speak differently from what he thinks, even when he has no intention of deceiving. A good man knows he has two natures...the internal and the external man. The internal is the real man. The external sometimes acts in harmony with the internal, and sometimes does not. We know from our own experience, from observation and history, that the internal and real character gradually gains the ascendancy, and brings the external, and even the body, into conformity with it to some extent...This work must continue to go on until the external and internal become one, and the whole being is perfectly homogeneous.

—Giles, *Ibid*

The road to excess leads to the palace of wisdom...for we never know what is enough until we know what is more than enough.

—William Blake

The best way to keep something bad from happening is to see it ahead of time...and you can't see it if you refuse to face the possibility.

—W.S. Burroughs

We are setting out to create new worlds, new beings, new modes of consciousness.

—W.S. Burroughs

We have a right to do what we want with our lives.

—*Things To Come*

There's nothing wrong with suffering, if you suffer for a purpose.

—*Things To Come*

Only very few of us can make a fire, catch a fish, skin a hare and build a decent shelter out of branches, in other words cope with our most fundamental needs. We prefer to leave things like this to the Boy Scout movement and others with special inclinations.

—Per Mollerup, *Design for Life*

Short is the pain, and long is the ornament

—Tattoo Chant

[In Mojave culture] almost everyone is tattooed, because a man or woman without marks on the face would be refused entrance to "the land of the dead."

—Taylor & Wallace, *Mojave Tattooing & Face-Painting*

Everyone should consider his body as a priceless gift...a marvelous work of art, of indescribable beauty, and mastery beyond human conception, and so delicate that a word, a breath, a look, nay, a *thought* may injure it.

—Nikola Tesla

SOURCES

BOOKS

Arnold Rubin, ed. *Marks of Civilizalion.* 9x12", 280 pp. Order from Museum of Cultural History, UCLA, 405 Hilgard Ave, LA CA 90024.

Ed Hardy. *Dragon Tattoo Design.* $53 ppd from Hardy Marks Publications, PO Box 90520, Honolulu HI 96835. (hardback book of flash for tattoo artists)

Douglas, Mary. All books, such as *Natural Symbols. Purity and Danger.*

Mauss, Marcel. All books, such as *The Gift. Sacrifice. Primitive Classification. A General Theory of Magic.*

Bataille, Georges. All books, such as *Death & Sensuality, Theory of Religion*, etc.

Riefenstahl, Leni. All books, such as *The Last of the Nuba, People of Kau & Vanishing Africa.*

Semiotext(e): all publications. SASE for calalog from Autonomedia, 55 So. 11th St, Brooklyn NY 11211-0568 (718-387-6471)

Burchett, George & Peter Leighton. *Memoirs of a Tattooist.*

Ebin, Victoria. *The Body Decorated.*

Brain, Robert. *The Decorated Body.*

Lenors & Virel. *Decorated Man.*

Parry, Albert. *Tattoo.*

Rondinella, G. *The Sign Upon Cain.* Order from Alterocca Editore srl, Via S. Marco 16, 05100 Temi, Italy

E. Royston Pike, *The Strange Ways of Man*

John Lame Deer & Richard Erdoes, *Lame Deer Seeker of Visions*

Scutt, R.W.B. & Christopher Gotch. Art, Sex & Symbol [U.K. title: Skin Deep

Morse, Albert. The Tattooists. $70 from 320 Miller Ave, Mill Valley CA 94941.

Hambly, W.D. *The History of Tattooing & Its Significance.*

Ray, Cindy. *The Story of a Tattooed Girl & How to Do Good Tattooing.* PO Box 34, Ivanhoe, Victoria, Australia.

Ebensten, H. *Pierced Hearts & True Love. London, Verschoyle, 1953.*

Sparrow, Phil. *The Tattoo Jungle.* Unpublished.

Tuttle, Lyle. *Tattoo 70.* San Francisco, 1970.

Zeis, Milton H. *Tattooing The World Over.* Rockford, Ill, 1968.

Japan Tattoo Institute, ed. *Japanese Tattoo Ladies & Japan's Tattoo Arts: Horiyoshi's World* vol. 1 & 2 . Order from Keibunsho, 3-37-7 Nakano, Nakono-ku, Tokyo Japan Y164

Bogdan, Robert. *Freak Show.* $32 from Univ of Chicago Press, Chicago 60637. Excellent; useful bibliography.

Virel, Andre. *Ritual & Seduction: The Human Body as Art.*

Monestier, Martin. *Human Oddities.* $16 from Citadel Press, 120 Enterprise Ave, Secaucus NJ 07094.

Richie, Donald & Ian Buruma. *The Japanese Tattoo.*

Mails, Thomas. *Sundancing at Rosebud and Pine Ridge.* $43 from *Augustana* College, Sioux Falls, South Dakota.

Richter, Stefon. Tattoo.

Skarifi. Write Coup de Grace, Kattenberg 122, 2200 Antwerp, Belgium for info.

Spider Webb. *Heavily Tattooed Men & Women; Pushing Ink.*

Fellman, Sandi. *The Japanese Tattoo.* $33 from Abbeville Press, 505 Park Ave, NYC 10022.

McCormick, E.H. *Omai.* Auckland/Oxford Univ Press.

Handy, W.C. *Tattooing in the Marquesas.* Kraus Reprint, 1978.

King, Michael. *Moko: Maori Tattoo in the 20th Century.*

Fish, Pat. *The Big Golden Book of Flash.* $40 from PO Box 77, Santa Barbara CA 93102.

Rosen, Michael. *Sexual Magic: The S/M Photographs.* $28 from Shaynew Press, Box 11719, SF CA 94101 .

Wroblewski, Chris. Photo books such as *Tattoo: Pigments of Imagination.*

Gatewood, Charles: *Forbidden Photographs.*

MAGAZINES

PFIQ (Piercing Fans Int'l Quarterly). See Jim Ward intro for ordering info. Sample issue $12 (plus "I am Over 21" signed statement).

Tattootime. Order from Re/Search.

Tattoo Historian. See Lyle Tuttle intro for ordering info.

Sandmutopio A Guardian & Dungeon Master. Sample issues $7 ppd (plus "I am Over 21" signed statement) from PO Box 11314, SF CA 94101-1314. Store at 285 Shipley, SF CA 94107 (415-978-5377).

Body Art. Blake House Studios, Blake End, Rayne, Braintree, Essex CM7 SSH, England. In USA order from Last Gasp, 2180 Bryant, SF CA 94110.

Magical Blend. Subscription $12 from PO Box 11303, SF CA 94101-7303. (415-673-1001)

Tattoo. $10 for 4 issues to *Tattoo,* Box 15107, Santa Ana CA 92705-0107. (213-374-7134)

Skin Two. 23 Grand Union Centre, Kensal Rd, London WI0 SAX, U.K. U.K. (01) 968-9692.

Tattoo Life Magazine. Write Bob McMahon, Rt. 8 Box 44L48 TA, Winchester, Winchester VA 22601. (703-667-9050)

Tattoo Advocate, $12 from Shotsie Gorman, 470 Haledon Ave, Haledon NJ 07508 (201-790-0429)

Tattoo International. Tattoo Club of Great Britain, 389 Cowley Rd, Oxford OX4 2BS, England. Send 4 IRCs for info.

Tattoo Gazette. Quarterly; 4 issues for $20 from Tattoo Society of New York, c/o Clayton Hats, 161 Essex St, NYC 10002.

Vague. BCM Box 7207, London WCIN 3XX, England.

Betty Pages. $4 from Pure Imagination, 88 Lexington Ave 9C, NYC 10016.

Arsenal #4. $15 from 1726 W. Jarvis Ave, Chicago IL 60626.

ZONE #3, 4, 5: Fragments for a History of the Human Body. $24 each ppd from Zone, 611 Broadway #838, NYC 10012.

VIDEOS

Emiko Mori's *Tattoo City* and Michael Stearns' *Tattooing Reality* (both on Ed Hardy & associates). *Stoney Knows How*—intv w/Stony St. Clair by Alan Govenar. Available from Tattoo Archive. *Signatures of the Soul,* good New Zealand tattoo video. Crazy Ace's *Colored People Invade San Diego* (documentary/intvws at '87 San Diego Tattoo Convention). Charles Gatewood's *Erotic Tattooing & Body Piercing, Parts 1 & 2; Weird San Francisco; Weird Amsterdam.*

FILMS

Irezumi (Spirit of Tattoo), Shocking Asia Part 2, The Yakuza, Mondo Magic, The Illustrated Man, Tattoo, The Rose Tattoo. All films of Robert Gardner (founder of Harvard's Film Study Center): *Dead Birds, Deep Hearts, Sons of Shiva, Rivers of Sand, Forest of Bliss.*

MAIL ORDER

Send $1 for Charles Gatewood's superior catalog of unusual books & Charles' intense tattoo/piercing videos. Flash Video, Box 410052, SF CA 94141.

Send large SASE for catalog of rare books, memorabilia and videos to Tattoo Archive (Chuck Eldridge), 2804 San Pablo, Berkeley CA 94702. (415-548-5895)

Tattoo Designs Catalog $6 from Spaulding & Rogers, Rt. 85-New Scotland Road, Voorheesville NY 12186. (518-768-2070)

Corset Catalog. $3 from BR Creations, PO Box 4201, Mountain View CA 94040 (415-961-5354). Note: some movies featuring corsets include *Wicked Lady, The Great Train Robbery, La Nuit de Varennes, The Pit & the Pendulum* with Barbara Steele, most Sophia Loren movies, *Nana, Picnic at Hanging Rock, Berserk, Beach Party, Frankie & Johnny, Calamity Jane, Pal Joey*

Send $10 for color catalog to National Tattoo Supplies, PO Box 2063, New Hyde Park, Long Island, NY 11040 (516-747-6953).

Send SASE for catalog to Lyle Tuttle, 839 Columbus, San Francisco CA 94133. (415-775-4991).

Society for Eradication of TV Newsletter, PO Box 1124, Albuquerque, NM 87103. Send SASE plus $5 donation.

Belier Press, PO Box 1234, Old Chelsea Station, NYC 10113. Send SASE for catalog.

Supergraphics, Box: 4489, Reading PA 19606-4489. Send SASE for catalog. Clasicos del S/M (John Willie books) Apartado de Correos 93020. 08080 Barcelona, Spain. Send 4 IRCs for catalog.

Movie Star News (Bettie Page videos), 134 W. 18th St, NYC 10011. Send $l for catalog.

Lyndon Distributors, PO Box 8146, Van Nuys CA 91409. Send SASE for catalog.

John Lyle, Harpford, Sidmouth, Devon EX10 ONH, U.K. $5 for catalog.

Loompanics book catalog $3 from PO Box 1197, Port Townsend, WA 98368

A Conversation with Raelyn Gallina, April 2009. Las Vegas

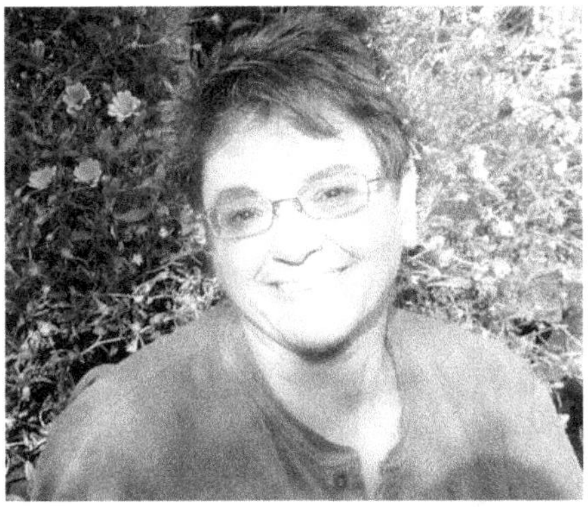

My name is Raelyn Gallina, I'm out of Oakland, California. I've been piercing and doing scarification since 1982—I'm the grandmother of piercing! I was asked to come [to APP Convention] last year as an honored guest and asked to offer a couple of workshops on anthropology; basically the history [laughs]—"*her*-story." And they asked me to come again this year as an "honored guest"—but I wouldn't have to work. They wanted me to come and just hang out. It was a little suspicious, but I admit I was totally surprised...

I was given the APP President's Award for being a forerunner in the body modification world when most of the people here at Conference were in diapers. While Jim Ward, Doug Malloy and Fakir were doing their thing with the boys in the gay SM communities, I was paralleling them in the lesbian SM communities and the women's leather groups, and *ripping it up,* right alongside. We don't get as much press as the boys, but I'm here to say, "I was there." We were doing it. We were blazing trails of blood [laughs]—lovely, *lovely* lesbian blood. And just pushing—really giving momentum to the body modification movement: piercing, especially scarification, and suspension. There you have it.

When we do modifications to our body, it allows us a great opportunity for transformation, change, empowerment, spiritual elevation—whatever you want.

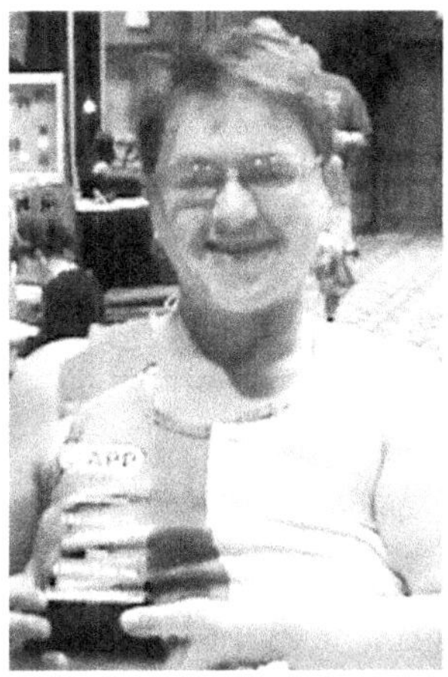

Vale: I particularly loved your talk last night [acceptance speech], which was trying to remind people that there ought to be a lot more depth, thinking, and compassion [in body modification work]—more bonding; something deeper than surface work.

Raelyn: Yes, and the opportunity is there every single time. You *can* give it meaning. *Anything* can be a ritual—you can turn any little everyday thing into a ritual that works for you and helps transform things in your life. Magic exists; we just have to use it and believe. And when we do modifications to our body, it allows us a great opportunity for transformation, change, empowerment, spiritual elevation—whatever you want.

I just heard this recently: We're spirit beings. **We are spirits on a human journey. We're not humans on a spiritual journey.** We're *already* spirits, and the thing is to get through the human experience while still remembering that we are spiritual beings that go on and on and *endure.* We have this body for the time being—so Glory in it. Protect it. Do all kinds of things with it. It's a great journey, and the more we can consciously use our human bodies for change and beneficial things, the better. It's a great vehicle.

Vale: Thank you very much, Raelyn, and congratulations on your amazingly well-deserved President's Award.

Raelyn: Girls are doing it for themselves. [laughs]

INDEX

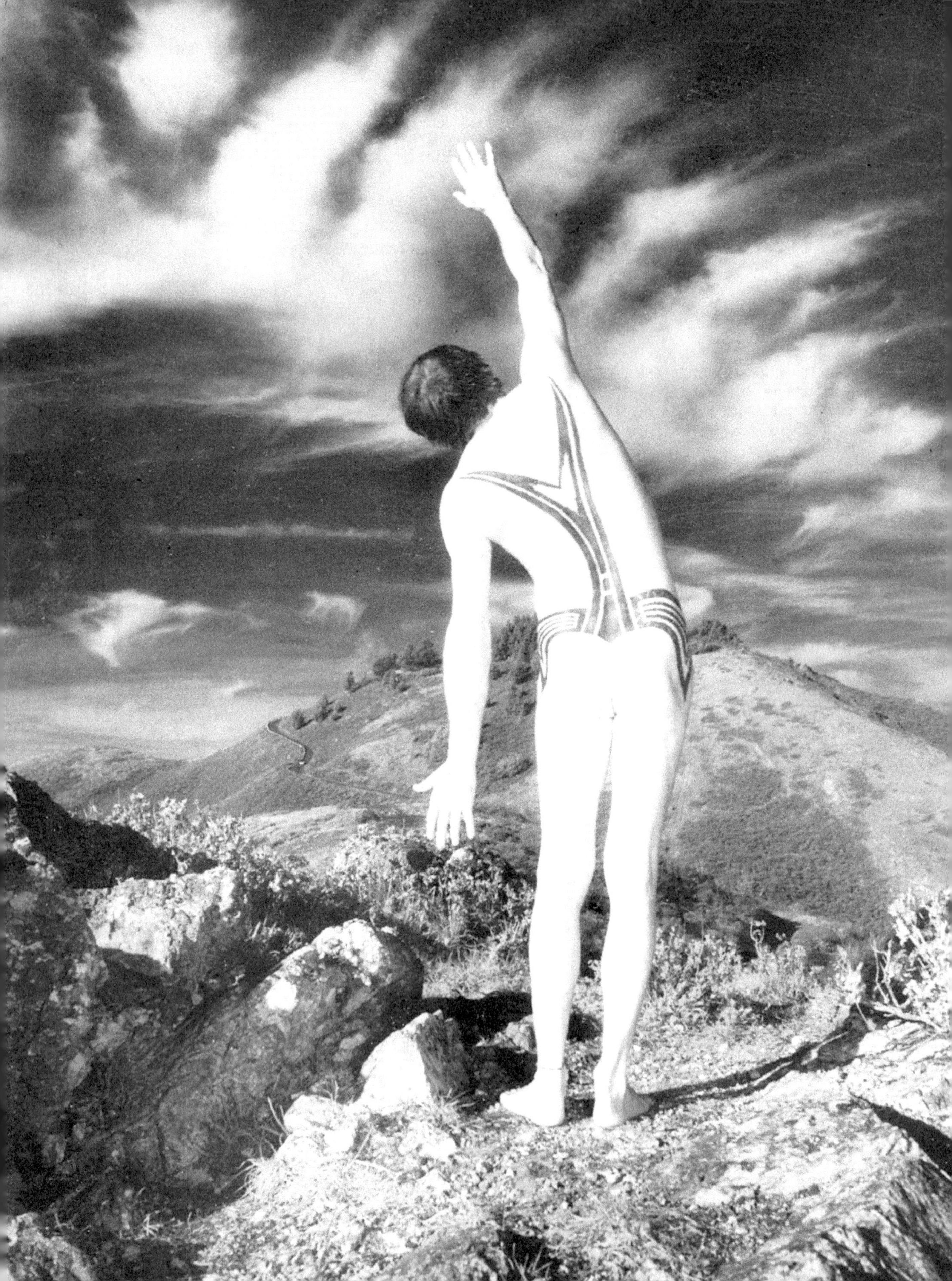

www.ingramcontent.com/pod-product-compliance
Lightning Source LLC
Jackson TN
JSHW052309160626
103893JS00005B/11
* 9 7 8 1 8 8 9 3 0 7 2 6 8 *